ADOLESCENCE

BY G. STANLEY HALL

LIFE AND CONFESSIONS OF A PSYCHOLOGIST

SENESCENCE

JESUS THE CHRIST IN THE LIGHT OF PSYCHOLOGY

RECREATIONS OF A PSYCHOLOGIST

MORALE

ADOLESCENCE

YOUTH

EDUCATIONAL PROBLEMS

FOUNDERS OF MODERN PSYCHOLOGY

ASPECTS OF CHILD LIFE AND EDUCATION

D. APPLETON AND COMPANY
New York London

ADOLESCENCE

ITS

PSYCHOLOGY

AND ITS RELATIONS TO

PHYSIOLOGY, ANTHROPOLOGY, SOCIOLOGY
SEX, CRIME, RELIGION

AND

EDUCATION

BY

G. STANLEY HALL, PH. D., LL. D.

PRESIDENT OF CLARK UNIVERSITY AND PROFESSOR OF
PSYCHOLOGY AND PEDAGOGY

VOLUME I

NEW YORK AND LONDON
D. APPLETON AND COMPANY
1931

Printed in the United States of America

PREFACE

THIS book is based on the author's Psychology, now in preparation, which should logically have been published first. The standpoint of the latter is roughly and provisionally indicated in Chapter X, with which it is hoped any reader with philosophic interests will begin. This point of view is further set forth in the last part of Chapter XVI, and some of its implications appear in Chapter XII, which should follow. That, recognizing fully all that has hitherto been done in this direction, the genetic ideas of the soul which pervade this work are new in both matter and method, and that if true they mark an extension of evolution into the psychic field of the utmost importance, is the conviction of the author. Although most of even his ablest philosophical contemporaries, both American and European, must regard all such conceptions much as Agassiz did Darwinism, he believes that they open up the only possible line of advance for psychic studies, if they are ever to escape from their present dishonorable capitivity to epistemology, which has to-day all the aridity, unprogressiveness, and barrenness of Greek sophism and medieval scholasticism, without standing, as did these, in vital relations to the problems of their age.

Idealism, metaphysics, and religion spring from basal needs of the human soul, and are indispensable in some form to every sound and comprehensive view of it, as well as necessary to a complete science. But these are now volatilized for both theory and practise by the present lust for theories of the nature of knowledge, which have become a veritable and multiform psychosis. To a psychology broad enough to include all the philosophic disciplines, this extravasation of thought, especially in a practical land like ours, presents a challenging problem. In academic isolation from the throbbing life of the great world, with but faint interest in or acquaintance with nature, afield or even in the laboratory, in habitual communion with the second-hand sources of knowledge found in books, in the solitude of the study, the sedentary and mentally pampered thinker has lost reality and devotes himself to a passionate quest of it as if it were a Golden Fleece or a Holy Grail to be rediscovered or a sacred sepulcher to be won from the paynim scientists. With little experience in willing and far less with the floods of feeling that have irrigated the life of the man in the past, the " experience " of the adult consciousness he so persistently analyzes is at best but a provincial oracle of the soul which is incalculably older, vaster, or more organized than it. These searchers still think in a pre-evolutionary age, and if they do not have recourse to pure apriorism or creationism are peculiarly prone to lapse to some savage type of thought like spiritism, telepathy, or transmundane irruption, and their interest in the soul is both impelled and guided by the imperious question of its survival after death, which is not, and probably never can be, a problem of science. It is they who have given us a bankrupt psychology without a soul. Beginning with Berkeley's ephebic dreamery about the existence of the external world, and Hume's satirical and not very sincere corollary of negation of the self, which Kant took in grim German earnest, they re-edit the latter with countless variants to find new patent ways out of an agnosticism that belongs, if anywhere, more to senescence than to adolescence. Just as infancy and senility have a certain correspondence, as does each stage of individual evolution and devolution, and as youth needs to anticipate the problems of old age and even of death, so the young need to feel by anticipation the great problems of reality, but not so seriously as to endanger losing their souls and the world which is so much easier to teach than how to find them again. Just as it is only a crippled belief in God that rests on theological arguments for his being, so at the age when the whole heart of youth goes out to reality, it is only those made prematurely old by the pedagogy of doubt that need the cheap, artificial confirmation of epistemology in order to face life with resolution and enthusiasm. The studies of the mind need new contact with life at as many points as possible. The psychic activities of childhood and youth and of the common average man, often the horror of previous philosophy and the actually as distinct from the theoretically practical, are worthy of all scientific honor.

While inanimate nature and even the lower forms of animal life are relatively stable, some of the latter having persisted from remote geologic ages, man is rapidly changing. His presence on the globe, his dominion over animals, his diffusion, and the historic period, are a series of increasingly recent events. While his bodily form is comparatively stable, his soul is in a transition stage, and all that we call progress is more and more rapid. Old moorings are constantly broken; adaptive plasticity to new environments—somatic, economic, industrial, social, moral and religious—was never so great; and in the changes which we hope are on the whole truly progressive, more and more human traits are too partially acquired to be permanently inherited. All this suggests that man is not a permanent type but an organism in a very active stage of evolution toward a more permanent form. Our consciousness is but a single stage and one type of mind: a late, partial, and perhaps essentially abnormal and remedial outcrop of the great underlying life of man-soul. The animal, savage, and child-soul can never be studied by introspection. Moreover, with missing links and extinct ethnic types, much, perhaps most, soul life has been hopelessly lost. Thus, the adult who seeks self-knowledge by introversion is banausic, and his system is at its best but one human document or return to the eternal but ever unanswered question what man can know, what he should do, and how he most truly feels. From this it follows that we must turn to the larger and far more laborious method of observation, description, and induction. We must collect states of mind, sentiments, phenomena long since lapsed, psychic facts that appear faintly and perhaps but once in a lifetime, and that in only few and rare individuals, impulses that, it may be, never anywhere arise above the threshold, but manifest themselves only in automatisms, acts, behavior, things neglected, trivial and incidental, such as Darwin says are often most vital. We must go to school to the folk-soul, learn of criminals and defectives, animals, and in some sense go back to Aristotle in rebasing psychology on biology, and realize that we know the soul best when we can best write its history in the world, and that there are no finalities save formulæ of development. The soul is thus still in the making, and we may hope for an indefinite further development. Perhaps other racial stocks than ours will later advance the kingdom of man as far beyond our present standpoint as it now is above that of the lowest savage or even animals. There are powers in the soul that slumber like the sleepers in myth, partially aroused, it may be, in great personal or social crises, but sometime to be awakened to dominance. In a word, the view here represents a nascent tendency and is in striking contrast to all those systems that presume to have attained even an approximate finality. But the twilight is that of dawn and not of evening. It is the morning hours of beginning and not that of completing the day of work, and this can appeal only to those still adolescent in soul.

Holding that the child and the race are each keys to the other, I have constantly suggested phyletic explanations of all degrees of probability. Some of these, I think, have been demonstrated so far as is now possible in this obscure and complicated domain. Realizing the limitations and qualifications of the recapitulation theory in the biologic field, I am now convinced that its psychogenetic applications have a method of their own, and although the time has not yet come when any formulation of these can have much value, I have done the best I could with each instance as it arose. Along with the sense of the immense importance of further coordinating childhood and youth with the development of the race, has grown the conviction that only here can we hope to find true norms against the tendencies to precocity in home, school, church, and civilization generally, and also to establish criteria by which to both diagnose and measure arrest and retardation in the individual and the race. While individuals differ widely in not only the age but the sequence of the stages of repetition of racial history, a knowledge of nascent stages and the aggregate interests of different ages of life is the best safeguard against very many of the prevalent errors of education and of life.

Modern conceptions, which increasingly make all mental

processes efferent in their psychophysical nature, suggest a now impending synthesis that may give to our practical age and land the long-hoped-for and long-delayed science of man. To help bring these tendencies to their maturity is the task to which organic thinkers should address themselves. Utilizing to the utmost the lessons of the past, they should free themselves alike from excessive subjectivisms and from the limitations of old systems and methods, and feel it their highest duty to enter upon the less critical and more constructive work of building larger philosophic mansions for the soul. If truth is edification, the highest criterion of pure science is its educative value. The largest possible aspect of all the facts of life and mind is educational, and the only complete history is the story of the influences that have advanced or retarded the development of man toward his completion, always ideal and forever in the future. Thus psychology and the higher pedagogy are one and inseparable. Not only the beautiful and the good, but the true, can have no other test of validity than that they appeal to and satisfy certain deep needs; and these are many. From this general view-point I have tried to show how truth about things of the soul, in an unique sense, is never complete or certain till it has been applied to education, and that the latter field is itself preeminent and unlike all other fields of application for either scientific or philosophic conclusions.

The years from about eight to twelve constitute an unique period of human life. The acute stage of teething is passing, the brain has acquired nearly its adult size and weight, health is almost at its best, activity is greater and more varied than ever before or than it ever will be again, and there is peculiar endurance, vitality, and resistance to fatigue. The child develops a life of its own outside the home circle, and its natural interests are never so independent of adult influence. Perception is very acute, and there is great immunity to exposure, danger, accident, as well as to temptation. Reason, true morality, religion, sympathy, love, and esthetic enjoyment are but very slightly developed. Everything, in short, suggests the culmination of one stage of life as if it thus represented what was once, and for a very protracted and relatively stationary period, the age of maturity in some remote, perhaps pigmoid, stage of human evolution, when in a warm climate the young of our species once shifted for themselves independently of further parental aid. The qualities now developed are phyletically vastly older than all the neo-atavistic traits of body and soul, later to be superposed like a new and higher story built on to our primal nature. Heredity is so far both more stable and more secure. The elements of personality are few, but are well organized and on a simple, effective plan. The momentum of the paleopsychic traits is great, and they are often clearly distinguishable from those to be later added. Thus the boy is father of the man in a new sense in that his qualities are indefinitely older and existed well compacted untold ages before the more distinctly human attributes were developed. Indeed, there are a few faint indications set forth in the text of a yet earlier age nodality or meristic segmentation, as if amid the increased instabilities of health at the age of about six we could still detect the ripple-marks of an ancient pubic beach now lifted high above the tides of a receding shore-line as human infancy has been prolonged. I have also given reasons that lead me to the conclusion that, despite its dominance, the function of sexual maturity and procreative power is peculiarly mobile up and down the age-line independently of many of the qualities usually so closely associated with it, so that much that sex created in the phylum now precedes it in the individual.

Rousseau would leave prepubescent years to nature and to these primal hereditary impulsions and allow the fundamental traits of savagery their fling till twelve. Biological psychology finds many and cogent reasons to confirm this view if only a proper environment could be provided. The child revels in savagery, and if its tribal, predatory, hunting, fishing, fighting, roving, idle, playing proclivities could be indulged in the country and under conditions that now, alas! seem hopelessly ideal, they could conceivably be so organized and directed as to be far more truly humanistic and liberal than all that the best modern school can provide. Rudimentary organs of the soul now suppressed, perverted, or delayed, to crop out in menacing forms later, would be developed in their season so that we should be immune to them in maturer years, on the principle of the Aristotelian catharsis for which

I have tried to suggest a far broader application than the Stagirite could see in his day.

These nativistic and more or less feral instincts can and should be fed and formed. The deep and strong cravings in the individual to revive the ancestral experiences and occupations of the race can and must be met, at least in a secondary and vicarious way, by tales of the heroic virtues the child can appreciate, and these proxy experiences should make up by variety and extent what they lack in intensity. The teacher art should so vivify all that the resources of literature, tradition, history, can supply which represents the crude, rank virtues of the world's childhood that, with his almost visual imagination, reenforced by psychonomic recapitulatory impulses, the child can enter upon his full heritage, live out each stage of his life to the fullest, and realize in himself all its manifold tendencies. Echoes only of the vaster, richer life of the remote past of the race they must remain, but just these are the murmurings of the only muse that can save from the omnipresent dangers of precocity. Thus we not only rescue from the danger of loss, but utilize for further psychic growth the results of the higher heredity, which are the most precious and potential things on earth. So, too, in our urbanized hothouse life, that tends to ripen everything before its time, we must teach nature, although the very phrase is ominous. But we must not, in so doing, wean still more from, but perpetually incite to visit field, forest, hill, shore, the water, flowers, animals, the true homes of childhood in this wild, undomesticated stage from which modern conditions have kidnapped and transported him. Books and reading are distasteful, for the very soul and body cry out for a more active, objective life, and to know nature and man at first hand. These two staples, stories and nature, by these informal methods of the home and the environment constitute fundamental education.

But now another remove from nature seems to be made necessary by the manifold knowledges and skills of our highly complex civilization. We should transplant the human sapling, I concede reluctantly, as early as eight, but not before, to the schoolhouse with its imperfect lighting, ventilation, temperature. We must shut out nature and open books. The child must sit on unhygienic benches and work the tiny muscles that wag the tongue and pen, and let all the others, which constitute nearly half its weight, decay. Even if it be prematurely, he must be subjected to special disciplines and be apprenticed to the higher qualities of adulthood, for he is not only a product of nature, but a candidate for a highly developed humanity. To many, if not most, of the influences here there can be at first but little inner response. Insight, understanding, interest, sentiment, are for the most part only nascent, and most that pertains to the true kingdom of mature manhood is embryonic. The wisest requirements seem to the child more or less alien, arbitrary, heteronomous, artificial, falsetto. There is much passivity, often active resistance and evasion, and perhaps spasms of obstinacy, to it all. But the senses are keen and alert, reactions immediate and vigorous, and the memory is quick, sure, and lasting, and ideas of space, time, and physical causation, and of many a moral and social licit and non-licit, are rapidly unfolding. Never again will there be such susceptibility to drill and discipline, such plasticity to habituation, or such ready adjustment to new conditions. It is the age of external and mechanical training. Reading, writing, drawing, manual training, musical technic, foreign tongues and their pronunciation, the manipulation of numbers and of geometrical elements, and many kinds of skill have now their golden hour, and if it passes unimproved, all these can never be acquired later without a heavy handicap of disadvantage and loss. These necessities may be hard for the health of body, sense, mind, as well as for morals, and pedagogic art consists in breaking the child into them betimes as intensively and as quickly as possible with minimal strain and with the least amount of explanation or coquetting for natural interest and in calling medicine confectionery. This is not teaching in its true sense so much as it is drill, inculcation, and regimentation. The method should be mechanical, repetitive, authoritative, dogmatic. The automatic powers are now at their very apex, and they can do and bear more than our degenerate pedagogy knows or dreams of. Here we have something to learn from the schoolmasters of the past back to the middle ages, and even from the ancients. The greatest stress, with short periods and few hours, incessant insistence, incitement, and little reliance upon interest, reason, or work done without the presence of the teacher, should be the guiding principles for pressure in these essentially formal and, to the child, contentless elements of knowledge. These should be sharply distinguished from the indigenous, evoking, and more truly educational factors described in the last paragraph, which are meaty, content-full, and relatively formless as to time of day, method, spirit, and perhaps environment and personnel of teacher, and possibly somewhat in season of the year, almost as sharply as work differs from play, or perhaps as the virility of man that loves to command a phalanx, be a martinet and drill-master, differs from femininity which excels in persuasion, sympathetic insight, story-telling, and in the tact that discerns and utilizes spontaneous interests in the young.

Adolescence is a new birth, for the higher and more completely human traits are now born. The qualities of body and soul that now emerge are far newer. The child comes from and harks back to a remoter past; the adolescent is neo-atavistic, and in him the later acquisitions of the race slowly become prepotent. Development is less gradual and more saltatory, suggestive of some ancient period of storm and stress when old moorings were broken and a higher level attained. The annual rate of growth in height, weight, and strength is increased and often doubled, and even more. Important functions previously non-existent arise. Growth of parts and organs loses its former proportions, some permanently and some for a season. Some of these are still growing in old age and others are soon arrested and atrophy. The old moduli of dimensions become obsolete and old harmonies are broken. The range of individual differences and average errors in all physical measurements and all psychic tests increases. Some linger long in the childish stage and advance late or slowly, while others push on with a sudden outburst of impulsion to early maturity. Bones and muscles lead all other tissues, as if they vied with each other, and there is frequent flabbiness or tension as one or the other leads. Nature arms youth for conflict with all the resources at her command—speed, power of shoulder, biceps, back, leg, jaw, —strengthens and enlarges skull, thorax, hips, makes man aggressive and prepares woman's frame for maternity. The power of the diseases peculiar to childhood abates, and liability to the far more diseases of maturity begins, so that with liability to both it is not strange that the dawn of the ephebic day is marked at the same time by increased morbidity but diminished rates of mortality. Some disorders of arrest and defect as well as of excessive unfoldment in some function, part, or organ may now, after long study and controversy, be said to be established as peculiar to this period, and diseases that are distinctly school- and city-bred abound, with apparently increasing frequency. The momentum of heredity often seems insufficient to enable the child to achieve this great revolution and come to complete maturity, so that every step of the upward way is strewn with wreckage of body, mind, and morals. There is not only arrest, but perversion, at every stage, and hoodlumism, juvenile crime, and secret vice seem not only increasing, but develop in earlier years in every civilized land. Modern life is hard, and in many respects increasingly so, on youth. Home, school, church, fail to recognize its nature and needs and, perhaps most of all, its perils. The cohesions between the elements of personality are loosened by the disparities of both somatic and psychic development, and if there is arrest at any stage or in any part before the higher unity is achieved there is almost sure to be degeneration and reunion on a lower level than before. One of the gravest dangers is the persistent ignoring by femininists of the prime importance of establishing normal periodicity in girls, to the needs of which everything else should for a few years be secondary.

The functions of every sense undergo reconstruction, and their relations to other psychic functions change, and new sensations, some of them very intense, arise, and new associations in the sense sphere are formed. Haptic impressions, appetite for food and drink, and smell are most modified. The voice changes, vascular instability, blushing, and flushing are increased. Sex asserts its mastery in field after field, and works its havoc in the form of secret vice, debauch, disease, and enfeebled heredity, cadences the soul to both its normal and abnormal rhythms, and sends many thousand youth a year to quacks, because neither parents, teachers, preachers, or physicians know how to deal with its problems. Thus the foundations of domestic, social, and religious life are oftenest undermined. Between religion and love God and nature have wrought an indissoluble bond so that neither can attain normality without that of the other. Secondary sexual qualities are shown to have an ever-widening range, and parenthood to mean more with every upward step of development. The youth craves more knowledge of body and mind, that can help against besetting temptations, aid in the choice of a profession, and if his intellect is normal he does not vex his soul overmuch about the logical character of the universe or the ultimate sanction of either truth or virtue. He is more objective than subjective, and only if his lust to know nature and life is starved does his mind trouble him by in-growing. There are new repulsions felt toward home and school, and truancy and runaways abound. The social instincts undergo sudden unfoldment and the new life of love awakens. It is the age of sentiment and of religion, of rapid fluctuation of mood, and the world seems strange and new. Interest in adult life and in vocations develops. Youth awakes to a new world and understands neither it nor himself. The whole future of life depends on how the new powers now given suddenly and in profusion are husbanded and directed. Character and personality are taking form, but everything is plastic. Self-feeling and ambition are increased, and every trait and faculty is liable to exaggeration and excess. It is all a marvelous new birth, and those who believe that nothing is so worthy of love, reverence, and service as the body and soul of youth, and who hold that the best test of every human institution is how much it contributes to bring youth to the ever fullest possible development, may well review themselves and the civilization in which we live to see how far it satisfies this supreme test.

Never has youth been exposed to such dangers of both perversion and arrest as in our own land and day. Increasing urban life with its temptations, prematurities, sedentary occupations, and passive stimuli just when an active, objective life is most needed, early emancipation and a lessening sense for both duty and discipline, the haste to know and do all befitting man's estate before its time, the mad rush for sudden wealth and the reckless fashions set by its gilded youth—all these lack some of the regulatives they still have in older lands with more conservative traditions. In a very pregnant psychological sense ours is an unhistoric land. Our very Constitution had a Minerva birth, and was not the slow growth of precedent. Our ideas of freedom were at the outset fevered by the convulsion of the French Revolution. Our literature, customs, fashions, institutions, and legislation were inherited or copied, and our religion was not a gradual indigenous growth, but both its spirit and forms were imported ready-made from Holland, Rome, England, and Palestine. To this extent we are a fiat nation, and in a very significant sense we have had neither childhood nor youth, but have lost touch with these stages of life because we lack a normal development history. It is not merely that we have no antiquity rich in material and spiritual monuments that is the best nursery of patriotism in the young, but our gallery of heroes is largely composed, not of glorious youth but of sages advanced in age or old in wisdom for their years. Our immigrants have often passed the best years of youth or leave it behind when they reach our shores, and their memories of it are in other lands. No country is so precociously old for its years. Few as these are, the senescence of the original American stock is already seen in abandoned farms and the infecundity of graduates, so that if our population had been unreplenished from abroad for the last century we should be to-day not merely stationary, like France, but retrogressive. In this environment our young people leap rather than grow into maturity. Our storm and stress strenuousness too often imparts at least the narrow nervous intensity of an individuation that is biologically antagonistic to genesis and that is less ephebic, as we fondly think it to be, than ephebeitic. We are conquering nature, achieving a magnificent material civilization, leading the world in the applications though not in the creation of science, coming to lead in energy and intense industrial and other activities; our vast and complex business organization that has long since outgrown the comprehension of professional economists, absorbs ever more and earlier the best talent and muscle of youth and now dominates health, time, society, politics, and lawgiving, and sets new and ever more pervading fashions in manners, morals, education, and religion; but we are progressively forgetting that for the complete apprenticeship to life, youth needs repose, leisure, art, legends, romance, idealization, and in a word humanism, if it is to enter the kingdom of man well equipped for man's highest work in the world. In education our very kindergartens, which outnumber those of any other land, by dogma and hyper-sophistication tend to exterminate the naive that is the glory of childhood. Everywhere the mechanical and formal triumph over content and substance, the letter over the spirit, the intellect over morals, lesson setting and hearing over real teaching, the technical over the essential, information over education, marks over edification, and method over matter. We coquet with children's likes and dislikes and can not teach duty or the spirit of obedience. In no civilized land is teaching so unprofessional or school boards at such a low level of incompetence. Nowhere are the great traditions of the race so neglected, the high school so oblivious of either the nature or the needs, or both, of the adolescent stage of life. The American college is half universitized with methods and matter prematurely specialized, and half bound to the recitation, marking methods and discipline of the school, while the apex of our educational system is still in Europe, where hundreds of our best graduates go yearly to find the advanced and special training we are still, in most departments, unable to supply.

In religion, which was grafted from an alien ethnic stock, we lack scientific sincerity. Statistics show more sects and more clergymen per capita of population than in any other land, and a rapidly progressive ignorance by the rising generation of the very Bible we profess to revere. Churches, charities, missions abound, but our slums are putrefying sores whose denizens anthropologists believe lower in the moral and intellectual scale than any known race of savages, and the percentages of juvenile crimes and the average age of first commitment grows steadily earlier. We have vastly simplified politics by separating Church and State and by our voluntary system, but we have also permitted a chasm to yawn between our secular and religious life, between science and theology, till even seminaries for the training of clergymen neglect and even suspect the study of nature as if God were a hypocrite and did one thing in his works and said another in his Word, when in fact each supplements and is an imperfect thing without the other. We try to impose not only our civilization, but our religion, upon lower races, even though they are thereby exterminated, and fail to study the nature and needs of even those we try to help.

All this is hard on youth, which was better understood in ancient Greece and Rome than now, for it is profoundly responsive to all these influences. Despite all this I am an optimist root and core, not merely because an evolutionist must hold that the best and not the worst will survive and prevail, but because in most, though not yet in all, of these fields I see clearly the beginnings of better things. Even in education and religion, the strongholds of conservatism, there are new and better ideals and efforts, and these are less exceptional and are growing in power and influence and are represented by more and better men. In vigor, enthusiasm, and courage we are still young, and our faults are those of youth. Because they have been great our suffering has been also great, and pain is the world's best teacher whose lessons are surest to be laid to heart. The very fact that we think we are young will make the faith in our future curative, and we shall one day not only attract the youth of the world by our unequaled liberty and opportunity, but develop a mental, moral, and emotional nurture that will be the best preparation for making the most and the best of them and for helping humanity on to a higher stage.

As for years, an almost passionate lover of childhood and a teacher of youth, the adolescent stage of life has long seemed to me one of the most fascinating of all themes, more worthy, perhaps, than anything else in the world of reverence, most inviting study, and in most crying need of a service we do not yet understand how to render aright. Socrates knew that there was no such companionship or inspiration. In ministering to it the higher instincts of parenthood culminate and age renews its youth. This should make teaching the most humanistic, the noblest, and the most satisfying vocation of man, as well as the surest safeguard against pessimism. These years are the best decade of life. No age is so responsive to all the best and wisest adult endeavor. In no psychic soil, too, does seed, bad as well as good, strike such deep root, grow so rankly, or bear fruit so quickly or so surely. To love and feel for and with the young can alone make the teacher love his calling and respect it as supreme. That it may directly and indirectly help the young to exploit aright all the possibilities of the years from fourteen to twenty-four and to safeguard them against the above insidious dangers is the writer's chief desire. Hence the book attempts a pretty full survey of pedagogic matter and method for the age treated, and also, to some extent, for earlier and later years. To motor education, grouped under four great divisions, and will-training, one of the longest chapters (III) is devoted. The last part of Chapter XV and Chapter XVI treats of the pedagogy of the English literature and language, history, drawing, normal and high schools, colleges and universities, and philosophy, and Chapter XII is devoted to that of nature and the sciences most commonly taught. Menstruation and the education of girls occupies two chapters (VII and XVII), hygiene, crime, and secret vice one each (IV, V, and VI), social and religious training have each a chapter (XV and XIV, respectively), and the education of the heart is described not only in XI, but in XV, XII, and elsewhere.

This is essentially the author's first book. It has grown slowly under successive repetitions and amplifications as a lecture course to graduate students. It constitutes the first attempt to bring together the various aspects of its vast and complex theme. In revising these lectures for publication, I have eliminated much that was technical and detailed and tried to bring the subject-matter of each chapter within the reach of any intelligent reader. In writing it, I have been most indebted, especially in the second volume, to my own pupils past and present. I have been throughout also under special obligation to the librarian of the University, Louis N. Wilson, who has for years had my themes in mind and not only obtained books difficult of access, but often found valuable references that I should not otherwise have known. Miss Florence Chandler has not only typographed most of the book and made the name index, but made me in countless ways a debtor to her intelligence and interest. Lastly, Miss Alice Thayer, A. B., has read the entire proof in both galley and page form, and brought her special training in psychology to bear in correcting many errors not only of commission but of omission. To all these my debt can never be repaid. Few authors have ever been more fortunate in their helpers, and I do not like to think what these volumes would have been without their aid.

G. Stanley Hall.

TABLE OF CONTENTS

CHAPTER I

GROWTH IN HEIGHT AND WEIGHT

Individual growth recapitulates the history of the race—Rate of prenatal growth in height and weight—Statistical methods—Prenatal growth in animals—Causes that favor and hinder it—Lessened rate at eight to twelve, also at seventeen and eighteen—Delay and compensation—Last stages of growth—Advantages of size—What is growth?—National differences—New genetic theories of retardation and the period of increment—Augmented size and power of the human race—A later, higher, new story superposed on the older foundations now represented in boyhood.

THE beginning of individual life, or the age of zero for all sexed animals, is when the male cell penetrates the ovum. Their attraction for each other, which Maupas thinks a relic of the psychochemic tropism of agamic generation, is the biological basis, as the karyonomic rejuvenation thus caused is the goal of love in the ascending stages of life. By their fusion in impregnation these two master cells, the bearers of heredity, acquire the momentum of growth, which next to love is perhaps the most interesting and important fact in the world of organic nature and the key to most of its problems. The new tensions and dominants, to use the terms of Reinke and Morgan, thus set free and given definite direction, begin to develop a new individuality, to which the parental one, which now begins to wane, is subordinated. With ontogeny in successive generations the immortal germ plasm puts on mortality, somewhat as lost limbs in lower or tissues in higher forms of life are regenerated. The marvelous phenomena of impregnation, in which pleasure, which all creatures seek, culminates and in the interest of which beauty, spring-time, blossoms, ornament, courtship in the animal world, and all physical and psychic secondary sexual qualities and even the life and death of the individual find their key and motive, thus start the long series of anagenic processes that end in complete maturity.

As the germ-cell begins to increase in size, its mass or substance does so, of course, at a faster rate than does its surface, so that, since all nutrition must first be absorbed from without, a limit is soon reached, and either equilibrium or death by starvation must ensue. This result, however, is avoided by cell division which begins at the nucleus and proceeds by very complex processes, which cytologists have lately made great progress not only in tracing but even in explaining. The first division results in two smaller daughter-cells of equal size, each of which grows in bulk and weight but does not separate to form each a new individual, as do the primitive unicellular organisms, but divides again, so that their numbers tend to increase in geometrical ratio. These successive generations of daughter-cells which constitute the adult body are thus all descended from a single ovum, and frequency of cell division mainly determines the rapidity of growth. The rate of the latter is high when the generations of cells succeed each other rapidly, and low if the intervals between successive divisions are long. The number of cells thus, as Minot has pointed out,[1] depends ideally upon the number of generations, each division effecting in some degree a rejuvenation, and an individual or biad being simply a group of cells produced from a single egg.

In this process the individual in a general way repeats the history of its species, passing slowly from the protozoan to the metazoan stage, so that we have all traversed in our own bodies ameboid, helminthoid, piscian, amphibian, anthropoid, ethnoid, and we know not how many intercalary stages of ascent. How these lines of heredity and growth along which all the many thousand species, extant and extinct, these viatica of the holy spirit of life, the consummate products of millennia of the slow travail of evolution, have been unfolded, we know scarcely more than we do what has been the impelling force, or will to live, which seems so inexhaustible and insistent. Certain it is that the cellular theory needs to be supplemented by assuming, both in the organism as a whole and in the species, powers that can not be derived from the cells. Probably, too, the original cause of phylogenetic evolution was no inherent and specific

[1] Minot, C. S. Ueber Vererbung und Verjungung, Biol. Centralbl., August 1, 1895. Growth as a Function of Cells, Proc. Nat. Hist. Soc., March 5, 1879. Also Senescence and Rejuvenation, Jour. of Physiol., 1891, No. 2.

nisus, but, as we know it, was due to a struggle for survival forced upon organisms by their environment.

The early stages of growth are telescoped into each other almost indistinguishably, so that phylogenetically the embryo lives a thousand years in a day, and the higher the species the more rapid relatively is the transit through the lower stages. This law of tachygenesis may perhaps be expressed somewhat as follows: Heredity, which slowly appears as a substitute for the external causes that have produced a given series of characters, tends to produce that succession with increasing economy and speed and also to become in a way more independent of the causes which originally determined it.

The human ovum, when ripe for impregnation, has a diameter of about 0.2 mm. Mühlmann[1] has averaged the four best measurements of the monthly embryonic growth in length. To find the prenatal monthly rate of growth in weight, he assumes Welcker's[2] estimate of 0.00008 milligram as the weight of a red blood-corpuscle measuring 0.007 mm; then an embryo of the above size would weigh 0.00228 milligram. Assuming with Mühlmann 0.003 milligram as its weight, these results appear in the following table:

Prenatal month.	1.	2.	3.	4.	5.	6.	7.	8.	9.	10.
Length of the embryo in mm. at the end of the month...	7.5	14.4	77	136	230	315	362	415	452	490
Monthly increase in per cent.	3,650	92	434	77	70	37	15	14	9	8

Prenatal Growth in Weight

Month.	0.	1.	2.	3.	4.	5.	6.	7.	8.	9.	10.
Absolute weight at beginning of each month in gr.	0,000003			12	88	284	634	1,218	1,834	2,235	2,717
Increase in per cent......					633	223	123	92	51	22	21

Thus at the end of the first month we have the enormous growth in length of 3,650 per cent. If we except the third month, when there seems to be another considerable outburst of growth in length, the rate of increase is less, though with oscillations in the ratio of decline each month up to birth. Weight, according to the above table, increases from impregnation to birth 905,600,000 fold. Here, too, the law of progressive decline is clear. During the first three months,

[1] Ueber die Ursache des Alters. Wiesbaden, 1900, p. 44 *et seq.*

[2] Zeits. f. rat. Med., vol. xx.

weight increases 400,000,000 per cent; during the next three, 5,182 per cent; and during the three preceding birth, but 252 per cent. Thus the new-born child is millions of times heavier than the ovum in which it started, while in the next twenty-five years the adult will become only about twenty times heavier than at birth. At the third month the cells must therefore have divided twenty-two times if we assume their size and weight equal. Such estimates, of course, are only approximate and more or less conjectural, but it is certain that the growth per cent steadily diminishes during each fœtal month. It is as if the nourishment of some of the cells began to suffer very early, and this may perhaps be ascribed to their differing remoteness from nutritive material. On Roux's hypothesis of a struggle for survival between the tissues, organs, and cells of the same body for the available food-supply, some have sought to explain even the development of cavities, folds, and divisions as due to atrophic degeneration of those cells far from the blood-supply. Indeed, Mühlmann goes so far as to say that there is no other cause in pathology for necrotizing processes, than imperfect nutrition. From Weismann's premise that multicellular organisms are differentiated from unicellular by the fact of death, he infers that this latter is due to the symbiosis of the cells, and says "the organism dies because it grows." Growth results in death, or "is constantly digging its own grave." He also infers that the function of cells is determined by their morphologic position in an organism, that it represents nothing more than a phenomenon of growth, and that current teleological points of view are irrelevant. He even reaches the surprising conclusion that some of the chief structural parts of the body, such as the skeleton, muscles, and nervous system, are products of defective nutrition, and their growth is really a regressive accumulation of inferior products. Folds, constrictions, hollows, the separation of organs one from another, which are phenomena of growth, may thus be due to the abortion or non-development of cells which are beyond the reach of food. The difference of distribution of nutritive material also causes great variations in the rate of growth of the different organs after they are once differentiated. Thus growth develops their diverse functions.

At birth the child is cast like a shipwrecked mariner by angry waves on a strange and unknown coast, and finds itself in a new and rigorous climate. Instead of the conditions of fluid pressure equal on all sides, it is now in a stereometric world. Its nascent senses are assailed by new stimuli; the alimentary canal now comes into full function; the lungs are first inflated with a gasp, the occurrence of which is one of the most easily established and important medico-legal facts, connected, perhaps, with the characteristic first note of the human voice, which philosophers since Kant have variously interpreted as a sign of pain, a shout of triumph and joy, or a purely mechanical insentient automatism. It is not strange, therefore, that the new-born child rarely gains, and often loses weight during the first few days, small and especially prematurely born infants usually losing more than large ones. Indeed, with all these profound readjustments, the marvel is that the loss is not greater.

At birth the average and maturely born child, about 19½ inches long, has a little over one-third the length of body it will attain when adult, but its weight must increase nineteen- or twentyfold. During the first year, it grows about nine inches in length and gains about thirteen pounds, or increases less than one-half its length, but much more than doubles its weight. In both respects the absolute gain of the first year is greater than it will be in any other year of life. During the second year the child should grow in height a trifle over five inches and gain four or five pounds, and by two and one-half years of age should have about one-half its adult height and nearly one-fifth its adult weight. From this point on to the prepubescent acceleration, which begins at eleven or twelve in girls and nearly two years later in boys, the percentage of growth in both height and weight is rather constant. There is perhaps a little increase at seven, and a certain and almost universal retardation, most marked about the tenth year, but extending over several years; this depression in the curve some have wrongly thought complemental to its elevation during the period of pubertal increase. Many children suffer slight and more or less prolonged diminution in both rates during dentition, while some show a retardation and others an acceleration, ascribed to the change of habits beginning with school life. At eighteen there is a decided abatement of the energy of growth and an increase of sickness, but one or two years later in boys, especially if under favorable conditions, there often comes a last period of increase, tapering off, some think, asymptoically, but generally with irregularities, a period imperfectly known but of the very greatest interest, to final height in the early twenties. Girls are usually slightly less than boys in both weight and height, and twins than single births. Despite Fasbender's [1] conclusions to the contrary, Boas finds that first-born children exceed those born later, first-born girls excel others from six to maturity, and first-born boys excel from five to fifteen, and perhaps later. The average superiority of the former is 10 mm. in height and 1.6 pounds, and that of the latter 7 mm. and 1.2 pounds.

A literature of some threescore very valuable memoirs and tabulations of human growth is now accessible,[2] to say nothing of a far larger number of miscellaneous records kept in schools, gymnasia, homes, institutions for special classes, etc. Boas has summed up more comprehensively than any one else averages for the rate of growth in height of American children, based upon five of the best special studies of large numbers, viz., in Boston,[3] St. Louis,[4] Milwaukee,[5] Worcester,[6] Toronto,[7] and Oakland, representing in all, 45,151 boys and 43,298 girls. With a very slight modification of the age, these results are presented in the following table, which explains itself:

[1] Zeits. f. Geburtshülfe, vol. iii, p. 286.

[2] Consult for descriptive bibliography as well as for the most comprehensive summary of results Growth of Children in Height and Weight, by Frederic Burk, Am. Jour. of Psy., April, 1898, pp. 253–326.

[3] The Growth of Children, by H. P. Bowditch. Eighth Annual Rep. Mass. State Board of Health.

[4] Growth of St. Louis Children, by William T. Porter. Rep. Acad. of Science of St. Louis, vol. vi, pp. 263–380.

[5] The Growth of Children, by George W. Peckham. Sixth Annual Rep. Wis. State Board of Health.

[6] Anthropometrische Untersuchungen über die Schulkinder in Worcester, Mass., von Gerald M. West. Archiv f. Anthropologie, vol. xxii, 1894, pp. 13–48.

[7] The Growth of Toronto Children, by Franz Boas. Rep. U. S. Com. of Ed., 1896–97, p. 1541.

TABLE I

Approximate average age.	Boys.				Girls.			
	Number of observations.	Average height for each year. Inches.	Absolute annual increase. Inches.	Perc'tage annual increase.	Number of observations.	Average height for each year. Inches.	Absolute annual increase. Inches.	Perc'tage annual increase.
5½...	1,535	41.7			1,260	41.3		
			2.2	5.3			2.0	4.8
6½...	3,975	43.9			3,618	43.3		
			2.1	4.8			2.4	5.5
7½...	5,379	46.0			4,913	45.7		
			2.8	6.1			2.0	4.4
8½...	5,633	48.8			5,289	47.7		
			1.2	2.5			2.0	4.2
9½...	5,531	50.0			5,132	49.7		
			1.9	3.8			2.0	4.0
10½...	5,151	51.9			4,827	51.7		
			1.7	3.3			2.1	4.1
11½...	4,759	53.6			4,507	53.8		
			1.8	3.4			2.3	4.3
12½...	4,205	55.4			4,187	56.1		
			2.1	3.8			2.4	4.3
13½...	3,573	57.5			3,411	58.5		
			2.5	4.3			1.9	3.2
14½...	2,518	60.0			2,537	60.4		
			2.9	4.8			1.2	2.0
15½...	1,481	62.9			1,656	61.6		
			2.0	3.2			0.6	1.0
16½...	753	64.9			1,171	62.2		
			1.6	2.5			0.5	0.8
17½...	429	66.5			790	62.7		
			0.9	1.4				
18½...	229	67.4						

The growth of 742 different Amherst students (classes 1885–1901) measured twice a year by Hitchcock, the American pioneer in this work, shows the following results for later years:

Age.	Number at each age.	Height.		Weight.	
		Actual in mm.	Per ct. increase.	Actual in kilos.	Per cent.
16..........	30	37.23	2.15	8.01	14.51
17..........	134	20.76	1.15	5.30	9.23
18..........	244	13.12	.70	4.56	7.41
19..........	153	7.99	.43	3.18	5.49
20..........	73	7.69	.50	3.31	5.29
21..........	49	6.40	.34	2.87	5.60
22..........	27	5.22	.29	3.98	5.34
23..........	12	4.92	.26	2.03	3.15
24..........	13	3.30	.16	1.92	3.02
25..........	7	4.28	2.42	3.67	6.18
Average.....	..	12.76	.70	4.19	8.45

The majority of observers find the most rapid growth in height from fourteen to fifteen. This is especially apparent in the latest, and in some respects, the most satisfactory, measurements, because all were made on the same 100 boys from thirteen and one-half to eighteen,[1] living under uniform conditions in a military school.

Burk has massed, from some of the data cited, the weights of 24,500 children of Boston, 34,500 children of St. Louis, and 9,600 children of Milwaukee, making 69,000 in all, in such a way that at each age the number of children from each city has been proportionately represented in the result in the following table:

TABLE II

Age.	Boys.			Girls.		
	Average for each age. Pounds.	Absolute annual increase. Pounds.	Annual increase. Per cent.	Average for each age. Pounds.	Absolute annual increase. Pounds.	Annual increase. Per cent.
6½......	45.2	...	...	43.4	...	...
7½......	49.5	4.3	9.5	47.7	4.3	9.9
8½......	54.5	5.0	10.1	52.5	4.8	10.0
9½......	59.6	5.1	9.3	57.4	4.9	9.3
10½......	65.4	5.8	9.7	62.9	5.5	9.6
11½......	70.7	5.3	8.1	69.5	6.6	10.5
12½......	76.9	6.2	8.7	78.7	9.2	13.2
13½......	84.8	7.9	10.3	88.7	10.0	12.7
14½......	95.2	10.4	12.3	98.3	9.6	11.9
15½......	107.4	12.2	12.8	106.7	8.4	8.5
16½......	121.0	13.6	12.7	112.3	5.6	5.2
17½......	.....	....	...	115.4	3.1	2.8
18½......	.....	....	...	114.9	...	...

The results embodied in the above tables are graphically presented in the chart on page 9.

N. V. Zak,[2] e. g., measured the height and chest girths of 1,434 pupils of Moscow Real-schools and 2,811 from classical *gymnasia*.. He finds that height decreases during the day slightly at eleven, much more at fourteen, and less at eighteen, while weight increases also most at fourteen. At every age

[1] P. Godin. La Croissance, pp. 224, Paris, 1903. His results are more fully discussed in the next chapter.

[2] In a volume in Russian, entitled Physical Development of Children in the Secondary Educational Institutions of Moscow. 1892, pp. 271. The chief points and tables have been translated for me by M. de Perott.

these boys are markedly taller than peasant boys. The pubertal increment of growth in height at from thirteen to fourteen is more rapid than that of English, Swedish, or Boston boys, but

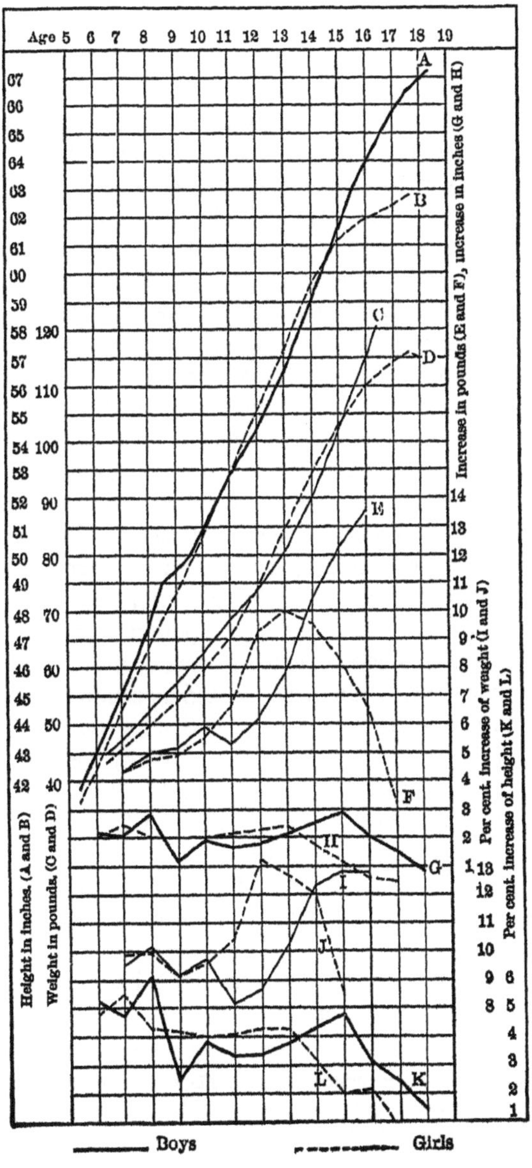

the decline of rate from sixteen on is most marked yet with a tendency to resume growth at twenty-one. Up to eighteen, the more years had been spent in school the greater the average height. The yearly increase in height fell off from nine to ten, and then slowly increased, reaching a marked maximum from thirteen to fourteen, and thereafter falling off more rapidly than it rose. Puberty began from one and one-half to two years earlier among the gymnasiasts than among the rural population, and Jewish boys began their increase in height earliest, and from thirteen to fourteen exceeded all others in rate, but were then overtaken by the Orthodox Russians, whose yearly increment thereafter exceeded to eighteen or nineteen.

Prince N. W. Viasemsky,[1] on measurements embracing 4,872 individuals, not only found periods of acceleration alternating with those of retardation, but thought the latter characteristic of the period of the development of the reproductive organs, which modify profoundly the equilibrium between assimilation and expenditure of energy. He conceived puberty as an acute crisis, and that bad heredity tended either to prematurity or retardation, as well as to intermittence. School had no influence upon those who were robust, but for the feeble it was helpful in approximating their manner of growth to that of those who were strong, or making it more regular. On the whole, he thought school retarded puberty, and also that a period of arrest was compensated by one of more rapid growth. He also found that, while there existed a certain correlation between different measurements, it was of a purely individual character and could not be expressed by any general formula, and that in his physical proportions man did not acquire his true type until this stage of life. The age of eighteen, he found unfavorable and critical in the development of the human organism, generally involving arrest and diminution of activity, as if the energies of growth were exhausted and needed reparation.

In Europe height and weight have been determined in most of the leading countries for yet larger numbers: In

---

[1] Ismenenia organisma v periode sformirovania, or modifications of the organism during the period of puberty from the age of ten to twenty. 278 tables. 43 diagrams. St. Petersburg, 1902.

England, for over 40,000;[1] in Denmark, on 17,134 boys and 11,250 girls;[2] in Freiberg, on 10,343 boys and 10,830 girls;[3] in Sweden, on 15,000 boys and 3,000 girls;[4] in Saalfeld, on 4,699 boys and 4,807 girls;[5] in Moscow, on 3,212 boys and 1,495 girls;[6] in Turin, on 1,048 boys and 968 girls[7] in Lausanne, on 2,000 children;[8] in Hamburg, on 515 boys;[9] in Gohlis, on 1,386 boys and 1,420 girls.[10] These references might be indefinitely extended.[11]

Unless we except the unscientific effort of Lange,[12] whose data include various races for height with little discrimination, and are not worked up according to the scientific methods of modern statistics, there has been no attempt to mass the measurements of all these 138,224 children, and indeed, this would have still less value than the above totalizing of returns from different American cities, on account of the still wider diversity of race and conditions.

---

[1] Report of the Anthropometric Committee of the British Association for 1883, Francis Galton; and Manual of Anthropometry, Charles Roberts. London, 1878.

[2] Report of the Danish Commission, Axel Hertel.

[3] Die Grössenverhältnisse der Schulkinder im Schulinspektionbezirk, Arthur Geissler und Richard Uhlitzsch. Freiberg, Zeits. des K. Sachs. Statistischen Bureaus, vol. xxxiv, 1888, pp. 28-40.

[4] Läroverkskomiténs Betänkande III. Bilage E. Redogörelse för den hygieniska undersökningen afgiven af komiténs ledamot Axel Key. Stockholm, 1885, i, p. 528, with appendix of several hundred tables and curves. Condensed by Burgerstein. Schulhygien. Untersuch. Leipzig, 1889.

[5] Die Körpergrösse und das Gewicht der Schulkinder des Kreises Saalfeld, Emil Schmidt. Archiv f. Anthropologie, vol. xxi, 1892-93, pp. 385-434.

[6] Die Schulhygiene auf der Jubiläumsausstellung der Gesellschaft für Beförderung der Arbeitsamkeit in Moskau, Fr. Erismann. Zeits. f. Schulgesundheitspflege, 1888, pp. 347-373, 393-419.

[7] Die Entwickelung des Menschen in den der Geschlechtsreife vorangehenden späteren Kinderjahren und in Jünglingsalter von 7 bis 20 Jahren, Pagliani.

[8] Körperlänge und Wachstum der Volksschulkinder in Lausanne, Combe. Zeits. f. Schulgesundheitspflege, 1896, pp. 569-589.

[9] Die Körperverhältnisse der gelehrten Schüler des Johanneums in Hamburg, L. Kotelmann. Zeits. des K. p. s. Bur., 1879.

[10] Messungen von Schulkindern in Gohlis-Leipzig, Arthur Geissler. Zeits. f. Schulgesundheitspflege, 1892, pp. 249-253.

[11] Consult on the whole question of growth in height and weight the admirable article and bibliography of Burk, Am. Jour. of Psychol., vol. ix, p. 315 *et seq.*

[12] Die normale Körpergrösse des Menschen, Emil von Lange. München, 1896. He has also constructed a somewhat elaborate *Skala-Messtabelle* for use in families and schools to show the variations within what he deems normal limits from birth to the twenty-fifth year.

From birth to three and one-half, and indeed up to five years, or the beginning of school life, we have measurements on relatively very few children. Toldt and Hecker are still our standards for length, and Schröder and Fehling for weight, during prenatal stages. While there have been many measurements at birth, Quetelet and Zeissing, Camerer, Dafner, and Schmidt-Monnard, the former based on only ten of each age and sex, and all on but very few, are our only authorities for growth during the first and second years. So, too, most of the studies of large numbers stop before the last stages of growth, for which we are perhaps still further from having reliable norms. The English commission and Pagliani began at three and one-half, Peckham at four and one-half, Bowditch, West, and Roberts at five and one-half, but most begin at six or seven, soon after the age of entering school, and at thirteen and one-half some of the most important of these measurements end. From the middle teens on to maturity there are far fewer numbers, so that data beginning for the pre-adolescent increment and the preceding lowered rate of growth are based on the largest numbers. Combe, Geissler, Uhlitzsch, and Landsberger stopped at thirteen, Carstadt and Hertel at sixteen, Gilbert and Erismann at seventeen, Bowditch and Peckham at eighteen, Pagliani, Porter, Kotelmann, Key, and Quetelet at nineteen or twenty. Those that continued weighed and measured small numbers, and even at eighteen results begin to be uncertain, while after twenty they become not only increasingly variable, but sometimes contradictory and even anomalous, some even suggesting a shortening of stature or else early mortality among tall people. Baxter's[1] study of over a million recruits, on the other hand, actually indicates an increase up to thirty-four.

From the standpoint of modern statistical theory, not only the methods of massing large results, but many of the more comprehensive studies of height and weight leave very much to be desired. There is often lack of uniformity in taking measurements, especially where this is done by teachers. Age determinations are often too inaccurate, and frequency of measurements vary. It makes a great difference

[1] Statistics of the Provost-General's Bureau, 2 vols., Washington, 1875.

also whether measurements through the successive years are taken upon the same or upon different children. As Boas, perhaps our best American authority on the treatment of these statistics, points out, "the younger groups contain many individuals who will not reach the adult stage, while the older classes contain only few individuals, who will die before becoming adults." Those who are remote from the average, whether too large or too small, approach pathological conditions and so are more likely to die, and where their measurements are included variations are greater, as is illustrated in the curious decrease in brain weights of males after twenty, due to the exceptional mortality of those with very large brains at about this age. Again, statistics of large numbers contain more of the poorer classes who are smaller at the same age, and among whom there is greater mortality, while the more favored classes found in high schools and colleges are larger. Perhaps, again, weak or small children go to school longer than those that are strong, or stay longer because more slowly promoted, so that the older school children will include an undue proportion of those who are dull and have been sickly. Again, if many children of slow growth should die during adolescence, this might affect the overlapping of the curves of boys and girls, for the amount and duration of the latter's superiority is smaller, the more favorable the conditions of life. Once more, there is a wide difference between a mean and a type. Children of the same racial stock, like, for instance, the tall Swedes, represent a type, as would the smaller Italians or the yet smaller Japanese, but the mean of the two races might find its analogue in an average between dogs and horses which would represent no individual. Every generalization of heterogeneous persons suppresses facts concerning individuals, and to seek a cause for every variation from an average is folly. A type, on the other hand, is a norm to which every individual in a really homogeneous group tends to approach or to vary from, and in a pure race the average persons should be most frequent, and around them others should be grouped closely as well as symmetrically. Any individual, although far from a miscellaneous average, may represent a type and illustrate some tendency away from the average in some new direction, or may even be a sport leading to a new type. Still again, race, climate, poverty or riches, which are known to cause difference for the same age, would almost violate the law of social type; and the theory of least squares has suggested many more or less complicated and interesting modes of treating statistics to determine their real significance so as not only to present, as e. g., by percentile grades, but even to evaluate, the different degrees of departures from the mean.

It is not strange, therefore, that some of the most valuable measurements are those made upon a single child or upon a very few. This method is perhaps best illustrated by Weiner's[1] measurement of the height of each of his four sons from birth to the age of twenty-five years. In the graphic illustration of these results on the opposite page, *A* represents the growth curve of the three older sons, and *B* the absolute annual increase; the heavy line is the oldest, the light the second, the dotted the third son; figures on the left apply to curves *A*, and on the right, to curves *B*. The fourth son, by a different mother, taller and older than the first, follows a different curve in both height and weight.

Camerer,[2] too, has studied his own children, and with the most exact methods, to determine their metabolism, although his best work has been done on infants. Landsberger,[3] followed a few boys for seven years.

It is, however, quite remarkable that whether individuals or large groups are studied, the main characteristics of the curves of growth remain the same for both height and weight, so that we have the following established results: first, as shown in every study since Quetelet, a marked prepubescent acceleration in both height and weight; second, precedence of girls in this accelerated growth by a year or two; third, a period of slightly diminished growth centering about the ages from eight or nine to ten or eleven; fourth, a gradual and probably irregular tapering off of growth in height at about eighteen or nineteen, and to a degree, of

[1] Das Wachstum des menschlichen Körpers, Christian Wiener. Karlsruhe, 1890.

[2] Untersuchungen über Massenwachsthum und Längenwachstum. Jahrb. f. Kinderheilkunde, 1893, pp. 249–293.

[3] Das Wachstum im Alter der Schulpflicht. Archiv f. Anthropologie, vol. xvii, pp. 229–264.

weight a few years later, concerning which much remains yet to be learned; and, fifth, as shown in many but not in all of

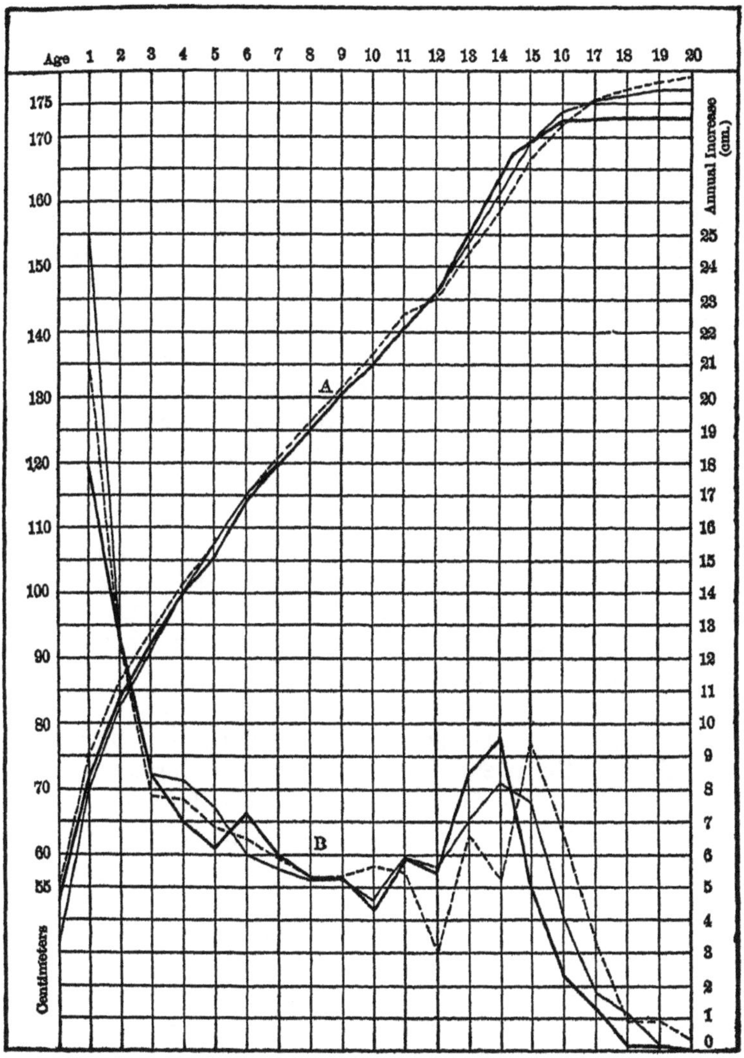

these studies, a very slight retardation near the period of school entrance with an acceleration shortly after. These are centers of interest for our purpose to be considered in some detail.

Bowditch [1] found that the relation of weight and height in growing children is such, that at heights below 58 inches, boys are heavier than girls in proportion to their stature; at heights above this, the reverse is the case. By a supplementary application of Galton's methods to his data still later, he [2] found that the period of pubescent acceleration of growth occurred at an earlier age in large than in small children, or that large children achieve their most rapid growth at an earlier age than small ones; that this growth period differs in larger boys from that in small boys in duration rather than in intensity, and that in girls this difference is not apparent. He also found that at eleven there is a remarkably slow growth in weight and height in both girls and boys, less, in fact, than for several years preceding or subsequent to it, and that in girls a similar but less marked period of retarded growth occurs at nine, but the rate of increase in weight decreases less. The period of female superiority in height was found to be less in tall than in short children, while the female superiority in weight was found to be more marked in heavy than in light children. The author concludes by desiderating annual measurements of not only growth but strength, especially during adolescence, besides annual school examinations, not only the purpose of recording power and size, but to find whether pupils are progressing physically under the environment of instruction, *régime*, etc.

The Milwaukee studies led to the conclusion that boys are taller till the twelfth and heavier till the thirteenth year, but from thirteen to fifteen girls are both taller and heavier; that after fifteen boys exceed in both weight and height, and that girls almost cease to grow at seventeen.

Key found that Swedish boys grow rapidly in the seventh and eighth year. From the ninth to the thirteenth year their rate of growth diminishes, and they may reach almost a standstill at the tenth year, which falls about midway between two periods of growth acceleration. The curve of increase at the fourteenth year is steep and for height, con-

[1] Boston Med. and Surgical Journal, October 19, 1872.

[2] The Growth of Children studied by Galton's Percentile Grades, by H. P. Bowditch. Twenty-second Annual Report Mass. State Board of Health, 1890, pp. 479–525.

tinues through four years, reaching its maximum at the fifteenth and ending with the seventeenth year. Weight increases during all this period, but at first not so fast, and reaches its maximum of rate at the sixteenth year, or one year later than the fastest growth in height. Swedish boys grow heavy fastest in the sixteenth and through a part of the seventeenth year. At seventeen, and on at least to twenty, boys grow in weight more than in height. At eighteen the curve of growth decreases rapidly to a much slower rate. Key's results showed that schoolboys pass through three distinct periods of growth: a moderate increase in the sixth and seventh years, a weaker growth from the ninth to the thirteenth year, and a much more rapid increase in height and weight from the fourteenth to the sixteenth year. The growth of his girls is also periodic, but comes a few years earlier than that of boys. Swedish pass American boys in height and weight in the nineteenth year. The period of growth begins earlier with the well-to-do than with the poorer classes, but is more rapid when it does come, with the latter. The period of diminished growth for girls is like all the other stages, earlier and less marked. Their year of minimum growth is nine. The great acceleration in growth-rate for height begins at the tenth year in Swedish girls from well-to-do families and lasts five years, reaching its maximum at the twelfth, or three years earlier than with boys. At fifteen the curve of growth falls, first slowly and then rapidly, and at seventeen nearly reaches zero. Growth in weight begins at twelve and lasts four years with the maximum at fourteen, which is the year of most vigorous growth in girls. Weight continues to increase rapidly during the seventeenth year, and sinks nearly to zero at twenty, when girls seem to have reached nearly the limit of their physical development. The first menstruation appears from one to two years after the maximum growth in height. For both sexes growth in height precedes that in weight. The superiority of girls over boys in both height and weight lasts five years, or from the twelfth to the seventeenth year, which is much longer than other observers have found. Danish girls, according to Hertel, increase in height most rapidly from twelve to fourteen, and boys from thirteen to sixteen; and in weight, girls increase most from twelve to fifteen, and boys from about thirteen to sixteen or seventeen, and before and after growth is less rapid.

There is much consensus among investigators that from eleven (Bowditch, Geissler, Uhlitzsch, Combe) or twelve, (Key, Hertel) till fourteen (Combe) or even sixteen (Key, Hertel), girls are taller than boys and are then overtaken by them. This is by some thought to be true of all races and classes of society. Only Lange, Quetelet, Liharzik, and Wiener, all of whom measured small numbers, think that in length of body girls remain always behind boys of the same age. Lange points out that the period of excess of girls over boys has been most marked by observers who have studied the hard-working classes, and that it may be exceptional if not abnormal and can not be called as yet established independently of mode of life and social station. While on the whole, the evidence seems to us to point pretty clearly to a more or less prolonged superiority of girls, the question as to whether they actually exceed boys is of much less import than that they have a period of rapid increment and that it precedes that of boys.

Only Quetelet, writing before modern refinements of method and dominated by mathematical theory, who, as we saw, measured only ten individuals of each sex for each year, failed to note this sudden outburst of growth in height or weight. It is, however, not only demonstrated by all careful studies within the last thirty years and patent to common observation, but it is found in savage man and has been observed in several species of animals. Prof. C. S. Minot tells me he noticed this in his elaborate weighings of guinea-pigs,[1] in which puberty occurs at the age of about four months. A much less marked post-pubertal retardation was also noticed. Prof. C. F. Hodge tells me he has noticed the acceleration in dogs, and Dr. Stewart also found it in rats and squirrels. Prof. A. H. Yoder, who weighed white rats daily for a long time, writes me: "I found they grew about three to four days and then rested about the same time. I also found there was an acceleration of growth at puberty.

[1] See also his Senescence and Rejuvenation, p. 133.

Besides physiological changes, the hair grows coarse and is often slightly tinged with brown, and there is a noticeable change in the motions and general appearance." Moon believes that "a corresponding fact is true in regard to horses and some other quadrupeds," and compares boys to Indian corn, which grows most in height when it "shoots and tassels," or reaches its age of puberty.

Of all single measurements, height is the most valuable. It is easily taken, is relatively constant, and not liable to much fluctuation. Along with weight it is the truest expression of the energy of growth, the best index of health, and gives a datum from which, by the use of current norms and standards, many other data can be approximately inferred. It is, moreover, the most distinctly human dimension, as man alone has assumed a fully erect attitude. Some anthropometrists think growth in height to be more or less antagonistic to growth in girth. Hall[1] formulates the following law: "When the vertical dimension of the human body is undergoing an acceleration of its rate of growth, the horizontal dimensions undergo a retardation of their rate of growth," and conversely. The two certainly vary independently, and excess of either may tend to arrest of the other. Height is usually quite complete before twenty-five, while weight may augment indefinitely afterward, and during the years when both are increasing, each appears to have its own season, and the maximum of one more or less coincides with the minimum of the other. Weighing, on the other hand, gives no index of qualitative change. Decay in the most important tissues may be compensated by fat or water, and weight may increase from imperfect elimination of waste. Height once attained can not be reduced save by the slight intervertebral compression of cartilage and muscle, relaxation of fatigue restored daily (more than half an inch, as Bishop and Bradford found by recumbency at night), and by old age; but weight is subject to diurnal and seasonal fluctuations and may be reduced fifty per cent by disease and regained,

[1] W. S. Hall. Changes in the Proportions of the Human Body during the Period of Growth. Jour. of Anthropol. Inst. of Great Britain and Ireland, 1895.

the brain, e. g., in progressive starvation remaining about as little diminished as the bones. Most tissues, however, are subject to many changes and increase slightly in weight with age, as the proportion of solid to fluid matter is augmented.

Imperfect nutrition checks growth in weight more than it does in height, but whether growth in either of these dimensions is preparatory for and conditions growth in the other; whether spring growth in height conditions the autumnal thickening of the body more than the latter conditions the former; whether height is a more vital growth than normal weight; whether we have here two manifestations of one and the same energy, or whether the fact of independent variability means that there are two distinct principles or tendencies, we do not know. If the number of individuals of a given age is distributed over uniform intervals of height and weight, as by the method of percentile grades, it will be seen that the age of greatest growth coincides with that of greatest mean variation from the average size. Although the range of individual deviations from any mean is great, very large or very small persons in both dimensions are extremely rare, and there is a limit beyond which every deviation becomes abnormal and unhealthful. In general, while growth in height is one of the most desirable expressions of vital energy, but few would deny that symmetry and proportion are of at least no less importance. Young people who grow very tall and fail to develop proportionately in thickness later are handicapped in the race of life. Porter well says that the lack of proper relations between height and other physical dimensions is itself ill health. Great height involves increased work for the heart and for the skeletal muscles, and a greater loss of heat, because the surface of the body is larger in tall than in short people of the same weight and bulk. Even on the average, the relation of surface to weight is only about three-eighths in the adult of what it is at birth. The exceptionally tall person, therefore, if not relatively developed in other dimensions, although he may have sufficient income of vitality to meet the demands of life, will fail under strain. Insurance companies discriminate against tall and slender men.

From May, 1882, to February, 1886, Malling-Hansen,[1] director of the deaf-mute institution at Copenhagen, daily weighed 130 of his boys, and for the last two years of that period, daily measured them with well-elaborated precautions to secure uniformity and accuracy. He found that the weight of an average boy from nine to fifteen passed three annual periods of change. The period of greatest growth was from August to the middle of December. During the second four and one-half months till the end of April, growth was of average rate, and it was least for the next three months ending with July. During the maximal period the daily gain was three times as great as in the middle period, while nearly all the gain of the latter was lost in the minimal period. For growth in height, the minimal period begins in August and lasts till near the end of November, the middle period lasts four months till the end of March, and the maximal period lasts four and one-half months to the middle of August. In the middle period the daily increase is twice, and in the maximal, three times as great as in the minimal period. Boys grow thick most slowly while they are growing tall fastest, and vice versa. Increase in weight varies with local temperature, so that all these changes the author ascribes ultimately to the sun.

According to these conclusions, spring growth in height leads with very slight autumnal incremeut in thickness, and a year or two later, the latter predominates and the former ceases. During the annual as distinct from the longer periodic changes in rate of increase, the season of most rapid growth in height is also the period of least growth in weight, and vice versa. To secure this later thickening of the body to due proportions, so as to prevent the wastes and dangers of tallness and slenderness, is one of the most important desiderata of hygiene and body training. To win back the due proportions between height and thickness and to correct those rarer cases when the converse relation exists, Malling-Hansen suggested that children who are in danger of remaining too short and thick go gradually south to warmer

[1] Perioden im Gewicht der Kinder und in der Sonnenwärme. Fragment III, A. Kopenhagen, 1888, pp. 208. Fragment III, B, Atlas 44 Taf.

climates toward the end of summer, when the period of maximal growth in weight comes, and so be removed from the influence of the maximal period of growth in thickness. Conversely, a tall, slender child must be removed from the influence of the maximal period of growth in height by being taken slowly north in April. Travel, he suggested, might thus be prescribed to control growth by following spring or autumn, as height or thickness respectively is desired. The practicability of this remains yet to be tested.

Again, adults probably tend to grow thin at the same period when children tend to grow tall, and also to grow thick when children grow heavy. By choosing the former period for cures, fleshy people can aid nature. School vacations should come at the time of the periods of most rapid growth. Even trees grow tall in May and thick in June, resting in one dimension while the other grows. Finally, children eat most in the winter, beginning in December, and reach a maximum in March, when growth in height begins, so that growth does not immediately follow an increase of food-supply.[1]

Camerer corroborates Hansen's facts of seasonal fluctuation, rejecting his cause. Wahl found that Danish children gained in weight during the summer half-year more than during the winter half-year, and that for children below school age there was also a slight difference in the same direction, which was, however, greatly accentuated at puberty. These conclusions do not quite agree with those of Wretkind, the first in this field, who found that girls over nine, in three Swedish schools, grew in weight relatively more in the three vacation months of summer than they did in the other nine months of the year, and this fact he ascribed to the retarding influences of the school. Vierordt[2] finds weekly or half-

---

[1] Hansen expended vast labor in connection with these studies to establish a curious but now quite discredited theory that growth periods in children, temperature changes in grown women, etc., correspond to a slight periodicity in temperature. This occurrence he thought world-wide and due to the revolutions of the sun every twenty-seven and one-half days, and he constructed an outline of the solar corona of a shape needed for his hypothesis. His own voluminous curves are, however, mostly twenty-five-day periods, while many of them can hardly be distinguished from the lunar periods of twenty-eight days.

[2] Physiologie des Kindesalters, von K. Vierordt. Gerhardt's Handbuch der Kinderkrankheiten, vol. i, pp. 228–236.

weekly periods repeating themselves, so that healthy children are constantly fluctuating.

Many studies show a diminished rate of growth in both height and weight during a few years preceding adolescence. In general, the decrease begins at six or seven and continues with various oscillations until about ten in girls and twelve in boys. Various observers find a period ending at the seventh or eighth year, when the brain has about ceased to grow in weight. Peckham and Vierordt make this age, which about coincides with second dentition, a period by itself. Up to its close, despite the fluctuations, there is relative uniformity of rate, and boys and girls differ but little. West found this age of retarded growth rather uniform, but thought the great diversities that begin with pubescent growth due to heredity and environment. Nearly all the best researches reveal this diminished rate of growth in height and also in weight. Even although the absolute increment is maintained during these minimal years, the percentage rate is usually diminished. The same retardation is also manifest in nearly all returns for weight, although it can not be determined whether height or weight have precedence in this retardation, and this holds for individual as well as mass measurements.

Vierordt thought he discriminated seven growth periods; Liharzik,[1] twenty-four; Zeissing, three; Cohn, two; Key and Lange, four. On Minot's assumption of senescence as a constantly increasing arrest of growth culminating in degeneration, these rhythms may be conceived as oscillations between two opposing tendencies. This author does not use his hypothesis, however, to account for rhythms, nor is there ground to urge that retarded growth at ten or eleven suggests senescence so much as a diversion of growth energy from other fields. It is a little as if the processes of assimilation made a sudden advance, extending their conquest over non-living substance, and then paused to organize the new acquisition; or else, if it be established that periods of increased food consumption precede growth increments by a considerable period, as if the ashes and cinders of the biological furnace are first removed with exceptional thoroughness to prepare for the extension of life's

[1] Das Gesetz des Wachstums und der Bau des Menschen, etc. Vienna, 1862.

combustion to new fuel, so that vitality is first thus raised to a higher level, itself an expensive process, and then the mass it animates is augmented. This is different from the decay of old age, when many cells die from overspecialization, in that it is not compensated and it also is arrest at the bottom rather than at the top of the scale of complexity. Even in the segmentation of the ovum, there is a rhythm of fast and slow and a marked oscillation about the sixth fetal month. Pauses may be to permit adaptation of new-grown cells, tissues, or organs to each other and to the environment. That the amount and time of retardation is exactly compensated during periods of augmentation is a theory that at present lacks confirmation, approximate as this may be for normal individuals. Moreover, there seem to be norms of rates and seasons of growth from which organisms can only with difficulty be much diverted without distinct compensatory tendencies. As in convalescence not only lost flesh but growth is often made up, so hardship, malnutrition, etc., may retard for a time, only to be followed by compensatory acceleration, all the more rapid if the delay has been prolonged up to a certain point, a point probably itself variable. As to whether causes that result in excessive and premature growth tend to react in stationary periods, the evidence is less clear. We also often see what seems to be an illustration of the law laid down by St. Hilaire, that growth in size and in function are inversely to each other, so that when either is progressing rapidly the other tends to be stationary, and the alterations here are often rhythmic, like those between growth in size and in weight.

Will retarded growth be made up or compensated for later? Key thinks that where children grow slowly owing to hard conditions during their earlier years, they will catch up later and end their growth with others who have been more favored. All who have weighed and measured large numbers in such a way that their results bear on this question, indicate, as we have seen, a certain elastic resilient tendency, at least to resume, if not to complete, interrupted or delayed growth, somewhat as the emaciation of disease is compensated. There is reason to believe that weight gained near the normal period for its most rapid increment is more likely to be retained permanently, especially if the muscles are mainly concerned, than if it is won later. We should infer that growth was most advantageous when it was most timely and when the latent energy of tissue-producing power was normal. The opinion which some have held that where one or even several generations have been kept down by hardship, their descendants tend to regain the former height of their race if conditions become favorable, rests on too slight evidence, and indeed seems to have been suggested by the phenomena of alternation of generations.

Concerning the later stages of growth, the data are insufficient and opinions are contradictory. Quetelet, influenced again, no doubt, in part by his mathematical formulæ of growth, thought both sexes might continue to grow a little in height till twenty-five, and in weight till perhaps thirty. Liharzik thought growth continued in both sexes till twenty-four or twenty-five, Villerme till twenty-three. Zeissing thinks twenty-one is the time of cessation in growth of both sexes. Venn finds moderate growth in height in male students at Cambridge, England, up to twenty-three, and in weight to twenty-four. Hall finds that boys drop to a very slow rate of increase in height at eighteen, but continue to grow at about that rate for three years; and that in weight, their rate of increase is retarded from eighteen to twenty and then starts up again. The Anthropological Committee concludes that after a retardation at eighteen, boys increase in weight at nineteen or twenty and continue to grow till twenty-three or twenty-four, and that girls pause at nineteen without entirely ceasing to grow, but go on a little more at twenty or twenty-one. Key finds not an entire cessation of growth, but a distinct retardation in weight and height at eighteen or nineteen, with indication of later increment. Roberts asserts an "entire cessation" of growth in the non-laboring classes of England at nineteen, but thinks in the artisan class, growth is more uniform and extends to the twenty-third year. Smedley [1] found that girls grew in height at

[1] Report of the Department of Child Study and Pedagogic Investigation, Chicago, No. 2.

a rather uniform but reduced rate from fourteen to seventeen, when they had practically attained their highest stature, and that from just before nineteen until after they were twenty, boys did not grow in height. Beyer thinks that the naval cadets at Annapolis for thirty years show an almost steady increase in weight from fifteen to twenty-three, amounting in all to thirty-seven pounds, and that growth in height shows marked retardation at eighteen; that then comes another increase, closing at twenty-one, and later a third increase, ending perhaps with growth of span of arms at twenty-three. He also infers that tall boys complete their growth earlier than short boys, but that tall and heavy boys are more likely to increase under the influence of gymnastics than those that are small, and that the ratio of increase in height and girth is different in these two classes. Lange thinks there may normally be an infinitesimal growth till senescence, and that it tapers off asymptotically, and one writer conjectures that by this increment, civilized man is slowly growing larger, and that we should so live as to keep on growing till the age of forty-nine, when Plato thought man attained his highest development. Early Amherst reports showed that students, as a rule, do not grow in height from eighteen to nineteen, but that some increase up to twenty-five. Several of the best American colleges report cases of growth of from one-third of an inch to a little over one inch in half a year after eighteen, a result that is ascribed to physical training. Large boys seem not only to achieve their adolescent growth earlier than small ones, but are more likely to keep on growing.

Dr. Edward Hitchcock, who still measures Amherst students and has made many reports, while admitting the meagerness of his numbers for the later years of growth, writes me: "I can only say that growth, in our observations, continues up to twenty-six years of age, whether longer or not our data do not show." Beyer, perhaps our most competent authority upon this point, writes me that in a list of height averages based upon 8,000 accepted recruits, it appears that while there is no increase from twenty-four to twenty-five (nearest birthday), there is an increment of one-tenth of an inch at the twenty-sixth year, but that the height then attained is not exceeded by any age up to thirty-five, which is as far as his work has been carried. He says we know "that exercise has been followed by a very slight increase in height in some rare instances at a late period in life," and suggests that, if poor personal hygiene or bad conditions prevented men from attaining predestined height during the usual periods of growth, the change to more favorable influences "may cause a reawakening of dormant, undeveloped centers and in this manner aid nature in making up for lost opportunities at a later period than is usual."

Dr. D. A. Sargent, of Harvard, whose data published and unpublished are of the highest value, writes: "Men usually cease growing in height at about twenty-three, but continue to increase in weight up to fifty. It is a question, however, whether most of the weight accumulated after twenty-five is not more or less abnormal. It may be, however, that this is nature's way of conserving the body's heat and storing up excessive carbon to meet the demands of advancing age."

Prof. J. W. Seaver writes me that from his data based on Yale men he can "not find an age when there is not a small increment in height or weight, although this is very small after twenty-three years of age. The growth curves of the mass taper off gradually, but those of individuals nearly all show spasmodic growth. As the periods of growth and rest come at irregular intervals in different individuals, I think they tend to neutralize each other in the mass. Persons taking the least exercise grow least, but the opposite is only partially true. The athletes grow more than 'high stand' men taking certain severer courses that are confining in their nature. These show slight or no average growth, the slight gain in the few being neutralized by the loss in the others."

From data and opinions so diverse, no inferences of scientific validity can be drawn, and we have little settled knowledge of the laws of growth after eighteen. That there is a general retardation about this age is probable. That there is a later upward tendency in weight in boys can hardly be doubted, and the same is probable to a much less extent in height. Growth seems also to have a far wider range of individual variation as its momentum diminishes near its terminal stages, than earlier in life. It is not unlikely, too, that as a spent ball is more easily stopped or turned, so the later stages of growth are more easily prevented by improper diet or hygienic conditions, excess or defect of exercise, excitement, overpressure in school, vice, or possibly they are transformed into some kinetic equivalent of function, reproductive, motor, or assimilative, etc.

It is hard to realize the complexity of processes involved in the term growth, and yet there is a point beyond which oversubtle methods of weighing and even measuring are mere pedantries. If a child lived in a glass case on the arm of a sensitive balance, and every respiration and all its insensible perspiration, as well as all food and secretions, could be weighed, measured, and chemically analyzed with the utmost accuracy, tentative determinations already made in this direction show that we might be able to estimate to an extent as yet by no means attained, how much loss of each kind was caused by emotional strain or by mental activity, and just when and under what functional and other conditions, growth occurred. But even this interesting physical biography could never tell us what organs were growing large or heavy, or what, if any, small, or which took up and vitalized the ingesta, and in which loss exceeded profit in the chemical bookkeeping of metabolism. The body contains matter in all degrees of organic assimilation, from food just taken and excrement, up to the most controlling parts of the cells in the highest tissues. Cell nuclei or nucleoli, leucocytes, or other invisible and hypothetical chemical components, perhaps brain-cells or the reproductive elements, or whatever else may be thought to be at the high-water mark of organization, and so most vitalized and dynamic, represent a very different level of life and are perhaps as much above simple and lower structures, like bone and connective tissue, as these are above fat, or fat itself above the chip pile of products of decomposition awaiting removal. Individuals differ immeasurably in their nutritive plane; and water and fat, urea and other low-level and waste products may accumulate by reason of imperfect elimination. Growth is really the formation of new cells, the development of cells from granules or, as is more common near the end of the growth period, the further increase in size of cells already well developed. It is these processes that are chiefly sought, and other factors included in growth in weight are not true growth but, in a sense and in varying degrees, errors to be overcome.

Of what actually goes on in the body, then, we know relatively little. No admittance is, as some one has said, the sign which nature hangs out to the physiologist. Could we weigh or measure the gain or loss on any of its higher planes, we might find very different laws of growth. We may conceive our ego as limited by the dermal surface and as scarcely even perforated by the twenty-two foot alimentary canal. We can not say just when the food we take becomes no longer a foreign substance to be acted on, but part of the true physical self, and endowed itself with assimilative power, nor can we say when tissues on the down road of decay cease to be so, any more than the psychologist can tell when the matter of apperception becomes an organ of it. The suggestion is obvious, however, that seasons of rest between growth periods may be times of the greatest qualitative improvement, when what we may call the higher digestion augments the complexity of structure and assimilative processes are carried on upon a higher plane, and all by the same growth impulse as its kinetic equivalent of augmentation in bulk. Of such changes, however extensive or important, determinations of the mass of the body as a whole can give no intimation. Of the laws and processes of growth in individual tissues and organs, our knowledge is but limited, and of those in chemical complexity, we know still less, and yet it is not improbable that these more specific and higher changes are more closely related to psychic development than is growth in height and weight. Mass, cytological change, and chemical complexity and functions, then, are the three factors or dimensions of growth, and many of the mysteries in which it is now shrouded will remain unsolved till we know more of the last two and of their relations. Studies of fatigue and all we know of metabolism indicate that the second factor is far more variable, especially within short periods, than mass, as well as far more closely associated with function.

The rate of growth is a result of many determinants. Race and heredity seem to decree for every individual being an approximate ultimate size, and the way in which total growth is distributed over the years in which it occurs, is one of the most characteristic expressions of heredity. This seems to prescribe and ordain almost with an aspect of fatality, as if every person and part strove to attain a certain size decreed by ancestral ids and determinants, which, although due to a less fundamental momentum than that which determines the species, is hard to modify much by training or even environment. In this factor many anthropologists are chiefly interested and many general and special anthropometric inquiries are undertaken in quest of purer and more aboriginal race types. The Patagonians, the North American Indians, especially the Mississippi tribes, and the Scotch are perhaps the tallest, with Swedes, Norwegians, and white Americans as close seconds; while the African dwarfs, Japanese, Eskimos, South Italians, Bushmen, West Africans, Malays, French, and Spaniards are among the shortest races of men. So far as we know not only after, but before puberty these relations are tolerably maintained. Next at least to hair and eyes, stature is thought to be fundamentally determined by race. Women more nearly attain the stature of men among savages than among civilized races, a fact against the theory of progressive equalization of the sexes. Natural as distinct from forced emigrants, Ripley [1] thinks taller than the "stay-at-homes." Long-headed or dolichocephalic races are taller than brachycephalic or broad-headed races, and the former seem to have been on the whole represented by the more energetic and civilized peoples, and, some anthropologists add, are characterized by more vigor of limb and energy of action. While city life tends to shorten stature, the city is fed by the tallest youth from the country. Most of the human race are between five feet and five feet ten inches, so that with all the causes of variation, the human species is quite uniform as compared with many animal types. According to Bowditch, American boys are taller and heavier than English boys of the non-laboring classes in public schools and universities, the superiority being somewhat greater in weight than in height. He also found that the greater height and weight of Amer-

[1] Racial Geography of Europe. New York, 1900.

ican over Irish children was due more to race than to occupation. Incidentally Peckham found that urban life tends to decrease stature and that intermarriages between Germans and Americans were advantageous because children tend to reach the height of the tallest parent.

While American boys are taller and heavier than others during pubescent years they excel only for a few years, and at nineteen are overtaken and surpassed by Swedish, Danish, and Dutch boys, while Belgian boys and those of northern Italy remain the smallest of those whose growth has been carefully studied. In the same way, Swedish girls excel those of other nationalities, both in height and weight, except during a few pubescent years. Key thinks for both sexes and in both height and weight, growth ceases earlier in Italy and America than elsewhere. Retardation by poverty is most marked in Italy and England, and least so in the United States. Racial influences upon both weight and height seem to assert themselves strongly at puberty.

It has long been held that increase of comfort increases stature and weight. Quetelet was the first to demonstrate this by comparing the measurements of factory children with those of others more favored. Key concludes that in nearly all lands "the weak period of development before puberty is lengthened for the poorer children to their cost," and that the prepubescent growth comes later but is more sudden, so that poor and well-to-do children end their growth about the same time. Some infer that boys are more influenced by this than girls, as they seem to be by many other of the factors of environment. Bowditch concluded that the superior size of children of American parentage in the Boston schools is partly due to the greater comfort and partly to race, but thinks the former more potent than the latter. In England, Roberts found that in the better classes, prepubescent growth began a year or two earlier than among laborers, and that the former were more variable in height and at least two inches taller. The anthropometric committee's study in England found that boys from the better classes at ten were 3.31 inches taller and 10.64 pounds heavier than industrial schoolboys, and at fourteen they were 6.65 inches taller and 21.85 pounds heavier. In Leipzig, children paying eighteen marks school-fees are superior in height to those paying nine marks, and *gymnasia* boys exceed those of the *Real* and *Burger* schools for the same reason. The same difference has been found very marked in Russia, Stockholm, and Turin. As Burk well points out, however, the poorer classes from ten to seventeen, the ages best studied, grow at quite as rapid and often a more rapid rate than those of the favored classes. Their absolute increment may be the same or even greater, but the conditions existed earlier and they were already smaller before observation began, so that defective nutrition may have its chief effects in the earlier years or even during embryonic life, but figures are, however, too small to warrant conclusions for these earliest years. Weight seems at least quite as much if not more affected by social condition than height, although its chief effects are manifested in both after the period of pubertal acceleration.

When we turn to the effects of different kinds of food upon growth, results are difficult of interpretation. Hansen studied in a deaf-mute asylum in Copenhagen the effects of a change of diet, from one consisting chiefly of black bread and beer to one made up of bread and milk and richer in albumen. The seventy boys together gained 105 pounds more under the new diet, but did it all in the six weeks from October eleventh to November twenty-second. All the rest of the six months' growth was unaffected, so that on the whole he thinks food had no effect and he urges that weight is no true index of essential growth. It has also been demonstrated in many cases that poor children brought into a better nutritive environment grow more rapidly than those who remain in unchanged conditions. In Russia, an elaborate experiment on the relative growth of weight in about fifty infants fed exclusively from the breast and those fed artificially, seemed on the whole rather favorable for the latter food, but this may have been because the former was scanty.

That perverse or defective nutrition tends to retard growth and to delay the characteristic growth periods and also that the final size attained is thus reduced, seems also established with great probability. Excessive functional activity probably has the same tendency, as growth and work, while mutually helpful up to a certain very variable point, become antagonistic beyond it. Disease retards, while health and growth go together. Some seasons make for growth and others for retardation. Combe thinks that boys born between September and February are shorter than those born between March and August, while girls born from December to May are shorter than those born during other seasons.

Thus we must conceive growth as due to an impulse which, despite its marvelous predeterminations, is exceedingly plastic to external influences, a few of which can be demonstrated and more have to be assumed. The Heraclitic fire of life as thus observed is like a sensitive flame burning now high, now low; swerving under various influences; its combustions or oxidizations now faster, now slower; always true to its own laws, but in its rhythms infinitely more delicately responsive to everything in the environment than we have dared to dream. To the inner assimilative and dissimilative processes, which physiological chemistry alone can ever hope to unravel and which underlie all morphologic and perhaps even functional changes, there is strong reason, as we shall see later, to ascribe a susceptibility of incredible fineness, due at bottom to the growth impulse in conflict with the vast variety of obstacles on which it impinges.

The effects of climate, which have been insufficiently studied, are sometimes difficult to separate from those of work and rest. Low temperatures involve kinetic energy to maintain heat, and larger quantities of food must be provided. Its indirect influence in affecting mode of life, food, etc., must be of itself great, while the earlier age of puberty in most warm climates would suggest earlier completion of growth. No doubt there is an optimum temperature most favorable to the highest human development and also a limit of variation beyond which retardation is caused. The studies of the effects of temperature upon the growth of lower animal forms are interesting here.[1]

[1] See also The Migratory Impulse *vs.* Love of Home, by L. W. Kline (Am. Jour. of Psy., October, 1898), which shows the inferior stature of the inmates of truant schools, and how low nutrition breeds discontent and the tendency to run away.

In view of all we know of the influences affecting growth, the problem whether ultimate size can be otherwise much controlled, except by avoiding certain known causes of arrest, need not concern us. Interesting as it is and despite Hansen's suggestion above of migration, it may seem to some to lie rather in the realm of some modern analogue of Plato's republic than in that of science. But Boveri found that each half of a fertilized ovum in lower forms produced a complete individual but of half size. Bizzozero, Yung, De Varigny, and others have found that by increasing heat and blood pressure, organs of growing animals could be greatly increased in size, and that the ultimate size of snails and tadpoles was increased with the size of the vessel containing them. The results of thyroid feeding; the greater size of plain dwellers as compared with their congeners among the hills, and of boys bred in the country over those in the city; all the results which Lamarckians claim for use and disuse, and those urged by physical trainers for college youth as the results of judicious exercise; the effects of the misery spots of the world; the increase of size claimed to follow the increased prosperity of a country; the tendency of offspring of mixed races toward the size of the tallest parent; and other facts of this order, suggest hopeful auguries for the future when man shall have more fully domesticated himself in the school of civilization; the home, city, and nation of Hygeia shall become a reality; and also all known principles of human stirpiculture in selecting partners and in marriage regimen shall be put in practise.

Is the race or are Americans growing? Dr. Anderson, the physical instructor of Yale, thinks that the Yale men of to-day average nearly an inch taller than those of twenty years ago, also that they are heavier and more muscular. Mr. Goldie, for thirty-four years gymnastic director at Princeton, says that thirty years ago the average student was five feet seven or seven and one-half inches tall and weighed about one hundred and forty pounds, whereas to-day the average student measures five feet eight or eight and one-half inches and weighs not less than one hundred and forty-five pounds, and goes so far as to predict that, if this rate of development is maintained, in 1950 the average student will be six feet tall and will weigh one hundred and sixty pounds. Prof. P. C. Phillips, of Amherst, thinks that the young women in our colleges to-day are "almost certainly an inch taller and four or five pounds heavier than they were ten years ago." "The young man of to-day," he says, "at every age is taller and heavier than the man previous to 1894, the difference as a rule amounting to an inch in height and three pounds in weight." The average height of the American soldier is five feet seven and one-half inches in his stockings. He is both heavier and taller and has larger chest girth than the soldier of any other country save only Scandinavia. Professor Donath's statistics suggest that in most European lands height and weight are slightly decreasing. These opinions we must accept with caution, for not only must measurements be very carefully correlated with age, often increasing in college, but with the fact that college environment is more and more favorable to growth, and we must also have homogeneous classes and races as a basis of comparison. Certainly an inch or even half an inch in twenty years, which would make five, or two and one-half inches per century, is quite incredible. If man has developed from a pigmoid and is still growing, it must be at a vastly slower, and probably with data at hand, an almost insensible rate.

Is a period of rapid growth advantageous or would it be better if the curve of height and weight were a straight line, as, previous to the measurements above described, it had been generally supposed to be? While this question can not be answered, it suggests important theoretical and practical considerations. If there were danger of stagnation or of becoming hidebound on the lower level of ten to twelve years, if an equilibrium within and without were liable to be established here, it is not impossible that there might be physiological advantage in growing part by part or by the method of what is known as nascent periods. If, for instance, the bones grow first and tense the muscles causing growing pains, as often occurs, the latter are thus stimulated to further growth. If fundamental joints and muscles grow first, then the apparatus of the finer accessory system is stimulated to restore the old proportion so that we can act as deftly when we are large as we do when we are small. Fat accumulation often precedes growth in height, especially in girls, as if the body were provisioning for an advance movement. Structure and function, body and mind, weight and height, may thus each act as a leverage for the increment of the other, if we assume a tendency always to restore the lost equilibrium, and after a fall, to find at-one-ment on a higher plane. Thus it may be that if we could measure kinetically all the energies of growth, their summation would still be represented by a straight line, and the height and weight augmentation be only an accident of our as yet inadequate knowledge and methods of measuring all the expressions of growth. On the other hand, phenomena like acromegalia and perhaps genius in one direction with defect in others, and many other morbid phenomena, indicate, as we shall see later, that growth may be disequilibrated and become so excessive in one part or function that others can not be brought into harmony with it or they may even retrogress because left too far behind in the intersystemic competition for nutriment or power.

Is the utmost possible growth desirable? This presents a vast but hitherto unsolved problem. On the one hand, Bohannon[1] has shown that children who are especially tall or heavy for their age are dressed and treated as if they were older, associate with those more mature, and more is expected of them on account of their size. They are more likely to be leaders, to have undue attention, and are so treated as to bring early maturity. Children unusually small of their age, on the other hand, often associate with and dress like those younger than they, and less is expected, so that retarded development often results. Thus, if Porter's inference, that large children are intellectually superior to small ones, is confirmed, it may be at least partly due to artificial, and not to natural causes, and the popular conception that rapid growth is likely to be attended by sluggish mentality may yet be true to nature.

The Chicago studies of Christopher and Smedley in general favor Porter's conclusions. Although often the best

[1] Ped. Sem., vol. iv, p. 3 *et seq.*

pupil in a room is the smallest and perhaps the youngest, these constitute a class by themselves, deserving, like all exceptions, special consideration. Christopher says: "Such children can not be considered normal, and I venture the assertion that the true explanation of them will be found to be of greater medical than pedagogical interest."

Porter found that children who make the best progress in their studies are on the average larger in girth of chest and width of head than children whose progress is less satisfactory. Successful pupils are larger than unsuccessful, but the comparative rate of growth, the age at which increase begins, and the point where girls most exceed boys is about the same for dull, mediocre, and precocious children, at least from seven to sixteen years of age.

Professor Beyer[1] concludes that "the relationship between physique and mental ability is such that the training of the one will indirectly and favorably influence the growth and development of the other, when the training of either is kept within physiological limits." He supports Porter's conclusion that "precocious children are heavier and dull children lighter than the mean child of the same age," against Boas, who states "in fact, an investigation which I have carried on in Toronto with the same object, but according to a different method, gives just the reverse results. The data were compiled by Dr. G. M. West, who found that the children pronounced by the teacher bright were less favorably developed than those called dull." Beyer[2] examined and marked 76 applicants for positions as navy-yard apprentices, and concluded that for them, weight has great significance in judging the physique of a young person and consequently his capacity for mental work, again supporting Porter's studies of precocity and dulness.

Desirable as generous size is, it has its limits. Large animals move slowly, are inexact, clumsy, with less fine control, so that size often seems at the expense of function. Galton found tall men somewhat less fertile than short men. Giants not only lack vigor of mind, body, or both, but are

[1] Jour. of the Boston Soc. of Med. Sciences, April, 1901.

[2] The Relation between Physique and Mental Work. Jour. of the Boston Med. Soc., February 20, 1900.

often marked by stigmata of degeneration or reversion, while restricted growth in both the brute and human world often coincides with great activity. It is not demonstrated that the largest brains as such are best, or that large views, great moods, and wide ideas are more natural in large bodies. Size has certainly great natural advantages not only among animals and savages, but among civilized races. It insures a certain natural prestige and authority and awakens in others the necessity of recognizing leadership, favors dominating manners, and inclines to the assumption of superiority and the subordination of others. Large men can put forth more strength absolutely than small men, but whether relatively, is very doubtful. It is a wide-spread opinion among army surgeons that small, slight men can endure hardships best; that large, muscular men are more likely to succumb to epidemics and to other diseases; that even slightly undersized, if sound, men are best for hard service. In many, if not most diseases incident to army life, and particularly fevers, large men are sick longer and are more liable to die. On the Greely expedition most of the large men died and nearly all the survivors were small. Well-proportioned "doughboys," or raw infantry of middle weight, are said to endure more time work, hunger, heat, and exposure than large athletic men, although the latter may put forth most active energy for a limited time.

Small as well as homely and insignificant men have a special motive to assert themselves functionally to offset their disadvantages of structure. Large men are more frequently found among natural, self-made pioneers, chiefs, bosses, captains of industry, and perhaps, though neither is demonstrated, experts and specialists are on the average smaller and possibly less handsome and well proportioned, frequent as the exceptions are. Small men certainly are apt to be quick in their rhythms, while large men move slowly in mind and body but carry more momentum. On the whole, perhaps we may conclude that in the economy of nature, height and weight much above the average are liable to be bought at too great a cost of function. As Beyer, whose opinion is entitled to great weight, writes me, the results of the battle of life "point to the average of the race as being the goal to strive for with regard to growth." On the other hand, as he adds:

"If we find the leaders of a race which is on the march to a higher plane of human development to be larger than the average or the fifty column in percentile grades, then the latter acquire a different significance; instead of being the fittest to survive they only do so by virtue of the protection afforded them by the superior qualities of the advanced guard, without which they would have to retreat with numerical losses. According to this same figure, those below the average would represent that portion of the population that is unable to keep up with the procession owing either to hereditary or accidental causes, and for whom we build hospitals, asylums, sanatoria, etc." Dr. Sargent writes me: "In my opinion, the greatest possible development of body, mind, or 'soul' is undesirable, inasmuch as neither condition can be attained in man, a composite being, without dwarfing or impairing the condition of the other two. For this reason, to quote your own language, 'physical culture should be chiefly directed to building up average dimensions' of the masses that are in our schools and colleges. By pursuing this method I think the best results may be eventually attained for the race if not for the individual."

In discussing the desirability of maximal growth we must reflect, on the one hand, that if the earlier stages of growth relatively represent what man has in common with animals, and its last stages raise him above them and make him most distinctively human, then this question must be answered in the affirmative, because the most perfect individual is the one most completely evolved. Certainly we want all that our heredity entitles us to, and perhaps a little extra for progress or even for selfishness of the Max Stirner type. Indeed, one might ask why man should stop growing at all, and not progress at least slowly to near the end of his life like extinct Saurians; as, indeed, his heart often does. On the other hand, as we have seen giants and monsters become unfertile and we are unable to bring at-one-ment between the greatest individual development and the highest interest of the race to which it should be subordinated. Possibly mankind may sometime learn the secret of progressively harmonizing the two. Meanwhile egoism can only say that maximal growth is desired if it is in every way proportionate and harmonious, and if it is chiefly growth of the best tissues, be they reproductive, cerebral, or muscular. To assert that maximimal mass growth for the individual or for our race in the future is desirable, would involve the evaluation of all the functions—physical and psychic—that make human life. Although growth upward out of the womb of nature is the one miracle of the world and its direction is the only clue to human destiny, yet progress and the highest human evolution may, for aught we know, be carried too far for other greater issues, so that on the whole we are hopelessly agnostic in the presence of this question. If it be found, as Beyer, Galton, and others think, that most of the present leaders of mankind are somewhat above the average height and weight on the percentile scale, so that the large people are bearing the burden of the forward march of humanity, it would indeed appear that those below the average size are followers and are somewhat sheltered and protected in the wake of these leaders, and if so, then the race is tending slowly but surely upward in size, and if the reverse be true it is tending downward.

According to current biological conceptions the soma or cells which make up the organs of the body, in contrast with those devoted to reproduction, become specialized for particular purposes, very gradually in the evolutionary processes and, somewhat in proportion as they do so, slowly lose reproductive power. In the mitosis involved in tachygenesis cells continue to divide, but with ever less rejuvenative energy. Even in the child, each cell can produce only a few generations of daughter-cells, and as differentiation and integration proceed, the momentum given to them at impregnation is gradually lost. In old age the body desiccates, specific gravity increases as does low-level connective tissue, and thus death or a corpse of lived-out organs is evolved. Even in maturity, body cells repair lost tissue in man and lost limbs in animals, as they recover from fatigue, etc. All this is in progressive contrast with the capacity for indefinite reproduction in the lowest forms of life and in the sexual elements in man which are relatively immortal, because these cells continue to multiply by division indefinitely.

From this familiar consideration it follows that in the

earlier processes of the evolution of the soma there must be many cells which have already acquired some definiteness by departure from the general type, and which although already more or less set apart for particular functions have not entirely lost the germinant expansion of the purely reproductive elements, and under certain conditions may revert to it. Many lower forms reassume growth if reproductive activity is checked, while the latter tends to arrest growth. Hard conditions favor early sexual maturity, and overnutrition, as is well known, may diminish reproductive vigor. Thus genesis and individuation beyond a certain point are in inverse ratio to each other. Giants and monsters among men and animals have low generative activity, while both precocity and early dissipation are unfavorable for growth. Hence we can insist that there is a sense in which the growth of the soma itself may almost be regarded as a secondary sexual quality, and growth can be conceived in a large way as a product of reproduction, or the latter as a special or primitive form of growth. From the flagella up, hunger and love preside over the evolution of the body. Special organs are developed either to reach food, hold it, digest it, etc., or else to reach or hold the female for impregnation or, irradiating more widely, with which to fight for mates or to charm them as by colors, wattles, antlers, plumes, and all the love antics of animal or human courtship. Not only this, but man's pristine and deepest psychic instincts are developed primarily to serve the rising generation by providing food, shelter, nursing, education, and instruction; and even the length of life, as Weismann has shown, is so adjusted as to be continued beyond the age of greatest fertility only just as long, on the average, as is necessary to bring the young to full maturity. Thus not only the form, organs, and functions of the adult, but his term of life is regulated to meet the necessities of reproduction and of education, which are in a sense a *continuum*.

Bearing these general considerations in mind, let us now proceed to inquire whether we can offer any explanation of the singular but almost universal retardation just before the pubescent outburst of growth, and of the great increment which follows it in the earliest teens. First, all measurements agree, as we have seen, that girls precede boys in the period of maximal growth if not in that of retardation just before. No one, to my knowledge, has seriously attempted to account for this interesting and challenging fact. Lange says it is accidental; several have vaguely intimated that it may have been nature's design that the human female, charged with larger functions and organs of reproduction than the male, was intended to be larger than he, as in the case of the queen bee and many other lower forms of life. She is anabolic, and should normally not have only preceded but exceeded man in height and weight through life, but from some unknown cause, this tendency is arrested and man reassumes the lead in the middle teens. This view is purely speculative and we need hardly consider it here, because this would make man an exception to the almost universal law of mammalian life, where the female is inferior in size.

We may, however, look in another direction for an at least hypothetical explanation. If man has developed from an animal stage of existence to savagery, it seems plausible from what we know of primitive races, phallicism, etc., that the female would at first be prematurely impregnated, at least as soon as she became attractive to the other sex, on account of the hypertrophied sex passion in the human male, and would have been forced to assume maternal functions before nature had completed her preparations therefor. Many of the institutions of higher and even of savage life, however, later came in that would tend to postpone fertilization. Thus we should have an early stimulus of the reproductive function followed phyletically by a more or less gradual postponement of it. With this delay, the cell development that had formerly gone to genesis would turn back to individuation, and the vitality that had made the fetus and decidua would now make for somatic growth. On this view, part of the sudden and early increment in girls is a trace of ancient but now deferred maternity due originally to premature male aggression, but now turned to personal augmentation by male restraint and female coyness. This view at least is entirely congruent to, and even favored by the above current biological conceptions, while anthropology is rich in facts that indicate progressive delay of motherhood with emergence from animal to higher human stages.

Natural selection suggests another partial explanation. Sexual desire normally develops progressively to a maximum during years of greatest fertility, while the instincts of female coyness and reserve are strongly developed earlier. Thus the largest and most vigorous girls would be able most successfully to resist fertilization, even in an age of animal violence, by not only their mates of near their own age of the opposite sex, who were coming to maturity and whom they would see most of, but also especially, if the advantages of the upright position in this respect be also considered, would have increased power to protect their chastity from older males. The weaklings who failed to do so would produce weak, because immature, offspring, while those who were large and strong would transmit this variation to their female children. Hence this augmentation, which now seems in the course of nature and without any direct advantage of utility, may in the past have performed a very important service for heredity in helping man on to a higher plane of greater maturity. The very size, due in part originally to too early maturity, may now be utilized as an instrument to prevent it.

Possibly, indeed, we may go back much further and suggest an ulterior explanation not only of this, but of far earlier stages of somatic growth. It may all be due to the momentum of ancient modes of reproduction, now superseded and abortive, but the tides of which still swell every tissue and cell, or as a kind of incipient internal incubation. All these energies that now enlarge the individual, formerly, and before the specialization of sperm and germ elements, proceeded to the very fecund formation of new generations by budding, division, etc. Now they are specialized and coordinated for functions, some more and some less directly auxiliary to a more effective and less wasteful method of insuring offspring and of bringing each to a more complete maturity. Nature and education thus may have a new biologic explanation and meaning, and a deeper import, as limitation in fecundity is supplemented by the later functions of parenthood, which are transfigurations of what was originally more primitive than sex itself, so that secondary sexual qualities were once primary but are now diverted to higher uses. The ministry of nursing, protecting, providing for, and teaching the young is thus performed by the same impulses, now sterilized and diverted, that once produced offspring. Thus the augmented individuality of adolescence is developed in the interest of the species for the sake of which sex itself originally arose, and to serve which art, science, and religion came into being, together with all the institutions which the powers acquired at this age have since created.

No explanation, however, of the stage of acceleration is complete without considering the lower plateau of growth at the age of from eight or nine to eleven or twelve, which precedes it. Some have argued that the later growth was a compensation for the preceding retardation and have even thought the two curves similar, though inverse. It has been urged that nature paused a while only to catch up later, and this has never been thought to demand any explanation save the commonplace view that first the organism husbands its resources to make a spring forward later. I think we must seek a cause for both these variations from a straight line of increment, and it is certain that the curves are not complemental, but that the later increase in rate is far more marked than the earlier decrease, and therefore can not be accounted for as merely making up for lost time.

The genetic explanation I propose here is the following: The period of retardation represents a relative balance between assimilation and expenditure and, what is far more important, between fundamental growth of the large bones and muscles and the accessory development of the smaller and more peripheral parts and functions. Indeed, the boy of ten or eleven is tolerably well adjusted to the environment of savage life in a warm country where he could readily live independently of his parents, discharging all the functions necessary to his personal life, but lacking only the reproductive function. In his instincts, amusements, and associations, his adjustment to such an environment is quite stable; his activity is at its greatest both in amount and variety, as studies to be later considered show. We shall later also see in how many of his ways he resembles the savage and how each furnishes the key for understanding both the good and bad points in the other's character. All this suggests on the recapitulation theory some long stationary period during which life had been pretty fully unfolded and could be led indefinitely and with stability and security in some not too cold Lemuria, New Atlantis, Eden, or other possible *cunabulum gentium.* This arrest may even suggest the age of senescence in some post-simian stage of ancestry. This short pause would thus be the present echo of a long phyletic stage when for many generations our prehuman forebears were pigmoid adults, leading short lives and dying at or before the pubic growth increment now occurs. It is no argument against this view that the boy of this age can not perpetuate his species, for this function is most of all mobile up and down the age scale by causes to some extent known and in some degree controllable.

Not only this, but hard conditions, like homelessness, imperfect food and health, and now sexual precocity develop strong tendencies to revert to or to remain in this stage. Kline has shown that truants are not only smaller but more akin to nomadic races than others; Dawson and many others, whose work will be later discussed, have pointed out how criminality is a product of augmentation of instincts normal at this age, but where the power to inhibit and repress does not develop, while the former grows to dangerous dimensions. Thus man, adult in years and stature, is constantly prone to drop to this lower level, development above which becomes a little more precarious than the preceding stages had been. The latter periods of growth are different and more insecure because newer and more unstable.

On this hypothesis we can perhaps inventory some of the influences which have contributed to the ascent of man to a more ample growth. First of all, selection favors large races and individuals; the latter would overcome others in the conflicts of sexual competition and win the most desirable wives as well as the best food and all other advantages that strength could procure. Moreover, as migration has led man west and north into more rigorous climates, the tallest and largest have preceded as they still continue to go west. Perhaps competition is at first more severe in new regions and in high latitudes, where, as we have seen, men are usually larger, or these may have been the more enterprising in leading such advances of the race, just as tall dolichocephalic men still now most frequently forsake the country for urban life. Again, the struggle with the saber-toothed tiger, the great cave bear, mastodon, Irish elks, gigantic sloths, and extinct vertebrates of the Quaternary age, may have been a factor in stimulating greater growth in man. The advent of the father to the family after the long period of matriarchate and perhaps the prolonged domestication of savage youth, who had before tended to become feral at the dawn of adolescence due to paternal influences and subjection, the growth of the home, all agencies that tended to defer marriage, as civilization with its arts increased, while numbers and intensified struggle slowly augmented; these and many other factors need not have come altogether, but only to have been unevenly distributed in order to constitute a curve of acceleration.

Once more, adolescence is a period of rich and polymorphic variations almost suggesting sports in all that pertains to both primary and secondary sexual qualities. Virchow states that variations often thought pathological are normal at this age. The organism reassumes its more primitive power of all-sided development as if ids or determinants essentially contrary were struggling for survival or prepotency among themselves in the same individual. These variables later become less independent and their range is reduced. This is all seen in the psychic field. The various equilibria of forces thus accurring, constitute the great opportunity for the environment and for education. Cope, Scott, Bateson, Dollo, De Vries, and others,[1] dissatisfied with the doctrine of gradual origin of species, have gathered facts from many fields suggesting that the variations which produce new species are sudden and discontinuous, and that these mutations, which may not be in only one but many directions at once, tend to show themselves in a species at certain periods separated by long intervals, when symptoms of a tendency to multiform variations, that are qualitative and not merely quantitative, arise and produce many individuals of a new kind within a short interval of time, so they can perpetuate themselves. The parent species then settles to its old lines,

[1] Cf. especially De Vries. Entstehung der Arten durch Mutation, 1901.

possibly later to suffer competition and even extermination by their transpeciated descendants. However this may be for plants and animals, such mutation periods suggest something like an adolescence of the species in which they occur, and are analogous to the changes that take place in both the body and soul of youth at this age of all-sided and saltatory development, when new traits, powers, faculties, and dimensions, which have no other nascent period, arise. Galton [1] supposes that his midparent contributes two-thirds the peculiarity in height and that any peculiarity tends to regress to mediocrity. Thus again we come upon a suggestion that adolescence abounds in cases that need special explanation not covered by general laws.

We must therefore regard the preadolescent increment of growth as representing not only a later stage in the phylogeny of modern man, but as marked off from previous stages, a little as the successive geologic strata are differentiated. Relatively to the periods that precede, man is now in a recent epoch, prolonged as it may have been, in which a new story has been added to his nature, so that he is now a super-man to his ancient forebears. A new being is born out of and superposed on the old, and in a new sense the boy is father to the man, and far older.

All this comports well with the greatly increased physical and mental instability which we find here. Young children grow despite great hardships, but later adolescence is more dependent upon favoring conditions in the environment, disturbances of which more readily cause arrest and prevent maturity. Not only is the range of variation in growth now increased, but there is far greater liability to reversion. As we advance to the later stages of adolescence, all these liabilities are greatly increased, as is the predisposition to sickness. The young pubescent, achieving his growth in the realm of fundamental qualities, dimensions, and functions, comes up to adult size at eighteen relatively limp and inept, like an insect that has just accomplished its last molt, and is therefore far more in the need of protection, physical care, moral and intellectual guidance; and in general, as will be considered later in

[1] Family Likeness in Stature. Proc. Royal Soc. of London, vol. xl, p. 42.

detail, this last great wave of growth throws the child up on to the shores of manhood or womanhood relatively helpless as from a second birth, rejuvenated, as if every cell in his body had striven to revive for the last time its failing reproductive potency. Through all these later stages of his growth, we can almost fancy that in the individual arrests and accelerations that make up its minor rhythms, we detect the ripple-marks on successive old shore-lines which represent once final stages of emergence to maturity, but which are now successively transcended.

This view will be strongly confirmed when we consider later the relatively independent character of boy life as compared with that of pubescence. Boys of ten lead a life with and for each other with less interest in adult life, yielding with what grace they may to the domination of "the Olympians," or adults, whose thoughts, purposes, and deeds often seem falsetto, unreal, and afar; but with adolescence, they become intensely susceptible to a wide range of adult influences. Possibly some of the perturbations in the curve of growth for earlier years may mark yet older eons of maturity. Our adolescent phenomena may sometime be represented by a series of oscillations between anagenic and catagenic processes, such as we now see in the perturbations at the age of six or seven, which suggest the ripple-marks of an old pubic beach, now at nearly every point submerged; so, too, our present period of maturity may sometime shrivel to a rudiment like the pause and finer adjustment at from nine to eleven or twelve, as childhood, youth, and apprenticeship to life become prolonged in some ascendent super-race of the future. How many accelerations and retardations in height and weight are traces of ancient nodes where new buds were once set off we can not now tell, but I think that an indefinite perspective of these may sometime be determined. The pedigree of the horse is now pretty well traced from the polydactylous hippops, the size of a rabbit, up through the Eocene orohippus, the size of a fox, the miohippus of the Miocence age, the size of a sheep, the archihippus and protohippus of the Pliocene, the size of an ass, etc., with every indication that at least its period of immaturity, if not its average age, has also increased. We can not prove that modern man was once adult at the size of the pigmy and that the boy represents the height and weight of our forebears in a remote past, any more than we can disprove that he sprung from some extinct anthropoid the size of our smaller apes. Indeed, in the processes of evolution large phylogenetic stages may be represented by smaller ontogenetic ones, and our childhood be analogous to a dwindled, rudimentary organ. Our ancestors may possibly have been, as an eminent anthropologist thinks, of Anakim size and perhaps have lived to a correspondingly great age. It is, of course, not demonstrably impossible that he may have had both a smaller stature and shorter life and then grown larger and lived longer than now, and again diminished, so that both increase and decrease in these respects may be atavistic or reversionary. However this be, two things seem more certain: first, that the relative size and age of reproduction must have been a factor, and, in some way not yet known, a concomitant variant; and, second, that at every stage, and especially since the period when the evolutionary struggle began to be predominantly psychic instead of physical, it is in psychic yet more than in physical rudiments that we must seek the key to unlock the enchanting but baffling mysteries of man's past in these respects, of which the soul, even more than the cells and organs, is full of dim echoes and reverberations.

Dominant in all these aspects of adolescence is the note of an equilibrium relatively less secure than what has preceded, of an old anchorage broken, of elements less harmonized, of coordinations yet incomplete, of adjustments to the environment less fine and less settled, of insecurity and ever-impending danger of mental or physical relapse, and at the same time, of the promises and potencies of a slow but ever higher development. Hence there is need of the most careful study of consummate practical wisdom, in providing the most favorable environment and eliminating every possible cause of arrest or reversion. This is indeed the practical problem of this book.

Could we solve the problems of adolescence, which these aspects of growth alone propound, and justly evaluate the cause of its great advance, we should thus best be able to settle the deeper problems of education in the large sense that considers it as coextensive with all the environment. Tentative as is now our knowledge, it is sufficient to generate a deep optimism in the hope that man is yet in the making, that the best things have not yet happened in his history, and that perhaps his present stage is at the same time the point of departure of a yet higher one related to all that adolescence now gives, as it is to the stages that have preceded. Assuming the bionomic law, infant growth means being loaded with paleoatavistic qualities in a manner more conformable to Weismannism, embryonic growth being yet purer, while the pubescent increment is relatively neoatavistic. From this it would seem to follow that the more complete and established the maturity before offspring are produced, the greater the probability of phyletic progress in successive generations. It would also seem to be probable that the environment, the influence of which is augmented somewhat in proportion as maturity is attained, would be felt by advancing the species, infinitesimally though it be in each generation, toward a more perfect development of its higher and later acquired powers. On Cope's view, the influence of the environment in producing acquired characters transmissible by heredity is greatest on the soma during adolescence.[1] At any rate, for those prophetic souls interested in the future of our race and desirous of advancing it, the field of adolescence is the quarry in which they must seek to find both goal and means. If such a higher stage is ever added to our race, it will not be by increments at any later plateau of adult life, but it will come by increased development of the adolescent stage, which is the bud of promise for the race.

[1] Primary Factors in Organic Evolution, p. 446.

CHAPTER II

GROWTH OF PARTS AND ORGANS DURING ADOLESCENCE

Change of Proportions—Growth of Bones; Arms; Legs; Thighs; Pelvis; Sitting Height and Trunk; Skull; Neck; Jaw; Teeth; Muscles; Heart; Veins and Arteries; the Blood; Changes in Circulation; Lungs and their Capacity; the Vital Index; Brain; Dermal and Intestinal Surfaces; Glands and their Action — Abnormalities of Growth; Harmonious Development and its Meaning.

WHEN, instead of considering the body as a whole, we now pass within it or seek to weigh and measure single parts and organs, we are confronted by yet more difficult problems. Many of these determinations can, of course, be made only on the cadaver, and the data are still far too few for many final conclusions. Even the external measurements of parts, limbs, joints, etc., are less numerous, too often less accurate and less accordant with each other than those of the body as a whole. Very significant and practical facts, however, are already established.

First: The parts do not grow in equal ratio. If they did so, the infant would become a monster adult with an enormous head, with legs and arms too short, the body, especially the belly, too thick, the trunk too long. The following table from Vierordt,[1] although known to be inaccurate in

	Fold.		Fold.
Testes	60	Kidneys	12
Muscles	48	Skin	12
Pancreas	28	Salivary glands	10.7
Skeleton	26	Spinal cord	7
Lungs	20	Thyroid gland	4.5
Stomach and alimentary canal	20	Brain	3.7
Milts	18	Eye	1.7
Liver	13.6	Suprarenal capsules	0.9
Ovaries	13	Thymus	.½
Heart	12.5		

some parts, is still as a whole the best we have to show how manifold the weight of certain organs increases from birth to maturity. The lungs, stomach, and milts only grow about

[1] Physiol. des Kindesalters, p. 254.

as much as does the body as a whole; while testes and muscles greatly exceed, the thymus, eye, etc., grow far less than the total body. Many rudimentary parts, not mentioned in the preceding table, of which Wiedersheim describes several score which make the body like an old curiosity-shop, decline, and some even vanish with increasing age, so that at maturity our component parts are normally very different in their relative size from what they are at birth. Were we able to construct an analogous table showing the relative increase of organs from the first intrauterine month to the mature fetus, we should find very different and greater changes as well as more in number. Where single parts continue to grow too fast or exceed their normal proportions, and others fall behind or cease to grow, we have data for the very interesting science of teratology, in which the due balance and harmony of growth has been disturbed, and some parts are hypertrophied and others atrophied.

This is also seen although in general to a less extent in external dimensions.

Growth in Lengths.	Age.						Total growth to 15th year.	Further growth.
	At birth.	0–3.	3–6.	6–9.	9–12.	12–15.		
Vertex to the orbital margin..	6	2.6	0.9	0.1	0	0	3.6	0.1
Orbital margin to the larynx..	6	4.4	1.9	0.2	1.1	0.6	8.2	1.5
Larynx to the axilla	3.9	4.7	1.4	0.7	1.3	1.4	9.5	2.2
Axilla to the crest of the ischium	8.3	6.8	1.7	0.5	1.3	2.1	12.4	4.5
Upper arm................	6.6	9.3	3.3	3.6	0.6	3.5	20.2	2.2
Lower arm................	7.5	8.0	4.4	4.6	...	2.3	....	...
Hand.....................	6.0	4.2	0.7	2.2	...	1.9	....	...
Sum of the above three	20.1	21.5	8.4	10.4	(1.3)	7.6	49.2	6.9
Ischial crest to the knee	15.2	14.7	9.3	7.9	4.9	8.1	44.9	6.1
Knee to the foot sole........	9.1	13.3	4.6	1.6	2.4	5.8	27.7	3.9
Length of foot.............	8.1	5	3	1.5	2.5	4	16	1.9

Growth in Breadths.	Age.					Total growth to 15th year.	Further growth.
	At birth.	0–3.	3–6.	6–9.	9–15.		
Head.........................	9.7	2.7	1.2	0.6	0.8	5.3	1.4
Neck.........................	6.6	0.6	0.8	0.8	0.3	2.5	2.8
Shoulders....................	13.7	9.3	3.8	5.2	4	22.3	14.4
Thorax at the level of the præcordia	10.5	5.5	2.6	3.8	3.6	15.5	5.2
Hips at the level of the trochanter.	10.5	1.8	2.4	4.0	2.8	17.3	6.2
Greatest breadth of calf..........	3.3	3.3	0.6	0.7	1.3	5.9	3.4
Greatest breadth of foot..........	3.3	2.7	1.4	0.6	1	5.7	0.6

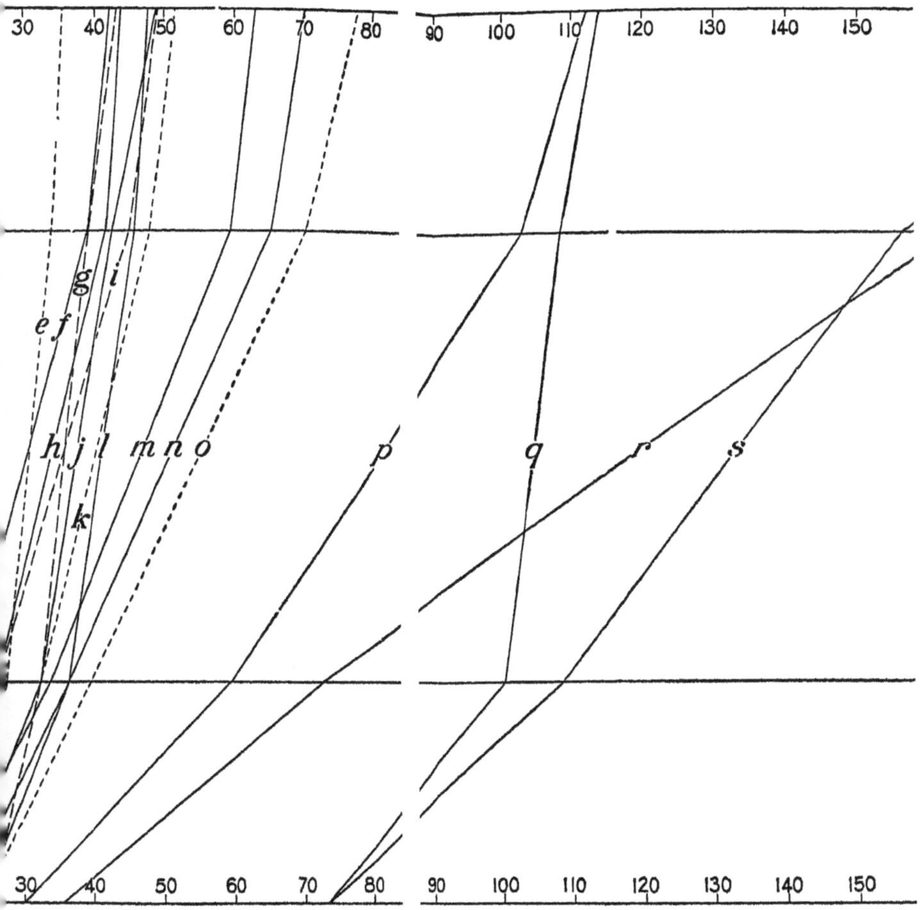

AVERAGE GR VTH MEASUREMENTS.

per half of head ; *d*, length of face ; *e*, transve e diameter of head ; *f*, head ; *g*, head diameter, front t epth of chest ; *k*, abdominal girth ; *l*, head len over ; *m*, upper arm ; *n*, breadth of male hip and sho ngth of arm ; *q*, head girth ; *r*, leg length ; *s*, orax expanded.

The table on page 52 (Zeissing-Vierordt) shows the absolute growth in length and breadth in centimeters.

The opposite chart is a combination of two from Vierordt (Physiol. des Kindesalters, pp. 271, 274) showing, on the basis of Liharzik's measurements, nineteen dimensions for four ages, viz.: at birth, one year and nine months, fourteen years and three months, and twenty-five. This is drawn to scale in such a way that, starting from the left vertical line the distances along the four horizontal lines are in each case one-fifth those of the average individual.

Dr. W. W. Hastings[1] concludes that "the nearer an individual approaches mean development in height, the more nearly will he conform to an absolute standard of symmetry in his entire development. But there is a typical development and standard of symmetry for each height of each age, a standard which is attainable and to which the muscular development of the individual of that height may be made to conform very closely through the aid of systematic physical training and general care of health."

A good picture of the growth of the body as a whole and of its special external dimensions is presented in the cut on page 54 from Godin,[2] who sought to determine the adolescent type at different pubescent years by 36,000 measurements on one hundred French schoolboys, followed individually from thirteen to eighteen years of age. By comparing the eighteen *points de repère* here represented by dots, the changes of proportion can be traced and measured on a millimetric scale.

Second: Few parts grow steadily, so that their development is represented not by straight lines but by curves which differ greatly one from the other in the same person and also differ in different individuals in whom the summative measures of gross height and weight may coincide. The brain, e. g., almost ceases to increase in size or weight before puberty, when reproductive organs, hips, and muscles then grow at an augmented rate. The age of most rapid growth in any

[1] See his Manual for Physical Measurements, with anthropometric tables for each height of each age and sex from five to twenty years, and vitality coefficients. 1902. The best manual of its kind.

[2] Recherches Anthropométriques sur la croissance des diverses parties du corps, Paris, 1903, pp. 242.

part is called its nascent period. While pubertal growth reaches more or less simultaneously nearly every part of the body, even its energies focus upon certain organs more than

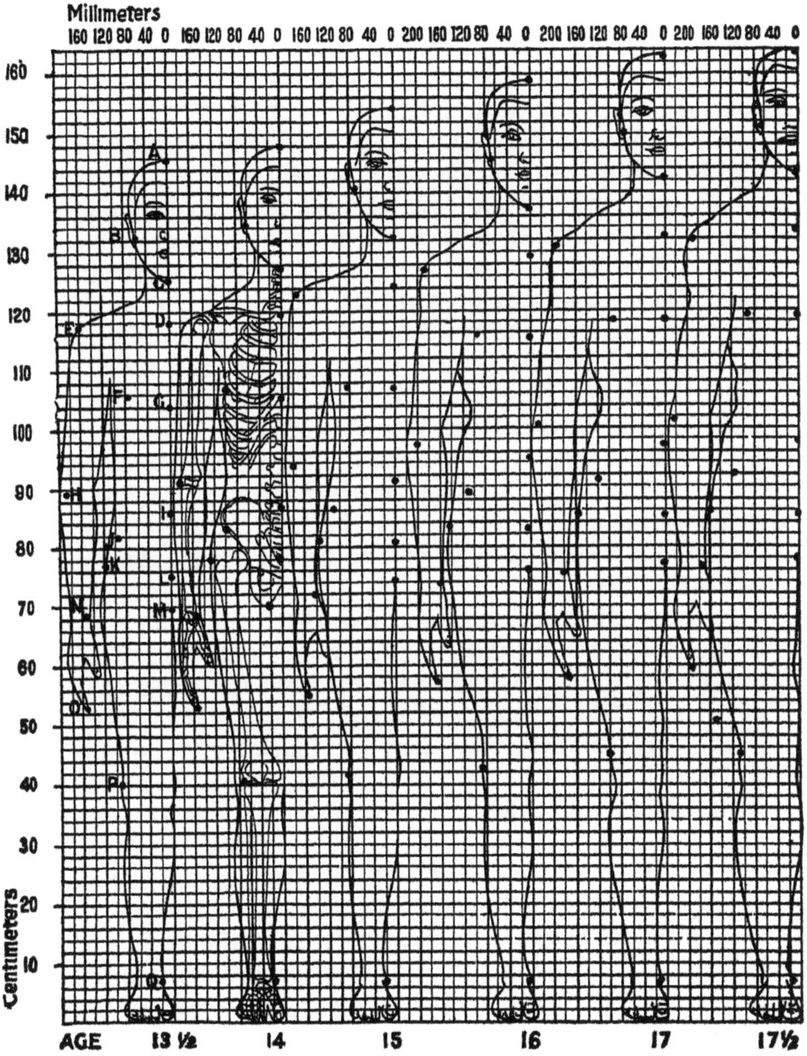

others, and not a few sequences, to be later noted, are established, and more detailed and accurate measurements will probably add to this number. To determine these periods, not only for different parts, but for different traits and powers of the soul, is one of the chief quests of genetic study, and where established, the result is fraught with most important practical results.

Third: Not only do different parts reach their maximal size at different ages, but some continue to grow well on into old age. A recent writer concludes that the kidneys are at their largest in the third decade, the muscles, skeleton, intestines, and liver in the fifth, the heart and lungs in the eighth; and from this it would seem almost as if each organ has its youth, maturity, and old age, and that these do not coincide either with each other or with the stages of body growth as a whole. The motor organs as the heaviest give to growth its chief character, so that what we call maturity is the period of their greatest development. The body-weight as a whole sinks in old age despite the growth of lungs, intestines, heart, and liver, chiefly because the muscles and bones decline. Man is therefore not old because all the parts of his body are old, but because his heaviest organs decline. There is therefore no absolute standstill of growth, and age is relative, some organs remaining young, and some achieving their highest rate of growth and nearly or quite ceasing before others attain their most rapid rate.

Fourth: It is well to remember that from a larger biological view, every higher animal is not only composed of organs phyletically old and new, but that the order of their development may even be changed. Basal and lapidary as is the great biogenic law that the individual recapitulates the growth stages of his race, the work of Appel, Keibel, Mehnert,[1] and many others has demonstrated abundant inversions of it. The heart, e. g., in the individual develops before the blood-vessels, but this reverses the phylogenetic order. The walls of the large vessels develop before the blood-corpuscles, while the converse was true in the development of the species. Ontogenetic age in all such cases is an index only of the intensity of cenogenetic energy. Retarded development of an organ, on the other hand, is an indication of regressivity, and many writers have collected cases showing

[1] See especially his Biomechanik. Jena, 1898.

that abbreviation and retardation of the different organs of a creature which is their bearer are ontogenetic processes that are constantly operative. The latter may affect the date of the first appearance of an organ, the differentiation of its tissues among each other, or the entire processes of growth of a part or all of them. Organs are progressive according to the degree of their vitality. The rapidity of the growth of a part is directly as the degree of development acquired by the phyletic process. Owing to this heterochrony, every animal, man included, is a mixture of high and low, new and old qualities, so that in certain respects not a few animals excel man, and we are slowly gaining and slowly losing traits. In general, we may say with Jordan that "if the history of an individual is an epitome of the history of the group to which the individual belongs, then adaptive characters appearing late in the growth of the individual must have appeared late in the history of the group." [1] But this is only a part of the fact, for as Hyatt [2] states the matter, "all modifications and variations in progressive series tend to appear first in the adolescent or adult stages of growth, and then to be inherited in successive descendants at earlier and earlier stages according to the law of acceleration, until they either become embryonic or are crowded out of the organization and replaced in the development by characteristics of later origin." Cope [3] has modified this law by suggesting that "the accelerations in the assumption of a character progressing more rapidly than the same in another character must soon produce a type whose stages were once the exact parallel of a permanent lower form; the condition of inexact parallelism." Hence he infers that acceleration has occurred in some traits and qualities, but also that, as each type has had its time of culminating perfection, retrogression and retardation have also occurred, till some characters have been lost. Thus in ontogeny or the development of the individual, we often have characters that occurred simultaneously in the ancestral organism appearing successively. Indeed, many variations of parts and functions, both those of excess and defect, may

[1] Jordan. Foot-notes to Evolution, p. 210.
[2] Smithsonian Contributions, No. 673, Preface, p. ix.
[3] Origin of the Fittest, p. 142.

have a morbid origin. Virchow, describing the differences between diathesis, Anlage, and variations, makes the former permanent, but holds that the latter especially may arise from a pathological inception.[1]

Weisbach [2] thinks, e. g., that the measurements of savages show that ape-like traits are not concentrated in any race, but are scattered among different races, and that some are found even among Europeans. Turner [3] infers that no one race is inferior or superior to all others in all traits. He finds, e. g., that while the Lapps and Eskimos most approach apes in the proportions of thigh to upper arm and of shaft of lower to upper limb, they are among all races one of the most widely removed from apes in the no less important ratio of forearm to upper arm and of leg to thigh. In other respects, the Fuegians are among the most ape-like of men, yet in pelvis and sacrum they rank high. While on the whole, in the important skeletal character of skull and pelvis, the Europeans are more removed from the general type of mammals, it is by no means as yet proved that the higher races have been derived by graded perfection of all structure from the black or any other existing race or from the Simian type. In some respects the so-called low races are more developed out of and even opposite to the pithecoid type than are the most civilized.

Fifth: In the present state of the question between preformation and epigenesis we shall assume that the earlier stages of life are more conformable to Weismannism, and the later to the views of Hertwig. The eozooic or paleoatavistic bases of heredity are the formative principles of fundamental organs, condition all others, and are constant and more independent of recent environment both in the time and degree of their development. But even if we assume the monophyletic origin of animal life, it will still follow that as maturity and on the whole death are longer delayed as we ascend the scale of being, more and more weight must be assigned to those qualities which are later acquired than to those which are

[1] Verh. Acad. Wiss. Berlin, 1896.

[2] Reise der Novara. Anthropol. Theil. 1867, p. 269.

[3] Voyage of the M. S. Challenger. Zool., vol. xvi. Bones of the Human Skeleton.

earlier and more stable. Even if we admit that the rudiments of all the chief characteristics possessed by the species lie dormant in the egg, this does not compel us to infer that there is no inherited congenital indefiniteness, to say that all is predetermined, that there are no latent energies to be not only set off but guided by stimulation, or that the only limitation, to the opening of new lines in all directions, previously fixed in the constitution of germ-plasm is that by developing some modes of reaction, certain others become impossible. All we need to assume is that there are neoatavistic factors, and that the later part of each individual life is more characterized by the evolution of acquired qualities. Prominent among the epigenetic elements are the effects of use, which increase from birth onward, while organs not needed tend to atrophy or become rudimentary as their functions cease. Not only the relations between these two functions, but recent biological discussions repeat, in many respects, those which Locke inaugurated concerning innate ideas, and the issue of the two discussions is also analogous. Each of these principles will have abundant illustrations in this chapter.

A. *The Growth of the Bones.*—To secrete solid substances is one of the primitive powers of animal organisms, as is seen in all of the siliceous and calcareous shell-made oozes (pteripod, globigerina, radiolarian, diatome, etc.) that cover so deeply the primitive ocean-bed upon which they are always snowing down, in the form of coral formations, molluscan shells, crustacea, articulata, the bony coats of insects, the carapaces of exoskeletal mammals, etc. Although this tegumentary framework is now represented in man only by hair, nails, and perhaps the dermal bones of the head and secondary or outer skull, suggestions and recrudescences of it are still often seen in abnormal and monstrous individuals, not only in defects of the endoskeleton, but in various forms of outer callosity

In vertebrates, the axial system is both ontogenetically and phylogenetically first to appear, and can be detected within the first month of fetal life. The development of the appendicular system of limbs of all kinds, first in the membranous and then in the bony stage, is later very gradual, and in general proceeds from the larger to the smaller bones, and from the central or fundamental to the distal or accessory part, the limb-fingers, toes, etc., coming after arm and leg bones. Here, too, the force of heredity is stronger and truer in the early stages, so that congenital deformities and insufficiency are more liable for the parts that develop late than for those that develop earlier. This general law, however, has frequent exceptions. The skull, as we go up the vertebrate scale, has grown at the expense of the cervical vertebræ, and strangely, the first bone in the embryo to ossify is commonly the clavicle, which has so important a function in expanding the shoulders in the erect position, frees the arms from locomotive functions, and gives them a power and range of lateral movement almost equal to that in the mesial plane.

Just before and after puberty there is a great increase in the growth of bones, and at the close of the adolescent ferment the skeleton is considerably extended and also much consolidated and joined together. This growth is much accentuated in the larger and especially in the longer bones, which have been chiefly measured. Kotelmann, Hall, and Moon have shown that they grow in thickness as well as in length, adding new periosteal layers. The motor apparatus in men, consisting of 223 bones and about 316 muscles, constitute by weight some $\frac{724}{1000}$ of the adult body, so that its increase is the chief factor of growth. Augmenting twenty-six fold from birth to maturity, the weight of the skeleton varies, with no yet fully determined law, from thirteen to twenty-three per cent that of the body, declining both relatively and absolutely in old age.[1] For the prepubertal stages of growth it is still impossible to give exact data. Mühlmann [2] can find but

Age.	Weight of the Entire Skeleton.	
	Absolute.	Relative.
16	8,436	23.7
23	8,651.7	13.8 (?)
30	11,464	20.6
33	11,080	15.9

[1] Vierordt. Daten u. Tabellen, p. 17.

[2] Ueber die Ursache des Alters. Wiesbaden, 1900, p. 150.

six careful attempts to weigh the skeleton at different ages, and from these constructs the table for males on page 59.

In the following cut, for which I am indebted to my colleague Professor Sanford, the skeleton of an infant is magnified to the approximate length of that of an adult, to show

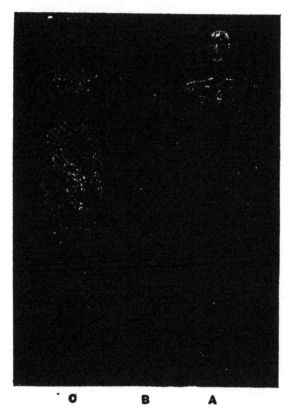

C B A

a, skeleton of an adult; *b*, skeleton of a new born infant on the same scale; *c*, the same infant's skeleton magnified photographically to approximate the length of the adult skeleton.

how monstrous maturity would be if the bones grew in equal proportions in all their dimensions. The skull and face would be enormous, the neck long, the shoulders low or almost absent, the thorax narrow laterally but deep from front to back like a quadruped, the arms and especially the legs short, the hips small and feeble, etc.

(*a*) *Sitting and Standing Height.*—Important and interesting is the relation between the growth of the upper and lower lengths of the body, or the trunk from the vertex to the hip, as compared with that of the leg. Unfortunately, there have been discrepancies in taking these measurements, so that results are as yet unsatisfactory. Zeissing[1] found individual differences here so great that the proportions of some children at four were like those of others at fourteen, while Liharzik thought this ratio so distinct for each period of life and so uniform for all that he could approximately determine the age by it alone. Landsberger[2] measured this relation only from the age of six to that of twelve years, and found the percentage of lower length to increase from 56.1 to 59.3 per cent of the entire length of the body.

While the middle of the body by length slowly descends with growth, the center of gravity descends relatively with growth, but ascends absolutely, and in the adult male is in the pelvis just above the hip-joint.[3] Weber found the center of gravity in a male body 166.92 centimeters long, to lie 8.77 centimeters above the axis of rotation of the head of the femur; 0.87 centimeter above the promontorium; 94.77 centimeters above the heel; 72.15 centimeters below the sinciput. According to Vierordt,[4] if the body were divided at the level of the crista of the ischium (the lower part of the hip-bone) and the total be divided into 1,000 parts—

At 8	the upper	body	will	measure	397,	and	the	whole	603;
At 13	"	"	"	"	382,	"	"	"	618;
At 60	"	"	"	"	369,	"	"	"	631.

Liharzik, who divided a little lower at the pubic symphisis, found that—

At 7½	the upper	length	was	63.5	centimeters,	and	the	lower	63.5	centimeters;
At 18	"	"	"	75	"	"	"	"	88	"
At 24	"	"	"	81	"	"	"	"	94	"

W. S. Hall[5] found that at nine years the height of the pubes was exactly equal to that of the body, and at twenty-

[1] Vierordt. Physiol. des Kindesalters, p. 267.

[2] Das Wachsthum ins Alter der Schulpflicht, p. 245.

[3] Ueber den Schwerpunkt des menschlichen Körpers. W. Braune u. O. Fischer. Leipzig, 1889.

[4] Daten u. Tabellen, p. 11.

[5] Jour. Anthropol. Inst., 1895.

three, when the middle of the body had moved down to that of the symphysis, it was fifty-one per cent.

Moon[1] concluded that at fifteen the limbs are relatively longer in proportion to the body than those of the man or the boy of eleven. In sitting height, or the length of the vertebral column, there is a retarded stage of growth relative to height during the entire period from eleven to fifteen. Later[2] he found that growth of sitting height was independent of the approach of puberty. This increases for a year or two before as well as afterward. In fine, the legs tend to outstrip the other components of height during early youth, but afterward increase more slowly; while the sitting height increases rapidly.

Bowditch[3] says "women appear to be relatively longer in body and shorter in the legs than men." By measuring 1,546 girls and 324 men, mostly college and normal students, he found the average sitting height to be 53.24 per cent of the total height without shoes. Sargent has made this a trifle less, viz., 52.7 per cent. Ranke[4] takes the relatively greater body length of woman for granted and infers that she is thus embryologically lower than man, and Huxley states that long thigh and forearm are distinctively human traits. Hitchcock,[5] however, compared measurements of 500 students each of Amherst (male) and Mount Holyoke and Wellesley (female), where the average age of entrance is nineteen, and found that while each sex had about 1.9 pound weight for every inch in height, and that while the females excelled a trifle in length of head and neck, the males were seven per cent taller and the male trunk was eleven per cent longer than that of the female, and that even the distance from pubis to navel was twelve per cent longer in the male. This surprising result, so contrary to the common opinion that the female trunk is rela-

[1] The Growth of Boys. Proc. Am. Ass'n for Advancement of Phys. Education, 1896.

[2] The Question of Growth at Puberty. Am. Phys. Ed. Rev., Sept., 1899.

[3] Beiträge zur Anthropol., p. 490. München, 1883.

[4] Arch. f. Anthropol., vol. xv, 1884, p. 171.

[5] Comparative Study of Measurements of Male and Female Students at Amherst, Mount Holyoke, and Wellesley Colleges. Journal of Physical Education, vol. i, p. 90.

tively the longest, can not yet be interpreted. It is possible that these girls are not average representatives of their sex, but more mannish. There is some reason to believe that relatively long-bodied women are higher and better mothers and that relatively long-limbed girls are decadent, as we shall see later.

Dr. G. M. West [1] concluded from the measurements of 3,250 Worcester school children that girls' sitting height began to rise rapidly at twelve, before which age it had been very slight, and rose for two years. From the fifteenth to seventeenth year inclusive, the growth of boys rises, but drops the next year. His curves suggest that up to the twelfth year in girls, and to the fifteenth year in boys, a large part of the growth in stature is made in the lower limbs, while after these ages it is made largely in the trunk. During all the period from five to eighteen the limbs of boys grow more rapidly than the trunk, while with girls, the period of greater comparative growth is divided about equally between the extremities and the trunk. The trunk is relatively longer in girls than in boys, except from the seventh to the tenth year, while after the thirteenth year, girls' bodies are relatively still longer. After the twelfth year the annual increase in sitting height is less than before, though boys maintain a more uniform rate during all the period of acceleration; while both sexes make greater annual growth after than before twelve, yet girls make the greatest absolute increase before, and boys after that period.

Porter [2] concluded from his measurements on 33,500 children that sitting height in girls attained its fastest rate of growth at thirteen and in boys at fifteen, and that the period during which girls exceed boys in size is longest in sitting height. Hrdlicka [3] found that the greatest length of lower limb in the sexes taken together was attained from the thirteenth to the sixteenth years, and that thereafter the body gains slightly on the limbs. He also suggested that the chief defect in the growth of badly nourished chil-

---

[1] Science, January 6, 1893.
[2] Acad. of Science, St. Louis, March, 1893.
[3] Special Report of New York Juvenile Asylum.

dren is found in the under growth of the lower limbs, but thought that colored children relatively excelled white in this respect.

Peckham [1] infers from the measurements of about 10,000 children from four to eighteen that the growth of the body and of the lower extremities takes place in such a way that the length of the body of the girl is less than that of the body of the boy until the tenth year and thereafter greater until the sixteenth year. From fifteen to eighteen the bodies of girls grow only two inches and the bodies of boys over four inches. For the lower extremities at nine years of age, those of the girls are longer (as compared with the boys), at eleven shorter, and from twelve to fourteen again longer. At fourteen the lower extremities of the girls almost cease growing, while those of the boys increase by four inches between the ages of fourteen and nineteen.

The Chicago measurements [2] showed that in sitting height girls at fifteen began to increase more slowly and at eighteen appeared to have reached their maximum, while the Chicago boys grew steadily in body length till after eighteen, and then at a rather uniform but reduced rate until twenty and a half, when this census ended. The last Chicago percentiles show that while girls' sitting height is growing rapidly from ten to fourteen and almost ceases from sixteen to eighteen, it increases rather faster than net height from thirteen to fourteen and decidedly more slowly from eight to ten. In boys from sixteen to seventeen, sitting height augments more than net height and from nine to ten distinctly less. In other words, increase in pubertal trunk growth in both sexes both begins later and, relatively to limb growth, continues longer.[3]

Daffner, who measured distances below and above the navel from ten to twenty-two, found that at birth the navel was 2.3 centimeters below the middle of the body; that between the age of one and one year and a half it was at the middle length; then the lower part began to exceed the upper, so that at ten it was 21 centimeters; at eleven, 22 centimeters;

[1] Sixth Report of the State Board of Health of Wisconsin.

[2] Report of the Department of Child Study and Pedagogic Investigation, Chicago, No. 2.

[3] Ibid., No. 3, 1900–'01.

at twelve, 14 centimeters; at thirteen, 28 centimeters; at fourteen, 31 centimeters; and at twenty-two, nearly 34 centimeters farther from the sole of the foot to the navel than from the navel to the crown of the head.

(*b*) *Arms and Legs, Thorax and Pelvis.*—The limbs probably originate polymerously as outgrowths of primitive body segments, and precede in their development the pelvic and pectoral girdles that support them. From approximate identity in the fish the fore and hind limbs diverge in structure and function, as we ascend the evolutionary scale. In the embryo the development of the bones of the limbs precedes those of both the above girdles, but whether the pubertal increment follows this order is not yet determined. From data compiled from the latest works on anatomy, the following seem to be the chief adolescent changes in the bones of the limbs:

The epiphyses of the humerus join the shaft at about twenty, the nucleus of the external condyle appears between thirteen and seventeen, that of the internal condyle joins the shaft at about eighteen and the other members at sixteen or seventeen. The superior epiphyses of the tibia join the shaft at seventeen or eighteen, and the inferior epiphyses at eighteen. The metacarpal bones and phalanges have epiphyses which join about twenty. The epiphyses of the clavicle appear about the eighteenth year and join the shaft about the twenty-fifth year. The coracoid process of the scapula, which ossifies from two centers which join from the sixteenth to the eighteenth years, assists the clavicle in rotating the fore limbs outward farther from the trunk and in giving them greater freedom of motion. The gradual recession of the shoulders from the head; the gradual transformation of a fore foot into a hand and the greatly increased contact with the environment thereby, the reduction of a prehensile to a human foot with growing mesial and degenerating external functions; the opposite bend of knees and elbows; the modification of the hip-bones for effective and varied motion, seem well-attested lines of evolution, but whether the pubescent bone changes are an advance along these lines or diversions from them, or neither, more genetic studies must yet determine.

Landsberger[1] found the span between the tips of the longest finger slightly less for most ages than body length. He also found that the forearm plus hand grew slightly less from six to thirteen than the upper arm. Quetelet[2] found it slightly longer, and Zeissing still longer. The "acromial breadth" of Landsberger or span minus length of arms increased regularly, but if this was measured from shoulder to shoulder in front, this anterior acromial breadth increased much faster.

In bone girths at the instep, elbow, and wrist, Sargent found boys from thirteen to sixteen to distinctly exceed girls; he also found that the length of the upper arm of girls from thirteen to sixteen is one-fifth of an inch less than that of boys, while the forearm and hand is three-fifths of an inch shorter.

W. S. Hall found that while the total height was increasing fastest the forearm was retarded, but, like the lower leg, at twenty-three resumed the same relations to total height that it had at nine. Moon says: "In length from shoulder to elbow, the rate of growth appears to increase after the age of twelve, while in length from elbow to tip there is little variation till the age of fourteen, when the growth is relatively quickened." In span of arms, Porter found a marked increase in boys at thirteen, which was greatest from fourteen to fifteen, slightly less from fifteen to sixteen, and diminishing to eighteen. The year of greatest growth for girls he found to be from twelve to thirteen, the time during which the span of girls exceeds that of boys, in the main coinciding with, but lasting a little less than their superiority in height. Sargent found that among men the stretch of arms of only 10 per cent was less than the total height, but that this was true of over 35 per cent of women.

In the legs the femur often has the greatest growth, both relatively and absolutely, and in giants and sometimes in acromegalia is generally the bone most in excess of the normal. The epiphyses join the shaft in the inverse order of their appearance. The small trochanter joins at seventeen, the great at eighteen, the head at nineteen, and those of its lower extremity are

[1] Untersuchungen über die Körperliche Entwickelung der Fabrikarbeiter in Zentralrussland. Tübingen, 1889, p. 94.

[2] Das Wachsthum im Alter der Schulpflicht.

solidified at about twenty. In the tibia the lower epiphyses join the shaft at eighteen or nineteen, and the upper about three years later. In the fibula the same process takes place at the lower and later, at the upper end of the shaft, but two or three years after the corresponding processes in the tibia. The cartilage of the patella is fully ossified only at puberty.

It has been often observed that the shin-bone or tibia is bent backward near its upper end and that its joint surface is inclined and enlarged; Henter[1] thinks this due to pressure in the fetal position. H. Charles[2] thinks that it is known to be caused by the habit of squatting or sitting on the heels, so common among primitive peoples; Retzius[3] finds it far more common in embryos than in adults, and thinks that these peculiarities are acquired characters inherited from an almost universal custom before chairs were used and found in the early stages of life in about all fetuses, but that it is gradually corrected among civilized races during growth.

W. S. Hall found that the increase in the height of the knee was relatively retarded during the three years when the modulus or total height was rapidly increasing, but at twenty-three it had the same relation to it as at nine. Comparing the thigh with the crus, the latter reached its limit at the end of the sixteenth year, while the former continued to grow for at least three years. Moon found growth in height of knee retarded from eleven to sixteen, while length of body was rapidly increasing, and perhaps also while the thigh was growing fastest. If it is among the first lengths to feel the pubertal increment, it resumes after a comparative pause, and is also among the last bone lengths to grow. Landsberger found that from six to twelve the length of leg increased from 60 to 80.6 centimeters. His figures agree very closely with those of Liharzik, although both are somewhat greater than the measurements of Zeissing and less than those of Quetelet. He, too, found leg growth greatest in the upper thigh.

Sargent found the difference in height between boys and

[1] Anat. Studies. Virchow Archiv, 1863.
[2] Jour. of Anat. and Physiol., April, 1894.
[3] Biol. Studies. Neue Folge, vii, p. 61.

girls from thirteen to sixteen to be largely due to the comparative shortness of the thigh-bone in girls. "Although the body length is greater than that in boys, the difference, as shown by the sitting height, is largely due to the greater length of neck and head in girls, as shown by the superiority in boys in the height of the sternum."

Sargent says that the mean girth of the knee is about the same in both sexes, but the girth of the calf is two-thirds of an inch greater in girls.

Moon measured bone girths of boys from eleven to fifteen, and found that for knee, ankle, instep, elbow, and wrist, there was relative retrogression from eleven to thirteen, and afterward an advance till fifteen. In these dimensions the boy at fifteen has grown relatively larger than the man, except in the case of the instep, but this increase puts him still farther from the proportions he will have when mature. W. S. Hall, too, found that from fourteen to eighteen joint girths increased faster than bone lengths. Sargent found that from thirteen to sixteen boys have the start of girls in length of foot by half an inch, and in stretch of arms, by fully two inches.

In the *os calcis,* the junction of the epiphyses and bone occurs at about fifteen or sixteen. The tarsal bones and even the metatarsals and phalanges show distinct progress in ossification about and soon after puberty. The instep is a trifle more arched, the sole some think distinctly broader, and the great toe seems to lose power of opposition and to become confirmed in its structure as well as in its function of supporting the body and springing. Jäger thinks certain changes in the form and position of the human foot are acquired and not inherited. At birth the foot is oblique, so that only the outer edge touches the floor; it is drawn upward from its right-angular position, so that the heel would first touch, and is very flat. When first used, it must be placed squarely down over all its surface, and the anterior metatarsi are also pressed against the basis of support. If thus every irritation of the periosteum, on which lateral growth is assumed to depend, and of the cartilaginous disks between the diaphysis and the epiphyses, on which longitudinal growth is known to depend, increases the production of bone substance, then the progressive changes in the form and position of the human foot must, he thinks, be explained as the results of experience and not of congenital influence.

After puberty two small epiphyses appear both in the head and tubercle of the ribs and join the main bone by the twenty-fifth year. The sternum ossifies progressively, beginning with the complete union of the third and fourth members of the body, leaving the cartilage below the manubrium to be ossified soon after puberty. The carcinoid process joins the body of the scapula, and epiphyses appear from the fourteenth to the sixteenth years, coalesce, and join the spine six or seven years later. If we regard the scapula, clavicle, and ribs as the thoracic girdle, it is phylogenetically sinking, owing, perhaps, to the upright position. Cervical ribs are now only found in man in abnormal cases and the upper rib is beginning to degenerate, but the decay at the lower part of the thorax is more rapid than at the upper part. Even the eleventh and twelfth ribs are rudimentary, and there are abundant traces of former supernumerary ribs below, where in the horizontal position they were needed to support the viscera. Thus as the thorax has flattened from front to back and broadened laterally as man became erect, a change also marked from infancy to maturity, the adolescent chest growth is mainly lateral, while its length becomes relatively less.

Marro's measurement of chest circumference shows little increase from ten to twelve years, then a development reaching its maximum rate at fifteen, but continuing to nineteen. For the total period from eleven to nineteen years the augmentation was from 0.62 to 0.76 meters. Kotelmann concluded that the circumference of the thorax, which in adults is one-half the length of the body, does not attain that relation until about nineteen, and grows most rapidly at puberty. Hrdlicka found it relatively deepest from front to back in infancy, and that it grew broad and flat with age up to the early teens. Porter found chest girths nearly equal from thirteen on for two or three years, but that boys excelled girls at all ages in chest expansion, girth of chest being usually about equal to sitting height.

The pelvic girdle, as if also in response to a downward tendency of the center of gravity, is, as it were, slowly creeping up the spine. At any rate, the trunk was once longer and the upper sacral vertebræ, the incorporation of which with the hip-bone is later than with the lower vertebræ, have left us now a trifle uncertain whether man has twenty-five or twenty-six presacral vertebræ. This relative approximation of the upper and lower bony girdle is easier because both are developed later than the skeleton of the limbs.[1]

The pelvic region, especially in girls, undergoes important pubertal changes. The iliac arches broaden, the Y cartilage, separating the three parts of the hip-bone, begins to ossify from several centers about the age of puberty, and the epiphyses about the crest of the ilium unite with the main bone at from twenty-three to twenty-five years of age. Complementary and intercalary bony points develop and join, especially the newly discovered cotyloid bone of Albinus between the pubis and the ilion, which join at eighteen. There is enlargement in like manner in the region of the symphysis pubis, and sometimes so great as to noticeably rotate the neck of the femur and toes outward in girls. The transverse diameter of the pelvis, which before is often less than the antero-posterior, now becomes greater and the inclination of the pelvis is decreased. These changes give firmer support to the large iliac and gluteal muscles, better sustain the viscera, and make balance easier, especially laterally, and may cause noticeable modification in posture and carriage. The five sacral and four coccygeal bones unite at from eight to ten years, but are fully fused into one at fifteen or eighteen. The sacrum and coccyx are often not completely joined at twenty-five, and the mobility of the latter, particularly its lower members, which is maintained very late in women, plays an important rôle in confinement. The female pelvis is broader horizontally relatively to that of the male. The dimensions of the iliac fossæ are less in the female, the distance of the os pubis is greater, and it has an inclination to the horizon of at least five degrees more than that of the male.

The development of the female pelvis is one of the most exact expressions of puberty, coinciding in time and following completely the growth and needs of the organs it contains. The parallel between the development of the two is as close as that of the sexual organs themselves and the

[1] Wiedersheim. Structure of Man, 1895, p. 32 *et seq.*

breasts. All the many points of differentiation from the male pelvis seem to be increasing in civilized lands, and pelvic dimensions increase with the degree of cephalization at birth, in which racial differences are so well pronounced. Sexual dimorphism is nowhere so marked in the pelvic region as in man. Complete pelvic development is rarely attained till well into the twenties for women, and is of profound importance for normal maternity. In this respect, the sexes seem to be growing unlike in many communities instead of alike, and from the mechanism of this part alone we see how every kind of physical training involving its activity should be modified for women during and after pubescence.[1] Sargent[2] found that the girth of hips from thirteen to sixteen is one and three-fourth inches larger in girls than in boys, and that they were more than two inches larger in the girth of thighs. From seven to twelve Landsberger found that the greatest breadth of hips increased from 18.2 to 21.9 centimeters.

(*c*) *Growth of the Head.*—The development of the face is a long, slow process, and to fully trace it we must begin as low down as the lamprey, where the skull appears. The fantastic faces of fishes and even ophidians, which often suggest so many kinds of ugliness to us, have very little expression. The head moves but little, independently, and the movements of jaws and eyes constitute the only expression. This is true even in birds. As we ascend the animal series, we see the snout slowly forming and developing to a nose, at first embryonic; the lips acquire increasing and independent mobility; the superciliary ridges, crests, brows, and eyebrows develop; the cheek-pouches, jaws, and, last of all, the nose and chin appear. In many animals, ear movements seem to be those most expressive of inner states of mind; in others, the tail; in still others, secretions—excretory, salivary, etc. The circulatory system becomes very expressive, and blushing, paling, and changes of heart rate respond to every flitting change in the psyche. Again, respiration is a delicate register, as is the voice. Pupils, patella tension, delicate

[1] Some of these later differences are very briefly summed up in Bierent's La Puberté, 1896. See chiefly, however, the standard texts on human anatomy, in which the above data are found.

[2] The Physical Development of Women. Scribner's Magazine, 1889.

changes in the timbre of the voice, in the depth and form of respiration, in the movement of the eye and all its adjacent parts, the posture of the head, the permanent expression and the range and kind of mobility of nostril, forehead, and mouth, constitute a very comprehensive repertory of expression, the development of which is an interesting chapter, the richness of which the superficial current treatises on expression in no wise suggest, but conceal.

Perhaps no part of the body has been so much measured and discussed as the skull. Its philogenetic origin and relation to the vertebra is a problem the solution of which Goethe suggested, and it seems to have perennial interest. Cranial capacity is measured in various ways. Török[1] enumerates 535 skull measurements. Benedict[2] insists that his many score of cathetometric determinations shall be made "with crystallographic exactness," and Rieger[3] sees in studies of skull dimensions a power of distinguishing ethnic stocks almost comparable to the value ascribed by phrenologists to its curves as exponents of mental and moral traits. While there is some reason to surmise that the long-headed races tend to excel the round- or broad-headed races in the competition seen in civilized, and particularly in urban life (Schlitz concluded that dark and long-headed pupils stood highest, although he found a mixture of long and broad heads superior to pure types), there are so few problems in this field yet solved that the very great number of craniometric measurements sometimes insisted on seem at present little more than an affectation.

The length of the face from the middle of the chin to the beginning of the hair Landsberger found to increase between six and thirteen years from 14.7 to 16.5 centimeters. Quetelet found it to increase between six and maturity from 16 to 18.6 centimeters, and to grow most rapidly during puberty. This dimension, therefore, increases more rapidly during school age than any other head measurement. While the face grows, the upper arch of the head remains almost stable. Porter

[1] Ueber einen universalen Kraniometer. Leipzig, 1888.

[2] Kraniometrie und Kephalometrie.

[3] Ueber die Beziehungen des Schädellehre zu Physiologie, Psychol., u. Ethnologie.

found that the height of face from the hair line to the point of the chin in boys, whose superiority was greatest at six, declining at eleven or twelve, underwent marked augmentation at thirteen, was increased still more from fourteen to fifteen, and was also marked from fifteen to sixteen; and that in girls there was a slight increase in the rate of this growth from twelve to fourteen, when till fifteen they equaled or exceeded boys, only to be surpassed by them in the next two years. He found that the superiority of boys decreased from six to thirteen, when girls, having undergone augmentation, almost equaled them for a time, only to be excelled still more by them after fourteen, the girls' development in this respect having nearly ceased at sixteen, when boys were still increasing rapidly. The distance from the root of the nose to the point of the chin in boys was distinctly augmented from fourteen to fifteen, while in girls this acceleration was from ten to thirteen or fourteen. In width of face, Porter found that boys' superiority over girls declined from thirteen to sixteen, when there was closest approximation, girls' faces growing broad rapidly from fourteen to fifteen, boys' too, showing distinct pubertal broadening. West found that in width of face boys excelled girls, but were almost equaled by them at twelve, from which age to twenty-one they increased steadily, except for a slight drop at nineteen, at a faster rate than girls, the latter reaching their maximum at eighteen.

Head form is relatively uninfluenced by climate and food, and is one of the clearest of all permanent, hereditary differences. The best of the head measurements is perhaps the ratio between length and breadth, above eighty being usually classed as brachycephalic or broad-headed, and below seventy-five being classed as dolichocephalic or long-headed. Ripley[1] concludes that the basal population of Europe in the stone age was composed of long heads, the Eskimos being a relict of the old Cromagnan stock. Round heads came in from Asia, slowly driving the long heads upland and producing the vast diversity in small space that characterizes the western part of the Old World. Since then nationality

[1] Popular Science Monthly, Feb., 1897, *et seq.*

and language have no longer been founded on race, the more relatively permanent mold of true and really pure types was broken, and the mixture caused a ferment which under the name of social and political progress tends toward progressive mediocrity. He concludes that America, being still further mixed and standing betwen the Asiatic breadth of skull and Western length, should persist in the serene impartiality of mongrels, be terrified at no conclusion, etc.

Beginning, then, at the vertex, and passing down, we note that there is a gradual increase in the breadth of the skull in both sexes; in girls at least to the eighteenth year, while in boys this development does not seem to be complete at twenty-one. This increase is most rapid in boys from fourteen to eighteen, and from about twelve to fifteen in girls. Growth in length of skull from the glabella to the farthest occipital point is greater not only absolutely but relatively, and the pubertal increment is more marked, being greatest from thirteen to fifteen in boys, but continuing at least till twenty, and being slower but more evenly distributed from twelve to eighteen in girls. In these measurements, but most in length, boys exceed girls at all ages; but in all, girls gain on, and most nearly approximate boys from ten to thirteen, and in all, the adolescent increment is distinct but not great.[1] From twelve to nineteen the average distance between the eyes increases from about fifty-two to sixty-two millimeters.

The diploe and sinuses of some of the bones of the skull are often found growing as late as, and even after puberty. The basi-occipital may be joined to the basi-sphenoidal bone by cartilage as late as the twentieth year, when ossification takes place and completes the union in about two years. The air-cells in the temporal bone are not developed till near puberty, and the stylohyoidal process grows with sudden rapidity at puberty, but only joins late in life. At this age, too, the spongy bones which appear at birth join the body of

[1] For these head and face measurements, see G. M. West, Anthropometrische Untersuchungen über die Schulkinder in Worcester, Mass., Arch. f. Anthropol., 1893, p. 13 *et seq.*

the sphenoid. The laminæ of the vomer, too, are completely united with it only at puberty.[1]

The greatest skull diameter from front to back, according to Quetelet, increases from six to maturity from 17.8 to 19.1 centimeters; according to Liharzik, from 17.5 to 21 centimeters; according to Landsberger, from 16.5 to 17.5 centimeters at the age of thirteen, when his measurements end. Landsberger holds that the growth of the skull is independent of that of body length and follows laws peculiar to itself. The greatest diameter of the skull from seven to thirteen he found to increase only from 14.6 to 14.7 centimeters, or almost nothing during school age.

The sagittal diameter of the head from the vertex to the middle of the chin, often called height of head, increases from thirteen to sixteen, and in girls is but one-fifth of an inch below that in boys. According to Landsberger, whose figures are slightly higher than those of Quetelet and less than those of Liharzik, it is from 20.7 to 21.7 centimeters.

Sargent found that the mean girth of the head in girls from thirteen to sixteen is but one-fifth of an inch below that in boys.

In length of head, West found boys always superior to girls, but their relative increase was greatest in this respect from eighteen to twenty. In width of head, he found boys to always excel, but to gain upon girls almost steadily from eighteen to twenty-one. Porter found that from fourteen to sixteen there was a marked augmentation in the increase of the length of head in boys; that in girls a similar augmentation began at twelve, and was still in force at sixteen. He found that while boys were superior to girls in length of head at all ages, they were much more so from six to eleven, and that from that age to fifteen girls gained almost steadily upon boys; and that almost the same was true for width of head, only the differences and gains were less marked.

In apes and lower races of men the sutures of the skull unite first in the frontal, then in the parietal, and last in the occipital region, while in civilized man this order is reversed.

---

[1] See Quain, Elements of Anatomy, 9th ed., vol. i, p. 68 *et seq.*; also Henle, Handbuch der Knochenlehre, *passim*.

Whether this is atavistic or developmental is uncertain. Wiedersheim thinks that an original independence of ossification centers inherited from lower ancestors may be sometimes retained in the interest of the progressive development of the anterior lobes. Venn's[1] measurements indicate a "small but decided" increase in head measurements after nineteen in all students, but this gain is distinctly more in honor than in poll men. Galton[2] found that 258 higher honor English university students had distinctly larger skulls than poll men, in the ratio of 241 to 230.5. But while, according to his computation, the brain of the former increased only three per cent during their college course, that of the poll men increased six per cent. In all cases the head grew after the age of nineteen. Honor men thus seemed more precocious. Measurements do not yet tell us in what part of the skull the later stages of growth are greatest, but by long-continued individual methods, starting from fixed points, this problem does not seem inaccessible. While the relation of the volume of the brain to the cranial capacity varies greatly, and may be twenty per cent less, it would seem a reasonable inference that in growing periods the correspondence is closer and that, as we know the brain to be erethic, pressure from within may be one cause of cranial growth late as well as early in the development period.

Dr. Warner[3] found that cranial abnormalities, including asymmetry, and also skulls too large or too small, were the most important defects in development. They were not only most numerous, but had the widest correlation with low nutrition, nervousness, ordosis, epicanthus, bad balance of head, overcorrugation or overmobility of frontal muscles, and even defects of speech and form of ear.

In what we may conceive as the long developmental struggle for existence between the cranial and the facial parts of the skull, the latter would prevail till massive jaws, teeth, and muscles at the entrance of the alimentary canal were overcom-

[1] Cambridge Anthropology, by J. Venn. Journal of the Anthropological Institute, November, 1888.

[2] Head Growths in Students of University of Cambridge, by F. Galton. Ibid.

[3] An Inquiry as to the Physical and Mental Condition of School Children, Brit. Med. Jour., March 12 and 19, 1892.

pensated in value for survival, by brain power.[1] Between eleven and twenty-five four pairs of permanent teeth are acquired in the lower jaw. Welcker's table of second dentition is as follows:

MONTH OF APPEARANCE.	Name of tooth.	Year of change.
	First molar tooth.	7
6–8 (under jaw first)	Inner incisors.	8
7–9 " " "	Outer "	9
12–15	Front premolars.	10
16–20	Eye-teeth.	11–13
20–24	Back premolars.	11–15
	Second molar teeth.	13–16
	Third molar teeth.	18–30

Daffner [2] concludes that the permanent incisors begin to appear at about six years and nine months of age; that the permanent eye-teeth and buccal teeth appear between eleven and twelve; that the permanent molars are cut early in the fourteenth year; and that the wisdom teeth appear on the average at about the age of twenty-one years and six months, although this age varies four or five years in different individuals. In general, these teeth appear first on the lower jaw. The deciduous teeth are more primitive in type, and the molars are less useful in warfare, but suggest a change of food habits, and involve greater length of jaw to make room for them and greater strength of muscle. Hence pubertal increase of the lower jaw, which is often specified in our returns, may perhaps be assumed. Increased prominence of the chin, breadth of lower jaw, propensity to chew, to bite hard things, or to perform feats of strength with the teeth and jaws, the frequency with which clenching the teeth is mentioned in our anger returns, which shows a great pubertal development of irascibility, teaches how clearly jaw tension, once a chief factor in battles, is still associated with pugnacity. This, too, is a theme inviting further research.

Our *questionnaire* returns also show that it is a very common impression that the lower jaw grows in size during pu-

[1] The Structure of Man an Index to his Past History, by G. R. Wiedersheim, 1895.

[2] Das Wachstum des Menschen. Leipzig, 1897. See also Vierordt. Physiologie des Kindesalters.

bescent years, most specifying that the chin becomes more prominent, others that it widens at the outer angle, grows deep, strong, and more firmly set. This change, I think, has been pronounced in boys under my observation, and has given the face an aspect of strength and character. It would be natural to expect that the growing width of the face in the molar region would involve increased width in the lower jaw, where the inferior ends of the same muscles are attached. No adequate measurements, however, have yet been published upon this point, although one careful memoir[1] shows that the lower jaw in man is heavier between twenty and forty-five than it is later, and that it is always heavier in man than in woman, both absolutely and relatively to the weight of the skull. Further research is also needed on this point. It may be here added that Dr. Schlitz,[2] in studying 1,413 children between twelve and fourteen in Heilbronn to determine race types, found that all measurements involving the chin formation were defective because of its imperfect development. The facial index, too, he thought unserviceable, because the face was not yet completely grown in length.

The nasion, or depression on the level of the eyes between the root of the nose and the beginning of the glabella above, is often said to fill out during puberty in a way to straighten the line joining nose and forehead. This is a thing so frequently specified by intelligent parents in our *questionnaire* returns that it deserves attention. Dr. F. Boaz has made this region an object of study by taking many drawings, using flexible strips of lead, plaster, etc., with Worcester school children.

That the nose itself grows is generally believed by those making returns, increase in length being most often specified, prominence next, and breadth least often.

Some think that the upper jaw comes forward in the region of the alveolar point, but more think that together with the upper lip it grows in vertical length. Some state that the

---

[1] Gurriesi e Masetti. Influenza del sesso e dell' età sur peso del cranio el della mandibola. Revis. Sperimen. di Frenatria, 1895.

[2] Correspondenz-Blatt für Anthropologie, September, 1899.

coronal suture now hardens; others that the vertical depth of the skull in the bregma region increases; others that the occipital point grows prominent or they think they first detect bilateral asymmetries, that the eyes come more to the front as if their sockets were more parallel as they were growing farther apart; that the palate grows more or less arched, etc. Such data indicate a wide range of individual variation, and the need of many further measurements. Their value is, of course, chiefly suggestive till confirmed by a large number of measurements.

Another change often specified in our returns is a marked increase in the volume of the neck, seen in its circumference and especially in the region of the opisthion. The growth in the circumference of the neck between six and twelve years increases from 24.9 to 27.9 centimeters. Sargent found the neck of girls from thirteen to sixteen about two-fifths of an inch smaller than that of boys. The popular impression of relation between fulness in the upper part of the neck and lower posterior skull, involving the occipital bone and the region of the atlas, on the one hand, and sex on the other, has found expression in many ways.[1] In Brittany and Algeria, two ends of a thread are held between the teeth and the loop is drawn tight over the back of the neck. If this loop can be made to pass over the head, the girl is declared fit to marry and the boy must pay taxes, bear arms, etc. Popular vagaries like those of Dr. Damm, a German therapeutist, who assumes that each nation has a normal life of one thousand years, and that progressive slenderness in the nape of the neck, which increases with ethnic age, is the best index of how far the senescence of a race, nation, family, or individual has proceeded, reflect the same vulgar notion. Whether changes really occur in this region which are related to the sex is doubtful, and that bone growth is involved is very improbable.

(*d*) *Abnormalities and Morbidities connected with Bone Growth, and its Hygiene.*—The increased volume of blood and physiological work which centers about the various bony epiphyses at this period of augmented growth, where ossification is taking place so rapidly at so many points and gradually fusing bones into solid individuality, is also increasing the

[1] The Child and Childhood in Folk-Thought. Alex. Chamberlain, p. 95.

proportion of solid matter in those parts of bones previously ossified. Bibra's opinion that the proportion of carbonate of lime in the bones increases toward nineteen, to diminish later, while that of phosphate of lime conversely decreases at that age and increases later, lacks confirmation. Although the bones, because they are the hardest parts of the body and the last to decay, are our chief data for interpreting the past of paleontology, they are nevertheless the framework of the body only in a mechanical and not in a morphological sense; their development is not only later than that of the soft parts, but is dominated by them. Bones, like all other tissues, are composed of cells, penetrated by nerves and blood-vessels, are very plastic both to the normal forces of growth and to external influences, and are subject to many diseases. Ossification may be premature or excessive, and the bones become too large, dense, or heavy. The processes of mineralization may even encroach on cartilages, arteries, heart, muscles, etc., until they decay from overcalcification, or they may invade the joints until they become rigid. On the other hand, bone growth by which the skeleton is completed may be deferred and insufficient in its later stages, and its parts, its connections, or both, may be arrested, while in a group of diseases of defect, bone-cells may be broken up and bone even discharged by suppurative processes, and again, bones may grow perversely in form, proportion, or chemical composition. In rickets, the skeleton grows into many irregular shapes, owing in part to abnormally compensated muscle tonus. Too much phosphate and carbonate of lime may make the bones so brittle as to cause spontaneous and recurrent fracture from the weight of the body. Defect of the mineral salts and excess of gluten and chondrin make them too soft and flexible. Finally, bones are not exempt from extremely well-marked types of invasion by micro-organisms.

If growth is excessive, there are often two kinds of so-called growing pains: First, that located in epiphyses or growing centers of the bones, which are supplied with nerves and may become the seats of inflammation. These pains may seem seated in the bones, limbs, and perhaps most often near the neck of the femur and tibia, although almost no part of the body is entirely exempt from them. Adolescent tarsalgia and arthralgia have been described. The rapid bone growth following fever may be attended with painful, though mild osteitis, periostitis, medullitis, and even hyperosteogenic exostosis, especially in boys between eleven and twenty-two. Second, the bones may grow faster than the muscles or the skin; the latter then suffer from abnormal tension and are stretched and perhaps bloodless, especially on the thighs, because growth in the various tissues involved is not proportionate. This, too, is often acutely painful.

Very interesting is the intimate relation between sex organs and bones, as seen in cases of osteomalacia consequent upon ovarian or testicular defect or removal, and still more so in acromegalia. In this disease the bones of the face and limbs, after having reached their normal size, continue to enlarge so as to greatly change the features and form. The hands and limbs are sometimes enormous. Changes in the thyroid gland, sex organs, and their functions and general nutrition are also common. Although these changes may be noticeable and become more rapid after thirty, they seem usually to originate at puberty, and by some, following Marie, are ascribed to disturbance in the pituitary body. It has been suggested that the normal growth of puberty is acromegalic, and that this process is a late recrudescence or continuation and excess of the rapid evolution of hands and feet, face, and limbs at the awkward age. I can find no more interesting case on record than one photographed and described at length by Marro,[1] of a precocious boy who, besides the large bones characteristic of this disease, was at nine years and six months of age practically a mature man in beard, voice, intelligence, etc., and who four months after semi-castration lost his beard and some other signs of abnormality.

Souza-Leite gives a brief history[2] of conceptions of acromegalia since it was first recognized at the Salpêtrière in 1886. It is, as the name indicates, a marked augmentation of the extremities, and often of the head. The rings, gloves, shoes, and hat are too small; the jaw, nose and cheeks enlarge; mus-

[1] La Purbeté, pp. 184, 185.

[2] Revue scientifique, 1890, p. 801 *et seq.*

cular force is at first increased and then decreased; the voice becomes deep, urination is profuse, and genital functions decline, and all these symptoms never occur in childhood, but always after puberty. After a long period of evolution it may remain stationary, but it rarely recedes. Patients generally grow feeble, rachitic, and perhaps die in syncope. Its chief activity is not only in the bones of the extremities, but at the extremity of the bones. The thymus, instead of disappearing as it should with youth, increases.

Excessive strain and tension at this period tend to various curvatures, lordosis, scoliosis, etc., so that too high pillows, sleeping in one position, ill-adjusted seats at school or on the bicycle, lacing, occupations that strain, confine, or require unnatural postures, are especially to be avoided at this age. It is necessary that the muscles should be used enough to keep them both flexible and growing with the bones, so that insufficient muscular development be avoided. They should not, however, be used enough to cause contractures, for unequal or abnormal tension may warp the bones. Children should never be made to feel ashamed of their height, which they often form crouching habits to conceal, but should be proud of it, and stand and sit as erect as possible, and habitual cross-legged attitudes should be avoided. The thorax suffers from such easily avoidable causes perhaps even more than the pelvis, which may be contracted in the coccygeal aperture by sitting too low down on the back; while many young people who might go through life with strong chests and good busts fail to develop them and remain on a lower plane of vitality, unable to breathe deeply and well. Brain-work, if excessive or ill directed, may cause modifications of muscular tenacity that affect bone growth and bodily form and symmetry generally. Normal muscle tensions are thus of great importance during these plastic, and therefore vulnerable, years.

So plastic are they that Jäger[1] thinks the following illustrative of Meyer's law that pressures and tensions exert great influence on the development of the human skeleton. The length of each vertebra in child and man he found to

[1] The Longitudinal Growth of the Human Bones, by Gustav Jäger. In his Problems of Nature. New York, 1897, p. 154.

increase steadily downward from the second cervical to the fifth lumbar (except from the second to the sixth dorsal, which he ascribes to the arms). Reckoning the body weight as nearly two pounds per inch, each vertebra would have less weight to sustain than the one above and more than the one below it. This increase is therefore ascribed to the stimulus of increased pressure.

Bone growth needs lime, and our returns abound in accounts of eating chalk, pencils, plaster of Paris, and even mortar. These appetites are most often specified when growth is most rapid, as after a fever. Some think these freaks of appetites are less in hard-water regions, and that bone growth is retarded if only soft water is used. Some physicians hold very strong views upon this subject. Perhaps at this stage of growth children need lime somewhat as cattle need salt; that their milk, etc., should have slight lime admixtures, and that all foods and drinks of acidulous character need such compensation. Perhaps the nicotine and other alkaloid habits, to which this age is so prone, may also owe part of their strength to nutritive needs, which might be better interpreted and thus lose their morbid character.

Interesting in this connection is the wide-spread belief in the western parts of this country that hard water causes sterility. Especially in soda regions we are often told that children are few, and many cases are cited where children in such places are born only to households where the water is distilled.

B. *Growth of Muscles.*—The epithelial muscle plates are developed from the primitive segments of the central wall of the mesothelium. These cells elongate in the direction of the embryonic axis, and from them the circa two hundred and forty skeletal or voluntary muscles arise. These show their characteristic structure early in fetal life, and fibrillation appears soon after. The details of the development of the muscles is one of the most obscure chapters of embryology. It seems clear, however, that both nerve and muscle fibers are well along in their development before they unite. In lower vertebrates the muscles are more or less segmented into myotomes by partitions and sclerotomes which cross them at each vertebra; but in man this is seen only in the deeper muscles nearest the spine. In general, the energy of the contraction of a muscle varies with the number, and its range with the lengths of its fibers. There is so wide a field of individual variation that Wiedersheim states that new muscles, not down in the text-books, can be found in nearly every human subject. He finds three classes of variations, viz., retrogressive and vestigial muscles, occasional or atavistic, and progressive or slowly developing muscles. Abnormalities are so frequent, and so completely connect man with normal apes, that he concludes that the chasm which separates them is entirely bridged so far as the muscular system is concerned, although this perhaps can not be so confidently stated of other systems. Variations are more frequent in the limbs than in the body, in the arms than in the legs, and in the hands than in the arms, suggesting here again that man breeds truer in the more fundamental than in the later acquired or accessory parts, which are less indispensable to life.

During pubescent growth the muscles increase in both length and thickness in both sexes, especially in boys, and their points of attachment to the bones become more pronounced. Oppenheimer thinks that at this period the muscular grows faster than any other tissue, unless it be fat in girls. Muscle growth is not only in the length and thickness of fiber, but it can no longer be doubted that new fibers are formed besides the primitive ones in animals and perhaps in man. In girls muscular growth is less pronounced, with the important exception of the uterine muscles, which acquire most of their development during these years.

In the human body of the adult male, considerably more than half the muscles, or 18,682 grams out of the total of 30,574 grams, are connected with the legs; 8,016 grams with the arms; and 1,708 grams with the back. The relation of the extensors of the forearm and head to that of the contractors is as 42 to 58.

We have no data to show just how much individual muscles grow with age. Several have attempted to determine the weight of the entire muscular system. Upon the six cases of Bischof and the much better work of Theile,[1] Mühlmann

[1] Theile. Nova. acta der Kaiserl. Leip. Akad. des Naturforscher. Halle, 1884.

concludes that at eight the muscles weigh 27.2 per cent of the entire body; at fifteen, 32.6 per cent; at sixteen, 44.2 per cent; at twenty-six, 45 per cent; and at none of the intermediate years he gives do they reach so high a proportion, but fall off slowly, and rapidly after forty-five, with the slight exception of the age of forty-two, when they reach the doubtful ratio or 49 per cent.

Of all the special measurements of growing boys in this respect the best are still the girths of arms and legs made by Kotelmann, as follows, the figures being centimeters:

Upper Arm

Age.	Extended.		Bent.	
		Yr. abs. increase		Yr. increase.
9	16.89	....	18.43	....
10	17.41	0.52	18.87	0.44
11	17.93	0.52	19.61	0.74
12	18.53	0.60	20.34	0.73
13	18.94	0.41	20.82	0.48
14	20.08	1.14	22.24	1.42
19	25.04	....	28.32	....

Lower Leg

Age.	Extended.		Bent.	
	Muscles of calf.	Yr. increase.	Calf.	Yr. increase.
9	24.65	....	26.38	....
10	25.42	0.77	27.26	0.88
11	26.23	0.81	28.00	0.74
12	27.08	0.85	29.14	1.14
13	27.65	0.57	29.62	0.48
14	29.30	1.65	31.45	1.83
19	34.60	....	36.94	....

These measurements were made on the left upper arm at the upper third of the biceps region, and at the upper third of the calf when both limbs were straight and also at their maximal flexion. The relatively less increase of the leg as compared with the arm he thought not normal, and ascribed to sitting in school. In muscle girths at hips, thigh, calf, biceps, and forearm, Moon found that "the boy at fifteen is relatively to height superior to the boy at eleven, and more nearly the equal of the man." The growth of these girths follows closely that of bone girths, only the period of acceleration begins a year earlier in the muscles of the leg—that is, at twelve instead of thirteen. In these muscle girths the boy is relatively to height inferior to the man.

Age.	Number of men measured.	Girths.					
		Right thigh.	Left thigh.	Right calf.	Left calf.	Upper right arm c'ntract'd	Upper right arm.
16	70	502	498	342	339	279	250
17	326	504	504	339	338	282	250
18	735	512	505	344	342	290	255
19	988	514	510	347	345	296	258
20	888	515	514	340	348	300	262
21	824	524	524	353	351	305	266
22	434	525	521	354	353	308	262
23	296	526	521	356	347	300	262
24	155	526	522	356	355	310	270
25	100	527	524	355	352	311	270
26	74	519	515	351	350	305	265
Total	4,890	3.5	4.1	3.1	2.9	6.6	4.9

Age.	Girths.			Breadths.				
	Upper left arm.	Right forearm.	Left forearm.	Neck.	Shoulder.	Nipples.	Waist.	Hips.
16	240	253	249	106	418	188	246	320
17	242	255	247	107	426	190	247	322
18	248	260	252	108	429	192	252	323
19	252	261	254	109	433	195	252	326
20	256	263	257	109	437	197	253	327
21	259	266	260	110	442	201	258	328
22	256	268	261	110	443	203	260	336
23	258	264	257	110	439	200	258	329
24	258	269	262	111	446	206	264	333
25	265	268	262	111	445	208	266	333
26	259	267	260	111	447	205	261	335
Total	5.9	2.5	2.6	4.0	3.9	4.4	3.2	3.2

The best data for showing the growth in the size of the larger voluntary muscles are those by Dr. Hitchcock, who has measured Amherst students for many years and who gathers into the above table the average girths and breadths found among the students for each age. The numbers are millimeters: In the lower line above I have added from the same authority the gain, of each student, in each of the dimensions named, during his four years in college, most of them eighteen on entering, and twenty-two on leaving. Comparing these figures with those available from five other American colleges, the difference in each respect is very slight, so that we have here the best account yet accessible of the growth of these muscles during the above years, a growth which is greatest in the upper arm, both flexed and relaxed. The neck, chest, and shoulder muscles seem here also to grow more than the waist and hip muscles, and those of the upper arm more than those of the thigh or calf. Although most of these measurements have been regularly taken on American college girls, I can learn of no treatment of the data to show growth.

Kotelmann's[1] measurement of boys in a Hamburg gymnasium between the ages of nine and twenty-one showed many interesting results. He found that the difference of girth between the relaxed and contracted muscles of the upper arm at the point of greatest expansion of the biceps constantly increased with age; also that this absolute increase was "distinctly greatest at the age of puberty and decreased more and more backward to nine and forward to twenty-one." Both bent and contracted, the relative increase of girth became annually greater to the age of fifteen, and less and less to twenty-one. He also found that while the growth of the muscles of the lower thigh as measured by girth increased, it was steadily less relatively to that of the upper arm with increasing years, or the older the pupil the more the rate of increase in the muscles of the lower extremities fell behind those of the upper; this he ascribed to sitting. When the difference in girth of thigh contracted and relaxed was measured, this disadvantage of the leg to the arm was still greater. These muscles were growing less contractile just at the age when those of the upper arm were growing most. Yet in each respect puberty was the age of most rapid relative and absolute annual increment, this being greatest at fourteen and less both before and after.

From the estimates of Wertheim,[2] it seems that the coefficient of elasticity of the muscles diminishes in a marked

[1] Die Körperverhältnisse der Gelehrtenschule. Berlin, 1879.

[2] Annales de Chimie et de Physique, vol. xxi, 1847, p. 385.

and rather steady way from infancy to old age, falling from 0.857 to 0.352; from twenty-one to thirty years in cohesion from 0.040 to 0.026 in kilograms pro 1 min.; and that for later years at least a marked decline in both these respects holds for the same qualities of nerves.

Sometimes the muscles grow in length more slowly than the bones, and then occur the "growing pains" so characteristic of this age, especially in boys, as we have seen. On the other hand, the muscles may grow more rapidly than the bones, and then the flexibility of joints often so extreme at this period of life is seen. The range of movements in joints is sometimes increased, though in some persons it is diminished. Sometimes muscular growth is not well distributed or is asymmetrical, and then new and perhaps abnormal positions of the body and limbs and new expressions of the face are seen. In morbid cases, arrest of growth of muscles may, like contractures, cause distortion of bones. Probably the most common disproportion in muscular development arises from the fact that the larger and more fundamental muscles, which move the greater joints, precede in their development the smaller, finer, or accessory muscles which move fingers, throat, lips, and make all the more delicate adjustments. This, along with the disproportion between bone and muscle growth, is one of the chief causes of the characteristic clumsiness of adolescent boys.

For the development of muscular function, see the next chapter, which is devoted to the subject.

C. *Growth of the Heart and Blood-Vessels.*—The heart, which seems to be phylogenetically a remnant of the primitive body cavity arising in vertebrates as a fissure in the mesoderm, according to Bütschli, begins its development in the embryo independently of the arteries and veins, and soon joins them, but not until after it has begun to beat. It is first a straight tube, and connects with the arterial system at its cephalic, and with the yolk or food supply at its caudal end. Gradually it becomes free, except so far as is needful for support, and begins its evolution toward the adult form by blending and twisting till all its chambers and valves are developed. The blood-vessels arise from a network in the area vasculosa, where groups of cells slowly aline themselves and become hollow. The first red blood-cells are probably proliferated and liberated cells from the endothelial lining of the vessels. These first elements of the blood slowly become flat, uniform, colored, and multiplied by division.

From their origin on to maturity the circulatory elements are probably the most variable of all the great anatomical systems, not excepting even the muscles. Indeed, variations in the form, position, and arrangement of the blood-vessels are so great that in all but the most fundamental respects it is often hard to tell what is normal and what is abnormal. Vascular variations constantly repeat not only fetal but prehuman animal arrangements. In general, the development is from fundamental to accessory, and arteries constantly compensate each other, not only in structure but in function, so that collateral circulation is easily developed, if not especially provided for as in many plexi, the circle of Willis, etc. Moreover, the heart continues to grow even to advanced age, although less rapidly after twenty-eight or thirty. Capillary changes are probably still more variable. Minot[1] goes so far as to say that "the immediate ancestors of the vertebrates had no capillary vessels, but only a few large afferent and efferent trunks with a few anastomoses," so that if variability and growth are inversely as either size or as ordinal development, a large field of unknown possibilities awaits exploration here. How much of this progressive capillary vascularity is pubertal we do not yet know.

This circulatory variability is nowhere so great as in those parts connected with the reproductive functions. We need but to instance the changes in the spermatic and ovarian blood-vessels as the testes and ovaries descend, the changes in the vaginal and uterine plexi, the pudic vessels, especially those going to and in the corpus spongiosum and the corpus cavernosum, the mammary, and most of all, the umbilical vessels, which are involved in both growth and function.

The mature heart ought to weigh about ten ounces in the male and eight in the female, or be from $\frac{1}{160}$ to $\frac{1}{170}$ of the weight of the body, and should be about the size of the tightly closed fist, increasing, according to Vierordt, to thirteen-fold

[1] Human Embryology, p. 229.

its size at birth in males and twelve-fold in females. Before puberty the volume of the heart is nearly the same in both sexes, but between fifteen and twenty Benecke found its volume to increase from an average of 160 to 225 cubic centimeters; this increase being from 25 to 30 cubic centimeters greater for males, but continuing only about one cubic centimeter per year for the next thirty years. This growth is not only in mass, but in the number of contractile fibers. Perhaps the best table here is that of Mühlmann, who, on the basis of Thoma's elaborate figures,[1] brings together the results of four elaborate measurements.

Age.	Body weight.	Weight of heart.	Rel. weight of heart.
	Gr.	Gr.	Per cent.
10	24,150	115	0.47
11	26,250	130	0.49
12	29,000	147	0.50
13	32,800	165	0.50
14	36,700	184	0.50
15	40,600	205	0.50
16	44,400	218	0.52
17	48,850	230	0.47
18	51,850	240	0.46
19	54,850	248	0.45
20	56,850	254	0.44
21	57,750	260	0.45
22	58,850	265	0.45
23	59,850	270	0.45
24	......	274	....
25	60,500	278	0.46

During the age of growth the increase of the heart keeps pace rather closely with that of the body, and this appears to be true for nearly all countries in Europe where these measurements have been made, and where the heart remains about 0.48 per cent of the body weight. This continued increase may be due to the fact that of all organs the circulatory are in the most favorable position to receive nourishment and oxygen from the blood. This increment may be so great as to seem almost pathological. After puberty hypertrophy of the heart is almost twice as frequent in males, and atrophy predominates in females. The heart now takes on the character and does the work of an adult organ, and normally

[1] Untersuchungen über die Grösse und das Gewicht der anat. Bestandtheile des menschl. Körpers. Leipzig, 1882.

responds well to the increased activity imposed upon it by the expansion of the circulatory area. If there be temporary hypertrophy, which seems beyond normal limits in certain dimensions, this is soon compensated in normal individuals, and development becomes proportional.

The frequency of heart-beats is reduced at adolescence, but here again data differ widely. One writer computed a falling of from eight to eleven beats per minute between the ages of ten and fifteen. Guy's figures are as follows:

Age.	Males.	Females.
8–12	79	92
14–21	76	82
21–28	73	80

Some conclude that there is a diminished, and some that there is an increased variation between minimal and maximal rates for a time. How much of the retardation is due to increased size of the heart, which sometimes grows in a saltatory way a fourth in a single year, how much to the temporary weakening of its power thus caused, how much to changed relations between general vascular capacity, or tension, and the total amount of blood, or to other causes, is unknown. It is, however, due more to increase in height than to age, for the pulse averages slower in tall than in short people. Volkmann and Ramenaux have given mathematical formulæ to express this retardation, and it has been found that the increase in frequency of heart-beats that follows the scale of decreasing stature, when carefully averaged for many cases, approximated the results obtained by calculation. Deductions of height, however, from the number of pulsations, even though they could be made with a far greater degree of accuracy than has yet been attained, for averages will be found, besides having a certain theoretical interest, to be of some value as a basis from which to measure the wide range of individual variations. Curiously, the ratio of diminished pulse to increasing height is nearly the same whether computed for the different stages of growth or for adults of different height.

The strength of the heart-beat measured by the force of its blow against the thoracic wall was found by Poatain[1]

[1] Clinique Medicale de la Charité. Paris, 1889.

to be greater at puberty. Whether the growth of this wall renders it more elastic or the heart-beat grows really stronger as it is reduced in frequency, whether there is a new relation slowly established between elasticity of its walls and the vigor or mode of its contraction, is unknown. The frequent palpitations and unaccountable variations in rate and mode of action and other functional disturbances, which often awaken a cardiac consciousness so disquieting, without any dangerous structural derangement, are among the more common experiences of this age, and are due, in part at least, to the change in size of the heart as compared with the lumen of the cardiac and other large arteries.

Although Gilbert's tests were only carried to the age of sixteen, his "data point very distinctly to the acceleration of the pulse during the age of puberty for both sexes, both in the curves of normal pulse and pulse subsequent to fatigue. This effect at puberty seems more marked for boys than for girls."

The blood-vessels can not be isolated for weighing, so that their circumference becomes the most important measurement. It is inferred that the growth of the larger vessels and that of the smaller capillaries in general coincide, although only the former have been measured. Vierordt's table is as follows:

Age.	Height.	Arteria pulmonalis.	Aorta ascendens.	Aorta thoracica.	Iliaca com. dextra.	Carotis com. dextra.	Subclavia dextra.
Years.	cm.	mm.	mm.	mm.	mm.	mm.	mm.
6–6⅚........	109	43	39	28	12	14.1	15.9
14½–16......	150	51	48	34	17	16.8	19.7
18–21........	164	59	54	41	20	17.8	22
24–31........	161	64	60	43	21	17.5	27
47–71........	171	67	73	54	27	20	29

The following is the best available table of diameters:

Age.	Arteria pulmonalis.	Aorta ascendens.	Aorta renalis.	Carotis communis dextra.	Subclavia dextra.	Renalis dextra.	Femoralis dextra.
Years.							
5–10.......	15.7	15.1	7.8	5.0	3.7	3.2	3.4
17–20.......	21.3	20.7	11.2	5.9	5.2	4.8	5.0
23–29.......	24.0	22.4	13.3	6.7	6.2	5.3	6.2

The arteries continue to grow in size till at least the age of sixty. The best of all measurements of them begins at the age of twenty.[1] The thickness of the arterial walls increases with age, but this probably occurs after the period of maximal increase of size, and involves diminished elasticity and erethism of most organs and tissues.

Of profound and far-reaching significance is the fact that before puberty the blood-vessels are large and the heart small. The latter now undergoes a great and often sudden relative increase. Landois says that from infancy to puberty the heart is small and the vessels relatively large, but in the adult, conversely, the heart is large and the arteries relatively narrow; so that there is a conversion of the relation existing between the size of the heart and the cross-section of the arterial system, taken as a whole. At birth the relation of heart to arteries is as 25 to 20; at the dawn of puberty it is as 140 to 50; and in full maturity it is as 290 to 61. The pulmonary artery is relatively large in infancy as compared with the aorta, but at puberty the two approximate the same diameter. Benecke[2] also thinks that before puberty the arterial system is larger relatively to the heart than afterward, and sums up his view by saying: "The larger the heart relatively to the vessels, the higher the blood-pressure, and the earlier this becomes the case, the earlier, stronger, and more complete is the development of puberty." A recent text-book sums up the matter by saying that the relation between the size of the heart and the width of the arteries is in children the reverse of what obtains in adults. "The ratio of the volume of the heart to the width of the ascending aorta before puberty is approximately as 56 to 20, while after puberty it is as 97 to 20." This means that there is almost double the volume to the heart's capacity, and as the arterial lumen is for a time unchanged, there is great increase of blood-pressure. This view is that the ratio of the weight of the blood to that of the body is increased after puberty.[3]

---

[1] Schiele-Wiegand. Virchow's Archiv, vol. lxxxii.

[2] Die anat. Grundlagen der Constitutionsanomalien der Menschen. Marburg, 1878.

[3] Exercise during Adolescence, by Walter Truslow. Am. Jour. of Physiology, III, 2, p. 114.

Arterial tension is also modified and blood-pressure is considerably augmented during adolescence, except in the lungs, where it is somewhat lowered in adults. Along with this goes, too, the slight increase of temperature at puberty, amounting on the average, according to the best estimates, to about $\frac{1}{2}°$ F. Vierordt's figures give for the ages between three and fourteen an increase of from 138 to 171 millimeters quicksilver; in adults it is 200, while the measurements that indicate the lowest results give a rise from three to thirteen years of from 97 to 113 millimeters. This suggests, especially when we consider the frequent anemia and chlorosis of this age, so common in girls, that while there is a distinct rise of pressure there is now, as in so many other respects, a widened range of variation not only between individuals and sexes, but in the same person at different times.

By the constant tension or tonicity of the walls of the arteries, which is maintained by the vaso-constrictor nerves, a high pressure of blood is always maintained in the arteries. As these divide toward the capillaries, the total cross-section of which is some six hundred times that of the aorta, pressure decreases and the rate of movement becomes very slight in the small and often negative in the large veins. Blood-pressure changes not only with every pulse-beat and respiration, but follows the longer and so far unexplained curves of Traube and Hering, and also the seasonal changes lately demonstrated by Zadek. With this increment of pressure at adolescence, together with a considerable increase of arterial caliber and the rise of temperature, is associated not only the increased metabolism and increased growth rate, but the necessity of mental and physical activity, the psychic intensity, need of excitement, and emotional prodigality so characteristic of the erethism of pubescent muscles, brain, stomach, and other organs, and the range of vascularity also widens. The importance of this action gives some countenance to the adage that a man's health and age are as that of the walls of his blood-vessels.

In the new-born child one-nineteenth of the body's weight is blood. This proportion decreases to one-thirteenth or one-fourteenth at maturity. It is never so variable in all its elements as at this age. About 29.2 per cent of all the blood is found in the muscles at rest, but this amount is, of course, greatly increased by their action; 29.3 per cent is found in the liver; 22.76 per cent in the heart, lungs, and great blood-vessels; 8.24 per cent in the bones; 6.3 per cent in the intestines; 2.1 per cent in the skin; 1.63 per cent in the kidneys; 1.24 per cent in the brain and spinal cord. In the very young child a very large part of the total quantity of blood circulates in the skin. In hemorrhage or anemia it may be, at any age, reduced or increased. In general, as Madden says in substance, a new balance is struck in the allotment of blood to the different parts of the body at this period, involving in some parts congestion and in others discharge, the last relieving the former. This is connected with an increase in the relative amount of blood and the increased power of producing it, with menstruation and all of the other profound changes of adolescence.

Tables show that with adolescent growth between the age of fourteen and maturity there is a retardation in the time of circulation of the blood, an increase of from 97.4 to 180 grams thrown out by one systole, and at the same time an increase of from 141 to 218 grams in the amount per second that passes the aorta. The work of the left chamber of the heart is still more increased from 0.3134 to 0.5668 kilometers, while the blood that circulates per minute through a kilogram of the body is reduced from 246 grams to 206 grams.

Of the many determinations of red and white blood-corpuscles, Schwinge's is the best. It is as follows for men:

	Red.	White.
1–10 yrs..................	4,516,000 per cubic mm.	12,940
10–20 "	5,225,000 " " "	8,711
20–30 "	5,278,000 " " "	7,915
30–40 "	5,063,000 " " "	5,882
40–50 "	5,455,000 " " "	6,554
50–60 "	5,397,000 " " "	8,576
60–70 "	5,003,000 " " "	8,541
70–80 "	5,478,000 " " "	10,165

Thus while the red or white corpuscles seem to hold their own or perhaps slightly increase with slight variation,

[1] Quain. Med. Dic.

the white corpuscles or leucocytes decrease in the thirties and forties, but increase again later.

The number of red blood-corpuscles per cubic millimeter is high at birth (5,368,000). It seems to decline at five or six years and perhaps to reach its maximum in the later teens and twenties; but all these determinations are still uncertain. The extinction coefficient of hemoglobin, which is very high during the first week of life, seems to rise with the development of puberty, as perhaps does the relative number of white to red corpuscles. The number of white corpuscles is enormously increased in leucocythemia and in the process of inflammatory reaction to certain inflective diseases, and by digestion, and, as like the red corpuscles they are constantly breaking down, their numbers may be very greatly reduced and their vigor impaired by age.

The ancient idea that blood is the best index of an eugenic race seems to have a certain confirmation in the studies that have been made on its specific gravity since Lloyd Jones's first important memoir[1] in 1887. According to Sörensen, beginning with about 1,050 in both sexes in the third year, this rises on the average in boys till the seventeenth year to 1,058, with little change thereafter till old age, when it falls. In girls it rises till the fourteenth year to 1,055, at seventeen drops a little, and remains some three points below that of man till about forty-five. The plasma alone, however, in woman has a slightly higher specific gravity than in man, with a distinct rise at puberty not seen in males. A sexual difference thus becomes evident at the dawn of adolescence. Menstruation both at its first onset and at each periodic return causes a slight reduction of the specific gravity of the blood. The period between fifteen and twenty-two, when variations in the specific gravity of the blood in girls are great and when it may fall very low, is called by Dr. Jones the age of anemia, and suggests that the chlorosis so characteristic of that period is an exaggeration of a state normal in old age. That specific gravity rises in women after the age of child-bearing is only another indication that this sexual difference is associated with the repro-

[1] On the Variations in the Specific Gravity of the Blood in Health. Journal of Physiology, 1887.

ductive functions. Variability in the quantity of serum, fibrin, alkali, carbonic acid, and hemoglobin, is known to be great, but so far these fluctuations have not been definitely associated with puberty.

D. *Growth of the Lungs.*—Lungs and chest share to a marked degree in the augmented development of adolescence. This is true whether inferred from girths of the chest expanded or contracted (which do not consider the movements of the diaphragm, which have not been measured), or by determining the weight of the lungs from the cadaver at different ages, or by recording the maximum amount of air that can be expelled into a spirometer. In the following table I have brought together averages from various tables, many of which are now at hand:

Age.	Weight of both lungs, boys.—Mühlmann.	Weight of both lungs, girls.	Volume of both lungs, boys.—Vierordt.	Capacity av. 4,890 students. —Hitchcock.	Vital capacity, boys, Chicago, 1900-'01.	Vital capacity, girls.	Chest girth in repose.—Hitchcock.	Chest girth full.	Moon. 100 boys. Lung capacity.	Beyer. Chest girths, 4,542 cadets. Inches.
9	357.6	371.7 }		....	1,500	1,325	...	...	....	.....
10	486.8	430.0 }	596.2	....	1,650	1,450	...	...	....	.....
11	465.8	490.0 }		....	1,800	1,600	...	...	1.80	.....
12	415.0	672.2	....	....	1,950	1,750	...	...	2.00	.....
13	458.7	.....	....	....	2,200	1,925	...	...	2.13	.....
14	698.1	507.5	....	....	2,450	2,100	...	...	2.36	.....
15	750.3	684.1	771.3	....	2,800	2,225	...	...	2.80	29.95
16	747.3	675.6	1,362.2	3.91	3,300	2,300	858	897	....	31.10
17	772.9	703.2	1,001.2	4.01	3,575	2,350	857	886	....	31.84
18	867.0	677.4	1,148.2	4.11	3,850	2,425	867	917	....	32.68
19	990.5	843.7	1,143.7	4.11	3,825	2,500	882	925	..	33.25
20	962.5	803.1	1,804.2	4.23	3,825	2,550	889	924	....	33.58
21	943.9	903.5	1,621.10	4.27	4.221	4,221	901	941	....	33.65
22	998.3	784.1 }		4.35	46	223	409	949	....	33.77
23	946.0	896.9 }	1,655.5	4.36	4,100	2,600	899	944	....	33.87
24	961.6	884.9 }		4.38	.....	.....	915	959	....	.....
25	994.9	875.1 }		4.38	.....	.....	917	957	....	.....
26	.....	.....	....	4.75	.....	.....	894	949	....	.....

Averaging records of Amherst students for twelve years, Hitchcock found that during their four years' course the increase was 7.1 per cent of their lung capacity on entering. It is certain that the lungs continue to grow in weight until old age. In youth they constitute from 1½ to 2 per cent of the body weight, while in mature years from 2½ to 3⅜ per cent. Thus they outgrow the body, especially the alveolar cells which are vigorous and growing in extreme age, when the elastic fibrous tissue has begun to degenerate. According to Smedley, girls increase most rapidly in vital capacity from twelve to fourteen, after which the increment is at a diminished rate and appears to end before twenty. Boys take a sharp start upward at fourteen, increasing most rapidly for two years thereafter, but continue a rather rapid rise till at least nineteen and a half. Smedley says that the difference between the greatest amount of air that can be expired after a forced inspiration into a wet spirometer has very marked increment during adolescence; is much greater in those trained to physical exercise; decreases with the amount of activity; and if taken in connection with size is an index of the rate of metabolism.[1] In boys the rate of annual increase in this respect reaches its first maximum at fourteen; shows a very slight decline at fifteen; and reaches its highest maximum at sixteen. Among all twelve-year-old children tested it was found to be much greater the higher their standing in the grades, and to be distinctly inferior in boys in a school for laggards.

In Chicago the greatest percentile differences in the vital capacity of boys is at sixteen, when it ranges from 2,400 to 4,200 cubic centimeters, and in girls at fifteen. In both, this is naturally just after the year of greatest aggregate measure.

Age.	Yearly increase.	Relation—	
		Of the circumference of the thorax to vital capacity.	Of body length.
9	...	26.9	13.8
10	94	27.6	14.3
11	157	29.1	14.2
12	155	30.5	15.6
13	93	31.4	15.9
14	226	32.8	16.8
15	261	....	....
16	495	....	....
17	301	....	....
18	...	....	....
19	...	43.5	23.3

[1] Report of the Department of Child Study and Pedagogic Investigation. Chicago, 1900. No. 2.

Increase of thoracic capacity, on which the strength of the body architecture is so dependent, seems from the measurements of Kotelmann, Roberts, Pagliani, Pesskoff, Erismann, Schnepf, and Wintrich to be of great significance, and to follow the curve of weight increment more closely than that of height. Correlating the figures of four of these writers, we have the results in the table on opposite page.

The normal enlargement of the heart at puberty is so great as to materially lessen the vital capacity. Careful measurements show, however, that this reduction is more than compensated by the enlargement of the thoracic space, due to growth, and more yet by increase in the surface of the pulmonary tissue, which in a man is about 200 square meters. Between twenty and thirty the right lung of the male, which is smallest at birth, becomes, according to Boyd, about one-third heavier than in the female. One of the now somewhat extended list of diseases, which are less liable to appear during pubescent acceleration of growth, is consumption, although whether adolescent development can regenerate pulmonary tissue already lost, as Lancaster[1] thinks, is a question which must for the present be left in abeyance.

The following is the interesting table of vital capacity from Pagliani:[2]

Years.	M.	F.	Circumference of thorax. Boys (cm.).
8	....	1,240	....
9	....	1,290	....
10	1,660	1,500	61.0
11	1,700	1,585	61.2
12	1,860	1,766	62.8
13	2,045	1,930	65.2
14	2,100	2,100	66.4
15	2,445	2,233	69.5
16	2,485	2,223	70.3
17	2,660	2,300	71.6
18	3,115	2,325	72.6
19	3,125	....	74.2

Kotelmann[3] found the circumference of the thorax at the nipple to increase most rapidly in the fifteenth year; next

[1] Lancaster. Psychology and Pedagogy of Adolescence. Ped. Sem., vol. v, No. 1, p. 61.

[2] Luigi. Sopra Alcuni Fattori dello Sviluppo Umano. Turin, 1876, p. 54.

[3] Die Körperverhältnisse der Gelehrtenschule. Berlin, 1879.

most rapidly in the year before and the two years after; and then to decline up and down the age scale to nine and twenty-one, and this both absolutely and relatively. This in adults is about half the height, but for boys chest girth is more than half the height and increasingly so to fourteen, and then approximates the adult norm. As compared with body weight, on the other hand, chest girth increases more and more slowly. He found that vital or lung capacity measured on the spirometer increases most rapidly during the sixteenth year, and declines absolutely and relatively up and down the age scale. However chest girth be taken—in inspiration, expiration, or rest—vital capacity increases more rapidly than it. This increases more rapidly than height, but slower than weight. The relation between chest girths in maximal inspiration and expiration decreases with age, showing progressively less elasticity.

Beyer's[1] table of chest circumference is as follows:

Age.	Cadets, 4,541.	Men, 3,445.
15	29.95	30.07
16	31.10	30.40
17	31.89	31.34
18	32.68	31.80
19	33.25	32.00
20	33.58	32.50
21	33.65	33.14
22	33.77	33.62
23	33.87	34.00

Moon's data for the ages below sixteen years are continued by the Amherst figures based on 742 students, where the same men in the classes from 1885 to 1901 were measured for three and one-half years:

Moon

Years.	Capacity of lungs.
11–12	1.80
12–13	2.00
13–14	2.13
14–15	2.36
15–16	2.80

[1] Beyer, H. G. The Value to Physiology of Anthropometric Tests and Measurements in the Form of Statistics and their Importance to Education. Reprinted from the Journal of the Boston Society of Medical Sciences, May, 1901, vol. v, pp. 482–495.

Amherst

Age.	Numbers.	Chest Repose.		Lung Capacity.		Lungs.
		Actual in mm.	Per cent.	Actual in liters.	Per cent.	
16.......	30	54.46	6.63	.59	17.37	1.31
17.......	134	39.70	4.76	.43	11.81	1.15
18.......	244	31.76	3.73	.32	8.30	1.33
19.......	153	23.56	2.71	.29	7.22	1.36
20.......	73	29.13	3.32	.26	6.78	1.40
21.......	49	19.46	2.20	.15	3.82	1.41
22.......	27	20.70	2.29	.15	3.61	1.47
23.......	12	13.08	1.50	.11	3.43	1.46
24.......	13	20.61	2.18	.13	3.39	1.44
25.......	7	25.85	3.01	.26	6.86	1.40
Average .	..	30.39	3.50	.31	8.36	1.22

Sargent found that while there was little difference in the natural chest of the sexes from thirteen to sixteen, boys show superior expansive power. In lung capacity he found girls from thirteen to sixteen to be seventy cubic inches behind boys, and far weaker in strength of expiratory muscles. Porter found that in the power of mean expansion of the chest, boys gained over girls almost steadily from eight, but with a slight gain in the rate of their superiority from twelve to seventeen. In chest girths he found the year of most rapid growth in boys to be from fourteen to fifteen, and that it continued to be rapid to eighteen. In girls, he found the years of greatest increase in chest girth to be from twelve to fourteen.

In vital capacity the Chicago boys increased steadily but little from six to twelve. The next two years showed a marked increase, and from fourteen to sixteen came the greatest rate of increase, followed by diminution during the next two years. In vital capacity, the increment of Chicago girls was manifest before eleven, greatest for the next three years, with progressive decline from fourteen, and especially from fifteen to seventeen.

Moon found that chest power, which increased but little from eleven to thirteen, underwent very marked increase between fourteen to sixteen, when his tests ended, as did lung power, although the latter was less marked. Strength of expiratory muscles and legs he found to develop earlier than those of back and forearm.

Landsberger's measurements show increase during the ages

from six to thirteen from 52.3 to 60.5 centimeters in the circumference of the body at the navel, but at a rate less and less each year than the height. Sargent found that girls from thirteen to sixteen were 1½ inch smaller at the waist than boys.

Zak[1] finds the circumference of the chest increasing fastest in the fourteenth and fifteenth years, viz., 4.1 and 3.6 centimeters respectively. An increased rate of chest girth began at thirteen and one-half, and from sixteen and one-half it was less rapid but marked to eighteen and one-half, when it became slow but continued to increase to twenty-two and one-half, when his census ended. At all ages after twelve it was greater absolutely than that of rural and peasant children, whose most rapid increment was later and continued a year longer, viz., to nineteen and one-half. Of thirteen of the best measurements made in various lands the Russian choir boys of Vasilyew excel all others from ten to fourteen, and the English boys of Roberts from fourteen to eighteen. Up to nineteen chest circumference is less than half the height and thereafter greater. From eleven to fourteen, both inclusive, it is nearly four centimeters less than half the height, this difference being greatest at thirteen. In factory boys and in all other classes this inferiority of chest girth to half height either did not exist or was less marked at all ages to seventeen. No measurements have shown such marked inferiority of chest development in school-going youth.

Ling wished young men to increase one hundred and fifty-four cubic centimeters semiannually for a few years, and there are cases where running has increased chest capacity over three hundred cubic centimeters in three months. Some think exercise also gives increased efficiency of a respiratory surface of a constant size. Deep breathing, however caused, no doubt acts against auto-intoxication, gives increased power to resist disease, is the root of endurance under effort, and is of great and hitherto unsuspected importance in determining the level or intensity of life, one of the chief variables with which the rate and completeness of normal oxidation of the blood is correlated. The ratio of lung capacity to weight is very properly called the vital index. Training largely consists in taking off weight and adding lung power. In the interests of effective

[1] Op. cit., p. 141 *et seq.*

respiration there is much to be said against the military position required at the command " attention," because it so restricts the action of the diaphragm.

Frequency of respiration, like so many other functions, is very dependent upon size. The rhinoceros breathes six, and the rat two hundred and ten times per minute. The human infant begins life with from thirty-five to forty-four, and at fifteen has settled to eighteen or twenty respirations per minute when at rest. For a score of years thereafter the rate normally varies but little.

Vierordt compiles the following interesting table showing the relation of vital capacity or the respiration content to height as follows:

Age.	cm.³ for 1 cm.	Height.
8–10	11.40	9–11
10–12	12.00	11–13
12–14	14.17	13–15
14–16	16.44	
16–18	20.65	
18–20	23.40	
20–25	23.25	
25–30	22.98	
40–50	21.00	

Hastings, on the basis of 5,496 children, gives the following interesting bases for comparison:

Age.	Lengths (cent.).		Breadths (cent.).			Depth (cent.) chest.	Girths (cent.) chest expansion.	Strengths lung capacity (liters).
	Height sitting.	Span of arms.	Head.	Chest.	Waist.			
5	59.32	102.44	14.21	18.10	16.52	12.39	3.42	.67
6	61.35	108.18	14.24	18.43	16.69	12.83	4.29	.83
7	64.08	114.28	14.33	18.92	17.14	12.91	4.58	.99
8	66.00	119.34	14.44	19.44	17.66	12.89	5.95	1.15
9	68.00	124.70	14.51	19.78	18.04	13.21	6.55	1.33
10	70.04	130.06	14.53	20.26	18.29	13.29	7.00	1.48
11	71.64	135.64	14.58	20.98	18.92	13.89	7.36	1.66
12	73.59	140.42	14.69	21.57	19.56	14.17	7.80	1.83
13	75.21	146.02	14.78	22.11	20.18	14.38	8.29	2.03
14	78.06	152.43	14.89	22.78	21.00	15.07	8.46	2.30
15	81.68	160.33	15.00	23.68	22.00	16 07	8.44	2.64
16	85.21	168.21	15.14	25.04	23.19	16.80	8.80	3.14

The blood is freed from certain impurities, especially carbon dioxide, by the lungs, where it is supplied with oxygen, which is the most immediate and imperative need of all creatures that breathe. A deep instinct demands an abundance of free air space all about, and if this is limited, a peculiar class of fears, viz., of narrow or close places, being choked, dreams of being buried alive, and other acute panics, constitute a complete psychosis by themselves, which I have elsewhere described,[1] may arise. The best age determination we have is still that of Gavarret for boys, in 1843, as follows:

Age.	Gr.	Age.	Gr.	Age.	Gr.
8	5	13	8.3	17	10.2
10	6.8	14	8.2	18	11.1
11	7.6	15	8.7	19	11.2
12	7.4	16½	10.2	20	11.2

The number of grams of carbon burned or exhaled from the lungs per hour depends largely upon the development of the muscular system. In girls Gavarret found it never to amount to quite seven grams per hour from the age of ten to forty-five, except at fifteen and nineteen in subjects with good muscles. This important difference between the sexes becomes much more marked at puberty, and menstruation may, as Marro suggests, tend to check this increment. From Scharling's table it would appear that while a girl of ten expires but 19.1 grams of carbonic acid per hour, or 0.88 gram per kilo of weight, a girl of nineteen expires 25.3 grams, or 0.45 gram per kilo of weight. A boy of nine expires 20.3 grams, or 0.92 gram per kilo of weight, while one of sixteen expires 34.3, or 0.59 gram per kilo of weight. These very diverse results can not yet be coordinated.

Although the female organism needs less air than the male, and needs it less imperatively, and although the adult woman produces but little more than one-half the carbonic acid evolved in the male body, both have about the same temperature. The frequency of respiration in the two sexes, however, does not vary greatly, the difference being found in respiratory capacity. The chief pubertal change is from the abdominal characteristic of all children to the costal type, which girls assume during adolescence. This view, which has long been held to be a natural difference, has, however, been lately challenged by studies upon savages and peasant women, which suggest that the difference may be due to corsets

[1] A Study of Fears, p. 132, Sec. III. Fear of Closeness.

or tight lacing. That corseted mature women breathe more frequently than men is clear, but the difference in respiratory type due solely to age and sex is probably less than has been hitherto taught. Landois thinks that the vesicular murmur of respiration, which is somewhat raucous in early childhood, grows softer at puberty, owing to the widening of the pulmonary alveoli.

E. *Growth of the Brain.*—According to the tables of Vierordt, the brain increases between twofold and threefold in weight during the first year of life; not far from ten per cent more during the second; no less and a little more during the third. During the fourth year alone it increases more than it will during all the rest of life, and is nearly done growing by the sixth year. After eight it will grow but little, although the body has only one-third its mature weight.[1] Increase, however, continues very slowly till about twelve or fourteen years of age, when it about reaches its maximal size, although recent minute determinations by Mies and Pfister indicate a very slight growth to between twenty and thirty. In old age it gradually loses weight and size. In the average man it begins to decline by fifty-five, according to Bischoff, while in eminent men it may actually increase to sixty-five before the senescent shrinkage and atrophy begins. Individuals, no doubt, differ widely in this respect. The brain nearly fills the skull, more completely in women and children than in adult men. Cranial capacity, however, may continue to increase till the volume of the brain lacks from ten to twenty-five per cent of filling it. Thus at the beginning of school life the brain has nearly ceased growing, and soon after, or, as some think, a few years before puberty, has reached its greatest weight. The skull continues to grow in length and breadth, at least till twenty, an increase that is divided between scalp, bone, and space inside, so that the size of the head is no sure index of the size of the brain. From birth to maturity the weight of the brain increases about three-and-a-half-fold and that of the spinal cord between sevenfold and eightfold. The cord becomes relatively to the brain twice as heavy between early infancy and manhood.

---

[1] Am. Text-Book of Physiol., p. 726 *et seq.* See Spitzka's Brain Weight of 96 Famous Men. Phil. Med. J., May 2, 1903.

The following table shows its absolute and relative growth in both sexes up to seventy, according to the data of Vierordt, correlated by Mühlmann with the results of other investigators and his own:[1]

Age.	Brain Weight.	
	Absolute.	Relative per cent.
8	1,377.6	6.38
9	1,425	6.06
10	1,408.3	5.59
11	1,359.9	5.04
12	1,415.6	4.88
13	1,486.5	4.49
14	1,289	3.47
15	1,490.2	3.62
16	1,435.1	3.16
17	1,409.2	2.84
18	1,421	2.64
19	1,397.2	2.43
20	1,444.5	2.43
21	1,412.1	2.31
22	1,348.3	2.14
23	1,397.3	2.16
24	1,424	3.3
25	1,430.9	2.16
29	1,356	2.29
30–40	1,365	2.14
33	1,362	2.11
40–50	1,357	2.13
42	1,225	2.00
53	1,480	3.50
50–60	1,360	2.19
60–70	1,319	2.20

In general terms, therefore, we may say the brain in most persons nearly or quite ceases to gain in weight at or before the dawn of adolescence, its declining increment almost suggesting insufficiency, and to one writer degeneracy. It has long been supposed that some important modulation in the method or direction of growth occurs at this important epoch, evolution of mass passing over to involution of texture. Changes in structural complexity may continue indefinitely; or, again, certain parts may diminish in mass and others increase in equal ratio; or, yet again, changes in chemical constitution may be characteristic of increasing age.

The processes of cell division in the brain seem to end

[1] Op. cit.

three or four months before birth. During the prepubertal period, according to the careful studies of Kaiser, the number of cells that pass from the small undeveloped stage to full maturity is nearly equal to that functioning at birth, so that the number of active cells nearly doubles by the end of the fourteenth year. In the boy of fifteen, the volume of cell bodies is already, on the average, one hundred and twenty-four times their size at birth, and by thirty will have increased to one-hundred-and-fifty-fold. New cells are perhaps not formed at all, but developed out of granules, many of which never do develop, but suggest possibilities in the neural elements yet unrealized. Donaldson [1] concludes that the amount of increase in the mass of individual nerve-cells "ranges between zero and fifty-thousand-fold," and assumes in the three-fourths of the total volume of the central nervous system, which he thinks is nerve tissue proper, that there are 3,000,000,000 cells, most of which are probably more or less developed. Thus Kaiser's increase in, e. g., the cervical enlargement of from 104,270 at birth to 211,800 at fifteen is really an increase in the number of developed cells, no intrinsically new ones being formed. Cells constitute but a very small part of the total brain, so that they can increase many fold and not greatly affect its total size or weight.

Cajal [2] has suggested that the energy of the division of cells in the embryonic period may be later transformed into the work of developing collaterals and finer processes, upon which he assumes not only the number of associations but the size of the cells depend.

Of prime importance for adolescence are these recent lines of study, of which the first is upon the tangential fibers which connect different parts of the cortex, with which the names of Vulpius,[3] Kaes,[4] and Flechsig are associated. After the projection system has penetrated the cortex, several systems of fibers among the cortical cells, themselves at right angles to the afferent and efferent fibers, slowly develop, some of them continuing to do so well on into the third or fourth

---

[1] Growth of the Brain. London, 1895.
[2] Archiv f. Anat., 1896, p. 191.
[3] Archiv f. Psych. u. Nervenkrank., 1892.
[4] Deutsche Wochenschrift, 10, 11, 1898.

decade of life at least. These, which Kaes calls the second and third association layers of Meynert, and the lamina of Baillaryer, all of which Vulpius calls the middle layer, begin an augmented development in the occipital and in parts of the parietal regions at about seventeen or eighteen years, and continue to increase in definiteness for at least two decades. This is best seen in the convexities of the convolutions, and less in their median and lower surfaces, except for radial fibers. They may represent Hughlings Jackson's highest level. These superradial or tangential fibers seem to grow steadily in caliber and perhaps in number from the age of eighteen on, the short fibers maturing earlier than the long ones. Kaes thinks the brain increases enormously in complexity after sixteen or seventeen, the brain of his man of thirty-eight being nearly twice as rich in fibers here as that of his boy of eighteen, and he holds that medullations and increase of brain power may continue at least till fifty. Kaes and Vulpius are in impressive agreement that the age of the later teens is epochful for the development of the middle layer, which then begins a new and prolonged period of growth. This causes increased thickness of the parietal and central regions, some in the temporal, and is probably followed by growth in the frontal regions last, all this occurring in regions that were far less rich in fibers in early adolescence. The development of these fibers seems to follow more closely than any other brain structure we know the growth of intelligence. They decline in numbers with old age; their growth is checked by poor nutrition, and they reach their maximum in the centers for sight and hearing by the end of the second year, while in the speech area they increase rapidly till the eleventh and slightly till the thirty-third year. Of the three layers of these fibers, the middle, although beginning in the ninth month and having the least fibers, makes no marked increase till the beginning of adolescence, and grows fastest during the years of early adult manhood and womanhood, continuing till thirty-eight at least. Kaes thinks there is an arrest in their rate of growth at about forty. The outer layer of tangential fibers is normally far smaller than the inner, save in idiots, where it is very large, as it also is in reptiles before the projection system is much developed, and of which it may have been a functional precursor. Kaes holds that these idiots revert to an ancient type, fibers closest connected with smell (which is the oldest cortical structure) being best developed. Perhaps the rule is that the finer the structure the later on in life it continues to develop.[1]

The second recent line of brain study bearing upon adolescence has been opened by Flechsig, which may be concisely summarized as follows: A considerable part of early growth of the brain before and after birth is due to the increase of medullation, myelinization, or the sheathing of the fibers, which is generally held to be the surest concomitant of the development of their function. The various bundles of fibers acquire this sheath not all together, but strand by strand. First come the fibers connecting adjacent centers in the spinal cord, which mediate reflexes of the same level or segment, which medullate the last part of the fifth fetal month. Next come the fibers connecting different vertical levels of the cord; then the sensory column of Gall and Burdach; then the pyramidal or volitional bundles. Nearly all the cord, save this column of fibers, is medullated by the time of birth, but the brain is very undeveloped; so that the new-born child is a spinal creature. Passing up, he finds three sheafs of sensory fibers connecting with the brain which mature at different times, and carrying tactile and kinesthetic sensations to the central convolutions, the latest of which connects with the speech centers. Of the senses judged thus by medullation, smell comes first and hearing develops last. Not only this method of reasoning, but the results of these researches are now more or less widely accepted.

The novel and even revolutionary part of the above publication of Flechsig, however, is his claim that, whereas it has generally been held that all parts of the cortex were connected with the lower centers of sense, two-thirds of it has no such connection. Only one-third of the gray cerebral mantle "has any direct connection with the processes which bring

---

[1] See F. Burk. From Fundamental to Accessory in the Development of the Nervous System and of Movements. Pedagogical Seminary, October, 1898, p. 8 *et seq.*

sense-impression to consciousness and excite the muscles and mechanism of movement." The rest of it, more or less detached from sense and motion, has the functions of reason, science, judgment, moral and esthetic feeling, etc. This two-thirds is reduced to one-half in the higher apes and in idiots, and vanishes in the rodents. It is almost inevitable to ask whether this higher two-thirds does not come into predominant function during adolescence, or, at least, if there is then an increased prepotence of it.

Again, Hughlings Jackson, as is well known, has long held that the central nervous system was made up of three superposed levels closely correlated, but maintaining so much independence that each might be more or less separately involved in an epileptic attack. His lowest level consists of the gray cells of the cord, medulla, and pons. If this only is involved in disease, the limb may be convulsed, or there may be respiratory spasms, etc., while the higher powers are not much affected. The next higher or mid-level receives sense-impressions indirectly from and its motor discharges are indirect through the lowest level, and comprises the basal ganglia, the centers for special sense, and the central convolutions of the cortex. The epilepsies of this level are more complex and widely irradiated, and instead of involving synchronous convulsions of remote parts, may progress regularly from one to another as they are structurally connected, and loss of consciousness, if it comes, is later, but more uncertain and incidental. So accurate was this view, and so exact can diagnosis by its aid now be, that many an operation in the lateral convolution is correctly indicated and successfully made. Jackson's highest level is connected with the second much as that is with the first, and may be said to approximately coincide with Flechsig's higher two-thirds of the brain front and back, which has no direct pyramidal connections. When epilepsy occurs here consciousness is lost at first in such an attack. In this scheme the simplest structures and functions are the oldest. The lowest stratum represents reflex movements of limbs, of eyes, tongue, digestion, etc., and the highest uses these same organs and motions for volition, gesture, facial expression, words, and emotion. The lowest is presentation, the middle layer is representation, to use the terms familiar in Scotch philosophy, and the top level is for re-representation.

Each of these structures has its nascent period when the energies of growth tend to focus not exclusively but only with more or less predominance upon it, and I think we may say that, at last, we seem to have within our reach some conception of what brain changes are involved in adolescence. It appears to be the period of acceleration for the mid-stratum of tangential fibers of Vulpius and Kaes, for Flechsig's two-thirds of the brain that lacks direct connection with the projection system, and for Jackson's highest level. Certain types of insanity are rare before puberty, because the child can not reason according to adult standards until fourteen, the age at which Aristotle would begin the education of reason. Before this comes the age of the spinal reflex and automatic nascency of the late prenatal life and the early months of infancy. Then comes the stage of controlled muscular actions—walking, plays—when drill, habituation, memory, and instinct culminate, which is associated with the mid-level regions of the brain. Lastly comes the age of rational thought, higher logical correlation, personal opinion and conviction, higher esthetic enjoyments, deliberate choice, and willed action. One common and now most interesting form of arrest here is to be discussed at length in Chapter IV. Each lower level, however, must have its full development, for it is a necessary condition for the unfoldment of the higher. Logical methods, on the other hand, if too early, tend to stultify and violate the law that fundamental must always precede accessory structures and functions.

Again, on this view, thought is more independent of muscular activity or motor innervation than we have considered it to be, and the sphere of gymnastic and motor education is perhaps more restricted. The field of sense-training and object-lesson methods are also limited. We can train the sense centers and cultivate eye and ear mindedness in the regions contiguous to the Rolandic fissure by manual or athletic culture, but all this only supplies the data and lays the foundation for the education of the highest level. The dawn of reason, marked by the appetency for crude logical processes, the shadowy grasping of new and great conceptions, and the silent reverie and dreams of dawning adolescence which we shall trace later when the senses and muscles are inert, may be the first psychic function of new neural parts. At first, their activity is tentative, intermittent, incidental, dim, and unformulated; but they are designed later to dominate more and more of life, and to subordinate, and in abnormal developments even to precede and arrest the lower levels.[1]

F. *Growth of Skin and Internal Tract.*—Of several careful measurements of the dermal surface, that of Meeh,[2] who laid on strips of paper to follow the folds and changes of level, is perhaps the best. Even this method was by no means exact. His table from the ages of nine to twenty-six is as follows:

Age. Yrs.	Mos.	Height in cm.	Weight in g.	Surface in cm.	No. of cm. surface to 1 kg. weight.
9	10.......	111.5	19,313	8,855	458
13	1½......	137.5	28,300	11,883	420
15	9¾......	152	35,375	14,988	421
17	9.......	169	55,750	19,205	344
20	7.......	170	59,500	18,695	314
26	3½......	162	62,250	19,204	308

[1] Copious and bewildering as is the recent literature upon the embryology of the brain, its structure and growth in lower animals, localization, and especially the anatomy of the adult brain, one examines not only most of the recent comprehensive text-books, Ramon y Cajal, van Gehüchten, Kölliker, Barker, Retzius, Edinger, etc., but the new neurological Jahresbericht and the files of the Centralblätt, almost in vain as yet for studies upon brain growth during youth which would seem to be more promising of practical results than work in any other field, and which must be ere long the center of the highest scientific interest when evolutionary lines of research attain the importance that belongs to them. Only Vulpius, Kaes, Flechsig, and Jackson shed distinct light on it. See Kaes, Archiv f. Psychiatrie u. Nervenkrankheiten, Bd. xxv, p. 695. Neurol. Centralblätt, Bd. x, p. 456, and Bd. x, p. 119; Bd. xiii, p. 410. München Wochenschrift, Bd. xliii, p. 100. Wiener med. Wochensch., 1895, pp. 1734–1770. Vulpius, Arch. f. Psych., 1891, p. 775. Edenger, Vorlesungen, 6th ed., 1900, p. 424. Flechsig. Gehirn u. Seele, 1896, p. 112. Études sur le Cerveau, 1898, p. 221. Neurolog. Cèntralblätt., 1894, p. 606; 1898, p. 977; 1899, p. 1000; and 1895, pp. 1118, 1177. Localization der Geistigen Vorgänge, Leipzig, 1896. Arch. Ital. de Biol., 1901, p. 30. Hughlings Jackson. Brit. Med. J., 1898, vol. i, p. 65. Apáthy's fibrillar theory that since 1897 invades the neuron doctrine; Dercum's ameboid make and break theory, 1896; Loeb's ion theory of neuron and muscle action, 1900, and many late studies in neuropathology, e. g., by Ceni, Babinski, Dejerine, and many others, have added a great and new charm to all this field.

[2] Zeits. f. Biologie, vol. xv.

There is a rapid decline in the relation of surface to weight between birth and maturity estimated at from about eight hundred and twelve to three hundred and one centimeters square per kilogram. The epidermis is quite unlike the corium, in that it continues to grow until at least sixty. It is more exempt from atrophic changes than the cutis.

As the skin covers the body from without, the mucous surface lines it within. Owing to its very many folds and the contraction and expansion of the intestines, its area can be determined with even less accuracy than that of the skin. Early determinations gave the conclusion that the growth of the intestines was relatively less than that of the mass of the body, but Mühlmann's careful weighings indicate that the converse is true, save perhaps for a very brief period in infancy. The mucous surface, however, probably continues to grow through life. This is especially true of the epithelial layer.

Men

Age.	Weight in grs.	Length.	Intestinal Weight.		Intestinal Length.		Intestinal as related to bodily weight.
			Abs. g.	Rel. per cent.	Abs. cm.	Rel. per cent.	
14	29,050	...	1,000	3.4	....	...	...
16	48,736	154	1,460	3.0	934	2.0	6.0
17	42,997	157	1,350	3.0	1,063	2.4	6.7
19	43,816	161	1,527	3.5	1,200	2.7	7.9
24	42,588	177	1,609	3.7	930	2.2	5.2

From six to twenty years the small intestine increases to about threefold and the large intestine to about fourfold its capacity at birth. The length of the latter grows from about one-sixth that of the former in infancy to one-fourth in maturity. The total length of the digestive canal, which is about five times that of the body in the adult, increases relatively less than stature, for at birth it is about six times the length of the body. In the adult its surface is almost equal to that of the body, while in the carnivorous dog it is half, and in the herbivorous horse nearly twice its body surface. We have little exact data, but it would appear from those at hand that at adolescence the absorptive surfaces of the canal increase less than the body surface, and if so, this suggests increased animal food in the past, at the phyletic correlate of this age. At the age of eleven or twelve the waist of boys is increasing more than their height, and in the average boy continues to grow till at least twenty-three. The area of chewing surface is slowly increased by the addition of the later molars, and as we saw there is increase in both length and strength of jaw.

Growth of Glands and Other Organs.—We shall never understand many of the deepest problems involving the relation of the mind to the body until we can write a new chapter of psycho-physiology on glandular psychology. Secretions and excretions, both internal and external, including the functions of what we may still call the sexual glands, although unlike others, they secrete only living cells, condition many psychic states in a way hardly less basic than they do all other physiological processes, and for fundamental feelings and instincts they are probably quite as important as the brain itself.

Kidneys.—Both the volume and the weight of the kidneys increase till well into the third decennium of life, but their growth relatively to that of the body weight begins to fall behind in the second year of life. Vierordt has compiled from various measurements of men the following table, which is more comprehensive than Benecke's:[1]

Age.	Weight of both Kidneys.	
	Abs.	Rel.
11	171.5	0.64
12	157.5	0.54
13	212.9	0.64
14	233.7	0.63
15	239.7	0.58
16	247.7	0.55
17	274.9	0.55
18	271.6	0.50
19	273.9	0.48
20	296.4	0.50
21	323.5	0.53
22	306.9	0.49
23	281.8	0.44

During most of the life of the individual the kidney cells simply replace their slight loss without growing, and after the third decennium usually begin to atrophy.

[1] Constitution und constitutionelles Kranksein des Menschen. Marburg, 1885.

Urea is known as the chief nitrogenous waste and product of the proteid element of food; it is chiefly prepared for elimination in the liver, the largest gland, and is provided with the richest blood supply. It is discharged thence into the blood and taken up again by the kidneys for final elimination. One of the most interesting and important chapters in modern physiology and another in practical medicine are devoted to the study of its history, and a well-marked group of diseases are traced to its accumulation. Despite several careful studies, we are still uncertain concerning its relations to adolescence. Uhle found a decrease of urea from eight to eleven years of age, and still more from thirteen to sixteen, at which latter age the amount secreted reached about the normal adult standard, which was about half that before six. Marro found a marked increase in urea and also in urine at about twelve in girls, and again at fourteen, with a later decline. Uhle and Mosler have shown that there is a marked diminution in phosphoric acid secreted in the urine at puberty, which they think combines with bases like lime to form bone, which grows so rapidly at this period. Marro[1] found a distinct augmentation of chlorin at fourteen and fifteen, and also of H_2SO_4 and of P_2O_5. As under the influence of the whip-stroke, which adolescence applies to growth, boys exceed girls in the amount of carbonic acid exhaled, so also they do in azotic urinal deposits. Physicians report occasional cases of albumen in the urine of adolescents to an extent that suggests Bright's disease, but these regulate themselves to normality later; even sugar may be excessive. On the whole, while many more determinations for different ages are needed before kidney secretions can be correlated with growth, it is highly probable that these, like so many other functions, have a wider range of average and also of individual variation within the limits of normality than at the age just preceding the growth increment or at any subsequent period save that of senescent involution, which is in so many ways an inverted picture of adolescence.

The increase in the amount of urine at different ages is shown in the following table:

[1] La Puberté, p. 20.

Age.	Amount in 24 hours.	To 1 k. weight.
8	822	40.2
9	1,205	53.6
10	1,866	65.7
11	1,205	46.9
12	1,201	43.5
13	1,012	36.9

Micturitional obscenities, which our returns show to be so common before adolescence, culminate at ten or twelve, and seem to retreat into the background as sex phenomena appear. The former are of two classes, fouling persons or things secretly from adults but often openly with each other, and less often ceremonial acts connected with the act or the product that almost suggests the scatological rites of savages, unfit for description here, but of great interest and importance for the psychic side of the recapitulation theory, and although rare, sometimes elaborately developed.[1] No less significant are the phenomena of what we may call urinophobia, sometimes developed at this age of fears, which remind us of the many centuries when urinomancy and urinoscopy vied with astrology as the chief factors in a physician's training. Many adolescents whose attention is called to the subject by the scare advertisements perhaps naturally scan their urine daily for years, suffer acute and generally secret fears as they find it now cloudy, turbid, with red or white deposits or with iridescent film, test its odors and imagine incipient, fatal, and offensive diseases; seek consolation by furtive comparisons with that of other persons; modify their diet, exercise, and general regimen; associate this with the yet more serious sex fears later described, and sometimes muster up courage to consult friends or throw themselves into the hands of quacks. Of one hundred and nineteen students, all but five confess to a period of mild or intense fear which a little incidental instruction would have shown to be groundless.[2]

The suprarenal capsules or adrenals are ductless glands largest in the fetus, where they exceed the kidneys themselves, and become steadily smaller at least to forty, according

[1] See Burke. Scatological Rites.

[2] See, e. g., Sprengel Geschichte der Arzneikunde, B. ii *passim* and B. iii, p. 314 *et seq.*

to Lorey, Bischof, and Schwann. Some now think they aid in removing the toxic products produced by the muscles during exercise.

The *liver* was thought to continue to grow well on into old age, but later determinations indicate that it grows relatively very slowly after fifteen, and from that age on to senescence has a weight progressively less compared to that of the body. The following is Mühlmann's table for males:

Age.	Weight of the Liver.	
	Abs.	Rel.
11	870.4	3.22
12	880	3.03
13	1,036	3.13
14	1,188	3.20
15	1,306	3.17
16	1,339	2.95
17	1,481	2.98
18	1,509.6	2.80
19	1,644.6	2.86
20	1,560.8	2.62
21	1,626.9	2.66
22	1,675	2.66
23	1,528.5	2.37
24	1,847.7	....

Its circulatory mechanism, so inadequate for oxidization and elimination, may account for the great amount of unoxidized material it contains and why it deposits fat and atrophies so easily. It receives only about the same amount of arterial blood as the kidneys, although it weighs about six times as much in the adult, and less than the milt, although it is a little over nine times heavier.

Ritter's analysis of the bile at different ages gives the following table:

Age.	Solid residuum.	Matter.		Natrium.	
		Organic.	Inorganic.	Glycochol acid.	Taurochol acid.
14	131.4	120.0	11.4	41.9	29.1
21	129.0	118.8	10.2	39.6	16.4
23	117.6	111.7	5.9	40.9	25.1
25	128.2	122.2	5.8	44.9	23.25

The salivary glands also increase in size and function. It has often been noted that their activity is augmented with intensity of the sexual life. In the almost epidemic outburst of venery, which travelers describe, as the arctic spring advances after the long winter night, not only is the liver stimulated so that constipation and jaundice cease and menstruation becomes more profuse and frequent, sometimes with hemorrhage from the mouth and nose, but saliva flows with great and offensive exuberance. When temperature rises, respiration becomes more frequent, bleeding is easier in this purest of all airs, when spring seems full of premature joy, and distils the wine of action, and when everything quivers with the wild passion of life after its long depressing winter.[1] The jaws increase in size and power, and there is a new propensity to bite, chew, smoke, and to taste various stimulants which act as ptyalagogues. *Questionnaire* returns also show an increased disposition now to spit with various artistic refinements and even competitions as to distance, accuracy, method, and amount, while idiots become offensive by drooling. The change in the sensitiveness and quality of tastes and appetites later discussed is also connected with adolescent hypersalivation. These and certain emotional phenomena also indicate a wide irradiation of glandular sympathy at this age.

The milt or pancreas continues to grow till old age. Mühlmann has compiled from seven measurements the following tables for males:

Age.	Weight of Milt.	
	Abs.	Rel.
11	71.3	0.26
12	76	0.24
13	86	0.26
14	70	0.19
15	145	0.35
16	153	0.34
17	145.6	0.29
18	176.2	0.33
19	166	0.29
20	186.2	0.31
21	168.1	0.27
22	148.9	0.24
23	153.7	0.24
24	177.4	....

[1] Cook. Some Physical Effects of Arctic Cold, Darkness, and Light. New York Medical Record, July 12, 1897.

The pancreas, like the spleen, develops from the wall of the intestinal tract; like that organ, it is under the control of special nerves, but it secretes alkaline as the spleen does acid products. Its maximal secretion is during the first hour after eating, and its minimal three or four hours later. The pubescent growth of both these glands is far greater than that of the body as a whole, so that some, so far unknown, significance for this age seems suggested.

The spleen grows yet more rapidly during adolescence. Roberts's table for males is as follows:

Age.	Spleen, oz.
4–7	1.85
7–14	3.03
14–20	5.14
20–30	7.19
30–40	7.12

The spleen is one of the most mysterious organs of the body. Unlike any other, it has its own local arrangement for maintaining circulation. After every meal it increases greatly in size, then contracts synchronously with digestive periods, and probably has a shorter rhythm of varo-dilation. It can be removed without serious danger. Probably it aids in the process of producing red blood-corpuscles, and possibly destroys old ones. Vierordt thinks it continues to grow till at least the forty-seventh year. It need hardly be said that the spleen has no more relation with the psychic quality which suggested its name and was once thought to be located in it than sweetbread has with sweetheart.

The sebaceous glands over the surface of the skin, which secrete in the new-born child the vernix caseosa, corresponding to the lanolin of sheep's wool, the oily matter of birds' feathers, cerumen or ear-wax, preputial smegma, etc., are more active at puberty. Their secretions about the hair-follicles increase, some think, with changed quality. They are often obstructed so that sebum accumulates, causing pimples or comedones. In the axillæ or armpits especially, these glands reveal their morphological affinity to those of the mammæ, and the frequent dryness and irritability of the hands and sometimes of the entire dermal surface, often noted in states of nervous weakness after coition, show their functional sympathy with testes and ovaries. Their odor is quite *sui generis*, and since Haller's description of this as due to the more volatile parts of this sperm diffused through the flesh, a popular conception widely diffused has ascribed genital odors to them in general, centering, however, in their peculiar secretions on the organs of sex, which are greatly modified by function and disease. Jäger's vague speculations on his discovery of the soul as a smell rested for its meager basis of fact largely upon exploitations of the facts connected with the action of these glands. Pornographic literature abounds in suggestions in this field; lewd people's dread of water, certain arts of breeders to secure cross-fertilization between species that normally do not mate at all, perfumes used to make birds sing, and a distinct odor ascribed to puberty in savage races by anthropologists may also be recalled here. Many of our returns specify moisture, clamminess, or, more rarely, dryness of the hand in adolescents, along with heat and coldness, when also the face very often becomes covered with indications of abnormality in these secretions. Modifications of dermal sensitiveness and itching, the passion for being stroked, patted, and caressed, and other erogenic phenomena connected with the sense of touch, to say nothing of laboratory tests of hepatic sensibility at this age thought to be connected with these secretions, intimate how deep is the *rapport* between them and the new functions of sex.

A man loses about as much sweat as he does urine, and these two sources of outflow are complemental. Each have nervous centers in the medullary region which are adjacent to each other. It must be remembered, however, that while urine is a true secretion, sweat is also a heat regulator. At puberty the amount of water imbibed and given out in both these ways is increased. Sweating is easier and more profuse, no doubt partly from the increased relative weakness that attends rapid growth. Many returns state that the odor of perspiration from underwear at this age is both stronger and different than heretofore. Whether these modifications are due to growth of the glands or modifications in the nervous control to which they are subject is unknown. Travelers and anthropologists have thought that characteristic national odors so marked that negroes, Chinese, and even Irish, Germans, and others can be distinguished by the aroma of their sleeping-rooms, underwear, etc., and which are far more marked at puberty, are partly sudoriferous.

Pigmentation, which Laycock ascribes to imperfect oxidation, undergoes more or less modification. Sometimes the hair slightly changes its hue, in such cases more commonly growing a shade darker; the eyes are often thought to change color, light eyes sometimes grow lighter and dark eyes darker; a few have thought they detected slight color modifications in the skin, although these may have been accounted for by changes of circulation which affected only complexion. Certain it is that the sex organs, the nipples, and aureola become distinctly darker. In mixed races, especially in mulattoes, testimony would indicate frequent modifications both ways.

As to whether the lachrymal glands share the general augmentation of the secretory function, we find no evidence save only the repeated statement that weeping is more frequent in girls for a few years after the dawn of puberty than before.

The following is Puech's table showing the average dimensions of the ovaries at different ages:

	Right.			Left.		
	Length.	Height.	Thickness.	Length.	Height.	Thickness.
New-born...	....	19.8	....	..	18.2	....
6–11 yrs....	26.7	9	4.4	24	8.4	4.5
13–15 "	29.6	15	10	25	14	8.3
19–35 "	36.5	18	13.7	35	16.7	13.1

Mühlmann, from a few determinations, gives their weight as follows:

Age.	Weight of both Ovaries.	
	Abs.	Rel.
3	1.0	0.007
18	21.2	0.041
70	2.9	0.009

He has also weighed the testes at different ages, with the following results:

Age.	Weight of Testes.	
	Abs. g.	Rel. per cent.
14	14.9	0.051
16	24.7	.....
17	35.0	.....
21	43.6	.....
22	44.5	.....
23	41.0	.....
24	27.7	0.065
25	38.4	.....

Some think that in contrast with the ovaries, which after the climacteric are reduced greatly, the testes continue to grow. That they do not share the general post-climacteric involution which comes later in men is not yet sufficiently established.

On the other hand, two secretory organs rapidly decline in size, one relatively and the other absolutely, during adolescence. The mysterious thymus gland, which is large at birth, is reduced one-half and sometimes to a vestige before puberty, and often vanishes between twenty-five and thirty-five. It has, however, no known connection with this age save perhaps through its relation with the thyroid gland higher up in the lower part of the neck. The latter has lately come to be of great and growing interest, through its relation with the blood and nutrition, which are known to be very important, although not yet well understood. At birth its weight is $\frac{1}{400}$, in maturity about $\frac{1}{1800}$, that of the body. After, but not before puberty, it can be extirpated without very great danger. It is larger in women than in men, swells considerably at the first and somewhat after all successive menstruations, also after the first coitus even in men. To measure the neck is a wide-spread test of virginity and also ceremonially of nubility, among rude and savage people. It enlarges also during pregnancy and lactation, so that its sympathy with the uterus is close. Exophthalmic goiter and myxedema, which involve extreme facial and other expressions resembling fear, seem to be based on thyroid troubles, and both diseases often occur during the later stages of puberty. After thyroidectomy the pituitary body often hypertrophies, and the suprarenal bodies are affected. Its connections with sexual functions, especially in the female, and its close and necessary relation with nutrition, which have in recent years given rise to a vast body of literature, are both accentuated by the fact that at the dawn of senescence this gland is peculiarly liable to degenerative disease.

Fat seems to decrease at puberty in vigorous boys. If it preexisted, it is often then used up as if it were reserve material accumulated for the sake of growth. Boys are often described in our returns as lean, spidery, scrawny, cadaverous, as having lost their plumpness of limb and feature and their good looks. This is partly due to the increased relative prominence of the joints and the points for muscular attachment. Not only are the curves and angles sharper, but the limbs are relatively longer as compared with the trunk than they were in childhood, and this adds to the general disharmony of proportions. A chapter might be written on the morphological ugliness of the boy.

While girls also often grow thin, the increase of cellular tissue in the mammary and the growth of the pelvic region in its horizontal expansion are in a sense complementary. The hips, thighs, limbs, shoulders, and arms round out into contours more or less beautiful, and with curves always predominating over angles, while not only on the bony prominences, but over, between, and in the fibers of the great muscles themselves, adipose and other intracellular tissue pads all parts and members into more or less rounded and graceful outlines.

The thickness of the subcutaneous adipose tissue shows, of all parts of the body, most irregular development. Kotelmann found it to increase up to nineteen years almost exactly as height increases and along with muscle growth. In relation to weight, it maintains a pretty constant relation of from three to nine per cent.

The temperature of the body is partly due to nutrition and partly to causes not yet explained. A large part of the total energy of life is consumed in producing bodily heat. Loss of heat varies considerably with the relation of surface to mass of body, which in the adult is only about three-eighths what it is at birth, although the determinations of the effects of sex and age upon calorification are not yet in complete accord.

The child at birth has a slightly higher temperature than the uterus of its mother. After a considerable fall it begins at about the second hour after birth to rise, and thereafter through childhood is on the average about 37.5° C., or about 0.3° more than the adult, nearly half a degree warmer awake than asleep. In general, however, temperature taken in rectum, mouth, and armpits rises a little between the ages of five and nine. Some think puberty is marked by a distinct rise, which has been estimated as high as 0.5° F. It then sinks slightly from the fifteenth to the twenty-fifth year, when adolescence is well established, and falls to a minimum at about the fiftieth. It is highest a few days before menstruation, and may vary normally 0.5° or even 1° F. Although sexual differences of temperature are not yet well established, present indications point to a slightly higher temperature in males, who also present greater individual variations. Children also vary much more within the limits of normal change than do adults. Other things being equal, the smaller the body the greater the changes caused by outer temperature.

Harmonious Growth.—There is no one fixed standard of proportion of parts or of beauty either in art or in anthropometry. Even Erismann's law that "During the development of puberty, the squares of the weights in different ages are related to each other as the fifth power of the length" is only an approximation. Man the measurer, who has in the past used his forearm (cubit, ell), his foot, his girth (yard from *gyrdon*), his length (fathom), his thumb (pouce), nail, hand, as standards and metric units, and has selected some dimension in many art canons—length of face, foot, palm, middle finger, ear, nose, etc.—as a modulus (so many times which gave the true dimensions of other parts), has always been and still is more autotypic than he knows, reproducing in his representation of the human form the type of his own race. Some of these schemes of proportion have been elaborately and even mystically wrought out in detail, treated mathematically, and applied even to architecture. The special part to which all the rest sustained occult relation has sometimes been thought to be able in some way to furnish a key to unlock the secrets of our being. Anthropometry, however, shows that a true type is something very different from all these normal figures. The modern head, e. g., is larger than the Greek canons permitted, and Fock lately proved that the only length of the upper arm that corresponded to the Apollo Belvedere was the Ethiopian type, thus suggesting an Egyptian origin of the Greek norm.[1] True beauty in the human form, the type of the divine, can not be absolute or uniform. Apollo does not inspire young men now to esthetic ideals of art, while the type or mean form of the fifty percentile line represented, e. g., in Sargent's casts, at the Chicago Exposition, of the average male and female collegian is positively repellant. Young men especially desire to develop individuality by departing more or less widely from standard forms without becoming distinctly disproportionate. Perfect symmetry of body, then, either in form or function, is rare and more or less asymmetry is the rule.

The bilateral halves of the body differ in size, strength, rapidity, and in temperature. The blood-vessels are of different size, the eyes are unlike in acuteness and in mobility, the two hemispheres of the brain, the number of fibers in the pyramidal decussation are unlike, while liability to disease is sometimes greater in one half of the body than in the other. It is impossible to make symmetrical movements with both hands, the preferred hand always making the greater excursion. Pages would be needed to simply enumerate the asymmetries in form and function of the right and left half of the body that have been specially studied.[2] Bolton [3] found that children were symmetrical until adolescence, and until early pubescent years when the shoulders or head tip slightly, the spine curves, the two sides of the face grow unlike, eyes, hips, feet, legs differentiate, the relative ambidexterity declines, and the disposition to lop and stoop in sitting and standing, to sleep on one side in preference to the other, and in general to specialize the two halves of the body, is augmented. The Am-

[1] See Robert Fletcher. Human Proportion in Art and Anthropometry. Cambridge, 1885.

Also W. S. Hall. Changes in the Proportions of the Human Body during the Period of Growth. Journal of the Anthropological Institute, 1895.

[2] See Bilateral Asymmetry of Function. G. Stanley Hall and E. W. Hartwell. Mind, xxxiii.

[3] Proceedings of the Colorado Teachers' Association. Session 1896.

herst measurements show that the right thigh, calf, instep, upper arm, forearm, breadth of shoulders and elbow tip are at this time greater than the left. These differences are greater in men than in women, and the differentiation of the bilateral structure and functions is accelerated at adolescence.

Dr. Hrdlicka [1] found among 1,000 children that the maximal number of abnormalities occurred at the age of from eight to nine, and then distinctly decreased, puberty tending to diminish them. Massive gums common in children are very rare after this age, and the nose, which may be low or broad before, then assumes ordinary proportions. The author says: "All habit abnormalities tend to increase in proportion as we advance from early childhood. From my observations on adults and adolescents outside of the institution, I think that after the age of fifteen or sixteen these abnormalities tend again to diminish, a certain proportion of them being spontaneously corrected." Genital irregularities, particularly adhesion of the prepuce, diminish rapidly after puberty.

Smedley's Chicago Report (No. 2) shows that the average number of growth abnormalities seen in pupils below grade is strikingly more than in those at or above grade, whether this difference be sought among children of different standing in the same school or whether the comparison be between the averages of higher grade and those of schools for backward children.

Dr. Francis Warner suggests that the same conditions that caused ill-proportioned development of the body may also have caused the tendency to ill balance of nerve-centers, and that even the converse of this may possibly be true. Overaction of the frontal muscles, e. g., may go with cranial defect, and the action of cause and effect may work either way or indeed both ways. Dr. Warner thinks that many of his new nerve signs or symptoms go with disproportioned growth. If this relation of past structure to present function be established, environment and education should have power to control to some extent the proportionality of growth, so that even reversions may be temporary. Girls,

[1] Special Report of Anthropological Investigation on 1,000 White and Colored Children of the New York Juvenile Asylum, pp. 117-172.

although less often abnormal than boys, seem more influenced by environment if they are defective. Disordered nerve states appear to go with defective bodily structure. It is a disadvantage, again, to be tall, broad, and heavy if the lungs, heart, or stomach are not proportioned to the increased size, which imposes a strain upon them, and they then become more liable to collapse. If the reproductive parts and all the complex apparatus connected with them, which are from their very intricacy so peculiarly liable to arrest by fatigue, excitement, low diet, etc., are subnormal, race deterioration is certain no matter how complete in other respects individual development may be.

From these data we see that sexual maturity involves changed relations of parts which for a time lessens their coordination and unity. Moreover, if we include rudimentary organs in our survey, we see that many parts are growing less and vanishing, especially in childhood. Some grow on into old age, and are even then at least relatively young. Structures vary in size more or less independently of each other, and the warring equilibrium of proportionate growth is more or less disturbed. Some parts are arrested or decline while others rapidly increase. Some vary directly with each other, some inversely. Such changes are far more numerous and more rapid in the infant, and still more so in the growth of the embryo; but in these respects they are analogous in their nature, although later growths are less predetermined, rapid, or transforming. At birth respiration, phonation, and a new mode of alimentation spring into function. In teething and weaning, new forms and qualities of food involve changes in salivation and many reflex disturbances. So puberty is not unlike a new birth, when the lines of development take new directions. The range of individuality in nearly all respects—size, strength, motion, mental ability, etc.—is greatly increased, extremes are wider apart, and average variations ampler, as seen in wider distributions among the percentile grades. This means increased plasticity and docility, so that powers of acquisition are increased and deepened. There is much reason to believe that the influence of the environment in producing acquired traits transmissible by heredity is greatest now, although perhaps the influence of experience upon the germ-plasm may be greatest a little later. Changes of ethnic development best occur now, and the point of departure for higher and more evolved forms is adolescence and not adulthood, just as upward steps in the development of the phylon have not been from the terminal types of earlier periods, but have started from stages farther back.

So, too, if the soul grows with every part of the body, its development is not continuous, uniform, or proportionate, but with successive nodes, the earlier stages ever a little more strange and alien to the newer, like dimly remembered past lives to a transmigrationist. The fact that coordinations are a little loosened, and that parts can vary more independently of each other and are freer from the control of the whole, make this the age of modification and plasticity more than the few years that precede or than all those that follow.

It is the age of reconstruction, when new determinants come to the front and also the point of departure for new lines of development. It is the age, too, when, if ever, previous tendencies to abnormality may be overcome both by nature and by treatment. The law of nascent periods, or the age curve of growth of each organ or faculty, is one of the first desiderata of genetic psychology; how to apply it, by what means and to what degree to stimulate each part in its stage of most and least rapid growth, and how to apportion training of mind and body between developing the powers that excel to a degree of specialized culture that corresponds to their hereditary possibilities, or educating the weakest parts and powers in order to improve proportion and symmetry, is one of the chief problems of individual pedagogy.

CHAPTER III

GROWTH OF MOTOR POWER AND FUNCTION

Educational value of special study in this field illustrated—Importance of muscle culture for the development of mind and morals, relations to sex, the lift and pull—Growth of biceps and "putting" power, pressing power of hands and knees, leg strength, grip and grasping, maximal rate of tapping, growth in accuracy, precision and inhibition, right- and left-hand power, fatigue, second breath, reaction time, reproduction of time intervals, fundamental and accessory power, mobility of children, automatic movements, their meaning and repression, control, motor efficiency, monotony, motor degeneration of modern man, tendencies to motor revival. I. Industrial training, monotechnic and trade schools and their results. II. Manual training, its defects, criticism of sloyd, arts and crafts movement, motor methods illustrated by telegraphy and drawing. III. Gymnastics: (*a*) ideal of doing everything possible with the body as a machine, the movement of Jahn; (*b*) ideal of volitional control; (*c*) ideal of economy in movement; (*d*) ideal of symmetry; calamity of rival systems, effects of exercise on strength, athletic records. IV. Play and sport—A new theory corrective of Groos, ancient Greece, the charm of play traced to the plylon, the doll, number of plays and games, team play records, rhythm, dancing, plays of conflict, the duel, student honors, military training, play and sex, cold baths and swimming, playgrounds, regimentation of plays and games and professionalism, play and work.

SOON after graduating from a college where the chief studies of the senior year were under a president who summed up the great questions of the universe in a finishing way that gave a sense of finality unfavorable to further progress, I went to Leipzig to work under the leading physiologist of Germany, full of the conviction that the study of the mind could best be approached through that of the body. After hearing my case, Professor Ludwig suggested that I begin by studying certain functions of one of nearly a score of the muscles—the gastrocnemius—of a frog's leg. The mild dissipation of a somewhat too prolonged general culture and a little taste for easy, breezy philosophical speculation caused at first a strong sense of repugnance from so small and mean a theme. When it was well under way, however, and with the daily and personal guidance of this master in devising methods of experiment, planning new instruments for record and stimulus, suggesting fertile possibilities, showing the details of all the technique, suggesting and placing in my hands new reading, etc., I found that I must know in a more accurate way than before certain definite points in electricity, which was the agent of stimulation; in mechanics, for the apparatus was complex, and there were possibilities of improvement and invention that might open up a new field of myological investigation; in the anatomy and physiology of other tissues for comparison; in chemistry in order to judge something of the effects of the artificial blood for constancy; and in mathematics in order to compute and analyze the contraction curve into its components and to construct and interpret the records and tables. As the year progressed the history of previous views were studied and broader biological relations were seen. When summer came I packed a large case of books and read with might and main at a little summer resort on the Baltic, and began a second year of research upon this muscle with the most eager curiosity and zest. I realized that the structure and laws of action of muscles were the same in frogs as in men, that such contractile tissue was the only organ of the will and had done all man's work in the world, made civilization, character, history, states, books, and words. As the work went on, I felt that the mysteries not only of motor education and morality, but of energy and the universe, centered in this theme, from the persistent study of which, although in the end I made but an infinitesimal contribution to the vast body of certain scientific knowledge in the world, I learned several great lessons, viz.: that any object, however unattractive, may be a key to the greatest themes; that narrow specialization is now hardly possible, since evolution and the doctrine of the conservation of energy and comparative methods of study in every field have given us again a true universe instead of a multiverse; I understood the meaning of a really literal education and of a special as distinct from a professional higher education, in a modern as opposed to a medieval sense, and I felt the *omne tutit punctum* of nature's organic unity as a profound conviction that the world is lawful to the core. In fine, in the presence of this tiny object I had gradually passed from the attitude of Peter Bell, of whom the poet says "a primrose by a river's brim a yellow primrose was to him, and it was nothing more," up to the standpoint of the seer who plucked a "flower from the crannied wall," and realized that could he but know what it was "root and all and all in all," he would know what God and man is.

The muscles are by weight about forty-three per cent of the average adult male human body. They expend a large fraction of all the kinetic energy of the adult body, which a recent estimate places as high as one-fifth. The cortical centers for the voluntary muscles extend over most of the lateral psychic zones of the brain, so that their culture is brain building. In a sense they are organs of digestion, for which function they play a very important rôle. Muscles are in a most intimate and peculiar sense the organs of the will. They have built all the roads, cities, and machines in the world, written all the books, spoken all the words, and, in fact, done everything that man has accomplished with matter. If they are undeveloped or grow relaxed and flabby, the dreadful chasm between good intentions and their execution is liable to appear and widen. Character might be in a sense defined as a plexus of motor habits. To call conduct three-fourths of life, with Matthew Arnold; to describe man as one-third intellect and two-thirds will, with Schopenhauer; to urge that man is what he does or that he is the sum of his movements, with F. W. Robertson; that character is simply muscle habits, with Maudsley; that the age of art is now slowly superseding the age of science, and that the artist will drive out with the professor, with the anonymous author of "Rembrandt als Erzieher"; that history is consciously willed movements, with Bluntschli; or that we could form no conception of force or energy in the world but for our own muscular effort; to hold that most thought involves change of muscle tension as more or less integral to it—all this shows how we have modified the antique Ciceronian conception *vivere est cogitari*, to *vivere est velle*, and gives us a new sense of the importance of muscular development and regimen.[1]

[1] See my Moral Ed. and Will-Training. Ped. Sem., ii., pp., 72-89.

Modern psychology thus sees in muscles organs of expression for all efferent processes. Beyond all their demonstrable functions, every change of attention and of psychic states generally plays upon them unconsciously, modifying their tension in subtle ways so that they may be called organs of thought and feeling as well as of will, in which some now see the true Kantian thing-in-itself the real substance of the world, in the anthropomorphism of force. Habits even determine the deeper strata of belief, thought is repressed action, and deeds, not words, are the language of complete men. The motor areas are closely related and largely identical with the psychic, and muscle culture develops brain-centers as nothing else yet demonstrably does. Muscles are the vehicles of habituation, imitation, obedience, character, and even of manners and customs. For the young, motor education is cardinal, and is now coming to due recognition, and for all, education is incomplete without a motor side. Skill, endurance, and perseverance may almost be called muscular virtues, and fatigue, yelleity, caprice, *ennui*, restlessness, lack of control and poise, muscular faults.

For men, as we saw in the last chapter, and for animals, the age of sexual maturity is marked by an outburst of muscular growth, and also by great changes in its direction and distribution. It is the age when males engage in conflicts for females and develop organs of combat and also of prehension. There is a very close and but little understood relation between sexual and motor vigor, and many new notions and kinds of activity arise. The definite determination of these changes is a new and very promising field of scientific activity. We first summarize the more important measurements of the motor changes typical of this age. Important as these are, they all leave much to be desired.

Most of the common strength tests made in gymnasia are hardly more available as data for scientific measurement than are athletic records, and yet from both, interesting and valuable facts can be gathered, and there have been a number of special studies of much worth.

Beginning with the lift, where the part played by back, legs, hips, and arms is not distinguished, Quetelet's table, where both hands were used, is as follows:

Age.	Men.	Women.	Annual Gain.	
			Men.	Women.
10	45	31	..	..
11	48	35	3	4
12	52	39	4	4
13	63	43	11	4
14	71	47	8	4
15	80	51	9	4
16	95	57	15	6
17	110	63	15	6
18	118	67	8	4
19	125	71	7	4
20	132	74	7	3
21	138	76	6	2
22	143	78	5	2
23	147	80	4	2
25	153	82	6	2
27	154	83	1	1

From this table it appears that the lifting power of girls from the ages of ten to twenty-seven, while constantly increasing, absolutely declines relatively to that of boys from 1.4 to 1.9; that this difference increases fastest from fifteen to eighteen, viz., from 29 to 51 kilograms. Both boys and girls gain most rapidly at sixteen and seventeen, but the gain of boys is more grouped about pubescent years, so that their increment curve is then greater, and also they continue to gain longer than girls.

Marro found the power to pull up on the Regnier dynamometer according to the following table of kilograms:

Age.	Boys.	Girls.
11–12	56.8	36.1
12–13	59.8	35.7
13–14	60.3	37.4
14–15	64.7	40.0
15–16	70.0	46.0
16–17	83.1	48.0
17–18	105.0	46.7
18–19	105.0	50.4

From this table it appears that from the sixteenth to the eighteenth years there is a sudden gain in boys and a less marked access of strength in girls in their sixteenth and nineteenth years.

Hitchcock measured 742 Amherst students on entering

college and the same men three and a half years later with the following results:

Age.	Number measured.	Actual number of units.	Per cent of gain.
16...........	30	1.60	32.28
17...........	134	2.16	33.74
18...........	244	1.48	26.56
19...........	153	1.50	27.69
20...........	73	1.79	20.32
21...........	49	1.34	21.61
22...........	27	1.25	18.51
23...........	12	1.83	21.88
24...........	13	.15	.70
25...........	7	.85	38.51
Average......	..	1.61	26.68

From this table it appears that boys who enter college at sixteen and seventeen gain most during the course, but that all gain much. These results must be connected with the fact that most of them practised gymnastics during their course.

Hitchcock's averages for 4,000 Amherst students' back lift showed greatest gain at seventeen and eighteen, with no gain but slight loss from sixteen to seventeen, and reduced gain at twenty-one, a sharp rise at twenty-two, and no increase from twenty-three to twenty-six. From seventeen to twenty-three the average gain runs from 128 to 156.2 kilograms. Moon found the greatest increase of strength of back from fifteen to sixteen (91 to 102 kilograms, when his table ends), and next most from fourteen to fifteen (82 to 91 kilograms). With Erismann,[1] the lifting power of arms and back, beginning with 82 at fourteen, reached 136 at nineteen, and then increased more slowly to a maximum of 151 at thirty-three, some eight or nine years later than the maximal clinching power. The greatest rate of gain was in the seventeenth and eighteenth years, and he thought strength generally increases fastest between fifteen and nineteen, but continues to gain at a diminishing rate to a maximum at from twenty-four to thirty-five, and then declines. Venn thought his pull, which was in large part a back movement, reached the maximum at twenty-three. Several observers

[1] Ueber die Körperliche Entwickelung der Fabrikarbeiter in Zentralrussland. Tübingen, 1889.

have expressed the opinion that for a time muscles of hips and back are not exceeded in growth rate by any others, whether measured by girth or strength.

The strength of the upper arms in the biceps region is remarkably augmented. According to Moon, at sixteen it is nearly fivefold what it is at eleven, and nearly doubles from fifteen to sixteen, increasing but very little from thirteen to fourteen. Hastings's measurements of 5,476 children are as follows:

Age.	Strength of forearm, r.	Strength of forearm, l.
	Kilos.	Kilos.
5	4.89	4.72
6	6.98	5.70
7	9.18	8.53
8	10.63	9.53
9	13.14	11.77
10	14.74	14.06
11	18.02	16.11
12	19.68	18.44
13	22.59	20.49
14	25.37	23.05
15	28.85	24.68
16	33.31	29.64

According to the Amherst tables, while strength in this part does not gain very rapidly after sixteen, it gains rather steadily to twenty-two. From sixteen to seventeen the forearm at Amherst is gaining on the upper arm, and reaches the highest point at twenty-three, suggesting that its period of strength increment may be a little later than the biceps, especially if we compare it with Moon's tables. The power to pull the body up at Amherst increased fastest from seventeen to eighteen, with years of low gain and often loss intervening, and reaching its maximum at twenty-three, as did dip. The latter increased by far the most rapidly from eighteen to nineteen, when pull not only did not increase, but fell off. It gained from twenty-one to twenty-two. There was also a year of loss in power to pull up.

Basing on the weight and the distance and height to which it was thrown, Vierordt computed the expenditure in "putting" for different ages, and found a great increase from the ages of ten to eighteen. This was both percentile and absolute for each two-year period. Roberts, Porter, and Gilbert have tested wrist and arm lifts from six and a half to nineteen years. From these researches the very significant result is reached that boys acquire about one-half of their sixteen-year-old strength after eleven.

Gilbert tested about fifty boys and fifty girls from six to nineteen in lifting from the wrist, and found that from six to ten this ability nearly doubled in both sexes. From ten to nineteen it increased nearly threefold in boys and nearly twofold in girls. From fourteen to seventeen it nearly doubled in boys. The lifting power of the arm was, of course, far greater (171.9 kilograms: 27 kilograms boys at nineteen), but here also boys exceeded girls at all ages, and at nineteen, as with the wrist, they lifted nearly twice the weight girls could. The mean variations increased most during the period of most rapid growth.

With the dynamometer, Kotelmann[1] found that the power of the hands to press together against each other was nearly twice that of the arms to pull apart in a horizontal direction; that the former increased relatively to the latter to fourteen, and from that age to twenty-one suffered relative but irregular decline. In both respects, "puberty is a marked turning-point." The pulling power of the arms rose steadily to fourteen, and then showed a great and sudden augment, and thereafter increased at a constantly slower rate to twenty-one. The same was true of this increment relatively. The muscles of the upper arm gain in strength more each year than does their girth, so that if the girth did not gain, this increase in power would be more each year up to twenty-one. At first the power of the arms to press together is nearly twice this power to pull, but the latter increases faster, so that at twenty-one the two are nearly equal. The clinching power of the hands is at all ages greater than the pressing power of the arms, and from ten to twenty-one the former gains upon the latter till at twenty-one it is one and three-fifths times greater.

Passing to the lifting strength of legs, Moon found that from eleven to sixteen boys increased from 125 to 213 kilograms, the greatest gain being at the thirteenth, fifteenth, and fourteenth years of 29, 24, and 23 kilograms respectively,

[1] Die Körperverhältnisse der Gelehrtenschule. Berlin, 1879.

as against 11 kilograms in the twelfth year. The Amherst tables show greatest average gain at eighteen, with another distinct increment at twenty-one and twenty-two, with decline after twenty-three. Vierordt, basing on Quetelet's tables of weight and the highest average leap for boys each age from ten to eighteen, calculated the amount of impulse or leg force for each two-year period. Beginning at ten to twelve with 25.61 kilometers, at twelve to fourteen it was 36.92; at fourteen to sixteen, 52.41; at sixteen to eighteen it was 72.67, showing marked absolute and some percentile gain. Moon found a marked increase between twelve and thirteen corresponding with the growth of muscle girth, but so much greater than the latter as to suggest that the nerve-centers controlling these muscles were developing faster than the muscles themselves. The increase in the strength of the legs is so rapid for Moon's boys that at fourteen and fifteen it surpasses that of men. The will is perhaps unable to excite the maximal contractive power of the muscles. Rivalry was found a potent stimulus in making these tests.

By placing a dynamometer between the knees, Kotelmann[1] measured the power to press them together. He found that the pressure power of the thighs shows a pubertal increment that becomes annually greater till the age of fifteen, and is then less, this increment being both relative and absolute. This increase is greater each succeeding year compared to the circumference of the thighs. The right adductors are slightly stronger than the left. In general, he found that the older the pupil the more the muscular development of the lower lagged behind that of the upper extremities. Sedentary life also gave the muscles of the leg less contractibility than that of the arms. The strength of the latter increased relatively to arm girth, while that of the legs declined. Both leg girth and power showed distinct puberal acceleration.

Vierordt doubts Kotelmann's conclusion that strength increases for a time faster than cross-section, falling back on the old law of their proportionality by Weber and even Bo-

[1] Die Körperverhältnisse der Gelehrtenschüler des Johanneums in Hamburg, von Dr. Med. u. Philos. L. Kotelmann. Zeitschrift des koniglich. preus. statistis. Bureau, 1879.

relli. He fails to recognize that a law true of the excerpted muscle under artificial stimulus can not be applied to muscles in normal connection with the nervous system, and that the independent increase in the disposable energy of the latter might account for Kotelmann's increase if it be real. Dr. Gulick, a leading authority on physical training, informs me that near the dawn of puberty there is a distinct decline in the power to climb and hang and otherwise move the body by the use of the hands. This comports well with the slow development of strength at the dawn of puberty just before the often sudden increment. This latter Bierent thinks directly due to the development and retention of seminal fluid. Amherst statistics show that tall students are best in the use of back, legs, and forearm, and short ones in lung power, dip, and pull up.

As far as any inferences can be based on these not entirely harmonious data, it appears that lifting power increases on the average fastest at sixteen, but hardly less rapidly at fifteen and seventeen, and reaches a maximum at twenty-three or twenty-four, with a decline in the rate of augmentation in the later teens. Biceps power also increases, fastest at fifteen or sixteen, and power to pull the weight of the body up increases fastest a little later, from seventeen to eighteen, power in forearm having its fastest increment later than biceps, and dip later than pull, as power of the arms to pull apart comes later than the power to press together. Wrist power augments very fast, about doubling from six to ten, and nearly doubles again from fourteen to seventeen, pull up, dip, and forearm reaching a maximum at about twenty-three, or soon after. If Moon can be relied on, there is an almost explosive growth of leg power from thirteen to fifteen, and the Amherst records suggest another marked augmentation at eighteen. All these directions of growth, perhaps especially that of leg power, seem not constant, but in periods of augmentation and diminution. Leg power seems to come first, then biceps and back, with forearm and power to repel later, and twenty-three is suggested as a culminating age. These inferences, however, are insecure. How this almost fulminating growth of leg and biceps power is related to phyletic flight, pursuit, modes of conflict, or sexual selection, is a suggestive but tantalizing and at present unsolvable problem. The rapid growth of locomotive organs suggests early migrations, and its selective advantages are conceivably manifold, and leg power is, as we shall see, very closely connected with sex. If sedentary life tends now to arrest its normal later development, its nascent period should be more utilized. That the power of pulling up the body and of otherwise moving it by the arms lags behind the growth of weight suggests that at this age, at least, the phyletic influence of anthropoid arboreal life has ceased, or perhaps has been surpassed by more rapid growth of weight, while the sudden biceps increment suggests manifold possible inferences to prehistoric acts and occupations at this stage of development. That such inferences are now little more than conjectural is freely admitted. At best they are only suggestive. But if facts in both the history of the development of the race and in that of the individual have their chief value as those of one series shed light on those of the others, suggestiveness even has an illustrative value, because present studies in psychogenesis indicate not only that this interval will be bridged, but that the arches that span it will some time bear a heavy traffic of scientific work and thought when they become the foundation of educational philosophy and practise.

The power of the hand to grip or squeeze is an interesting and significant measurement. The infant, like the ape, grasps with the fingers acting together, pressing inward upon the palm. The young child seizes a water glass, e. g., by inserting all the fingers in the glass and squeezing it against the palm, the root of the thumb remaining outside and useless, and in climbing anthropoids use the hand as a hook. Slowly and relatively late in the child and the race is the thumb opposed. The dynamometer measures, although in part only, its power of acting against the fingers. This power, although well developed before, undergoes its most rapid acceleration in the teens. This, all tests show, although they differ from each other in many details. In Quetelet's table the greatest annual increase for boys' right hand is from fourteen to fifteen, and the next greatest increase is the year before and the year after, but with a continued but diminishing rate of increase to thirty. Kotelmann's table ends at fourteen, but the greatest increase is the last year shown. Pagliani[1] found the greatest increase from thirteen to fourteen years, but with marked annual increment to nineteen, when his table ends. Porter found the maximal increase from fourteen to sixteen. Chicago boys increased most rapidly from fourteen to sixteen, but continued to increase to twenty-one. Grigorescu,[2] in testing ten boys of each age, found that from ten to thirteen strength of grip increased only from 42 to 48 pounds, but that at fourteen it ran up to 59, and at fifteen to 72. Venn[3] found that the mean squeeze of the two hands increased from nineteen to twenty-four only from 82 to 87.3 pounds, and thought that the power to both squeeze and to pull reached its maximum at about twenty-three to twenty-four, and then slowly declined. Erismann,[4] in testing 4,642 factory workmen of different ages in central Russia, found grip to increase in form most rapidly at sixteen and seventeen. After nineteen it increased more slowly to a maximum at twenty-four to twenty-five, and then slowly declined, so that at the age of fifty-eight it equaled the strength of eighteen.

Age.	Numbers.	Grip.	
		Actual in kilos.	Per cent.
16	30	6.23	21.23
17	134	6.50	10.80
18	244	5.74	15.53
19	153	5.32	14.77
20	73	4.72	14.24
21	49	5.29	13.15
22	27	5.33	14.30
23	12	7.37	18.82
24	13	.50	1.73
25	7	3.42	9.20
Average	..	5.62	15.77

[1] Sopra Alcuni Fattori dello Sviluppo Umano. Turin, 1876, p. 54.

[2] Zeits. f. Schulgesundheitspflege, 1892, p. 127. See also Compte Rendu de la Société de Biologie, July 4, 1891.

[3] Cambridge Anthropology. Journal of Anthropology Institute, November, 1888, p. 151.

[4] Untersuchungen über die Körperlehre Entwickelungen des Russischen Arbeites, 1889, p. 94.

Erismann sums up by saying that in general the most rapid development of physical power occurs between the ages of fifteen and nineteen. From nineteen on the increase is slower, and twenty-six seems to be a stationary period. The maximum of greatest possible development of energy occurs from twenty-four to thirty-five; the maximum of lifting power comes a little later than that of the power to squeeze with the hands and also lasts longer. After thirty-five there is a gradual decline, which should not be marked before fifty. Although there is a remarkable coincidence between growth in weight and the pressure power of the hands, this parallelism is somewhat disturbed after eighteen, pressure power growing fastest, while from fourteen to eighteen weight increases fastest. Lifting power is far greater, and is in general related to power to squeeze as 2½ to 1.

In general, we can say that boys almost double their eleven-year-old strength of dynamometer grip by the time they are sixteen. This is nearly the case with girls. Neither will ever double again, but boys will more than treble their eleven-year-old strength and girls will not. Erismann found a remarkable parallelism between increment in squeezing strength and in weight, except between fourteen and eighteen, when the former fell behind. Porter also noted this coincidence. Kline[1] concluded that the available power of a sudden squeeze was in proportion to the habitual vigor and energy of mental power and activity. Feré[2] thought that the educated and intelligent classes excelled the lower classes in this respect, even though the latter be muscle workers. It is now pretty well established that civilized man has greater strength of hand as tested thus than savages, and that adult men excel women by about one-third. If we compare numbers and methods there are indications that somewhat favor fifteen as the year of fastest growth, with fourteen and then sixteen as ages of next fastest increment. After this wave there is a period of less rapid augmentation, with probably another lesser wave of increased rate in the very early twenties. The first period of increment seems to come later in the laboring classes, if Erismann's figures are typical. Per-

[1] Ped. Sem., Jan., 1898.
[2] Rev. Philos., vol. xli, p. 623.

haps grip precedes biceps. This would indicate greater power to cling and hang than to move about, as Robinson found in very young infants, where this power may be surprisingly developed. Grip is perhaps the most generalized form of hand power, and the phyletic correlate of its pubescent increment is probably without suggestion of arboreal life, but reminiscent of the later development of hand power in the race. The words grasp, apprehend, comprehend, etc., in their etymologies suggest the close relation between mental and manual ability, and remind us of Huxley's statement that man excels the higher anthropoids no more in varied powers of mind than he does in those of the hand.

The greatest number of taps that can be made in a given brief time interval is an important determination for the development of accessory muscular control. The time between two successive taps in such a series is from four to six times greater than between successive vibrations that the ear can distinguish before sound-waves fuse into a note or than the successive impulses that cause a tetanic muscular contraction, and comes nearer that of a simple reaction time. This measurement is very important, and marks one of the factors of motor ability. Not only for children, but even for adults further tests are greatly needed. How rapidly two like simple volitional contractions can follow each other is perhaps the best index we have of will time, and is not much behind the rate of most rapid clear articulation of successive syllables. The maximal adult rate of wagging the forefinger does not vary much from that of trotting the leg, whispering the sounds *t* and *k*, vibrating the head or lower jaw, but none of them have been tested for children.

The best determination of maximal tapping rate at different ages yet made is that of Bryan.[1] This he sought to ascertain for each of the six joints from finger-tip to shoulder, clamping the other joints in each test. He found that rate increased almost steadily from the age of six to sixteen in boys, but that for girls there was a falling off at fourteen or fifteen, with indication of a subsequent rise. The shoulder was the

[1] On the Development of Voluntary Motor Ability. American Journal of Psychology, Nov., 1892.

slowest joint for all ages after seven. At six elbow and wrist were both decidedly ahead of both shoulder and finger, the chief tests of which latter were made with the knuckle-joint. At sixteen the finger had overtaken the fastest joint, while the shoulder had not, suggesting advance of this power down the arms with advancing age. The central or fundamental movements of the shoulder matured earlier than the more accessory wrist. The lowest mean rate was 17.5 taps in five seconds in shoulders of girls at the age of six, and the fastest was at the age of sixteen in the right wrist of boys, viz., 35.9. The rate of the shoulder increases most slowly, of the elbow slightly faster, and that of the wrist and fingers yet more rapidly. At six the finger-joint in boys is slowest, but at sixteen it has surpassed the elbow. Wrist and finger movements do not grow much ahead of those of the shoulder till the eleventh year, when they develop at a rate relatively much faster.

Puberty thus seems to mark the chief stage of nascency for increased rate of this finger movement, a point of great and obvious importance for many kinds of hand training. There is some indication that this development is not continuous, but that years of rapid growth are interspersed with years of slow growth. This is also suggested in Gilbert's [1] results. He found, in testing the greatest number of taps that could be made in five seconds, that from the ages of six to nine girls excelled, but for the next ten years boys surpassed them, most so from fourteen to fifteen. During the whole period of thirteen years, boys increased from 22 to 36.7 taps. The mean variation was greatest for girls at ten and for boys at thirteen, and there was great difference in fatigue. In his New Haven [2] studies, he found that there was a steady increase of both sexes to twelve; then a year of decline for boys and two for girls; after which there was a steady increase of the greatest number of taps per second to sixteen for girls and seventeen for boys.

In Chicago from thirty to fifty children of each sex and of each age from eight to eighteen tapped as rapidly as possible for thirty seconds, and it was found that for every age

[1] Studies in Psychology. Univ. of Iowa, 1897.

[2] Researches on the Mental and Physical Development of School Children. Studies from the Yale Psy. Lab. vol. ii.

except eleven, girls were slightly inferior in rate to boys. Boys' greatest increment was in the thirteenth year, while the tenth, thirteenth, and fifteenth were also years of rapid gain. The continuity of development seemed to be slightly more constant with girls.

That there is a more rapid increase in this power at or near adolescent years seems clear, but it is also undoubted that this power increases rapidly before puberty, and perhaps it would be found to increase fastest earlier yet. Much depends upon the length of time the tapping is continued, and this effort is intense and always very rapidly fatiguing, especially for the young, in whom it would probably be found that tapping for two, five, ten, and twenty seconds would show a rate greatly reduced as the periods lengthen. From available data it would seem that this pubertal increment is much less than for grasping, but it is easy to conceive that the latter may have had greatly increased value at this age in phyletic development, but this is not so apparent for tapping. To infer from this movement ancient modes of paddling, scratching, digging, or masturbation, as one writer suggests, etc., may seem to some a hazardous conjecture, but perhaps hardly more so, when the factor of thumb opposition is considered, than to see in grasping a survival and development of a power so highly unfolded in arboreal life. It must not be forgotten, however, that complete as they are both are elemental movements when compared with all the manifold activities into which they enter in all the historic stages of human life.

Accuracy of movement is a very different function and marks the volitional control of the will, and the inhibition of irrelevant spontaneous, reflex, or automatic movements. It involves conscious effort and attention. The same motions performed with precision by the lower reflex centers are often at first performed very imperfectly by the higher conscious and self-directed powers. Exactness is one of the chief products of skill and practise, and is probably more indicative of mental development than the preceding kinds of muscular action. Motor education here is most liable to cause the evils of precocity, and fatigue has special dangers.

Many methods have been devised for testing muscular control and precision of movement in adults, but we have as yet few studies which follow the changes in these respects up the school grades. The ataxiagraph, in which a pen attached to the head writes on a frictionless horizontal plate above the involuntary swayings of the body standing, showed, according to Hancock,[1] a marked increase of steadiness from the age of five to seven, but even at the latter age, despite the shortness of the body of children, it was greater both laterally and vertically than Bullard and Brackett,[2] or Hinsdale[3] found with adults. The automatograph, which consists of two glass plates with marbles between them so that the upper plate moves without friction and writes unconscious movements when the hand is placed on it, showed a marked gain between five and seven in ability to hold the hand still, but at the latter age these movements were several fold greater than with adults. The tremograph, a thimble attached to a pivoted lever moving freely in all directions, showed that children could not hold the index-finger still for half a minute, and that in this kind of control, although there was much gain from five to seven, they were at the latter age still further behind adults. Hancock's conclusions were that by young children "fine and completed movements are made with difficulty. Efforts to keep quiet produced strong symptoms of nervous irritation. Movement is inhibited only in part, and awkward swayings and twitchings result. Children in normal healthy growth show a lack of coordination and control paralleled only by ataxic, choreic, and paralytic patients." Girls were steadier than boys before puberty, the left hand less than the right, and the ring-finger less than the others.

In testing the influence of voluntary inhibition by an apparatus in which a hammer threatened to strike the eye, but was arrested just in front of it by a glass, Partridge[4] counted in 583 boys and 557 girls from the ages of five to fifteen the number of winks necessary before such control was gained as

[1] A Study of Motor Ability. Ped. Sem., vol. iii, 1894.

[2] Boston Med. and Surg. Journal, vols. i and ii of 1888.

[3] The Stature of Man. Oregon Med. Journal, vol. xciii.

[4] Experiments upon the Control of the Reflex Wink. Am. Jour. of Psy., Jan. 1900, vol. xi, pp. 246 and 247.

entirely inhibited the reflex wink. He found that this was reach much sooner by boys than girls, but his tables showed in general a marked diminution with the boys from eleven or twelve onward in the number of trials before complete control, indicating the increased dominance of volition over reflex impulses at this age.

Precision of movement may be measured as to force, as in holding a weight or pressing a dynamometer steadily so as to maintain a constant muscular tension, or as to direction, as in making regular movements, as in drawing a straight line, or writing in ink of one color over letters in another, etc. The best tests with regard to age have so far been made only in the latter class. This is unfortunate when we consider the great importance of accuracy, the many devices which have been applied to adults, and the ease with which these and other methods might be used for the study of the young.

Kinesthetic sensation, and delicacy of touch and perhaps of eye, are closely connected with precision of movement. Gilbert,[1] on averaging results of one hundred children for each age from seven to seventeen, found that lifted weights were distinguished more finely and with a nearly steady increase of accuracy in judgment with increasing age, and that at thirteen for girls and fourteen for boys this discrimination reached its highest point; that it fell off at fifteen and sixteen; and was slowly increasing at seventeen, but had not regained for either sex its maximal sensitiveness.

Bryan[2] applied two tests which gave significant results. Children placed a metallic stylus in the open arms of a platinum V-shaped figure forming an acute angle of 2.2½ degrees and sought to bring the point to the apex of the V without contact with the arms, failure to do so being electrically recorded. These writing movements were made up, down, and with both hands. In all cases, as the apex was approached and the task became harder, the absolute number of errors increased, but fewer errors in proportion to

[1] Researches in the Mental and Physical Development of School Children. Studies from Yale Psy. Lab., vol. ii.

[2] On the Development of Voluntary Motor Ability. American Journal of Psychology, Nov., 1892.

the space were made. The most striking result was the great rate of gain between the ages of six and eight and the relatively slight gain in early pubescence. Curiously, too, in these tests the average superiority of the right hand over the left was greatest at six and eight, and rather steadily declined up to sixteen.

Bryan's second test for accuracy was a modified clinical test for ataxia, viz., putting a sharp metallic point in a small hole several times without touching the edge. Here the gain between six and eight was less striking, the mean deviations were larger, and the decrease in their absolute size between six and sixteen was much greater than in the V movements.

From both tests it appeared that accuracy improved much faster during the first two or three years after the age of six than later. This was especially true of the right hand. Although the right hand is superior, the left improves between six and sixteen by a greater absolute amount. This is true for both sexes, and there was slight difference between the sexes. That nearly half the gain from six to sixteen often takes place in the first two years, and that puberty has an almost relatively retarding effect, suggests again that periods of increase in strength alternate with those of control and perhaps at certain stages have an almost inverse ratio. This is of the greatest significance for motor education, suggesting that for a few years the stress should incline to the larger sthenic or coarser strength forms of development, and that precision should have less relative emphasis. Motor activities involving accuracy, which may be accentuated during years that precede puberty, should now yield somewhat to those involving fundamental rather than accessory development. The dangers involved in a violation of this rule will be described later.

There are many facts that seem to suggest that in adolescence the right hand precedes the left, and is not usually quite overtaken, so that this predominance is greater after puberty. If this be so, the relation of the two hands in man is somewhat analogous to the relation between the male and female body in muscular development.

Quetelet found that the left hand was always behind the

right in strength of grip from one-sixth to one-eighth or less, but that it was most behind it at sixteen and at the two years preceding and following, and that at twenty and twenty-one the difference between them was again increased, this difference being greater in boys than in girls. In girls he found the predominance of the right hand was more marked in the early teens than before or after.

In the first Chicago Report on Child-Study Investigation, Christopher found "that marked differences in the strength of the two hands does not occur in boys till after fourteen, and in girls till after thirteen," and that twelve-year-old pupils in the seventh and eighth grades showed much more marked increment of strength in the right hand than those in the grades below. Thus unidexterity, although developed before school age, increases rapidly during early adolescent years, and as there appears to be some connection between unidexterity and speech, which is innervated from the same hemisphere as is the preferred hand, Smedley raised the interesting question whether the pubescent increase in unidexterity does not parallel the change of voice. He found that with the increment in both sexes, the superiority of the right hand over the left was more and more marked with increase of age and strength. "The curve representing the strength of the boy's left hand runs nearly parallel to that representing his growth in weight, and in the earlier years of adolescence the curve representing the strength of the right hand gradually approaches the curve of weight." The strength of grip in the right hand increased most rapidly in girls at thirteen and in boys at sixteen, after which the rate of increase rapidly declined. Of twelve-year-old pupils, it was found that those in the higher grades excelled those in the lower, and also that this was much more marked in the right hand than in the left.

The brightest Chicago pupils were more decidedly unidextrous than the average pupils; the latter more so than the dull, and they yet more so than pupils of the Reform School. This was found to be the case both on the basis of strength tests and on those of the greatest number of taps, the left hand more nearly approaching the right in both these respects the lower in the above order the pupils stood.

With accuracy alone the case is different. Bryan found that with his tests the right hand improves faster the first two or three years after the age of six than later. This, too, indicates that precision or control follows a different law than growth in strength or speed. Education of one side causes indirect education of the other, as Scripture and others have shown. For thirteen days, e. g., Miss Brown at Yale squeezed a mercury dynamometer bulb, and thereby increased the strength of her right hand from 28 to 48 points, while the left hand, without exercise, showed a gain of 12 points. Miss Smith daily inserted a needle-point into a small hole, so that error was electrically recorded, 200 times a day for ten days, and reduced her error from 39 to 12 per cent. Meanwhile the untrained left hand fell from 50 to 24 per cent.

Here, as in the vast body of clinical, anatomical, physiological, and popular literature on the subject, the problem of bilateral asymmetry is suggestive yet tantalizing. Attention has more influence on the favored side. Up to a certain point excess of development of one side tends to bring up the other, and beyond this variable and indeterminable point, to increase at the expense of the weaker side. This disparity has great practical advantages in skill, tools, etc., and can not be called a deformity because nature gives nowhere any intimation that perfect parity of form or function was intended. This form of specialization must have some biological advantages analogous to those of nascent periods for different organs and parts, as if the difficulties in growth were economically overcome when the energies were focused, and then when a point of higher development was reached in one direction, this was a stimulus to proportionate growth in related parts. The vicarious performance of the functions of one half of the body by those of the other suggests analogies with cases where fundamental muscles do the work of those that are accessory. Probably in legs, and perhaps in other parts and functions, adolescence involves a marked increase of disparity in the dual halves of the body.[1]

Of the power of adolescents to resist fatigue we still know very little that can be called scientific. Periods of rapid

[1] See Bilateral Asymmetry of Function. Hall and Hartwell. Mind. xxxiii.

growth are commonly thought to be marked by increased fatiguability, but fatigue has very different forms. Some individuals have great power to suddenly summon their resources for a very concentrative and intense effort, which leaves them soon exhausted, while others, lacking this summative power, resist fatigue by endurance under long-sustained effort. The power to summate and power to plod rarely go together, but seem to be usually distinct diatheses. There is much to suggest that early adolescence develops in the direction of spurty rather than in that of sustained effort, or that the latter comes later. The known changes in circulation, the conjectured modification of the nervous centers, phyletic analogy with the longer than diurnal rhythms of work and rest elsewhere discussed, and common observation as well as the general concept of plasticity to be shaped by culminative stresses that break out new ways across old ones—all these suggest this temporal primacy of erethic over plodding increment.

The ergogram pictures a very specific form of fatigue and shows a very wide range of individual differences. In Chicago the ergograph was loaded with seven per cent the weight of the individual and lifted with the right middle finger forty-five times in ninety seconds. From six to twelve years of age both boys and girls increase quite steadily, girls' absolute endurance and also their rate of increase being less than boys'. From twelve and a half to eighteen and a half boys increase much more rapidly than before, gaining fastest from fourteen to seventeen. In Chicago girls, the ergograph increment began at ten and was greatest from twelve to fourteen, with subsequent marked decline, the gain from fourteen to eighteen being hardly equal to half that of from twelve to fourteen. In endurance, as measured by ergograms as well as in the strength of grip, "boys surpass girls at all ages, and this differentiation becomes very marked after the age of fourteen, after which girls increase in strength and endurance but very slightly, while after fourteen boys acquire almost exactly half of their total power in these two directions," these curves being almost identical with those of vital capacity.[1] Muscular differentiation of the sexes practically begins at thirteen.

[1] **Child Study Report, No. 2. Chicago, p. 72.**

Fatigue was tested by tapping forty-five seconds and comparing the number of taps for the last five seconds with those for the first five. There was a loss of power to resist fatigue at eight years, then a steady increase to twelve for girls and thirteen for boys, with a year of subsequent loss followed by another of gain, both reaching their maximum at fifteen and showing some diminution thereafter. It was found also that "muscle sense, force of suggestion, voluntary motor ability, fatigue, lung capacity, reaction, reaction with discrimination and choice, time memory—all give clear indications of a marked change in the development of this period [puberty]." [1]

One of Christopher's most interesting charts shows that the extremes of strength between the weakest and strongest pupils are almost twice as great in the two upper grades as in those below. This greatly increased range of individual variation in early puberty was no less marked in vital capacity and in resistance of fatigue as tested by the ergograph. In vital capacity, still more in strength, and most of all in endurance as tested by the ergograph, the difference between the extreme individuals increases very rapidly up the grades, sometimes becoming from three or four to six or eight times in the seventh and eighth grades what it was in the first, and being in these respects much greater than the similar but marked differentiation between extremes in weight and height.

Partridge,[2] in his study of second breath, had one hundred and sixty-eight cases of overplay, abandon to mental or physical effort, the most striking of which were between the ages of fifteen and twenty, although his data demonstrated nothing concerning age except that the phenomenon is very common at this stage. The descriptions of it in his returns by girls, and especially by boys, in whom it seems more common, is far more graphic and detailed at this age than before or after. When one runs, skates, dances, works, the breath is short and the next effort seems almost impossible. If one still persists, a point is soon reached when all fatigue has passed away and there is as great freshness as at first. The same is true of study late at night beyond the

[1] Studies from the Yale Psy. Lab., vol. ii, p. 40.

[2] Second Breath. Ped. Sem., April, 1897, vol. iv, pp. 372–381.

usual hour of sleep. At a certain point sleepiness ceases and one can easily work with perhaps increased clearness and facility far into the night, although later there may be marked signs of reactionary exhaustion. The same is found in the so-called warming-up curve in lifting weights with the finger. The height of the lift declines with every successive pull by a rather regular curve until the weight does not leave its support at all, but if the effort is continued at each rhythmic interval it is soon lifted, it may be, as high as before, with perhaps several successive periods of recovery and loss. Erethic states in general, very likely physiologically akin to those of inspirationists and ecstatics, are probably connected with the erethic or erectile function of circulation, and quite likely this is an important one in the education of adolescents, which is, however, not yet adequately known.

One of the most fruitful of the methods of experimental psychology has been that of time reactions. The discovery of Helmholtz fifty years ago that the time of a stimulus-wave along a nerve-fiber not only marked an epoch in demonstrating that psychic processes were not timeless nor even with electrical velocities, but relatively very slow, opened one of the most voluminous chapters in psycho-physics. By means of this method-instrument we not only determine the completeness of reflex organization, but measure with precision the time required to discriminate forms and colors, to make associations, to recognize, classify, make a choice, etc. In general this time is inversely as complexity and practise, and these studies reveal the very composition of the habit-plexus, the ruts most worn by repetition in thought. That so far most of these studies have been confined to adults is unfortunate, for the reconstructions and mobilizations of this age, with its new interests, suggest that the chief triumphs of this method are to be achieved in applying it to mapping out the psycho-physic organization of the stages of childhood and youth, and that it has a great examination function in the future. All of value yet done here is briefly told.

Herzen[1] found a marked reduction of reaction time for both girls and boys at puberty. His table is as follows:

[1] Le Cerveau. Paris, 1887, p. 97.

Age.	Boys.	Girls.
5–10	Foot, .548 Hand, .538	Foot, .535 Hand, .525
10–15	Foot, .343 Hand, .336	Foot, .400 Hand, .350
After 15	Foot, .318 Hand, .283	Foot, .400 Hand, .365

From this it appears that young girls react quickest, and Marro[1] thinks that they often reach a high point and are either arrested rather suddenly in rate or often decline from a high point which they can not maintain and develop no further through life. This, he says, may be due to the lowered rate of oxidation characteristic of this age, and which, if marked, may cause hysteria, or it may be due to the greater distraction of attention which makes the concentration of mind necessary for this test now harder.

At Chicago, quickness of reaction to a signal was found to increase rapidly to eight years, when for a year the increment was less, followed by another rise for both sexes to twelve. Then there was no gain for boys to fourteen and little for girls; a rapid increase of both to sixteen, with no gain the following year.

The time of thought required for a reaction, plus the two mental processes of discrimination and choice, showed a rather steady increase to ten; then a positive loss for a year to twelve in girls; then a rather steady increase to thirteen in boys, followed by a year of loss. Girls increased rapidly from thirteen to fourteen, and boys from fourteen to fifteen, after which the rate of increase was less for girls and very slight indeed for boys.

Here, too, may be mentioned the studies of Seashore,[2] who found that children were able to reproduce small time intervals of about five seconds pretty accurately at all ages from six to fifteen. Intervals of ten seconds were shortened to 8.2, those of twenty to 14.4, and those of thirty to 13.5. From eight or nine years on the improvement in reproducing the longer intervals rapidly increased.

[1] La Puberté, p. 37

[2] Studies in Psychology. University of Iowa, 1899.

Adolescence marks a new relation to time and space. The temporal and spatial horizon is enlarged; greater wholes are more adequately judged; more complex members of each are grouped into unity; the relation of wholes and parts is better seen. This we shall see more fully in the chapters on mental development.

To understand the momentous changes of motor functions that characterize adolescence we must consider other than the measurable aspects of the subject. Perhaps the best scale on which to measure all normal growth of muscle structure and functions is found in the progress from fundamental to accessory. The former designates the muscles and movements of the trunk and large joints, neck, back, hips, shoulders, knees, and elbows, sometimes called central, and which in general man has in common with the higher and larger animals. Their activities are few, mostly simultaneous, alternating and rhythmic, as of the legs in walking, and predominate in hard-working men and women with little culture or intelligence, and often in idiots. The latter or accessory movements are those of the hand, tongue, face, and articulatory organs, and these may be connected into a long and greatly diversified series, as those used in writing, talking, piano-playing. They are represented by smaller and more numerous muscles, whose functions develop later in life and represent a higher standpoint of evolution. Those smaller muscles for finer movements come into function later and are chiefly associated with psychic activity, which plays upon them by incessantly changing their tensions, if not causing actual movement. It is these that are so liable to disorder in the many automatisms and choreic tics we see in school children, especially if excited or fatigued. General paralysis usually begins in the higher levels by breaking these down, so that the first symptom of its insidious and never interrupted progress is inability to execute the more exact and delicate movements of tongue or hand, or both. Starting with the latest evolutionary level, it is a devolution that may work downward till very many of the fundamental activities are lost before death.

Nothing better illustrates this distinction than the difference between the fore foot of animals and the human hand. The first begins as a fin or paddle or is armed with a hoof, and is used solely for locomotion. Some carnivora with claws use the fore limb also for holding as well as tearing, and others for digging. Arboreal life seems to have almost created the simian hand and to have wrought a revolution in the form and use of the forearm and its accessory organs, the fingers. Apes and other tree-climbing creatures must not only adjust their prehensile organ to a wide variety of distances and sizes of branches, but must use the hands more or less freely for picking, transporting, and eating fruit, and this has probably been a prime factor in lifting man to the erect position, without which human intelligence as we know it could have hardly been possible. "When we attempt to measure the gap between man and the lower animals in terms of the form of movement, the wonder is no less great than when we use the term of mentality."[1] The degree of approximation to human intelligence in anthropoid animals follows very closely the degree of approximation to human movements.

The gradual acquirement of the erect position by the human infant admirably repeats this long phylogenetic evolution.[2] At first the limbs are of almost no use in locomotion, but the fundamental trunk muscles with those that move the large joints are more or less spasmodically active. Then comes creeping, with use of the hip muscles, while all below the knee is useless, as also are the fingers. Slowly the leg and foot are degraded to locomotion, slowly the great toe becomes more limited in its action, the thumb increases in flexibility and strength of opposition, and the fingers grow more mobile and controllable. As the body slowly assumes the vertical attitude, the form of the chest changes till its greatest diameter is transverse instead of from front to back. The shoulder-blades are less parallel than in quadrupeds, and spread out till they approximate the same plane. This gives the arm freedom of movement laterally, so that it can be rotated one hundred and eighty degrees in man as contrasted to one hundred degrees in apes, thus giving man the command

[1] F. Burk in From Fundamental to Accessory. Pedagogical Lessons, vol. i, p. 29.
[2] Creeping and Walking, by A. W. Trettien. Am. Jour. of Psychol., Oct., 1900.

of almost any point within a sphere of which the two arms are radii.

On the principle of heterogeny, by which movements as well as structures are carried on, but transferred to higher levels, grasping was partly developed from and partly added to the old locomotor function of the fore limbs; the jerky automatisms as well as the slow rhythmic flexion and extension of finger and hand, early aimless reflexes, survivals of arboreal and perhaps even earlier aquatic life, are coördinated, and the bilateral, simultaneous, and rhythmic mode of movements so characteristic of larger fundamental parts is supplemented by superposed systems of exact and complex serial activities, which are less determined by heredity as ancestral currents grow shallow and uncertain near the end of the growth period. In a sense, a child or man is the sum total of his movements or tendencies to move, and nature and instinct chiefly determine the basal, and education the accessory parts of our activities.

The entire accessory system is thus of vital importance for the development of all of the arts of expression. These smaller muscles might almost be called organs of thought. Their tension is modified with the faintest change of soul, such as is seen in accent, inflection, facial expressions, handwriting, and many forms of so-called mind-reading, which, in fact, is always muscle-reading. The day-laborer of low intelligence, with a practical vocabulary of not over five hundred words, who can hardly move each of his fingers without moving others or all of them, who can not move his brows or corrugate his forehead at will, and whose inflection is very monotonous, illustrates a condition of arrest or atrophy of this later, finer, accessory system of muscles. On the other hand, the child, precocious in any or all of these later respects, is very liable to be undeveloped in the larger and more fundamental parts and functions. The full unfoldment of each is, in fact, an inexorable condition precedent for the normal development to full and abiding maturity of the higher and more refined muscularity, just as conversely the awkwardness and clumsiness of adolescence mark a temporary loss of balance in the opposite direction. If this general conception be correct, then nature does not finish the basis of her pyramid in the way Ross, Mercier, and others have assumed, but lays a part of the foundation, and, after carrying it to an apex, normally goes back and adds to the foundation to carry up the apex still higher, and if prevented from so doing, expends her energy in building the apex up at a sharper angle till instability results. School and kindergarten often lay a disproportionate strain on the tiny accessory muscles, weighing altogether but a few ounces, that wag the tongue, move the pen, and do fine work requiring accuracy. But still at this stage prolonged work requiring great accuracy is irksome and brings dangers homologous to those caused by too much fine work in the kindergarten before the first adjustment of large to small muscles, which lasts until adolescence, is established. Then disproportion between function and growth often causes symptoms of chorea. The chief danger is arrest of the development and control of the smaller muscles. Many occupations and forms of athletics, on the contrary, place the stress mainly upon groups of fundamental muscles to the neglect of finer motor possibilities. Some who excel in heavy athletics no doubt coarsen their motor reactions, become not only inexact and heavy, but unresponsive to finer stimuli, as if the large muscles were hypertrophied and the small ones arrested. On the other hand, many young men, and probably more young women, expend too little of their available active energy upon basal and massive muscle work, and cultivate too much, and above all too early, the delicate responsive work. This is, perhaps, the best physiological characterization of precocity, and issues in excessive nervous and muscular irritability. The great influx of muscular vigor that unfolds during adolescent years and which was originally not only necessary to successful propagation, but an expression of virility, seems to be a very plastic quantity, so that motor regimen and exercise at this stage is probably more important and all-conditioning for mentality, sexuality, and health than at any other period of life. Intensity and for a time a spurty diathesis is as instinctive and desirable as are the copious minor automatisms which spontaneously give the alphabet out of which complex and finer motor series are later spelled by the conscious will. Mercier and others have pointed out that, as most skilled labor, so school work and modern activities in civilized life generally lay premature and disproportionate strains upon those kinds of movement requiring exactness. Stress upon basal movements is not only compensating, but is of higher therapeutic value against the disorders of the accessory system; it constitutes the best cure or prophylactic for fidgets and tense states, and directly develops poise, control, and psycho-physical equilibrium. Even when contractions reach choreic intensity the best treatment is to throw activities down the scale that measures the difference between primary and secondary movements and make the former predominate.

The number of movements, the frequency with which they are repeated, their diversity, the number of combinations, and their total kinetic quantum in young children, whether we consider movements of the body as a whole, fundamental movements of large limbs, or finer accessory motions, is amazing. Nearly every external stimulus is answered by a motor response. Dresslar[1] observed a thirteen months old baby for four hours, and found, to follow Preyer's classification, impulsive or spontaneous, reflex, instinctive, imitative, inhibitive, expressive, and even deliberative movements, with marked satisfaction in rhythm, attempts to do almost anything which appealed to him, and almost inexhaustible efferent resources. A friend has tried to record every word uttered by a four-year-old girl during a portion of a day, and finds nothing less than verbigerations. A teacher noted the activities of a fourteen-year-old boy during the study time of a single school day,[2] with similar results.

Lindley[3] studied 897 common motor automatisms in children, which he divided into 92 classes: 45 in the region of the head, 20 in the feet and legs, 19 in the hands and fingers. Arranged in the order of frequency with which each was found the list stood as follows: fingers, feet, lips, tongue, head, body, hands, mouth, eyes, jaws, legs, forehead, face, arms, ears. In the last five alone adolescents exceeded children, the latter excelling the former most in those of head and mouth, legs and

[1] A Morning Observation of a Baby. Ped. Sem., Dec., 1901.

[2] Kate Carman. Notes on School Activity. Ped. Sem., March, 1902.

[3] A Preliminary Study of Some of the Motor Phenomena of Mental Effort. Am. Jour. of Psy., vol. vii, p. 491.

tongue, in this order. The writer believes that there are many more automatisms than appeared in his returns.

School life, especially in the lower grades, is a rich field for the study of these activities. They are familiar as licking things, clicking with the tongue, grinding the teeth, scratching, tapping, twirling a lock of hair or chewing it, biting the nails (Bérillon's onychophagia), shrugging corrugations, pulling buttons or twisting garments, strings, etc., twirling pencils, thumbs, rotating, nodding and shaking the head, squinting and winking, swaying, pouting and grimacing, scraping the floor, rubbing hands, stroking, patting, flicking the fingers, wagging, snapping the fingers, snuffling, squinting, picking the face, interlacing the fingers, cracking the joints, finger plays, biting and nibbling, trotting the leg, sucking things, etc.

The average number of automatisms per 100 children Smith found to be 176, in adolescents 110. Swaying is chiefly with children; playing and drumming with the fingers is more common among adolescents; the movements of fingers and feet decline little with age, and those of eyes and forehead increase, which is significant for the development of attention. Girls excel greatly in swaying, and also, although less, in finger automatism, and boys lead in movements of tongue, feet, and hands. Such movements increase with too much sitting intensity of effort, such as to fix attention, and vary with the nature of the activity willed, but involve few muscles directly used in a given task. They increase up the kindergarten grades and fall off rapidly in the primary grades; are greater with tasks requiring fine and exact movements than with those involving large movements. Automatisms are often a sign of the difficulty of tasks. The restlessness that they often express is one of the commonest signs of fatigue. They are mostly in the accessory muscles, while those of the fundamental muscles (body, legs, and arms) disappear rapidly with age; those of eye, brow, and jaw show greatest increase with age, but their frequency in general declines with growing maturity, although there is increased frequency of certain specialized contractions, which indicate the gradual settling of expression in the face.

Often such movements pass over by insensible gradation

into the morbid automatism of chorea, and in yet lower levels of decay we see them in the aimless palpation of the sick, in pselaphesis, carphology, and floccilation. In idiots[1] arrest of higher powers often goes with hypertrophy of these movements, as seen in head-beaters (as if, just as nature impels those partially blind to rub the eyes for "light-hunger," so it prompts the feeble-minded to strike the head for cerebrations), rockers, rackers, shakers, biters, etc. Movements often pass to fixed attitudes and postures of limbs or body, disturbing the normal balance between flexors and extensors, the significance of which as nerve signs or exponents of habitual brain states and tensions Warner has so admirably shown.

These non-volitional movements of earliest infancy and of later childhood are thus sure to become centers of intense and deep scientific interest in the near future. They are one of the richest of all the paleopsychic fields. I think we may regard most of them as rudimentary impulses to do acts which in some prehuman stage were of all-conditioning importance for life. They are not anticipatory of future useful activities, as Groos says they are, so much as relics of past forms of utilities now essentially obsolete. Ancient modes of locomotion, prehension, balancing, defense, attack, sensuality, etc., are all rehearsed, some quite fully and some only by the faintest mimetic suggestion, flitting spasmodic tensions, gestures, or facial expressions. These motor odds, ends, and titbits often suggest therotropic or regressive acts of an almost saurian age, like the swimming movements of young infants, old modes of climbing, hitting, fighting, hunting. A few that were once accessory now seem fundamental, but with more the converse seems true. Each one of them is rich in suggestions now tantalizingly unverifiable. When we approach the origin of vertebrate life, they are mementoes of the highest scientific value, and in their sign language, which now seems jargon, genetic psychology will one day read its title clear to pedigrees that are lost, while their further record and analysis by the refined methods now available is one of the richest of the many new fields opened by child study. They are motor analogues of the stray, segregated psychoses that

[1] G. E. Johnson. **Psychology and Pedagogy of Feeble-Minded Children. Ped. Sem.**, Oct., 1895.

make the subconscious activities now beginning to be studied. Both are largely vestigial and perhaps semiferal. They are the partly lapsed and unreclaimed, partly virgin and never cultivated Bad Lands of the state of Man-Soul, and if their area becomes too extensive or their growth too rank and noxious, may become a source of danger, but they always suggest larger possibilities of human nature when we know how to make motor education utilize them aright. Thus it is with movements a little as Taine thought it was with impressions and ideas, which tend to grow to delusional intensity unless checked and balanced by others and wrought into the thought plexus of true perception and reason. This view I believe to be essentially new, and if true, its practical applications are important and its theoretical implications yet more so.

Abundance and vigor of these movements are desirable and even a considerable degree of restlessness is a good sign in young children. Many of what are now often called nerve signs and even choreic symptoms, the fidgetiness in school on cloudy days and often after a vacation, the motor superfluities of awkwardness, embarrassment, extreme effort, excitement, fatigue, sleepiness, etc., are simply the forms in which we receive the full momentum of heredity, and mark a natural richness of the raw material of intellect, feeling, and especially of will. Hence they must be abundant. All parts should act in all possible ways at first and untrammeled by the activity of all other parts and functions. Some of these activities are more essential for growth in size than are later and more conscious movements. Here as everywhere the rule holds that powers themselves must be unfolded before the ability to check or even to use them can develop. All movements arising from spontaneous activity of nerve cells or centers must be made in order even to avoid the atrophy of disease. Not only so, but this purer kind of innateness must often be helped out to some extent in some children by stimulating reflexes; a rich and wide repertory of sensation must be made familiar; more or less and very guarded, watched and limited experiences of hunger, thirst, cold, heat, tastes, sounds, smells, colors, brightnesses, tactile irritations, and perhaps even occasional tickling and pain to play off the vastly complex function of laughing, crying, etc., may in some cases be judicious. Conscious and unconscious imitation or repetition of every sort of copy may also help to establish the immediate and low-level connection between afferent and efferent processes that brings the organism into direct *rapport* and harmony with the whole world of sense. Perhaps the more rankly and independently they are developed to full functional integrity, each in its season, if we only knew that season, the better. Premature control by higher centers, or coördination into higher compounds of habits and ordered serial activities, is repressive and wasteful, and the mature will of which they are components, or which must at least domesticate them, is stronger and more forcible if this serial stage is not unduly abridged.

But, secondly, many, if not most, of these activities when developed a little, group after group, as they arise, must be controlled, checked, and organized into higher and often more serial compounds. The inhibiting functions are at first hard. In trying to sit still the child sets its teeth, holds the breath, clinches its fists and perhaps makes every muscle tense with a great effort that very soon exhausts. This repressive function is probably not worked from special nervous centers, nor can we speak with confidence of collisions with " sums of arrest " in a sense analogous to that of Herbart, or of stimuli that normally cause catabolic molecular processes in the cells, being mysteriously diverted to produce increased instability or anabolic lability in the sense of Wundt's *Mechanik der Nerven.* The concept now suggested by many facts is that inhibition is irradiation or long circuiting to higher and more complex brain areas, so that the energy, whether spontaneous or reflex, is diverted to be used elsewhere. These combinations are of a higher order, more remote from reflex action, and modified by some Jacksonian third level, or perhaps in part by Vulpius' transverse layer. Action is now not from independent centers, but these are slowly associated, so that excitation may flow off from one point to any other and any reaction may result from any stimulus.

The more unified the brain the less it suffers from localization, and the lower is the level to which any one function can exhaust the whole. The tendency of each group of cells to discharge or overflow into those of lower tension than themselves increases as correspondence in time and space widens. The more one of a number of activities gains in power to draw on all the brain, or the more readily the active parts are fed at cost of the resting parts, the less is rest to be found in change from one of these activities to another, and the less do concentration and specialization prove to be dangerous. Before, the aim was to wake all parts to function; now it is to connect them. Intensity of this cross-section activity now tends to unity, so that all parts of the brain energize together. In a brain with this switch-board function well organized, each reaction has grown independent of its own stimulus and may result from any stimulation, and each act, e. g., a finger movement of a peculiar nature, may tire the whole brain. This helps us to understand why brain-workers so often excel laborers not only in sudden dynamometric strength test, but in sustained and long-enduring effort. In a good brain or in a good machine, power may thus be developed over a large surface, and all of it applied to a small one, and hence the dangers of specialization are lessened in exact proportion as the elements of our ego are thus compacted together. It is in the variety and delicacy of these combinations and all that they imply, far more than in the elements of which they are composed, that man rises farthest above the higher animals, and of these powers later adolescence is the golden age. The aimless and archaic movements of infancy, whether massive and complex or in the form of isolated automatic tweaks or twinges, and perhaps even the still more microkinetic gleanings of fibrillary formications, are thus, by slow processes of combined analysis and synthesis, involving changes as radical as any in all the world of growth, made over into habits and conduct that fit the world of present environment.

But, thirdly, this long process carried out with all degrees of completeness may be arrested at any unfinished stage. Some automatisms refuse to be controlled by the will, and both they and it are often overworked. Here we must distinguish constantly between (1) those growing rankly in order to be later organized under the will, and (2) those that have become feral after this domestication of them has lost power from disease or fatigue, and (3) those that have never been subjugated because the central power that should have used them to weave the texture of willed action—the proper language of complete manhood—was itself arrested or degenerate. With regard to many of these movements these distinctions can be made with confidence, and in some children more certainly than in others. In childhood, before twelve, the efferent patterns should be developed into many more or less indelible habits and their colors set fast. Motor specialties requiring exactness and grace like piano-playing, drawing, writing, pronunciation of a foreign tongue, dancing, acting, singing, and a host of virtuosities, must be well begun before the relative arrest of accessory growth at the dawn of the ephebic regeneration and before its great afflux of strength. The facts seem to show that children of this age, such as Hancock[1] described, who could not stand with feet close together and eyes closed without swaying much, could not walk backward, sit still half a minute, dress alone, tie two ends of a string together, interlace slats, wind thread, spin a top, stand on toes or heels, hop on each foot, drive a nail, roll a hoop, skate, hit fingers together rapidly in succession beginning at the little finger and then reversing, etc., are the very ones in whom automatisms are most marked or else they are those constitutionally inert, dull, or uneducable.

In children these motor residua may persist as characteristic features of inflection, accent, or manners; automatisms may become morbid in stammering or stuttering, or they may be seen in gait, handwriting, tics or tweaks, etc. Instead of disappearing with age, as they should, they are seen in the blind, as facial grimaces uncorrected by the mirror or facial consciousness, in the deaf as inarticulate noises, and they may tend to grow monstrous with age as if they were disintegrated fragments of our personality, split off and aborted, or motor parasites leaving our psycho-physic ego poorer in energy and plasticity of adaptation, till the distraction and anarchy of the individual nature becomes conspicuous and pathetic.

At puberty, however, when muscle habits are so plastic, when there is a new relation between quantity or volume of motor energy and qualitative differentiation, and between volitional control and reflex activities, these kinetic remnants strongly tend to shoot together into wrong aggregates if right

[1] A Preliminary Study of Some of the Motor Phenomena of Mental Effort. American Journal of Psychology, July, 1896, vol. vii, pp. 491–517.

ones are not formed. Good manners and correct motor form generally, as well as skill, are the most economic ways of doing things, but this is the age of wasteful ways, awkwardness, mannerisms, tensions that are a constant leakage of vital energy, perhaps semi-imperative acts, contortions, quaint movements, more elaborated than in childhood and often highly unæsthetic and disagreeable, motor coordinations that will need laborious decomposition later. The avoidable factor in their causation is, with some modification, not unlike that of the simpler feral movements and faulty attitudes, carriage, and postures in children, viz., some form of overpressure or misfit between environment and nature. As from the years of four to eight there is great danger that overemphasis of the activities of the accessory muscles will sow the seeds of chorea, or aggravate predispositions to it, now again comes a greatly increased danger, hardly existing from eight to twelve, that overprecision, especially if fundamental activities are neglected, will bring nervous strain and stunting precocity. This is again the age of the basal, e. g., hill-climbing muscles, of leg and back and shoulder work, and of the yet more fundamental heart, lung, and chest muscles. Now again the study of a book, under the usual conditions of sitting in a closed space and using pen, tongue, and eye combined, has a tendency to overestimate the accessory muscles. This is especially harmful for city children who are too prone to the distraction of overmobility at an age especially exposed to maladjustment of motor income and expenditure, and it constitutes not a liberal or power-generating, but a highly and prematurely specialized, narrowing, and weakening education unless offset by safeguards better than any system of gymnastics, which is at best artificial and exaggerated.

As Bryan well says, "the efficiency of a machine depends so far as we know upon the maximum force, rate, amplitude, and variety of direction of its movements and upon the exactness with which below these maxima the force, rate, amplitude, and direction of the movements can be controlled." The motor efficiency of a man depends upon his ability in all these respects. Moreover, the education of the small muscles and fine adjustments of larger ones is as near mental training as physical culture can get, for these are the thought-muscles and movements, and their perfected function is to reflect and express by slight modifications of tension and tone every psychic change. Only the brain itself is more closely and immediately an organ of thought than are these muscles and their activity, reflex, spontaneous, or imitative in origin. Whether any of them are of value, as Lindley thinks, in arousing the brain to activity, or, as Müller suggests, in drawing off sensations or venting efferent impulses that would otherwise distract, we need not here discuss. If so, this is of course a secondary and late function—nature's way of making the best of things and utilizing remnants.

With these facts and their implications in mind we can next pass to consider the conditions under which the adolescent muscles best develop. Here we confront one of the greatest and most difficult problems of our age. Changes in modern motor life have been so vast and sudden as to present some of the most comprehensive and all-conditioning dangers that threaten civilized races. Not only have the forms of labor been radically changed within a generation or two, but the basal activities that shaped the body of primitive man have been suddenly swept away by the new methods of modern industry. Even popular sports, games, and recreations, so abundant in the early life of all progressive peoples, have been reduced and transformed, and the play age, that once extended on to middle life and often old age, has been restricted. Sedentary life in schools and offices, as we have seen, is reducing the vigor and size of our lower limbs. Our industry is no longer under hygienic conditions, and instead of being out of doors, in the country, or of highly diversified kinds, it is now specialized, monotonous, in closed spaces, bad air, and perhaps poor light, especially in cities. The diseases and arrest bred in the young by life in shops, offices, factories, and schools increase. Work is rigidly bound to fixed hours, uniform standards, stints and piece-products, and instead of a finished article, each individual now achieves a part of a single process, and knows little of those that precede or follow. Machinery has relieved the large basal muscles and laid more stress upon fine and exact movements that involve nerve strain. The coarser forms of work that involve hard lifting, carrying, digging, etc., are themselves specialized, and skilled labor requires more and more brain-work. It has been estimated that "the diminution of manual labor required to do a given quantity of work in 1884 as compared with 1870 is no less than 70 per cent."[1] Personal interest in and the old native sense of responsibility for results, ownership and use of the finished products, which have been the inspiration and soul of work in all the past, are in more and more fields gone. Those who realize how small a proportion of the young male population train or engage even in amateur sports with zest and regularity, how very few and picked men strive for records, and how immediate and amazing are the results of judicious training, can best understand how far below his possibilities as a motor being the average modern man goes through life, and how far short in this respect he falls from fulfilling nature's design for him.

For unnumbered generations primitive man in the nomad age wandered, made perhaps annual migrations, and bore heavy burdens, while we ride relatively unencumbered. He tilled the reluctant soil, digging with rude implements where we use machines of many man-power. In the stone, iron, and bronze age, he shaped stone and metals, and wrought with infinite pains and effort, products that we buy without even knowledge of the processes by which they are made. As hunter he followed game, and when found, he chased, fought, and overcame it in a struggle perhaps desperate, while we shoot it at a distance with little risk or effort. In warfare he fought hand to hand and eye to eye, while we kill "with as much black powder as can be put in a woman's thimble." He caught and domesticated scores of species of wild animals and taught them to serve him; fished with patience and skill that compensated his crude tools, weapons, implements, and tackle; danced to exhaustion in the service of his gods or in memory of his forebears, imitating every animal, rehearsing all his own activities in mimic form to the point of exhaustion, while we move through a few figures in closed spaces. He dressed hides, wove baskets which we can not reproduce, and fabrics which we only poorly imitate by machinery, made pottery which set our fashions, played games that invigorated body and soul. His courtship was with feats of prowess, and skill, and meant physical effort and endurance.

[1] Encyclopædia of Social Reform, 1898, p. 1095.

Adolescent girls, especially in the middle classes, in upper grammar and high school grades, during the golden age for nascent muscular development, suffer perhaps most of all in this respect. Grave as are the evils of child labor, I believe far more pubescents in this country now suffer from too little than from too much physical exercise, while most who suffer from work do so because it is too uniform, one-sided, accessory, or under unwholesome conditions, and not because it is excessive in amount. Modern industry has thus largely ceased to be a means of physical development and needs to be offset by compensating modes of activity. Many labor-saving devices increase neural strain, so that one of the problems of our time is how to preserve and restore nerve energy. Under present industrial systems this must grow worse and not better in the future. Healthy natural industries will be less and less open to the young. This is the new situation that now confronts those concerned for motor education, if they would only make good what is lost.

Some of the results of these conditions are seen in average measurements of dimensions, proportions, strength, skill, and control. Despite the excellence of the few, the testimony of those most familiar with the bodies of children and adults, and their physical powers, gives evidence of the ravages of modern modes of life that, without a wide-spread motor revival, can bode only degeneration for our nation and our race. The number of common things that can not be done at all; the large proportion of our youth who must be exempted from many kinds of activity or a great amount of any; the thin limbs, collapsed shoulders or chests, the bilateral asymmetry, weak hearts, lungs, eyes, puny and bad voices, muddy or pallid complexions, tired ways, automatism, dyspeptic stomachs, the effects of youthful error or of impoverished heredity, delicate and tender nurture, often, alas, only too necessary, show the lamentable and cumulative effects of long neglect of the motor abilities, the most educable of all man's powers, and perhaps the most important for his well-being. If the unfaithful stewards of these puny and shameful bodies had again, as in Sparta, to strip and stand before stern judges and render them account, and be smitten with a conviction of their weakness, guilty deformity, and arrest of growth, if they were brought to realize how they are fallen beings, as weak as stern theologians once deemed them depraved, and how great their need of physical salvation, we might hope again for a physical renaissance. Such a rebirth the world has seen but twice or perhaps thrice, and each was followed by the two or three brightest culture periods of history, and formed an epoch in the advancement of the kingdom of man. A vast body of evidence could be collected from the writings of anthropologists showing how superior unspoiled savages are to civilized man in correct or esthetic proportions of body, in many forms of endurance of fatigue, hardship, and power to bear exposure, in the development and preservation of teeth and hair, in keenness of senses, absence of deformities, as well as immunity to many of our diseases. Their women are stronger and bear hardship and exposure, monthly periods and childbirth, better. Civilization is so hard on the body that some have called it a disease, despite the arts that keep puny bodies alive to a greater average age, and our greater protection from contagious and germ diseases.

The progressive realization of these tendencies has prompted most of the best recent and great changes motorward in education and also in personal regimen. Health- and strength-giving agencies have put to school the large motor areas of the brain, so long neglected, and have vastly enlarged their scope. Thousands of youth are now inspired with new enthusiasm for physical development, and new institutions of many kinds and grades have arisen, with a voluminous literature, unnumbered specialists, specialties, new apparatus, tests, movements, methods, and theories, and the press, the public, and the church are awakened to a fresh interest in the body and its powers. All this is magnificent, but sadly inadequate to cope with the new needs and dangers, which are vastly greater.

In the lower realms of culture, sects have arisen, each with its own creed and cult, and perhaps its own publications, schools, apparatus, etc., and each blind and perhaps hostile to the merits of others. Some make deep breathing central, others relaxation and passivity, to get all the unconscious tensions out of the muscles and joints, group by group, with special exercises, postures, etc., to this end. Some years ago a laughing cult, with giggle classes and a so-called philosophy of happiness, flourished in a number of our cities. Others aim chiefly at Delsartian grace, emotional expression, and gesture. One schemelet cultivates classic poses and recommends those of famous statues of antiquity, in the attitude of some of which the pupil must always be found. Yawning has a cult and a little literature all to itself, and so has artificial crying and laughing and stretching. There are several health-lift, chest-expanding systems and apparatus, and trainers with secret methods explained only to pupils. I have a book-shelf full of graded class and personal exercises for both sexes, all with copious directions and reasons, collections of plays and games, new and old, edited and arranged according to principles superior to what has been known hitherto. Sometimes the diaphragm, or the regulation of the bowels, the liver, sex, and lungs are chiefly had in view; these apparently for the most part by adult authors, who have suffered, and found relief, and who benevolently offer their cures as preventives to the young. Here the rankest weeds show the richest soil of need and opportunity.

Higher up the scale of ameliorative efforts are far more sane and beneficent methods, and we must glance at a few of the best and most typical, following the order: (1) industrial, (2) manual training, (3) gymnastic, and (4) sports and play games.

I. Industrial education is now imperative for every nation that would excel in agriculture, manufacture, and trade, not only because of the growing intensity of competition, but because of the decline of the apprentice system and the growing intricacy of processes, requiring only the skill needed for livelihood. Thousands of our youth of late have been diverted from secondary schools to the monotechnic or trade classes now established for horology, glass-work, brick-laying, carpentry, forging, dressmaking, cooking, typesetting, bookbinding, brewing, seamanship, work in leather, rubber, horticulture, gardening, photography, basketry, stock-raising, typewriting, stenography and bookkeeping, elementary commercial training for practical preparation for clerkships, etc. In this work not only is Boston, our most advanced city, as President Pritchett [1] has shown in detail, far behind Berlin, but German

[1] The Place of Industrial and Technical Training in Public Education. Technology Review, January, 1902.

workmen and shopmen are slowly taking the best places even in England, and but for a high tariff, which protects our inferiority, the competitive pressure would be still greater. In Germany, especially, this training is far more diversified than here, always being colored if not determined by the prevalent industry of the region and more specialized and helped out by evening and even Sunday classes in the school buildings, and by the still strong apprentice system. Frœbelian influence in manual training reaches through the eight school years, and is in some respects better than ours in lower grades, but is very rarely coeducational, girls' work of sewing, knitting, crocheting, weaving, etc., not being considered manual training. There are now over 1,500 schools and workshops in Germany where manual training is taught; twenty-five of these are independent schools. The work really began in 1875 with v. Kaas, and is promoted by the great Society for Boys' Handwork. Much stress is laid on paper and pasteboard work in lower grades, under the influence of Kurufa of Darmstadt. Many objects for illustrating science are made, and one course embraces the Seyner water-wheel.[1]

In France it is made more effective by the equal salaries of teachers everywhere, thus securing better instruction in the country. Adolescence is the golden period for acquiring the skill that comes by practise, so essential in the struggle for survival. In general this kind of motor education is least of all free, but subservient to the tool, machine, process, finished product, or end in view, and to these health and development are subordinated, so that they tend to be ever more narrow and special. The standard here is maximal efficiency of the capacities that earn. It may favor bad habitual attitudes, muscular development of but one part, excessive large or small muscles, involve too much time or effort, unhealthful conditions, etc., but it has the great advantage of utility, which is the mainspring of all industry. In a very few departments and places this training has felt the influence of the arts and crafts movement and has been faintly touched with the inspiration of beauty. While such courses give those who follow them marked advantage over those who do not, they are chiefly

[1] See an article by Dr. H. E Kolk, Education, Dec., 1902.

utilitarian and do little to mature or unfold the physical powers, and may involve arrest or degeneration.

Where not one but several or many processes are taught, the case is far better. Of all work-schools, a good farm is probably the best for motor development. This is due to its great variety of occupations, healthful conditions, and the incalculable phyletic reenforcement from immemorial times. I have computed some threescore industries[1] as the census now classifies them, that were more or less generally known and practised sixty years ago in a little township, which not only in this but in other respects has many features of an ideal educational environment for adolescent boys, combining as it does not only physical and industrial, but civil and religious elements in wise proportions and with pedagogic objectivity, and representing the ideal of such a state of intelligent citizen voters as was contemplated by the framers of our Constitution.

Contrast this life with that of a " hand " in a modern shoe factory, who does all day but one of the eighty-one stages or processes from a tanned hide to a finished shoe, or of a man in a shirt-shop who is one of thirty-nine, each of whom does as piece-work a single step requiring great exactness, speed, and skill, and who never knows how a whole shirt is made, and we shall see that the present beginning of a revival of interest in muscular development comes none too early. So liberal is muscular education of this kind that its work in somewhat primitive form has been restored and copied in many features by many educational institutions for adolescents, of the Abbotsholme type and grade, and several others, whose purpose is to train for primitive conditions of colonial life. Thousands of school gardens have also been lately developed for lower grades, which have given a new impetus to the study of nature. Farm training at its best instils love of country, ruralizes taste, borrows some of its ideals from Goethe's pedagogic province, and perhaps even Gilman's pie-shaped communities, with villages at the center irradiating to farms in all directions. In England, where by the law of primogeniture holdings are large and in few hands, this training has never flourished, as it has greatly in France, where nearly every

[1] See my Boy Life in a New England Town. Proc. Am. Antiquarian Society, October, 1890.

adult male may own land and a large proportion will come to do so. So of processes. As a student in Germany I took a few lessons each of a bookbinder, a glassblower, a shoemaker, a plumber, and a blacksmith, and here I have learned in a crude way the technique of the gold-beater and old-fashioned broom-maker, etc., none of which come amiss in the laboratory, and I am proud that I can still mow and keep my scythe sharp, chop, plow, milk, churn, make cheese and soap, braid a palm-leaf hat complete, knit, spin and even "put in a piece" in an old-fashioned hand loom, and weave frocking. But this pride bows low before the pupils of our best institutions for negroes, Indians, and juvenile delinquents, whose training is often in more than a score of industries and who to-day in my judgment receive the best training in the land, if judged by the annual growth in mind, morals, health, physique, ability, and knowledge, all taken together. Instead of seeking soft, ready-made places near home, such education impels to the frontier, to strike out new careers, to start at the bottom and rise by merit, beginning so low that every change must be a rise. Wherever youth thus trained are thrown, they land like a cat on all-fours and are armed *cap-à-pie for* the struggle of life. Agriculture, manufacture, and commerce are the bases of national prosperity, and on them all professions, institutions, and even culture, are more and more dependent, while the old ideals of mere study and brain-work are fast becoming obsolete. We really retain only the knowledge we apply. We should get up interest in new processes like that of a naturalist in new species. Those who leave school at any age or stage should be best fitted to take up their life work instead of leaving unfitted for it, aimless and discouraged. Instead of dropping out limp and disheartened, we should train "struggle-for-lifeurs," in Daudet's phrase, and that betimes, so that the young come back to it not too late for securing the best benefits, after having wasted the years best fitted for it in profitless studies or in the hard school of failure. By such methods many of our flabby, undeveloped, anemic, easy-living city youth would be regenerated in body and spirit. Some of the now oldest, richest, and most famous schools of the world were at first established by charity for poor boys who worked their way, and such institutions have an undreamed-of future. No other so well fit for a life of respectable and successful muscle work, and perhaps this should be central for all at this stage. It develops the muscular activities rendered necessary by man's early development, which were so largely concerned with food, shelter, clothing, making and selling commodities necessary for life, comfort and safety. The natural state of man is not war, but peace, and perhaps Dawson[1] is right in thinking that three-fourths of man's physical activities in the past have gone into such vocations. Industry has determined the nature and trend of muscular development, and youth, who have pets, till the soil, build, manufacture, use tools, and master elementary processes and skills, are most truly repeating the history of the race. This, too, lays the best foundation for intellectual careers. The study of pure science, as well as its higher technology, follows rather than precedes this. In the largest sense this is the order of nature, from fundamental and generalized to finer accessory and specialized organs and functions, and such a sequence best weeds out and subordinates automatisms. The age of stress in most of these kinds of training is that of most rapid increment of muscular power, as we have seen in the middle and later teens rather than childhood, as some recent methods have mistakenly assumed, and this prepolytechnic work, wherever and in whatever degree it is possible, is a better adjunct of secondary courses than manual training, the sad fact being that according to the best estimates only a fraction of one per cent of those who need this training in this country are now receiving it.

II. Manual training has many origins, but in its now most widely accepted form it came to us more than a generation ago from Moscow, and has its best representation here in our new and often magnificent manual-training high schools and in many courses in other public schools. This work meets the growing demand of the country for a more practical education, a demand which often greatly exceeds the accommodations. The philosophy, if such it may be called, that underlies the movement, is simple, forcible, and sound, and not unlike Pestalozzi's "*keine Kentnisse ohne Fertigkeiten*," in that it lessens the interval between thinking and doing; helps to give control, dexterity, and skill an industrial trend to taste; interests many

[1] Am. Phys. Ed. Rev., June, 1902.

not successful in ordinary school; tends to the better appreciation of good, honest work; imparts new zest for some studies; adds somewhat to the average length of the school period; gives a sense of capacity and effectiveness, and is a useful preparation for a number of vocations. These claims are all well founded and this work is a valuable addition to the pedagogic agencies of any country or state. As man excels the higher anthropoids perhaps almost as much in hand power as in mind, and since the manual areas of the brain are wide near the psychic zones, and the cortical centers are thus directly developed, the hand is a potent instrument in opening the intellect as well as in training sense and will. It is no reproach to these schools that, full as they are, they provide for but an insignificant fraction of the *circa* sixteen millions or twenty per cent of the young people of the country between fifteen and twenty-four.

When we turn to the needs of these pupils, the errors and limitations of the method are painful to contemplate. The work is essentially manual and offers little for the legs, where most of the muscular tissues of the body lie, those which respond most to training and are now most in danger of degeneration at this age; the back and trunk are also little trained. Consideration of proportion and bilateral asymmetry are practically ignored. Almost in proportion as these schools have multiplied, the rage for uniformity, together with motives of economy and administrative efficiency on account of overcrowding, have made them rigid and inflexible on the principle that as the line lengthens the stake must be strengthened. This is a double misfortune, for the courses were not sufficiently considered at first and the plastic stage of adaptation was too short, while the methods of industry have undergone vast changes since they were given shape. There are now between three and four hundred occupations in the census, more than half of these involving manual work, so that never perhaps was there so great a pedagogic problem as to make these natural developments into conscious art, to extract what may be called basal types. This requires an effort not without analysis to Aristotle's attempt to extract from the topics of the marketplace the underlying categories eternally conditioning all thought, or to construct a grammar of speech. Hardly an attempt worthy the name, not even the very inadequate one of a committee, has been made in this field to study the conditions and to meet them. Like Froebel's gifts and occupations, deemed by their author the very roots of human occupations in infant form, the processes selected are underived and find their justification rather in their logical sequence and coherence than in being true norms of work. If these latter be attainable at all, it is not likely that they will fit so snugly in a brief curriculum, so that its simplicity is suspicious. The wards of the keys that lock the secrets of nature and human life are more intricate and mazy. As H. T. Bailey well puts it in substance, a master in any art-craft must have a four-fold equipment: 1. Ability to grasp an idea and embody it. 2. Power to utilize all nerve, and a wide repertory of methods, devices, recipes, discoveries, machines, etc. 3. Knowledge of the history of the craft. 4. Skill in technical processes. American schools emphasize chiefly only the last.

The *de facto* result is thus a course rich in details representing wood and iron chiefly, and mostly ignoring other materials; the part of the course treating of the former, wooden in its teachings and distinctly tending to make joiners, carpenters and cabinet-makers, that of the latter iron in its rigidity and an excellent school for smiths, mechanics, and machinists. These courses are not liberal because they hardly touch science, which is rapidly becoming the real basis of every industry. Almost nothing that can be called scientific knowledge is required or even much favored, save some geometrical and mechanical drawing and its implicates. These schools instinctively fear and repudiate plain and direct utility, or suspect its educational value or repute in the community because of this strong bias toward a few trades. This tendency they even also fear less often because unfortunately trade-unions in this country sometimes jealously suspect it and might vote down supplies, than because the teachers in these schools were generally trained in older scholastic and even classic methods and matter. Industry is everywhere and always for the sake of the product, and to cut loose from this as if it were a contamination is a fatal mistake. To focus on process only, with no reference to the object made, is here an almost tragic case of the sacrifice of content to form, which in all history has been the chief stigma of degeneration in education. Man is a tool-using animal, but tools are always only a means to an end, the latter prompting even their invention. Hence a course in tool manipulation only, with persistent refusal to consider the product lest features of trade-schools be introduced, has made most of our manual-training high schools ghastly, hollow, artificial institutions. Instead of making in the lower grades certain toys which are masterpieces of mechanical simplification, as tops and kites, and introducing such processes as glass-making and photography, and in higher grades making simple scientific apparatus more generic than machines to open the great principles of the material universe, all is sacrificed to supernormalized method.

As in all hypermethodic schemes the thought side is feeble. There is no such control of the work of these schools by the higher technical institutions as the college exercises over the high school, so that few of them do work that fits for advanced training or is thought best by technical faculties. In most of its current narrow forms, manual training will prove to be historically as it is educationally extemporized and tentative, and will soon be superseded by broader methods and forgotten and obsolete, or cited only as a low point of departure from which future progress will loom up.

Indeed in more progressive centers, many new departures are now in the experimental stage. Goetze at Leipzig, as a result of long and original studies and trials, has developed courses in which pasteboard work and modeling are made of equal rank with wood and iron, and he has connected it even with the kindergarten below. In general the whole industrial life of our day is being slowly explored in the quest of new educational elements, and rubber, lead, glass, textiles, metallurgical operations, agriculture, every tool and many machines, etc., are sure to contribute their choicest pedagogical factors to the final result. In every detail the prime consideration should be the nature and needs of the youthful body and will at each age, their hygiene and fullest development, and next, the closest connection with science at every point should do the same for the intellect. Each operation and each tool—the saw, knife, plane, screw, hammer, chisel, draw-shave, sandpaper, lathe—will be studied with reference to their orthopedic value, bilateral asymmetry, the muscles they develop, and the attitudes and motor habits they favor; and uniformity, which in France often requires classes to saw, strike, plane up, down, right, left, all together, upon count and command, will give place to individuality.

Sloyd has certain special features and claims. The word means skilful, deft. The movement was organized in Sweden a quarter of a century ago as an effort to prevent the extinction by machinery of peasant home industry during the long winter night. Home sloyd was soon installed in an institution of its own for training teachers at Nääs. It works in wood only, with little machinery, and is best developed for children of from eleven to fifteen. It no longer aims to make artisans, but its manipulations are meant to be developmental, to teach both sexes not only to be useful but self-active and self-respecting, and to revere exactness as a form of truthfulness. It assumes that all and especially the motor-minded can really understand only what they make, and that one can work like a peasant and think like a philosopher. It aims to produce wholes rather than parts like the Russian system, and to be so essentially educational that, as a leading exponent says, its best effects would be conserved if the hands were cut off. This change of its original utilitarianism from the lower to the liberal motor development of the middle and upper classes and from the land where it originated to another, has not eliminated the dominant marks of its origin in its models, the penates of the sloyd household, the unique features of which persist like a national school of art, despite transplantation and transformation.[1]

Sloyd at its best tries to correlate several series, viz., exercises, tools, drawing, and models. Each must be progressive, so that every new step in each series involves a new and next developmental step in all the others, and all together, it is claimed, fit the order and degree of development of each power appealed to in the child. Yet there has been hardly an attempt to justify either the physiological or psychological reason of a single step in any of these series, and the coordination of the series even with each other, to say nothing of their adaptation to the stages of the child's development. This, if as

[1] This I have elsewhere tried to show in detail. Criticisms of Manual Training and Mechanic Arts in High Schools. Ped. Sem., June, 1902.

pat and complete as is urged, would indeed constitute on the whole a paragon of all the harmony, beauty, totality in variety, etc., which make it so magnificent in the admirer's eyes. But the "45 tools, 72 exercises, 31 models, 15 of which are joints," all learned by teachers in one school year of daily work and by pupils in four years, are overmethodic, and such correlation is impossible in so many series at once. Every dual order, even of work and unfoldment of powers, is hard enough, since the fall lost us Eden, and woodwork, could it be upon that of the tree of knowledge itself, is incompatible with enjoying its fruit. Although a philosopher may see the whole universe in its smallest part, all his theory can not reproduce educational wholes from fragments of it. The real merits of sloyd have caused its enthusiastic coryphei to magnify its scope and claims far beyond their modest bounds, and although its field covers the great transition from childhood to youth, one searches in vain both its literature and practise for the slightest recognition of the new motives and methods that puberty suggests. Especially in its partially acclimatized forms to American conditions, it is all adult and almost scholastic, and as the most elaborate machinery may sometimes be run by a poor power-wheel, if the stream be swift and copious enough, so the mighty current that sets toward motor education would give it some degree of success were it worse and less economic of pedagogic momentum than it is. It holds singularly aloof from other methods of efferent training and resists coordination with them, and its provisions for other than hand development are slight. It will be one of the last to accept its true but modest place as contributing certain few but precious elements in the greater synthesis that impends. Indian industries, basketry, pottery, bead, leather, bows and arrows, bark, etc., which our civilization is making lost arts by forcing the white man's industries upon red men at reservation schools and elsewhere, need only a small part of the systemization that Swedish peasant work has received to develop even greater educational values, and the same is true of the indigenous household work of the old New England farm, the real worth and possibilities of which are only now, and perhaps too late, beginning to be seen by a few educators.

This brings us to the arts and crafts movement, originating

with Carlyle's gospel of work and Ruskin's medievalism, developed by William Morris and his disciples at the Red House, checked awhile by the ridicule of the comic opera Patience, and lately revived in some of its features by Cobden-Sanderson, and of late to some extent in various centers in this country. Its ideal was to restore the day of the seven ancient guilds and of Hans Sachs, the poet cobbler, when conscience and beauty inspired work and the hand did what machines only imitate and vulgarize. In the past, which this school of motor culture harks back to, work was indeed praise for which our degenerate age lacks even respect. Refined men and women have remembered these early days, when their race was in its prime, as a lost paradise which they would regain by designing and even weaving tapestries and muslins; experimenting in vats with dyes to rival Tyrian purple; printing and binding by hand books that surpassed the best of the Aldines and Elzevirs; carving in old oak; hammering brass; forging locks, irons, and candlesticks; becoming artists in burned wood and leather; seeking old effects of simplicity and solidity in furniture and decoration, as well as in architecture, stained glass, and to some extent in dress and manners; and all this toil and moil was *ad majorem gloriam hominis* in a new socialistic state, where the artist and even the artisan who does take his rightful place above the man who merely knows. The day of the mere professor, who deals in knowledge, is gone, and the day of the doer, who creates, has come. The brain and hand, too long divorced and each weak and mean without the other, use and beauty, each alone vulgar, letters and labor, each soulless without the other, are henceforth to be one and inseparable, and this union will lift man to a higher level. The workman in his apron and paper hat, inspired by the new socialism and the old spirit of chivalry as revived by Scott, revering Wagner's revival of the old *Deutschenthum* that was to conquer *Christenthum*, or Tennyson's Arthurian cycle—this was its ideal; even as the Jews rekindled their loyalty to the ancient traditions of their race and made their Bible under Ezra; as we begin to revere the day of the farmer-citizen, who made our institutions, or as some of us would revive his vanishing industrial life for the red man.

Although this movement was by older men and women and

had in it something of the longing regret of senescence for days that are no more, it shows us the glory which invests racial adolescence when it is recalled in maturity, the time when the soul can best appreciate the value of its creations and its possibilities, and really lives again in its glamour and finds in it its greatest inspiration. Hence it has its lessons for us here. A touch, but not too much of it, should be felt in all manual education, which is just as capable of idealism as literary education. This gives soul, interest, content, beauty, taste. If not a polyphrastic philosophy seeking to dignify the occupation of the workshop by a pretentious Volapük of reasons and abstract theories, we have here the pregnant suggestion of a psychological quarry of motives and spirit opened and ready to be worked. Thus the best forces from the past should be turned on to shape and reenforce the best tendencies of the present. The writings of the above gospelers of work not only could, and should, but will be used to inspire manual-training high schools, sloyd and even some of the less scholastic industrial courses, but each is incomplete without the other. These books and those that breathe their spirit should be the mental workshop of all who do tool, lathe, and forge work, who design and draw patterns, carve or mold, or of those who study how to shape matter for human uses, and whose aim is to obtain diplomas or certificates of fitness to teach all such things. The muse of art and even of music will have some voice in the great synthesis which is to gather up the scattered, hence ineffective elements of secondary motor training, in forms which shall represent all the needs of adolescents in the order and proportion that nature and growth stages indicate, drawing with this end supreme, upon all the resources that history and reform offer to our selection. All this can never make work become play. Indeed it will and should make work harder and more unlike play and of another genus, because the former is thus given its own proper soul and leads its own distinct, but richer, and more abounding life.

I must not close this section without brief mention of two important studies that have supplied each a new and important determination concerning laws of work peculiar to adolescence.

The main telegraphic line requires a speed of over seventy letters per minute of all whom they will employ. As a sending rate this is not very difficult and is often attained after two months' practise. This standard for receiving rate is harder and later, and inquiry at schools where it is taught shows that about seventy-five per cent of those who begin the study fail to reach this speed and so are not employed. Bryan and Harter[1] explained the rate of improvement in both sending and receiving, with results represented for one typical subject in the following curve.

From the first, sending improves most rapidly and crosses the dead-line a few months before the receiving rate, which

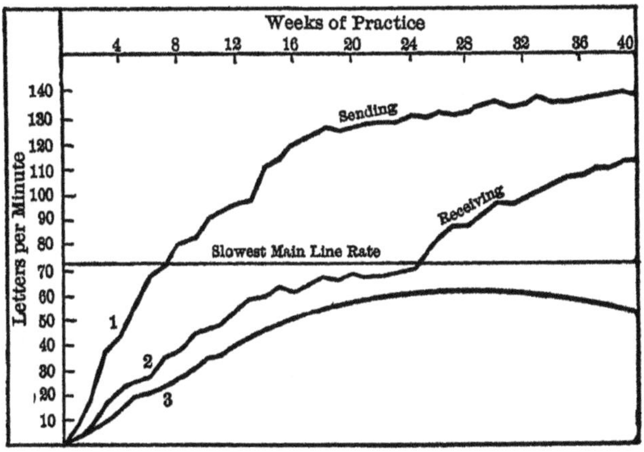

may fall short; curves 1 and 2 represent the same student. I have added line 3 to illustrate the three-fourths who fail. Receiving is far less pleasant than sending, and years of daily practise at ordinary rates will not bring a man to his maximum rate, but he remains on the low plateau with no progress beyond a certain point. If forced by stress of work, danger of being dropped, or by will power to make a prolonged and intense effort, he breaks through his hidebound rate and permanently attains a faster pace. This is true at each step, and every advance seems to cost even more intensive effort than the former one. At length, for those who go on, the rate of receiving, which is a more complex process, exceeds that of sending, and the curves of the above figure would cross if produced. The expert receives so much faster than he sends that

[1] Studies in the Physiology and Psychology of the Telegraphic Language. Psychological Review, vol. iv, p. 27, and vol. vi, p. 345.

abbreviated codes are used, and he may take eighty to eighty-five words a minute on a typewriter in correct form. The motor curve seems to asymptotically approach a perhaps physiological limit, which the receiving curve does not suggest. This seems a special case of a general though not yet explained law. In learning a foreign language, speaking is first and easiest, and hearing takes a late but often sudden start to independence. Perhaps this holds of every ability. To Bryan this suggests as an hierarchy of habits, the plateau of little or no improvement, meaning that lower order habits are approaching their maximum but are not yet automatic enough to leave the attention free to attack higher order habits. The second ascent from drudgery to freedom, which comes through automatism, is often as sudden as the first ascent. One stroke of attention comes to do what once took many. To attain such effective speed is not dependent on reaction time. This shooting together of units distinguishes the master from the man, the genius from the hack. In many, if not all skills, where expertness is sought, there is a long discouraging level, and then for the best a sudden ascent, as if here too, as we have reason to think in the growth of both the body as a whole and in that of its parts, nature does make leaps and attains her ends by alternate rests and rushes. Youth lives along on a low level of interest and accomplishment and then starts onward, is transformed, converted, the hard becomes easy, the old life sinks to a lower stratum and a new and higher order, perhaps a higher brain level and functions are evolved. The practical implication here of the necessity of hard concentrative effort as a condition of advancement is reenforced by a quotation from Senator Stanford to the effect of early and rather intensive work at not too long periods in training colts for racing. Let-ups are especially dangerous. He says, "It is the supreme effort that develops." This, I may add, suggests what is developed elsewhere, that truly spontaneous attention is conditioned by spontaneous muscle tension, which is a function of growth, and that muscles are thus organs of the mind; and also that even voluntary attention is motivated by the same nisus of development even in its most adult form, and that the products of science, invention, discovery, as well as the association plexus of all that was originally determined in the form of consciousness, are made by rhythmic alternation of attack, as it moves from point to point creating diversions and recurrence.

The other study, although quite independent, is in part a special application and illustration of the same principle.

At the age of four or five, when they can do little more than scribble, children's chief interest in pictures is as finished products; but in the second period, which Lange calls that of artistic illusion, the child sees in his own work not merely what it represents, but an image of fancy back of it. This, then, is the golden period for the development of power to create artistically. The child loves to draw everything with the pleasure chiefly in the act, and he cares little for the finished picture. He draws out of his own head, and not from copy before his eye. Anything and everything is attempted in bold lines in this golden age of drawing. If he followed the teacher, looked carefully and drew what he saw, he would be abashed at his production. Indians, conflagrations, games, brownies, trains, pageants, battles, everything is graphically portrayed, but only the little artist himself sees the full meaning of his lines. Criticism or drawing strictly after nature breaks this charm, since it gives place to mechanical reproduction in which the child has little interest. This awakens him from his dream to a realization that he can not draw, and from ten to fifteen his power of perceiving things steadily increases and he makes almost no progress in drawing. Adolescence arouses the creative faculty and the desire and ability to draw are checked and decline after thirteen or fourteen. The curve is the plateau which Barnes has described. The child has measured his own productions upon the object they reproduced and found them wanting, is discouraged and dislikes drawing. From twelve on, Barnes found drawing more and more distasteful, and this, too, Lukens found to be the opinion of our art teachers. The pupils may draw very properly and improve in technique, but the interest is gone. This is the condition in which most men remain all their lives. Their power to appreciate steadily increases. Only a few gifted adolescents about this age begin to develop a new zest in production, rivaling that of the period from five to ten, when their satisfaction is again chiefly in creation. These are the artists whose active powers dominate.

Lukens [1] finds in his studies of drawing, that in what he calls his fourth period of artistic development, there are those "who during adolescence experience a rebirth of creative power." Zest in creation then often becomes a stronger incentive to work than any pleasure or profit to be derived from the finished product, so that in this the propitious conditions of the first golden age of childhood are repeated and the deepest satisfaction is again found in the work itself. At about fourteen or fifteen, which is the transition period, nascent faculties sometimes develop very rapidly. Lukens [2] draws the following interesting curve.

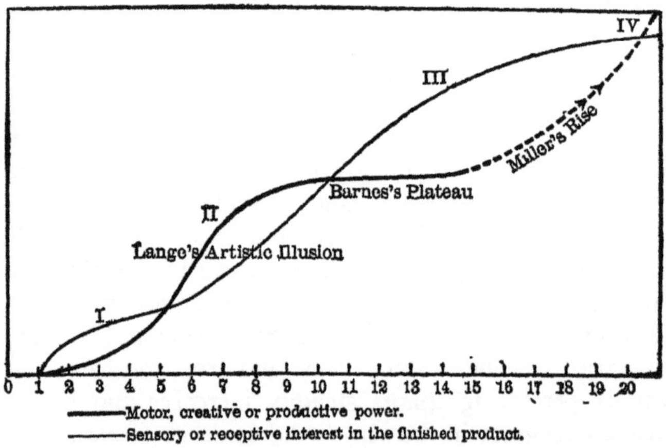

The reciprocity between the power to produce and that to appreciate, roughly represented in the above curve, very likely is also true in the domain of music, and may be, perhaps, a general law of development. Certain it is that the adolescent power to apperceive and appreciate never so far outstrips his power to produce or reproduce as about midway in the teens. Now impressions sink deepest. The greatest artists are usually those who paint later, when the expressive powers are developed, what they have felt deepest and known best at this age, and not those who in the late twenties, or still later, have

[1] A Study of Children's Drawings in the Early Years. Ped. Sem., October, 1896. See also Das Kind als Kunstler, von C. Götze. Hamburg, 1896. Drawing in the Early Years. Proceedings of the Nat'l Educ. Assoc., 1899. The Genetic *vs.* the Logical Order in Drawing, by F. Burk. Ped. Sem., September, 1902.

[2] Die Entwickelungsstufen beim Zeichnen. Die Kinderfehler, vol. ii, p. 166.

gone to new environments and sought to depict them. All young people draw best those objects they love most, and their proficiency should be some test of the contents of their minds. They must put their own consciousness into a picture. At the dawn of this stage of appreciation the esthetic tastes should be stimulated by exposure to, and instructed in feeling for, the subject-matter of masterpieces and instruction in technique, detail, criticism, and learned discrimination of schools of painting should be given intermittently. Art should not now be for art's sake, but for the sake of feeling and character, life, and conduct; it should be adjunct to morals, history, and literature; and in all, edification should be the goal, and personal interest, and not that of the teacher, should be the guide. Insistence on production should be eased, and the receptive imagination, now so hungry, be fed and reënforced by story and all other accessories. By such a curriculum, potential creativeness, if it exists, will surely be evoked in its own good time. It will, at first, attempt no commonplace drawing-master themes, but will essay the highest that the imagination can bode forth; it may be crude and lame in execution, but it will be lofty, perhaps grand, and if it is original in consciousness it will be in effect. Most creative painters before twenty have grappled with the greatest scenes in literature or turning points in history, representations of the loftiest truths, embodiments of the most inspiring ideals. None who deserve the name of artist copy anything now, and least of all with objective fidelity to nature, and the teacher that represses or criticizes this first point of genius, or who can not pardon the grave faults of technique inevitable at this age when ambition ought to be too great for power, is not an educator but a repressor, a pedagogic philistine committing, like so many of his calling in other fields, the unpardonable sin against budding promise, always at this age so easily blighted. Just as the child of six or seven should be encouraged in his strong instinct to draw the most complex scenes of his daily life, so now the inner life should find graphic utterance in all its intricacy up to the full limit of unrepressed courage. For the great majority, on the other hand, who only appreciate and will never create, the mind, if it have its rights, will be stored with the best images and sentiments of art, for at this time they are best remembered and sink deepest into heart and life; now, although the hand may refuse, the fancy paints the world in brightest hues and fairest forms; and such an opportunity for infecting the soul with vaccine of ideality, hope, optimism, and courage in adversity, will never come again. I believe that in few departments are current educational theories and practises so hard on youth of superior gifts, just at the age when all become geniuses for a season, very brief for most, prolonged for some, and permanent for the best. We do not know how to teach to see, hear, and feel when the sense centers are most indelibly impressible, and to give relative rest to the hand during the years when its power of accuracy is abated and when all that is good is idealized farthest, and confidence in ability to produce is at its lowest ebb.

Finally, our divorce between industrial and manual training is abnormal, and higher technical education is the chief sufferer. Professor Thurston, of Cornell, who lately returned from a tour of inspection abroad, reported that to equal Germany we now need: "1. Twenty technical universities, having in their schools of engineering 50 instructors and 500 students each. 2. Two thousand technical high schools or manual-training schools, each having not less than 200 students and 10 instructors." If we have elementary trade-schools, this would mean technical high schools enough to accommodate 700,000 students, served by 20,000 teachers. With the strong economic arguments in this direction we are not here concerned; but that there are tendencies to unfit youth for life by educational method and matter shown in strong relief from this standpoint, we shall point out in a later chapter.

III. Under the term gymnastics, literally naked exercises, we here include those denuded of all utilities or ulterior ends save those of physical culture. This is essentially modern and was unknown in antiquity, where training was for games, for war, etc. Several ideals underlie this movement, which although closely related are distinct and as yet by no means entirely harmonized. These may be described as follows:

A. One aim of Jahn, more developed by Spiess, and their successors, was to do everything physically possible for the body as a mechanism. Many postures and attitudes are assumed and many movements made that are never called for in life. Some of these are so novel that a great variety of new apparatus had to be devised to bring them out, and Jahn invented many new names, some of them without etymologies, to designate the repertory of his discoveries and inventions that extended the range of motor life. Common movements, industry, and even games, train only a limited number of muscles, activities, and coordinations, and leave more or less unused groups and combinations, so that many latent possibilities slumber, and powers slowly lapse through disuse. Not only must these be rescued, but modern progressive man has new nascent possibilities that must be addressed and developed. Even the common things that the average untrained youth can not do are legion, and each of these should be a new incentive to the trainer as he realizes how very far below their motor possibilities most men live. The man of the future may, and even must, do things impossible in the past and acquire new motor variations not given by heredity. Our somatic frame and its powers must therefore be carefully studied, inventoried, and assessed afresh, and a kind and amount of exercise required that is exactly proportioned, not perhaps to the size but to the capability of each voluntary muscle; thus only can we have a truly humanistic physical development, analogous to the training of all the powers of the mind in a broad, truly liberal, and non-professional or non-vocational educational curriculum. The body will thus have its rightful share in the pedagogic traditions and inspirations of the renaissance. Thus only can we have a true scale of standardized culture values for efferent processes, and from this we can measure the degrees of departure, both in the direction of excess and defect, of each form of work, motor habit, and even play. Many modern Epigoni in the wake of this great ideal, where its momentum was nearly spent, feeling that new activities might be discovered with virtues hitherto undreamed of, have almost made fetiches of special disciplines, both developmental and corrective, that are pictured and lauded in scores of manuals. Others have had expectations no less excessive in the opposite direction and have argued that the greatest possible variety of movements best developed the greatest total of motor energy. Jahn especially thus made gymnastics a special art, and inspired great enthusiasm of humanity, and the songs of his pupils were of a better race of man and a greater and united fatherland. It was this feature that made his work unique in the world, and his disciples are fond of reminding us of the fact that it was just about one generation of men after the acme of influence of his system that, in 1870, Germany showed herself the greatest military power since ancient Rome, and took the acknowledged leadership of the world both in education and science.

These theorizations even in their extreme forms have been not only highly suggestive but have brought great and new enthusiasms and ideals into the educational world that admirably fit adolescence. The motive of bringing out latent, decaying, or even new powers, skills, knacks, and feats, is full of inspiration. Patriotism is aroused, for thus the country can be better served; thus the German Fatherland was to be restored and unified after the dark days that followed the humiliation of Jena. Now the ideals of religion are invoked that the soul may have a better and regenerated somatic organism with which to serve Jesus and the Church. Exercise is made a form of praise to God and of service to man, and these motives are reenforced by those of the new hygiene which strives for a new wholeness-holiness, and would purify the body as the temple of the Holy Ghost. Thus in Young Men's Christian Association training schools and gymnasiums the gospel of Christianity is preached anew and seeks to bring salvation to man's physical frame, which the still lingering effects of asceticism have caused to be too long neglected in its progressive degeneration. As the Greek games were in honor of the gods, so now the body is trained to better glorify God, and regimen, chastity, and temperance are given a new momentum. The physical salvation thus wrought will be, when adequately written, one of the most splendid chapters in the modern history of Christianity. Military ideals have been revived in cult and song to hearten the warfare against evil within and without. Strength is prayed for as well as worked for, and consecrated to the highest uses. Last but not least, power thus developed over a large surface may be applied to athletic contests in the field, and victories here are valuable as foregleams of how sweet the glory of achievements in higher moral and spiritual tasks will taste later.

The dangers and sources of error in this ideal of all-sided training are, alas, only too obvious, although they only qualify its paramount good. First, it is impossible to thus measure the quanta of training needed so as to rightly assign to each its modicum and best modality of training. Indeed no method of doing this has ever been attempted, but the assessments have been arbitrary and conjectural, probably right in some and wrong in other respects, with no adequate criterion or test for either save only empirical experience. Secondly, heredity, which lays its heavy ictus upon some neglected forms of activity and fails of all support for others, has been ignored. As we shall see later, one of the best norms here is phyletic emphasis, and what lacks this must at best be feeble, and if new powers are unfolding, their growth must be very slow and they must be nurtured as tender buds for generations. Thirdly, too little regard is had for the vast differences in individuals, most of whom need much personal prescription.

B. In practise the above ideal is never isolated from others. Perhaps the most closely associated with it is that of increased volitional control. Man is largely a creature of habit, and many of his activities are more or less automatic reflexes from the stimuli of his environment. Every new power of controlling these by the will frees man from slavery and widens the field of freedom. To acquire the power of doing all with consciousness and volition mentalizes the body, gives control over to higher brain levels, and develops them by rescuing activities from the dominance of lower centers. Thus *mens agitat molem.* This end is favored by the Swedish *commando* exercises, which require great alertness of attention to translate instantly a verbal order into an act and also, although in somewhat less degree, by quick imitation of a leader. The stimulus of music and rhythm are excluded because thought to interfere with this end. A somewhat sophisticated form of this goal is sought by several Delsartian schemes of relaxation, decomposition, and recomposition of movements. To do all things with consciousness and to encroach on the field of instinct involves new and more vivid sense impressions, the range of which is increased directly as that of motion, the more closely it approaches the focus of attention. By thus analyzing settled and established coordinations, their elements are set free and may be organized into new combinations, so that the former is the first stage toward becoming a virtuoso with new special skills. This is the road to inner secrets or intellectual rules of professional and expert successes, such as older athletes often rely on when their strength begins to wane. Every untrained automatism must be domesticated, and every striated muscle capable of direct muscular control must be dominated by volition. Thus tensions and incipient contractures that drain off energy can be relaxed by fiat. Sandow's "muscle dance," the differentiation of movements of the right and left hand, one, e. g., writing a French madrigal while the other is drawing a picture of a country dance, or each playing tunes of disparate rhythm and character simultaneously on the piano, controlling heart rate, moving the ears, crying, laughing, blushing, moving the bowels, etc., at will, feats of inhibition of reflexes, stunts of all kinds, proficiency with many tools, deftness in sports—these altogether would mark the extremes in this direction.

This, too, has its inspiration for youth. To be an universal adept like Hippias suggests Diderot and the encyclopedists in the intellectual realm. To do all with consciousness is a means to both remedial and expert ends. Motor life often needs to be made over to a greater or less extent, and that possibilities of vastly greater accomplishments exist than are at present realized, is undoubted, even in manners and morals, which are both at root only motor habits. Indeed consciousness itself is largely and perhaps wholly corrective in its very *raison d'être*. Thus life is adjusted to new environments, and if the Platonic postulate be correct, that untaught virtues that come by nature and instinct are no virtues, but must be made products of reflection and reason, the sphere and need of this principle is great indeed. But this implies a distrust of physical human nature as deep-seated and radical as that of Calvinism for the unregenerate heart, against which modern common sense, so often the best muse of both psycho-physics and pedagogy, protests. Individual prescription is here as imperative as it is difficult. Wonders that now seem to be most incredible, both of hurt and help, can undoubtedly be wrought, but analysis should always be for the sake of synthesis and never be beyond its need and assured completion. No thoughtful student fully informed of the facts and tentatives in this field can doubt that here lies one of the most promising fields of future development, full of far-reaching and rich results for those as yet far too few experts in physical training, who have philosophic minds, command the facts of modern psychology, and whom the world awaits now as never before.

C. Another yet closely correlated ideal is that of economic postures and movements. The system of Ling is less orthopedic than orthogenic, although he sought primarily to correct bad attitudes and perverted growth. Starting from the respiratory and proceeding to the muscular system, he and his immediate pupils were content to refer to ill-shapen bodies of most men about them. One of their important aims was to relax the flexor and tone up the extensor muscles and to open the human form into postures as opposite as possible to those of the embryo, which it tends so persistently to approximate in sitting, and in fatigue and collapse attitudes generally. The head must balance on the cervical vertebræ and not call upon the muscles of the neck to keep it from rolling off; the weight of the shoulders must be thrown back off the thorax; the spine be erect to allow the abdomen free action; the joints of the thigh extended; the hand and arm supinated, etc. Bones must relieve muscles and nerves. Thus an erect, self-respecting carriage must be given, and the unfortunate association, so difficult to overcome, between effort and an involuted posture must be broken up. This means economy and a great saving of vital energy. Extensor action goes with expansive, flexor with depressive states of mind; hence courage, buoyancy, hope, are favored and handicaps removed. All that is done with great effort causes wide irradiation of tensions to the other half of the body and also sympathetic activities in those not involved; the law of maximal ease and minimal expenditure of energy must be always striven for, and the interests of the viscera are never lost sight of. This involves educating weak and neglected muscles, and like the next ideal, often shades over by almost imperceptible gradation into the passive movements by the Zander machines. Realizing that certain activities are sufficiently or too much emphasized in ordinary life, stress is laid upon those which are complemental to them, so that there is no pretense of taking charge of the totality of motor processes, but the intention is principally to supplement deficiencies, to insure men against being warped, distorted. or deformed by their work in life, to compensate specialties and perform more exactly what recreation to some extent aims at.

This wholesome but less inspiring endeavor, which combats one of the greatest evils that under modern civilization threatens man's physical weal, is in some respects as easy and practical as it is useful. The great majority of city bred men, as well as all students, are prone to deleterious effects from too much sitting, and indeed there is anatomical evidence in the structure of the tissues, and especially the blood-vessels of the groins, that at his best man is not yet entirely adjusted to the upright position. So a method that straightens knees, hips, spine, and shoulders, or combats the school-desk attitude, is a most salutary contribution to a great and growing need. In the very act of stretching, and perhaps yawning, for which much is to be said, nature itself suggests such correctives and preventives. To save men from being victims of their occupations is often to add a better and larger half to their motor development. The danger of the system, which now best represents this ideal, is inflexibility and overscholastic treatment. It needs a great range of individual variations if it would do more than increase circulation, respiration, and health, or the normal functions of internal organs and fundamental physiological activities. To clothe the frame with honest muscles that are faithful servants of the will adds not only strength, more active habits and efficiency, but health, and in its material installation this system is financially economic. Personal faults and shortcomings are constantly pointed out where this work is best represented, and it has a distinct advantage in inciting an acquaintance with physiology and inviting the larger fields of medical knowledge.

D. The fourth gymnastic aim is symmetry and correct proportions. Anthropometry and average girths and dimensions, strength, etc., of the parts of the body are first charted in percentile grades and each individual is referred to the apparatus and exercises best fitted to correct weaknesses and subnormalities. The norms here followed are not the canons of Greek art, but those established by the measurement of the largest numbers properly grouped by age, weight, height, etc. Young men are found to differ very widely. Some can lift 1,000 pounds, and some not 100; some can lift their weight between twenty and forty times, and some not once; some are most deficient in legs, others in shoulders, arms, backs, chests. By photography, tape, and scales, each is interested in his own bodily condition and incited to overcome his greatest defects, and those best endowed by nature to attain ideal dimensions and make new records are encouraged along these lines. Thus this ideal is also largely though not exclusively remedial.

This system can arouse youth to the greatest pitch of zest in watching their own rapidly multiplying curves of growth in dimensions and capacities, in plotting curves that record their own increment in girths, lifts, and other tests, and in observing the effects of sleep, food, correct and incorrect living upon a system so exquisitely responsive to all these influences as the muscles. To learn to know and grade excellence and defect, to be known for the list of things one can do and to have a record, or to realize what we lack of power to break best records, even to know that we are strengthening some point where heredity has left us with some shortage and perhaps danger, the realization of all this may bring the first real and deep feeling for growth that may become a passion later in things of the soul. Growth always has its selfish aspects, and to be constantly passing our own examination in this respect is a new and perhaps sometimes too self-conscious endeavor of our young college barbarians, but it is on the whole a healthful regulative, and this form of the struggle toward perfection and escape from the handicap of birth will later move upward to the intellectual and moral plane. To kindle a sense of physical beauty of form in every part, such as a sculptor has, may be to start youth on the lowest round of the Platonic ladder that leads up to the vision of ideal beauty of soul, if his ideal be not excess of brawn, or mere brute strength, but the true proportion represented by the classic or mean temperance balanced like justice between all extremes. Hard, patient, regular work, with the right dosage for this self-cultural end, has thus at the same time a unique moral effect.

The dangers of this system are also obvious. Nature's intent can not be too far thwarted, and as in mental training the question is always pertinent, so here we may ask whether it be not best in all cases to some extent, and in some cases almost exclusively to develop in the direction in which we most excel, to emphasize physical individuality and even idiosyncrasy, rather than to strive for monotonous uniformity. Weaknesses and parts that lag behind are easiest overworked to the point of reaction and perhaps permanent injury. Again, work for curative purposes lacks the exuberance of free sports, and it is not inspiring to make up areas, and therapeutic exercises imposed like a sentence for the shortcomings of our forebears bring a whiff of the atmosphere of the hospital, if not of the prison, into the gymnasium.

These four ideals, while so closely interrelated, are as yet far from harmonized. Swedish, Turner, Sargent, and American systems are each, most unfortunately, still too blind to the other's merits and too conscious each of the other's shortcomings. To some extent they are prevented from getting together by narrow devotion to a single cult, aided sometimes by a pecuniary interest in the sale of their own apparatus and books or in the training of teachers according to one set of rubrics. The real elephant is neither a fan, a rope, a tree nor a log, as in the fable the blind men contended, each thinking the part he had touched to be the whole. This inability of leaders to combine causes uncertainty and lack of confidence in and of enthusiastic support for any system on the part of the public. Even the radically different needs of the sexes have failed of recognition from the same partizanship. All together represent only a fraction of the nature and needs of youth. The world now demands what this country has never had, a man who, knowing the human body, gymnastic history, and the various great athletic traditions of the past, shall study anew the whole motor field, as a few great leaders early in the last century tried to do; who shall gather and correlate the literature and experiences of the past and present with a deep sense of responsibility to the future; who shall examine martial training with all the inspirations, warnings, and new demands, and who shall know how to revive the inspiration of the past animated by the same spirit as the Turners, who were almost inflamed by referring back to the hardy life of the early Teutons and trying to reproduce its best features; who shall catch the spirit of, and make due connections with, popular sports past and present, study both industry and education to compensate their debilitating effects, and be himself animated by a great ethical and humanistic hope and faith in a better future. Such a man, if he ever walks the earth, will be the idol of youth, will know their physical secrets, will come almost as a savior to the bodies of men, and will, like Jahn, feel his calling and work sacred, and his institution a temple in which every physical act will be for the sake of the soul. The world of adolescence, especially that part which sits in closed spaces conning books, groans and travails all the more grievously and yearningly, because unconsciously, waits for a redeemer for its body. Till he appears, our culture must remain for most a little hollow, falsetto, and handicapped by school-bred diseases. The modern gymnasium performs its chief service during adolescence and is one of the most beneficent agencies of which not a few but every youth should make large use. Its spirit should be instinct with euphoria, where the joy of being alive reaches a point of high, although not quite its highest, intensity. While the stimulus of rivalry and even of records is not excluded, and social feelings may be appealed to by unison exercises and by the club spirit, and while competitions, tournaments, and the artificial motives of prizes and exhibitions may be invoked, the culture is in fact largely individual. And yet in this country the annual *Turnerfest* brings 4,000 or 5,000 men from all parts of the Union, who sometimes all deploy and go through some of the standard exercises together under one leader. Instead of training a few athletes, the real problem now presented is how to raise the general level of vitality so that children and youth may be fitted to stand the strain of modern civilization, resist zymotic diseases, and overcome the deleterious influences of city life. The almost immediate effects of systematic training are surprising and would hardly be inferred from the annual increments tabled earlier in this chapter. Sandow was a rather weakly boy and ascribes his development chiefly to systematic training.

We have space but for two reports believed to be typical. Enebuske reports on the effects of seven months' training on young women averaging 22.3 years. The figures are based on the 50 percentile column.

	Lung capacity.	Strength of legs.	Strength of back.	Strength of chest.	Strength of r. forearm.	Strength of l. forearm.	Total strength.
Before training ...	2.65	93	65.5	27	26	23	230
After six months..	2.87	120	81.5	32	28	25	293

By comparing records of what he deems standard normal growth with that of 188 naval cadets from sixteen to twenty-one, who had special and systematic training, just after the period of most rapid growth in height, Beyer concluded that the effect of four years of this added a little over an inch of stature, and that this gain was greatest at the beginning. This increase was greatest for the youngest cadets. He found also a marked increase in weight, nearly the same for each year from seventeen to twenty-one. This he thought more easily influenced by exercise than height. A high vital index or ratio of lung capacity to weight is a very important attribute of good training. Beyer [1] found, however, that the addition of lung area gained by exercise did not keep up with the increase thus caused in muscular substance, and that the vital index always became smaller in those who had gained weight and strength by special physical training. How much gain in weight is desirable beyond the point where the lung capacity increases at an equal rate, is unknown. If such measurements were applied to the different gymnastic systems, we might be able to compare their efficiency, which would be a great desideratum in view of the unfortunate rivalry between them. Total strength, too, can be greatly increased. Beyer thinks that from sixteen to twenty-one it may exceed the average or normal increment fivefold, and he adds, "I firmly believe that the now so wonderful performances of most of our strong men are well within the reach of the majority of healthy men, if such performances were a serious enough part of their ambition to make them do the exercises necessary to develop them." Power of the organs to respond to good training by increased strength probably reaches well into middle life.

It is not encouraging to learn that, according to a recent writer,[2] we now have seventy times as many physicians in proportion to the general population as there are physical directors, even for the school population alone considered. We have twice as many physicians per population as Great Britain, four times as many as Germany, or 2 physicians, 1.8 minister, 1.4 lawyer per thousand of the general population; while even if all male teachers of physical training taught only males of the military age, we should have but 0.05 of a teacher per thousand,

---

[1] See H. G. Beyer. The Influence of Exercise on Growth. Am. Phys. Ed. Rev., 1896, p. 76.

[2] J. H. McCurdy. Association Seminar, March, 1902.

or if the school population alone be considered, 20 teachers per million pupils. Hence, it is inferred that the need of wise and classified teachers in this field is at present greater than in any other. But fortunately while spontaneous, unsystematic exercise in a well-equipped modern gymnasium may in rare cases do harm, so far from sharing the prejudice often felt for it by professional trainers, we believe that free access to it without control or direction is unquestionably a boon to youth. Even if its use be sporadic and occasional, as it is likely to be with equal opportunity for out-of-door exercises and especially sports, practise is sometimes hygienic almost inversely to its amount, while even lameness from initial excess has its lessons, and the sense of manifoldness of inferiorities brought home by experiences gives a wholesome self-knowldge and stimulus.

In this country more than elsewhere, especially in high school and college, gymnasium work has been brought into healthful connection with field sports and record competitions for both teams and individuals who aspire to championship. This has given the former a healthful stimulus although it is felt only by a picked few. Scores of records have been established for running, walking, hurdling, throwing, putting, swimming, rowing, skating, etc., each for various shorter and longer distances and under manifold conditions, and for both amateurs and professionals who are early accessible. These in general show a slow but steady advance in this country since 1876, when athletics were established here. In that year there was not a single world's best record held by an American amateur, and high-school boys of to-day could in most, though not in all lines, have won the American championships twenty-five years ago. Of course, in a strict sense, intercollegiate contests do not show the real advance in athletics, because it is not necessary in order for a man to win a championship that he should do his best, but they do show general improvement.

We select for our purpose a few of those longest kept. Not dependent on external conditions like boat-racing, or on improved apparatus like bicycling, we have interesting data of a very different order for physical measurements. Intercollegiate data down to present writing—revised to December,

1902—are as follows: For the 100-yard dash, every annual record from 1876 to 1901 is 10 or 11 seconds, or between these, save in 1896, where Wefers' record of $9\frac{3}{4}$ seconds still stands. In the 220-yard run there is slight improvement since 1877, but here, too, the record of 1896 (Wefers, $21\frac{1}{5}$ seconds) has not been surpassed. In the quarter-mile run, the best record was in 1899 (Long, $49\frac{2}{5}$ seconds), but in 1891 this was nearly equaled (Shattuck, $49\frac{1}{2}$ seconds). The half-mile record, which still stands, was made in 1890 (Dohm, 1 minute $57\frac{1}{2}$ seconds); the mile run in 1895 (Orton, 4 minutes $23\frac{2}{5}$ seconds). Hurdling under fixed conditions shows more steady improvement, the best record being in 1900 for the 120-yard race, and in 1898 for the 220-yard race. The running broad jump shows a very steady improvement, with the best record in 1899 (Kraenzlein, 24 feet $4\frac{1}{2}$ inches). The running high jump shows improvement, but less, with the record of 1897 still standing (Windsor, 6 feet 3 inches). The college record for pole vaulting, corrected to January, 1902, is 11 feet $10\frac{1}{2}$ inches (Clapp); for throwing the 16-pound hammer in a seven-foot circle, 54 feet $4\frac{1}{2}$ inches (Plaw); for putting the 16-pound shot, 44 feet $8\frac{1}{2}$ inches (Sheldon); the standing high jump, 5 feet $1\frac{1}{2}$ inches (Crook); for the running high jump, 6 feet $5\frac{5}{8}$ inches (Page); for the one mile run, 4 minutes $23\frac{2}{5}$ seconds (Orton). We also find that if we extend our purview to include all kinds of records for physical achievement, that not a few of the amateur records for activities involving strength combined with rapid rhythm movement are held by young men of twenty or even less.

In putting the 16-pound shot under uniform conditions the record has improved since the early years nearly 10 feet (best at present writing, fall, 1902—in 1900 Beck, 44 feet 3 inches). Pole vaulting shows a very marked advance culminating in 1899 (Clapp, 11 feet 5 inches). Most marked of all perhaps is the great advance in throwing the 16-pound hammer. Beginning between 70 and 80 feet in the early years, the record is now 154 feet 4 inches (Plaw, 1900). The two-mile bicycle race also shows marked gain, partly, of course, due to improvement in the wheel, the early records being nearly 7 minutes, and the best, including 1901, being 5 minutes $18\frac{1}{5}$ seconds (Goodman, 1894). Some of these are world records, and more exceed professional records. These, of course, no more indicate general improvement than the steady reduction of time in horse-racing suggests betterment in horses generally.

In Panhellenic games as well as at present, athleticism in its manifold forms was one of the most characteristic expressions of adolescent nature and needs. Not a single time or distance record of antiquity has been preserved, although Grassberger [1] and other writers would have us believe that in those that are comparable ancient youthful champions greatly excelled ours, especially in leaping and running. While we are far from cultivating mere strength, our training is very one-sided from the Greek norm of unity or of the ideals that develop the body only for the sake of the soul. While gymnastics in our sense, with aparatus, exercises, and measurements independently of games, was unknown, the ideal and motive were as different from ours as was its method. Nothing, so far as is known, was done for correcting the ravages of work, or for overcoming hereditary defects, and until athletics degenerated there were no exercises for the sole purpose of developing muscle.

On the whole, while modern gymnastics have done more for the trunk, shoulders, and arms than for the legs, it is now too selfish and ego-centric, deficient on the side of psychic impulsion, and but little subordinated to ethical or intellectual development. Yet it does a great physical service to all who cultivate it, and is a safeguard of virtue and temperance. Its need is radical revision and coordination of various cults and theories in the light of the latest psycho-physiological science.

Gymnastics allies itself to biometric work. The present academic zeal for physical development is in great need of closer affiliation with anthropometry. This important and growing department will be represented in the ideal gymnasium of the future—First, by courses, if not by a chair, devoted to the apparatus of measurements of human proportions and symmetry, with a kinesological cabinet where young men are instructed in the elements of auscultation, the use of calipers, the sphygmograph, spirometer, plethysmograph, kinesometer to plot graphic curves, compute average errors, and tables of percentile grades and in statistical methods, etc. Second, anatomy,

[1] Gymnastik der Alten Helenen.

especially of muscles, bones, heart, and skin, will be taught, and also their physiology, with stress upon myology, the effects of exercise on the flow of blood and lymph, not excluding the development of the upright position, and all that it involves and implies. Third, hygiene will be prominent and comprehensive enough to cover all that pertains to body-keeping, regimen, sleep, connecting with school and domestic and public hygiene —all on the basis of modern as distinct from the archaic physiology of Ling, who, it is sufficient to remember, died in 1839, before this science was recreated, and the persistence of whose concepts are an anomalous survival to-day. Mechanico-therapeutics, the purpose and service of each chief kind of apparatus and exercise, the value of work on stall bars with chest weights, of chinning, use of the quarter-staff, somersaults, rings, and inometer, clubs, dumb-bells, work with straight and flexed knees on machinery, etc., will be taught. Fourth, the history of gymnastics from Greece to the present is full of interest and has a very high and not yet developed culture value for youth. This department, both in its practical and theoretical side should have its full share of prizes and scholarships to stimulate the seventy to seventy-five per cent of students who are now unaffected by the influence of athletics. By these methods the motivation of gymnastics, which now in large measure goes to waste in enthusiasm, could be utilized to aid the greatly needed intellectualization of those exercises which in their nature are more akin to work than play. Indeed, Gutsmuth's first definition of athletics was "work under the garb of youthful pleasure." To so develop these courses that they could chiefly, if not entirely, satisfy the requirements for the A. B. degree, would not only be to coordinate the work of the now isolated curriculum of the training-schools with that of the college and thus broaden the sphere of the latter, but besides its culture value, which I hold very high, such a step would prepare for the new, important, and as we have seen very inadequately manned profession of physical trainers. This has, moreover, great but yet latent and even unsuspected capacities for the morals of our academic youth. Grote states that among the ancient Greeks one-half of all educations was devoted to the body, and Galton urges that they as much excel us as we do the African negro. They held that if physical perfection was cultivated, moral and mental excellence would follow, and that without this national culture rests on an insecure basis. In our day there are many new reasons to believe that the best nations of the future will be those which give most intelligent care to the body.

IV. Play, sports, and games constitue a more varied, far older, and more popular field. Here a very different spirit of joy and gladness rules. Artifacts often enter but can not survive unless based upon pretty purely hereditary momentum. Thus our first problem is to seek both the motor tendencies and the psychic motives bequeathed to us from the past. The view of Groos that play is practise for future adult activities is very partial, superficial, and perverse. It ignores the past where lie the keys to all play activities. True play never practises what is phyletically new, and this, industrial life often calls for. It exercises many atavistic and rudimentary functions, a number of which will abort before maturity, but which live themselves out in play like the tadpoles tail, that must be both developed and used as a stimulus to the growth of legs which will otherwise never mature. In place of this mistaken and misleading view, I regard play as the motor habits and spirit of the past of the race, persisting in the present, as rudimentary functions sometimes of and always akin to rudimentary organs. The best index and guide to the stated activities of adults in past ages is found in the instinctive, untaught, and non-imitative plays of children which are the most spontaneous and exact expressions of their motor needs. The young grow up into the same forms of motor activity, as did generations that have long preceded them, only to a limited extent, and if the form of every human occupation were to change to-day, play would be unaffected save in some of its superficial imitative forms. It would develop the motor capacities, impulses, and fundamental forms of our past heritage, and their transformation into later acquired adult forms is progressively later. In play every mood and movement is instinct with heredity. Thus we rehearse the activities of our ancestors, back we know not how far, and repeat their life work in summative and adumbrated ways. It is reminiscent, albeit unconsciously, of our line of descent, and each is the key to the other. The psycho-motive impulses that prompt it are the forms in which our forebears have transmitted to us their habitual activities. Thus stage by stage we reenact their lives. Once in the phylon many of these activities were elaborated in the life and death struggle for existence. Now the elements and combinations oldest in the muscle history of the race are re-represented earliest in the individual, and those later follow in order. This is why the heart of youth goes out into play as into nothing else, as if in it man remembered a lost paradise. This is why, unlike gymnastics, play has as much soul as body, and also why it so makes for unity of body and soul that the proverb " man is whole only when he plays " suggests that the purest plays are those that enlist both alike. To address the body predominantly strengthens unduly the sarcous elements, and to overemphasize the soul causes weakness and automatisms. Thus understood, play is the ideal type of exercise for the young, most favorable for growth, and most self-regulating in both kind and amount. For its forms the pulse of adolescent enthusiasm beats highest. It is unconstrained and free to follow any outer or inner impulse. The zest of it vents and satisfies the strong passion of youth for intense erethic and perhaps orgiastic states, gives an exaltation of self-feeling so craved that with no vicarious outlet it often impels to drink, and best of all realizes the watchword of the Turners, *frisch, frei, fröhlich, from.*

Ancient Greece, the history and literature of which owe their perennial charm for all later ages to the fact that they represent the eternal adolescence of the world, best illustrates what this enthusiasm means for youth. Jäger and Guildersleeve, and yet better Grassberger, would have us believe that the Panhellenic and especially the Olympic games combined many of the best features of a modern prize exhibition, a camp-meeting, fair, Derby day, a Wagner festival, a meeting of the British Association, a country cattle show, intercollegiate games, and medieval tournament; that they were the " acme of festive life " and drew all who loved gold and glory, and that night and death never seemed so black as by contrast with their splendor. The deeds of the young athletes were ascribed to the inspiration of the gods, whose abodes they lit up with glory, and in doing them honor these discordant states found a bond of unity. The victor was crowned with a simple spray of laurel; cities vied with each other for the honor of having given him birth, their walls were taken down for his entry and immediately rebuilt; sculptors, for whom the five ancient games were schools of posture, competed in the representation of his form; poets gave him a pedigree reaching back to the gods, and Pindar, who sang that only he is great who is great with his hands and feet, raised his victory to symbolize the eternal prevalence of good over evil. The best body implied the best mind; and even Plato, to whom tradition gives not only one of the fairest souls, but a body remarkable for both strength and beauty, and for whom weakness was perilously near to wickedness and ugliness to sin, argues that education must be so conducted that the body can be safely entrusted to the care of the soul and suggests, what later became a slogan of a more degenerate gladiatorial athleticism, that to be well and strong is to be a philosopher—*valare est philosophari.* The Greeks could hardly conceive bodily apart from psychic education, and physical was for the sake of mental training. A sane, whole mind could hardly reside in an unsound body upon the integrity of which it was dependent. Knowledge for its own sake, from this standpoint, is a dangerous superstition, for what frees the mind is disastrous if it does not give self-control; better ignorance than knowledge that does not develop a motor side. Body culture is ultimately only for the sake of the mind and soul, for body is only its other ego. Not only is all muscle culture at the same time brain-building, but a book-worm with soft hands, tender feet, and tough rump from much sitting, or an anemic girl prodigy, "in the morning hectic, in the evening electric," is a monster. Play at its best is only a school of ethics. It gives not only strength but courage and confidence, tends to simplify life and habits, gives energy, decision, and promptness to the will, brings consolation and peace of mind in evil days, is a resource in trouble and brings out individuality.

How the ideals of physical preformed those of moral and mental training in the land and day of Socrates is seen in the identification of knowledge and virtue, "*Kennen und Können.*" Only an extreme and one-sided intellectualism separates them and assumes that it is easy to know and hard to do. From the ethical standpoint, philosophy, and indeed all knowledge, is the art of being and doing good, conduct is the only real subject of knowledge, and there is no science but morals. He is the best man, says Xenophon, who is always studying how to improve, and he is the happiest who feels that he is improving. Life is a skill, an art like a handicraft, and true knowledge a form of will. Good moral and physical development are more than analogous, and where intelligence is separated from action the former becomes mystic, abstract, and desiccated, and the latter formal routine. Thus mere conscience and psychological integrity and righteousness are allied and mutually inspiring.

Not only play, which is the purest expression of motor heredity, but work and all exercise owe most of whatever pleasure they bring to the past. The first influence of all right exercise for those in health is a feeling of well-being and exhilaration. This is one chief source of the strange enthusiasm felt for many special forms of activity, and the feeling is so strong that it animates many forms of it that are hygienically unfit. To act vigorously from a full store of energy gives a reflex of pleasure that is sometimes a passion and may fairly intoxicate. Animals must move or cease growing and die. While to be weak is to be miserable, to feel strong is a joy and glory. It gives a sense of superiority, dignity, endurance, courage, confidence, enterprise, power, personal validity, virility, and virtue in the etymological sense of that noble word. To be active, agile, strong, is especially the glory of young men. Our nature and history have so disposed our frame that thus all physiological and psychic processes are stimulated, products of decomposition are washed out by oxygenation and elimination, the best reaction of all the ganglionic and sympathetic activities is aroused, and vegetative processes are normalized. Activity may exalt the spirit almost to the point of ecstasy, and the physical pleasure of it diffuse, irradiate, and mitigate the sexual stress just at the age when its premature localization is most deleterious. Just enough at the proper time and rate contributes to permanent elasticity of mood and disposition, gives moral self-control, rouses a love of freedom with all that that great word means, and favors all higher human aspirations.

In all these modes of developing our efferent powers, we conceive that the race comes very close to the individual youth, and that ancestral momenta animate motor neurons and muscles and preside over most of the combinations. Some of the elements speak with a still small voice, raucous with age. The first spontaneous movements of infancy are hieroglyphs, of most of which we have as yet no good key. Many elements are so impacted and felted together that we can not analyze them. Many are extinct and many perhaps made but once and only hint things we can not apprehend. Later the rehearsals are fuller, and their significance more intelligible, and in boyhood and youth the correspondences are plain to all who have eyes to see. Pleasure is always exactly proportional to the directness and force of the current of heredity, and in play we feel most fully and intensely ancestral joys. The pain of toil died with our forebears; its vestiges in our play give pure delight. Its variety prompts to diversity that enlarges our life. Primitive men and animals played, and that too has left its traces in us. Some urge that work was evolved or degenerated from play, but the play field broadens as with succeeding generations youth is prolonged, for play is always and everywhere the best synonym of youth. All are young at play and only in play, and the best possible characterization of old age is the absence of the soul and body of play. Only senile and overspecialized tissues of brain, heart, and muscles know it not.

Gulick[1] has urged that what makes certain exercises more interesting than others is to be found in the phylon. The power to throw with accuracy and speed was once pivotal for survival, and non-throwers were eliminated. Those who could throw unusually well best overcame enemies, killed game, and sheltered family. The nervous and muscular systems are organized with certain definite tendencies and have back of them a racial setting. So running and dodging with speed and endurance, and hitting with a club, were also basal to hunting and fighting. Now that the need of these is less urgent for utilitarian needs, they are still necessary for perfecting the organism. This makes, for instance, baseball racially familiar, because it represents activities that were once and for a long time necessary for survival. We inherit tendencies of muscular coordination that have been of great racial utility. The best

[1] Am. Phys. Ed. Rev., June, 1902.

athletic sports and games are composed of these racially old elements, so that phylogenetic muscular history is of great importance. Why is it, this writer asks, that a city man so loves to sit all day and fish? It is because this interest dates back to time immemorial. We are the sons of fishermen and early life was by the water's side, and this is our food supply. This explains why certain exercises are more interesting than others. It is because they touch and revive the deep basic emotions of the race. Thus we see that play is not doing things to be useful later, but it is rehearsing racial history. Plays and games change only in their external form, but the underlying neuro-muscular activities, and also the psychic content of them, is the same. Just as psychic states must be lived out up through the grades, so the physical activities must be played off, each in its own time.

The best exercise for the young should thus be more directed to develop the basal powers old to the race than those peculiar to the individual, and it should enforce those psycho-neural and muscular forms which race habit has handed down rather than insist on those arbitrarily designed to develop our ideas of symmetry regardless of heredity. The best guide to the former is *interest*, zest, and spontaneity. Hereditary momenta really determine, too, the order in which nerve centers come into function. The oldest, racial parts come first, and those which are higher and represent volition come in much later.[1] As Hughlings-Jackson has well shown, speech uses most of the same organs as does eating, but those concerned with the former are controlled from a higher level of nerve-cells. By right mastication, deglutition, etc., we are thus developing speech organs. Thus not only the kind but the time of forms and degrees of exercise is best prescribed by heredity. All growth is more or less rhythmic. There are seasons of rapid increment followed by rest and then perhaps succeeded by a period of augmentation, and this may occur several times. Roberts' fifth parliamentary report shows that systematic gymnastics, which, if applied at the right age, produce such immediate and often surprising development of lung capacity, utterly fail with boys of twelve, because this nascent period has not yet come. Donaldson showed that if the eyelid of a young kitten be forced open prematurely at

[1] The Influence of Exercise upon Growth, by Frederic Burk. Am. Phys. Ed Rev., 1899, p. 340.

birth and stimulated with light, medullation was premature and imperfect; so, too, if proper exercise is deferred too long, we know that little result is achieved. The sequence in which the maturation of levels, nerve areas, and bundles of fibers develop may be, as Flechsig thinks, causal; or, according to Cajal, energy, originally employed in growth by cell division, later passes to fiber extension and the development of latent cells; or, as in young children, the nascent period of finger movements may stimulate that of the thumb which comes later, and the independent movement of the two eyes, their subsequent coordination, and so on to perhaps a third and yet higher level. Thus exercise ought to develop nature's first intention and fulfil the law of nascent periods, or else not only no good but great harm may be done. Hence every determination of these periods is of great practical as well as scientific importance. The following are the chief attempts yet made to fix them, which show the significance of adolescence.

The doll curve reaches its point of highest intensity between eight and nine,[1] and it is nearly ended at fifteen, although it may persist. Children can give no better reason why they stop playing with dolls than because other things are liked better, or they are too old, ashamed, love real babies, etc. The Roman girl, when ripe for marriage, hung up her childhood doll as a votive offering to Venus. Mrs. Carlyle, who was compelled to stop, made sumptuous dresses and a four-post bed, and made her doll die upon a funeral pyre like Dido, after speaking her last farewell and stabbing herself with a penknife by way of Tyrian sword. At thirteen or fourteen it is more distinctly realized that dolls are not real, because they have no inner life or feeling, yet many continue to play with them with great pleasure, in secret, till well on in the teens or twenties. Occasionally single women or married women with no children, and in rare cases even those who have children, play dolls all their lives. Gales's [2] student concluded that the girls who played with dolls up to or into pubescent years were usually those who had the fewest number, that they played with them in the most realistic

[1] A Study of Dolls, by G. Stanley Hall and A. C. Ellis. Ped. Sem., Dec., 1896, vol. iv, pp. 129–175.

[2] Studies in Imagination, by Lillian H. Chalmers. Ped. Sem., April, 1900, vol. vii, pp. 111–123.

manner, kept them because actually most fond of them, and were likely to be more scientific, steady, and less sentimental than those who dropped them early. But the instinct that "dollifies" new or most unfit things is gone, as also the subtle points of contact between doll play and idolatry. Before puberty dolls are more likely to be adults; after puberty they are almost always children or babies. There is no longer a struggle between doubt and reality in the doll cosmos, no more abandon to the doll illusion; but where it lingers it is a more atavistic rudiment, and just as at the height of the fever, dolls are only in small part representatives of future children, the saying that the first child is the last doll is probably false. Nor are doll and child comparable to first and second dentition, and it is doubtful if children who play with dolls as children with too great abandonment are those who make the best mothers later, or if it has any value as a preliminary practise of motherhood. The number of motor activities that are both inspired and unified by this form of play and that can always be given wholesome direction is almost incredible, and has been too long neglected both by psychologists and teachers. Few purer types of the rehearsal by the individual of the history of the race can probably be found even though we can not yet analyze the many elements involved and assign to each its phyletic correlate.

In an interesting paper Dr. Gulick [1] divides play into three childish periods, separated by the ages three and seven, and attempts to characterize the plays of early adolescence from twelve to seventeen and of later adolescence from seventeen to twenty-three. Of the first two periods he says, children before seven rarely play games spontaneously, but often do so under the stimulus of older persons. From seven to twelve games are almost exclusively individualistic and competitive, but in early adolescence "two elements predominate—first, the plays are predominantly team games, in which the individual is more or less sacrificed for the whole, in which there is obedience to a captain, in which there is cooperation among a number for a given end, in which play has a program and an end. The second characteristic of the period is with reference to its plays, and there seems to be all of savage out-of-door life—hunting, fishing, stealing, swimming, rowing, sailing, fighting, hero-

[1] Some Psychical Aspects of Physical Exercise. Pop. Sci. Mo., 1898.

worship, adventure, love of animals, etc. This characteristic obtains more with boys than with girls." "The plays of adolescence are socialistic, demanding the heathen virtues of courage, endurance, self-control, bravery, loyalty, enthusiasm."

Croswell[1] found that of 2,000 children familiar with 700 kinds of amusements, those involving physical exercises predominated over all others, and that "at every age after the eighth year they were represented as almost two to one, and in the sixteenth year rose among boys as four to one." The age of the greatest number of different amusements is from ten to eleven, nearly fifteen being mentioned, but for the next eight or nine years there is a steady decline of number and progressive specialization occurs. The games of chase, which are suggestive on the recapitulation theory, rise from eleven per cent in boys of six to nineteen per cent at nine, but soon after decline, and at sixteen have fallen to less than four per cent. Toys and original make-believe games decline still earlier, while ball rises steadily and rapidly to eighteen, and card and table games rise very steadily from ten to fifteen in girls, but the increment is much less in boys. "A third or more of all the amusements of boys just entering their teens are games of contest—games in which the end is in one way or another to gain an advantage over one's fellows, in which the interest is in the struggle between peers." "As children approach the teens, a tendency arises that is well expressed by one of the girls who no longer makes playthings but things that are useful." Parents and society must, therefore, provide the most favorable conditions for the kind of amusement fitting at each age. As the child grows older, society plays a larger rôle in all the child's amusements, and from the thirteenth year "amusements take on a decidedly cooperative and competitive character, and efforts are more and more confined to the accomplishments of some definite aim. The course for this period will concentrate the effort upon fewer lines," and more time will be devoted to each. The desire for mastery is now at its height. The instinct is to maintain one's self independently and ask no odds. At fourteen, especially, the impulse is in manual training to make something and perhaps to cooperate.

[1] Amusements of Worcester School Children. Ped. Sem., September, 1899, vol. vi, pp. 314–371.

McGhee[1] collected the play preferences of 15,718 children, and found a very steady decline in running plays among girls from nine to eighteen, but a far more rapid rise in plays of chance from eleven to fifteen, and a very rapid rise from sixteen to eighteen. From eleven onward with the most marked fall before fourteen, there was a distinct decline in imitative games for girls and a slower one for boys. Games involving rivalry increased rapidly among boys from eleven to sixteen and still more rapidly among girls, their percentage of preference even exceeding that of boys at eighteen, when it reached nearly seventy per cent. With adolescence specialization upon few plays was markedly increased in the teens among boys, whereas with girls in general there were a large number of plays which were popular with none preeminent. Even at this age the principle of organization in games so strong with boys is very slight with girls. Puberty showed the greatest increase of interest among pubescent girls for croquet, and among boys for swimming, although baseball and football, the most favored for boys, rose rapidly. Although the author does not state it, it would seem from his data that plays peculiar to the different seasons were most marked among boys, in part at least, because their activities are more out of doors.

Ferrero and others have shown that the more intense activities of primitive people tend to be rhythmic and with strongly automatic features. No form of activity is more universal than the dance, which is not only intense but may express chiefly in terms of fundamental movements, stripped of their accessory finish and detail, every important act, vocation, sentiment, or event in the life of man in language so universal and symbolic that music and poetry seem themselves to have arisen out of it. Before it became specialized much labor was cast in rhythmic form and often accompanied by time-marking and even tone to secure the stimulus of concert on both economic and social principles. In the dark background of history there is now much evidence that at some point, play, art, and work were not divorced. They all may have sprung from rhythmic movement which is so deep-seated in biology because it secures most joy of life with least expense. By it Eros

[1] A Study in the Play Life of Some South Carolina Children. Ped. Sem., December, 1900, vol. vii, pp. 459–478.

of old ordered chaos, and by its judicious use the human soul is cadenced to great efforts toward high ideals. The many work-songs to secure concerted action in lifting, pulling, stepping, the use of flail, lever, saw, ax, hammer, hoe, loom, etc., show that arsis and thesis represent flexion and extension, that accent originated in the acme of muscular stress, as well as how rhythm eases work and also makes it social. Most of the old work-canticles are lost, and machines have made work more serial, while rhythms are obscured or imposed from without so as to limit the freedom they used to express. Now all basal, central, or strength movements tend to be oscillatory, automatically repetitive, or rhythmic like savage music, as if the waves of the primeval sea whence we came still beat in them, just as all fine peripheral and late movements tend to be serial, special, vastly complex, and diversified. It is thus natural that during the period of greatest strength increment in muscular development, the rhythmic function of nearly all fundamental movements should be strongly accentuated. At the dawn of this age boys love marching, and as our returns show there is a very remarkable rise in the passion for beating time, jigging, double shuffling, rhythmic clapping, etc. The more prominent the factor of repetition the more automatic and the less strenuous is the hard and new effort of constant psychic adjustment and attention. College yells, cheers, rowing, marching, processions, bicycling, running, tug-of-war, calisthenics and class gymnastics with counting, and especially with music, horseback riding, etc., are rhythmic; tennis, baseball and football, basket-ball, golf, polo, etc., are less rhythmic, but are concerted and intense. These latter emphasize the conflict factor best brought out in fencing, boxing, and wrestling, and lay more stress on the psychic elements of attention and skill. The effect of musical accompaniment, which the Swedish system wrongly rejects, is to make the exercises more fundamental and automatic, and to proportionately diminish the conscious effort and relieve the neuro-muscular mechanism involved in fine movements.

Adolescence is the golden period of nascency for rhythm. Before this change many children have a very imperfect sense of it, and even those who march, sing, play, or read poetry with correct and overemphasized tempo, experience a great broadening of the horizon of consciousness, and a marked, and, for mental power and scope, all-conditioning increase in the carrying power of attention and the sentence-sense. The soul now feels the beauty of cadences, good ascension, and the symmetry of well-developed periods, and all, as I am convinced, because this is the springtime of the strength movements which are predominantly rhythmic. Not only does music start in tempo, the drum being the oldest instrument, but quantity long took precedence of sense and form of content, both melody and words coming later. Even rhythmic tapping or beating of the foot (whence the poetic feet of prosody and meter thus later imposed on monotonous prose to make poetry) exhilarates, makes glad the soul and inspires it to attack, gives compulsion and a sense of unity. The psychology of rhythm shows its basal value in cadencing the soul. We can not conceive what war, love, and religion would be without it. The old adage that "the parent of prose is poetry, the parent of poetry is music, the parent of music is rhythm, and the parent of rhythm is God" seems borne out not only in history, but by the nature of thought and attention that does not move in a continuum, but flies and perches alternately, or on stepping-stones and as if influenced by the tempo of the leg swinging as a compound pendulum.

Dancing is one of the best expressions of pure play and of the motor needs of youth. Perhaps it is the most liberal of all forms of motor education. Schopenhauer thought it the apex of physiological irritability and that it made animal life most vividly conscious of its existence and most exultant in exhibiting it. In very ancient times China ritualized it in the spring and made it a large part of the education of boys after the age of thirteen. Neale thinks it was originally circular or orbicular worship, which he deems oldest. In Japan, in the priestly Salic College of ancient Rome, in Egypt, in the Greek Apollo cult, it was a form of worship. St. Basil advised it; St. Gregory introduced it into religious services. The early Christian bishops, called præsuls, led the sacred dance around the altar, and only in 692, and again in 1617, was it forbidden in church. Neale and others have shown how the choral processionals with all the added charm of vestment and intonation have had far more to do in Christianizing many low tribes, who could not understand the language of the church, than preaching. Savages are nearly all great dancers, imitating every animal they know, dancing out their own legends, with ritual sometimes so exact that error means death. The character of people is often learned from their dances, and Molière says the destiny of nations depends on them. The gayest dancers are often among the most downtrodden and unhappy people. Some mysteries can only be revealed in them, as holy passion-plays. If we consider the history of secular dances, we find that some of them, when first invented or in vogue, evoked the greatest enthusiasm. One writer says that the polka so delighted France and England that statesmen forgot politics. The spirit of the old Polish aristocracy still lives in the polonaise. The gipsy dances have inspired a new school of music. The Greek drama grew out of the evolution of the tragic chorus. National dances like the hornpipe and reel of Scotland, the *Reihen* of Germany, the *rondes* of France, the Spanish tarantella and *chaconne,* the strathspey from the Spey Valley, the Irish jig, etc., express racial traits. Instead of the former vast repertory, the stately pavone, the graceful and dignified saraband, the wild *salterrelle,* the bourrée with song and strong rhythm, the light and skippy bolero, the courtly bayadere, the dramatic plugge, gavotte, and other peasant dances in costume, the fast and furious fandango, weapon and military dances; in place of the pristine power to express love, mourning, justice, penalty, fear, anger, consolation, divine service, symbolic and philosophical conceptions, and every industry or characteristic act of life in pantomime and gesture, we have in the dance of the modern ballroom only a degenerate relict, with at best but a very insignificant culture value, and too often stained with bad associations. This is most unfortunate for youth, and for their sake a work of rescue and revival is greatly needed, for it is perhaps, not excepting even music, the completest language of the emotions and can be made one of the best schools of sentiment and even will, inoculating good states of mind and exorcising bad ones as few other agencies have power to do. Right dancing can cadence the very soul, give nervous poise and control, bring harmony between basal and finer muscles, and also between feeling and intellect, body and mind. It can serve both as an awakener and a test of intelligence, predispose the heart against vice, and turn the springs of character toward virtue. That its present decadent forms, for those too devitalized to dance aright, can be demoralizing, we know in this day too well, although even questionable dances may sometimes work off vicious propensities in ways more harmless than those in which they would otherwise find vent. Its utilization for and influence on the insane would be another interesting chapter.

Very interesting scientifically and suggestive practically is another correspondence which I believe to be new, between the mode of spontaneous activity in youth and that of labor in the early history of the race. One of the most marked distinctions between savage and civilized races is in the longer rhythm of work and relaxation. The former are idle and lazy for days, weeks, and perhaps months, and then put forth intense and prolonged effort in dance, hunt, warfare, migration, or construction, sometimes dispensing with sleep and manifesting remarkable endurance. As civilization and specialization advance, hours become regular. The cultured man is less desultory in all his habits, from eating and sleeping to performing social and religious duties, although he may put forth no more aggregate energy in a year than the savage. Women are schooled to regular work long before men, and the difficulty of imposing civilization upon low races is compared by Bücher [1] to that of training a cat to work when harnessed to a dogcart. It is not dread of fatigue but of the monotony of method that makes them hate labor. The effort of savages is more intense and their periods of rest more prolonged and inert. Darwin thinks all vital function bred to go in periods, as vertebrates are descended from a tidal ascidian (Descent of Man, i, p. 204 *et seq.*). There is indeed much that suggests some other irregular rhythm more or less independent of day and night, and perhaps sexual in its nature, but not lunar and for males. This mode of life not only preceded the industrial and commercial period of which regularity is a prime condition, but it lasted indefinitely longer than the latter has yet existed; during this early time great exertion, sometimes to the point of utter exhaustion and collapse, alternated with seasons of almost vegetative existence. We see abundant traces of this

[1] Arbeit. u. Rithmus. Leipzic, 1896.

psychosis in the muscle habits of adolescents, and I think in student and particularly in college life, which can enforce regularity only to a limited extent. This is not reversion, but partly an expression of the nature and perhaps the needs of this stage of immaturity, and partly the same instinct of revolt against uniformity imposed from without, which rob life of variety and extinguish the spirit of adventure and untrammeled freedom, and make the savage hard to break to the harness of civilization. The hunger for fatigue too can become a veritable passion and is quite distinct from either the impulse for activity for its own sake or the desire of achievement. To shout and put forth the utmost possible strength in crude ways is an erethic intoxication at a stage when every tissue can become erectile and seems, like the crying of infants, to have a legitimate function in causing tension and flushing, enlarging the caliber of blood vessels, and forcing the blood perhaps even to the point of extravasation to irrigate newly growing fibers, cells, and organs which atrophy if not thus fed. When maturity is complete this need abates. If this be correct, the phenomenon of second breath, so characteristic of adolescence, and one factor in the inebriate's propensity, is an ontogenetic expression of a rhythm trait of a long racial period. Youth needs overexertion to compensate for underexertion, to undersleep to offset oversleep at times. This seems to be nature's provision to expand in all directions its possibilities of the body and soul in this plastic period when without this occasional excess powers would atrophy or suffer arrest for want of use, or larger possibilities would not be realized without this regimen peculiar to nascent periods. This is treated more fully elsewhere.

Perhaps next to dancing in phyletic motivation comes personal conflicts, such as wrestling, fighting, boxing, dueling, and in some sense, hunting. The animal world is full of struggle for survival, and primitive warfare is a wager of battle, of personal combat of foes contesting eye to eye and hand to hand, where victory of one is the defeat and perhaps death of the other, and where life is often staked against life. In its more brutal forms we see one of the most degrading of all the aspects of human nature. Burk[1] has shown how the most bestial of these instincts survive and crop out irresistibly in boyhood,

[1] Teasing and Bullying. Ped. Sem., 1896, p. 336.

where fights are often with desperate abandon. Noses are bitten, ears torn, sensitive places kicked, hair pulled, arms twisted, the head stamped on and pounded on stones, fingers twisted, and hoodlums sometimes deliberately try to strangle, gouge out an eye, pull off an ear, pull out the tongue, break teeth, nose, or bones, or dislocate jaws or other joints, wring the neck, bite off a lip, and torture in utterly nameless ways. In unrestrained anger, man becomes a demon in love with the blood of his victim. The face is distorted, and there are yells, oaths, animal snorts and grunts, cries, and then exultant laughter at pain, and each is bruised, dirty, disheveled and panting with exhaustion. For coarser natures, the spectacle of such conflicts has an intense attraction, while some morbid souls are scarred by a distinct phobia for everything suggestive of even lower degrees of opposition. These instincts, more or less developed in boyhood, are repressed in normal cases before strength and skill are sufficiently developed to inflict serious bodily injury, while without the reductives that orthogenetic growth brings they become criminal. Repulsive as are these grosser and animal manifestations of anger, its impulsion can not and should not be eliminated, but its expression transformed and directed toward evils that need all its antagonism. To be angry aright is a good part of moral education, and non-resistance under all provocations is unmanly, craven, and cowardly.[1] An able-bodied young man, who can not fight physically, can hardly have a high and true sense of honor, and is generally a milk-sop, a lady-boy, or a sneak. He lacks virility, his masculinity does not ring true, his honesty can not be sound to the core. Hence, instead of eradicating this instinct, one of the great problems of physical and moral pedagogy is to rightly temper and direct it.

Sparta sedulously cultivated it in boys and in the great English schools, where for generations it has been more or less tacitly recognized, it is regulated by custom, and their literature and traditions abound in illustrations of its man-making and often transforming influence in ways well appreciated by Hughes and Arnold. It makes against degeneration, the essential feature of which is weakening of will and loss of honor. Real virtue requires enemies, and women and effeminate and

[1] See my Study of Anger. American Journal of Psychology, vol. x, 1899.

old men want placid, comfortable peace, while a real man rejoices in noble strife which sanctifies all great causes, casts out fear, and is the chief school of courage. Bad as is overpugnacity, a scrapping boy is better than one who funks a fight, and I have no patience with the sentimentality that would here pour out the child with the bath, but would have every healthy boy taught boxing at adolescence if not before. The prize-ring is degrading and brutal, but in lieu of better illustrations of the spirit of personal contest I would interest a certain class of boys in it and try to devise modes of pedagogic utilization of the immense store of interest it generates. Like dancing, it should be rescued from its evil associations and its educational force put to do moral work, even though it be by way of individual prescriptions for specific defects of character. At its best, it is indeed a manly art, a superb school for quickness of eye and hand, decision, force of will, and self-control. The moment this is lost stinging punishment follows. Hence it is the surest of all cures for excessive irascibility and has been found to have a most beneficent effect upon a peevish or unmanly disposition. It has no mean theoretic side of rules, kinds of blow and counters, arts of drawing out and tiring an opponent, hindering but not injuring him, defensive and offensive tactics, etc., and it addresses chiefly the fundamental muscles in both training and conflict. I do not underestimate the many and great difficulties of proper purgation, but I know from both personal practise and observation that they are not unconquerable.

This form of personal conflict is better than dueling even in its comparatively harmless German student form, although this has been warmly defended by Jacob Grimm, Bismarck, and Treitschke, while Paulsen, Professor of Ethics, and Schrempf, of Theology, have pronounced it but a slight evil, and several Americans have thought it better than hazing, which it makes impossible. The dark side of dueling is seen in the hypertrophied sense of honor which under the code of the corps becomes an intricate and fantastic thing, prompting, according to Ziegler,[1] a club of sixteen students to fight over two hundred duels in four weeks in Jena early in this century.

[1] Das Deutsche Student, 1895, p. 88. See also H. D. Sheldon: History and Pedagogy of American Student Societies, N. Y., 1901, p. 31 *et seq.*

It is prone to degenerate to an artificial etiquette demanding satisfaction for slight and unintended offenses. Although this professor, who had his own face scarred on the *mensur*, pleaded for a student court of honor, with power to brand acts as infamous and even to expel students, on the ground that honor had grown more inward, the traditions in favor of dueling were too strong. The duel had a religious romantic origin as revealing God's judgment, and means that the victim of an insult is ready to stake body, or even life, and this is still its ideal side. Anachronism as it now is and degenerating readily to sport or spectacle, overpunishing what is often mere awkwardness or ignorance, it still impresses a certain sense of responsibility for conduct and gives some physical training, slight and specialized though it be. The code is conventional, drawn directly from old French military life, and is not true to the line that separates real honor from dishonor, deliberate insult that wounds normal self-respect from injury fancied by oversensitiveness or feigned by arrogance; so that in its present form it is not the best safeguard of the sacred shrine of personality against invasion of its rights. If, as is claimed, it is some diversion from or fortification against corrosive sensuality, it has generally allied itself with excessive beer-drinking. Fencing, while an art susceptible of high development and valuable for both pose and poise and requiring great quickness of eye, arm, and wrist, is unilateral and robbed of the zest of inflicting real pain on an antagonist.

Bushido,[1] which means military-knightly ways, designates the Japanese conception of honor in behavior and in fighting. The youth is inspired by the ideal of Tom Brown "to leave behind him the name of a fellow who never bullied a little boy or turned his back on a big one." It expresses the race ideal of justice, patriotism, and the duty of living aright and dying nobly. It means also sympathy, pity, and love, for only the bravest can be the tenderest, and those most in love are most daring, and it includes politeness and the art of poetry. Honor is a sense of personal dignity and worth, so the *bushi* is truthful without an oath. At the tender age of five the *samurai* is given a real sword, and this gives self-respect and responsi-

[1] Bushido: The Soul of Japan. An exposition of Japanese thought, by Inazo Nitobé. Philadelphia, 1900.

bility. At fifteen, two sharp and artistic ones, long and short, are given him, which must be his companions for life. They were made by a smith whose shop is a sanctuary and who begins his work with prayer. They have the finest hilts and scabbards, and are besung as invested with a charm or spell, and symbolic of loyalty and self-control, for they must never be drawn lightly. He is taught fencing, archery, horsemanship, tactics, the spear, ethics and literature, anatomy, for offense and defense; he must be indifferent to money, hold his life cheap beside honor, and die if it is gone. This chivalry is called the soul of Japan, and if it fades life is vulgarized. It is a code of ethics and physical training.

Wrestling is a form of personal encounter which in antiquity reached a high development, and which, although now more known and practised as athletics of the body than of the soul, has certain special disciplinary capacities in its various forms. It represents the most primitive type of the struggle of unarmed and unprotected man with man. Purged of its barbarities, and in its Greco-Roman form and properly subject to rules, it cultivates more kinds of movements than any other form—for limbs, trunk, neck, hand, foot, and all in the upright and in every prone position. It, too, has its manual of feints, holds, tricks, and specialties, and calls out wariness, quickness, strength, and shiftiness. Victory need involve no cruelty or even pain to the vanquished. The very closeness of body to body, emphasizing flexor rather than extensor arm muscles, imparts to it a peculiar tone, gives it a vast variety of possible activities, developing many alternatives at every stage, and tempts to many undiscovered forms of permanent mayhem. Its struggle is usually longer and less interrupted by pauses than pugilism, and its situations and conclusions often develop slowly, so that all in all, its character among contests is unique. As a school of posture for art, its varieties are extremely manifold and by no means developed, for it contains every kind of emphasis of every part and calls out every muscle group and attitude of the human body; hence its training is most generic and least specialized, and victories have been won by very many kinds of excellence.

Perhaps nothing is more opposed to the idea of a gentleman than the *sæva animi tempestas* of anger. A testy, quarrelsome, mucky humor is antisocial, and an outburst of rage is repulsive. Even non-resistance, turning the other cheek, has its victories and may be a method of moral combat. A strong temper well controlled and kept in leash makes a kinetic character; but in view of bullying, unfair play, cruel injustice to the weak and defenseless, of outrageous wrong that the law can not reach, patience and forbearance may cease to be virtues and summary redress may have a distinct advantage to the ethical nature of man and to social order, and the strenuous soul must fight or grow stagnant or flabby. If too repressed, righteous indignation may turn to sourness and sulks, and the disposition be spoiled. Hence the relief and exhilaration of an outbreak that often clears the psychic atmosphere like a thunderstorm, and gives the peace that passes understanding so often dilated on by our correspondents. Rather than the abject fear of making enemies whatever the provocation, I would praise those whose best title of honor is the kind of enemies they make. Better even an occasional nose dented by a fist, a broken bone, a rapier-scarred face, or even the sacrifice of an occasional life of our best academic youth than stagnation, general cynicism and censoriousness, bodily and psychic cowardice, and moral corruption, if this indeed be, as it sometimes is, its real alternative.

So closely are love and war connected that not only is individual pugnacity greatly increased at the period of sexual maturity, when animals acquire or develop horns, fangs, claws, spurs, and weapons of offense and defense, but a new spirit of organization arises which makes teams possible or more permanet. Football, baseball, cricket, etc., and even boating can become schools of mental and moral training. First, the rules of the game are often intricate, and to master and observe them effectively is no mean training for the mind in controlling the body. These are steadily being revised and improved, and the reasons for each detail of inner construction and conduct of the game require experience and insight into human nature. Then the subordination of each member to the whole and to a leader cultivates the social and cooperative instincts, while the honor of the school, college, or city, which each team represents, is confided to each and all. Group loyalty in Anglo-Saxon games, which shows such a marked increment in coordination and self-subordination at the dawn of puberty as to constitute a distinct change in the character of sports at this age, can be so utilized as to develop a spirit of service and devotion not only to town, country, and race, but to God and the Church. Self must be merged and a sportsmanlike spirit cultivated that prefers defeat to tricks and secret practise, and a clean game to the applause of rooters and fans, intent only on victory, however won. The long, hard, fight against professionalism that brings in husky muckers, who by every rule of true courtesy and chivalry belong outside academic circles, scrapping and underhand advantages, is a sad comment on the character and spirit of these games, and eliminates the best of their educational advantages. The necessity of intervention, which has imposed such great burdens on faculties and brought so much friction with the frenzy of scholastic sentiment in the hot stage of seasonal enthusiasms, when fanned to a white heat by the excessive interest of friends and patrons and the injurious exploitation of the press, bears sad testimony to the strength and persistence of warlike instincts from our heredity. But even thus the good far predominates. The elective system has destroyed the class games, and our institutions have no units like the English colleges to be pitted against each other, and so, as colleges grow, an ever smaller percentage of students obtain the benefit of practise on the teams, while electioneering methods often place second best men in place of the best. But both students and teachers are slowly learning wisdom in the dear school of experience. On the whole, there is less license in " breaking training " and in celebrating victories, and even at their worst, good probably predominates while the progress of recent years bids us hope.

Finally, military ideals and methods of psycho-physical education are helpful regulations of the appetite for combat, and on the whole more wholesome and robust than those which are merely esthetic. Marching in step gives proper and uniform movement of legs, arms, and carriage of body, the manual of arms, with evolution and involution of figures in the ranks, gives each a corporate feeling of membership, and involves care of personal appearance and accouterments, while the uniform levels social distinction in dress. For the French and Italian and especially the German and Russian adolescent of the lower classes, the two or three years of compulsory military service is often compared to an academic course, and the army is called, not without some justification, the poor man's university. It gives severe drill, strict discipline, good and regular hours, plain but wholesome fare and out-of-door exercise, exposure, travel, habits of neatness, many useful knacks and devices, tournaments and mimic or play battles; these, apart from its other functions, make this system a great promoter of national health and intelligence. Naval schools for midshipmen, who serve before the mast, schools on board ship that visit a wide curriculum of ports each year, cavalry schools, where each boy is given a horse to care for, study and train, artillery courses and even an army drill-master in an academy, or uniform, and a few exterior features of soldierly life, all give a distinct character to the spirit of any institution. The very fancy of being in any sense a soldier opens up a new range of interests too seldom utilized, and tactics, army life and service, military history, battles, patriotism, the flag, and duties to country, should always erect a new standard of honor. Youth should embrace every opportunity that offers in this line, and instruction should greatly increase the intellectual opportunities created by every interest in warfare. It would be easy to create pregnant courses on how soldiers down the course of history have lived, thought, felt, fought, and died, how great battles were won and what causes triumphed in them, and to generalize many of the best things taught in detail in the best schools of war in different grades and lands.

Play and Sex.—A subtle but potent intersexual influence is among the strongest factors of all adolescent sport. Male birds and beasts show off their charms of beauty and accomplishment in many a liturgy of love antics in the presence of the female. This instinct seems somehow continuous with the growth of ornaments in the mating season. Song, tumbling, balking, mock fights, etc., are forms of animal courtship. The boy who turns cartwheels past the home of the girl of his fancy, is brilliant, brave, witty, erect, strong in her presence, and elsewhere dull and commonplace enough, illustrates the same principle. The true cake-walk as seen in the South is perhaps the purest expression of this impulse to courtship antics seen in man, but its irradiations are many and pervasive. The presence of the fair sex gives tonicity to youth's muscles and tension to his arteries to a degree of which he is rarely conscious. Defeat in all contests is more humiliating and victory more glorious thereby. Each sex is constantly passing the examination of the other, and each judges the other by different standards than its own. Alas for the young people who are not different with the other sex than with their own!—and some are transformed into different beings. Achievement proclaims ability to support, defend, bring credit and even fame to the object of future choice, and no good point is lost. Physical force and skill, and above all, victory and glory, make a hero and invest him with a romantic glamour, which, even though concealed by conventionality or etiquette, is profoundly felt and makes the winner more or less irresistible. The applause of men and of mates is sweet and even intoxicating, but that of ladies is ravishing. By universal acclaim the fair belong to the brave, strong, and victorious. This stimulus is wholesome and refining. As is shown later, a bashful youth often selects a maiden onlooker and is sometimes quite unconsciously dominated in his every movement by a sense of her presence, stranger and apparently unnoticed though she be, although in the intellectual work of coeducation girls are most influenced thus. In athletics this motive makes for refinement and good form. The ideal knight, however fierce and terrible, must not be brutal, but show capacity for fine feeling, tenderness, magnanimity, and forbearance. Evolutionists tell us that woman has domesticated and educated feral man and taught him all his virtues by exercising her royal prerogative of selecting in her mate just those qualities that pleased her for transmission to future generations and eliminating others distasteful to her. If so, she is still engaged in this work as much as ever, and in his dull, slow way man feels that her presence enforces her standards, abhorrent though it would be to him to compromise in one iota his masculinity. Most plays and games in which both sexes participate have some of the advantages with some of the disadvantages of coeducation. Where both are partners rather than antagonists, there is less eviration. A gallant man would do his best to help, but his worst not to beat a lady. Thus, in general, the latter performs her best service in her true rôle of sympathetic spectator rather than as fellow player, and is now an important factor in the physical education of adolescents.

How pervasive this femininity is, which is slowly transforming our schools, is strikingly seen in the church. Gulick holds that the reason why only some seven per cent of the young men of the country are in the churches, while most members and workers are women, is that the qualities demanded are the feminine ones of love, rest, prayer, trust, desire for fortitude to endure, a sense of atonement—traits not involving ideals that most stir young men. The church has not yet learned to appeal to the more virile qualities. Fielding[1] asks why Christ and Buddha alone of great religious teachers were rejected by their own race and accepted elsewhere. He answers that these mild beliefs of peace, non-resistance, and submission, rejected by virile warrior races, Jews and ancient Hindus, were adopted where women were free and led in these matters. Confucianism, Mohammedanism, etc., are virile, and so indigenous, and in such forms of faith and worship women have small place. This again suggests how the sex that rules the heart controls men.

Too much can hardly be said in favor of cold baths and swimming at this age. Marro quotes Father Kneipp, and almost rivals his hydrotherapeutic enthusiasm. Cold bathing sends the blood inward partly by the cold which contracts the capillaries of the skin and tissue immediately underlying it, and partly by the pressure of the water over all the dermal surface, quickens the activity of kidneys, lungs, and digestive apparatus, and the reactive glow is the best possible tonic for dermal circulation. It is the best of all gymnastics for the nonstriated or involuntary muscles and for the heart and blood vessels. This and the removal of the products of excretion preserve all the important dermal functions which are so easily and so often impaired in modern life, lessen the liability to skin diseases, promote freshness of complexion, and the moral effects of plunging into cold and supporting the body in deep water is not inconsiderable in strengthening a spirit of hardihood and reducing overtenderness to sensory discomforts. The exercise of swimming is unique in that nearly all the movements and combinations are such as are rarely used otherwise, and are perhaps in a sense ancestral and liberal rather than directly preparatory for future avocations. Its

[1] The Hearts of Men, chap. xxii.

stimulus for heart and lungs is, by general consent of all writers upon the subject, most wholesome and beneficial. Nothing so directly or quickly reduces to the lowest point the plethora of the sex organs. The very absence of clothes and running on the beach is exhilarating and gives a sense of freedom. Where practicable it is well to dispense with bathing suits, even the scantiest. The warm bath tub is enfeebling and degenerative, despite the cold spray later, while the free swim in cold water is most invigorating.

Happily, city officials, teachers, and sanitarians are now slowly realizing the great improvement in health and temper that comes from bathing and are establishing beach and surf, spray, floating and plunge summer baths and swimming pools; often providing instruction even in swimming in clothes, undressing in the water, treading water, rescue work, free as well as fee days, bathing suits, and, in London, places for nude bathing after dark; establishing time and distance standards with certificates and even prizes; annexing toboggan slides, swings, etc.; realizing that in both the preference of youth and in healthful and moral effects, probably nothing outranks this form of exercise. Such is its strange fascination that, according to one comprehensive census, the passion to get to the water outranks all other causes of truancy, and plays an important part in the motivation of runaways. In the immense public establishment near San Francisco, provided by private munificence, there are accommodations for all kinds of bathing in hot and cold and in various degrees of fresh and salt water, in closed spaces and in the open sea, for small children and adults, with many appliances and instructors, all in one great covered arena with seats in an amphitheater for two thousand spectators, and many adjuncts and accessories. So elsewhere the presence of visitors is now often invited and provided for. Sometimes wash-houses and public laundries are annexed. Open hours and longer evenings and seasons are being prolonged.

Prominent among the favorite games of early puberty and the years just before are those that involve passive motion and falling, like swinging in its many forms, including the May-pole and single rope varieties. Mr. Lee reports that children wait late in the evening and in cold weather for a turn at a park swing. Psychologically allied to these are wheeling and skating. Places for the latter are now often provided by the fire department, which in many cities floods hundreds of empty lots. Ponds are cleared of snow and horse plowed, perhaps by the park commission, which often provides lights and perhaps ices the walks and streets for coasting, erects shelters, devises space economy for as many diamonds, bleachers, etc., as possible. Games of hitting, striking, and throwing balls and other objects, hockey, tennis, all the courts of which are usually crowded, golf and croquet, and sometimes fives, cricket, bowling, quoits, curling, etc., have great "thumogenic" or emotional power.

Leg exercise has perhaps a higher value than that of any other part. Man is by definition an upright being, but only after a long apprenticeship.[1] Thus the hand was freed from the necessity of locomotion and made the servant of the mind. Locomotion overcomes the tendency to sedentary habits in modern schools and life, and helps the mind to helpful action, so that a peripatetic philosophy is more normal than that of the easy chair and the study lamp. Hill-climbing is unexcelled as a stimulus at once of heart, lungs, and blood. If Hippocrates is right, inspiration is possible only on a mountain-top. Walking, running, dancing, skating, coasting are also alterative and regulative of sex, and there is a deep and close though not yet fully explained reciprocity between the two. Arm work is relatively too prominent a feature in gymnasia. Those who lead excessively sedentary lives are prone to be turbulent and extreme in both passion and opinion, as witness the oft-adduced revolutionary disposition of cobblers.

The play problem is now fairly open and is vast in its relation to many other things. Roof playgrounds, recreation piers, schoolyards and even school-buildings, open before and after school hours; excursions and outings of many kinds and with many purposes, which seem to distinctly augment growth; occupation during the long vacation when, beginning with spring, most juvenile crime is committed; theatricals, which according to some police testimony lessen the number of juvenile delinquents; boys' clubs with more or less self-government of the George Junior Republic and other types, treated in another chapter; nature-study; the distinctly different needs and pro-

[1] See A. W. Trettien. Creeping and Walking. Am. Jour. of Psy., vol. xii, p. 1 *et seq.*

pensities of both good and evil in different nationalities; the advantages of playground fences and exclusion, their disciplinary worth, and their value as resting places; the liability that "the boy without a playground will become the father without a job"; the relation of play and its slow transition to manual and industrial education at the savage age when a boy abhors all regular occupation; the necessity of exciting interest, not by what is done for boys, but by what they do; the adjustment of play to sex; the determination of the proper average age of maximal zest in and good from sand-box, ring-toss, bean-bag, shuffle-board, peg-top, charity, funeral play, prisoner's base, hill-dill; the value and right use of apparatus, and of rabbits, pigeons, bees, and a small menagerie in the playground; tan-bark, clay, the proper alternation of excessive freedom, that often turns boys stale through the summer; the disciplined "work of play" and sedentary games; the value of the wash-board in rubbing and the hand and knee exercise of scrubbing, which a late writer would restore for all girls with clever and Greek-named play apparatus; as well as digging, shoveling, tamping, pick-chopping, and hod-carrying exercises in the form of games for boys; the relations of woman's clubs parents' clubs, citizens' leagues and unions, etc., to all this work—such are the practical problems.

The playground movement encounters its chief obstacles in the most crowded and slum districts, where its greatest value and success was expected for boys in the early teens, who without supervision are prone to commit abuses upon property and upon younger children,[1] and are so disorderly as to make the place a nuisance, and who resent the "fathering" of the police, without, at least, the minimum control of a system of permits and exclusions. If hoodlums play at all, they become infatuated with baseball and football, especially punting; they do not take kindly to the soft large ball of the Hull House or the Civic League, and prefer at first scrub games with individual self-exhibition to organized teams. Lee sees the "arboreal instincts of our progenitors" in the very strong propensity of boys from ten to fourteen to climb in any form; to use traveling rings, generally occupied constantly to their fullest extent; to jump

[1] Constructive and Preventive Philanthropy, by Joseph Lee. New York, 1902, chap. x and xi.

from steps and catch a swinging trapeze; to go up a ladder and slide down poles; to use horizontal and parallel bars. The city boy has plenty of daring at this age, but does not know what he can do and needs more supervision than the country youth. The young tough is commonly present, and though admired and copied by younger boys, it is, perhaps, as often for his heroic as for his bad traits.

Dr. Sargent and others have well pointed out that athletics afford a wealth of new and profitable topics for discussion and enthusiasm which helps against the triviality and mental vacuity into which the intercourse of students is prone to lapse. It prompts to discussion of diet and regimen. It gives a new standard of honor. For a member of a team to break training would bring reprobation and ostracism, for he is set apart to win fame for his class or college. It supplies a splendid motive against all errors and vices that weaken or corrupt the body. It is a wholesome vent for the reckless courage that would otherwise go to disorder or riotous excess. It supplies new and advantageous topics for compositions and for terse, vigorous, and idiomatic theme-writing, is a great aid to discipline, teaches respect for deeds rather than words or promises, lays instructors under the necessity of being more interesting, that their work be not jejune or dull by contrast; again the business side of managing great contests has been an admirable school for training young men to conduct great and difficult financial operations, sometimes involving $100,000 or more, and has thus prepared some for successful careers. It furnishes now the closest of all links between high school and college, reduces the number of those physically unfit for college, and should give education generally a more real and vigorous ideal. Its obvious dangers are distraction from study and overestimation of the value of victory, especially in the artificial glamours which the press and the popular furor give to great games; unsportsmanlike secret tricks and methods, overemphasis of combative and too stalwart impulses, and a disposition to carry things by storm, by rush-line tactics; friction with faculties, and censure or neglect of instructors who take unpopular sides on hot questions; reaction toward license after games, spasmodic excitement culminating in excessive strain for body and mind, with alternations of reaction; "beefiness";

overdevelopment of the physical side of life, and, in some cases, premature features of senility in later life, undergrowth of the accessory motor parts and powers, and erethic diathesis that makes steady and continued mental toil seem monotonous, dull, and boresome.

The propensity to codify sports, to standardize the weight and size of their implements, and to reduce them to what Spencer calls regimentation, is an outcrop of uniformitarianism that works against that individuation which is one of the chief advantages of free play. This, to be sure, has developed old-fashioned rounders to modern baseball, and this is well, but it is seen in the elaborate Draconian laws, diplomacy, judicial and legislative procedures, concerning "eligibility, transfer, and even sale of players." In some games international conformity is gravely discussed. Even where there is no tyranny and oppression, good form is steadily hampering nature and the free play of personality. Togs and targets, balls and bats, rackets and oars are graded or numbered, weighed, and measured, and every emergency is legislated on and judged by an autocratic martinet, jealous of every prerogative and conscious of his dignity. All this separates games from the majority and makes for specialism and professionalism. Not only this, but men are coming to be sized up for hereditary fitness in each point and for each sport. Runners, sprinters, and jumpers,[1] we are told, on the basis of many careful measurements, must be tall, with slender bodies, narrow but deep chests, longer legs than the average for their height, the lower leg being especially long, with small calf, ankle, and feet, small arms, narrow hips, with great power of thoracic inflation, and thighs of small girth. Every player must be studied by trainers for ever finer individual adjustments. His dosage of work must be kept well within the limits of his vitality, and be carefully adjusted to his recuperative power. His personal nascent periods must be noted, and initial embarrassment carefully weeded out.

The field of play is as wide as life and its varieties far outnumber those of industries and occupations in the census. Plays and games differ in seasons, sex, and age. McGhee[2]

[1] C. O. Bemies. Physical Characteristics of the Runner and Jumper. Am. Phys. Ed. Rev., 1900, p. 235.

[2] A Study in the Play Life of some South Carolina Children. Ped. Sem., 1900, p. 459.

has shown on the basis of some 8,000 children, that running plays are pretty constant for boys from six to seventeen, but that girls are always far behind boys and run steadily less from eight to eighteen. In games of choice boys showed a slight rise at sixteen and seventeen, and girls a rapid increase at eleven and a still more rapid one after sixteen. In games of imitation girls excel and show a marked, as boys do a slight, pubescent fall. In those games involving rivalry boys at first greatly excel girls, but are overtaken by the latter in the eighteenth year, both showing marked pubescent increment. Girls have the largest number of plays and specialize on a few less than boys, and most of these plays are of the unorganized kinds. Johnson [1] selected from a far larger number 440 plays and games and arranged the best of them in a course by school grades, from the first to the eighth, inclusive, and also according to their educational value as teaching observation, reading and spelling, language, arithmetic, geography, history, and biography, physical training, and specifically as training legs, hand, arm, back, waist, abdominal muscles, chest, etc. Most of our best games are very old, and Johnson thinks have deteriorated. But children are imitative and not inventive in their games, and easily learn new ones. Since the Berlin Play Congress in 1894 the sentiment has grown that these are of national importance and are preferable to gymnastics both for soul and body. Hence we have play-schools, teachers, yards, and courses, both for their own value and also to turn on the play impulse to aid in the drudgery of school work. Several have thought that a well-rounded, liberal education could be given by plays and games alone on the principle that there is no profit where there is no pleasure or true euphoria.

Play is motor poetry. Too early distinction between play and work should not be taught. Education perhaps should really begin with directing childish sports aright. Froebel thought it the purest and most spiritual activity of childhood, the germinal leaves of all later life. Schooling that lacks recreation favors dulness, for play makes the mind alert and its joy helps all anabolic activities. Says Brinton, "the measure of value of work is the amount of play there is in it, and the measure of value of play is the amount of work there is in it."

[1] Education by Plays and Games. Ped. Sem., 1894, p. 97 *et seq.*

Johnson adds that "it is doubtful if a great man ever accomplished his life work without having reached a play interest in it." Sully [1] deplores the increase of "agolasts" or "non-laughers" in our times. In merry old England [2] every one played games, and laughter, their natural accompaniment, abounded. Queen Elizabeth's maids of honor played tag with hilarity, but the spirit of play with full abandon seems taking its departure from our overworked, serious, and tense age. To requote Stevenson with variation, as *laborari,* so *ludere,* and *joculari orare sunt.* Laughter itself, as Kühne long ago showed, is one of the most precious forms of exercise, relieving the arteries of their tension.[3]

The antithesis between play and work is generally wrongly conceived, for the difference is essentially in the degree of strength of the psycho-physic motivations. The young often do their hardest work in play. With interest, the most repellent tasks become pure sport, as in the case Johnson reports of a man who wanted a stone pile thrown into a ditch and, by kindling a fire in it and pretending the stones were buckets of water, the heavy and long-shirked job was done by tired boys with shouting and enthusiasm. Play from one aspect of it is superfluous energy over and above what is necessary to digest, breathe, keep the heart and organic processes going, and most children who can not play, if they have opportunity, can neither study nor work without overdrawing their resources of vitality. Bible psychology conceives the fall of man as the necessity of doing things without zest, and this is not only ever repeated but now greatly emphasized when youth leaves the sheltered paradise of play to grind in the mills of modern industrial civilization. The curse is overcome only by those who come to love their tasks and redeem their toil again to play. Play, hardly less than work, can be to utter exhaustion, and because it draws upon older stores and strata of psycho-physic impulsion its exhaustion may even more completely drain our kinetic resources, if it is too abandoned or prolonged. Play can do just as hard and painful tasks as work, for what we love is done with whole

[1] An Essay on Laughter, 1892, p. 427 *et seq.*

[2] See Brandt's Antiquities.

[3] See Professor Allin's and my Psychology of Tickling, Laughing, and the Comic. Am. Jour. of Psy., vol. ix, p. 1 *et seq.*

and undivided personality. Work, as too often conceived, is all body and no soul, and makes for duality and not totality. Its constraint is external, mechanical, or it works by fear and not love. Not effort but zestless endeavors is the tragedy of life. Interest and play are one and inseparable as body and soul. Duty itself is not adequately conceived and felt if it is not pleasure, and is generally too feeble and fitful in the young to awaken much energy or duration of action. Play is from within from congenital hereditary impulsion. It is the best of all methods of organizing instincts. Its cathartic or purgative function regulates irritability, which may otherwise be drained or vented in wrong directions, exactly as Breuer[1] shows psychic traumata may, if overtense, result in "hysterical convulsions." It is also the best form of self-expression and its advantage is variability, following the impulsion of the idle, perhaps hyperemic, and overnourished centers most ready to act. It involves play illusion and is the great agent of unity and totalization of body and soul, while its social function develops solidarity and unison of action between individuals. The dances, feasts, and games of primitive people, wherein they rehearse hunting and war and act and dance out their legends, bring individuals and tribes together.[2] Work is menial, cheerless, grinding, regular, and requires more precision and accuracy and, because attended with less ease and pleasure and economy of movement, is more liable to produce erratic habits. Antagonistic as the forms often are, it may be that, as Carr says, we may sometimes so suffuse work with the play spirit, and *vice versa*, that the present distinction between work and play will vanish, the transition will be less tragic and the activities of youth will be slowly systematized into a whole that better fits his nature and needs; or, if not this, we may at least find the true proportion and system between drudgery and recreation.

The worst product of striving to do things with defective psychic impulsion is fatigue in its common forms, which slows down the pace, multiplies errors and inaccuracies, and develops

[1] Breuer and Freud. Studien über Hysterie. Wien, 1895. See especially p. 177 *et seq.*

[2] See a valuable discussion by H. A. Carr. The Survival Value of Play, Colorado Investigation, November, 1902.

slovenly habits, ennui, flitting will specters, velleities and caprices, and neurasthenic symptoms generally. It brings restlessness, and a tendency to many little heterogeneous, smattering efforts that weaken the will and leave the mind like a piece of well-used blotting-paper, covered with traces and nothing legible. All beginnings are easy, and only as we leave the early stages of proficiency behind and press on in either physical or mental culture and encounter difficulties, do individual differences and the tendency of weak wills to change and turn to something else increase. Perhaps the greatest disparity between men is the power to make a long concentrative, persevering effort, for *In der Beschränkung zeigt sich der Meister.* Now no kind or line of culture is complete till it issues in motor habits, and makes a well-knit soul texture that admits concentration series in many directions and that can bring all its re sources to bear at any point. The brain unorganized by training has, to recur to Richter's well-worn aphorism, saltpeter, sulfur, and charcoal, or all the ingredients of gunpowder, but never makes a grain of it because they never get together. Thus willed action is the language of complete men and the goal of education. When things are mechanized by right habituation, there is still further gain, for not only is the mind freed from further and higher work, but this deepest stratum of motor association is a plexus that determines not only conduct and character, but even beliefs. The person who deliberates is lost, if the intellect that doubts and weighs alternatives is less completely organized than habits. All will culture is intensive and should safeguard us against the chance influence of life and the insidious danger of great ideas in small and feeble minds. Now fatigue, personal and perhaps racial, is just what arrests in the incomplete and mere memory or noetic stage. It makes weak bodies that command, and not strong ones that obey. It divorces knowing and doing, *Kennen* and *Können,* a separation which the Greeks could not conceive because for them knowledge ended in skill or was exemplified in precepts and proverbs that were so clear cut that the pain of violating them was poignant. Ideas must be long worked over till life speaks as with the rifle and not with the shotgun, and still less with the water hose. The purest thought, if true, is only action repressed to be ripened to more practical form. Not only do muscles come before mind, will before intelligence, and sound ideas rest on a motor basis, but all really useless knowledge tends to be eliminated as error or superstition. The roots of play lie close to those of creative imagination and idealism.

The opposite extreme is the factitious and superficial motivation of fear, prizes, examinations, artificial and immediate rewards and penalties, which can only tattoo the mind and body with conventional patterns pricked in, but which lead an unreal life in the soul because they have no depth of soil in nature or heredity. However precious and coherent in itself, all subject-matters thus organized are mere lugs, crimps, and frills. All such culture is spurious, unreal, and parasitic. It may make a scholastic or sophistic mind, but a worm is at the root and, with a dim sense of the vanity of all knowledge that does not become a rule of life, some form of pessimism is sure to supervene in every serious soul. With age a civilization accumulates such impedimenta, traditional flotsam and jetsam, and race fatigue proceeds *pari passu* with its increasing volume. Immediate utilities are better, but yet not so much better than acquisitions that have no other than a school or examination value. If, as Ruskin says, all true work is praise, all true play is love and prayer. Instil into a boy's soul learning which he sees and feels not to have the highest worth and which can not become a part of his active life and increase it, and his freshness, spontaneity, and the fountains of play slowly run dry in him, and his youth fades to early desiccation. The instincts, feelings, intuitions, the work of which is always play, are superseded by method, grind, and education by instruction which is only an effort to repair the defects of heredity, for which, at its best, it is a vulgar, pinchbeck substitute. The best play is true genius, which always comes thus into the world, and has this way of doing its work, and all the contents of the memory pouches is luggage to be carried rather than the vital strength that carries burdens. Gross well says that children are young because they play, and not *vice versa*; and he might have added, men grow old because they stop playing, and not conversely, for play is, at bottom, growth, and at the top of the intellectual scale it is the eternal type of research from sheer love of truth. Home, school, church, state, civilization, are measured in one supreme scale of values, viz., whether and how, for they aid in bringing youth to its fullest maturity. Even vice, crime, and decline are often only arrest or backsliding or reversion. National and racial decline beginning in eliminating one by one the last and highest styles of development of body and mind, mental stimulus of excessive dosage lowers general nutrition. A psychologist that turns his back on mere subtleties and goes to work in a life of service has here a great opportunity, and should not forget, as Horace Mann said, "that for all that grows, one former is worth one hundred reformers."

CHAPTER IV

DISEASES OF BODY AND MIND

Physical and mental ailments and diseases of adolescence a new field of pathology—Neglect of age determination between childish and the better defined diseases of maturity—*Minderwerthigkeit*—Disparate growth of psychic elements loosens cohesion—Health tables from schools—Prevalent disorders—Death rate and morbidity—Indigestion and changes of appetite—Heart troubles and their psychic effect—Curvatures—Consumption—Stuttering—Eye defects—Chlorosis—Typhoid fever—Nerve signs—Sleep—Catatonia—Hebephrenia—Age of first insanity—Tables—Circular and periodic troubles and epilepsy—Melancholy—Idiocy—Hysteria and sex-psychoses—Anxiety—Impulsiveness—Neurasthenia—Folly of doubt and *Grubelsucht*—General paralysis—Special views of many authors—Modern concepts and forms of dementia præcox by Wille, Marro, Kraepelin, Trommer, Ilberg, Seglas, Serieux, Serbski, Christian, etc.—Criticisms of Kraepelin—Ten traits in normal youth exaggerated in dementia præcox—Genius and insanity—Some general causes of precocious decay.

UNTIL recent years there has been a remarkable gap in the medical literature and knowledge concerning health and disease during adolescence. Pediatrics, which treats of the diseases of infancy and early childhood and which has lately become a prominent specialty, usually leaves the child at eight or ten, and in the text-books of Heneoch, Stenzl, Spitzner, Burns, Strümpell, and Möbius, or other standard authors or in the files of the special journals devoted to children's diseases, one finds little attention paid to even the early stages of puberty. So too the diseases of senescence and the menopause, although not a specialty, have a copious and valuable literature. A striking illustration of this relative neglect and ignorance by the profession of the morbific peculiarities of pubescent life is seen in the fact that until well within the last decade, writers often inferred morbidity from mortality tables and many were thus strangely misled, because early adolescence, while the most healthful period of life, if measured by death rates, which are then lowest, is most prone to many ailments, and is therefore marked by a high percentage of ill health.

The general reason for this neglect is that medicine has been chiefly concerned with the study and practical treatment of pronounced diseases and has not yet come to rest on the broad basis of biology, which is its natural and scientific foundation. Practitioners too have been occupied, both at home and in hospitals, with grave cases and have had little time and less motive to consider preventive medicine or the more general problems of regimen and hygiene, personal, domestic, or public. Perhaps occupation with flagrant symptoms tends to give diminished interest, if not distaste, for the milder and incipient manifestations of disease which require sharper diagnosis and a higher quality of mind to detect; and this perhaps could only be overcome by some such philosophic device as having physicians insure the health of their patients, be mulcted, if they are ill, and lose caste if they become so by their neglect. Again, during nearly all its history, medicine has chiefly busied itself with the diseases of adults in whom the same disorders are often expressed by very different symptoms, and which have different prognosis, relations to heredity, treatment, etc. Plato may have had some degree of justification in urging that the ideal doctor must himself not be too well, but must have been schooled by experiences of sickness in his own person to rightly understand the diseases of his patients. If this be so, the treatment of adolescents would be hardly less difficult than that of children, and would be quite as different, because maturity means the obliteration of nearly all traces, physical and mental, of this stage of metamorphosis and transition. Another cause of the hitherto inadequate recognition of the general abnormalities of adolescence is that its sexual and a certain few salient nervous phenomena, which alone have a copious literature, have absorbed attention to the neglect of the other and far more numerous symptom groups peculiar to this age.

The recent advance of interest and knowledge in this latter direction has come for the most part from special studies of large numbers by statistical methods. Some of these researches have concerned health and sickness generally, have selected a group of chronic, acute, or contagious diseases, or else they have specialized upon eye, ear, curvature, circulatory, digestive, or other troubles. In looking over this recent literature one is struck by the following facts: First, that age tables have been too often neglected. Five- and even ten-year periods only instead of single years are sometimes shown, or children are grouped by the class in school which they attend, and the numbers studied are generally far too few to show reliable age proclivities. Secondly, wherever these latter are plotted on a sufficiently broad basis of numbers, for almost every trouble grave and slight, there are indications that there is some characteristic modification of the curve at or near puberty, whatever the nature of the trouble. These data of age liability are now seen to be so fundamentally important that it can be said with confidence that we have no adequate scientific knowledge of any youthful disease, unless this has been presented. It must be recognized that our knowledge of but relatively few of these diseases yet conforms satisfactorily to this criterion. As puberty approaches, most of the diseases to which childhood is most prone, like meningitis, scarlatina, diphtheria, acute bronchitis, and a number of epidemics decrease, while rheumatism, disorders of bones, muscles, nerves, heart, and circulation increase. Goubert[1] concludes that diathesic diseases (as opposed to those like dysentery, typhoid, etc., due to bad hygiene) decrease, although his tables are based on death rates. Recurrent circular and periodic troubles are especially liable to begin at puberty. The characteristic adult diseases to which youth is now becoming liable, without having ceased to be exposed to those of childhood, are often more simple with less evolved symptoms. Illusions are less systematized than they will be later, when mental phenomena are more complex and more developed. Insanities are more emotional, and Moreau's *état mixte,* which is neither health nor sickness, but on or near the border line that separates them, indicates how in this transition stage youth is still exposed to most early diseases, although their assault is with diminished violence, while most adult troubles are beginning to lay hold upon him but can not yet exert their full power. This is, as we shall see later, also the age of incipiency for what Prichard was the first to characterize as moral insanity, and for the *Minderwerthigkeit* of Koch, Trüper, and others, a term which designates anomala or antinomia of character and conduct which are not normal nor yet insane, but suggest the difficulty and liability of failure to

[1] Les maladies des enfants à Paris, 1891, p. 95 *et seq.*

pass successfully and completely to the adult stage. Brethean[1] was one of the first to recognize this aspect of these critical years during which the resistance of different parts of the organism to morbid influences varies greatly. The diseases he thought most liable to appear at this stage are chlorosis, anemia, goiter, hysteria, epilepsy, and a peculiar form of chorea. The point of departure for each, if not its cause, he found in the physical changes which characterize sexual evolution, but he thought that many symptoms which do not develop into complete morbid entities had their root in the digestive perturbations peculiar to this age.

That nutritive processes are influenced by climate, seasons, and geographical location, has often been pointed out. Military statistics show that the size of adults varies greatly in different parts of this country, suggesting thus that growth may also be very sensitive to outer conditions. Such considerations led Dr. Bowditch to inquire if the accurate determination of the normal rate of growth of children would not throw light on the nature of the diseases to which they were subject and also guide to proper curative measures. Dentition is known to retard growth. Many special cases seem to show that loss of weight or arrest of growth, at the age when it should be most rapid, is a danger-signal of peculiar value because it precedes all others. Loss of weight may precede by months the characteristic cough of consumption, and the advent of other especially constitutional and inherited diseases, and even measles may be thus heralded by some loss of weight. This is an argument for weekly weighings, but it must not be inferred that diminution of growth is always a morbid symptom, as this is subject to oscillation the curves and limits of which are not yet sufficiently understood.[2]

As we know more of adolescence, it will probably be apparent that many, if not indeed most of its minor disorders are due to disproportionate development. If increase in height is too rapid and excessive, not only growing pains in the limbs due to failure of the muscles to develop *pari passu* with the

---

[1] De la Puberté chez la Femme. Paris, 1865, p. 38.

[2] See I Fattori della Statura Umana. Arch. di Statistica. Rom., 1877.—Bowditch. The Relation between Growth and Disease. Transactions of the Am. Med. Ass'n, 1881.

bones, but venous disturbances, particularly varicosities in the legs, now so common, and even aortic disorders may be caused, to say nothing of curvatures and torsions, because young people become self-conscious and perhaps ashamed of their sudden height, and the fully upright posture is hard to maintain. Acromegalia, or excessive development of the limbs or bones of the face, probably illustrates this same disturbed equilibrium. Some headaches and eye troubles have here their cause. Closely related too, no doubt, are some forms of heterotopy and still more heterochrony or anomalous changes in the direction or order of the various growth stresses. We must probably here too invoke the principle laid down by Roux that different organs and tissues or determinants compete for the available nutritive material in the blood, and some for a time get ahead of others in this internal struggle for survival among the different parts or independently variable growth units. If functions or tissues that ought to develop at the age of twenty appear at fifteen, or earlier, we have here on a small scale what, if excessive, constitutes, from an evolutionary standpoint, the very interesting body of facts treated in teratology. We shall later see how this principle must be appealed to in genius, in some aspects of insanity and crime as well as in sexual and mental precocity. Its more restricted range is a matter of common observation as seen in children, who are precocious and belated in one or many respects.[1] We know too from the fact of tachygenesis as described by Cope, and also from the manifold data which already have a rich literature showing how ontogeny often reverses the order of phylogeny, that there is great temporary plasticity and interchange of forces here, the brain and eye—e. g., appearing in the human embryo far earlier than their place in the phyletic sequence. Assuming that our personality is compound and made up of many elements, as Hirt suggests, into which disease, traumata, hypnotism, etc., may partially resolve it, as seen in the phenomena of multiplex personality, we must regard the adolescent stage as especially characterized by either a loosening of the bonds between the manifold factors of our ego, somatic and psychic, or else by a sudden and independent growth of single elements which

[1] Baur, Die körperliche und geistige Früh- und Spätentwickelung. Zeits. f. Schulgesundheitspflege, 1899, p. 707.

leaves their former associative bonds relatively weakened, or perhaps by both together. The fact that the growth factors are increased, some more and some less, and thus brought into new relations with each other, makes this the most favorable field for the genetic study of character and temperament, whether mental, as seen in the now recognized difference of eye, ear, motor-minded, etc., or emotional and active, as seen in the dominance of different classes of temperaments, so apparent in the observation of individual and particularly of peculiar and exceptional children or adults. Thus again, as from so many standpoints, we come to the suggestion of ancestral prepotencies struggling with each other for predominance, checking and favoring each other in a way that suggests the Herbart-Taine concepts of collisions and impacts at all angles, with sums of arrest and reenforcements. These perhaps when we understand the laws of heredity we shall find due in part to the mingling of different ancestral stocks, the elements of which are more or less compactly knit together in proportion to the time in which they have been associated in the phylum, as we trace man's ancestral tree backward and downward further toward its earliest roots.

Clouston suggests that the tissues that mature slowly are most liable to be affected by hereditary disease, and others have intimated that growth energy itself may do harm unless rightly distributed and proportioned, so that each determinant gets its full share of this momentum, so that height be not at the expense of weight, or the nervous system left arrested, immature, etc. We have seen in Chapter II that boys are more likely than girls to grow unsymmetrically, and there are many cases where even bilateral symmetry, especially of limbs and shoulders, is lost for a time and then regained, as if boys grew first, and most on one side and then on the other. Indeed all the facts that support the doctrine of nascent periods show that for a time growth tends to focalize upon one group of qualities and then upon another, and the newer developments even in brain anatomy suggest, as we saw, a difference between the period of development for the projection system, which reacts through the senses and muscles to the outer world, and the associative functions which combine these capsular and sensory centers with each other into new and higher unities.

Dr. Hertel[1] examined 3,141 boys in 14 schools in Copenhagen, and found 1,900 healthy, 978 sickly, and 236 uncertain. 18 per cent were sickly on entering school; after two years this number increased to 30 per cent; and just before puberty, had reached 40 per cent, when it dropped to 30, where it remained for a few years. Of 1,211 girls between the ages of five and sixteen, 640 were healthy, 433 sickly, and the rest not returned. The percentage of sickness for girls rose rapidly from the first to the third school year, from 12 to 32 per cent. From twelve to sixteen sickness increased till the ill outnumbered the well by 10 per cent, except at fourteen, when there was a slight change for the better. At about twelve and one-half years there was a sudden increase of illness due, as he thought, to the impending development of adolescence. Before puberty he found scrofulous diseases most common, and after it anemia, nervousness, headache, and eye diseases. Hertel says: "We must put aside all illusions and confess that the present generation of young girls is weakly, anemic, and nervous to an extraordinary degree." He scores the ignorance and stupidity of teachers about health, when they are possessed by the demon of education, which is causing an appalling national invalidism as well as juvenile serfdom. The best pupils he thinks are thus often made the slowest and most vacant minded. From thirteen to fifteen great reduction of school work for both sexes, but chiefly for boys, should be insisted on. No one should be allowed to go to school at all without nine hours of sleep and a hearty appetite, for even presence in school impairs nutrition, arrests growth, starts neurotic habits, and especially checks the development of the highest powers, which are the last to unfold. He almost agrees with Dr. Pilger, who had urged that the youth of Germany had degenerated mentally, morally, and physically, and who thought that only a few exceptional boys should be allowed to attend school at all after eighteen. Teachers, he says, are incompetent to judge of the health of pupils and could hardly be trusted for unbiased opinions were they competent. All nervous girls need very careful individual study and the greatest degree of consideration at this period. Household duties, if moderate, are a good regulator. Girls must be taught to endure disappointment, to relish the common

[1] Overpressure in the High Schools of Denmark. London, 1885.

homely joys of life, to be content and hopeful as they now rarely are, to avoid extreme fatigue, excitement or exposure, high diet, etc. He concludes by recommending, as better means against threatened decadence, a health report book for each child, such as Hornemann had proposed.

Soon after the first publication of Hertel, the Danish Government in 1882 appointed a commission which examined 16,889 boys and 11,225 girls, and found 29 per cent of the boys and 41 per cent of the girls sickly, the highest per cent—nearly 50—being reached at the age of twelve and thirteen.

In 1885 Key published the report of a Swedish commission, of which he was the head,[1] and which was chiefly devoted to examining the health of 15,000 boys in the Swedish middle schools and 3,000 girls in private schools. Key's studies were made in March and April, and showed a far greater percentage of poor health than in Denmark, where Hertel's data were gathered in the fall. At the beginning of the school year, children are more lively, stronger, and more healthful than in winter. Toward spring and near the end of the school year, morbidity reaches its maximum, so that the school is then most detrimental to health.

Eliminating all acute and all chance illness and studying only chronic troubles, states, and feebleness, special curves were constructed by Key for pallor or anemia, headache, nearsightedness, other eye troubles, nosebleed, loss of appetite, scrofula, nervousness, spinal curvature, and other slow diseases. The high percentages of these diseases and their generally rapid increase were alarming. Over 13 per cent of the boys suffered from frequent headache and nearly 13 per cent were anemic. From the first to the second school year, 5 per cent of illness increased to 36 per cent, and in the fourth school year reached 40 per cent. There was a great increase in the percentage of illness near the beginning of puberty. As soon as this is well begun, the rate of illness sinks term by term. The increment of weight has closer relation to health than height, for these

[1] Läroverkskomiténs Betänkande III. Stockholm, 1885, 2 vols. With elaborate tables. This is greatly condensed and most of the elaborate tables are omitted by Burgerstein in a work entitled, Schulhygienische Untersuchungen, 1899. See also Key: Die Pubertäts Entwickelung, Verhandl des Internat. Med. Congres zu Berlin. Vol. i, 1890, p. 67 *et seq.*

diseases decrease almost *pari passu* with increase of weight. Just when weight is increasing fastest, there is least liability to illness; but as the growth rate declines, the sickness rate rises steadily to a second maximum in the nineteenth or twentieth year. The seventeenth is the healthiest of all years for boys, yet the eighteenth is sickly. When the body grows slowly at an age when it should grow fast, it offers least resistance to disease, and while children are growing fast they are least liable to these illnesses. The weak period just before puberty seems exceptionally liable to disease. While in general the results agree with Hertel's, they still lack confirmation in other lands, although there is no reason to think them peculiar to Sweden and Denmark.

Key's studies of girls were based on those from the upper classes of society, but he found 61 per cent more or less sickly. Of these, 36 per cent were anemic and nearly the same number had habitual headache, 10 per cent had spinal curvature, and 5 per cent scrofula. This illness curve rises to its maximum of nearly 65 per cent in the thirteenth year. Illness of girls continues to increase awhile after the beginning of the period of puberty, but soon slowly ceases to rise and then falls, although at no age under 60 per cent, to rise again after the period of increase weight growth is passed. That these girls, whose health is so impaired at the beginning of the increment period, do not decidedly improve during its later stage is a ground for the gravest apprehension, and shows according to Key that modern methods of educating girls are radically and dangerously wrong, perhaps in being too much like the methods applied to boys. It is not safe, however, to reason directly from the pubertal phenomena of one sex to those of the other.

Hertel,[1] who later compared the results of the two commissions in two very suggestive articles, drew many practical conclusions, and found that of children who studied more than the normal time, 7 per cent more were ill than of those who worked less than this time. Key determined the average time devoted to study by 2,000 Stockholm *Gymnasium* pupils, living under uniform conditions, and found that over 5 per cent more

[1] Neure Untersuchungen über den allegemeinen Gesundheitszustand der Schuler und Schulerinen. Schulgesundheitspflege, 1888. Nos. 6 and 7, pp. 16?–183; 201–215.

of those who studied over this average were ill than of those who devoted less time to study. In lower classes this difference was between 7 and 8 per cent, for young children have less power to resist disease than pubescents. The injury caused by excessive brain work in the latter class, although less manifest in actual sickness, is probably no less insidious, and is thus very likely greater and its evils more lasting. Rousseau long ago suggested the crude corrective of withholding Émile from study till he was twelve, but surely, says Key, after that age the school is very liable to squander in childhood the vigor of the future man. Key thought younger school children should sleep from eleven to twelve hours, and that in children of all ages, and perhaps especially during puberty, the need of the system for sleep is very rarely met in modern civilized lands. The time spent in bed is by no means the same as that in sleep, although so estimated. The latter decreases in almost exact proportion as the time given to study increases. Instead of decreasing steadily, as children go up the classes and study harder, the amount of sleep should increase with the growth of mental activity until the body is mature, and should be distinctly augmented at puberty.

In about 2,000 children in Lausanne, Combe[1] found the percentage of morbidity (chiefly anemia, headaches, catarrhs, indigestion, and respiratory troubles) as follows, from which, comparing annual increase in height, he inferred that morbidity and growth increased together. To this we have added, in the lower row of figures, the results of Nesteroff's[2] test of 216 boys in a Moscow gymnasium.

Age	8	9	10	11	12	13	14	15	16	17	18	19	20
Boys, per cent ill	64	43	42	40	33	29	34	..	..	..	..	..	..
Girls	88	75	60	60	68	61	39	..	..	..	..	..	..
Moscow boys	..	29	58	57	100	61	57	46	50	59	67	64	25

The diseases of the Russian children in the lower row in the order of frequency—nervous troubles being excluded—were throat troubles, 15 per cent; general disturbance of digestion, 10 per cent; sight, 8; chronic lung trouble, 7; spinal

[1] Körperlänge u. Wachsthum, etc. Zeits. f. Schulgesundheitspflege, 1896, p. 569.

[2] Die moderne Schule u. d. Gesundheit. Zeits. f. Schulgesundheitspflege, 1890, p. 213 *et seq.*

curvature, 6 per cent. Of all these children 71 suffered from nervous troubles, which increased very steadily from 8 per cent on entering to 69 per cent at the end of the eighth year. During Nesteroff's four years' record he found that each pupil needed a doctor on the average about five times a year, most often for colds and nervous troubles, and that there were two ages of maximal illness, viz., twelve and seventeen.

Zak[1] finds among 4,245 Moscow secondary pupils the following percentage of nervousness:

Age...............	10	11	12	13	14	15	16	17	18	19	20
Nervous..........	8.3	20	16.6	20	25	9	33	66.6	55.5	77.7	42.8

Lesgaft found very frequent swelling of the veins of the seminal cord among the St. Petersburg pupils, especially in the middle and higher grades.

Dr. Schmidt-Monnard,[2] a specialist in children's diseases, investigated the chronic disorders of 5,100 boys and 3,200 girls as to anemia, chlorosis, headache, nervousness, sleeplessness, defect of appetite, digestive troubles, nosebleed, chronic inflammation of the cornea, and abnormal refraction of the lens. In the middle schools among 2,100 boys, he found nine and twelve the most sickly years, where morbidity from all causes reached 30 and 35 per cent respectively, and that sleeplessness culminated at the age of twelve. Among 1,900 girls in the same class of schools, the year of maximal sickness for all diseases was thirteen, where it reached nearly 50 per cent; at the same period headaches reached 30 and nosebleed 8 per cent and sleeplessness reached its maximum, while as with the boys morbidity decreased materially the year after its maximum. In higher private schools for girls, sickness increased rapidly from the twelfth to the fifteenth year, when it reached 57 per cent, and slightly increased for the two following years, as did nervous troubles, while sleeplessness at sixteen had reached nearly 10 per cent. In the *Real* schools and *Gymnasia,* the maximum of 40 per cent was reached at seventeen for those who had no afternoon session, and the maximum of over 70 per cent was reached at sixteen for those who studied after-

[1] *Op. cit.*, p. 9.

[2] Die chronische Kränklichkeit in unseren mittleren und höheren Schulen. Zeits. f. Gesundheitspflege, 1897, pp. 593 and 666.

noons, while headaches alone considered culminated at seventeen and sleeplessness at eighteen. The differences in all ages were strikingly in favor of those who did no evening work.

Schmidt-Monnard also attempted to compare normal with actual hours of sleep for each age for boys.

Age	7	10	14	18–20
Normal	12	11½–12	11	8½–9
Actual	11–11¼	10–10½	9–9¾	7½–8

Cephalgic congestion increases with brain-work, and thus causes school headaches, or as Charcot called it *cephalgia adolescentium,* and nosebleed. Key and Becker have shown that this increases in the upper *Gymnasia* classes, and while there are other etiological factors, overpressure is one, though perhaps not the chief. Both pain and hemorrhage are greatly increased by the neuropathic diathesis.

In a study of the death rates in the school population of Boston, which for the years 1885 and 1890 numbered 70,000 between the ages of five and fifteen when the average annual number of deaths was 471, Dr. Hartwell[1] found that the period from ten to fifteen, which was characterized by the most rapid increase in height and weight, was also that in which the fewest deaths occurred. For girls the year of lowest death rate or power to resist disease was the twelfth; for boys the thirteenth. These years were thus at once the period of accelerated growth and of accentuated specific intensity of life, or in other words, this is the period at which Boston school children attain and pass the flood-tide of growth as measured by their power to resist death. Acceleration of growth and life intensity begin, culminate, and decline about a year earlier for girls than for boys. This result was presented in the table comparing Bowditch's result for weight and height with the specific intensity of life for 1875, 1885, and 1890. For our purposes it is compared in the following table with other standards and the age of least mortality, which ranges from eleven to fourteen:

[1] See Report of the Director of Physical Training of Boston. School Document No. 8, 1894, p. 46 *et seq.*

AGE.	Probability of dying at each age. Farr, 50 years ago. England.	Death rate per 1,000 (England and Wales, 1881-'90).		Dying in each year of age (Mass. Life Table, 1893-'97).		Annual mortality per unit at each year of age (Mass. Life Table, 1893-'97).		Death rates of Boston children, 1875, 1885, 1890.	
		M.	F.	M.	F.	M.	F.	M.	F.
8	.....	...	...	...	...	......	......	9.5	9.6
9	.....	...	...	...	...	......	......	7.1	8.1
10	5,735	2 0	1.7	123	120	.00326	.00349	6.3	5.1
11	5,207	1.8	1.6	110	113	.00292	.00306	5.0	5.2
12	4,933	1.8	1.7	104	113	.00277	.00307	3.8	3.2
13	4,891	2.0	2.0	111	123	.00297	.00336	3.9	4.3
14	3,040	2 4	2 4	135	146	.00362	.00400	5.2	6.2
15	5,359	2.9	2.9	159	172	.00428	.00473	4.9	5.8
16	5,811	3.4	3.5	181	195	.00489	.00539	5.6	5.7
17	.....	...	...	...	...	......	......	6.6	6.6

Journal of Adolescence, October, 1900, pp. 55–56.

The following table[1] shows the mortality of each age and sex in Prussia on the basis of 1,000 inhabitants:

YEARS.	Males, 1891-'95.	In the country, 1876-'81, male.	City, 1875-'81, male.	Female, 1891-'95.	Country, 1876-'81, female.	City, 1876-'81, female.
0– 1	225.0	....	....	192.0	....	....
1– 2	64.0	64.0	82.0	63.0	62.0	79.0
2– 3	26.3	33.5	39.0	25.4	32.0	39.0
3– 5	14.3	20.5	23.5	14.0	20.0	24.0
5–10	5.8	9.1	9.7	6.0	8.9	9.8
10–15	2.9	4.0	3.8	3.2	4.3	4.1
15–20	4.8	5.1	5.4	3.8	4.6	4.6
20–25	5.9	7.9	7.8	5.2	6.0	6.7
25–30	7.1	7.3	10.0	6.2	7.7	8.8
30–40	10.8	9.1	14.3	8.2	9.6	11.0
40–50	18.3	14.3	21.8	11.2	11.9	13.1
50–60	30.0	25.0	33.5	18.4	21.0	21.5
60–70	55.3	50.0	59.0	40.5	47.0	43.5
70–80	112.0	112.0	115.0	94.0	108.0	99.5

Symonds found for his table of American Life Insurance Societies that mortality is less for girls than for boys in the period preceding and following puberty in the ratio of 1.68 to 1.18.

The expectation of life for men at different ages[2]

[1] Compiled from several tables in the Deutsche Vierteljahrschrift f. öff. Gesundheitspflege, Bd. 3, 1899. Supplement, pp. 50–53.

[2] Monatsblätter für die Vertrauensärzte der Lebensversicherungsbank Gotha I. 1886. No. 2., p. 15.

Completed year of life.	Number living.	Number of those dying next year.	Probability of death.	Average duration of life in years.
25	10,000	53	.00532	38.66
26	9,947	54	.00543	37.87
27	9,893	55	.00556	37.07
28	9,838	56	.00569	36.28
29	9,782	57	.00584	35.48
30	9,725	59	.00600	34.69

In the chart on p. 251, from Engelman,[1] curve A represents the percentage of morbidity for prepubescent Danish girls from Key and Hertel, as we have no good and comprehensive American data. It is adapted to American girls by giving it the same relation to the period of prepubertal development, here averaging 13.8 years (indicated by the short vertical line near the bottom), that it bears to the time of first menstruation in Denmark, which is 1½ years later. *B* is Hartwell's curve of life intensity or the power to resist lethal influences, which is an expression of the nutritive activity of the organism during its period of greatest and most rapid growth, and is based on the ratio of the number living to the number dying. This curiously enough conforms generally to the curve of morbidity. *C* is the mortality curve, which is almost diametrically opposite that of morbidity, i. e., just during those years from eight or nine to thirteen or fourteen, when American girls are most likely to be sick they are least liable to die. *D* is the curve of growth in weight, and *E* represents the percentage of stuttering as indicating augmented nervous excitability.

We now pass to consider the special morbidities of adolescence. Very prominent among the physiological disturbances of this age are those of indigestion and disorders of the alimentary canal, and especially of the stomach. The rapid bone growth requires more lime, the blood needs iron, the increased metabolism more oxygen and more fats for heat, perhaps the brain more phosphorus, the muscles require more protein and muscle work more inogen and myosin to break down, and normally the food supply is increased with height and weight, and the chemical bookkeeping of income and expenditure readjusted. Gamgee suggests that the ingesta may

[1] The American Girl of To-day; Pres. Address. Gynecological Soc., 190●.

be raised to a plane of higher complexity. However this be, the body in general may be conceived as a machine for the con-

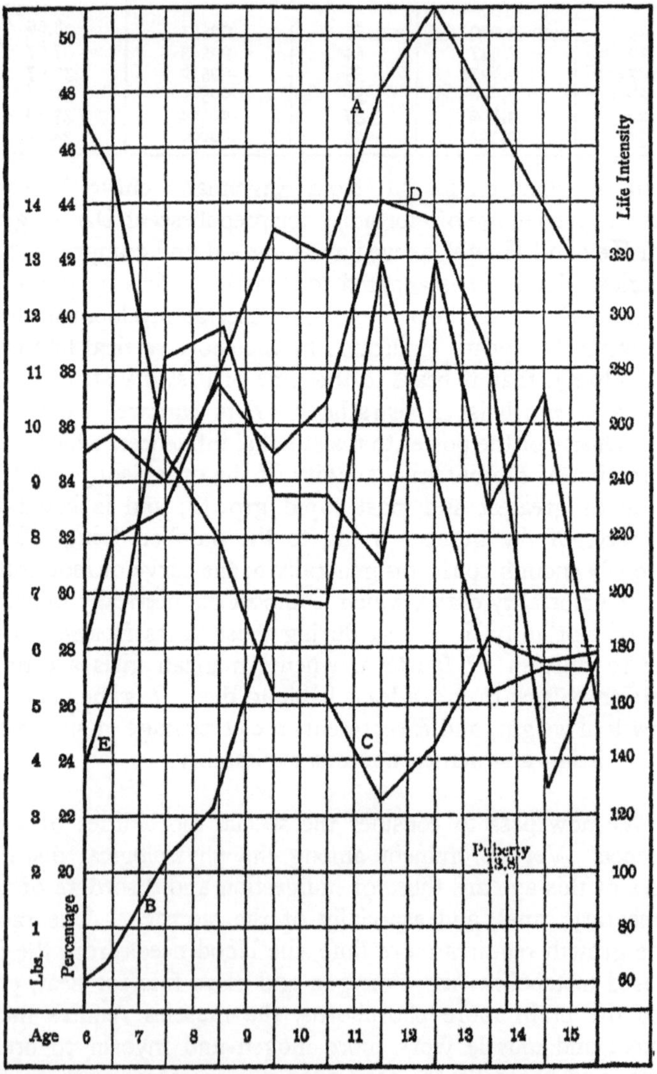

servation of energy which it receives originally from the sun, from which its every element came, and of which we are all children, and indirectly from chlorophyl, which is our kinetic basis like a bent bow. In a high sense every organ is a digestive organ, even the brain itself, and thought perhaps has a digestive function. Man is what he eats and what he does with it, through all the intricate formulæ of physiological chemistry.

There is a sense in which the basal will to live is simply the will to eat and in which this latter is the basis of psychology. Nearly three-fourths of the total energy of the body, expressed kinetically, probably goes to digestion and half the struggle of life is for food. The very cells of our embryo, as they grow large so that their surface diminishes relatively to their content, must divide or die of starvation. Most of the movements of every form of life that has ceased to be sessile are to get food; organs of locomotion are to get to it or to escape being eaten by enemies. In the primitive struggle for survival, when two hostile creatures meet, one is destined to be the food of the other. The first fear is that of being devoured; the first form of property is accumulated food. Almost every living being is the food for some other, even the organs of our body struggle in rivalry for the food which the blood brings, and every form of disease and death itself is caused by cutting off the food supply from some group of cells. Sleep is to feed and build up again the nuclei of cells, which under the microscope are seen to have been worn away by activity, and to remove the chip pile of dead matter. Fungoid growths are low level metabolisms, where the excreta or clinkers in the human furnace are not removed. What we call hunger is the massed and unconscious desire of every cell for the food it needs, and death in every form may be in a sense said to be due to progressive local or general starvation.

These general considerations, which I conceive to be the basis of the new genetic psychology of the future, may serve to give us due appreciation of the special importance for adolescence of the general law that there is a trophic or nutritive background to everything and to suggest that the profound metamorphoses of puberty involve adjustments far more radical than are usually imagined. Almost all returns to our food *questionnaires,* to be elsewhere more fully reported on, show that the appetite, which, if natural, is like a compass pointing to the true pole of our somatic needs, is often gravely disturbed at this period. Nearly all report changed appetite. Foods, very prominent in the habitual dietaries before, are now neglected and new favorites arise. This change is especially marked with regard to sweets, acids, fruits, meats, and stimulants. There is a new tendency to experiment, not only with new dishes, but often with things strange and even offensive. Boys dare each other to taste, eat, or swallow offensive and sometimes harmful things, or force their mates to do so, sometimes with disastrous results, not infrequently suggesting the nauseous anthropological chapter of scatology. Boys sometimes affect or boast of their achievements in eating, and girls affect daintiness, become exceedingly discriminating in sweetmeats, bonbons, summer drinks, etc. Boys have eating and drinking matches and duels, and intemperance very generally takes its rise here. Lancaster reported ninety-one spontaneous reconstructions of appetite in his returns. It is irregular, fasting and feasting perhaps alternate, strange whims or picæ arise with sometimes extreme dislike of some one and passionate fondness for other kinds of foods. Taste seems to acquire a more inward and independent quality of its own, and junkets dainty-mouthed and perhaps stealthily, on titbits. Girls in particular become squeamish, fastidious, and lickerish, and perhaps develop a sweet tooth of disproportionate dimensions. It is never so hard to establish a well-balanced dietary, and yet this is the nascent period for it. Perverse tastes may grievously interfere with health, and the rectification of appetite may be hard just in proportion as plasticity of this age passes into settled bad eating habits of later life.

I am convinced that one of the causes of diseased cravings, which may lead to wrong food habits and to intemperance, is due to the fact that the normal changes of appetite for both quality and quantity of food are perversions of normal appetite so often unnoticed and unmet. Now judicious oversight, perhaps eked out by a little wholesome authority, does more to push the psycho-physic organism on to pass safely over the immature stages and dangers of arrest and to come to full maturity with a real maximum of utilized nutrition, than almost any other influence. Very many of the failures of middle and later life are due to avoidable errors of diet, and the arrest thus caused. We know that many larvæ and embryos of the lower forms stop at various stages of immaturity, if food is not abundant and fit, taken properly at due intervals, etc. Not malaria, as Morel thought, but perverted appetites, sometimes aided by adulterations and bad cooking, are one of the causes of human degeneration, because man, who ought to be polyphagous and can only with increased difficulty adopt a new food after the period of sex development, is really not fed according to his physiological needs. This is not only the cause of many breakdowns among pupils and students, anemias and most of the maladies of malnutrition so common at adolescence, but of that disquiet, weakness, and lust for stimulants, which in part directly and in part indirectly causes the appetite for drink, by producing either the extreme fatigue under only normal strain, that often has recourse to it, or else this craving is due to lack of proper exercise which so strongly prompts to the quest of artificial excitement.

The wisdom teeth too are now forming, and the chin and lower jaw and the muscles of mastication are growing. Biting sticks, toothpicks, pencils, etc., is an automatism, the curve of which now undergoes a marked rise. The propensity for gum chewing, which partially gratifies this instinct, may contribute to digestive troubles by provoking salivary secretions, which are not utilized for digestion, and which thus introduce an element of discord into the manifold symphony of these processes.

Dr. Pitt[1] describes slight cardiac failure, shortness of breath, dyspnœa, palpitation, and other symptoms of cardiac dilation at puberty. The languor and feeble pulse, discomfort, and other symptoms which attend it rarely last long and ought soon to be compensated by growth. The heart, as we saw, nearly or quite doubles in size during the development of puberty, and this increase may all be within a year or may be extended over several. Dr. Pitt's tables of the normal volume of the heart at different ages and its rate of growth are of great value. The area of the pulmonary artery grows from 52 c. mm. at the age of thirteen to 61 c. mm. at fourteen, and the volume of the heart from 120 to 215 c. cm. during the same years. While the heart during its most rapid growth in the first year of life increases only 15–16 c. cm., during puberty it increases from 95–115 c. cm.

[1] On Cardiac Dilation at Puberty and its Frequent Occurrence in Girls. British Medical Journal, 1886.

Dr. E. Kisch, of Prague, in a valuable article describes the heart troubles of pubescent girls somewhat as follows: The most common form is nervous palpitation, which often and sometimes in violent form precedes by a few weeks or months the first menstruation, and generally ceases as these periods become well established. Diminution of appetite, indigestion, constipation, flatulence, irritability, inertia, and sleeplessness often occur, due in part to reflex excitation from the uterus and in part to oversensitiveness of the psyche. Another form of heart distortion is seen in cases of great delay of first menstruation or in long continued irregularity of this function, and seems to be due to the chlorotic composition of the blood. A third and far rarer form is seen where unusually rapid growth has just preceded menstruation, and in girls who are not anemic or nervous, but strikingly lean and slender. It goes with a sense of fulness, short breath, and hypertrophy of the left ventricle, and this is due to a circulatory storm incident to puberty, which obliges the heart to act against increased resistance. These cases are most frequent among the non-laboring classes, and are aggravated by garments in the least degree tight about the waist.

Irregularity of heart action or arhythmia is far more common among children than was previously supposed. It is usually transient and may be due to many causes; it becomes serious only as senescence approaches.[1] It is most frequent in anemic children who are growing rapidly at puberty and seems often due to relatively narrow arteries and overpressure, and hypertrophy may follow. Chronic heart troubles often begin in insufficiency of action, while arrhythmia appears only late in valvular diseases. Nervous heart troubles are due to imperfect development of the neural regulative apparatus. Idiopathic heart irregularities seem more common among boys than among girls. Sometimes the pulse at puberty is exceptionally slow, and sometimes very rapid for a season. Loss of a beat by deep inspiration may occur. Irregularity may be for a time habitual during sleep, while fright, worms, bowel trouble, a cold bath, nausea, etc., may produce this same effect. Guidi [2] has called special attention to the frequency of

[1] O. Heubner. Herzarythmia im Kindesalter. Zeit. f. Klin. Med., 1894, p. 492.
[2] Arch. Ital. di Pediatria, 1892.

palpitation in growing school children between fifteen and eighteen.

Very many children now become morbidly conscious of their heart, anxiously feel their pulse, count the beats, and not a few in our returns work themselves into a state of high tension, fearing that they are doomed to die and that the heart may cease to pulsate at any moment. This might almost be called a characteristic phobia of adolescence. In extreme cases for months, and even years, the fingers are on the wrist on every occasion, and ingenious methods of concealing this watch from others are invented. Especially at night, when after reclining its beats are slightly feebler and at longer intervals, this chronic solicitude may occasionally reach a sudden panic that the end has come, and this starts it bounding again. Some read medical books, devise pretexts for comparing rate and intensity with that of their friends, imagine twingings, gurgles, stoppages, and obstructions, dread violent exercise, modify their regimen, all this perhaps without betraying their fears to any one, and entirely outgrowing them later. One boy of fourteen never dared lie on his back or left side; another feared to take a deep breath and felt it necessary for his safety to assume a peculiar bending attitude in sitting or standing. Usually, however, these solicitudes, although very common, are slight and transitory.

Many studies have lately been made of the forms of scoliosis, or spinal curvature, peculiar to adolescents. Eulenburg had found that of 300 cases of scoliosis, most occurred between six and fourteen, and of these 53 per cent between seven and ten, 23 per cent between six and seven, and 12 per cent between ten and fourteen. Krug found that of 181 cases, most or 35 per cent occurred between thirteen and thirteen and three-quarters years; that next to most, or 28 per cent, occurred from eleven to eleven and three-quarters years; that 27.5 per cent occurred between twelve and twelve and three-quarters years; and that 5 per cent of the rest occurred between fourteen and sixteen and three-quarters years of age. Its advent is so slow and insidious that it is often unnoticed for years, or it is thought to be merely a bad habit of posture. The same leg is crossed over the other instead of reversing the position. In standing the weight is chiefly on one foot and perhaps always the same, rather than equally divided or alternating. One elbow is leaned on, the head is tipped to one side, vicious attitudes are assumed in writing, studying, etc. Heiser [1] recommends the use of the scoliometer at this age to detect the beginnings of asymmetry of function. Most frequent is right dorsal, and next comes left lumbar curvature. Both may be either cause or effect of habitually sitting with more pressure on one flank than on the other. Whether the various scolioses, including cyphosis and lordosis, are primitive and purely hereditary, still admits of some doubt. The deformity of the thorax is often attended by and perhaps causes irregularities of heart beat, respiration, and digestion. More or less torsion of the spine and muscular insufficiency are often causes, and osseous theories alone are at least inadequate to explain most cases, as are the muscular, nervous, or ligamentary theories so often exploited in connection with orthopedic methods. Most of the latter now agree in disapproving of corsets and all constant physical restraints of the freedom of motion, save in extreme cases, because immobility enfeebles. The accentuation of these asymmetries at adolescence is to be expected from the rapidity of growth under unfavorable conditions of heredity, environment, or habit, for one side of the body develops more nervous innervation and muscular tension, or more rapid metabolism, than the other, and the equilibrium which characterizes perfect normality and health is upset. Finer modern measurements show that nearly all persons are more or less unsymmetrical.

The great work of Alexander James [2] shows that the greatest mortality for consumption occurs from the ages of twenty-five to thirty. If we assume with Clouston that infection with this disease began on the average five years earlier, we could infer that consumption begins under twenty-five, and this would agree with James's law that "tubercular deposit tends to occur in various tissues at periods when the excessive nutritive power required for growth is becoming or has become exhausted." Clouston [3] adds that "lung tubercle first shows itself in any de-

[1] La Scoliose Essentielle des Adolescentes. Paris, 1897.

[2] Pulmonary Phthisis.

[3] The Neurosis of Development, p. 91.

gree in 14 per cent of persons living near the beginning of reproductive power, viz., fifteen years of age. It doubles its virulence about twenty, reaching 34 per cent, and gets to 38 per cent at twenty-five and to 40 per cent at thirty, thus killing most of its victims during the developmental ages and reaching its maximum just at the age of completed development." Clouston has described a special kind of mental disease, which he calls phthisical insanity, beginning during or just after adolescence, when he thinks the body is in a state of reduced nutritive condition favorable to tubercular infection. This innutrition he deems one form of trophic neurosis, and thinks the special pulmonary innutrition, that admits of the tubercle bacillus finding a nidus in the lungs, results in a developmental failure in the epithelium of their alveoli. He bases this inference very largely upon the coincidence of the maximal age of infection for both. Suggestive in this regard are the mortality tables for tuberculosis for the different ages and sexes in Prussia calculated in percentages on a basis of 10,000 inhabitants, as follows:[1]

Age.	10–15		15–20		20–25		25–30		30–60	
	M.	F.	M.	F.	M.	F.	M.	F.	M.	F.
1895	4.99	8.77	16.65	17.51	27.04	21.94	29.08	26.84	41.02	29.87
1896	4.77	8.30	15 74	17.34	26.81	22.17	25.81	25.31	36.81	29.33
1897	4.99	9 04	15.54	16.64	27.21	22.49	25.92	25.15	37.60	27.75

Stuttering is a spastic disorder of coordination in the muscles of speech and is most liable to occur at pauses or initial consonants, especially if they are explosive. The three factors of expiration and vowel production by action of the vocal cords and consonantal activity of lips and tongue, which are involved in articulation, are not harmonized, and tonic or clonic cramps occur. The impediments may sometimes all remit and speech be normal for a time, but they are aggravated or often caused by mental tension and bad training. Stammering differs from stuttering in lacking the spontaneous by-movements and in being a failure of pronunciation rather than of speech, while the latter is a kind of chorea of the muscles of utterance, and breathing is usually at fault. It is especially liable to occur at the age when mechanical reading is taught, and the speech

[1] Jahresbericht auf die Fortschritte u. Leistungen auf dem Gebiete der Hygiene, 1898. Supplement, p. 48.

processes long circuited from ear and mouth to eye and hand. It is favored by shyness and fatigue in the child, and by too great urgency on the part of the teacher, so that the child acquires a speech consciousness. Both are very contagious and with proper initial training could probably be very greatly reduced. Hartwell's valuable table [1] shows that averaging the six best German studies of 252,312 children, in all 1.12 per cent were stutterers, as against 0.77 per cent among Boston children and 1.57 per cent among Russians. Next to the age of second dentition, the onset of puberty is most susceptible to this form of nervous disturbance. He found the largest percentages in girls at seven, twelve, and sixteen, and in boys at eight, thirteen, and sixteen; and finding that these ages nearly corresponded with those of the highest specific intensity of life or immunity from death, he concluded that the irritability of the nervous system of which stuttering is an expression was bound up with the nutritive activity, which resisted lethal influences. He advocates special breathing exercises at this age.

Dr. Cullack[2] thinks many of the weaknesses and other eye troubles peculiar to puberty really originate in the sexual modifications of that period, especially in girls. Eye strain and retino-choroiditis, hemorrhage of the eye, etc., he describes as due to nature's seeking an outlet at this age which elsewhere is denied it or is found to be inadequate. These troubles he found are often removed when menstruation is normally established. Clouston, too, holds several visual neuroses to be essentially developmental neuroses.

The following table, adapted from Seggel,[3] who tested two or three times a year for sixteen years, is perhaps the best for German schools, and shows clearly the increased rate of myopia during adolescent years. Key on the other hand found that at fourteen and again at seventeen the increase of myopia was lessened. Other tables have shown no difference, so that on the whole we must infer that if the influence of puberty on near-sightedness is not yet conclusively established, a rather steady increase through the period of sexual maturation is certain.

---

[1] Rep. of Director of Physical Training. Boston, 1894, p. 69, *et seq.*

[2] The Eye at the Age of Puberty. Gaillard's Med. Jour., New York, beginning June, 1885.

[3] Eulenberg u. Bach. Schulgesundheitslehre, 1900, p. 669 and 771.

	Age.	Class.	Per cent of short-sighted.	Per cent increase.
Volksschule	6	1	2.8	...
	7	2	4.6	1.8
	8	3	7.8	3.2
	9	4	11.7	3.9
	10	5	12.1	0.4
	11	6	15.3	3.2
Gymnasia	12	I	17.0	1.7
	13	II	22.5	4.5
	14	III	29.7	7.2
	15	IV	36.0	6.3
	16	V	41.7	5.7
	17	VI	47.7	6.0
	18	VII	51.5	3.8
	19	VIII and IX (boys only)	68.0	16.5

Key gives the following statistics showing the age liability of Swedish girls to greensickness or chlorosis:

Age	7	8	9	10	11	12	13	14	15	16	17	18	19	20	21
Per cent of pupils having greensickness	18.8	15.4	18.3	23.8	31.9	32.7	39.7	38.2	33.3	40.2	41.4	40.6	39.6	48.0	63.6
Yearly increase in weight	2.0	7.5	4.2	5.5	5.5	8.8	8.2	11.5	9.0	66.2	6.6	3.7	2.4	0.6	?

Both Bunge and Marro found a slight excess of iron in the blood during early pubescent years, which they conjectured was nature's way of providing against the special liability to chlorosis and to anemia at this age.

Among the many miscellaneous nosological peculiarities of adolescence we may probably reckon increased liability to typhoid fever, Ziemsen's percentage being as follows: Between the ages of sixteen and twenty may be found 19 per cent of all cases; between twenty-one and thirty, 58 per cent; and between thirty-one and forty, 16 per cent. In malaria several writers have urged that tertian, quotidian, and other intermittent, periodic, and recurrent forms were more liable at and soon after puberty.

Berillon[1] concludes that onychophagia, or nail-biting, reaches its maximum frequency at about the age of greatest danger of masturbation.

Both Ireland[2] and Kind think that if idiots can remain in

[1] Monograph on the subject, 1894.

[2] Mental Affections of Childhood and Youth, 1898, p. 356.

schools for their benefit only four to five years, they will receive most profit between the ages of twelve to sixteen.. Some writers think this age prone to a type of cataleptic lethargy,[1] to simulation of diseases, and to many psychic contagions. Partridge [2] found that morbid blushing was prone to begin or to become greatly intensified at this age.

Dermal eruptions and muddy complexions, characteristics of several of the many skin diseases, are now common, especially with abnormalities of menstruation during the years of its first establishment.

While the suicide curve rises, there is also a new and offsetting horror of death not felt before. Clouston's "barking cough of puberty" has been often recognized by subsequent writers.[3]

Troubles that seem minor now may become grave later, and it is probable that this is the sprouting garden of many more chronic and hereditary troubles that become fatal later than is recognized; so that the germs of death are now taking root like tares among the forces of the budding vernal life; all this makes adolescence a process of assay and ordeal for the alloy of morbid predisposition. Now the robust often become delicate, or *vice versa*.

Liveing thinks megrim in girls has three periods of onset, each about equally liable, from seven to thirteen, at the dawn of puberty, and during adolescence.

Warner, whose very suggestive studies were made with singular disregard of age, with little apparent consideration of the work of other writers on related lines, and, I think, without a single indication that he had considered any work not written in English, found that of 100,000 London school children,[4] 9,777 had defects in development of various kinds and 8,323 were otherwise defective or sick, leaving only 81,900 without visible defect or not reported dull. Of all 10,355 showed nerve signs.

---

[1] See a valuable characterization by Rothmann and Nathanson in the Arch. f. Psychiatrie, 1899, pp. 283-319.

[2] Blushing. Ped. Sem., Apr., 1897, vol. 4, pp. 387-394.

[3] Neurosis of Development. 1891, p. 66.

[4] Report on Scientific Study of Mental and Physical Conditions of Childhood. London, 1895.

Warner found cases of developmental defect more frequent in males, but under the effects of their environment more apt to be harmful to girls than to boys. The former were more liable to acquire nerve disorders, mental dulness, and low nutrition.

Combe thought girls more prone to eye defects than boys in the proportion of twenty-one to twenty-seven, and about seven per cent more so in the city than in the country.

Most determinations of the time either actually given or needed for sleep at different ages show, as we saw, a decline near puberty, and most of our returns show that for a time sleep was at first restless and perturbed and afterward settled into a state described as better or worse, as if there were a new adjustment or balance struck between the processes of restoration and of expenditure. The sexual organs now often make themselves felt in dreams of a new character, and the advent of this new function is sometimes first announced in sleep. Greenwood thinks the function of dreams is to enlarge our imaginative knowledge of the fields of life, and Manacéine thinks that where mental development is not highly advanced dreams are more likely to be racial rather than personal. Spitta, Radistock, De Santis, and others have suggested that some diseases make their first symptomatic advent into consciousness in dream life, and many have held that some "nocturnal syndrome" may be the bud of a second personality; that dream life may enforce or check tendencies in the waking consciousness; that the latter is often brightened, darkened, predisposed, or rendered averse to many things by reason of the psychic activities of sleep; or that dreaming is, in Wundt's phrase, a "normal temporary insanity," and may even affect the form of permanent insanity if the latter come later. The spontaneous dreams not due to the momentum of waking life are often thought to have more or less value as a revelation of individual character.

However all this may be, I am convinced that the dawn of adolescence is marked by much emotional intensification of dream life, and that at no age is its influence so important upon the moods and dispositions of waking consciousness. Somnambulism often first appears at this age and trancoidal states of inner absorption midway between sleeping and waking are now most frequent. The new emotional life seems if not to create and project, at least to take command of mental imagery and association, and indeed this may be a part of nature's method of making the intellectual sphere better fit that of instincts. In some of our cases, dreams are so intense as to be one cause of the chronic fatigue and even morning tire common in the teens. Sometimes young people wake with the soul suffused with a sense of nameless and unaccountable rapture from nearly or quite forgotten dreams, or perhaps with a new and strong predisposition toward some person of the other sex unattractive before, which lingers hours and perhaps days before it fades. These presentiments and previsions of love, which often first arise spontaneously and naturally in sleep, seem to illustrate the old trope that the stars of other and larger systems come out best when the sun of our own personal consciousness has set. Indeed in the reverie and day dreaming common at this stage, when the soul transcends its individual limitations and expatiates over the whole field of humanity, past, present, or future, it is perhaps quite as near the world of our habitual, but generally unremembered dreams, as it is to the waking world of memory. In the new horizon now opening to the mind, unconscious cerebration generally has a larger rôle and for a time is more uncontrolled by the consciousness, over into which it shades by imperceptible gradations. Many psychic processes are so absorbing as to be almost a narcosis akin to the dreamy states that Crichton-Browne characterizes, so that if at first the soul falls to sleep with a great drop from waking life, the two states are later brought into manifold *rapport* and perhaps linked into unity.

Warner thinks the hours of work and sleep should be as follows:

Age.	Hours of work per week.	Hours of sleep per night.
Between 8–9	15	12
" 8–10	20	11½
" 10–11	25	11
" 11–12	30	10½
" 12–14	35	10
" 14–15	40	9½
" 15–17	45	9
" 17–19	50	8½

Our returns show great reason for believing that near the dawn of sexual life there is not only a new balance struck between the processes of repair and anabolism and those of katabolic expenditure of energy, but that there is a marked tendency to irregularities in sleep. Sometimes a sense of fatigue, lassitude, and sleepiness, rarely narcoleptic, may supervene, and the time of actual sleep for days, weeks, or greater periods be prolonged, but wakeful tendencies and special aversions to retire and to sleep follow and alternate. Some rebel at this period against the necessity of losing so much time from the life of active consciousness, dread night, and rejoice every morning on waking up that they have a long day before sleep is again imperative. There are almost always spells of sitting up late and sometimes, though far more rarely, of preposterously early rising to utilize the maximum of time. Normal adolescent boys especially wish to explore night out-of-doors, to rove about perhaps with adventurous or romantic thoughts, and on moonlight nights particularly there is a pathos about the necessity of rest. A part of this suggests an atavistic recrudescence of what may have been in primitive man the need of watchfulness, the custom of predatory adventures or amatory excursions of ancient courtships by night, still reverberating in the attenuated form of periods of nocturnal restlessness. The child's fever of early candle-light is metamorphosed by puberty into the youth's impulse to use darkness as a motive of abandon and license, as if the responsibilities of the day could be dispensed with by night in roving nocturns of riotous freedom analogous to the start on falling to sleep, due to the sudden removal of the habitual cerebral repression upon the lower spinal and midbrain centers. This passion to occasionally be out or to work late nights shades down the psycho-physical scale into increased dream activity and power to work evenings. The wonted irregularity of the diurnal rhythm, no matter how well established before, is now like every other function for a time disturbed.[1]

Passing now to the mental and nervous troubles, the profound effect of adolescence in producing disturbances of the

[1] See Reactions to Light and Darkness, by G. S. Hall and T. Smith. Am. Jour. of Psy., Jan. 1903, pp. 21–83.

nervous system and of the mind is recognized in many a custom and belief of savages, and has been recorded through the entire history of medicine. Hippocrates describes a girl who at the dawn of pubescence saw a vision, leaped and tried to throw herself into a well and then to hang herself, deeming death more desirable than life. Such cases in his day dedicated fine articles of cloth to the goddess Diana, usually on the advice of soothsayers. The Arab physicians noted the predisposition of pubescents to fall into religious melancholy. The Middle Ages abounded in ecstatics and *convulsionaires*, which religious leaders honored and knew well how to utilize, so great was the popular superstition and reverence for them. In the great delusions which Hecker, McKay, and others have described, in the children's crusade in witchcraft, stigmatization, animal magnetism, the dancing and sweating manias, trance, lycanthropy, demonology, and especially in revivals and other great religious movements, and in the general conceptions of insanity down into the present century, we detect disposition, humors, enthusiasm, and fanaticism, St. Medardisms, frenzies, and calentures, and sometimes somatic symptoms which were clearly marked with pubic and adolescent features, without the need of assuming that the world was in a more juvenile stage than now. It was, however, reserved for recent decennia to make these phenomena objects of scientific investigation, and although great progress has been made there are still many observations that will grow clear only with advancing knowledge of the more nearly normal metamorphoses of this stage of life. It is striking to note the cases where the predispositions peculiar to this age exist in greatly magnified form. Many of the most successful malingerers, simulators, and even dissimulators, that often defy both judicial and medical experts; the most preposterous impostors famous in history, from Alexander of Abonuteichos[1] to modern spirit mediums; the great seeresses from Joan of Arc to Katherine Emreich, who was spontaneously marked with the sacred stigmata of the cross, if we may accept the medical opinion on which Gabriel Max based his idealization of her in a painting as the "ecstatic virgin"; telepathic girls, like the Creery sisters, who for years misled the best members of the English Society of Psychic

[1] Zeller. Vortr. u. Abh. II., pp. 154–188.

Research; the most dithyrambic of the boy preachers; the visionaries who communicate most familiarly with the other world and its denizens; patients that puzzle the doctors with weird new symptoms and often victimize them, as the recent history of hypnotism and hystero-epilepsy illustrates in an anthology of striking cases—all these have been adolescents in whom the tendencies and characteristics normal to this age are here seen only in persistent or exaggerated forms.[1]

Rich as is the story of many of the early religious sects and of the great delusions and superstitions of the Middle Ages, fascinating as are several periods and departments of the history of medicine as told in Sprengel's monumental volumes, and copious as are the illustrations of these phenomena in a great science yet to be developed which I may call the pathology of religion, the careful and fruitful study of ephebic psychosis is of recent date.

Psychoses and neuroses abound in early adolescent years more than at any other period of life. This causes great emotional strain, which some have described as a kind of repressed insanity that is nevertheless normal at this period. To keep down morbid impulses is often a very difficult matter in this age of stress. There is an intense antagonism betwen egoistic and racial motives. One writer [2] would almost have us believe that the relative reduction of the individual involves a latentizing of energy which builds up the great organs involved in reproduction which are not now used but only prepared for the future. This expenditure of energy is not immediate, but the race ought to carry the day and accumulate energy not immediately spent. On this view pubescence to-day probably involves great waste of energy that should be stored up into active channels, and hence a tendency toward slow progressive race failure. This is also the most plastic period of life as seen in the very wide differentiation of size, brightness, dulness, etc. Thus in a sense the child is not completely born until he has

[1] Sorcellerie, Magnétisme, etc., par Paul Regnard. Paris, 1887. Das Wahnsinn in den vier letzen Jahrhunderten. Tr. from Calmeil by Dr. R. Leusbuscher. Halle, 1898. See also Gurney's Phantasms of the Living. Early Proceedings of the English Psychic Research Society. Lourdes, Anon. Paris, 1894. Delbrück: Pathologische Lüge und Schwindler. 1891. Hecker: Epidemics of the Middle Ages.

[2] W. S. Christopher: Adolescence from the Physical Standpoint. Trans. of the Ill. Soc. for Child Study. July, 1902, p. 196 *et seq.*

achieved this great revolution and established a law of division between stored and used energy.

In 1838 Esquirol and Morel discussed whether the weak-mindedness that sometimes supervenes in youth was acquired or constitutional; this condition Pinel had noticed in 1809. Schneider, in his voluminous discussion of the neuralgias of puberty in 1842, declared that the involutions which belong to old age might occur earlier, but in a long article of Hecker's [1] in 1871, on the basis of fourteen cases in his own asylum at Görlitz, we have the first description of a mental disease peculiar to adolescence, for which he proposed the name hebephrenia, or the insanity of puberty. He assumed that in a disease so mild, relatively few cases needed asylum treatment, and those few are seen there only in the later stages. As the symptoms are so protean, it was not strange that its features were not very exactly defined or that its existence as a morbid entity especially in other lands was regarded as one of the most questionable products of the German school of clinicians. Hecker conceived it as a psychic crippling that tended strongly to eventuate in some degree of imbecility, but in other respects he found it hard to distinguish between what was general in its nosology and what was due to individual difference of character. Moreover, the symptoms are not stationary, but all rapidly progressive toward either recovery, or, more commonly, to psychic decay. He sought to connect its abnormal manifestations with the ordinary phenomena of the *Flegel* or *Lummeljahre* of boys and the *Backfisch* age of girls with its fanaticism, romanticizing, overtension, and superlativeness. At first there was crass rawness, angularity of thought and movement and a dissociation that threatened the integrity of the ego, and later, at the age of eighteen or nineteen, came a tendency to collect and concentrate. The strife of opposite moods leads to dysthymia or else to a passion for simulation, which is the easiest form of the coexistence of two different states.

In another epoch-making work, which has ever since and especially in the last few years been much discussed by German clinicians, Kahlbaum [2] described a symptom group which he

[1] Virchow's Archiv, vol. 53, p. 394.

[2] Klin, Abhand. Ueber psych.—Krankh. Heft I. Berlin, 1874.

named catatonia, or the insanity of tension, and illustrated its various phases by twenty-six cases. He distinguished it from atonic melancholy, some phases of which resemble it, in that the depressive is prone to be followed by an excited stage, and there is danger of terminal psychic impairment. Sometimes thought stagnates, or there is a rapid flux of ideas, incessant repetitions, use of diminutives, patheticism, a strained intellectual effort, religious exaltation, etc. He thought it related to the preaching mania found among the *convulsionaircs* described by Culmeil, Leubuscher, and Jessen, and found it most common among the children of teachers, and often associated with sexual abnormalities; he also thought that it was most frequent from the dawn of puberty to early middle life, and that heredity was a less dominant influence in its causation than in most other forms of psycho-neural disease. The characteristic features of pronounced cases are an immobility that resists efforts to produce passive movements and the state of waxy flexibility characteristic of catalepsy. In this state, repetition of movements, or in the acute form, of words often occurs, and monotony or motor inhibition is very typical.

For years, while alienists often referred to the subject, little additions were made to the knowledge of these psychoses. In 1880 Fick [1] urged that hebephrenia is a disease of degeneration and that all affected by it are more or less idiotic. It may be latent during infancy and crop out only when more activity is demanded. The process of renewal of the ego that then takes place is the first serious strain to which the psychophysical organism is subjected. It differs from other mental diseases, all of which may occur at this age, in being an arrest of development caused by a degenerative basis, and we may conclude that wherever there is hereditary mental defect, hebephrenia is the most common of all psychic diseases. Save in the absence of characteristic cramp it differs little from catatonia and verbigeration. Favorite special phrases, obstinate silence, peculiar attitude, refusal of food are common to both; but the latter is often curable, the former is almost hopeless.

[1] Beiträge zür Kentniss des Jugendirreseins. Allg. Zeits. f. Psychiatrie, 1880, p. 490–520.

During the tumult of the first stages of puberty, which often threatens decomposition of the personality, and before the new orientation, the psycho-physic organism is peculiarly sensitive. The critical faculties are often hardly able to supply reductives of extravagant impulses or of visions, etc. Ideas flow rapidly but are very superficial, and so great is the vulnerability, that outside influences which would be ordinarily healthful, may break up the slow progress toward reorganization and leave their mark in exaggerated religiosity, or paranœic symptoms and perversions of many kinds. Especially in natures of morbid heredity, the soul seems to lapse to a lower plane and ordinary prudence and judgment are superseded. Clouston said that if fifty such individuals were on a savage island, they would not sow or reap and would die of hunger.

Seppelli [1] found that out of 6,000 insane only 400 cases, or less than seven per cent, became so between twelve and twenty-two years of age. For these he laid great stress upon heredity, particularly from the mother, and also upon precocious mental work and emotional strain. He also found that melancholia was rarer than mania, but that such cases frequently took on a circular and periodic character, and easily passed to stupor or even dementia. There were frequent signs of degeneration, perversions of the ethical sentiments, some cases of hysterical and moral insanity, but none of Kahlbaum's hebephrenia.

Hammond [2] thought puberty a more efficient cause of insanity in girls than in boys. While the latter have no sudden physical sign like menstruation to mark the advent of puberty, he judged that delayed spontaneous emissions in rare cases may be like a delayed first period in girls, a cause of mental alienation. He opined "reasoning mania" to be most common in boys of this age. The subject is ready with specious excuses for bad conduct. He runs away, is spied on, thinks every woman is in love with him. Emminghaus [3] held that hereditary forms of insanity most frequently develop between beginning puberty and the twentieth year; he said that girls

---

[1] Della psicosi della puberta. Atti del V. Congresso della Soc. Fren. 1886, p. 321.

[2] Treatise on Insanity, p. 112 *et seq.*

[3] Psycho-pathology, p. 321, also p. 307.

inherit it most often, and that while they are most commonly affected by the insanity of the mother, they are more intensely influenced by it in the father than are boys. In girls he thinks melancholy more common and that it easily develops under proper conditions into acute nostalgia, and religious and moral perversity. Maudsley[1] described as a common trait of this period the craving of something objective to attach to, which inclines the mind to idealize unfit persons, or even to create imaginary ones. Girls are most prone to it because the affective overtops the intellectual life. Sex organs are larger and more dominant, and woman's range of activity is more limited, society insists on more conventionalities and restrictions, and their periodicity constantly obtrudes this part of their natures. Pertness, self-conceit, and caprice are largely automatic, so that they are only "involuntary wilful." Dr. Campbell Clark[2] agrees with Trousseau that chlorosis is a nervous disease, originating at puberty, that anemia and menstrual irregularities are sequential to it, and that it colors nearly all the insanities of early womanhood, and distinctly diminishes sexual feeling. Regis and Berkhan thought pubertal insanity more often depressive than maniacal, and Levinstein thinks puberty a frequent cause of melancholy in females, and that at this period and in senescence the latter sex predominates, while in advanced age both are equally liable. Blanford and Clouston held mania far more common at puberty than melancholy.

Out of 1,800 insane, Clouston[3] found 230 between fourteen and twenty-five years of age; 49 between eighteen and twenty; 157 between twenty-one and twenty-five years of age. Fink[4] reported that of 1,892 inmates of the Wurzburg Hospital 228 were under twenty-nine, 12.5 per cent males and 11.5 per cent females. Cullerre[5] found in France that 4.7 per cent of all were between fourteen and twenty, and 8.8 per cent between twenty and twenty-five. Hagen's[6] figures on the age of the first attack of insanity were as follows:

[1] Pathology of Mind, p. 449.

[2] Journal of Mental Science, 1888, p. 385.

[3] Alienist and Neurologist, 1892. Quoted from Wille, pp. 403-405.

[4] Beiträge zür Kentniss des Jugendirreseins, Bd. 2.

[5] Traité pratique, Paris, 1890.

[6] Psychiat Untersuchungen, 1876.

Inmates.	16 Males.	11 Females.	Total, 27.
To 15	25	7	32
16–20	79	90	169
21–25	115	100	215
26–30	126	105	271
31–35	114	106	270
36–40	132	64	196

All of these tables show a marked increase during puberty. The danger is always more grave if the accented physical symptoms are severe, as bodily weakness, palpitation, headache, chorea, irregular menstruation. Females are on the whole more disposed than men because the changes are greater and because nutritive complications like anemia and chorea are more common. The great effect of heredity is shown by Hagen, who estimates that of cases inheriting mental abnormalities forty-two per cent of all first occur between sixteen and twenty. Savage holds that while psychoses are readily transmitted, if those who inherit them reach puberty safely they are more likely to recover than those attacked for the first time at this age without heredity. Too strict or too negligent education before the age of personal responsibility, overwork with the brain, which tends to overlabile equilibrium, are as bad for the cultivated as abnormalities of nutrition are for the lower classes, and are also prominent causes. The state of overirritability of brain often produced by high pressure can weaken all bodily functions and arrest growth. Matusch[1] holds that grave symptoms at puberty portend serious and perhaps similar complications at senescence. Regis thinks that puberty is less dangerous in girls, because when once regularly established menstruation has a curative effect that makes distinctly for sanity. Circular and periodic psychoses usually begin in these years, and Wille thinks seventy per cent and Clouston, sixty-six per cent recover. Brosius urges that these pubertal abnormalities may mark a fortunate episode during which earlier hindrances to psychic development may be obviated. Changes may be advantageous and permanent. Many of these psychoses are very fugitive and the recuperative power is greater than in later life.

[1] All. Zeit. f. Psych. Bd. 46.

A good estimate of age liability was lately compiled on a basis of 116 men and 107 women as follows:[1]

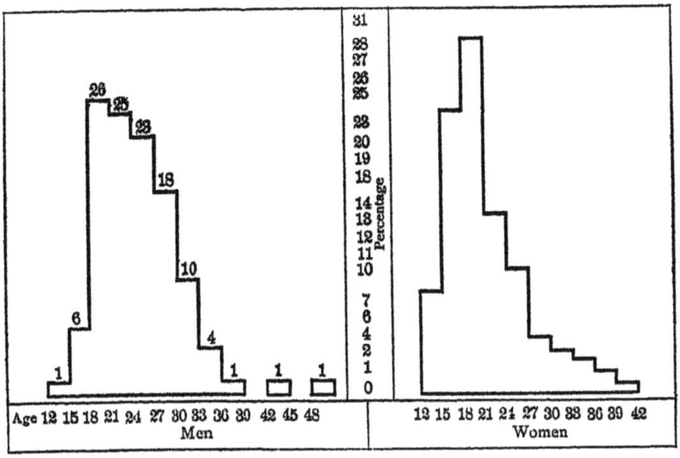

Schüle,[2] on the other hand, not only doubts the existence of this disease, but still more that of a katatonic motility neurosis and would preserve the adjective form of the word as a collective or heuristic term for many kinds of symptoms of motor stimulus and inhibition. It also lacks a psychic character of its own such as, e. g., epilepsy, hysteria, etc., have, from which other troubles can be clearly distinguished.

Marro[3] tabulated the age of the first appearance of insanity in 1,649 males and 1,257 females in the asylum at Turin during the decennium 1886–'95, and presents his results in the table on p. 273, in which, however, he included idiots and cretins, and all forms of arrested or perverted development. The age of most rapid increase is from about sixteen to twenty, and at twenty-five the age of greatest liability is already passed.

Some special forms of insanity are particularly prominent at this age. The epileptic neurosis tends to discharges of explosive or fulminating violence, which by undue forcing of

[1] Gustav Aschaffenburg: Die Katatoniefrage. Allg. Zeits. f. Psychiatrie, 1897, p. 1021.

[2] Zur Katatonie-Frage. Ibid, pp. 512–552. See also Nolan, who accepts Aschaffenburg. Jour. of Mental Science, Oct., 1892, p. 531.

[3] La Puberta, p. 233.

nascent nerve tracts do great damage to unstable nerve systems. In its grave forms it is a kind of universal spasm and much depends on the momentum of the discharge, whether it originates in the higher areas and begins with loss of consciousness, or whether it begins in more basal and reflex centers and spreads upward to these later. There are, therefore, as many epilepsies as there are seats of the difficulty, and in its milder forms it shades down to a yawn, hiccough, sneeze, momentary shudder, a faint lapse of consciousness seen in *petit mal,* etc. In the preparoxysmal stage there are various symptoms—gloom,

restlessness, dread, confusion, delusion, and just before the fit comes various auræ or warnings, the nature of which is of great significance. There may be flashes of light, subjective sensations of touch, taste, smell, or hearing, or of organic life. After the convulsion there is a stage of exhaustion and confusion, and hysterical symptoms are often complicated throughout. In the epileptic state instincts, impulses, or automatic acts, often complicated, may appear without full consciousness in subsequent memory, and this makes the medico-legal relationships of the disease difficult. Scientifically, epilepsy is one of the most interesting and instructive of diseases, still more so as it is easy to feign.[1]

Of fifty-eight cases of epilepsy observed by Sieveking,[2] forty were first developed before the age of twenty-one, and he

[1] For a good characterization of this state, see Bevan Lewis's Text-Book of Mental Diseases, p. 221.

[2] On Epilepsy, etc. London, 1858, p. 92.

says that it appears that "the greatest proclivity to epilepsy is to be found in the period of puberty, a fact upon which there is scarcely any difference of opinion among writers," although the age of greatest mortality from this cause comes a little later. Reynolds,[1] from his own and other cases, concluded that "the period of first arriving at puberty is in regard to age the most powerful predisposing condition to epilepsy"; that the proclivity of females before ten was slightly greater than males; that from ten to twenty there was little difference; that after twenty-one nearly four times as many males as females were attacked; and that although no age is exempt, the probability of becoming epileptic is less each decennial after twenty. J. Langdon-Down[2] quotes approvingly West's conclusion, that "it is usually with development of the sexual system that hysteria shows itself," and Trowbridge[3] thinks it often closely associated with chorea.

Of 1,288 cases collected by nine French authorities, 486 begin between the tenth and twentieth years. Gowers's 1,450 cases were distributed as follows:[4]

Under 10	422	30–39	87
10–20	665	40–49	31
20–29	224	(21 cases later.)	

Between ten and twenty nearly one-half of the total number of cases or 46 per cent occurred. More specifically these cases when tabulated for each year show that those appearing the first year are 5½ per cent of the whole, that the number falls at three, and reaches a minimum at five. "From this there is a considerable rise at seven, the commencement of the second dentition, then a fall at eight, and from this a maximum is reached at fifteen and sixteen, at each of which 84 cases or 5¾ per cent of the total number occur. From this period we have a rapid fall to twenty-one, when only 22 per cent of the whole occurred," and from here on there is a general decline. The maximum number for males is at thirteen, and for females at sixteen. In the second decade the females are 18 per cent and

[1] Epilepsy: its Symptoms, Treatment, etc. London, 1861, p. 126 *et seq.*

[2] On some of the Mental Affections of Childhood and Youth. London, 1887.

[3] Relations between Chorea and Epilepsy, Alienist and Neurologist, Jan., 1892, p. 45.

[4] A. M. Hamilton. Pepper's System of Medicine. p. 470.

in the third 12 per cent in excess of the males. The maximum of hereditary cases occurred one year earlier than that for non-hereditary cases. The percentage of hereditary cases distinctly declines with age. The hysteroid or coördinated form of the convulsions is greater at every age for females. With them this form reaches its maximum in the second decade and after adolescence it is about twice as frequent. Cases traceable to exciting causes are most frequent in males after ten, and of these causes fright, excitement, and anxiety are most common and mostly occur early in life, while the prospect of cure is somewhat better in cases that commence under ten than in those that commence between ten and twenty. Those beginning under twenty are considerably less curable than those beginning later.[1]

Donath [2] seeks to establish an epileptic impulse to wander off, posiomania, and some of his most interesting cases were adolescents. A fourteen-year-old boy started off, in an epileptic state, seven times in three years to make long journeys, while a less impulsive girl of nineteen took money and made other preparations for such trips. Hypnosis recalled the normal consciousness. Dénommé [3] has given the literature of such cases.

Bruns holds that while in young children hysteria is about as frequent among boys as girls, that " the nearer puberty approaches the more girls preponderate." [4] The childish form of hysteria is most common between seven and fourteen. That it is not a disease of overculture, he thinks proved because the most severe cases are found in country children. This has especially been the case in the epileptoid and also in the contagious forms. In its causation, most writers, and especially those of the Charcot school, have perhaps assigned too predominant a rôle to heredity both for its direct and homologous forms. However, as Clouston thinks, much depends on

---

[1] Gower's Epilepsy, pp. 13, 15, 244.

[2] Der epileptische Wandertrieb. Arch. f. Psychiatrie, 1899.

[3] Des impulsions morbides à la déambulation au point de vue médico-légal. Lyon, 1893.

[4] Die Hysteria im Kindesalter. Samml. zwangloser Abh. der Nerven und Geisteskrankheiten. 1897, vol., p. 26.

whether we "go on Charcot's lines and look out for local anesthesias and irregular motor symptoms chiefly, or take in perverted conduct and character or diminished control," abnormal feelings, etc. At or soon after puberty its character becomes more distinguishable for chorea, its provocations change in both kind and degree, and hypnotism is less helpful.

The literature and history on early symptoms of hysteria is well digested up to 1880 by Smidt[1] and Emminghaus[2] emphasizes its slight and transient forms and its relations to epilepsy and catalepsy, chorea, etc. Moreau,[3] on the other hand, ascribes little influence to first menstruation, while Klein out of fifty-eight hysterical children, found all between ten and fifteen.

The age distribution of first attacks of hysteria by the two best French authorities is as follows:

	Landouzy.	Briquet.
Under 10	4	66
10–15	48	98
15–20	105	140
20–25	80	71
25–30	40	24
30–35	38	9
35–40	15	9

In a recent study of the dreams of hysterics and epileptics, De Santis found that those of the former were most frequently of pain, next of fear, and were less often erotic. Dreams of large animals predominate, while in alcoholism those of tiny animals or microzooscopic dreams were most frequent. With his epileptics, who are mostly men, the dreams are usually brief and simple as opposed to the complex and romantic character of those of the hysterical patients. At bottom both are regarded as determined by sex, which often rises to great prominence in dream life at puberty.

Janet finds a peculiar cerebral exhaustion frequent at puberty, which he describes as "a special moral weakness consisting in the lack of power on the part of the feeble subject to gather and condense his psychological phenomena and assimi-

[1] Arch. f. Kindeskrankheiten. N. S. Vol. 15, p. 1 *et seq.*

[2] Die Psychischen Störungen des Kindesalters. 1887, p. 276 *et seq.*

[3] Das Irrsinn im Kindesalter. 1889, p. 291.

late them to his personality." He summarizes his views as follows: "There is, above all, an age which in this respect is particularly critical—the age of puberty. We speak here not of physical puberty, which has, however, a great influence, but of a state which comes a little later and which might justly be called moral puberty. It is an age slightly variable according to countries and surroundings, when all the greatest problems of life present themselves simultaneously; the choice of a career and the anxiety about making a living; all the problems of love, and for some the religious problems. These are preoccupations which invade the mind of young people and completely absorb their feeble power of thought. These thousand influences manifest a psychological insufficiency which remains latent during the less difficult periods. In a mind predisposed by hereditary influences, this psychological insufficiency develops, takes a special form, and presently manifests itself by an ensemble of symptoms which we call hysteria." [1] Although the primitive meaning of the word hysteria has much changed, he would preserve the word, because "it has so great and so beautiful a history." He conceives it as mental diseases of brain fag characterized by reduced nutrition and various moral symptoms, especially weakened synthesis, a contracted field of consciousness, and a tendency to complete and permanent division of personality. This weakened synthesis favors the development of parasitic ideas which manifest themselves in many forms, sometimes apparently only physical.

Janet finds that obsessions and psychasthenias manifest themselves most frequently between sixteen and twenty, although his predecessors in these statistics found that the years from eleven to fifteen were most liable. All authors admit the enormous influence of puberty upon all troubles of this class. Du Saulle held that those who were hereditarily predisposed could not go through puberty without grave dangers. Falret held that very frequently something like a bifurcation then took place, some suffering arrest and tending toward debility, and another class toward reasoning manias and phobias. Baillarger declared that doubting mania almost always made its *début* at the epoch of puberty. Janet adds that the development of the monthly periods with the female is often marked by phobias

[1] The Mental State of Hystericals, by Pierre Janet. N. Y., 1901, p. 526.

and obsessions.[1] Many young people at this age lose courage, live as if a veil were spread over their entire personality, grow indifferent, apathetic, easily fatigued, and agitated. Some of Janet's cases show very clearly the dangers either of precocity or of unwonted delay of puberty. In the former case there is sometimes terror at the new physical developments peculiar to this age, attempts to obliterate every trace of them and aversion to every thought of marriage, while in cases of abnormal retardation, agitation and anxiety predominate.

Sexual psychoses are plainly coming to play a greatly increased rôle in the psychology of the present and the future. They imply unique coördination between the cerebrospinal and the sympathetic system, and involve both in all their interrelations as do no other phenomena, are especially prominent in the sexual epochs of adolescence, marriage, menopause, etc., and are rejustifying the lately suspected appropriateness of the etymology of the term hysteria. The work of Gattel, Mobius, Breuer, Freud, Scott, Ellis, Moll, Geddes, and many others show the wide irradiation of this function into normal and abnormal psychic life. Although we can not agree with Mobius that all hysteria is of ideational origin, much of it doubtless is, and much depends upon the balance between overexcitation and repression of sexual functions. Far more than has hitherto been suspected depends upon the maintenance of normal tension in this sphere, and nothing is so vicarious, protean, and polymorphic in its expressions. Psychic lesions here readily become physical lesions, and *vice versa*. Mental pain becomes acute and local neuralgia, moral disgust becomes nausea, anxiety becomes contraction or cramp if shunted downward, and so through a long list of psycho-physic kinetic equivalents which with all their wealth of symbolism is yet to be fully worked out. Such metamorphoses constitute the mystery of the domestic demon of hysteria, and account for many adolescent symptoms.

Strong and sudden impressions amounting to psychic lesions or traumata, especially in women, particularly in this instable period, and above all in the sex sphere, are thus liable to entail long, very complex, and obscure results. Prompt, normal,

[1] Les Obsessions et la Psychasthénie, par P. Janet. Vol. 1, p. 613. See also Vol. 2, by F. Raymond and P. Janet, Paris, 1903, pp. 33, 253, 370, 470.

and adequate reactions to such experiences there is now great reason to believe are often necessary to prevent such morbid transformation. Excessive stimuli must be reacted on and their effects must stream out in some normal channel, or else they will become seated and act as a foreign body with long persistence and transference, and gradually, when perhaps lapsed almost beyond the reach of recall, accrete into a subconscious, nascent, alien kind of personality, subcharged it may be with emotional and motor intensity. At this stage they may break out in many kinds of anomalous discharges of accumulated morbidities of a hysteroid or epileptoid nature, while the ideational factors are more or less hidden from consciousness and beyond volitional control. Excessive repression may arouse a "*Gegenwille*" when control is fatigued, so that the patient does impulsively or imperatively the exact opposite of what is willed.

It is upon this general conception that an interesting theory and cure has been developed.[1] Hysterical patients are questioned as to the original cause of their troubles, and where it is more or less forgotten, light hypnosis is evoked till they can live over again and with the greatest detail and emotional intensity all the circumstances of the inception of their troubles, and state it or act it out with dramatic fervor. This "talking cure" opens a normal outlet of a confessional sort, although with no priestly absolution, and in many cases completely restores from hysteria, even though it be pronounced and has endured for years. The nature of these psychic causes (and in all but one of the cases reported it is a sexual shock) is such as to preclude reaction or confessing, and abnormal susceptibility, and perhaps fright, causes a changed consciousness with a highly affective content. Suppression makes it more deeply seated, involves perhaps temporary local paralysis, convulsions, or anesthesia in some other sphere, while the new symptoms and lapse of time before the new effects dissociate them from this cause, make them perhaps migratory disturbances appearing in different spheres successively, or else they accrete into sensor-motor groups and unfold as another submerged consciousness. In order to pluck out these raised sorrows it is necessary on this theory to reproduce their *status nascendi* with hallucinating

[1] Studien ueber Hysterie. Dr. I. Breuer und S. Freud. Wien, 1895.

clearness and vividness, and to give vent and outlet through speech and natural gesture, inducing trancoidal states if questionings fail, for language may be an adequate reflex. Expression relieves the tension and reestablishes poise and peace.

Whether as a therapeutic theory this be more or less partial, it is highly suggestive of the need at adolescence, when all the adjustments between sex and mentation are mobilized, of shelter from all forms of shock that are so liable and may be so disastrous, and of the need of wise mentors and advisers whose character invites the fullest confidence to forefend the dangers of a too cryptogamic development that in our civilization are so many and great. What part of the intensity of pubescent years, of its occasional proneness to confessionism and secrecies, of its frequent eccentricities and anomalous acts, is nature's effort to relieve strains of this sort, and how many of its reticences aggregate the evils of excessive repression, we do not know, but there is great reason to look to sex for the key to far more of phenomena of both body and soul at this as at other periods of life, than we had hitherto dreamed of in our philosophy.

Sidis, White, and Parker have described some exquisite symptoms which are most frequent at this age, the importance of which, unlike Janet, they do not adequately appreciate. Some of Sidis's work, nevertheless, is suggestive and important here. Especially is this true of the great stress he lays upon "reassociation or synthesis and dissociated symptoms or groups in the active, personal consciousness," and this synthesis which he is able to effect by hypnosis is therapeutic. He also rightly claims that functional psychoses and insanities, especially where disaggregation has not gone too far, should be more carefully studied by psychopathologists. He imagines dissociations somehow correlated with disaggregation of the neuron system in a way hardly consistent with the very timely precautions of

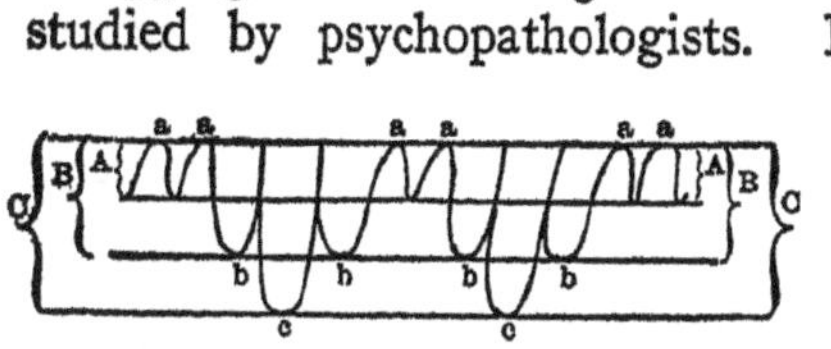

J. V. Kries,[1] concerning inferences either way between psychic processes and neural structure or function. Pedagogically helpful, nevertheless, is his diagram illustrating the new rela-

[1] Ueber die materiellen Grundlagen der Bewusstseinserscheinungen. Tübingen, 1901, p. 54.

tions between consciousness and the various subconscious strata, which are so peculiarly liable to occur at this age.

Here the waves on the upper line *a a* may stand for the usual stream of consciousness. The waves *b b* illustrate eruption into the first lower, and the waves *c c* into the second lower stratum. Thus *a b c b a* would represent a psychopathic cycle. The second, third, and fourth horizontal lines would represent various thresholds. If the *b* waves were omitted and the third stratum reached by leaping the second, we should have the germs of a dual personality. This, as Sidis adds, is analogous to what we find in biology, where a species is developed by eliminating intermediary variations and the survival of the last link of the series after the missing ones are gone. The above figure is reproduced here, however, chiefly to illustrate something quite different, viz., the tendency at adolescence to what may be called transliminal modes of psychic action. The horizontal lines, representing thresholds, might be multiplied, we know not how far, and new thought plexuses, which run up and down what was before a pretty well fixed series of limitations, may even become habitual, upper levels being submerged and lower ones denuded, so that psychic adolescence might be conceived as the indefinite distortion of these line levels and the gradual establishment of very different ones, so that what were at first waves illustrating dips deep down into unconsciousness become shorter waves of the *a a* form.[1]

Down [2] says "as puberty approaches attacks of mental aberration assume a special character; there is frequently unnatural introspection and a critical hyperconscientiousness becomes prominent." He describes five good and studious children who from eleven to thirteen became moody; had conscientious scruples as to their motives; could never make positive statements; grew anxious lest they might not have conveyed the precise idea intended; became confused or anxious about moral standards, and detailed things in a non-sequential way. One boy was troubled when he saw a dirty beggar, man or boy, lest he should contaminate his mother by thinking of her immediately afterward. All these mental disquietudes, he says,

[1] Psychopathological Researches, by Boris Sidis. 1902. Chapter IV. The Psychogenetic Law.

[2] Mental Affections of Childhood and Youth. London, 1887, p. 93 *et seq.*

are increased if there is any sexual deviation. Destructive energies are vented; there is a passion for creating astonishment and consternation by mischief, great cleverness in concealing delinquencies by lies, no natural affection and no conscience; yet even these cases after the wrench of these years of transition is passed often settle down to respectable and tolerably useful lives. Some are "idiot savants" and draw, paint, reckon, remember preternaturally well, but they may also have a passion for theft or setting fires, are cruel and have various malformations. Most standard writers like Ireland, Seguin, Warner, Voisin, Sollier, Henderson, and many others, who treat of mental defects in the young ignore puberty.

Arno Fuchs[1] well urges that our conceptions of mentally and morally defective youth are obscured and confused because writers have so generally failed to distinguish between the pre- and the post-pubertal age. He says that while the stadium of puberty is revolutionary for the normal persons, it is still more so for defectives. "Idiots animalize, imbeciles become violent, egoistic, coarse, and vulgar, and the weak-minded grow unsettled in their moral feelings and are without resistance to sensations that now erupt within them." Abnormal children often sink in the new sphere of sexual feeling or, if not this, emerge from the pubertal storms that rage through their inner being with profoundly changed characters. Thus descriptions and treatment, valid on one side of this line, are invalid on the other side of it, and this painstaking, judicious, and unusually competent writer expressly limits himself to the earlier period and insists that both his admirable descriptions of individual cases and his methods of treatment have no application to the pubertal and subsequent stage of development. In this he sets a most suggestive example for pedagogues, as well as for experts in this field, who should learn to profit by it.

When in 1828 Kaspar Hauser mysteriously appeared at the Nuremberg gate, a well formed and featured defective in the teens, it was a challenge to German savants to explain him. He was no idiot with phenomenal memory, no prodigy in arithmetic or music, no *homo sapiens ferus*, did not slaver or

[1] Schwachsinnige Kinder. Gütersloh, 1899, p. 298.

ruminate, was fairly well nourished, had no eclampsic symptoms or stigmata of degeneration, was not ineducable or irresponsible, and it was easy to interpret his few words and acts as expressions of peculiar sagacity. The interest he excited was profound and wide-spread and he was studied as no other representative of his class has ever been.[1] That he was extremely conscious of the interest he excited and of the many interpretations put upon his acts and traits as an animal boy or a disguised prince, a truant schoolboy, the victim of "a crime against a human soul," as his chief defender designated his wrongs, that he was vain, egotistic, a subtle and oft-confessed liar with a passion for deception, makes him, whatever else he was, a very unique adolescent defective. Many children, thought normal before, are first found wanting at this age. They are neither silly nor half-witted, but can no longer fully profit by school. Their minds develop irregularities, their educability ceases; perhaps they need to be sifted out of school for both its good and for their own; they begin to suffer in disposition from being teased by those more intelligent than themselves, and become dead weights in their classes because their brief period of docility is ended. Some, as Langdon Down says, "may by careful management be tided over the climacteric period of puberty and then all may go well."

Masselon [2] emphasizes the incapacity to systematize ideas and the effacement of images. The three chief traits of adolescent mental enfeeblement, according to this writer, are the retardation of psychic processes, the progressive effacement of memory, and the weakening of the power of mental synthesis. Aboulia, he describes, as due to weakening of desires. Negativism often alternates with docility. The twelve cases that he fully describes well illustrate the fundamental nature of the above characterization. Sollier[3] bases his classification of idiots and imbeciles on the degree of attention and deems its impor-

---

[1] For the fullest summary of this case and the voluminous literature upon it, see A. v. d. Linde: Kaspar Hauser; Eine neugeschichtliche Legende. Wiesbaden, 1887, 2 vols.; and the True Story of Kaspar Hauser, by the Duchess of Cleveland. London, 1893; also, The Story of K. H., by E. E. Evans. London, 1892.

[2] Psychologie des déments précoces. (Thèse de Paris.) Paris, 1902.

[3] Psychologie de l'Idiot et de l'Imbecile. Paris, 1901.

tance cardinal. Its preoccupation and instability is inversely as educability and disciplinability.

Many crimes and immoralities of early adolescence are from a blind impulse on which consciousness does not act at all. In the psychic evolution of the sexual impulse there is often at first a period of general perturbation before the brain reacts on the sex organs. In idiots and in cases of retarded development this stage may be distinct and prolonged. Itard watched with the greatest interest for the first manifestation of this instinct in the young savage of Aveyron[1] whom his studies have made so famous among feral men. Congenitally good-natured, he developed periods of turbulence, agitation, and almost desperation, when he would break out in tempests of rage, scream, bite, scratch, bleed at the nose and ears, and could be only slowly and with great difficulty tranquilized. At times he showed preference for the female sex and would sit beside some one and take her hand, but as his general excitement grew he would move away to another. Other idiots at this period stroke or lick the hair, embrace the head and take out hairpins; one held a girl down in a frenzy of erotic excitement but attempted nothing more, being ignorant of the ways and means of satisfaction. Beginning with fifteen there is a marked increase in the number of congenital idiots who are sent to asylums owing to the increase of general perturbations which become dangerous at this age. This diffused excitement is often attended by orgasms but with no knowledge of sex. There is activity and general disturbance reacting into depression. I have myself received written accounts of four weak-minded boys between eighteen and twenty-one described as nearly normal but with entire failure of development in the sexual organs. In two of these cases spells of great excitability and of apathy were described as having developed since the normal age of puberty. This stage may, as Marro suggests, correspond to that of prepuberty.

Many psychiatric studies have seemed to establish a "neurosis of anxiety" as a quite distinct symptom group of psychic abnormality. It has a vast variety of expressions and is readily associated with somatic disturbances like palpitation, sweating, dizziness, tremors, congestion, paresthesias. The attacks of

[1] Itard. Rapports et memoires sur le sauvage d'Aveyron. Paris, 1893.

anxiety may supervene slowly or very suddenly, and may be mild or very acute. Freud[1] was the first to insist that all forms of morbid anxiety were closely associated with the *vita sexualis,* and always arose in cases of retention of the *libido.* This might occur in adolescents and was common where sexuality was excessively or abnormally frustrated or restrained, whether after or before normal experiences. Löwenfeld[2] doubted this on the basis of six cases, and Binschwanger does not ascribe very great prominence to sexual causes. Gattel,[3] however, made a very careful individual study of one hundred cases and concludes that anxiety always results from some of the many forms of retention, whether overrestraint, abstinence, or imperfect exercise of the function, and that neurasthenia on the other hand is always due to the opposite cause of excess and especially to masturbation. These troubles occurred at the age of greatest reproductive activity, and as would be expected, the anxiety neurosis was relatively more common in women than in men. If this be true, a normal sexuality, wide as are its individual differences, is necessary to steady life between these two grave disturbances, either of which may originate in the individual without the aid of hereditary predisposition, and if the sexual life is absolutely normal the physician must be slow to diagnose a real neurosis. Perhaps no recent studies suggest so strongly the fundamental importance for health of all vital and social functions of normal sexual life.

Magnan's lowest group of sexual perverts he calls spinal. I knew a young dement in a Baltimore hospital, whose intelligence was almost entirely obliterated, who grew more and more perturbed through the week, but was always quiet and docile after the Sunday visit of his wife, and whose whole condition was determined by the degree of sexual tension, of the nature of which he seemed to have lost all knowledge. In normal adolescence, if entirely uninstructed, the evolution of this function begins as something entirely new in the experience of the individual, but so strong that it will more or less dominate the life. At first it is a widely irradiated physiological increase of activity, then come local voluptuous sensations due to spon-

---

[1] Neurol. Centralblatt, 1892.

[2] München med. Wis. Abh., 1895, No. 13.

[3] Die sexuale Ursache der Neurasthenie in den Neurosen, 1898.

taneous activity of hitherto unused organs, while it is pure sensuousness as a general psychic tonus, but as yet without knowledge. Instinct has not yet associated these gratifications definitely with the other sex. I believe that it is in this stage of development that sexual perversions of certain classes are rooted. Indeed it seems hardly going beyond the facts of sex fetishism now well established by Moll, K. Ebbing, Tarnowski, and others, to draw the momentous inference that *the sexual glow may come to be associated with almost any act or object whatever and give it an unique and otherwise inexplicable prominence in the life of the individual,* and that even the Platonic love of the eternally good, beautiful, and true is possible because of this early stage of indetermination and plasticity. This hypothesis I suggest as the key to many such phenomena to be later described.

Venturi[1] described two forms of pubertal perversions which he deems true insanity. The first is cortical chorea due to defective genital development, manifested in erotic delirious impulsiveness, fixed ideas, melancholia and mania, pyromania, neurasthenia, doubt and agaraphobia. This he thought closely related to absence or undue delay of seminal discharge, defective ovulation, and particularly to onanism. The second is hebephrenia, which occurs later, between eighteen and twenty-three, and reflects difficult psychic evolution and irregular emancipation of social life and is often attended by katatonic symptoms.

Dr. Edes[2] thinks the "New England invalid" a somewhat unique type and that her troubles arise from a relative impairment or non-development of the reproductive functions or organs. No specialist can escape such a case, for she has an ailment for every organ. After the surgeon has removed all he can, she returns to the general practitioner, needing only to be "built up." It is hard enough for him to hear her tale of symptoms, but for the members of her own household to hear the tensions, borings, thrillings, accusations of selfishness, and the more trying confessions of repentance, ostentatious resignation of one doomed to be eternally misunderstood, the craving for sympathy, etc., there is no escape or consolation. Dr.

[1] Le degenerazioni sessuali. Turin, 1892, p. 320 *et seq.*

[2] The New England Invalid. Shattuck Lecture, 1885, by R. T. Edes, M. D.

Edes classifies one thousand of his patients as follows: Malingerers, exaggerators, constitutional neurotics, hysterically excitable, neuromuscular, confirmed neurominetics, tense neurasthenics, limp neurasthenics, melancholics, and his characterization of each class is of interest and value, not merely as a medical treatise, but as a culture study. A large proportion of these cases are teachers and older pupils; they study not to know but to pass examinations, not because they are interested, but because others have done so; their aim is for the glorification of their sex, that they may show that girls are equal to boys and see in the curriculum an enemy to be put behind. Sometimes such patients seem to grow proud of their own cases, and love to recite their symptoms as if to defy the doctor to cure them, until he may develop the tact to make them think that their restoration would be still more phenomenal and interesting.

The pleasure-pain threshold is easily upset and depression or hilarity may be excessive and unbalanced. While we reserve adolescent suicide for more special treatment in the next chapter, we must not fail to note here the frequency of the melancholy that chiefly predisposes to it. This in general may be conceived as due to two groups of causes, first trouble, disease from objective influences. Misfortunes may follow so fast as to kill the joy of life in the most healthful and buoyant temperaments. The second cause is hereditary weakness or predisposition. Where this is not too controlling it may appear in the early discouragement that easily loses heart and gives up the battle of life with very inadequate cause, but this may be so fateful and dominant that the love of life succumbs with no trace of objective motivation. As hyperemia or melancholy is no longer regarded as a morbid entity but a symptom with a wide variety of morbid accompaniments, that may reach morbid intensity, we have no good statistical data concerning its frequency, and various forms of it are discussed in several chapters of this work. It must suffice here to note that in its milder forms no psychic symptom is more common at some stages of adolescence and that its liability is increased in a marked degree at the early teens, although it reaches morbid intensity more often later in life. In youth it has certain marked features, especially in suddenness and intensity of onset. Its impulsive and passionate forms predominate, and reactions to sanity are far more probable with health and heredity in favor of recovery, and less so if the latter is the chief causative factor. Youth is easily plunged into despair, but reemerges with resilience if the stock and blood are good. Degrees and symptoms that would be grave in mature life are not only more easily cured, but, other things being equal, are less hopeless.

In his careful study of the subject, Mairet[1] argued that lypemaniac stupidity in certain cases can have absolutely no other cause than puberty, especially when its onset is during this period. This malady is usually to be found in nervous accidents and in troubles of general nutrition and circulation. Its symptoms are very variable, but in the vast majority of cases there is maniacal agitation, sensory perversion, fears, visual hallucinations, etc. He notes the frequency of cases where excited and active states suddenly supervene after a period of stupidity. The insanity of pubescence involves arrest of intellectual development and the maniacal symptoms may be either choreic, impulsive, or hysterical. The stupid form is often complicated in its prodromal stage with chloro-anemia, and sometimes connected with physical fatigue, palpitation, and cerebral erethism, anomalies of character, alternations of excitement and depression. Its *début* is sometimes sudden, febrile, and delusional, and then a stage of stupor often follows in which the muscles are relaxed, circulation sluggish, the temperature low, menstruation suspended, and sensation dull. In this state abrupt outbreaks of perturbation may occur with great incoherence. The choreic form may be simple or hallucinatory. In these cases the mania is not subordinated to the chorea as has been usually assumed, but rather both are branches of the same trunk, the former acting on the mind, the latter on the muscles; both alike are caused by puberty, which is at least the chief pathogenetic agent and which gives to these morbid symptoms its own peculiar physiognomy. Its onset is usually sudden.

A single case of a young man in some respects typical, and

[1] Folie de la Puberté. Am. Med. Psych., 1888, p. 337, 368; 1889, pp. 27, 34, 209, 356.

for the account of which I am indebted to Dr. C. P. Bancroft, of the New Hampshire Asylum, must here suffice to illustrate

1

2

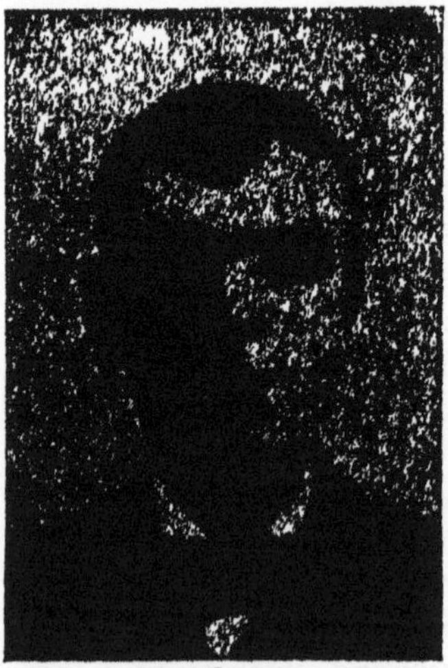

3

4

the resiliency of youth against heavy odds. The melancholy began shortly before he was twenty, and eighteen months prior to commitment. There was an history of insanity in both parental lines; he had attempted suicide both with a razor and with Paris green. Later every possible suicidal effort was made—refusing food, cutting his throat, dashing his head against the wall, throwing himself down a lightshaft—but all without fatal effect, or even serious injury. Slowly he began to respond to dietic and medical treatment. The recovery progressed rapidly. The first picture represents his state November 1, in the height of the attack, the second December 16, when improvement began, the third convalescence, and the last January 31, when he was discharged recovered.

Neurasthenia was first characterized and named by a brilliant American physician who was prematurely cut off at the point of his highest promise.[1] European experts, who have lately widely enlarged our knowledge of it, grant his priority, and often speak of it as especially an American disease. Cowles,[2] who has given us several careful studies, describes it as morbid irritability, depression, weakness, introspection, apprehension, and inattention, in which often the sense of fatigue is itself fatigued so that the victims of it constantly overdo, because this usual check is gone. It is a kind of pathological fatigue following civilization and the intense and competitive life of struggle. It may be due to regressive metabolism caused by the accumulation of autotoxins and ptomaines, and it is to be treated by rest-cures, heightened elimination, and abundant and nutritive food. Kaan[3] has shown how imperative ideas and anxiety, a sense of inner conflict and emotional perturbation, may be due to neurasthenia, and that although this state has no hallucinations and may last a lifetime, it never issues in dementia. It is most often connected with fears of storms, water, height, dread of standing, being poisoned, contact, impotence, of doing improper things, especially of an obscene or sacrilegious character, of being laughed at, of blushing, etc. Although neurasthenia falls chiefly in a somewhat later stage of life, not only do its symptoms very commonly begin to appear at puberty, but Binswanger,[4] who has up to date

[1] G. M. Beard. Neurasthenia. New York, 1888.

[2] Neurasthenia. Shattuck Lecture. Boston, 1891; and The Mental Symptoms of Fatigue. N. Y. State Med. Ass'n, 1893.

[3] Die neurasthenische Angst-effect, 1893.

[4] Neurasthenie. 1896, p. 336.

given the fullest exposition of it, describes a special pubertal form, which although not very frequent is more prone to degeneration. He says that neurasthenic symptoms occurring at puberty are often strongly suggestive of mental instability and imperatively call for such care as may prevent the development of actual insanity. He draws special attention to the parallelism between fatigue and the symptoms of neurasthenia, and thinks that the latter is overfatigue due to congenital weakness of nerves, and is peculiarly liable to become a settled diathesis during the period of sex evolution. Saville[1] thinks that although any age could be affected, "young male adults were slightly predisposed."

Dr. Scholz[2] characterized "pubertal weak-mindedness" as real retrogression rather than as arrested development. The latter he designated as imbecility. The former develops often rather suddenly, and without acute symptoms, in individuals of previously fairly good health. It may be attended by much psychic irritability of expansive form resembling hebephrenia, or it may have a more depressive and paranœic character. It can proceed to any stage of mental decay and may occur without hereditary predisposition. What cerebral changes accompany it is unknown, but puberty is the causal occasion or basis to which this psychosis owes many of its peculiar symptoms.

Again, that the insanity of doubt, which Legrand du Saulle,[3] Kovalevski,[4] Cowles,[5] and many since have studied under various names, with its *Grübelsucht*, hyperscrupulosity, imperative and oft-repeated repetition of the commonest acts, misophobia, oiko-, claustro-, agara-, acu-, sito-, and all the score of instinctive phobias, etc., is characteristic of the later stages of adolescence there can be no question, although age statistics have been strangely neglected by the authorities. Baillarger,[6] however, collected twenty interesting cases of one form

[1] Neurasthenia. London, 1899, p. 48.

[2] Ueber Pubertalsschwachsinn. Allgemeine Zeits. f. Psy. u. Psy. Gerichtl. Med., 1897. Hefts 5-6.

[3] La Folie du Doute. Paris, 1875.

[4] Journal of Mental Science, 1887, p. 209; 1888, p. 524.

[5] Insistent and Fixed Ideas. Am. Jour. of Psy., Feb. 1888, vol. 1, pp. 222-270.

[6] Folio du doute. Arch. Clin. des Mal. Mentales. Paris, 1881.

of a malady thus connected which is prone to make its *début* at puberty. We can not here consider all disorders. It is probably not too much to say that very nearly if not quite every psychosis or neurosis of defect or excess, if not manifest before puberty, will appear or at least begin its incubation at this time; these beginnings the statistics of insanity always place too late because the early stages are not seen by physicians and appear at institutions still later during the ephebic period. If they do not, it can be said that the tension of this period is safely and healthfully passed and maturity well achieved; that then there follows a stage of relative immunity during which much can with impunity be both done and endured, and which only exceptional strain, shock, organic lesion, or other external non-infectious cause or else early senescent decline, can destroy.

At variance with the older view,[1] there is now some indication that general paralysis of the insane has a distinct tendency to begin between the ages of thirteen and sixteen, although its curve rises higher at a later age. Since the valuable monograph of Alzheimer,[2] who collected forty-one well-described cases, Lührmann, Infeld, Hoch, and Stewart[3] have collected many more. Most of these, of course, but not all, are asylum cases. They were not idiots or infantilists, but had developed intelligence, and retrogressed toward dementia as the disease progressed. From fifteen to sixteen is the most common age of onset. This dreaded disease makes puberty a critical period, especially if there is any syphilitic or luetic taint. The sexes seem, so far as an opinion can be based on the above limited number of cases, to be about equally liable—a fact which differentiates the adolescent form of this disease in a very marked manner from the vast preponderance of cases among males in adult life. Although some ninety per cent of all are syphilitic, this taint is nearly always inherited and not acquired. The psychic symptoms are progressive dulness, apathy, and perhaps stuporose states in children who have been normal or

[1] E. G. W. I. Mickle: General Paralysis of the Insane, p. 249.

[2] Alzheimer: Die Frühform der Allg. Prog. Paralysis. Allg. Zeits. f. Psych., 1895, p. 583.

[3] See especially P. Stewart: General Paralysis of the Insane during Adolescence. Brains. Spring Number. 1898, p. 39 *et seq.*

even supernormal in intelligence. In adolescents the grandiose ideas so characteristic of this disease in adults are absent, and delusion and hallucination if they exist at all are mild and "never of the extravagant type met with in adults." Growth and especially sexual devlopment is arrested, and there are congestive attacks and perhaps the fibrillary tremors of tongue, face, and fingers, with slovenly, slurring articulation, weakness of limbs, an ataxic or sometimes a spastic gait. The post-mortem brain changes do not differ from those found in adults.

Maudsley's conception of adolescent insanity [1] rests on the general conception that reason is an apparatus of restraint, superposed upon intense and brutal impulses, and that in characteristic outbreaks this curb is broken, and all the bonds between the many wild factors of our nature which constitute the ego are also ruptured, so that all that later ages of civilization and even higher barbarism have superposed is gone and dehumanization ensues. All the high social reflexes being lost, diffidence and reserve give place to pertness, self-will, turbulence, aimless iteration, etc. This is illustrated by tickling and by the sex act, both of which begin in volition and go on to convulsion and orgasm, as they pass from cerebral down to spinal control. The progress from capricious acts to catalepsy is analogous. The "jumpers," who when suddenly told to jump or seize a hot iron or a friend's throat, or do any other absurd or even criminal act, obey convulsively and on the instant; frights that result in fascination and perhaps imitation of the cause, especially if it is with animals, illustrate the same boulepsy. Again, from each act of the body impressions are pouring in upon the brain, and the muscle sense should give tone to the will; but among the insane its disorder is connected with the sense of motor impotence. The abdominal organs normally contribute an euphoria of a peculiar intensity, and no one with abdominal disease can be cheerful, while those with thoracic complaints commonly are so. The sex organs, too, contribute their own contingent to the brain and to the sum of somatic feelings; and the latter respond to every change of the former. The tumultuous changes which occur in pubescent insanity are conditioned by changes either of unusual amount or rapidity in

[1] See Pathology of Mind, pp. 145 and 387.

these functions, and if the brain is weak it can not bear the strain thus imposed.

In the transition from the grub to the butterfly state, the female is most liable to become psychologically upset, because her reproductive organs and functions are not only larger, but the changes are more rapid. In her, Maudsley thinks love and religion are most often blended. In trances, stupors, or contortions, girl lunatics are most prone to symptoms of erotomania, or even nymphomania. There is almost sure to be alternation from depression to excitement, and *vice versa,* in adolescent insanity. Frequent and repeated oscillations, especially the occurrence of lucid intervals, is a bad sign. Menstruation predisposes women to this cyclic upsetting of equilibrium. If instead of slowly lapsing to dementia, the patient recovers, she is unconcerned about previous attack, and "the two selves, the sane and insane, pursue their respective courses apart." In depression there are the usual fears of being suspected of ill-doing, of being followed, watched, poisoned, wrongly dieted, slandered, and of being guilty of things never done. Although the symptoms seem superficial and histrionic, they are as real as the limited strength of mind and brain can make them, and the suicidal impulses may be carried out. Feelings that are not directed normally to love, marriage, and motherhood are always liable to devastation, and timely and happy wedlock may improve such cases. All adolescent insanities imperatively require change of surroundings, and too much sympathy is often the very food they feed and grow strong on. Here, too, belong the religious fasters, ecstatics, feigners of strange diseases and interesting symptoms, the diabolically clever liars and false accusers, mischievous tricksters, and moral imbeciles of divers types.

Wille,[1] whose one hundred and thirty-five cases seem to bear out his view, holds that there is no specific pubertal insanity, but that puberty gives a peculiar character to other psychoses, all of which may occur at this period, yet, as we should expect, with a special prevalence of atypic and mixed forms. Instead, therefore, of regarding set symptoms and laying stress on the mode of termination, he well urges that psychiatry should take account not only of causes, but of characteristic changes in the

[1] Die Psychosen der Pubertätsalters. Leipzig, 1898, p. 218.

course of diseases, and that this should be true not only of those which occur at puberty or the age of sexual evolution, which he places between fourteen and twenty-three, but at the age of involution or senescence. He classifies his cases (during the preceding fifteen years at the asylum of Basle) as follows:

		Cases.	Females.	Males.
Simple psycho-neuroses.	Melancholy	21	15	6
	Mania	29	18	11
	Acute dementia	9	8	1
	Acute hallucinations / Insanity	3	..	..
	Confusion	10	7	3
	Paranœa	4	2	2
Organic psychoses.	Primary chorea, dementia	9	3	6
	Combined neuro and toxic psychoses	37	8	29
	Heredity	9	3	6
	Hereditary weakness	4	1	3
		135	65	70

Common hebephrenic traits, Wille thinks, are present and color all these diseases, which become typical somewhat according to the degree of development toward adult life at which they occur. Superficiality, stupid jests, and jollity in the midst of lamentation and world pain, the most bizarre turns of thought, theatrical reference to a spectator, fanaticism, the sharpest contrasts and conflicts of owlish wisdom and fatuity, selfishness and altruism, idle distraction and great concentrative energy, savagery and tenderness, hypersensitiveness and obtuseness, growth and development concentrated upon any organ and function, so that there is hypertrophy here and atrophy there, sex organs and instincts enormously and prematurely developed or arrested, exotic virtue and brutal crime, exaggerated selfishness and no less extreme generosity and self-abnegation, resistance to authority and exceptional plasticity, fantastic views of life, abhorrence of work or, above all, of regularity in occupation, lunacy with misleading lucid intervals, impulsiveness, scrupulosity and reflection on trifles which may be paranœic—all these occur in different cases and a surprising number may follow each other in one individual. Krafft-Ebing, who held that great need of activity and self-confidence were often combined with chorea and catalepsy, that exaltation and a sense of greatness alternated with a deep sense of demerit and unworthiness; Regis, who thought that pubescent insanity was more often moral, showing itself in morbid acts and impulses rather than in the intellectual sphere; Savage, who compared the abnormalities of this age with those of early childhood, although holding the former to be more pronounced, and thought dysmenorrhea never so liable to produce intellectual weakness; Blanford, who deemed that violence was more characteristic than illusions, and that irregular and uncontrolled and perhaps choreic movements were rarely absent; Trowbridge, who emphasized the distinction between simple psychic neuroses of short duration and true psychoses, and thought the latter only incurable—all these and other conclusions may be legitimate inferences from different groups of cases, but can not yet be final.

Marro [1] does not accept a distinct pubertal form of insanity. He found that at this period the exigencies of growth had greatly reduced both the albumin and the salts of the blood, and conceives that at this their nascent period sex organs and nerve centers come into the closet *rapport;* that the mind is being rapidly developed; that sense is evolving into affection; that the nervous hyperesthesia is peculiarly exposed to influences from the gradually unfolding sex functions, and that very slight causes may upset sanity. In his twenty-eight fully described cases, fatigue, a glass sliver in the toe, constipation, toothache, and failure to pass examinations, a mild flogging, etc., caused symptoms of the utmost variety, nearly always transitory although often acute, that threatened the ultimate integrity of the whole psychic organism. These "phenomena of first reflexion" are often forms of epilepsy, and indeed the period of fifteen to sixteen has few others. The intelligence, always more or less radically changed, is easily and permanently injured by too intense and extreme perturbations of feeling or of conscience, but much of this is needed to deploy and stretch out the soul to its full dimensions. In the erratic acts of these cases, scratching, biting, screaming, chanting, butting, running aimlessly about, stripping off clothing, eroticism, spasmodic hilarity, pugnacity, exhibitionism, passionate vagrantism and vagabondage, solitude and soliloquy, self-torture, praying, shouting, obscene and profane words, taciturnity, anorexia and polyphagia, filthy acts, etc., we seem to see the vigor and variety

[1] La Puberta, p. 101 *et seq.*

of the elements that compose our nature and which are normally broken and harnessed to service of common sense, escaped from control, and suggesting in an unmistakable way the subhuman origin of the crude material of human nature. Many of these are given us in great abundance at adolescence, and the problem of moral and religious education is whether we can thoroughly civilize these barbaric and bestial proclivities and bring them into the harmony and unity of completed character.

Marro[1] describes the morbid congenital instability at this age as follows: " When we consider young people with hereditary taints, the picture may represent considerable variety. At one time they are torpid, obtuse, taciturn, without expansion, little given to society, indifferent to affection, but petulant, irritated, the reaction has no measure, they cease from their state of torpor to give way to outbursts of an unbounded violence, entirely disproportioned to the injury received. At other times they are unquiet, turbulent, without physical and moral firmness, always in motion without determined aim, incapable of attention and reflection, dominated by instantaneous impulses which they do not know how to resist, incapable of persevering in any occupation; impelled by whims which follow each other without any plausible motive to explain the first sympathy and the following aversion; they are always inclined to lamentation, tormented by a sense of ill-feeling which spoils their pleasures and magnifies the difficulties which they are about to face. The instinctive impulses and moral impressions find in them little or no power of resistance, and, according to the particular conditions of life and special circumstances, they become so many candidates for prison or the insane asylum."

In Marro's middle period of adolescence, from sixteen to twenty, the psychic changes predominate. There is great and frequent alternation of mood from grave to gay, extreme exaggeration, little power of resistance. In abnormal cases this is the age of gastric catarrh, sudden alterations of body temperature, nutritive disturbances particularly favored by masturbation, epigastric sensations of weight, hardness, heat, etc., chloroses, sitophobia, abnormal urinal deposits, and perhaps inflammation in parts not predisposed to it, auditory and visual

[1] La Puberta, p. 218.

hallucination, erotic and religious delusion, and a general lack of horizon for consciousness.

Marro examined 1,643 males and 1,257 females in the lunatic asylum of Turin. Of those between the ages of twelve and fourteen he found only a few cases of psychoneuroses, and still fewer epileptics. Between fourteen and seventeen was the age of most epilepsies, which abound also during the next few years. From twenty to twenty-three for males and from twenty to twenty-two for females was the age of most psychoses, and by twenty-five these had nearly ceased. Boys were more prone to melancholia and girls to mania, the latter acquiring less power to check reflexes. The moral perversions of boys are prone to take the form of cruelty and crime, while girls are more liable to shameless and erotic perversity, and egoism and self-satisfaction is common to both sexes. He found direct morbid heredity in one hundred and forty-five cases between eleven and twenty-five, ancestral heredity in fifty-four cases, and that paternal was to maternal heredity as eight to five. The effects of old age in the father was found in forty-one per cent and in the mother in twenty per cent of the adolescent cases. Heredity made itself felt more at this period than later, especially from the father, and more so the earlier it appeared. Of psychic causes he found fear and other affections and thwartings of the instincts of self-preservation, which were relatively more prominent before puberty, to give place to insults and other injuries of self-respect, religious feelings, love, etc. Failure in examination sometimes reacted into almost maniacal exaltation and defiance, and the alienation seemed to be a natural evolution aided by no external cause.

He[1] describes interesting typical cases; one of a bright student of sixteen, whose character seemed to change till he became visionary and fantastic, who wrote to the king and queen claiming to be their son, but was at once sequestered, severely lectured, and recovered. Another began with an extravagant dream of pistons working disharmoniously within him, which was continued for four years, with illusions of dual personality. He had an exaggerated sense of mental and physical inefficiency, passed just before intended marriage to aversion to his

[1] La Puberta, p. 164 *et seq.*

bride, alternating from passion to repugnance. Another slowly became a stutterer and feared that every act of his might have fatal consequences. A girl had delirium of sin, tried to give herself to God so passionately that no other could be thought of, and so intense was this eroticism, where religion took the place of sex, that gastric and respiratory symptoms often supervened during a long period of abnormal pubertal evolution. Another girl developed causeless hatred for her mother, grew gushy, sentimental, and familiar to partial strangers, was excitable, dirty, flushed and pale by turns, and became too religious. Another gave himself up to extreme self-abuse on the view that he must thus rid his system of a poison, and often before others as a sign of contempt for them, etc.

Most of the psychoses of this period appear as symptoms of exhaustion, so that prolonged repose in bed may do great good. Moral and physical development go hand in hand at this age as at no other, and it is very rare to find anomalies of one without those of the other. Marro lays chief stress upon disciplinability and sociability, and to these adds the power of continuous work and the power to pursue a predetermined line of conduct. These for defectives and criminals should be chiefly cultivated. The perfection of the organism and the solidity of moral qualities can not be divorced. If there is rapid growth in mind, while the secondary sexual qualities do not develop in proportion, the critical period is not yet passed and there is danger. Prevision for self and for others is cultivated by economy. He commends Dr. Wine's system of marks to teach those exposed to these dangers proper care of their own natures and interests, to say nothing of those of others.

Dr. Pickett [1] has tabulated cases of one hundred and sixty-seven young men, obtaining personal histories wherever this was possible. He concludes that from the standpoint of prognosis the puberty modifications of insanity are first a tendency to dementia as if the potentiality of mental life were exhausted. Only one-fourth of Pickett's cases left the hospital restored, and even they remained more or less psychic cripples. His paranœics were a little older than the others, or as Bevan Lewis said, "the delusional cases are older than merely maniacal ones."

[1] A Study of the Insanities of Adolescence. Jour. of Nervous and Mental Disease, Aug., 1901.

This suggests that age braces the hysterical temperament and increases the assertiveness of the individual, "so that one who at sixteen sinks into catalepsy under a burden of imagined troubles would, if he had escaped until he reached the age of thirty, have risen above his persecutions in the form of egoistic delusions, solely on account of the change in temperament wrought by mature age." He believes that hebephrenia today "includes those cases of dementia præcox which are not distinctly paranœic, and not katatonic; it is a group of the unclassified members of dementia præcox." "To omit all reference to the peculiar types of adolescence seems like rejecting our birthright—an heritage of the labors of master workmen in the field of psychiatry.

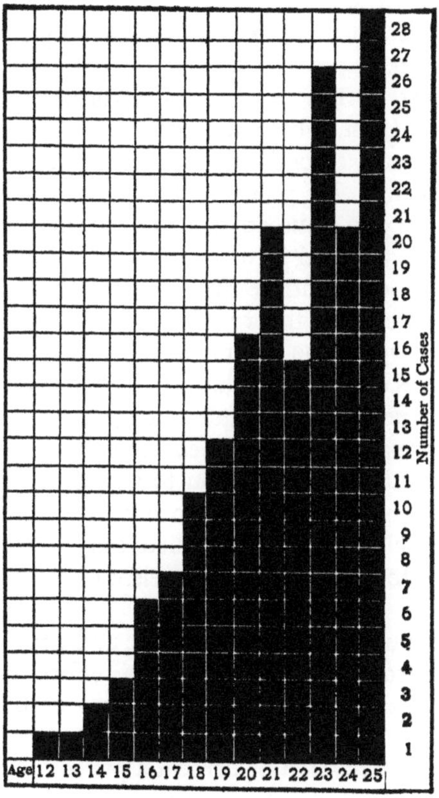

His age table is as shown in the adjoining diagram.

According to Sérieux,[1] who traces its history to Morel, the various forms of precocious dementia are followed after variable time by a special state of psychic enfeeblement. The delirious ideas are slowly attenuated and perhaps entirely lost, so that at its termination the patient has very little in body and mind that is not stereotyped. He distinguishes four distinct forms: simple, delirious, katatonic and paranœic—and three periods, that of its *début*, characterized

[1] La Démence précoce. Rev. de Psychiatrie, June, 1902.

by general neurasthenia, hysteria, perhaps preoccupation and other neuropathic manifestations; the second is acute or delirious, perhaps with ideas of greatness, persecution, hallucination, excitement, etc., and the third is terminal dementia. The clinical species or groups and the distinction between primary and secondary symptoms is a work of the future, but the tendency is now everywhere to substitute clinical species with well-determined stages of evolution for merely symptomatic groups. This alone can give a natural in place of an artificial classification.

V. Serbski [1] would restrict the term to those forms that have the following traits: First, where the onset is not later than the adolescent period, and, second, where there is distinct development of enfeeblement. He points out the important fact that it may be secondary to some other acute psychic disease and lays little stress on physical signs. It is very hard to diagnose and especially to differentiate from secondary dementia of adolescence. Kraepelin's theory of autointoxication by products of the sexual organs, he deems mistaken.

J. Seglas [2] agrees with Kraepelin that katatonic symptoms are of psychic origin and not, as Kahlbaum thought, simple muscular spasms. They are automatic, independent of the consciousness of the patient, and without relation to any illusions or delusions, but automatisms can only be corollaries. The substratum always is insufficiency of cohesion between the elements of personality. He, too, holds that negativism goes well with aboulia.

To Kraepelin belongs much credit for the great and growing interest in this subject, due to a serious effort to clear up the previous confusion. In the later editions of his text-book, and especially in the sixth,[3] he gives a brilliant and comprehensive clinical characterization of dementia præcox, including most of the abnormal symptoms of this age that issue in degeneration, on the basis of 296 cases and under three forms —hebephreniac, katatonic, paranoid. The age liability of his

[1] On the Question of Dementia Præcox. Jour. of Mental Pathology, Vol. 2, No. 4. Abstracted from a paper published in Russian, Jan., 1902.

[2] Démence précoce et Katatonie. Nouvelle Iconographie de la Salpêtrière, 1902, No. 4.

[3] Psychiatrie, 1899, vol. ii, ch. 5. Die Dementia Præcox, pp. 137–214.

cases is represented in the following cut, but of the first form seventy-two, of the second sixty-eight, of the third forty per cent, and of all together over sixty per cent occur before the twenty-fifth year. Its manifestations are extremely diverse and include symptoms of almost all other insanities. In the hebephreniac form the development is toward final stupidity more or less pronounced, with subacute, more often than acute, mental disturbance. The katatonic form is more likely to be characterized by negativism, stereotyped movements, and suggestibility of expression and acts, while the paranœic type, which he has added later, is marked by delusions, sometimes slightly systematized, especially in older cases, and by sensory illusions, which may persist for years along with tolerable sanity in other respects. In the most youthful cases the progress is toward simple dementia, while in katatonic and especially paranœic forms illusions are more likely to play the dominant rôle in the later adolescent stages; for this difference he can offer no explanation, but illusions seem germane to the somewhat later age, which he found a little more prone to them when will and ideation are more developed. The degeneration, which marks all form of this disease, he thinks can not be explained as mere arrest, for he strangely asks what do we conceive to be arrested, and so he proposes autointoxication, perhaps due to sexual elements as a chemical agent, to account for the fact and the rapidity of deterioration. Kraepelin's former student, Trömmer,[1] has summarized these views with additional clinical details and theoretical suggestions, while

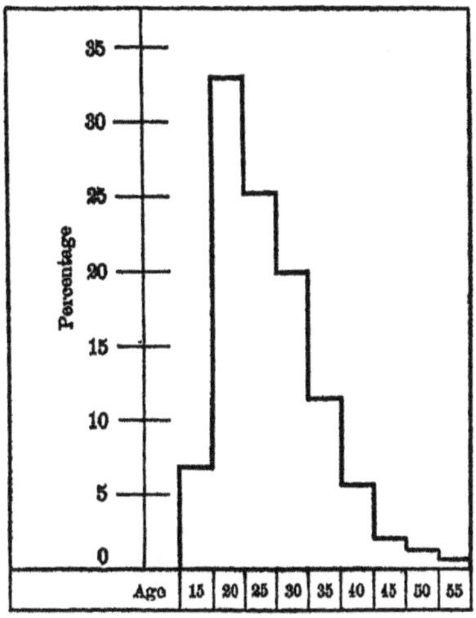

[1] Das Jugendirresein, von E. Trömmer. Samm. Abh. Nerven- und Geisteskrankheiten, Vol. 3, Part 5. Halle, 1902.

Ilberg,[1] whose twenty cases began on the average at twenty-one and a half years, perhaps best describes the earlier stages of the disease.

As to the frequency of dementia præcox, we have the following very diverse data:

Hecker	found	14	cases	among	500	insane,	or	3.0	per	cent.
Schüle	"	5	"	"	600	"	"	.3	"	"
K. Ebing	"	12	"	"	5,000	"	"	.25	"	"
Sterz	"	12	"	"	1,000	"	"	1.2	"	"
Finck	"	17	"	"	1,900	"	"	.84	"	"
Tschisch	"	14	"	"	688	"	"	2.03	"	"
Scholz	"	6	"	"	530	"	"	1.13	"	"
Christian	"	100+	"	"	2,000	"		....		
Kraepelin	"	296	"	"	....	"	"	14.15	"	"
						(5–6 hebephreniac and katatonic and the rest paranœic forms.				
Meyer	"	151 men, 173 women, simple and paranœic. 51 men, 40 women, Katatonic.			2,159			....		

Kraepelin's work in this field has proved a very fresh and invigorating stimulus to younger alienists. It marks some advance from an artificial toward a natural system in a field where, unlike that of most somatic diseases, temporary symptoms are protean and misleading, so that it is difficult to diagnose to the basal processes, because in its relatively long duration there are so many phases that are hard to differentiate from other morbid types, especially neurasthenia, which it often resembles, although the latter cases are more readily controlled intellectually by physicians and less prone to issue in mental weakness. Some of its manifestations suggest general paralysis, but this more affects the memory and brings special defects. The latter trouble, which now has a well-established pathology, is one of the best differentiated of diseases, while dementia præcox has far more varied forms and less specific symptoms, and its neural pathology, despite several hopeful tentatives, remains yet to be

[1] Das Jugendirresein, von G. Ilberg. Volkmann's Samm. Klin. Vort. No. 224, 1898. See also: Ueber Hebephrenie, etc., von Daraskiewicz. Dorpat, 1892; De la Démence Précoce des Jeunes Gens, von J. Christian. Ann. Méd.-Psychol., 1899. Beginning Jan.–Feb., 1899, and continuing through five numbers; Die Katatonie, von Tschisch. Monatsch. f. Psychiatrie u. Neurologie, 1899. See also a convenient compend in a small volume by G. Deny and P. Roy. La Démence Précoce, Paris, 1902, p. 96.

developed. As compared with epilepsy, too, its symptoms are far less sharply marked, while its relations with all the problems of psychic development constitute so vast a field that no single investigator can repeat here the triumphs of Hughlings Jackson, although many think that it should now take its place with these two morbid symptom groups as already next best established. Dr. Adolf Meyer, our most competent American authority, says in a personal letter that " the adaptation to the sexual life of the adult age is very often a prominent difficulty in these cases," and that " the disorder is frequently foreshadowed in the teens or may come on before in rare cases, but the majority develop mental derangement between twenty and twenty-five." In general, periodic types of insanity seem more endogenous to the third decennium of life; paranœa to the third and fourth; general paralysis to the fourth and fifth; melancholia to the climacteric; and senile dementia to a still later stage of life. To fully understand these, as well as the diseases most liable to earlier periods of life, now under consideration, we must have as a basis the fullest possible knowledge of the normal life in each age.

While no alienist has so carefully studied, presented, and grouped clinical symptoms on a basis of so many cases as Kraepelin, and while, in showing from this standpoint the peculiar liability of the transformation stage of adolescence to fail of achieving psychic maturity and to lapse toward dementia, he has made a contribution of great value to our knowledge of this age, neither these nor his experimental studies have enabled him to escape the fallacy of modern psychiatric specialization and recognize the larger relations of the morbid to the normal changes of which most of the former are only exaggerated forms. In this respect the broader and robust common sense of Maudsley, the more numerous and comparative methods of Marro, and in some respects even the conservatism of Wille, show sounder psychological insight. Hughlings Jackson's genius, which as some one has said makes even his guesses more valuable than many a man's demonstrations, while shown in his theory of levels, has contributed no less to establish his type of epilepsy by tracing its diathesis through all its gradations up into experiences common in every normal life. This is always possible and must always be the clinician's goal, and just in proportion as normal psychology is developed on a sound empirical and genetic basis, it will become the indispensable clue to guide and the shibboleth and touchstone by which to test every conclusion of the alienist, who even without the genius of insight will walk sure-footed just in proportion to his knowledge of it.

The terms dementia præcox, insanity of youth, primary dementia, hebephrenia, and katatonia are all partial and none of them are entirely satisfactory. These troubles do not by any means invariably issue in dementia, but if all did, the processes that produced and preceded the lesions, and not their effect, should furnish a truly scientific principle of characterization and nomenclature. Hegel said of Schelling's *absolute*, as many since might have said of Hartmann's *unconscious*, that it was not a true philosophic principle, because " all cows look alike in the dark," meaning that a purely negative principle can never be an adequate explanation. We may say the same of dementia præcox, which faintly suggests the propriety of giving to general paresis, which almost always has a fatal termination, a designation like thanatic dementia, based upon this fact. Early mental death is a result of the morbid processes we have here to study, but so it is of others. With senile dementia both the facts and the propriety of the name are very different.

There are two missing links indispensable to a full acquaintance with the many forms of precocious mental decay; first and chiefly, knowledge of the actual changes during the stage of puberty and later adolescence, which go on within the limits of sanity. This age has often been characterized as that of mental and moral inebriation and of psychic madness, and from my studies of its phenomena I am convinced that nearly all of its symptoms can be paralleled in the inner and outer life of youth who do not lapse toward the terminal imbecility, but develop to sane and efficient maturity. Here we may demand that the normal psychologist shall help to contribute a sound basis to the student of disease, while the alienist, who deals only with salient, flagrant, or ostensive instances where natural tendencies are " writ large " and who does not know the genetic and natural history of the soul, can not solve the most fascinating problems presented by clinical pictures.

The other gap is the absence of record or available knowledge of the early stages in the development of the disease before cases come to asylums, for of this disease even more than of many others it is certain that, if all were known, its manifestations would be found to be numerous in proportion as they are mild, and that the vast majority who are slightly impaired by the ferment of this storm and stress period of life never come under any kind of medical observation. For one, I incline to the opinion that just in proportion as these gaps are filled, we shall have less need of recourse, with Kraepelin, to toxic or to other chemical causes. Since in both these fields and in the disease itself, sexual factors often play a very important rôle, a leading contingent of our knowledge of these cases must come with every advance in the psychology of sex, now so lamentably undeveloped and till lately neglected. On the other hand, the paradigms of premature decay reveal a body of phenomena of the highest importance for normal genetic psychology, and it should already be asserted that no parent, judge, family or army physician, and especially no teacher, should be ignorant of these morbid forms, which in their mild degrees are so common and the key to so much that is normal, but which are generally concealed to others and often unconscious to self.

Dr. Meyers[1] suggests that like alcohol this may be nature's way of weeding out the unfit, and that as general paresis is now by many traced to infection, so early dementia may be in part due to preventable causes. He protests against the frequent acceptance of hereditary tendencies or fatalism which even the young sometimes now use as an excuse for their bad conduct. He would distinguish sharply between forms due to constitutional inferiority and poor endowment and those due to adolescence itself and its disharmonies of thoughts, habits, and interest. This cause of stunting and perversion is less due to overwork or stress of diseases of metabolism. He says:

"Before all I miss a sense for actuality, a living with life as it is and an enjoying of the opportunities that are within reach. Where flights of thought rise above indifference in such individuals, they naturally suffer from not being adapted to actuality. In the ambitious we see the features of day-dream rather than of strength. Virtue and social emotions remain abstract and in exalted words. Many of these weaklings become conscious of the con

[1] Address at Child Study Section of the New England Association, July, 1903.

trast between their words and their nature. They become self-conscious, suspicious of being discovered, and drift into solitude. Abnormal hankerings fail to be corrected there by a healthy spirit of social and other activity; the touch with actuality is lost more and more, and over a shock or some disappointment or a setback in general health the poor frame of judgment gives way, and the person loses balance. The eagerness with which hypnotism, mesmerism, mystic powers, and the unreal are elaborated into delusions and depended upon for explanation of the peculiar sensations connected with disordered circulation, nervous heart, the nervous excitability shown by increased reflexes, feelings of uneasiness and anxiety, and unusual intestinal and sexual sensations, seem sto me to show the great danger of all half-understood things which are not brought to the test of actuality. An aversion to actuality seems to lie in the trend of much modern teaching.

"The emphasis of nature study does perhaps much to bring a healthy turn into education. But we need more; we need greater wholesomeness in the training for human relations and aspirations; a better knowledge of what is likely to rouse a sound interest even in those who are naturally careless and indifferent and otherwise tickled merely by the sensational or by what gratifies crude emotions; we need a preparation for actual life, not for dream existence. What is called 'new thought,' though to a large extent a mere revival of the food for the eternal gullible, does much good where it incidentally encourages healthy instinct. But it is like strong wine, a questionable article of food, sometimes a useful drug, but really unfitting one for a good digestion and assimilation of what makes man the master of nature. Too many suffer from the effects of intoxication or the untimely use of these mental stimulants.

"The greatest stumbling-block is undoubtedly that which stands in the way of the development of sexual maturity in that broad and lofty sense of becoming the originators of a better race. That which in actuality is the center of the highest altruistic possibilities of mankind is allowed to be a social playground of chance, fed by dime novels and literature of doubtful adventures; fashions in dress and in social customs usher the young precociously into a world in which even too many adults fail. Abnormal responses lead to abnormal seclusiveness, and quack literature nurtures a fear and hopelessness, and frequently wrecks the chances of a timely reconstruction.

"Do not let us say that this is merely one of nature's methods of weeding out the unfit. Among the 25,000 persons who are to-day in the public and private institutions of New York State alone, there are many brilliant hopes buried, largely owing to a lack of knowledge of what some people need in the way of social and personal hygiene. Remember that some of the most illustrious members of the race have been dangerously near the borderland of insanity and seem to have been great although they showed obvious traces of the same misled instincts that have completely wrecked others. Are such people not worth our help? Should not the home, the press, and the school mind some of the dangers and shape their ethics and methods accordingly?

"This is the practical lesson to be drawn from the theory of degeneracy which is spread into immature minds as a doctrine of fatalism, so that even high-school pupils excuse themselves in some such way as: 'I can't help this. It is hereditary in the family.' Part of this may be sadly true. But it is the duty of pedagogy and of psychiatry to distinguish what is to be accepted with fatalism from what is open to correction. We have faith in gymnastics for the correction of physical defects. Let us devise more efficient gymnastics which lead us to heartily enjoy actuality, to instinctively shrink from anti-social ideas and abnormal friction, and to get time for an unsophisticated growth."

Many of the phenomena are those of overaccentuation of processes normal at puberty, which I have for years called *ephebeitic*, although this term can with less propriety be applied to many of the negative symptoms of defect. The germs of many of these disturbances lie in the common faults of childhood, which are now studied under the name of pedagogical pathology, to be treated in the next chapter. Some are the premature Phaethon flights of genius spoiled by the heat of its own fermentation, and others are definite symptom groups seen in the schoolroom and not always yet incompatible with its work.[1] Conformably to this view-point we must seek the key to these perversions by addressing ourselves to the larger, underlying, and preliminary problem of determining the natural forms of psychic and somatic transitions from childhood to maturity, and study what puberty and adolescence really mean as developmental stages of human life, which it is the purpose of this work to investigate.

Adolescence begins with the new wave of vitality seen in growth; in the modifications of nearly every organ; the new interests, instincts, and tendencies; increased appetite and curiosity, so that, as elsewhere described, it is a physiological second birth. The floodgates of heredity seem opened and we hear from our remoter forebears, and receive our life dower of energy. On the other hand, the expenditures of energy are greatly increased, so that it is a crucial period for the recomposition of all the hereditary forces. Passions and desires spring into vigorous life, but with them normally comes the evolution of higher powers of control and inhibition. The momentum of inheritance may be insufficient, and Binschwanger conceived the psychic morbidities of this age as due to exhaustion or lack of capital. Thus, while on the other hand the will to live is greatly reenforced, there is often an overcompensation of waste from debilitating causes, so that the higher plateau that should be attained by the knitting together of all the new and old factors of personality under the law of prepotence may not be reached, and nature may seem to refuse or be inadequate to this final step. New prepotencies give a new direction and a new distribution of the factors of organic and psychic evolution, and

[1] See many of these in Spitzner, Psychogene Störungen der Schulkinder, Leipsic, 1899.

just as an infant who grew equally in all directions would be a monster, so the pubescent who developed all the faculties which are normally given at this age without due subordination and unity would be at once many kinds of both criminal and lunatic. Indeed, one need accept in detail none of the current theories of the nature of genius to understand that it largely consists of keeping alive and duly domesticating by culture the exuberant psychic faculties, of which this is the nascent period, and that just as domestic animals and plants easily revert to wildness, so our faculties if not duly recomposed and harmonized to the new and higher life of altruism must retrograde. Personality is always more or less multiplex and at best is a kind of moving equilibrium of forces which check each other, so that adolescence means a new system of tensions where many a nisus, innervation, and tendency is offset by others, and all in the normal mind are so well integrated that their separate elements are commonly lost to consciousness, which shows only resultants and diagonals of composition of many forces. The adult knows nothing of the crude raw forms in which psychic data are so copiously given at this age. Youth is a period of associations between many factors and contents of life, and this conception is the only cue which can aid us in threading the labyrinthine mazes of this aggregate of diseases.

Roux's conception of a competitive struggle among the different organs or tissues of the body for nutrition in order to explain excessive or premature growth of bone, sexual parts, limbs, etc., with complementary defect elsewhere, is also suggestive here and has some explanatory power in the psychological interpretation of these phenomena. Early adolescence brings sudden spring freshets of growth impulse in all directions, and these initial momenta, now given like an inheritance turned over to a ward on attaining his majority, are at first more or less incoordinated in all, and in defectives especially prone to be perverted and unbalanced, so that we have the obvious picture of offsetting deficiencies, each of which tends to intensity almost inversely as the strength of the other. As Taine has shown, every concept or presentation strongly tends to become vivid until it reaches delusional intensity, so that sanity is a complex system of mutually arrested and repressed illusions. Herbart, despite the fantastic, mechanical, and mathematical affectations of his system, deserves credit for the effort of attempting to work out the sum of arrests which ideas acting and reacting upon each other produce, with all the various degrees of contradiction from diametrical up to perfect agreement and reenforcement. At this stage of life, the earlier consciousness of childhood is to a great extent deciduous and a new one is being slowly organized. Youth tends to do everything physically possible with its body considered as a machine in the tentative, to explore every possibility of action and innervation, and to give the soul a newer and higher control. It is plastic to every suggestion; tends to do everything that comes into the head, to instantly carry out every impulse; loves nothing more than abandon and hates nothing so much as restraint. It is the age that can withstand no dare or stump; loves adventure and escapade; tends to let every faculty go to its uttermost; and seems to have a special tendency, as the previous curve of morbidity, which here reaches its highest point, shows is true of somatic troubles, to every psychic disease. There is over-innervation and tonicity, which may issue in any fulminating and furibund manifestation, and which responds to all new and intensified impulsions from within and suggestions from without.

We see traces of these molimena of nature toward a higher level, this hunger for a fuller and larger life even in the midst of degenerative phenomena. Youthful dements wrestle with great problems and ideas; their delusions are of royalty, celestial and infernal beings, telepathy, hypnotism, spiritism, great inventions, the highest themes of politics and religion, but their powers are inadequate and they grow mentally dizzy, confused, and incoherent. Again, as if they unconsciously felt the need of control, we see the reticence normal to this age of concealment, when the soul strives to segregate itself and protect and nurse a new individuality, overdone to taciturnity or reflected in constrained acts and postures; or the new impulses to action may crop out in exaggerating or fantastically varying the most common movements of walking, eating, dressing, speech, writing, etc. In many of the rich clinical details which Kraepelin has so admirably gathered, it is easy to see the germs of genius of many kinds, for this is the crude ore of which the great productions of art, invention, heroism, and moral and religious reform would be made if the processes of elaboration and the supreme Greek virtue of temperance or avoidance of excess were adequate. The soil is always rich to profusion, insemination abundant, choice exotics and all the flora of culture strike root, but weeds are rank and choke them, and decay may be the direct resultant of superfetation. There are spots or periods of excessive fecundity offset by intervals or desert areas of arrest or decay; hence the psychic diseases of youth abound in surprises and contrasts.

Sometimes intellectual defect first appears. The student can not command his attention or fails to comprehend, understand, and associate, and despite every effort falls behind his mates; is oppressed with a sense of weakness and inability to meet the expectations or ambitions of friends and parents. Here probably belong most of the two hundred and eighty-nine Prussian school children who committed suicide between 1883 and 1888, from fear of examinations, punishment, non-promotion, etc.[1] In these cases the first outcrop of disease often appears to be depressive or melancholic. Sometimes impulsion fails and the subject grows apathetic, indifferent, loses interest, and does not respond to ordinary ambitions for his own future, all inner impulse and spontaneity abate, and he ceases to care. The leading motive of life and the mainspring of all high endeavor is gone. Then, sometimes, the very absence of the tensions previously felt has the psychical action of a vacation, and produces an exalted and hilarious state of mind. Whichever the prodromal stage of incubation, there is always great strain or anxiety at first, generally reflected in loss of flesh, which is gained later when the weakened faculties and decimated activities settle to some kind of adjustment on a lower plane.

As many of the more specific psychic traits of puberty are more fully considered in later chapters, it will serve our purpose to enumerate here only a few.

1. Inner absorption and reverie is one marked characteristic of this age of transition. Who has not had spells of mental involution and absent-mindedness, when thoughts went "wool-gathering" and the soul was haunted by automatic presenta-

[1] Schungesundheitslehre. (Eulenberg u. Bach). 1900, p. 1143.

tions that take the reins from the will and lead us far away in a rapt state, now reminiscent, now anticipatory, into a world of dreams or ghosts? As we muse and brood, we seem to lapse to some unknown past that "hath elsewhere had its setting," of which "the present seems a mere semblance," or to peer far into the future and "see the beauty of the world and all the glory that shall be." In these weird seizures, we lose touch with the world and move about "in a world not realized." Sometimes these states suggest the intellectual aura or voluminous mentation of epilepsy, and the day-dreamer goes about dazed like a somnambulist, and should be admitted to be legally irresponsible, because every act proves an alibi for attention. This may be the germ of some ancillary personality and lead to a double housekeeping of consciousness, or it may be incipient lunacy and suggest Lamb's remark to Coleridge, that no one knows the grandeur of fancy till he has been crazy. It may issue in the exotic and traditional states so religiously revered in the case of neurotic girls, and constitutes, as Partridge[1] has shown, one of the charms of many drugs and intoxicants. This preliminary expatiation of the soul over a vast realm, actual and possible, of life and mind, somewhere within which it will lay down the limits of its personality, is good for the strong and healthful, but dangerous for weak or *belastet* youth in this callow, pin-feather age. When we are wise enough to control "mental metabolism," we may be able to prescribe the place and function of these "voluminous mental states" to fit each individual need. The normal soul always soon comes back to the world of reality, perhaps wakes with a start, or may slowly ebb back, and is as powerless to revisit this subthalamic realm at will as it is to see stars or sea phosphorescence in sunshine.[2] As Browne has well shown, if this efflorescence of meditativeness or introspection has been too rank, prolonged, or frequent, the subject may fall to thinking on emerging from them, as Blood did on emerging from the influence of drugs, or Davy from the long inhalation of dilute gas, or the hashish eater, that nothing is real but thought, feeling, and sensation, and thus he

[1] Studies in the Psychology of Alcohol, by George E. Partridge. Am. Jour. of Psy., April, 1900, vol. ii, pp. 318-376.

[2] See James Crichton-Browne's Dreamy Mental States. Cavendish Lecture, 1895. London.

may be predisposed to become an adept in the occultism of epistemology, if not solipsisism; or he may lose the certainty or even sense of his personal identity and pinch himself to know if he is awake, wonder if he really lives, who he is, and where, and if the actual world is really real.

2. Puberty is the birthday of the imagination. This has its morning twilight in reverie, and if brilliant and vivid, supplements every limitation, makes the feeble athletic, the beggar rich, knows no limitations of time or place, and is, in a word, the totalizing faculty. In its world all wishes are actualized, and hundreds of our returns, elsewhere reported, show that in many sane children, their own surroundings not only shrivel but become dim and shadowy compared with the realm of fancy. This age is indeed sadly incomplete without illusions, and if the critical faculties which are later to slowly decompose them are not developed, the youth is rapt, apart, perhaps oblivious of his environment, and unresponsive to its calls, because his dreams have passed beyond his nascent and inadequate power of control and become obsessions. Many states that become trancoidal and absorptive are best described as the drunkenness of fancy, a state which may become habitual and passionate, but which, true to its secret nature, is unrevealed to others save in certain katatonic attitudes and a clumsiness to mundane reactions, such as Plato ascribes to the true philosopher. Here, near the verge of normality, belong many of the long-continued stories, imaginary companions, fancied but perhaps zoologically impossible animals, and romances, of which the maker is always the center, which are at this time intensely real, but, obeying the law of all psychic phenomena of pubescence, are transitory, so that scenes are always soon shifted for another play.

The ingenuous youth sees visions or dreams dreams somewhat according as he is ear- or eye-minded. The optical centers are especially sensitized to new harmonies of form and especially color; the mode of thought is pictorial and by images; and the ear now feels music and harmony, is attuned to sound, and is amazingly sensitive to voices, tone-color, inflections, etc. Both the auditory and optic areas come into new connections with thought, and speech music, phonisms, photisms, and probably number forms and exceptional psychic structures are now developed. Thought and the two higher senses are never so vivid and intense because they are just ready to bifurcate, each to lead its own life, so that the two are now peculiarly liable to be confused, intellectual processes to take sense forms, and *vice versa.* It is for this reason that hallucinations, false sight, and especially hearing, is most common; but in brains tainted by morbidity the faculty for discriminating mental from sense-forms is undeveloped, and dreamy conditions may become habitual, so that we see here the natural budding of insane perceptions. Perhaps the persistence in colleges of that form of critical philosophy, which devotes itself to discriminating the real from the phenomenal in sense-perception, is a hypertrophied relic of a long travel of the race to maintain this distinction for the practical purposes of life and is necessary for those who require years of sanifaction to fully recover from the strain of pubic aberrations. Our returns give abundant illustration of an attitude of early pubescence when the gracious lies of fancy shade by strictly imperceptible gradations into the clear light of objective fact.

3. As the child's absorption of objects slowly gives place to consciousness of self, reflectiveness often leads to self-criticism and consciousness that may be morbid. He may become captious and censorious of himself or others. Ultimate questions that present the mysteries of things—why was I born? who made God? what is soul, matter, good?—press for answers. Conscience becomes so oversensitive that "anxiety about doing right exhausts the energy that should go to action, trifles are augmented to mountains, or debate with oneself as to what is right is carried so far as to paralyze decision," and the "natural hue of resolution is sicklied o'er with the pale cast of thought." [1] Such boys rewrite a page rather than erase a false cross or dot, will never use a caret, stop in plowing if a single weed is missed, or in harvesting if a single head of wheat is lost. Details are exaggerated, irritability and pride of appearance and ideals of absolute perfection are seen. A girl

[1] G. A. Coe: The Morbid Conscience of Adolescents. Trans. Ill. Soc. for Child Study. III, 2, p. 99.

would never take a pin or pick a flower without asking, or saying thank you for each flower. The slightest hint or frown of disapproval by others causes depression. A youth could never decide the smallest matter promptly without arguing the pros and cons. Another was horrified at flitting fancies of crimes he might possibly commit. Sometimes imperative ideas crop out or uncontrollable fears arise. Others struggle intensely with secret religious doubts. Innocent things are sometimes magnified into sins of deepest dye. "Should I become a minister, a missionary, have a warm bed when others have a cold one, etc.," and even more trivial queries may become morbidly intense. The avoidance of fatigue, an adviser who really understands the case, and fit religious training, are cardinal needs. To love and care for these awkward, often unattractive neophytes is a specialty, and I believe is one of the types of genius which is never found among those who have exterminated in themselves too successfully the impulsion of youth.

4. Another trait is the overassertion of individuality. This is germane to a state of nature when the child no longer needs the parental protection but, in primitive life and warm countries, breaks away and shifts for himself. Hitherto he has been the center in his environment, has been fed, sheltered, and taught, and with all the flush of morning, and springtide hopes, goes out to maintain subsistence, and ultimately to become the center of another family; all this before the longer apprenticeship to life which civilization has enforced was known. It is the time for large views and plans; life problems now press upon him; ambition and self-affirmation are never of such high selective value. His ego must be magnified and all in the new environment subordinated to it. Strife and labor, intensified and prolonged, are imperative. It is now or never, the impulsiveness of youth can not wait and its ambition is never so exorbitant. Now, instead of head hunting, winning a new name, wrestling alone with spirits or other of the drastic initiations of savages, the civilized and more sedentary youth must vent his intensification of personal feeling in dreams of greatness—and who has not at this season been prince, millionaire, hero, walked with the great of earth or heaven, in reverie? Perhaps the very repressions of modern life have given added color and

range to the ideal. The youth's powers are now tested, and who knows but he may become the greatest among men? The whole soul is now protensive, and there is no life but in the realm of the possible, for the real is not yet. The sane man burns or distils these vaporings, and they are unsuspected to those about him, and fade like shadows as the sun of reality rises, or are relegated to the realm of poetry and fiction. But if the reductives are undeveloped, or the energy of production overintense, they appear as delusions of greatness, so common and so manifold in precocious dementia, or they may culminate in impudence, contradiction, and perhaps even in aggressiveness of the born criminal type, or may repel others by excessive irritability which becomes almost senile in pettishness and negativism, that is not only chronically cross, but that refuses to conform to every suggestion of friends by a contrary impulse so well characterized by Tarde in his Opposition Universelle.

5. Again, in this age, when everything is most uncertain, imitation reaches its acme, if we include its psychic as well as its merely attitudinal and motor forms. Youth must ape positions, expressions, gait, and mien in order to understand, and the new psychology of imitation shows that it is the basis of the social instinct of which also this age is the springtime. Every peculiarity is mimicked, and parodied, whether of phraseology, manner, or mood. Every youth has a more or less developed stock of phrases, acts, and postures, expressive of mimetic love, anger, fear, many occupations or vocations of infancy and old age, of the other sex, and he is plastic and suggestible to an amazing degree to everything of this kind in his environment. He catches the idiosyncrasies, accents, and inflections of teachers and fellow pupils, and reenacts incidents; a little older, he is bemastered by the style of great authors he has read, and is an adept at dialect and the personation of national types. Thus when the precocious dement apes other patients, perhaps following them about the wards to do so, as he is prone to in echopraxia, or repeat words in echolalia, or illustrates the automatism to command, so that any psychic influence about him may become a source of contagion, he is only an extreme type of what belongs to this age as one of its most integral traits, and

merely lacks the higher power of coordinating it with the opposite motive of self-affirmation and independence.

6. Partly its imitative, and partly its pragmatic nature makes youth dramatic, fond of assuming rôles and poses, of affectations and mannerisms, of attitudes and special movements, gestures, perhaps stereotyped, that may become as significant as slang. Normally these rôles succeed each other and seem to be circumnutations of the instinct to explore all the possibilities of life in feeling and expression, as well as aids to sympathetic comprehension of situations and types of character. But just as speech may lose its higher function and lapse to not only slang but even interjectional forms, so poses may slowly become fixed postures, and even contractures, or a limited repertory of stereotyped acts may develop on a basis of the natural automatisms of Lindley.[1] These manifestations are another of the characteristics of this degeneration.

7. Youth is the age of folly. Its self-consciousness makes it peculiarly susceptible to criticism and suspicion that all its acts and sayings may be ridiculous. This is especially felt for the sentiments new-born at this age. Hence, partly to disguise these, and partly from the very different propensity of lapsing to the lower plane of banality, we have silliness as a marked feature of adolescent witlings. College songs, the absurdities of cork minstrelsy, the infantilism of Mother Goose, the eccentricities of enfeebled intelligence, so strongly entrenched on the variety stage, with its exaggerated oddities, freakishness, and idiocies, foolish and funny acting, with every kind of grimace, have frequent illustrations in the lives of normal youth, with whom all this is spontaneous and intentional. This tendency is deep-seated in our organism, as I have elsewhere [2] tried to show. But we have in the early dements copious illustrations of the ebullitions of unpremeditated and unrepressed folly, the most fatuous manifestations of which we should only laugh at were there but the power of voluntary self-restoration.

[1] Some Mental Automatisms. (With G. E. Partridge.) Ped. Sem., July, 1897, vol. v, pp. 41–60.

[2] The Psychology of Tickling, Laughing, and the Comic. Am. Jour. of Psy., Oct., 1897, vol. ix, pp. 1–41.

8. Youth normally comes into a new attitude toward speech at puberty. The vocabulary is enlarged; meanings are readjusted; words seem different; there is always a new speech consciousness; interest in new terms shows that in some cases we have loquacity which becomes almost verbigeration; diaries and letters, and even stories and treatises are scribbled at great length. We often observe, too, an inverse ratio between thought and speech, so that as the former becomes scanty and indefinite the stream of words flows more copiously and smoothly; and conversely, as meanings deepen the vocabulary becomes more select and the lapse of speech and pen more restrained. In other normal types the mass of new inner experiences of thought, motive, and sentiment prompt concealment and reticence, and the subject becomes dumb-bound, silent, and perhaps seems to brood, or the range of expression is very confined and narrow. Both these tendencies have asylum outcrops in Forel's "word-salad" or Krafft-Ebing's "word-husks" on the one hand, or in mumbling and taciturnity, even speechlessness, on the other.

9. Normally this is the social age where friendships, interests, and sympathies with others ought to be at their strongest and best; but many a normal youth is shy, solitary, bashful, and inclines to withdraw from the world and nourish his individuality in isolation. It is the age when, whatever we may hold regarding adult life, Godfernaux's[1] conception of the dominance of sentiment over thought is not only true, but an admirable characterization. No stage of life is so prone to religious perturbations, which tend to become erratic as well as extreme. Speculation is trying its callow wings; sense solicitations are incessant and pervasive; competition makes tense every power of mind and body; the other sex, which had hardly existed before, now turns on its subtle magnetism and establishes a new polarity; art, science, and literature reveal their inner charm; the great elective system of the manifold vocations beckons in many directions at once; adult life, which had before seemed hazy and afar, because boyish interests expand horizontally along their own age level, now becomes a cynosure of fascinating absorp-

[1] Le Sentiment et la Pensée, 1894.

tion; a limbo of new temptations beckons or impels to the indulgence of passion or in the loss of orientation to truth, duty, health; all the possible permutations and combinations of error are illustrated in the aberrations of this formative period, so that the acceptance of any classification or systemization of its phenomena would be premature, and therefore unfortunate, for both knowledge and practise.

10. Even in graver cases orientation in time and place may be unimpaired; school knowledge may be tolerably well preserved; the memory plexus, although in parts distorted and shot through by veins or delusionary eruptions, may be tolerably maintained and many old skills intact. Unfavorable as the prognosis is for mental restoration at any stage, it is extremely favorable for life. The temperature fluctuates between wide extremes and may become exceptionally low; the heart and arteries, which normally undergo such rapid changes at this stage, are often modified in their action, and perhaps cyanosis or dermography show the disorders of circulation. Pain, and especially megrim, most common in girls of fourteen or fifteen, reflects vaso-motor irregularities. Excessive wakefulness and sleepiness, gormandizing or persistent refusal of food, which, like sadness and jollity, may alternate, exhibit the larger periodicities, while repetition, chewing, dancing, rocking and swaying show the disturbances of the shorter rhythms, to both of which this period is normally strangely susceptible.

As these troubles have far more mild than grave forms, we probably see the effect of their taint in hoodlums, rowdies, hoboes, vagrants, vagabonds, dudes, spendthrifts with no money sense, ne'er-do-wells, egoists, cases of moral insanity, juvenile criminals, and hosts of people whose early life promised well, but who disappoint the expectation of fond parents and friends and drop into contentment with very humble stations, the limited duties of which they just manage to perform. Fornelli[1] has described with great vividness the disappointed expectations concerning children, which is one of the sad observations of the school-teacher. We see them in the gilded

[1] Die Kinderfehler, 1901, pp. 208 and 241.

youth who live for the moment; who can never have serious thoughts of the future; who are selfishly unmindful of others' rights, interests, convenience, pleasures; who live to eat, drink, dress, and study girls.

While we are familiar with the dangers of the overstimulation of school to produce precocity, we greatly need to be reminded that the school may also be a distinct cause of arrested development, which follows directly from injudicious methods of teaching, as Dr. W. T. Harris [1] has shown. If wonted to a habit that belongs to a lower stage of development, as by oversevere drill in sense-perception or mechanical memory, the child is thereby held back on a lower plane and the normal growth of classification and the search for cause, that ought to come next, will be prevented. This is the effect of overthoroughness, excessive devotion to detail, or incessant analysis of processes that never ought to be dissected, because thus we take apart what should grow together to ever higher unities. Memory is often inversely as thought, and incessant appeals to sense also distract from it. Baur [2] concisely characterizes the causes and effects of premature and belated development of mind and body.

Many writers since Lelut and Nisbet have recognized a certain close analogy between genius and insanity. Both are prone to eccentricity; often have a disordered emotional basis or an insane temperament; are likely to produce inferior children; to occur in the same family, etc.[3] Whether mattoids or sports, geniuses are always the apotheosis of adolescence. At this age all may be said to be normally geniuses, some in slight and some in high degree, some for a flitting moment and some for life. Then at least the approximation to genius is closest, and those who blossom into full the efflorescence of creativeness do so by virtue of the energy that nature gives only then. Plato said delusions may be good if from the gods, and at the genius period of youth many a great man has been

---

[1] Education, April, 1900.

[2] Körperlich u. geistige Früh- und Spätentwickelung. Zeitsch. f. Schulgesundheitpflege, 1899, p. 707.

[3] Radestock: Genie und Wahnsinn, 1884, p. 76; Joli: Psychologie des Grandes Hommes, 1883; Lombroso; The Man of Genius; Windelband: Pathologie der Genie in Hölderlein; Morselli: Genie Neurosi, 1892; Hirsch: Genie und Entartung, 1894, p. 340.

more or less melted and perhaps remolded by the heat of his own soul. According to the severe and minute criteria of the Lombroso school, perfect sanity is a painfully limited, commonplace, and stupid thing, which very few of the great and good of the world have enjoyed. Like every conception based on averages, it is lacking in all individualizing traits, and has lost sight of variation. More than almost any other writer on abnormalities, this author lacks all appreciation of adolescence, which always involves more or less psychic inebriation. He fails to see that excess of normal vitality not only safely can but must explore the beginnings of many morbidities, both to know the more varied and intense possibilities of human life and to evoke the sanifying correctives, etc.

Genetic psychology, both morbid and normal, urgently needs better tables of age liability of all psycho-neural diseases; and for its larger development and truer and deeper insight, psychiatry needs them no whit less, while at present both are handicapped—the one by the speculative and introspective tradition of philosophic schools and outgrown problems, and the other by too exclusive attention to clinical symptoms. The old prejudices between these departments should now give place to a new and cooperative unity.

Among the chief external causes of the diseases of this age are all those influences which tend to precocity, e. g., city life with its earlier puberty, higher death rate, wider range and greater superficiality of knowledge, observations of vice and enhanced temptation, lessened repose, incessant distraction, more impure air, greater liability to contagion, and absence of the sanifying influences and repose of nature in country life. At its best, metropolitan life is hard on childhood and especially so on pubescents, and children who can not pass these years in the country are robbed of a right of childhood that should be inalienable, and are exposed to many deleterious influences which jeopardize both health and morals. Civilization with all its accumulated mass of cultures and skills, its artifacts, its necessity of longer and severer apprenticeship and specialization, is ever harder on adolescents, and even in a republic the submerged fraction of the population not adequate to achieve success in its ever fiercer competitions, who drop limp and exhausted in body and soul to a condition acknowledged by many anthropologists to be essentially inferior to that of most of the lowest savages, increases, and institutions for defectives and those who live on charities multiply. Modern industrialism makes poverty ever more unendurable. When we add to these predisposing causes the small and decreasing families, the later marriages, so that more and more are born of post-mature parents and thus physiologically tend to precocity; the over-nurture of only children who are so prone to be spoiled and ripened still earlier by unwise fondness; the mixture of distinct ethnic stocks that increase the ferments of adolescence by multiplying the factors of heredity and so increasing its instability, we no longer wonder that many in these most vulnerable years make more or less complete shipwrecks at every stage of these hothouse demands, which in the entire life of our race are so recent.

Under these provocations, some instincts spring into activity with a suddenness that is almost explosive, and so prematurely, that as, e. g., with sex and drink, the strong and complex psychic mechanism of control has no time to develop and forbidden pleasures are tasted to satiety, till the soul has sometimes not only lost its innocence before it understood what purity and virtue really mean, but life is *blasé,* a burnt-out cinder, admiration, enthusiasm, and high ambitions are weakened or gone, and the soul is tainted with indifference or discouragement. An English alienist gives as one of the chief traits of sanity what he terms tension—i. e., strong passions held in strong control, as if it were a kind of potential necessary for great achievement or great endurance; and physiologists have conceived inhibition, and even the brain itself, as a regulator of reflexes, as a method of storing up energy for either outer or inner work, so that if this is lacking there is incessant leakage, since the repose of good manners checks the waste of the many automatisms—giggling, swaying, grimacing, imperative impulses to say or do, expression of feelings of anger, pride, selfishness, fear, etc., and, in a word, tames man, who at this stage is ever prone to lapse to feral traits or even animalism. Not only will, but attention, means repression in all but the one direction to which all available energy is focused. As the decapitated animal plays off a convulsive "clotted mass of motion," the stimuli to many if not all of which were before present but repressed, and as the somnolent man starts as he falls asleep because the repressions of the higher zones which act in waking are removed in this "psychic decapitation"; so if these superior levels are not developed, reflex susceptibility not only to the environment but responsive expressiveness to every inner impulse is instant. The patient dramatizes every chance suggestion, creeps, yells, gallops, jabbers, spits, sings, lisps, whispers, utters or does nameless obscenities at any time, place, or in any presence, is made drunk by minimal drams because he is constitutionally near to inebriation by loss of higher impulsions and the intensification of lower ones. His talk is shot through by cross-thoughts that make verbal incoherence or "Bill Prattisms";[1] movements to one purpose are diverted to another; and flightiness, chaos, balderdash, and galimatias dominate sense and sentence. Or again, the mechanism runs down and there are incessant repetitions; movements are slow and clumsy as if weights were attached to the limbs as in Kraepelin's athetoid ataxia; and in rare cases there are poses resembling the waxy flexibility of catalepsy and perhaps even resulting contractures.

Judgment and even common sense begin in and rest on associations that reflect the ever irradiating correspondences in time, place, and cause. These processes are as different from those above as associate fibers (both ends and the entire course of which are within the brain) are from the projective system of afferent and efferent, or sensory and motor fibers. These functions, whatever their neural basis, come into dominance later than the sensori-motor activity of the internal capsule. Their cerebral elements may for our purpose here be roughly said to connect different brain areas, and thereby to establish psychic unity among the discrete factors of our personality. Now contradictions and inconsistencies begin to be eliminated, and thought harmonizes and knits into unity the elements of psychic life. We balance, compare, infer, and reason, and the brain, or at least the soul, acts more as a whole. We criticize our acts; apply logical and ethical tests; deliberate, plan, act to a purpose, and hear from outlying regions of our psychophysic plexus. Of these faculties, as of so many others, adolescence is the nascent period, and their failure to develop marks an

[1] Bill Pratt. The Saw-Buck Philosopher. Williamstown, 1895.

important characterization of juvenile degeneration. The city of "Man-soul," without any such government and regulative function, becomes a wild mob of lawless passion, desires, or blinder impulses and impressions, till from sheer anarchy, with no other specific agency, it speedily lapses to lower plateaus, where the surviving elements fall into some crude *modus vivendi*, which constitutes a chance personality very different from any earlier stage of development. One thing is certain, that if Morel's[1] pessimistic vaticinations are true and our race is to degenerate again, it will not be through ignorance of our idolatrized school knowledge, by impiety, war, pestilence, luxury, or even vice, or by the shortening of adult life as shown in tables of average longevity, or even by the abatement of adult activity, or all of these together, but it will be by the progressive failure of youth to develop normally and to maximal maturity and sanity, and these other proximal causes will be deleterious just in proportion as they affect this. If regeneration is ever to lift us to a higher plane, the adolescent nisus will be its mainspring.

[1] Traité des dégénérescences physiques, intellectuelles et morales de l'espèce humaine, et des causes qui produisent ces variétés maladives, pp. 700 with an atlas. Paris, 1857.

CHAPTER V

JUVENILE FAULTS, IMMORALITIES, AND CRIMES

Increase of youthful crime—Age statistics—Forms of juvenile crime—Causation—Degeneration and the criminal types—Nature and genesis of crime—Its biologic aspect—Children's faults—School conduct and punishments—Relations to weather—Truancy and the migratory instinct—The psychology of lying and its forms—Anger in adolescence—Revenge—Envy and jealousy—Fighting, psychic rudiments and atavism—Bullying and torturing—Spontaneous social organization of gangs and clubs—The Mafia and Camorra—Theft and its psychology—Pyromania—Alcoholism—Prostitution—Rape and age of consent—Suicide and its motivation and frequency in youth—Pauperism and crime—Contagion of vice and crime—Relation of crime to the menstrual period—Schemes of classification of crime—Punishment and juvenile penology—Its theory and practise in different ages and lands—Age of responsibility in ancient and modern times—Reformatories—Probation and conditional sentences—Flogging—Degrees of corrigibility and recidivism—The larger view—Suggestions for academic ethics.

In all civilized lands, criminal statistics show two sad and significant facts: First, that there is a marked increase of crime at the age of twelve to fourteen, not in crimes of one, but of all kinds, and that this increase continues for a number of years. While the percentages of certain grave crimes increase to mature manhood, adolescence is preeminently the criminal age when most first commitments occur and most vicious careers are begun. The second fact is that the proportion of juvenile delinquents seems to be everywhere increasing and crime is more and more precocious. Although vice is very different from crime, and although but a relatively small proportion of all offenders are caught and sentenced, the number of convictions affords one of the best indexes of the general state of morality at any age. Hence the significance of these facts for ethics, sociology, genetic psychology, and for the efficiency of education and religion, as well as for the success of a form of civilization, is profound and complex. We shall take space here for only a few of the most typical statistical illustrations of the above facts.

In Italy, where crime is so abundant and so well studied, an average for the year 1886, which I choose as typical, shows the following percentage frequency by ages:

	Men.	Women.
Below 14	1.29 per cent	1.41 per cent.
Between 14–18	6.04 "	6.02 "
" 18–21	13.29 "	10.05 "
" 21–35	46.91 "	39.38 "
" 35–50	23.29 "	30.94 "
" 50–70	8.40 "	11.63 "
Over 70	0.68 "	0.57 "

The age of maximal criminality in men in Italy is about twenty-five, but as this is the age of most active maternity in woman her age of greatest crime is about thirty-five. Rossi found that of 46 criminals 40 began their criminal career before twenty-six, and that their abuse of wine and their sexual precocity was hardly less marked. In India young children are often most expert in crime. N. David found that of 43,835 sentenced German criminals, 41 per cent were under twenty-one years of age. Corré [1] shows that in France, from 1876–'80 there were as many sentences for youth between sixteen and twenty-one as between twenty-one and forty, and for the next five years very nearly the same ratio was maintained, although severer penalties predominated for the older criminals. The increment of crime with age he shows by the following table, giving the distribution of 7,475 cases of young delinquents:

	Boys.	Girls.	Total.
Before 8	14	6	20
8–10	159	37	196
11–12	425	117	542
12–14	1,214	269	1,483
14–16	1,739	409	2,148
16–18	1,765	385	2,150
18–20	714	209	923
Over 20	3	8	11

Sikorski, commissioned by the Russian Government to study the pupils of the military gymnasium who presented

[1] Crime et Suicide. Paris, 1891, p. 307.

anomalies of character, that made their education difficult, found these distributed by ages as follows:

11 years	2.5	per cent.
12 "	6.1	"
13 "	23.7	"
14 "	20.0	"
15 "	21 0	"
16 "	6.2	"
17 "	1.2	"

In the 58 juvenile reformatories of the United States, according to the eleventh census of 1890, there were 14,846 inmates, of which 3,311 were females. The average age of both sexes was 14.23; of the males 14.09, and of the females 14.71 years. The lowest average for both sexes is found in the South Central States for children of foreign parents, and is 12.49 years; and the highest in the South Atlantic States for children of unknown nativity, when it is 16. Most of these institutions receive offenders from five to twenty-five. The following table shows the distribution between the ages of seven and twenty-one:

Age.	Males.	Females.
7	63	27
8	143	59
9	260	78
10	466	116
11	265	127
12	1,182	189
13	1,478	290
14	1,769	381
15	1,751	466
16	1,626	543
17	921	480
18	420	234
19	213	96
20	103	57
21	25	15

The above figures must not, of course, be interpreted to mean a decline in criminality after puberty, for the proportionate number of convictions continues to rise, but older criminals are not sent to reformatories, but to prisons and other institutions. The rise of these numbers to 15 shows the real pubescent increment of crime, which augments pretty steadily during all the earlier and later periods of adolescence, not only in number but in gravity. Jolly[1] ascribes the growing precocity in crime seen in most countries to the many causes in modern life which hasten maturity, and says that the great majority of criminals first convicted are adolescents. Juvenile crime has lately become a more or less independent department of penology and presents many new problems of absorbing interest and prime importance. To determine with certainty the increase in precocity, the age tables of prisoners should be compared with those of the population at large, and the number of each age in prison divided by the total number of each age. This calculation, Mr. F. H. Wines lately wrote me, has not yet been made in this country. In Russia, however, crime between fourteen and twenty-one has increased much faster than the relative growth of the population. In Germany, from 1871 to 1890, the rural population decreased from 63 to 53 per cent. The large cities increased from 4.8 to over 10 per cent, and cities of all lesser sizes increased. This Schultz[2] thinks favorable for youthful crime. He finds at this stage of life a growing distaste for both discipline and knowledge, and especially for religion, from which he infers only a gloomy future. In the German empire since 1892, when 46,496 juvenile convicts were reported, this class had increased 50 per cent in 1895. About 40 per cent of the annual convictions in England are of those under twenty-one. In 1886 the number convicted between eighteen and twenty-one years was 16 per cent of the prison population of England, while 6 per cent were between fifteen and eighteen, and 3 per cent between twelve and fifteen.[3] In Austria, in 1890, the number of juvenile offenders from eleven to fourteen for the ten years ending 1895 averaged 693 yearly, and those from fourteen to twenty averaged 5,729, a total of 21.82 per cent of all convicts. In this country the average age of all juveniles in reformatories was 14.23 years. Of these 6,930 were for offenses against society, of which 4,515 were against property, petty larceny being the predominating form of crime. In the New York reformatory 94 per cent were for offenses against property as against 87 per cent in the

[1] La France Criminelle, p. 179 *et seq.*
[2] Giftquellen für die ländliche Jugend. Leipzig, 1896.
[3] Drähms: The Criminal. 1900, p. 272 *et seq.*

English reformatories. From eighteen to twenty-four, according to Drähms, is the criminal age in England, the number of commitments reaching its maximum between sixteen and twenty-one; while the average age in this country is a little over two years later.

Of about 200,000 boys and girls in the *Gemeinde* schools of Berlin,[1] in the year 1899, 298 boys and 37 girls were convicted by the courts of some offense against law. Of the boys 35 were twelve years of age; 140 were thirteen; and 123 were thirteen or over. Of these 232 were convicted of stealing and the rest were distributed among 17 different rubrics. Only 108 of the boys were imprisoned; 199 were reproved by the judge, and 3 were fined. Most of the imprisonments were for a month or less, and only 9 for over six months.

Ferri [2] says that there is a continual increase of precocious criminals in Italy, and that precocity is most frequent in those natural crimes and offenses common among born criminals. He finds increased frequency among females of precocious crimes against person, and among males against property, and that precocity is closely attended by relapse which follows its own laws at this age as it does later in life. Born, like habitual, criminals generally confine themselves mostly to serious crimes, while occasional criminals are prone to minor offenses. A distinguished French magistrate finds that in fifty years the criminal percentage of the population in France has passed from 227 to 552 for every 100,000 inhabitants, an increase of 33 per cent, and that this increase is most marked among young persons, and he concludes that the recent free obligatory and lay education has not supplied the place of the old system of apprenticeship.

Corré and others give many representative cases of grave crime in early puberty in strongly motive temperaments before knowledge and power of control have developed. A young nurse, e. g., having no sense of the value of life poisoned a child with phosphorus from matches in order that she might go out and seek amusement. A boy of fourteen stabbed a playmate who had reproached him. Another of the same age killed

[1] Pädagogische Zeitung, March 28, 1901.
[2] Criminal Sociology, p. 32.

a comrade to rob him of ten centimes, and another violated and strangled a girl of nine, imagining an elaborate romance to escape the police. One of nine killed his brother of eight to get his new shoes. Another shot his two sisters, aged fourteen and sixteen, because jealous of the preference shown them by his parents. Emulation of crimes of acquaintances or of those heard or read of is often a motive. Two boys plotted and killed an old man "to amuse themselves." Eleven boys banded together to steal and rob, partly for sheer mischief, stealing nothing of value. Two boys of fifteen fought a duel with pistols, with seconds of the same age. A lad of eighteen stabbed a strange girl who refused his advances in the street. Such cases could easily be multiplied indefinitely from the current chronicles of crime. Dr. Wigan in his unpublished writings, as quoted by Winslow, gives an account of crimes committed without any object by young people from sixteen to eighteen. These are often crimes against people for whom they have had no animosity. Many of these cases had epistaxis. Winslow gives interesting cases of latent insanity in adolescence. Such children are by turns sad, and grow wild and ungovernable. They can neither apply themselves nor submit to rules. Some are successively apathetic and volatile. Sometimes there are spasmodic attacks after a long incubation period. In some cases the strangeness is manifested only in inability to assume any fixed position in life. Alienation in youth is serious because so often hereditary. Moral insanity, which sometimes precedes and sometimes comes out at puberty, is characterized by incapacity for education, distaste for family life, marked peculiarities of character, extreme cleverness in certain directions, bad sexuality and criminality. The more passionate and instinctive men are, the more they resemble children in these respects and the more egoistic they are.

As to the nature of juvenile crime in general, Drähms estimates it as in the proportion of fifteen to one against property, and all statistics show that crimes against persons reach their maximum later. Marro[1] constructs the curve on the next page to show this relation.

In Germany it was found that of 30,902 thieves, 45 per cent

---

[1] La Puberta, p. 224.

were under twenty-one. Out of every 100,000 inhabitants, 29 were convicted under twelve; 261 between twelve and sixteen; 321 between sixteen and twenty-one; 245 between twenty-one and thirty; about one-fourth of convicted thieves were under sixteen; and about one-third of all those convicted of breaking and entering were between eighteen and twenty-one. Between twelve and fifteen theft leads all other forms of crime; between twenty-one and twenty-five crimes against persons predominate; while offenses against public morals are rare at twenty. Sometimes when the sexual impulse has been delayed and breaks out suddenly, it leads to suicide and crime; but more frequently sex acts indirectly at first and crimes due to jealousy come relatively late in adolescence.[1]

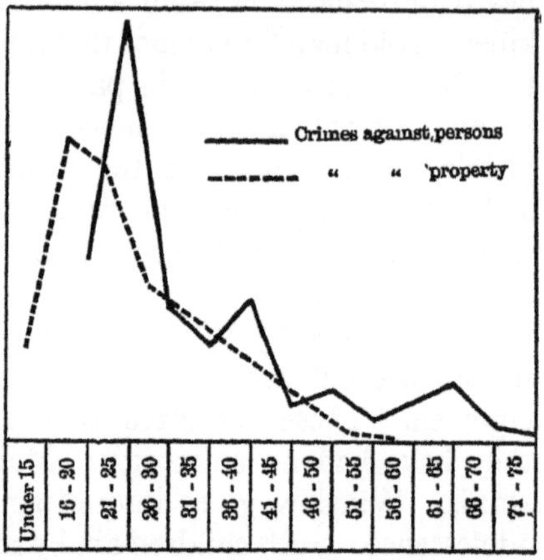

In a table Marro presents the following per cents:[2]

	Normal.	Criminals of all classes.	Murder.	Crimes against persons.	Crimes against property.	Theft.	Fraud.	Insanity.
Before 26............	8.8	10.9	2.9	13.5	2.7	15.5	2.8	17.0
26–40............	66.1	56.7	44.1	45.9	66.6	57.2	60.0	47.0
After 40............	24.9	32.2	52.9	40.5	30.5	27.1	37.1	36.0

Morrison[3] estimates that more than one-half of the children below fourteen sent to corrective institutions are for offenses such as truancy, begging, incorrigibility and refractory disposition, which he would group as nomadic, or at least with a strong factor of vagrancy, and that to reformatory schools,

[1] Wille: Pubertäts Psychose, p. 3 *et seq.*
[2] La Puberta, p. 344.
[3] Juvenile Offender, pp. 64–71.

from fourteen to sixteen, hardly one-tenth are sent for such offenses. Here more serious theft commonly leads. Morrison says "crimes of violence against the person are not half so numerous among young children under sixteen as they are among youths between sixteen and twenty-one. Crimes against morals are between three and four times more numerous among youth between sixteen and twenty-one as among the juvenile population under sixteen. Crimes in the nature of burglary, house-breaking, and shop-breaking and the like are four times more frequent among youths over sixteen than among juveniles under that age." Juveniles are not seriously addicted to drink, but there are more indictments among them in proportion to the juvenile population than there are among those between thirty and forty, when the influence of drink is far greater. Instead, therefore, of drink and crime going together, as is often said, "there is less indictable crime among the drunken than among the sober section of the population." Although the size and intelligence of children prevent them from becoming criminals except in the way of vagrancy or petty theft, we must not regard these offenses as less grave, because it is thus that every criminal career begins, and the effort of society should be to prevent this evolution into the habitual class.

The following table according to the census of 1890 shows the cause of condemnations in the juvenile reformatories of this country:

	Boys.	Girls.	Total.
Assassination, murder	232	58	290
Violation of morals	213	193	406
Theft	4,136	711	4,847
Lying and vagabondage	1,260	305	1,565
Disobedience of parents	1,055	278	1,333
Other crimes	138	11	148

I have also computed the table on p. 333 from the census of 1890 (Crime and Pauperism, Part II, pp. 586–569), arranging the years in order of frequency.

From this table it appears that of the above offenses, truancy is the first juvenile offense to be punished by sentences to these institutions, and that these cases constitute the youngest class, more of whom are thirteen than any other age. Fourteen is the maximal age for incorrigibility and malicious mischief and trespass; fifteen for petty larceny, vagrancy, disorderly conduct

Both sexes. Age.	Incorrigibility.	Petit larceny.	Vagrancy.	Larceny.	Burglary.	Truancy.	Disorderly conduct.	Assaults, all sorts.	Public intoxication.	Fornication.	Grand larceny.	Malicious mischief and trespass.	Total.	Females.
7	5	1	2	....	....	1	....	....	...	1	....	....	10	1
8	21	8	19	1	1	5	3	....	...	3	1	1	63	5
9	80	23	34	8	2	15	5	1	....	2	....	2	172	25
10	148	45	52	23	10	36	11	2	....	3	2	8	340	33
11	269	104	84	42	23	53	21	7	1	3	9	5	621	56
12	401	222	130	85	25	93	43	17	....	8	8	13	1,045	89
13	532	286	159	116	44	106	66	26	1	10	11	8	1,365	142
14	645	426	195	154	66	84	86	35	1	21	22	29	1,764	255
15	591	499	203	155	105	57	94	44	7	28	30	16	1,829	309
16	598	485	185	167	124	29	67	43	8	41	36	13	1,796	380
17	385	266	130	105	75	20	50	37	7	50	24	11	1,160	338
18	196	88	62	57	39	3	31	14	4	26	15	2	537	168
19	95	31	32	34	17	3	6	6	2	13	12	3	254	67
20	66	12	19	14	3	1	2	3	2	5	4	2	133	43
21	14	1	4	3	3	...	1	3	1	1	1	1	33	10
Total	4,046	2,497	1,310	964	537	506	486	238	34	215	175	114	11,122	1,921
of which females =	918	225	214	187	152	147	13	54	17	16	5	3	......	......

and assaults; sixteen for larceny, burglary, and public intoxication; and seventeen for fornication. Thus from about twelve to fifteen, and even from fifteen to twenty, crimes against property are more frequent, and these are in close connection with the primal instinct of self-conservation; while crimes against persons, except rapes, attain their maximal from twenty-one to twenty-five, and these are due to self-esteem and to an exaggerated sense of personality. The general instability of this period so often emphasized in defectives is seen in frequent change of occupation, which Marro estimates to be more than twice as common among the disequilibrated as among the normal. This is common among criminals. Crimes against property among the degenerates, he thinks, reach their maximum between twenty-one and twenty-five.

Juvenile crime shows thus the great difficulty which youth finds in making adjustment to the social surroundings, and so far as the law takes cognizance of it, it very often begins as the outcrop of the vagrant instinct which the requirements of the modern school bring out in a strong light. Next and closely connected with the reversion to nomadic life, in the evolution of the antisocial life of crime, comes resistance to the institution of property. In passing from home to the new conditions of industrial life with its severer code, control is increasingly difficult, and this epoch for the boy is not unlike that of the sudden emancipation of the negroes in the South, when, instead of being members of the planter's family where pilfering was treated leniently or punished at home, they found themselves liable to arraignment and imprisonment for every petty theft. Third, and later, as a rule, are evolved crimes against person.

Taking 1883 as a typical year, Corré[1] presents the following instructive table:

	Boys.	Girls.	Total.
Under 8 years	14	36	20
8–10 "	159	37	196
10–12 "	425	117	542
12–14 "	1,214	269	1,483
14–16 "	1,739	409	2,148
16–18 "	1,765	385	2,150
18–20 "	714	209	923
Above 20 "	3	8	11

In turning now more specifically to the cause and nature of adolescent crime, we confront the vast field of modern criminology, a whole new university department, which comprises both science with a myriad of details and new methods and a philosophy opening from a new standpoint into the largest problems of society, morals, biology, pedagogy, and life and mind generally. Unsatisfactory as his school is as a finality, we must ascribe great and epoch-making significance to Lombroso for first attempting the greater fundamentality so necessary and so inevitable. He intimates that even some plants have criminal traits, and finds them in abundance in the rage and slaughter of carnivorous animals; in their war-waging cannibalism; in their murders for love and luxury; in their destruction of the newly born and the aged; in their slyness and cunning; in thefts and in the outcasts from their social organisms, etc. Savages for him are essentially criminal, and he greatly exaggerates their cruelty, abortions, robbery, slaughter for vengeance, ambition, greed, etc., ignoring the fact that modern anthropology finds most savages amiable, kindly, and virtuous, often according to standards like, as well as others unlike, our own. Far sounder and more helpful is his suggestion that normal children often

[1] Crime et Suicide. Paris, 1891, p. 309.

pass through stages of passionate cruelty, laziness, lying, and thievery. He reminds us that their vanity, slang, obscenity, contagious imitativeness, their absence of moral sense, disregard of property, and violence to each other, constitute them criminals in all essential respects, lacking only the strength and insight to make their crime dangerous to the communities in which they live. We are told that to magnify the soul of the child before its more animal instincts are reduced to due proportion and control by conscience and reason, would give us the most truculent and menacing forms of criminality; just as to magnify all parts and organs of the infant's body in equal proportion would, as we have seen, product deformity and monstrosity.

He finds that criminals in general, tested anthropometrically, have smaller brains, larger jaws, less facial expression; are more prone to certain hyperemias, to asymmetries, prognathism, defects of the ear; are particularly prone to have their bodies tattooed with various symbolic devices, love sententious phrases or obscene images, to which adolescents have a special predilection; that their periodicities are perturbed; their general sensibility is below, and their disvulnerability above the normal; they are generally lacking in pity; their life is short; mancinism is more common among them; in most mental tests they are inferior; they are very proud of their accomplishments and achievements in crime; make revenge a virtue; are carnal in their love; and are often highly religious in an atavistic way. The chief lesion in criminal psychology, according to the Lombroso school, concerns not so much the intelligence as the sentiments. Criminals are generally of a very bright and buoyant humor, and fond of all kinds of revelry and raillery. Thieves perhaps are most inferior, and among the most highly specialized types of delinquents, who become very expert and professional, and have such instinctive horror of murder that they can not kill even to save their own lives. An interesting trait of mind is their fondness for symbolic and hieroglyphic signs, which have been made a study, as they are portrayed upon their bodies, on prison walls, in their letters, etc., and which are psychologically akin to their argot.

Degenerate children are neurotic, irritable, vain, lacking in vigor, very fluctuating in mood, prone to show aberrant tendencies under stress, often sexually perverted at puberty, with extreme shyness or bravado, imitative, not well controlled, "dashing about like a ship without a rudder, fairly well if the winds be fair and the sea be calm, but dependent on the elements for the character and the time of the final wreck." Invention, poetry, music, artistic taste, philanthropy, intensity, and originality, are sometimes of a higher order among these persons, but desultory, half-finished work and shiftlessness are much more common. With many of them, concentrated, sustained effort, and attempts to keep them to it, are impossible. Their common-sense perception of the relations of life, executive or business faculty and judgment, are seldom well developed. The memory is now and then extraordinary. They are apt to be self-conscious, egoistic, and morbidly conscious. They easily become victims of insomnia, neurasthenia, hypochondria, neuroticism, hysteria, or insanity. They offend against the proprieties of life and commit crime with less cause or provocation than other persons. While many of them are among the most gifted and attractive people in their community, the majority are otherwise, and possess an uncommon capacity for making fools of themselves, and of being a nuisance to their friends and of little use to the world." [1] They are often very imitative; their feelings are fervid but shallow; intense and sudden likes and dislikes, and frequent alternations between love, enmity, and indifference occur. When the body is well made, nervous disorders are less frequent, but often occur with normal physical development. Nerve strain may affect nearly every organ and process. Talbot agrees with Ewald in thinking that mercyism or cud-chewing, bulimia or bovine appetite, acoria or lack of satiety in eating, and a certain kind of catarrh may be directly due to this cause.

What Demoor [2] calls degenerate evolution exists everywhere in both the biological and the social field. Often the adult stage is suppressed, especially in pedogenesis, where sexual organs ripen and function prematurely. When the social organism is decaying, it does not readily and completely disappear, but drags a trail of *débris* from the past, and degen-

[1] Degeneracy: Its Causes, Signs, and Results, by E. S. Talbot. London, 1899, p. 155. [2] Evolution by Atrophy. New York, 1899.

erate forms soon lose the power to reacquire the conditions normal to their more perfect ancestors, as Magnan has shown; so that the degenerate condition is not attained by simply going backward down the line of ascent, but is a new point of departure, and retrogression is therefore a somewhat misleading term. The nauplius, which was originally a crustacean leading an independent and free swimming life when it is a parasite on the crab, which is its host, loses legs and senses, and can by no cultivation or environment regain the original nauplius form.

Another of the most extreme biological degenerations is that of the sea-squirt, which in its larval state is a vertebrate, but when it matures is only an ascidian. Lancaster shows how many organisms slide down the phyletic scale and react to an ever less complex environment. The idiot brain may be arrested in a stage very similar to that of the anthropoid or even the saurian. In giantism the human skeleton may revert to a state that suggests that of the gorilla. This is also illustrated in some of the degenerate families that have been studied and laboriously traced, in whom the power of self-help is hopelessly gone. A good illustration of this principle is seen in the descendants of a family stem explored back to about 1790, and some indeterminable time after that represented by thirty families with sixty-two individuals. In the sixth generation a total of 1,750 persons was traced of an estimated total of 5,000, and with an amazing percentage of vice, crime, pauperism, and disease, with thousands of pages of history in charity society records, and with the cost to the communities in which they lived of probably several hundred thousand dollars.[1] The same is true of other notorious families, so many of which have lately been studied, e. g., the Jukes, the Binswangers, Margarets, Aubry's Kerangal family, which Zola made the basis of his Rougons-Macquarts.

We saw in Chapter II that many monstrosities are due to arrest of some part or organ. Cleft palate, wide-open sutures, caudal appendages, etc., are normal at certain stages of embryonic development, and many structures regularly occurring in the lower members of the group to which man belongs may persist in him even up to maturity. We know, too, that certain

[1] The Tribe of Ishmael, by O. C. McCulloch. Proc. Nat. Conference of Charities, Buffalo, 1888.

races of men are ascendant, and others, like the Bushmen and Australians, are decadent stocks. Thus, not only species, including man, but his various organs and functions are evolving or retrograding to some extent independently of each other. From this biological point of view we should expect that exceptional characters and conduct would be found correlated with bodies marked by anomalies, disproportions, lack of symmetry, and stigmata of degeneration and hypertrophy. Such general considerations led to and have been justified by the results of criminal anthropometry. Poverty and crime are closely correlated with starvation of body and of mind, so that both are prone to arrest, and both heredity and environment cooperate in producing modifications of physical structure and psychic powers. Dawson [1] found among boys and girls in reformatory institutions a tendency to shorter stature, lighter weight, diminished strength in the muscles of the hand, greater sensitiveness to pain, small, broad heads, broad faces, deformed palates and skulls, defects of sight and hearing, dulness of touch, and inferiority in attention, memory, and association. Degeneration of mind and morals is usually marked by morphological deviations from the normal. Face, jaws, mouth, nose, arms, feet, legs, trunk, neck, head and its parts may be too small or too large in proportion to the rest. Among functional deviations are abnormal innervation on one side or of special muscles or of vaso-motor nerves, developmental irregularities in dentition, in learning to walk and sit, enuresis, inclination to epileptic and other attacks, incongruity between age and appearance; while the psychic stigmata following Meyer's [2] classification are abnormal habits, ideations, actions, sex psychoses, emotional attitudes, egoism, disequilibration, imperative ideas, associated movements, explosive activity, periodicity, etc. Clouston says all sorts of postponement of developmental processes and all forms of asymmetry about the head and face should be considered as moral danger-signals.

Criminals are much like overgrown children—egoistic, foppish, impulsive, gluttonous, blind to the rights of others, and our passions tend to bring us to childish stages. Goethe de-

[1] A Study in Youthful Degeneracy, by George E. Dawson. Ped. Sem., Dec., 1896, vol. iv, pp. 221–258.

[2] American Journal of Insanity, Jan., 1896.

clared that every one has committed crimes, and it is a frequent remark in the literature of the new criminology that every one would be in prison if he had his just deserts, and that if all laws were exactly enforced there would soon be none outside its walls to enforce them. Brouardel describes the Paris gamin as loving orgy, excitement, and mischief, even his playfulness being full of peccadillos, precociously bright and active from about eight to thirteen, but at sixteen plump, lazy, effeminate in form and habits and often partially or completely *blazé* or sexually impotent. Taverni describes the youth of criminal children as marked by resistance to lessons. They are refractory to the moral environment and without response to educational influences; almost always morally blind and often very superstitious; generally with good appetites and sleeping well, etc. Dr. Wines wrote me, "With regard to the kind of temptation which exerts the greatest influence over the child's mind, I am of the opinion that the criminal habit commences in most young persons either with illicit sexual indulgence or with extravagance and the contracting of debts." The power of self-control is latent and undeveloped, and its necessity must be slowly learned. If he is degenerate or of a criminal type, or if his surroundings are unfavorable, the young criminal fails to acquire this power and falls a victim to the same appetites and impulses which all normal persons feel, but repress. Perhaps the animal part of his nature is abnormally and congenitally disproportionate to the intellectual, so that there is no inner opposition to the gratification of his desires. But growing insight shows the futility of crime and leads to prudence, so that the percentage of criminals at heart in early life is lessened during later adolescence. Indeed it seems very clear that much of the art of living consists in self-control, the development of which in the individual is the unconscious but perhaps primary purpose of family, church, state, laws, customs, and most social institutions, and that the "progress of the world and the advance of personal liberty is just in proportion as the power of self-control has been developed in the community at large." If this is so, magnanimity and a large indulgent parental and pedagogical attitude is the proper one toward all, and especially toward juvenile offenders.

Low as the intelligence of criminals often is when measured

by conventional or educational standards, they are almost always unusually sly and cunning, childish, and even animal. Parasites on society like those on animal bodies need a peculiar kind of adaptation, and we may perhaps say that their intelligence is on a low plane, but is extremely well developed. This has been well brought out by Ferriani.[1] It is the insight of the street boy highly developed, and those accomplished in crime often have a well-developed philosophy of life, strange and bizarre to normal minds, but full of fascination and with standpoints, facts, and dialects which are remarkably adapted to survival, but perhaps on the whole not so very much nearer that of culture and refinement than to the sagacity of the higher animals. The contagion of this psychosis for a mind innately criminal is great. The young offender soon comes to feel himself an enemy of society; to regard legitimate business as legalized theft and robbery; religion as a cloak for hypocrisy; clergymen as paid to preach or labor with prisoners; doctors kill or cure as is for their interest; lawyers are licensed robbers or cunning knaves; purity is a mere pretense; the world is ruled by selfishness; the courts or justice shops are shams; and those who prey upon the weaker sides of human nature know the foibles of even the good only too well. The seasoned young criminal feels himself superior to the plodder who labors legitimately because he lacks the wit or adroitness to do otherwise. All who live comfortably seem to him rich, and all the rich are so by robbery of the poor, who may thus justly take, if they can, their own. Man wants only a bottle, pipe, a mistress, warmth, clothing, and food; and this the world owes every one. His view he profoundly believes to be the right and true one, but society outvotes and the police can overpower him. Hence it is well sometimes to sham virtues, penitence, and even religion. We have not yet in all the interesting literature of criminology any adequate presentation of what may be called the philosophy of feral mankind, who live in the midst of civilization but are undomesticated by it, and until we have we can not realize the infatuation which the first contact with it has at a certain stage upon the minds of youth not duly fortified against it.

Extreme views of the abnormality of crime may well make

[1] Schlaue und glückliche Verbrecher. Berlin, 1899.

us pause, when we reflect on its relativity. Socrates and Jesus were criminals according to the legal standards of their day. We confine and kill those who in the days of Abraham and Ulysses or in positions of power and influence would be heroes. Of the ten chief crimes of the Hebrews of old, only one is now a crime. Many of the knights and barons of the Middle Ages were brigands, but were not then outlawed by public sentiment as abnormal. There is deep and wide-spread feeling in every community that in extreme hunger all things belong to all. The thought of killing our own fathers or children is monstrous, but we kill the fathers and children of other people with impunity in war. Many of our greatest criminals would have been normal and perhaps eminently useful citizens in other ages and places. Judged by severe and inner standards of morals, most of us have committed every crime. None can read such histories of crime as Pike or Pelham without realizing how large an area of conduct, now thought legitimate, has been punished as crime, and even how much that was once forbidden is now allowed. There is a pregnant truth in the saying that every society has just the kind and number of criminals that it deserves. Ideally we can well conceive that a state might be constructed to produce within large limits any percentage of crime required, just as almost any degree of mortality could be controlled by hygienic arrangements. Morally, too, it is a truism that no act in itself may not become either extremely virtuous or extremely vicious, according to its setting in circumstances and environment. It is from this point of view that the question of pure criminal types should be approached. The refinements of the Bertillon measurements, it will then be seen, are just as likely to differentiate a butcher, tailor, drummer type of man, as a thief and murderer type, each with more or less well marked and characteristic physical and psychic traits. Several forms of crime require supernormal powers of body and mind, and it seems an insufferable and provincial assumption that our conventionalities, our moral ideas, and still less our laws are so exact and perfect, that all who transgress them are monsters. Vice and crime are so manifold and diversified, so highly colored with genuine human interests, and open such wide fields of originality and differentiation of human varieties, that it is no wonder that the feral traits of primal man often seem so attractive to children and even to women, compared to the more monotonous, tamed, and toned down humdrum life of good citizenship. There is a certain fascination, even for adults, in reading the chronicles of crime which often stir the blood more than romance, because truth is stranger than fiction. They awaken in every candid heart the confession that it might have consented to, if not have committed, most of the recorded moral aberrations, and suggest a regret that modern youth prefers the stories of more corrupting private vices to the more roistering crimes of old, which certainly had more blood and iron in them. Effrontery, audacity, supercleverness in committing crime, escaping detection, or evading punishment always win a certain admiration, especially in youth. When we have an ideal system of teaching ethics at this stage, we shall have learned how to utilize criminology which can be turned to far higher ethical utility than the current theories about the abstract nature of goodness or the hedonistic calculus, and just in proportion as civilization and practical sociology become developed, they will enable the state and community to utilize most of the energy now wasted in crime by devising more wholesome and natural expressions for the instincts that now motivate it. One thing is certain that the great body of crime is not to be essentially reduced by criminal codes, however skilfully drawn, but only by bettering the individual and social conditions of the community at large.

The greatest need of the penologist and the criminologist is the further study, by expert methods, of individual cases and their relations to the social environment. We must fathom and explore the deeper strata of the soul, personal and collective, to make our knowledge really preventive, and recognize the function of the psychologist, pedagogue, and the physician, which should be far more prominent for youth than for older offenders. If the ideal pauper is feeble and idiotic, the ideal criminal is a brave man in the prime of life, who plans and executes great crimes and not only escapes detection, but convinces the community that he is not only honest, but noble.[1] The fact is that "crime and honesty run in the lines of greatest vitality, and the qualities that make contrivers of crime are substantially the same that will make men successful in honest pur-

[1] See Dugdale: The Jukes, pp. 47 and 53.

suits." Burglary, e. g., requires a strong body, a cool head, presence of mind, a high degree of physical, and what in a better cause would be called moral courage. Wherever there is vitality and especially growth, there can be reform or interchangeability of careers, for many criminals have the qualities that are essential to success in normal careers, and need only a new direction and sphere of effort. Here we need not only the pettifogging pedagogy of school methods, but the largest educational philosophy based on a study of physical and mental character, which can measure the decay of will which lapses so much easier and earlier than, e. g., erotic passion in unregulated characters; which can learn the means of developing the element of continuity lacking in criminals; that can take large views of life and estimate the difference between the formative influences of precept and example which predominate in youth and those of experience and social compulsion, which become more efficient factors of conduct after twenty; that understands how the development of character, like everything else, is in the line of least resistance; which can study and compare the modes of drawing off energy from vice to industry; and which can metamorphose character during the later stages of adolescence to a degree hitherto unsuspected, if prison life has not broken down independence and institutionalized character. Families like the Jukes, which have now been studied in half a dozen leading countries, are marked by great vitality, ignorance, and poverty. The social damage they inflict, measured by the cost of police and prison alone, is vast, and Dr. Guy estimates their probable mental unsoundness as thirty-four times that of the average in communities. Dr. Bruce Thomson, who studied their diseases, says that in all his experience he never has seen such an accumulation of morbidities as their post-mortem examinations reveal. Few die of one disease, and often almost every organ is tainted, and he adds that although their intellects are inferior they are all excessively cunning. Arrested development perhaps tends to produce fitfulness of character, and if we accept the estimate that "for small crimes there are about 100 to 150 offenses to one conviction, and for big jobs five offenses to one conviction," we shall realize the magnitude of the problem.

The relations of crime to atavism, heredity, moral anomala,

insanity, degeneration, temperament, sex, race, age, climate, food, ignorance, vice, sin, misery, imitation, society, passion, free-will, constitute problems vast enough for any academic department. When we add to these themes those of penology and treatment generally, to say nothing of anthropometry, we shall find that we are dealing with almost all the diseases of society and the state besides many that center in the person. Perhaps no single writer has treated these latter themes in a broader and more thorough way than Proal, whose broad philosophy of the relations between crime and suffering and whose special study of suicide are both admirable illustrations of the spirit and method proper for such work (and are worthy the academic coronation which the former received),[1] from their suggestive, comparative standpoint of law and ethics. He has little sympathy with the many theories that would separate legal and moral responsibility, or with the excessive solicitude which extreme determinists feel for criminals. Attenuated responsibility has its place, and he defends remorse from the criticisms now so often made against its legitimacy; would reserve a large place for premeditation among the motives of crime; criticizes the extreme Darwinistic theory of race purgation by the death penalty; everywhere vindicates the utility, necessity, and virtue of free-will; and insists upon the rigor of social and moral expiation which, however, should never pass the exigencies of public security, but should always be effective for intimidation and prevention.

We are here concerned with the great field of criminology only so far as it sheds a rather direct light upon juvenile crime, and this especially requires us to consider more fully its embryology in childhood, and as was also the case with insanity, to dwell upon its relation to normal moral life. For this purpose, we find in the newly opened field of pedagogical pathology suggestive beginnings that must hereafter be considered with care and interest. This, which in some sense originated in Strümpell's publication of that name in 1890, was not much advanced by the arid Herbartian conceptions which he used, but it was reserved for Kraepelin, Demoor, Bauer, and

[1] La Crime et la Peine. Paris, 1894, pp. 548; Le Crime et le Suicide Passionnels. Paris, 1900.

especially Ufer, Trüper and the contributors to their journal devoted to the faults of children to really develop here a center of great interest. Strümpell found 314 faults mentioned and realized that "crimes are faults writ large and idiocy is but the extreme of dulness." Siegert[1] groups children of problematical nature into the following sixteen classes: the sad, the extremely good or bad, star-gazers, scatter-brains, apathetic, misanthropic, doubters and investigators, reverent, critical, executive, stupid and clownish, naive, funny, anamnesic, disposed to learn, and *blasé;* patience, foresight, and self-control, he thinks, are chiefly needed.

An unique and interesting study was undertaken by Közle[2] by collecting and studying thirty German writers on pedagogical subjects since Pestalozzi, and cataloguing all the words they use describing the faults of children. In all, this gave 914 faults, far more in number than their virtues. These were classified as native and of external origin, acute and chronic, egoistic and altruistic, greed, perverted honor, self-will, falsity, laziness, frivolity, distraction, precocity, timidity, envy and malevolence, ingratitude, quarrelsomeness, cruelty, superstition, and the latter fifteen were settled on as resultant groups, and the authors who describe them best are quoted.

Bohannon[3] on the basis of *questionnaire* returns classified peculiar children as heavy, tall, short, small, strong, weak, deft, agile, clumsy, beautiful, ugly, deformed, birthmarked, keen and precocious, defective in sense, mind, and speech, nervous, clean, dainty, dirty, orderly, obedient, disobedient, disorderly, teasing, buoyant, buffoon, cruel, selfish, generous, sympathetic, inquisitive, lying, ill-tempered, silent, dignified, frank, loquacious, courageous, timid, whining, spoiled, gluttonous, and only child.

Marro[4] tabulated the conduct of 3,012 boys in gymnasial and lyceal classes in Italy from eleven to eighteen years of age (see next page). Conduct was marked as good, bad, and indifferent, according to the teacher's estimate, and was good at eighteen in 74 per cent of the cases; at eleven in 70 per cent;

---

[1] Problematische Kindernaturen. Leipzig, 1889.

[2] Die pädagogische Pathologie in der Erziehungskunde des 19 Jahrhunderts. Gütersloh, 1893, p. 494.

[3] Peculiar and Exceptional Children. Ped. Sem., Oct., 1896, vol iv, pp. 3-60.

[4] La Puberté. Tafala Graf. I, p. 52.

at seventeen in 69 per cent; and at fourteen in only 58 per cent. In positively bad conduct, the age of fifteen led, thirteen and fourteen were but little better, while it improved at sixteen, seventeen, and eighteen. In general, conduct was good at eleven; declined at twelve and thirteen; sank to its worst at fourteen; and then improved in yearly increments that did not differ much, and at seventeen was nearly as good as at eleven, and at eighteen four points better.

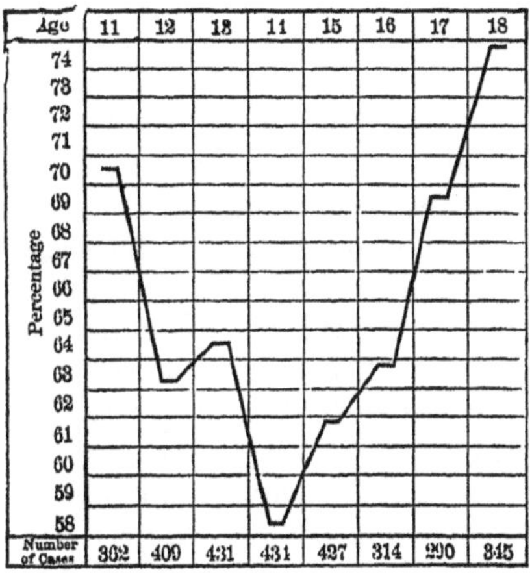

He computed also the following percentage table of the causes of punishments in certain Italian schools for girls and boys near pubescent ages:

	Boys.	Girls.
Quarrels and blows	53.90	17.4
Laziness, negligence	1.80	21.3
Untidiness	10.70	24.7
Improper language	.41	14.6
Indecent acts and words	1.00	.24
Refusal to work	.82	1.26
Various offenses against discipline	19.00	19.9
Truancy	9.60	.0
Plots to run away	1.70	.0
Running away	.72	.0

Mr. Sears[1] reports in percentages statistics of the punishments received by a thousand children for the following offenses: Disorder, 17⅓; disobedience, 16; carelessness, 13⅓; running away, 12⅔; quarreling, 10; tardiness, 6⅔; rudeness, 6; fighting, 5⅓; lying, 4; stealing, 1; miscellaneous, 7⅓. He names a long list of punishable offenses, such as malice, swearing, obscenity, bullying, lying, cheating, untidiness, insolence, insult, conspiracy, disobedience, obstinacy, rudeness, noisiness, ridicule; injury to books, building, or other property; and analyzes at length the kinds of punishment, modes of making it

[1] Home and School Punishments. Ped. Sem., March, 1899, vol. vi, pp. 159-187.

fit the offense and the nature of the child, the discipline of consequences, lapse of time between the offense and its punishment, the principle of slight but sure tasks as penalties, etc.

Triplett [1] attempted a census of faults and defects named by the teacher. Here inattention by far led all others. Defects of sense and speech, carelessness, indifference, lack of honor and of self-restraint, laziness, dreamy listlessness, nervousness, mental incapacity, lack of consideration for others, vanity, affectation, disobedience, untruthfulness, grumbling, etc., follow. Inattention to a degree that makes some children at the mercy of their environment and all its changes, and their mental life one perpetual distraction, is one which teachers, of course, naturally observe. Children's views of their own faults and those of other children lay a very different emphasis. Here fighting, bullying, and teasing lead all others; then come stealing, bad manners, lying, disobedience, truancy, cruelty to animals, untidiness, selfishness, etc. Parents' aspect of this subject Triplett found still different. Here wilfulness and obstinacy led all others with teasing, quarreling, dislike of application and effort, and many others following. The vast number of faults mentioned contrasts very strikingly with the seven deadly sins.

In a suggestive statistical study on the relations of the conduct of children to the weather, Dexter [2] found that excessive humidity was most productive of misdemeanors; that when the temperature was between 90 and 100 the probability of bad conduct was increased 300 per cent, when between 80 and 90 it was increased 104 per cent. Abnormal barometric pressure, whether great or small, was found to increase misconduct 50 per cent; abnormal movements of the wind increased it from 20 to 66 per cent; while the time of year and precipitation seemed to have almost no effect. While the effect of weather has been generally recognized by superintendents and teachers and directors of prisons and asylums, and even by banks, which in London do not permit clerks to do the more important bookkeeping during very foggy days, the statistical estimates of its effect in general need larger numbers for more valuable determinations. Temperature is known to have a

[1] A Study of the Faults of Children. Ped. Sem., June, 1903, p. 200 *et seq.*

[2] The Child and the Weather, by Edwin G. Dexter. Ped. Sem., April, 1898, vol. v, pp. 512–522.

very distinct effect upon crime, especially suicide and truancy. Workmen do less in bad weather, blood pressure is modified, etc.[1]

In his study of truancy, Kline[2] starts with the assumption that the maximum metabolism is always consciously or unconsciously sought, and that migrations are generally away from the extremes of hot and cold toward an optimum temperature. The curve of truancies and runaways increases in a marked ratio at puberty, which probably represents the age of natural majority among primitive people. Dislike of school, the passion for out-of-door life, and more universal interests in man and nature now arise, so that runaways may be interpreted as an instinctive rebellion against limitations of freedom and unnatural methods of education as well as against poor homes. Hunger is one of its most potent, although often unconscious causes. The habitual environment now begins to seem dull and there is a great increase in impatience at restraint. Sometimes there is a mania for simply going away and enjoying the liberty of nomadic life. Just as good people in foreign parts sometimes allow themselves unwonted liberties, so vagrancy increases crime. The passion to get to and play at or in the water is often strangely dominant. It seems so fine out of doors, especially in the spring, and the woods and fields make it so hard to voluntarily incarcerate oneself in the schoolroom, that pubescent boys and even girls often feel like animals in captivity. They long intensely for the utter abandon of a wilder life, and very characteristic is the frequent discarding of foot and head dress and even garments in the blind instinct to realize again the conditions of primitive man. The manifestations of this impulse, if read aright, are grave arraignments of the lack of adaptability of the child's environment to his disposition and nature, and with home restraints once broken the liabilities to every crime, especially theft, are enormously increased. The truant, although according to Kline's measurements slightly smaller than the average child, is more energetic and is generally capable of the greatest activity and usefulness

---

[1] Psychic Effects of the Weather, by J. S. Lemon. Am. Jour. of Psy., Jan., 1894, vol. vi, pp. 277–279.

[2] Truancy as Related to the Migrating Instinct, by L. W. Kline. Ped. Sem., Jan., 1898, vol. v, pp. 381–420.

in more out-of-door vocations. Truancy is augmented, too, just in proportion as legitimate and interesting physical exercise is denied.

The vagrant, itinerant, vagabond, gadabout, hobo, and tramp, that Riis has made so interesting, is an arrested, degenerate, or perverted being who abhors work; feels that the world owes him a living; and generally has his first real nomad experience in the teens or earlier. It is a chronic illusion of youth that gives " elsewhere " a special charm. In the immediate present things are mean, dulled by wont, and perhaps even nauseating because of familiarity. There must be a change of scene to see the world; man is not sessile but locomotor; and the moment his life becomes migratory all the restraints and responsibilities of settled life vanish. It is possible to steal and pass on undiscovered and unsuspected, and to steal again. The vagabond escapes the control of public sentiment, which normally is an external conscience, and having none of his own within him thus lapses to a feral state. The constraint of city, home, and school is especially irksome, and if to this repulsion is added the attraction of a love of nature and of perpetual change, we have the diathesis of the roadsman already developed. Adolescence is the normal time of emancipation from the parental roof, when youth seeks to set up a home of its own, but the apprentice to life must wander far and long enough to find the best habits in which to set up for himself. This is the spring season of emigration, and it should be an indispensable part of every life curriculum, just before settlement, to travel far and wide, if resources and inclination permit. But this stage should end in wisely chosen settlement where the young life can be independently developed, and that with more complacency and satisfaction because the place has been wisely chosen on the basis of a wide comparison. The chronic vagrant has simply failed to develop the reductives of this normal stage.

Crime is cryptogamous and flourishes in concealment, so that falsehood not only facilitates but certain types of lies often cause and are caused by it. The beginning of wisdom in treatment is to discriminate between good and bad lies. My own study[1] of the lies of 300 normal children, by a method care-

[1] Children's Lies. Am. Jour. of Psy., Jan., 1890, vol. iii, pp. 59–70.

fully devised in order to avoid all indelicacy to the childish consciousness, suggested the following distinct species of lies. It is often a well-marked epoch when the young child first learns that it can imagine and state things that have no objective counterpart in its life, and there is often a weird intoxication when some absurd and monstrous statement is made, while the first sensation of a deliberate break with truth causes a real excitement which is often the birth pang of the imagination. More commonly this is seen in childish play, which owes a part of its charm to self-deception. Children make believe they are animals, doctors, ogres, play school, that they are dead, mimic all they see and hear. Idealizing temperaments sometimes prompt children of three or four to suddenly assert that they saw a pig with five ears, apples on a cherry-tree, and other Munchausen wonders, which really means merely that they have had a new mental combination independently of experience. Sometimes their fancy is almost visualization and develops into a kind of mythopeic faculty which spins clever yarns and suggests in a sense, quite as pregnant as Froschmer asserts of all mental activity and of the universe itself, that all their life is imagination. Its control and not its elimination in a Gradgrind age of crass facts is what should be sought in the interests of the highest truthfulness and of the evolution of thought as something above reality, which prepares the way for imaginative literature. The life of Hartley Coleridge, by his brother, is one of many illustrations. He fancied a cataract of what he named " jug-force " would burst out in a certain field and flow between populous banks, where an ideal government, long wars, and even a reform in spelling, would prevail, illustrated in a journal devoted to the affairs of this realm—all these developed in his imagination, where they existed with great reality for years. The vividness of this fancy resembles the pseudo-hallucinations of Kandinsky. Two sisters used to say, let us play we are sisters, as if this made the relation more real. Cagliostro found adolescent boys particularly apt for training for his exhibition of phrenological impostures, illustrating his thirty-five faculties. He lied when he confessed he had lied, said a young Sancho Panza, who had believed the wild tales of another boy who later admitted their falsity. Sir James Mackintosh, near puberty, after reading Roman history, used to fancy himself the Emperor of Constantinople, and carried on the administration of the realm for hours at a time. His fancies never quite became convictions, but adolescence is the golden age of this kind of dreamery and reverie which supplements reality and totalizes our faculties, and often gives a special charm to dramatic activities and in morbid cases to simulation and dissimulation. It is a state from which some of the bad, but far more of the good qualities of life and mind arise. These are the noble lies of poetry, art, and idealism, but their pedagogic regimen must be wise.

Again with children as with savages, truth depends largely upon personal likes and dislikes. It is for friends, and lies are felt to be quite right for enemies. The young often see no wrong in lies their friends wish told, but may collapse and confess when asked if they would have told their mother thus. Boys best keep up complotted lies and are surer to own up if caught than girls. It is harder to cheat in school with a teacher who is liked. Friendships are cemented by confidences and secrets, and when they wane, promises not to tell weaken in their validity. Lies to the priest, and above all to God, are the worst. All this makes special attention to friendships, leaders, and favorites important, and suggests the high value of science for general veracity.

The worst lies, perhaps, are those of selfishness. They ease children over many hard places in life, and are convenient covers for weakness and vice. These lies are, on the whole, judging from our census, most prevalent. They are also most corrupting and hard to correct. All bad habits particularly predispose to the lie of concealment, for those who do wrong are almost certain to have recourse to falsehood, and the sense of meanness thus slowly bred, which may be met by appeals to honor, for so much of which school life is responsible, is often mitigated by the fact that falsehoods are frequently resorted to in moments of danger and excitement, are easily forgotten when it is over, and rarely rankle. These, even more than the pseudomaniac cases mentioned later, grow rankly in those with criminal predispositions.

The lie heroic is often justified as a means of noble ends. Youth has an instinct which is wholesome for viewing moral situations as wholes. Callow casualists are fond of declaring that it would be a duty to state that their mother was out when she was in, if it would save her life, although they perhaps would not lie to save their own. A doctor, many suggested, might tell an overanxious patient or friend that there was hope, saving his conscience perhaps by reflecting that there was hope, although they had it while he had none. The end at first in such cases may be very noble and the fib or quibble very petty, but worse lies for meaner objects may follow. Youth often describes such situations with exhilaration as if there were a feeling of easement from the monotonous and tedious obligation of rigorous literal veracity, and here mentors are liable to become nervous and err. The youth who really gets interested in the conflict of duties may reverently be referred to the inner lie of his own conscience, the need of keeping which as a private tribunal is now apparent.

Many adolescents become craven literalists and distinctly morbid and pseudophobiac, regarding every deviation from scrupulously literal truth as alike heinous, and many systematized palliatives and casuistic word-splitting, methods of whispering or silently interpolating the words "not," "perhaps," or "I think," sometimes said over hundreds of times to neutralize the guilt of intended or unintended falsehoods, appear in our records as a sad product of bad methods.

Next to the selfish lie for protection, and of special psychological interest for adolescent crime, is what we may call pseudomania, seen especially in pathological girls in their teens, who are honeycombed with selfishness and affectation and have a passion for always acting a part, attracting attention, etc. The recent literature of telepathy and hypnotism furnishes many striking examples of this diathesis of impostors of both sexes. It is a strange psychological paradox that some can so deliberately prefer to call black white and find distinct inebriation in flying diametrically in the face of truth and fact. The great impostors, whose entire lives have been a fabric of lies, are cases in point. They find a distinct pleasure not only in the sense of power which their ability to make trouble gives, but in the sense of making truth a lie and by decreeing things into and out of existence.

Ferriani [1] personally studied 500 condemned juveniles with

[1] Minderjährige Verbrecher. Berlin, 1895, p. 118.

reference to their lying habits, and found that their falsehoods were distributed in the following nine classes: 472 lied from instinct and weakness; 401 for self-defense; 360 vanity in getting the better of others; 231 imitation; 387 selfishness; 195 jealousy, envy, and revenge; 488 fancy; 370 laziness; 29 nobility of soul. Lies of fancy thus exceed all others, and those due to instinctive weakness and self-protection follow hard after. The lively mind of a child always sees the marvelous side of things, while weakness and fear always tempt to concealment in order to ward off blame or punishment.

Heinroth took the largest view of this subject in his mental pathology, when he conceived all diseases and sin a lie, because it was a perversion of man's true nature, which in these was falsely expressed, while Nordau [1] finds a more sensational verisimilitude in enumerating the many conventionalities which modern society has devised in its many courtesies, customs, and transparent hypocrisies. The sense of truthfulness comes hard and late, and everything depends upon distinguishing the radically different forms of falsehood and applying the remedy fit for each. Robust truth-speaking, which scorns pretense, false beliefs, fears, shames, and hopes, will never act a part or fill a place in life for which one's nature is not fitted; which finds none of the titillation that neurotic constitutions derive from mendacity; which instinctively shuns extravagance, even in the use of superlatives; that wants to be taken for what it really is by nature and heredity—this is a high attainment and psychologically not unworthy the grand old, but often abused term of regeneration.

Anger [2] is not yet sufficiently studied by psychologists, but the large vocabulary in the English language designating its states is itself enough to show it a strange and unique thing in human nature. A friend with whom we have lived for years grows pale or red on some provocation; clinches the fists; becomes rigid; breathes stertorously; emits perhaps some barbaric and inhuman cry; has horripilation; shudders, twitches, stamps,

---

[1] Conventionelle Luege. See also La Criminalité Comparée, ch. iv, civilization et mensonge, etc.

[2] See my Study of Anger. Am. Jour. of Psy., July, 1899, vol. x, pp. 516–591.

taps, writhes, paws, or assumes some strange attitude or posture; may butt his or her own head against hard objects; makes faces; often bites; in many of our returns the person scratches, pinches, pulls, kicks, hugs, strikes, and possibly kills; says cruel biting things in a hard, strange voice, and afterward is weak, limp, perhaps nauseated, bilious, sick; full of regrets and it may be apologies, and new resolves never again to fall into such a state of abandon. Anger is indeed a brief insanity, a *sava animi tempestas,* a furor suggesting epilepsy or the eruption of an alien spirit. It makes man a savage beast to his fellow man. The etymology of the words designating it are strangling, writhing, bursting, tearing, swelling, yelling, crushing, biting, boiling, inflammation, convulsion, conflagration, storm, rabies, rancid, acidity, etc.

Both forensic medicine and psychiatry have dealt much with the *iracundia morbosa,* and many have thought that the anger mania furnished an irresistible impulse which obliterated psychic freedom. Friedreich thinks the storm of this passion may temporarily quite obstruct the power of self-direction, and Fuerbach says "murder in the moment of passion is a crime possible for the noblest natures," and urges that crimes committed in sudden anger should always have special study. When Job was tempted to curse God and die; when we are goaded to desperation by disasters and misfortunes following swiftly and blighting all we care for; when the criminal in solitary confinement breaks out, yells, smashes, tears clothes and bedding; when the Malay runs amuck, stripping off all clothing, perhaps greasing his body, and stabbing every one in reach till he is killed or stunned, because pain, grief, and gloom have made him sick at heart—we see what this frenzy may be. The *Berserker* rage in the Viking Age sometimes vented itself in tremor, gnashing of the teeth, frothing at the mouth, howling, and perhaps, like Orlando Furioso, venting frenzy upon inanimate things. Some insane monarchs, whom Ireland has described, seem to have been chronically in this stage, as if, like Mohammed Toghlac, who had a passion for bloodshed and torture, their object was to exterminate the whole human race. Ivan the Terrible was simply a human tiger, in one case causing some 27,000 children to be slain before his anger was placated.

Anger seems sometimes to be glad, spontaneous, breaking

out with no known cause, but is generally provoked by crossing or thwarting a strong purpose, by contradiction, invasion of the sacred sphere of self, limitation of freedom, wounded pride, jealousy, personal antipathies to dress, habits, automatisms; at adolescence nearly if not quite all these causes are more keenly felt, and yet anger in normal cases, after a first period of intensification, slowly becomes more suppressed and internal. The motives of jealousy and wounded personal dignity increase in the greatest ratio. With puberty, our returns show also a marked increase in realizing the injury wrought by outbreaks and a great effort at self-control by many methods and devices. Those who are angry, with an utter abandon, and were spitfires before, begin to realize both the danger and the ugliness of temper, and with girls who have been violent before there is always a very powerful apparatus of repression which comes into operation at puberty. The young woman's life is far more subjective and in the teens she almost always learns to control the more violent physical outbreaks, but may become whining, peevish, or use her tongue in place of her fists. Anger is often so vigorously suppressed outwardly that it strikes in and vitiates the general disposition. In the main there is an increase of self-feeling, and mortifications, imagined and real, are never so stinging; so that for both sexes, between increased susceptibility on the one hand and increased control on the other, there is a new psychic tension which may now become a potent factor in the life. Indignation is restrained, deferred, and when vented is far more dangerous, not only because of the increased physical strength, but of the increased deliberation with which vengeance is executed. Anger should be a great and diffused power in life, making it strenuous, giving zest and power to the struggle for survival and mounting to righteous indignation. Its culture requires proper selection of objects and great transformation, but never extermination. The healthy and complete male especially will never be an entirely peaceful creature, and cowardice and the loss of courage will always mean some degree of psychic emasculation. It was for this reason in part that I advocated boxing in Chapter III as an essential part of the physical education of adolescents, because it affords a wholesome vent for anger, the psychology of which shows that it must find or make some way of escape for its energy, and that physical effort is the most instinctive, while it also teaches the control of temper because any loss of it is almost sure with a skilful antagonist to be punished by a stinging blow, against which loss of control always weakens the guard.

The instinct of revenge, however, is very deep-seated, and not entirely eradicable. In abnormal cases it is instantaneous and perhaps unconscious. I have myself talked with perhaps a score of youthful murderers under sentence of death, who I believe were in every way as good by nature as I am, but who in an instant of fulminating anger struck the fatal blow, possibly harder than they knew or because a weapon was at hand, and killed, it may be, their best friend with a regret no less than if sudden death had come without their agency, and with a self-reproach equal to that which they would have visited upon any wretch who had slain their friend. When we reflect that the entire administration of criminal law up to recent date was based upon vengeance, we can not wonder that its impulse is so strong and passionate in the heart of man, and when we read the horror of some American lynching scenes, we realize that collective man can with impunity be as vindictive as those on whom we inflict the worst punishments.

Thus, like nearly everything else in the soul, the power of indignation is greatly deepened and strengthened in adolescence, and the problem of rightly directing and habituating it is an important theme in juvenile criminology. All boys develop a greatly increased propensity to fight at puberty, and although most of them while pretending to give way completely seem very terrible in their rage, perhaps threatening everything if they are made mad, as if anger were a demoniacal possession, they nevertheless do not quite lose the power of discriminating where they hit and how, lest too great injury should be done. Anger, and even hate, uncaused at this age, is sometimes almost spontaneous and even against every motive. However, this stage passes as if it were slowly realized that "to kick against nothing is wrenching." Those whose tempers are strong and show no trace of this inhibition become dangerous; while those who morosely sulk, brood, and nurse their anger till it corrodes the soul, who can never forget or forgive, who are taciturn and malevolent—in these the seeds of injury may slowly grow to preposterous and even insane dimensions. The spasmodic type is far more complex, and simple prophylactics, like abundant food and exercise, are sometimes sufficient. Either type of this morbidity is augmented by humoring or indulgence, helped by drastic or judicious treatment, and although neglect may have its efficacy as a mode of treatment in children, the impulse must now be taken vigorously in hand. Plain talks, one writer suggests, with a careful and judicious use of profanity in rebuking this damnatory and diabolical instinct, may be effective in minor cases, but the infliction of the common legal penalties usually has very slight efficiency.

Envy and jealousy constitute another prominent factor in juvenile crimes. Of ninety-seven offenses by minors due to this impulsion, Ferriani finds that with both sexes insults were most frequent; next followed severer injuries, then light ones, false accusations and libels, attempted or successful murder. Marro[1] found these instincts more frequent in young women than in young men in the ratio of 17 to 1½. It is hard for girls to admit that others are more beautiful, witty, cultured, than themselves, and rivalry often drives them to extreme and even desperate acts. Vents of this passion are often secret and underhanded. If it be true that, as in matters of the heart in general, women are more susceptible to this passion than men, it may well be doubted whether, if it be broadly interpreted, man in his own sphere is not as liable to it. A friend reports an authentic case of a normal and sweet girl seen secretly dancing on the fresh grave of her nearest friend, singing exultantly, "I am so glad she is dead and I am alive." When food and dress were limited and communities small, this passion must have been more intense. It is probably the most direct expression of the struggle for survival and competition for all that is best in the world. Its roots strike deep into the animal world, and it is the rich soil in which prejudices have their recognized growth. It gives momentum to cruelty and self-consciousness, and is often secretly undermining the best friendships. Indeed Lombroso and Ferrero insist that no permanent friendship between two adolescent girls can withstand its influ-

[1] La Pazzia nelle Donne, 1893. See La Jalousie, ch. 8, in Proal's Le Crime et la Suicide, 1900.

ence, and that it is always made conjectural and uncertain by it. Many a noble and even great man has confessed that mingled with profound grief for the death and misfortune of their best friends, they were often appalled to find a vein of secret joy and satisfaction, as if their own sphere were larger or better. It would seem as if this feeling must have had its culminating development in a past where communities were smaller, and where the means of subsistence were so limited that every cause that lessened numbers meant increased supply.

However this may be, we find that with puberty begins an age of great intensification of rivalry for the favor of the other sex expressed in animal battles, showing off, and all the intricate processes of sexual selection. It is in this sphere that rivalry becomes most intense, and the dawn of first love is always marked, if not directly measured, by the growth of jealousy.

Some of the psychic rudimentary organs, which in degenerates often develop into crime, are seen in the teasing and bullying so common among children. It is perhaps almost normal at a certain stage of human life to take pleasure in hectoring, plaguing, pecking at, worrying, etc., often perhaps to test the temper or cry point. Burk has collected many interesting data and proposed a provisional classification for these phenomena.[1] Children stone, pinch, slap, pull the hair and clothes of those younger or weaker than themselves until they confess that they are beaten and beg for mercy. Jesse Pomeroy, the notorious pubescent murderer and torturer, could give no better reason for cutting the throat of one of his girl victims than to see what she would do. If children were to grow up with all their psychic propensities developed in due proportion from such a state, some of them would be insane, but most of them would be criminals. The fighting instinct, which is so strongly reenforced by the dawn of sexuality; the egoistic assertion of tyrannical power; the appropriation of property; the compulsion of service, and obedience of those weaker by bullying and sometimes under awful threats of torture or of the black man, who is invoked for many a form of juvenile spoliation; the tormentor who makes himself especially aggravating by insisting upon do-

[1] Teasing and Bullying, by Frederick Burk. Ped. Sem., April, 1897, vol. iv, pp. 336–371.

ing precisely that which is most objectionable to the victim, e.g., threatening those peculiarly timid of snakes, fire, etc., with these objects, barring the passage, jerking away chairs as others are about to sit in them; all these illustrate the strange teasing instinct often almost irresistible even in those incapable of rancor and who are overflowing with general good-will. This is also the motive in threatening and almost performing forbidden and perhaps heinous acts, in taking and hiding property, calling nicknames, twitting of personal peculiarities, arousing disappointment by practical jokes, exciting shame or envy. Burk enumerates from his empirical data a long list of modes by which the tormentor expresses his joy at the suffering of his victim, and suggests that these aggressions into the rights of other personalities may be broken neurological fragments or parts of old chains of activity involved in the pursuit, combat, torture, and killing of men and enemies. They may be regarded more as crystallized instincts than as conscious voluntary activities, as the causelessness of some and the purposelessness of others indicates. If they may be fragments of old reflex arcs, it is vain to seek any well-defined conscious motive. "Do they in some covert or concealed way, acting beneath the subliminal range of consciousness, aid in the development of useful activities, or are they merely a dead and useless weight continually serving as a drag to civilization," as if they were first intentions of nature? Lombroso deliberately assumes that criminal instincts are general in children. This is an easy explanation of some of the deeper problems of crime, but must not be interpreted as an indictment of childhood. There is a sense, however, in which this can be heartily granted without the slightest shock to modern ethical conceptions of the nature of right and wrong, and their relations to each other.

The child torturer is only an extreme and abnormal development from the arrant teaser. The latter lacks acute and tender sympathy for the sufferings of his victim over which he even comes to gloat, but his pleasure passes into pain when the distress reaches a certain point. The tormentor, on the other hand, lacks this check. Where cruelty is abnormally developed in adolescent years so that there is rapture in inflicting extreme pain, where the most bizarre torments are inflicted with no apparent motive, it is not enough to say that there is mere lack of sympathy, although this is true. We wish to be the cause of psychic states in others, to be an agent and exercise power, and Ireland holds that the insanity of power is a form of hypertrophied egoism. But we must reflect that primitive man was at enmity with most of mankind, his own family and race being excepted. The savage is a good father, perhaps husband and tribesman, with a kindly nature, but all his virtues are expended on those nearest him, and for all others he has suspicion, enmity, and bitter hostility. In the torturer the boundary between these two sentiments is disturbed. Just as there is individual love, so there is instinctive individual hate. He places the neighbor in the same position as the alien and enemy, whom he would capture and torture. Most can only love a few, and the diffusion and irradiation of fraternal sentiments outward toward ever larger portions and finally to the whole race is a matter of very slow and painful growth. Perhaps now even the best of us still need to keep alive the faculty of hate for what is bad rather than for strangers. At any rate I can conceive no other clue by which to explain the sad facts of certain types of juvenile torturers than the atavistic one.

Sheldon's interesting statistics show that among the institutional activities of American children,[1] predatory organizations culminate from eleven to fifteen, and are chiefly among boys. These include bands of robbers, clubs for hunting and fishing, play armies, organized fighting bands between separate districts, associations for building forts, etc. This form of association is the typical one for boys of twelve. After this age their interests are gradually transferred to less loosely organized athletic clubs. Sheldon's statistics are as follows:

Age	8	9	10	11	12	13	14	15	16	17	Total
No. of predatory societies.	4	5	3	0	7	1	1	3	1	0	25 = Girls
	4	2	17	31	18	22	(11)	7	1	0	111 = Boys

Innocent though these predatory habits may be in small boys, if they are not naturally and normally reduced at the beginning of the teens and their energy worked off into athletic societies, they become dangerous. "The robber knight, the

[1] Am. Jour. of Psy., July, 1898, vol. ix, pp. 425-448.

pirate chief, and the savage marauder become the real models." The stealing clubs gather edibles and even useless things, the loss of which causes mischief, into some den, cellar, or camp in the woods, where the plunder of their raids is collected. An organized gang of boy pilferers for the purpose of entering stores had a cache, where the stolen goods were brought together. Some of these bands have specialized on electric bells and connections, or golf sticks and balls. Jacob Riis says that on the East Side of New York, every corner has its gang with a program of defiance of law and order, where the young tough who is a coward alone becomes dangerous when he hunts with the pack. He is ambitious to get "pinched" or arrested and to pose as a hero. His vanity may obliterate common fear and custom as his mind becomes inflamed with flash literature and "penny dreadfuls." Sometimes whole neighborhoods are terrorized so that no one dares to testify against the atrocities they commit. Riis even goes so far as to say that "a bare enumeration of the names of the best-known gangs would occupy the pages of this book."[1] The names are sufficiently suggestive—Hell's kitchen gang, stable gang, dead men, floaters, rock, pay, hock gang, the soup-house gang, plug uglies, back-alley men, dead beats, cop beaters and roasters, hell benders, chain gang, sheeny skinners, street cleaners, tough kids, sluggers, wild Indians, cave and cellar men, moonlight howlers, junk club, crook gang, are some I have heard of. Some of the members of these gangs never knew a home, were found perhaps as babies wrapped in newspapers, survivors of the seventy-two dead infants Riis says were picked up on the street in New York in 1889, or of baby farming. They grow up street arabs, slum waifs, the driftwood of society, its flotsam and jetsam, or plancton, fighting for a warm corner in their resorts or living in crowded tenement-houses that rent for more than a house on Fifth Avenue. Arrant cowards singly, they dare and do anything together. A gang stole a team in East New York and drove down the avenue, stopping to throw in supplies, one member sitting in the back of the wagon and shooting at all who interfered. One gang specialized on stealing baby carriages, depositing their inmates on the sidewalk. Another blew up a grocery store because its owner refused a gift they demanded. Another tried

[1] How the Other Half Lives. 1890, p. 229.

to saw off the head of a Jewish pedler. One member killed another for calling him "no gent." Six murderous assaults were made at one time by these gangs within a single week. One who is caught and does his "bit" or stretch is a hero, and when a leader is hanged, as has sometimes happened, he is almost envied for his notoriety. A frequent ideal is to pound a policeman with his own club. The gang federates all nationalities. Property is depreciated and may be ruined if it is frequented by these gangs or becomes their lair or "hang-out." A citizen residing on the Hudson procured a howitzer and pointed it at a boat gang, forbidding them to land on his river frontage. They have their calls, whistles, signs, rally suddenly from no one knows where, and vanish in the alleys, basements, roofs, and corridors they know so well. Their inordinate vanity is well called the slum counterpart of self-esteem, and Riis calls the gang a club run wild. They have their own ideality and a gaudy pinchbeck honor. A young tough, when arrested, wrenched away the policeman's club, dashed into the street, rescued a baby from a runaway, and came back and gave himself up. They batten on the yellowest literature. Those of foreign descent, who come to speak our language better than their parents, early learn to despise them. Gangs emulate each other in hardihood, and this is one cause of epidemics in crime. They passionately love boundless independence, are sometimes very susceptible to good influence if applied with great wisdom and discretion, but easily fall away. What is the true moral antitoxin for this class, or at least what is the safety-valve and how and when to pull it, we are now just beginning to learn, but it is a new specialty in the great work of salvage from the wreckage of city life. In London, where these groups are better organized and yet more numerous, war is often waged between them, weapons are used and murder is not so very infrequent. Normally this instinct passes harmlessly over into associations for physical training, which furnishes a harmless outlet for these instincts, until the reductives of maturer years have perfected their work.

The Mafia is a secret association of malefactors that most abound throughout nearly the whole extent of Sicily. It has no laws, meetings, chiefs, or regular organization, but has great power and is incarnate like an instinct in the Sicilians. It has a clan for the city and one for the country. The urban Mafioso steal, assassinate, etc., while those in the country are brigands who go in bands of ten or a dozen, often on horseback, and are masters of the district which they infest. It is invisible, and any one condemned by it is usually killed within twenty-four hours. So great is the terror it inspires, that judges rarely condemn a convict, so that an almost unheard-of social decomposition is caused. It extends through all classes of society, and many whom no one suspects are members and may secretly do all its bidding. The bands share all profits and separate. This association has novices, usually called Sgaraglioni, who must prove their audacity and vow to God secrecy. First, they pay a tribute and are protected. If their conduct is disapproved or contrary to brigand customs, they are declared infamous.

The Camorra, another criminal organization of Italy, has a hierarchy, a highly developed *esprit du corps*, and is not without humanitarian aspirations. Like the Mafia, it can be traced back to the confusion caused by the fall of the Roman empire and the subsequent mixture of races. The Camorra has novitiate degrees. First and lowest are the Giovanne di Agarro. These youth have little to do but collect assessments and to serve the higher officers. They then become Giovanni d' Onore and can take part in the criminal activities of the Camorra and profit by its operations. The third stage is that of Camorrista who have received a baptism of blood. Those who attain the latter grade wear an elegant uniform. The society has its own vocabulary and something like a jury, and is much younger than the Mafia. Both sanction and execute the vendetta.[1] These societies form thus perhaps the most remarkable of all schools of crime, and account for the high rate of homicide, especially in Sicily.

The earliest form of theft is due to ignorance of what ownership is and means. Primitive man under the tribal organization had most things in common, and isolation was such that where every community was surrounded by unappropriated land and all the fruits of nature and animals of the

[1] Le Brigandage en Italie, by A. Dubarry. Paris, 1875, p. 369 *et seq.*

hunt, individual possession had a very limited sphere. Poaching was impossible, for there were no preserves. Possession was all the ten points of law. Children are reared in a communal state in all good homes. Most things necessary to satisfy their needs are their own to take and use. Food, clothing, and shelter are theirs by the right of their dependent state, and it is a long, hard curriculum to understand the *meum, tuum, suum,* of civilized life. Slaves newly emancipated have found this a hard lesson to learn, as the census of the causes of imprisonment of the colored race in the South shows. The city child, who takes edibles freely at home, has to learn that it can not do so from the stand of the street vender. Hence petty larceny, as nearly all statistics show, constitutes more than half the earliest crimes of youth. There is a deep instinct that things belong to those who most need or can best use them, and the finer conceptions of the sacredness of personal property come as a later stage of evolution. Theft in childhood is generally to satisfy immediate wants and desires, and it is interesting to see how edibles, or thefts of money to procure them, predominate.

Later comes theft by fraud and stealth, with a more or less developed sense of its nature. Thieving is literally furtiveness, and in civilized society, particularly in the country, exploitation of orchards and gardens is to some extent licensed and is often perpetrated in a jocose way, where the pleasure lies in the superior cleverness, stealth, or fraud of the invader of these rights. Thieving becomes often a passion gratifying the love of adventure and is celebrated in song and story. This, too, is no doubt an atavistic note of the ancient rights of the common. Even the frauds of the accomplished and adult swindler are often condemned less severely by public sentiment because of the unconscious traces in the human soul of the old days when things belonged to those who were shrewdest to get them. Robbers and footpads are very few in numbers until later adolescence, partly by reason of lack of strength and confidence, but then some of the boldest and most hardy crimes against person appear in connection with the forcible appropriation of property.

Marro says that house thieves predominate among children under fifteen years of age, and the innate disposition to steal to gratify sense and vanity shows a very marked increase in the beginning of the teens. Carrara says that in all times and by every race thievery is most incurable, and that women are less often reformed than men. Curiously enough the latter are especially prone to steal during menstruation. Ferriani [1] thinks that boys under fourteen are more likely to be recidivists because they lack circumspection, and their thefts are petty, but that from fourteen on, in place of many little disconnected thieveries larger plans are made; that repetitions are more common in the city than in the country, and in England than elsewhere. Youth rarely steals from avarice, and only gradually develops into the oily tactician or "flash" man. Theft slowly develops specialization, and all thieves develop great ingenuity in lying. Theft to satisfy passion, vice, and self-indulgence is far more common than to satisfy necessities, and the daily rhythm of life is upset and periods of idleness alternate with those of great energy. Moreover, it is often a passion with young adepts to corrupt others. The secret dialect, jargon, or cant of the thief, which is so interesting, is akin to that of the vagrant and the mendicant, and has been repeatedly made the object of philological study. The thief's life is no less often jolly and rollicking than is that of the beggar, and most thieves can beg and most beggars steal. In England and in Italy schools for instruction in thievery have been devised, and the excitement and uncertainty of life and the fresh possibilities of each day, which may end in a feast and debauch or in prison, have a certain great and natural charm. It was precisely in those days when the severest penalties were meted out to thieves, that it was necessary to chain cups, knives, forks, books, etc., and even now theft is less severely condemned by the moral sense of the community than most other crimes.

The thief has been described by the Lombroso schools as marked by certain physical and psychic qualities almost as if thieves constituted a special species of mankind. Those who have sought to trace the embryology of crime have found it among animals. MacDonald [2] holds that simple theft is marked by certain anthropometric proportions. While this may be the case in older countries, where this crime has become

[1] Minderjährige Verbrecher. Berlin, 1896, p. 267.

[2] Le Criminel type. Paris, 1894, p. 39 et seq.

more of a profession, one can not visit American prisoners or inspect the faces of Byrnes's[1] collection without the conviction that in this country criminals against property are often men of fine and even distinguished form, feature, and appearance, whom it is doubtful if all the measurements of the Bertillon system of identification could distinguish from the honest classes of the business community. No class of crimes is more relative than those against property. When the old English law was striving to exclude all middle men, regrating, which was simply buying up the market and waiting for a rise in price, was severely punished and forestalling was a penal offense, as were many other practises now common. Many letters of marque and reprisal were only licensed piracy. A serf or villein who went where he was not told was held to have stolen himself.[2]

The incendiaries, especially of the pyromaniac type, are commonly adolescents. This passion begins in the strong instinct to gaze into the fire; in the pleasure in seeing it grow, its tongues fork out and reduce combustibles to smoke and cinders. With the adult, this often has a soporific and almost hypnotic power and stimulation to fancy. A bonfire suggests jubilation and feasting, and is glorious at night, bidding defiance to darkness. Perhaps all men have the germs of fire-worshipers in them, and of all chemical processes this is the most fascinating. Some have thought it an epoch in an infant's life when it develops a passion for striking matches or throwing things into the fire to see them burn. This is the germ from which pure pyromania, if there is such a thing, springs, of which the instinct of the boy to run to fires is only the normally repressed form. Despine[3] thinks the monomania of burning for its own sake is a neuropathic inheritance which usually emerges at this age, and he distinguishes it from incendiaries for vengeance, avarice, jealousy, etc. Often, when the fire is kindled, the youthful incendiary runs for help, strives to put it out, and really pities those who suffer, not at all to disguise his crime, but because his human sympathies are aroused. This is very

---

[1] Professional Criminals of America. N. Y., 1886.

[2] L. O. Pike: History of Crime in England.

[3] Psychologie Naturelle. Vol. iii, p. 133.

different from the cases where hallucinatory voices command to burn and in early youth may even be innocent.

Another juvenile motive for setting fires is the love of the excitement caused, the rattle of the engines and the spouting of the water, the rescue of property and perhaps persons, the breathless crowds, the danger and novelty of which makes the nerves tingle. Youth thus often magnifies its own causative efficiency. It can not construct, but can destroy, and thus puts itself in the place of fate for helpless victims. This motive shades into the former and others, and strikes perhaps a root back into the psychic soil, where traces of ancient experiences of plunder, devastation, nightly foray, still exist. At any rate, this is radically different from the secret habits of revenge and hate, although even these may prompt incendiarism in youth.

The psychology of alcohol has become a new and interesting theme which must be more fully explored and carefully studied before we know the ethics of temperance. The intoxication habit is polygenetic. Religious intoxication cults abound both among civilized and savage races, on the theory that whatever makes the nerves crepitate brings the soul into communion with the gods, stimulates visions, expels diseases and bad spirits. Partridge,[1] who has best summed up this theme, shows how common the use of intoxicants has been in puberal rites among the American Indian tribes. All festivities, even death, are celebrated by intoxicants to produce artificial excitement. Primitive drinking was periodic or in modern terms dipsomaniacal, and not the steady drinking of the drunkard. Almost no tribe is known that has not had some stimulant or narcotic. Spencer holds that temperance first arose by offering a part of the drink to the gods. Samuelson holds that in every nation just before the time of its highest culture intoxication was prevalent, and in Greece the Dionysian orgies and the ecstatic dithyrambs of wine-flushed revelers preceded the golden age of the Greek intellect. All stimulants and narcotics in small doses or in their initial effects stimulate and later in large doses tend to narcosis, although whether intoxication is the paralysis of higher controlling cells or the direct

[1] Studies in the Psychology of Alcohol. Am. Jour. of Psy., April, 1900, vol. 1., pp. 318–376.

stimulus of lower ones is not known. The pleasure of intoxication is the widened range and increased intensity of emotional life; the sense of larger vitality; exhilaration, carelessness, confidence, and wider social feelings. Inebriety is more common in spring and early summer, and least in the fall and winter, and many interesting weekly and monthly curves have been traced. In general, Partridge concludes, "that drinking does not begin during school life, but in the great majority of cases the first drink is taken after the boy has left school and begun to associate with older men. The beginning was almost always social." Many habitual drinkers would feel disgraced to drink otherwise than socially. Our language has scores of words and phrases[1] designating inebriate states, which suggests how interesting they have always been, most of them, however, being terms of contempt or signifying exaltation—such as artificial, bended, breezy, canonized, cozy, electrified, fresh, glided, glorious, heady, irrigated, inspired, loaded, mellow, ossified, plowed, queered, salted, shot, touched, etc. Intoxication has been much besung for its abandon and pleasure, from the days of Anacreon to the quatrains of Khayyam and modern student and other bibulous songs.

At no time of life is the love of excitement so strong as during the season of the accelerated development of adolescence, which craves strong feelings and new sensations, when monotony, routine, and detail are intolerable, and when the breakings out both of students and prisoners in cells are most common.[2] Prison literature shows that the sudden spells of rage, above spoken of, when convicts feel that they must shriek, smash everything, tear their clothes, butt their heads against the wall until they are exhausted, are most common in the later teens and early twenties, at the age when in normal youth the craving for strong and new sensations is most instinctive. Among primitive people and especially males, life generally has a rhythm of days or even weeks, in which a spell of unusual energy and activity is succeeded by one of apathy. Indeed the impulse for intense states of mind has perhaps been useful in man's *excelsior* push upward to ever higher forms of

---

[1] Op. cit., p. 345.

[2] Nowhere better described than in the remarkably graphic and detailed biography of Jane Cameron, a typical female convict described by F. W. Robinson.

psychic life, and also has been in *rapport* with sexual impulse and tension. The passion for strong sensations then at adolescence favors greater capacity and aids mental development, and intoxication is a psycho-kinetic equivalent and aberrant expression of man's upward impulsion. Some writers have even thought that stimulants have been on the whole useful in making wider variations of life, preserving self-feeling, and keeping off pain. There is really no opposition between the view that craving for stimulants is an expression of neurasthenia, and the view of Beard [1] that the most energetic liberty-loving and religious people with the greatest passion for independence and procreation are also those most given to intoxication, so that intemperance is a by-product of mental evolution.

"Brain-workers," says an experienced friend of prisoners,[2] "provide the most hopeless cases of dipsomania. Increased brain power, more brain work, more brain exhaustion, more nervous desire for a stimulant, more rapid succumbing to the alcohol habit, these are the stages that can be noted everywhere among those who have had more 'schooling' than their fathers. Australia consumes more alcohol per head than any other nation. In Australia primary education is more universal than in England, and yet there criminals have increased out of all proportion to the population."

Rylands [3] accounts for the passion of drink in those who hate the taste of liquor and yet take it to excess by "a condition of pathological unrest or a diseased and overpowering mental and physical uneasiness, which it is impossible to describe, but which demands relief even at the price of adding to the trouble."

Mr. Partridge found that in 65 cases the age at which the first drink was taken was in all but four cases before twenty-two, and sixteen led all other ages. In the curve on the next page, based on 498 cases of inebriety, 443 males and 55 females, he shows the time when the drinking habit was formed.

Most habits are formed between fifteen and twenty-five, and the drinkers career usually closes in about twenty-five years,

---

[1] Stimulants and Narcotics.

[2] Prisons and Prisoners, by J. W. Horsley. London, 1898, p. 50.

[3] Crime: Its Causes and Remedy, by L. G. Rylands. London, 1889, p. 92.

either by the exhaustion of the desire or by death. It coincides nearly with the vigor of sexual life, etc., and very few cures take place under twenty-five.

The psychology of prostitution has constantly attracted more and more attention since the epoch-making work of Parent-Duchatelet.[1] Ferriani[2] undertakes a rough analysis of the causes in 10,422 cases, which are as follows, in order of prevalence: General vice and depravity, 2,752; loss of husband and parents or other supporter of a family and from other causes of misery, 2,139; seduction by lovers, 1,653; by patrons, employers, and others upon whom they were dependent, 927; desertion by husbands, parents, etc., 794; luxury, 698; incitement of those loved or others, not members of the family, 666; by parents, husbands, or other members of their family, 400; to support children, parents, or poor or sick members of their family, 393. Despine[3] first and later Ferriani best undertook to analyze the sense of shame or instinctive modesty, and both regard its loss as one of the chief causal factors. Everything, like family life in one room, familiarity with obscene or *risque* phrases, stories, pictures, etc., tends to break it down and thus precludes its emphatic normal accentuation at puberty, so that an effective barrier against vice is lost. Self-respect is another and more complex preventive agent, and whatever diminishes a proper *amour propre* and a sense of personal dignity predis-

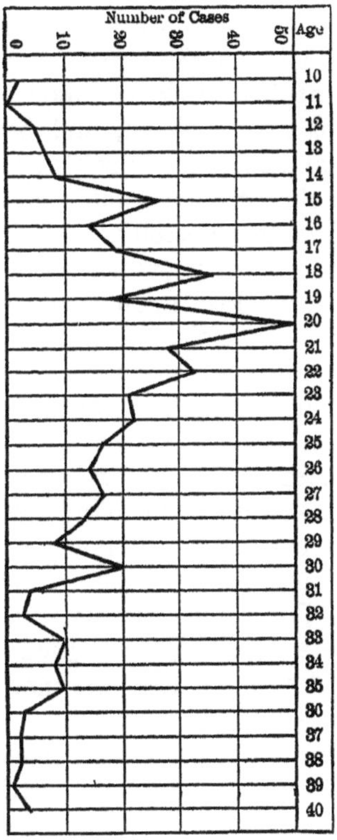

[1] De la Prostitution dans la ville de Paris. Bruxelles, 1832.

[2] Minderjährige Verbrecher. Berlin, 1896, p. 169.

[3] Psychologie Naturelle, vol. iii, p. 207 *et seq.*

poses to the fall of virtue. Lack of the power of foresight or of making what is really known of bad consequences effective in preventing them; shallow, excessive, and easily inflammable vanity; idleness and distaste for effort and labor; unattractive homes; excessive or premature development of sense, with objective knowledge and images of its modes of gratification—all these preform the soul; while an easy conscience that makes lying facile; a love of gormandizing and gratification of the appetite; turbulent and mobile dispositions that upset poise and regularity; the normal rhythms of day, week, and month; slovenly and untidy habits of dress and regimen, and bad body keeping generally; a sentimental disposition which passes over by ready and easy stages into the passional state, when control is temporarily lost and with it responsibility; a disposition to emotional prodigality and intensity (which favors the amorous obscession which can focus love upon a person whose unworthiness is a measure of its intensity)—this is the psychic foundation and background upon which the colossal and, according to all statistics, now increasing and ever more youthful evil of prostitution is built. Many recent writers insist that the victim of the seducer need not be immoral and is often pure and innocent, and that the entire responsibility rests with him and with society, which is excessively, if not hypocritically, cruel to the least lapse in girls, and will take no account of mitigating circumstances. The results of this social condition for young girls are well described by Augagneur,[1] Ferriani,[2] Lombroso,[3] Berry,[4] Taxil,[5] and Ascher,[6] and many others.

Sighele thinks that in many communities there are certain families from which corrupting influences irradiate among the young, which directly tend to this vice. Some hold that most girls, who do not come from good hereditary stock or good homes, have a period of intense and precocious passion which exposes them to peculiar dangers during the earliest teens, be-

[1] La Prostitution des Filles Mineures.

[2] Entartete Mutter. La Infanticida.

[3] La Donna Delinquente.

[4] Les Petits Martyres.

[5] La Corruption, Fin-de-Siècle.

[6] Grundsätze der vorbeugenden und der correctionellen Erziehung. Wien und Leipzig, 1880.

cause unprotected by knowledge which comes later, although pleasure in vice soon fades and changes to disgust. Others minimize the passional element or emphasize "psychic laziness," ascribe the chief causes to vanity, the reading of romance, or lay stress upon other factors. Much as we have lately learned, there is still no department of vice so little understood. This theme has a singular fascination to many minds, and for the most diverse reasons. To many it seems paradoxical that these girls should cling with such passionate devotion to faithless lovers and endure their blows and abuses. Their extreme pity and sympathy for each other, and sometimes for children, animals, and even relatives, stands out in glaring contrast with the general moral callousness which not only public sentiment, but the new criminology assigns them. Although adepts in hypocrisy, and most of them clever in simulating a modesty and shame which they know nothing of, they have not only an honor, but an honesty and frankness to their friends which is sometimes extreme and admirable. Some of them are very religious in both the formal and emotional meaning of that term, and not a few cherish the tenderest sentiments toward their abandoned home, parents, and the memories of their youth. Their psychology, too, affords the evolutionist profound matter for reflection in its suggestiveness of conditions of ancient polyandrous forms of society as well as being symptomatic of almost every imperfection in modern social conditions. Its problems will never be understood from the study of woman's nature alone, nor from that of the present status.

In Paris, where statistics are best, the minimum age of inscription in the police registers for prostitutes is sixteen years. Richard's[1] tables give the number for each age up to twenty years of age, which is the age of majority. Venereal disease is at no age so active. When the number actually registered is considered in connection with the reluctance of judges to convict on first offense, and with the fact that the vice does not naturally become habitual at first, and that if it does it is not usually known to the police for some time, it must be inferred, as Roussel has urged, that the moral abandonment of young girls in large cities is far greater than any data show, and also probably considerably earlier.

[1] La Prostitution à Paris. Paris, 1890, p. 192 *et seq.*

In his valuable study of rapes, Tardieu[1] shows that these crimes are increasingly upon young girls, and that particularly in the cities the age of victims is diminishing; that they are much more common in May, June, and July than in any other quarter, and least so in November, December, and January. The age of 632 victims was distributed as follows: Under thirteen years of age, 435; from thirteen to fifteen, 90; from fifteen to twenty, 84; above twenty, 9; age not given, 14. The age of consent by the law of 1863 was placed at thirteen years. Corré presents a very instructive curve, showing that violations of young girls have increased almost steadily since 1830, and in a ratio which outstrips that of any other crime.[2]

Lord Hale defines rape to be "the carnal knowledge of any woman above the age of ten years against her will, and of a woman child under the age of ten with or against her will." This is common law of England, and hence has arisen the term "age of consent." In general, force has always been assumed by courts prior to this age, whereas after it the question of consent or force is a matter for the decision of the jury. Thus the higher this age is placed and therefore the longer the severer punishment is in force, the greater the protection for girls. H. L. Bullock, the director of this movement, writes me January 9, 1901, "when we began this phase of our work about twenty years ago, the age of consent was not above ten years in any State." But when the facts were known and a distinct movement made, legislators have raised this age little by little, rarely over two years at a time, twenty-one years being the age the Purity Leagues seek, despite the legal entanglements that sometimes follow from marriage contracts made under eighteen. Long ago Dr. Roberts[3] had urged that the mind of young girls are so unstable and their consciences so elastic that our laws fixing the "age of consent" needed change. Although the average age of first menstruation is perhaps not far from fourteen, there is an individual variation of five or six years, and this and the younger limit of the marriage age have to be considered. This is especially true when we reflect that everything indicates that the majority of the 230,000 women in this

[1] Étude Médico-Légale sur les Attentats aux Moeurs. Paris, 1878, p. 22.
[2] Crime et Suicide. Paris, 1891, p. 362.
[3] Physical Maturity of Women. Lancet, July, 1885.

country, who are known to professionally invite lust and the large additional number that yield to it, begin their downward career before the above age, which it is sought to fix. All these considerations too, of course, enforce the great desirability of protecting immaturity from all libidinous and lewd suggestion, and our consciences may well be stirred when Mr. Comstock assures us that nearly fifty American papers are excluded from Canada as indecent.

The following table of the age of consent is revised to 1900:

10	years.	Miss., N. C., S. C.
11	"	None.
12	"	Ind. Ter. (for Indians), Ky., Nev., Va., W. Va.
13	"	None.
14	"	Ariz., Conn., Ga., Ill., Ind., N. Mex., Vt., Wis.
15	"	Iowa (raised from 13), Neb.
16	"	Ala. (raised from 10), Ark., Cal. (raised from 14), Del. (raised from 7 with death penalty now lightened), D. C., Ind. T. (for whites), La., Me. (raised from 14), Mass., Minn., Mont., N. H. (raised from 13), N. D. (raised from 14), Ohio, Ore., Pa., R. I., S. D., Tenn., Tex. (raised from 15).
17	"	None.
18	"	Col., Fla (raised from 17 for seduction), Idaho, Md. (raised from 14), Mich., N. J. (raised from 16), N. Y., Utah (raised from 13), Wash. (raised from 12), Wyo.
19	"	None.
20	"	None.
21	"	Mo.

The statistics of suicide constitute one of the chief themes of social dynamics. No crime is more completely dependent upon food, business, season, time of day, climate, age, sex, etc. These statistics are among the most sensitive of many indexes of social well or ill being. The ancients, especially the Stoics, assumed that any one had a right to make away with himself if he did not choose to live. It is only in modern times that suicide has generally been considered as a crime. The motives of suicide, although generally difficult to ascertain, constitute one of the most interesting of all psychological problems. It seems paradoxical that by an act of free-will, one should be able to negate the will to live, and some philosophers have thought it the most courageous of acts to overcome the repugnance to suicide by a sense of duty and have refused to be convinced that this act could with any justice be called self-murder. When, however, present life seems mean and painful and a glorious life beyond the tomb completely assured, it is easy for the soul "to fling the dust aside, and naked on the air of heaven ride." Hume and Schopenhauer justified it even as an experiment or a question put to nature, although a clumsy one, because "it abolishes the identity of the consciousness which should receive an answer."

There is a kind of reciprocity between life and death. In ages and races that have been eminent and successful, present existence has seemed delightful, and when, e. g., Rome fell and the hope of the race went out, suicide became an epidemic. For one falsely accused of a vile act, for a drunkard coming out of a debauch and realizing that he can never be cured, or for a criminal under sentence of death, suicide is not hard; nor is it for those badly equipped by nature, cheated by heredity, whose life is a neural torture. Hartmann's three stages of illusion suggest another paradox. He postulates a primal age when all men in their youth hoped to be happy before they died. Gradually as this was seen to be impossible, a second stage supervened when man placed his hope of anticipated happiness in another world. This slowly faded, and evolution left him no hope for himself, but only that his remote posterity might attain felicity here. This third recourse of optimism, however, is only a dream, for man and earth are both moribund. The race must sink with bubbling groans into unknown depths at last. This bankruptcy of all that is ideal leads him to renew the suggestion of Novalis, that the only true philosophy in it is for man to fix upon a moment, perhaps a few generations hence, when the whole human race will be educated to an agreement to commit suicide with a one, two, three, all together, in order that the energy which man has monopolized from the earth may flow back into and rejuvenate it, and a higher, better race more worthy to survive be evolved ions hence. This view, it may be said in passing, is perhaps a worthy counterpart to the ethics of Mailander's book, which finds the supreme motive to morality in pity for God called absolute, who has somehow been treacherously induced to break out into the creation of worlds as measles erupt in pimples, and who is therefore not happy and blessed but miserable, and whom it is man's highest duty to rescue from his transcendent negative eudæmonism. From this standpoint the only philosophy is that of negation, and virtue for both the individual and the race is progressive self-immolation. This is the most pretentious metaphysics that suicide has ever had.

One of the most common psychological motives to suicide among young children is to punish others who will be grieved at their death. Anger in bodies too puny to inflict physical harm upon those who have injured or insulted them can thus wound and punish those who love more acutely than in any other way. In many cases a scolding, a slight punishment, an affront to the sense of honor or self-feeling, which may be hypersensitive and act from causes purely imaginary, may be the only provocative. A youth flies to suicide as a mode of revenge where resentment is strong and intellectual realization of what life and death mean is inadequate. These young suicides now think, say, or perhaps write, that a friend or relative who has done him harm will be sorry for it, and life is sacrificed because revenge seems in the passionate state sweeter yet. This motivation is both more common and persists later in life with the female than with the male sex.

The next cause of juvenile suicide, more common at adolescence than in childhood, is due to disillusion. Early youth is always and necessarily more or less under the influence of great expectations. Life is mainly in the future. Its high achievements and successes are more apparent than the tedious means by which they are attained. The world is ideal, and possibilities are vast. Imagination is never so nearly an intoxication. All this is greatly increased in a country where the dominant educational ideals and methods require that every boy and girl should be trained so as to be ready to fill the high stations, and where the latter seem so accessible. Never have so many been educated above their sphere or above any destiny which their capacities enabled them to fill. Youth has never been so inebriated with lofty dreams and visions. Schooling has never so incapacitated youth for the humdrum of daily bread-winning work. Civilization at its best stimulates none to such fever of hope as it does youth. Thus when the protected and hyperstimulated stage of schooling is ended and the sterner realities of life are faced, there is always a critical period. Girls who return to plain homes with high school diplomas, youth who must begin at the bottom of the ladder of business along with few who have had their advantages and perhaps where their precious education is disparaged and seems of little avail, find themselves tempted and their mettle tested. Many feel that they are inadequate to the duties of life; some are moreover worried by an evil conscience; weakened in fact or fancy by dissipation; strained, it may be, by having to pass through the stages of religious readjustment of the creed of childhood; find life tedious, monotonous, and disappointing, and are thus inclined to *ennui* and even melancholy. In almost all lives this change comes as a critical stage, and to weak natures it seems tragic and may be nursed into a sense of misery and a desire to give up the fight and die. Occasionally there is recourse to stimulants or sometimes life is abandoned to pleasure for the sake of its distraction, and not infrequently there is real hereditary or induced insufficiency of health or positive defect which can justify only gloomy forebodings. The mind has been cultivated and the will weakened by inaction, so that when everything depends upon energy it collapses in despair. As the demands of life become complex and severe with advancing culture and civilization, the need of specialization and drudgery, this breaking in to the harness of business, profession, and the conventions of society seems unreal or cruel fate, against which the soul rebels. All these conditions are copiously illustrated in the lives of adolescent suicides, and rare is the earnest soul who has not at this stage at least coquetted with thoughts of self-inflicted death.

One of the ablest professors of philosophy I know told me how in the teens the burden and the mystery of life led him to purchase a pistol, go into the woods, load it, place its cold muzzle against his temple, and then meditate on what would happen if he pulled the trigger, which he never really intended to do. Another friend told me how he had devised a scheme of going to an obscure pond in Germany that he had seen as a boy, and weighting his body and leaping in, after every possible precaution that no clue whatever should be left behind. I have before me the printed, but not yet published, record of a brilliant youth who hung himself in his closet just before he was nineteen, and left behind an elaborate journal of his states of mind—his thrilling sensitiveness to everything in nature, of which he was passionately fond; his sense of inadequacy to meet the demands of life; his failure to find what he was born for; his alternations of dreamy sloth and energy; "the unutterable loneliness of the universe." Of thirty-seven seniors in a New England college, ten had toyed with suicide at some previous period of their lives, and all but one seemed to belong to this class.

Later yet comes the love motive in suicide. Love seems more closely associated with thoughts of death in youth than in maturer years. It involves the far-off anticipation of the life of another generation for the sake of which the individual is developed, while the actual culmination is rare. While the thanatic sentiments rarely issue in violence to self, wounded anger that another is preferred, mortification aggravated by suddenness of refusal or bereavement, breeds chagrin in which sometimes the first motive of punishing the loved one appears, but more often the utter wretchedness of loss, the bitter pang of jealousy that another and perhaps hated rival is to possess what he had hoped for, breeds an impulse to escape life because it is full of psychalgia.

Youth very rarely commit what may be called philosophic suicides, which may be noble and in every way justifiable if there is no escape from a lingering and painful death for self or others, and where it is certain for both friends and self to bring real relief. Thus, like every other crime, circumstances may justify this and even turn it into a virtue, where refusal is craven cowardice. This Stoic philosophy has been the resource of many of the greatest souls of the world, but rarely occurs at this stage of life.[1]

Taking all countries together, the greatest number of suicides usually occurs between the ages of forty and fifty. The prevalence of male suicides over those of females is least in youth. In England women who commit suicide between fifteen and twenty exceed by more than one-tenth the men. This is ascribed to the more sudden and energetic development of puberty, the youth of man lasting longer than that of woman. In the great cities, the curve of youthful suicides rises to a great height. From twenty-three or twenty-four criminality gradually diminishes, and suicides increase for twenty years.

In France[2] we have the following table:

---

[1] Morselli: Suicide, p. 310.

[2] Suicide in France, 1889. Rev. Ser., 1893, p. 636.

	Male.				Female.			
Under 6 yrs.	56	suicides, or	5	per cent.	21	suicides, or	10	per cent.
6–21	242	"	5	"	150	"	10	"
21–25	291	"	5	"	130	"	7	"
25–30	436	"	7	"	115	"	6	"
30–40	915	"	14	"	241	"	14	"
40–50	1,077	"	17	"	306	"	17	"
50–60	1,293	"	20	"	332	"	19	"
60 and over.	2,008	"	32	"	486	"	27	"

For twelve years—1885–'96—the age of suicides for all Italy foots up as follows:

Males.				Females.			
Age	10–15	15–20	All ages	Age	10–15	15–20	All Ages
	222	865	15,838		80	397	3,763

Proal[1] states that for many years the number of suicides of the young has steadily increased. For instance, in 1880 there were 55 cases under sixteen and 267 under twenty-one years of age, whereas in 1892 these numbers had risen to 87 and 475 respectively. This he assigns to the precocity of contemporary youth in love and libertinage. Jealousy, which plays a very important rôle in youthful love, is also a prominent cause.

Corré[2] computes from three authors the following sad table, showing the age of child suicides:

Age.	Moren, 1871–'75.	Bataile, 1876–'80.	Macé, 1877.	Macé, 1881.
7	1	1		
8	3	4		
9	3	4		
10	5	..	33	34
11	11	21		
12	21	40		
13	22	66	..	..
14	42	...	20	33
15	67	103	31	52
Below 16	175	240	84	119
At 16	...	...	57	81

[1] Le Crime et le Suicide Passionnels. Paris, 1890, p. 35. See also Julliard's Les Despérés, ch. i, Le malheur universel et l'aspiration à la mort, 1897.

[2] La France Criminelle, p. 313.

De Sanctos and B. Vespa have gathered the age statistics of suicides in different countries for the quinquennium 1889–'93 to show its relation to adolescence, as follows:

France......	Under ..16 yrs.. 8–100	16–21.. 45–100	31-25...... 80–100
Switzerland..	" ..20 " ..44	20–30..169	20–60......599
Belgium.....	" ..16 " ..13	16–29..138	25–40......236
Holland.....	" ..20 " ..33	20–50..501	50 and over.451
Prussia	Up to...15 " ..12	15–20.. 69	20–25...... 96
Bavaria	" ...20 " ..86	21–30..159	31–40......155
Würtemberg.	From 10–20 " ..85	21–40..319	41–60......407–10
England	Under ..15 " .. 5	15–20.. 40	20–25...... 63–100
Scotland	" ..15 " .. 3	15–20.. 31	20–25...... 59
Ireland......	" ..20 " ..18	20–25.. 95	25–35......161
Sweden	" ..15 " .. 4	15–20..122	20–25......122
Norway.....	" ..15 " .. 4	15–25.. 52	25–35......114
Denmark....	" ..15 " ..11	15–20.. 43	20–30......114
Spain	Up to...15 " ..13	16–25..257	26–35......178
Japan.......	" ...16 " ..26–10	16–20.. 73–10	20–30......213–10

Leffiingwell[1] shows that in England and Wales for the ten years ending 1887, suicides were most frequent in the quarter July to September, least so in January to March; that for the eight years ending in 1887, May, June, and July led all months in the number of lunatics admitted to the asylums of Scotland, while least were in the winter months. Murders, too, are most frequent in the hottest season and least so in the coolest, with more in the spring than in the fall. The same was true of crimes against person and also of those against chastity. He found illegitimacy in the United Kingdom most prevalent where thrift and prosperity were most general, and least where poverty prevailed. It was most common where elementary education was most diffused, and least among illiterate communities. Religion seemed one of the most potent agents against unchastity.

There is one stage of life, and only one, where the rate of suicide among females exceeds that of males, viz., from fifteen to twenty years of age. This is probably due to the evolution of sex life, which is more trying than the analogous change in boys. From this point on, the excess of male suicides over female increases steadily, with a slight remission from forty-five to fifty-five, during the climacteric. During the second five years of life, suicide has always been rare, but of late seems steadily increasing. At the dawn of puberty it has an increase

[1] Illegitimacy and the Influence of Seasons upon Conduct. London, 1892.

more marked than at any other quinquennium, although it generally reaches its maximum at about fifty. Most adults who take their own lives resist the impulse for some time, but with adolescents it is more apt to be sudden and unpremeditated.[1]

Suicide may be committed for trivial causes, and often by blind and sudden impulse. A girl of fourteen killed herself because reproved; a boy of the same age because he was punished; another because a far older actress did not return his love; a girl of twelve because she quarreled with her friend; one of fourteen killed her playmate to spite the mother of the latter; and another, so as not to be parted from a companion who had just died. Several German children of from thirteen to sixteen have slain themselves after becoming slightly infected with pessimism from disgust of life. Sometimes these young persons commit suicide because inspired by imitation to slay themselves in the ways they have read of in the journals, or because they have to go to work regularly, although the mitigation of the apprentice system is thought by some to have lessened this tendency.

In his history of the statistics of child suicide, Baer[2] has shown conclusively that during the last few decades this has increased in Great Britain, Italy, France, and Germany. Although still much less for girls under sixteen than for boys, the increase of the former has been greater than with the latter, although youth suicides have not increased as rapidly as those of adults. The effect of puberty, Baer shows to be a very marked increase, and he believes that an increased number of youthful suicides escapes the official statistician because of the strong tendency of parents and friends to assign and even to believe that cases which admit of doubt are due to accident or other causes. Mental disorders, although often the cause of child suicides, are more difficult to detect than with adults, and this is probably true both where the act is planned and where it is sudden and instinctive. Most surely morbid, perhaps, are those cases where the method of suicide is exceptional. Abnormal degeneration is a frequent cause, constitutional and infective diseases, psychopathic weakness of the brain manifesting itself in violent, stormy, obstinate, and peculiar conduct.

[1] Suicide and Insanity, by S. A. K. Strahan. London, 1893, chap. ii.

[2] Der Selbstmord im kindlichen Lebensalter. Leipzig, 1901.

No better statistics of cause can be found than those of Prussia from 1884–'98, when 963 children from ten to fifteen committed suicide, as follows:

Cause.	Boys.	Girls.
Regret, shame, and conscience	240	75
Vexation and strife	72	23
Mental disease	55	21
Passion	19	3
Satiety of life	13	3
Bodily suffering	14	4
Grief	11	2
Vice	6	3
Cause unknown	275	62

If we look to the larger environment, the absence of calm, slow, and natural development is especially seen in industrial and city life. In the narrower environment of the home, we find in the lowest classes poverty, mistreatment, hunger, and especially child labor, enforced in the German empire for more than half a million children out of eight and one-third million under fourteen years of age. Next to this comes the precocity favored by the environment of wealthy children and the luxury and superfluity of physical enjoyment, early habituation to the theater, dance, and society, which leaves them indifferent to more innocent pleasures, so that the seeds of religion, philanthropy, justice, truth, beauty, patience, and good-will to others are not implanted, and selfishness is overgrown.

The school is thought to be largely responsible for child suicides with its overpleasure, anxieties, and strain upon the memory. This is natural because this is the school age. For the five years ending 1888 there were 289 suicides of school children, of whom 49 were girls. Of the 210 in the lower schools, 45 boys and 23 girls committed suicide from fear of punishment. Of the 76 boys in the higher schools, the causes in order were:

Fear of examinations and unknown, 15 each.

Wounded honor and insanity, 11 each.

Other school causes and satiety with life, 5 each.

Unhappy love, 4.

While suicide in youth bears a very small proportion to suicide of adults, and while few inferences can be drawn from such meager statistics, there is a growing belief that the school's share of responsibility is much less than has been thought. In 1883, seventeen heads of institutions for the insane reported to the Prussian Minister of Education that insanity was no more common among the pupils of the middle schools than among others of their age, and that perhaps mental training was a production rather than a cause of insanity, while very rarely indeed was the school a cause of suicide. Even if unknown causes be charged up against the school, the absolute number is very small. On the other hand, we know that examinations are a great strain. Dr. Ignatieff [1] found that seventy-nine per cent of pupils lost weight and hence concluded that "examinations in their effect upon the youthful organism were like a grave disease which resulted in serious disturbances of nutrition and the tissues," especially the brain. Dr. Kosinzoff [2] from more data found that three-fourths of the children lost weight during examinations, and that this was most marked in the higher classes.

Unrequited love already plays its rôle here, often with extreme sentimentality. A typical case is that of a fourteen-year-old girl whose sister seemed more attractive to the boy of her choice than she. A letter was left behind wishing her sister and her lover long-married happiness, bequeathing them her skates and directing that she be buried in a white dress, with hair combed smooth, and her Bible and hymn-book in her hand upon her breast. A girl of twelve decided to freeze to death for love, because Edouard loved a richer girl than she, and wished to be buried where ultimately he would lie.

The power of imitation as a suggestive motive in adolescent suicides is often seen; so is vanity which can not be gratified; so is experimentation with nooses and pistols to see how the approach to death feels.

In the literature, child suicide has almost always been described as something not only pathetic but anomalous and monstrous, because occurring at an age when the love of life is supposed to be strongest. A few writers have recognized the fact that for very young children it may be favored by

[1] Der Einfluss der Examina auf das Körpergewicht. Zeits. f. Schulgesundheitspflege, 1898, p. 240.

[2] Ibid., 1899, p. 205

ignorance of what death really means, or the vivid imagery of the attractiveness of another life. While superstition more often makes it dreaded, it may cause it to seem attractive. The fact is, however, that more or less dwelling upon death and suicide is probably the rule rather than the exception with children in the early teens. Anger, love, and religion especially predispose to reveries of death. Children often have spells of musing upon how they would feel or look to others as corpses or during the act of death. They imagine themselves lying in the coffin and fancy the remarks that their relatives and friends would make about them. Often heroic sacrifices of life are planned, generally without great emotional depth. In one census sixty per cent confessed to these experiences.[1] In another where eleven children, and in another where fifty answered, all confessed these fancies which culminate in early adolescence. The cause is found in the fact that up to this period life has been more or less self-centered and served by others, but now begin premonitions of the subordinations of the ego to a life of service. Love, specifically, and altruism, generally, favor it. Plato defined philosophy as dwelling upon death, meaning that familiarity with ideas lessens the hold of the soul upon individual and personal objects and is a kind of diffusion motive.

If this can be assumed as a normal stage of development, the problem of suicide in youth in seen in a new aspect, for it is only a rarely culminating expression of a very general tendency which can hardly in itself be called pathological. Precocity, whether of feeling, will, or intellect, aggravates it because it brings the motives which limit individuation before the latter is complete. To assume the responsibilities, ideas, amusements, and passions of adults, when character is plastic and unformed, gives an unconscious sense of having been robbed of the just rights and immunities due to childhood, and makes demands upon its feeble powers which can not be met. From these prematurities, childhood should be protected. Reflection should not come too soon lest the heart be poisoned by negations. Passion must not be roused before the powers which control it are developed. "Other-worldness" should not be too intense. Care, partizanship, sensibility, vanity, and every specialization which interferes with harmony and symmetry

[1] **Scott: Old Age and Death. Am. Jour. of Psy., vol. viii, p. 98** ***et seq.***

of all-sided development predispose to morbid states which tend to renunciation. A committee of Swiss physicians lately petitioned for a law to prohibit the printing of suicides to avoid suggestion. A school system, which intensifies rather than shelters the young from the intense desires, ambitions, worries, and mortifications of life, is a forcing machine and a perversion of the purposes and etymology of the very word school.

Bartley[1] in his chapter on youth, or the third age of a pauper, or the period of life between the school age and that of matrimony, thinks it especially marked by a desire for independence, and that a good, strong, average lad has no wants beyond his mere food and dress. He is generally let alone by the church and his employer takes no care of him, and unless he is very exceptional he will follow the well-beaten track of spending every penny he earns, dressing like a swell, resenting advice, and in a reckless way passing the heyday of youth, during which he might with proper guidance lay the foundations of future independence and comfort. Young persons of this class never look ahead; rarely or at least reluctantly contribute to the support of their parents, almost never to their grandparents; and are often gotten up extravagantly when their parents are on the parish. Utterly reckless carelessness of youth in money matters, this writer thinks especially characteristic of those who will join the million paupers on the parish rolls of England. Adolescents of both sexes, if able-bodied, rarely receive either outdoor or indoor relief, but their life is a preparation for pauperism in that they carefully avoid learning any habits which will prevent it, and systematically live from hand to mouth and for present and immediate enjoyment, with no forethought. They perhaps justify the folly of doing nothing to provide for a rainy day by the argument that only thus are they sure of receiving the benefit of what they earn. Thrift, on the other hand, at this age is one of the greatest antidotes to drink, and the duty of inculcating it should be brought home to parents and teachers. Crime indicates in general more vigor and vitality than does pauperism, although the latter is more fixed and hereditary. Crime is misdirection and amenable to

[1] The Seven Ages of a Village Pauper. London, 1874, p. 81.

discipline, while pauperism is hopeless and often diseased, more persistent among men than among women, most common with the youngest child of a family, etc.[1]

Corré [2] holds that the more pronounced is civilization, the more critical the epoch of puberty becomes when heredity and predispositions appear, and when prostitution is enormously augmented. The adolescent, he seems to think, has always at the bottom of his nature the dross of villainy; is prone to idleness, and has a weak side for low pleasures; is jealous, vindictive, liable to drink and debauchery; and if criminal is sometimes very grossly so, and his cruelty is restrained by no sentiment of pity or shame. He describes the bands of precocious malefactors that often pillage gardens and furnished but unoccupied houses, and do not scruple to commit crimes of violence, if necessary for their safety or even for their pleasure. After giving a long list of flagrant crimes, he declares that "such facts repeated every day in the newspapers give us but a feeble idea of the criminality of minors" or those who are débutantes in adolescence and have the wit to escape police vigilance. The motives of their crimes seem usually very inadequate, and adolescents at present have a singular incapacity to endure the least effort or restraint. Corré enumerates youthful murders and tortures inflicted for no other reason than that the victim was displeasing, troublesome, that the young criminal felt romantic and wished to do something signal, or to imitate some outrage which had been read of.

Bonjean [3] thinks that in this age children strongly tend to revolt against their parents and that the latter are culpable for the consequent progressive disorganization of the family and its social results. His elaborate tables show that with some slight exceptions vagabondage, mendacity, theft, destruction of property and rebellion have steadily increased in the department of the Seine during recent decades, although for the few later years of his review the number of arrests had slightly decreased. This he believes to be chiefly due to the laxity of justice, and he holds that impunity and impenitence go together,

[1] A. H. Bradford: Heredity and Christian Problems, p. 142 *et seq.*

[2] Crime et Suicide. Paris, 1891, p. 309.

[3] Enfants révoltés et Parents coupables. Paris, 1895.

especially with minors. We can not "sterilize the bouillon of culture of the microbes of vice and crime" except by wholesome parental correction, and our problem he conceives to be how to transform youth with dangerous tendencies, which if uncorrected will make them parasites of society, into useful members of it. This he deems the gravest aspect of the decay of the family and its cult in France.

Sighele[1] lays great stress upon moral contagion of all degrees from suggestion *à deux* to psychic epidemics of crime, and shows how a crowd is a medium in which the microbe of evil develops more readily than that of good. In large and small bodies, whether parties, sects, or mobs, mimetism and psychic ferment may lead to a kind of moral drunkenness in which the most degenerate, foolish, and even criminal influences dominate, and where a spirit of extreme cruelty may dictate acts which every individual member of the group would abhor. Sudden and unpremeditated crimes, which are selfish, without reflection, and therefore not entirely responsible, indicate almost a kind of hypnotic state. Collective masses are especially prone to barbarism of an atavistic kind, and instability and caprice often increase almost directly as numbers.

The reading of romance has great influence upon the development of youthful passion. Werther has created a distinct psychosis known as Wertherism, just as Anthony has produced Antoninism. Stendhal not only admires passional crime, but almost revels in murder because it indicates energy. He admires aptitude for violent and dangerous action, loves the beautiful color of blood, salutes assassins, thinks it a bad sign that France has less passional crimes than other nations. Barrés eulogizes Spain because it can be at once exalted and fierce, mystic and cruel. Some of these "professors of energy"[2] consider crime, especially phrenetic, often "not as an insanity but as a sane idea, almost a duty or at least a noble protestation." Lacenaire declares that all assassins are courageous and have admirers and disciples.

Those who commit crimes by irresistible impulse are very rare, and their offenses are mostly against persons, so Lombroso calls occasional criminals criminaloids. We have abundant

[1] La Foule Criminelle. Paris, 1901. Second edition, radically revised.

[2] Proal, op. cit., p. 464.

classifications based upon the curative and defensive influences of punishment, but less upon organic, and fewest on psychological characteristics. In most countries, the grave crimes are steady and constant, and minor crimes are marked by steady increase; it is especially these which civilization has made and not correctionalized. Although there are often rapid oscillations of crimes in unstable lands, like Ireland, there is an increase in the aggregate, according to Ferri's law, of criminal saturation. He says it is with penal laws as with steam, compression increases the expansive force, for crime and punishment belong to two very different spheres.

Lacassagne has prepared an interesting criminal calendar to show the monthly and other periodicities of crime, how those against person are in direct proportion to the elevation of the temperature and the length of the day; those against property to the length of the night and low temperature. Garraud and Bernard[1] have shown that offenses of chastity against children, which have been very steadily increasing and at a rapid rate since the beginning of the second quarter of the last century, are most frequent in the month of June, and least so in November, following thus the law of rut in the animal world and of fecundation in plants. Ferri has traced the variations in crime which follow the thermometer; others find the price of corn and cereals a standard, according to which they can predict its amount. It follows wars, hard and flush times, humidity, altitude, urban or city life, with concomitant variations as Oettingen[2] has shown statistically, so that all cosmic influences affect ethics in a way which to many seems to threaten human freedom. In suicides these telluric, seasonal, finerstial, diurnal, and social causes seem so contributory as to challenge faith in human freedom.

Crime[3] is often committed in or near the menstrual state, and Krafft-Ebbing, Westphal, Tuke, Pelmann, Mabille, Philoindicus, Bartel, Ball, Kirn, Hugo Miller, Girand, and others

---

[1] Des Attentats à la Pudeur et des Viols sur les Enfants.

[2] Die moralstatistik in ihrer Bedeutung für eine Socialethik. Erlangen, 1882, p. 700 *et seq*.

[3] For a thoroughly detailed state of two typical cases, see The Menstrual State and Menstrual Psychoses, by Prof. P. I. Kovalevsky, in the Arch. de Psychol., Khartkof., 1894, i, pp. 73–131.

have collected many cases, illustrative of the nerve and soul storms that break out near this period or are connected with its delay, suppression, or excess. Excitement, rising sometimes to mania, depressing states shading toward suicide, tics, aches, tensions, flaccidities, pains local and general, imperative ideas, impulsive acts as violence to others, setting of fires, perversion of appetite, præcordial anxiety, sleeplessness, delusion of persecution, nervous coughs, irritability, etc., and crimes done in epileptoid and more or less unconscious states, fear and vague dreads, aptly characterized by Cowles as fear of fear, religious states of consciousness of abnormal intensity or kind, a series of such phenomena more or less pronounced and repeated with great uniformity every twenty-eight days for years, or as in other cases so protean that no two periods are alike, sometimes preceding, sometimes during, and sometimes after the flow itself, gravely complicate all classes of legal responsibility.

Tarde, who thinks that most of the traits peculiar to criminals are due to the professional exercise of crime, and who thus magnifies the acquired in comparison with the instinctive and hereditary factors, would by no means ignore the connection between negroid, mongoloid, mattoid, or epileptoid types of crime.

Ferri makes three great types of delinquents with two minor varieties. All have the common traits of impulsiveness of abnormal action with either absence or feebleness of resistance. These are as follows: (1) Criminals by birth or instinct with hereditary absence of moral sense, without feeling for the suffering of their victims, with cynicism, indifference, and absence of remorse afterward, and with improvidence of the consequence of their actions. (2) The insane criminal, a variety of the preceding class. In these cases there may be good conduct preceding the crime, but with a fixed idea of repulsion to it and with efforts to subdue it, and great fury in the accomplishment of the act itself. The victims may be chosen from among friends with no obvious motive, such as vengeance or cupidity. (3) The criminal of passion, personal or social, involving love, anger, honor, and followed often by a sincere and deep regret. (4) The occasional criminal, a variety of the passional, characterized by feebleness of the moral sense and with a constitution which makes him the victim of circumstances. (5) The habitual criminal, an intermediate type often developed from the occasional criminal, with the moral sense finally effaced owing to an imperfect constitution or unfavorable environment.

Lombroso finds two general types of criminals—first, those impelled by causes external to their own organization, whether occasional or habitual, and here he includes those led to crime by passion. A second class comprises criminals by organic defects and includes: (I) Those with acquired defects, whether due to special diseases, paralysis, hysteria, or to common diseases like consumption, syphilis, or those caused by senility, drugs, alcohol, or those with an insane taint, monomania, melancholia, acquired epilepsy, etc. (II) Criminals by internal organic defect, and of these he makes four subdivisions: (1) Epileptic, degenerative, asymmetrical, those with obtuse touch and pain sense, color blind, lascivious, irascible, hyperreligious, delirious, impulsive, ferocious. (2) Moral imbeciles, often macrocephalic, without beard and with abnormalities of nose, ears, hair, etc., with a psychic character like that of epileptics, but less pronounced. (3) Criminals with innate psychotic traits, mattoids, idiots, cretins, monomaniacs, but not quite imbeciles. (4) Born criminals, thieves, assaulters, violators, etc., each with their own peculiar traits.

Marro's categories are three: (1) Criminals by external causation, whether predisposing or determining. These are usually lazy, quarrelsome, and perhaps vagabonds, neuropathic, precocious, consumptive or alcoholic, with few marks of somatic degeneration, with no grave lesions of sensation or motility. They are impulsive and affectionate, with average intellect, may be very religious, and are usually curable. (2) Criminals in whom external or internal causes counterbalance, many recidival thieves, participants in graver crimes, with bad heredity, cupidity of wealth and pleasure, frequent deformities of skull and face, rickety, with frequent alternations of sensibility and intelligence, now normal and now defective, with precocious malice, feeble will, and doubtful courageability. (3) Criminals in whom internal causes predominate markedly over external: (*a*) where the internal causes are hereditary, prone to crimes of luxury, incendiarism, wounds without premeditation, crimes in unusual age or youth, with special susceptibility to seasonal changes and to momentary impulses, often blond and sanguine in temperament, with signs of arrested development in body, obtuse senses, dementia, ignorance, and rarely curable; (*b*) criminals in whom the predominant internal causation is morbid, thieves committing rapine and depredation, murder with premeditation, of delinquent parentage, addicted to alcoholism, fondness for orgy and vengeance, with physical development usually normal but the facial bones excessively large, lesions and scars not uncommon, fierce physiognomy, tattooing, deformities of the skull, exaggerated reflexes, low sensibility and a high degree of tolerance for alcohol, intelligence perhaps normal but moral sense degraded, suicidal tendencies, cynicism, and usually incorrigibility; (*c*) criminals who are such by coincidence of internal causes and those morbidly acquired, murderers and assassins, drunkards, epileptics, prone to exalted and rapt states, mental lesions, etc., these constituting the most dangerous and incurable types of all.[1]

The extreme severity of penalties in the past, the cross, stake, torture chamber, the lash, the scavenger's daughter, the iron maiden, mutilations, branks, stocks, hulks, the arena, early prisons, transportations, penal colonies, etc., indicated not that man had a deeper sense of the sinfulness of sin in the past than now, but that these were relics of a yet more barbaric and cruel age when man could readily become a wolf to his fellow man. No animal has equaled man in ferocity, and yet we must believe that in their time many of these abominations were necessary for the devlopment of society. Sometimes the latter went down and the worse elements terrorized over the best. So falsely has the line between the *licet* and the *non-licet* often been drawn, that our sympathies are frequently with the great but wicked, and sometimes even with those who have deemed it a shame not to be infamous; with those who have regarded temptation as an inspiration; or with heroes like Hercules and Ulysses, if not most of the great in antiquity, perhaps including even Jesus, who, if they undertook to live out their lives in any modern metropolis, would speedily find their way to prison.

[1] See A. Corré: Les Criminels. Paris, 1889.

Prison psychology, it may be said in passing, is yet to be written, but the glimpses of it which we have in penological literature are interesting. Some convicts wear a mask consistently through their entire term. They are more or less adaptable to all the rules, to moral and even religious influences, and the chaplain often has hopes of them, but is utterly deceived. All idealize their past, and often slowly evolve romances about it that are tissues of criminal idealization and which make the old life attractive by a lurid and diabolical glamour. When they go out all the prison life seems pallid and unreal and like a long nightmare. The day of release is one of palpitating anticipation, and the best resolutions wilt in a moment, like hothouse plants when exposed where they are unacclimated. They revert with organic fatality to a freedom which is the liberty of wild beasts. The sex tension is often extreme and may generate erotic illusions and hallucinations. Some cynics say every one will lie about sex because it is simply impossible to tell the truth, and it is certain that prisoners evolve the most false and lascivious images and stories. Here we see the crankiness and freakiness so characteristic of the masturbators, who always have some kink in their social relations, and the moralization of the debauchee, who as he approaches eviration prates of how women and wine relax all moral fiber and of the honor of wives, mothers, daughters as a tissue of moonshine that vanishes and leaves not a rack behind when passion finds freedom. We find strange paradoxes in the prison world—murderers who are in for life are proverbially the best behaved, while those who are the best men outside often have the worst prison records. The most heartless assassin is often most tender to sweetheart and mother, or agonizes over sparrows he had tamed, and almost dies if they do. The whole heart of a prisoner in solitary confinement may go out to a tender plant that grows between the paving-stones of his yard, as did that of Pellico, who watched and tended it daily as a mother ministers to a puny child. Some women, amenable enough outside, can not be subdued, and will literally die rather than be tamed. Some nurse revenge and plan a vendetta. Some, previously virtuous, take a revengeful delight in degrading themselves. Some harlots pray daily for pardon for sins that they charge up to cruel circumstances and for dear ones in a home they love, but never wish to see again. Some break out, scream, and smash everything, not always periodically, but whenever many crosses accumulate and reach a saturation point, as when the Malay runs amuck. To all not fully in their confidence, nearly all prisoners lie, till one inexperienced would think prisons were built for the pure and innocent. It is not well, as I have learned from much experience with prisoners, in addressing them collectively to speak of courts of *justice,* and many have a deep feeling that religion is a sham and virtue either an ideal or a pretense. Not only men but women pall in a schoolgirl mash, but women can not organize or complot. Thieves are sometimes enthusiastically in love with their vocations, and regard all business as thievery and without principle. Some become political reformers, and one bequeathed his hair for plaster, his bones for lime, his skin for a drumhead to arouse the people against their oppressors, and his intestines for fiddle strings to enliven their hearts.

The new penology is no longer actuated by vengeance, and does not look at the moral gravity of the offense, but solely at the protection of society, which must, not so much punish, as protect itself. "Judge not" is its maxim. In place of the old prison, which was a moral pesthouse and incubator of crime by contagion, we have the moral hospital, the director and officers of which become in a sense compurgators for working such reforms in the prisoner that he will be no longer dangerous to society. The special type of crime no more classifies it than do the specific acts of a lunatic indicate his form of insanity. Courts, too, have changed, and it is now a commonplace that if punishment is sure it need not be half as severe to work the same deterrents as if its severity were doubled on one-half the offenders, while the other half escaped. Justice now is asking with great earnestness after the state of mind and body of the accused. Individual study, which begins with the external details of the Bertillon system, is now postulated for all the deeper and more inward instincts, history, heredity, etc., while preventive education, which is perhaps the very best test of any pedagogic system, has led penologists and criminologists last of all to focus their attention upon juvenile crime as needing special consideration and as most susceptible to all reformatory influences.[1]

---

[1] Ferriani. Minderjährige Verbrecher. Strafgesetzgebungen, p. 30, and Ueber du Bestrafung, p. 409; F. H. Lowe's Punishment and Reformation, ch. xiii and xiv.

Despine[1] conceives natural psychology as that of instinct, and this he would characterize for each age, sex, race, etc. The intellect he regards somewhat in the sense of Horwicz, as an instrument to express and to aid in the modification of the deeper and all-dominant instincts. We think as we feel. The young often can not think a thing without saying or even doing it, so that even dissimulation may be a form of self-control. These instincts include sentiments and passions, but the mind being made to serve it, can not act against instinct, at least, unless there is a special moral sense, which is lacking in malefactors, so that they can have no free-will, and therefore no guilt, and thus moral treatment and not penalty is necessary. Superposed culture may even stand in the way of real psychic development, and ignorance is as good a point of departure as Cartesian doubt. In his final and summary statements he quotes approvingly Janet's dictum, that in philosophy ignorance is favorable to invention; and Lemoine's argument, that the thought of a man of good sense, who is ignorant although knowing that he is so, is an admirable point of departure for the most precise and profound philosophic researches.

On this view, rigorously applied, we should have to accept perhaps the most drastic of all the cures of crime and degeneration generally, which is that suggested by McKim.[2] His plan is "the gentle removal from this life" of defectives and degenerates, committers of heinous crimes or chronic recidivists for less grave crimes, and all others whose bodily and mental characters and ancestry show them to be hopelessly incorrigible. Idiots, and especially moral imbeciles, most epileptics that are hopelessly degenerate, and perhaps the worst habitual drunkards, should be selected for extinction, though not without a physical and mental examination. The essential question should be, to what degree the candidate is dangerous to society. Great discretion should always be used. Perhaps nocturnal house-breakers, who are more ruthlessly regardless of human rights than almost any others, should be included. Such have forfeited self-ownership and should come under the absolute control of the state, which should administer gentle and painless death. "In the United States," he says, "we have

[1] Psychologie Naturelle. 3 vols. Paris.

[2] Heredity and Human Progress, by W. Duncan McKim. N. Y., 1900.

gone up from 1,449 murders in 1886, to 14,000 murders in 1896, an average of 38 murders a day," so that unless some drastic remedy is adopted we shall soon come to live in shambles. Ultimately, his cure would so purify society that the cure itself would be no longer necessary. The world is hardly ready yet for this method.

Moral responsibility has generally been interpreted to begin at the age when right and wrong can first be distinguished. There is, of course, no exact, but only an arbitrary age, when it can be said to begin, and none when it can be said to be complete, and yet legislation has to assume an age for both, which differs much in different lands.

In Roman law, the child was entirely exempt from penalty up to its seventh year, and between this stage, called *infantia,* and puberty, there were two stages, *infantiæ proximi* and the *pubertati proximi.* Circumstances and the nature of the act decided whether the punishment should approximate that of the child or the adult. Canon law fixed this at seven years of age; the law of Italy at eight; Austria, Holland, and Sweden at nine; Germany at eleven; and England at sixteen. French law later decreed that when an offender had not yet reached the tenth year, it should be especially investigated, whether or not he acted with "discernment." In 1851 Prussia copied this determination, and most German states followed, although Thuringia fixed upon the twelfth, and Nassau and Austria upon the fourteenth year as the age below which children, unless there were special inculpating circumstances, should not receive public punishment.[1] The criminal code of the new German empire now excludes from legal responsibility, but not from guilt or from moral responsibility, those below twelve, while for those between twelve and eighteen legal responsibility is made conditional. This code gives a distinct place to reproof and admonition for first offenses.

In 1833 Wichern, aided by his mother, founded the Rauhe Haus, near Hamburg, for poor and exposed children, with the fundamental idea of the family. As his institution grew, he did not enlarge the house already in use, but built a second, and later still other houses, and thus grew an institution which has

[1] Die Lehre von den jugendlichen Verbrechern im gemeinen deutschen Strafrecht und Strafprozessrecht: Hans von Slupecki, Tübingen, 1895.

set the pattern for very many others. Wichern was a great believer in the power of the Word of God and in music. Every birthday in the house must be commemorated, and no teacher who could not enter into the plays of childhood was considered fit to come in contact with them. In France the Colonie Penitentiare Agricole of Mettray, founded by Demetz, was the pattern upon which many others were developed, though none of them were equal in elaborate organization to it. These marked an epoch in methods of juvenile reformation.

In most German states, legal responsibility begins with the completion of the twelfth year, but up to the eighteenth mitigating circumstances are often taken into account. This period is divided into two equal parts at fifteen, and for both these periods crime increased at a greater rate than the population for the decennium ending 1890, when 15,654 children for the younger, and 26,346 for the older triennium were in various houses of detention. In 1890 out of 381,450 prisoners, 103,641 were between twelve and twenty-one. For offenders during both these periods, petty thefts led all other offenses, and then came in order, concealment, bodily injury, graver thefts, damage to property, insults, falsification of documents, threats, incendiarism, etc.[1] In most countries, ten or twelve years marks the beginning and sixteen (France) or eighteen years (Germany) the completion of responsibility for young delinquents. Before this age special houses of detention for juvenile offenders have, in most civilized lands, been provided. As has often been pointed out, the power to know good from evil is a very different thing from the power to do the right that is recognized, and the former may be a small factor in the restraint of what Despine was the first to describe as the passional state, or in overcoming hereditary predisposition. Before the first age children are supposed to be irresponsible, and in some cases, after the latter the severest penalties, such as death and deportation, are rarely inflicted. Special penalties for this youthful period only sometimes exist as reproof in Germany or custody at large in Italy. Not only are judges usually lenient, but in the actual infliction of penalties early age is a ground of mitigation, and special courts, often with privacy, are instituted, and educational con-

[1] Was können die Schule und die Behörden thun, die Zunahme der jugendlichen Vergehen und Verbrechen zu verhüten? W. Pfeifer. Gütersloh, 1894.

ditions are often enforced in houses of detention for all under a certain age. In Germany youthful offenders are often sent to reform schools for a definite period after the completion of the sentence of confinement, and the duration of this compulsory education is left to a special board, which makes it dependent upon the progress and conduct of the pupil.[1]

The right of the state to assume the educational functions of the parents wherever there is grave danger of moral desolation, whether the child has done a penal act or not, is now generally insisted upon in Germany. Aschrott[2] pleads for raising the age of legal responsibility to the end of the fourteenth year, and for compulsory education of all youth beween fourteen and eighteen, who thus come under the control of the state.

Rylands concludes that "there is one way, and one only, by which embryo criminals may be caught and dealt with before inherited tendencies have had time to develop or evil example to make itself felt, and that is for the State to take under its own absolute control all children found in the streets without visible means of subsistence, or who seem to be neglected by their parents. If the State is to interfere in the matter at all, it can not logically stop short of this." Enforced habits of regular industry are his panacea.

Reddersen[3] deems it indispensible for the reduction of crime and the development of virtue and civilization, that all bad and stupid or recalcitrant children, even one of which may sap a teacher's energy, should be removed at once from the school before they poison the spirit of an entire class. In their growing numbers and abandon, he sees the chief cause of the progressive feralization of our youth. Perhaps, he thinks, a restoration of some of the stern *patria potestas* of ancient heathen Rome might be a wholesome tonic, but pleads that the moral education of the child is not a subjective private right of the parent, but his first and highest ethical duty to the child, to society, and to the state. If he fail, the latter must intervene.

---

[1] Holtzendorff u. Jagemann: Handbuch des Gefängnisswesens. Vol. ii, p. 320.

[2] Die Behandlung der verwahrlosten und verbrecherischen Jugend und Vorschläge zur Reform P. F. Aschrott. Berlin, 1892.

[3] Die Behandlung verwahrloster Kinder und jugendlicher Verbrecher. Bremen.

Appelius [1] has drawn up a rather elaborately motivated scheme of a new law for the punishment of juvenile criminals, according to which the local administration may transfer any child up to the age of sixteen to some educational establishment or to a family, and there compulsory education may be continued up to eighteen. Decision in this important matter must be based upon a careful examination, made by experts, and at which also the father or guardian must be heard. Imprisonment for less than a year must be severely solitary. Those sentenced for more than a year may be released provisionally under certain conditions. When imprisonment and education are combined, the first may be reduced one-half at discretion. Actual crime need not have been done to cause committal to these institutions.

Krohne [2] lays down the following principles: Reform schools should never be connected with youthful prisons. The former should be collective and patterned as far as possible after the family. In such schools, not only the sexes, but the different confessions should, if possible, be separated. The life, food, etc., should be plain and severe, but not actually without enjoyment to which children have a right. Both hand-work and field-work should be provided, and the preponderance of one over the other should be an individual problem. Very careful personal records, measurements, and observations should be kept for each child, special attention should be given to health, and all should be in an atmosphere of religion. Music and drawing should predominate, and communication with outside friends should be determined by individual considerations. The officers of these schools should first of all be good teachers, and all those connected with female institutions should be women.

Hartmann [3] insists upon brief sentences to very strict supervision, labor, or study, as the case may be, for juveniles, and would go to any extent to prevent the contagion of crime from contact with older criminals. He devised, in juvenile houses of detention, the following stages of discipline: re-

[1] Die bedingte Verurtheilung und die anderen Ersatzmittel für kurzzeitige Freiheitsstrafen. Cassel, 1891. See also Die Behandlung jugendlicher Verbrecher und verwahrloster Kinder. Berlin, 1892.

[2] Lehrbuch des Gefängnisskunde. Stuttgart, 1889.

[3] Carl C. Hartmann: Der jugendliche Verbrecher im Strafhause. Hamburg, 1892.

proof; refusal of the free hour in the court; refusal of the right to converse upon walks; removal, in whole or in part, of the disposition of products of their own industry in overtime work; forbidding the latter; forbidding letter-writing; no reception of visits; forcing to sleep on a hard board; refusal of light; isolation; arrest; dark cell; and fetters.

In England "there appears to be a very general conclusion that, both on grounds of mercy and expediency, the short and sharp punishment of a whipping with a birch rod may in many cases be even preferable."[1] This is said to conform to "the double characteristic of all good repression of crime—the minimum of punishment with the maximum of intimidation." Humanity especially requires, this report claims, a vigorous and uncompromising suppression of the cruel and ruffian class of young scuttlers, who have increased in English cities, and who are intolerable nuisances, known in Australia as larrikins, in the United States as hoodlums, and in Sweden as young leaguers. No trifling is suitable for this class, who require either flogging, a cell, or prolonged industrial discipline. These young men are intrusive in public places of recreation, and their language is often exceedingly offensive, particularly to women and to children. Vigorous exercise and games are also recommended. Probation officers can do little with these juvenile ruffians.

In England, reformatories are for older youth who have actually committed felony and undergone brief preliminary imprisonment, and are distinguished from industrial schools for younger offenders mostly under twelve, who have not been imprisoned. To the former, children under sixteen may be sentenced, at the magistrate's option, from two to six years, after they have been imprisoned ten days or longer.[2] On entering the school the superintendent has a serious talk, telling the young culprit that the prison has punished his fault, and that now he has a chance to reform, learn a trade, etc. To the industrial school, children who beg, as well as criminals, may also be sent, but only by order of a judge. In France, parents who wilfully neglect their children or whose bad con-

[1] Juvenile Offenders. A Report based on an inquiry by the Committee of the Howard Association, 1898. London, p. 8.

[2] The State and its Children, by Gertrude M. Tuckwell. London, 1894.

duct causes them to be taken in charge by the state, thereby forfeit all right and control, and can not even visit their children, whom the state has taken for its wards, unless their character shows improvement.[1] This principle is in successful operation in many States in this country. When children, trained in these institutions or by the boarding-out principle, complete their stay, their instructors seek to find for each one a patron or special friend in the neighborhood, who may be willing to find him employment and give him some kindly oversight, and become a not merely nominal godfather or godmother. In the day feeding-school system, four hours of lessons, five of manual industry, and three good meals constitute each day's routine, but if the child does not attend the forenoon school, dinner is forfeited, and if the afternoon work is missed he has no supper. This has the advantage of helping without breaking up the family life. Some religious instruction is insisted on in almost all English reformatory institutions. In 1896 there were in Great Britain 30,104 boys and 24,845 girls in her 48 reformatory and 144 industrial schools.[2]

The Massachusetts probation system is as follows: It was developed by citizens who visited the police court to seek out offenders who could be released, for whom they became sureties to the court, and whom they endeavored to reclaim. After some years of experiment, in 1878 a law was passed requiring the appointment of a probation officer. This, in 1891, was made mandatory in every town and by each police and district court. In 1898 the appointment of these officers was given to the Superior Court. It is now proposed to provide a Bureau of Records to coordinate the work of these officers and the police, and allow probation for all persons fined, if they need time for payment, which may be in instalments and to these officers. This would keep out of prison many who should never go there.[3] Upon this plan, a judge is empowered on the request of an agent to commit any person under the age of seventeen,

[1] Penological and Preventive Principles, by William Tallack. London, 1889, p. 356 *et seq.*

[2] See Fortieth Report of these institutions in the Parliamentary Blue Book for 1897.

[3] For detailed working of this system, see The Charities Review, April, 1900, p. 84 *et seq.*

convicted before him to the charge of the Board of Health, Lunacy, and Charity, until he or she shall attain the age of twenty-one, but with authority to discharge him at any time. The board has great power in such cases. The child may be left with a warning under the supervision of a parent, who is usually fined a small sum; but if there is no improvement in this state of probation, the child is removed from home. More than three-fourths of the children committed are thus returned. The board can remove the child from the parent and commit it to a State school, which is not a criminal institution, and to which no magistrate has the power to commit. The child may be sent to a reformatory or boarded out, with or without payment, in carefully selected homes; orphans may be placed for adoption, but only after trial; or the board can appoint a guardian with full parental powers up to twenty-one, nullifying the power of the real parents.[1] Thus it is sought to lift these youth out of the criminal and pauper class by means of agents, who are unpaid ladies and gentlemen of intelligence, and are thus made the arbiters of the children's fate.

Juvenile criminals, as a class, are inferior in body and mind to normal children, and despite the extravagances of the Lombroso school, they are no doubt more likely to be defective or abnormal, and their social environment is no less inferior. As to their treatment Morrison [2] thinks them more likely to be unjustly judged by courts than adults, and commends societies for their legal defense, which shall study each case and bring all circumstances before judges. A special office for this purpose has been created in Michigan and elsewhere. In England, up to 1847, juvenile crime was punished as severely as when committed by the most hardened criminals. The very severity of the penalties caused judges often to let children go free. The antiquated practise of fixing a minimum penalty for each offense should be banished from all penal codes for children and offenders in early adolescence, and the largest discretion given to the court. We must also commend the Belgian system of conditional sentence, by which the law warns before it strikes, and which often saves youth from the brand of con-

[1] Children of the State, by Florence Davenport-Hill. N. Y., 1899, p. 226.

[2] Juvenile Offender, p. 189 *et seq.*

viction. A sentence is conditional, when, if there is no fresh offense within a given time, it is not executed, and statistics show that such an impending sentence is more deterrent than actual imprisonment. Fining, too, is for many cases of juvenile delinquency one of the best of legal penalties. It is unique in that it can be made good if error is discovered. Moreover, it is economical to the state and is more and more taking the place of imprisonment. Of course it chiefly falls on the parent, but may be paid in instalments. The alternative sentence of, e. g., ten dollars for ten days should be so modified that five days and five dollars can be accepted, instead of as now requiring the whole fine to escape a single day of confinement. Fining in work to be done for the city is found wise in some places, and industrial schools, for day work only, in others.

There is very much to be said in favor of corporal punishment for young offenders. Although gradually passing into disuse with capital and other severe forms of punishment, flogging is still a part of the criminal law in England, Scotland, Norway, Denmark, and several colonies.[1] Flogging usually has special safeguards in the form of medical examiners, laws regulating the form and size of the rod, etc., the number of strokes, the presence of friends and parents. Save in Great Britain the prevailing sentiment is probably against it, but there is much to be said in favor of it for certain offenses among boys in the early teens and younger. Dermal pain is far from being the pitiful evil that sentimental and neurasthenic adults regard it, and to flog wisely should not become a lost art, whether with criminals or in normal families, although of course other very different influences should supplement it. Imprisonment is, as a rule, the severest penalty for the young. To be deprived of liberty of motion and contact with the social and material world is bad enough, but such isolation at this age brings temptation to a special form of vice, while the contagion of crime among prison associates and the stigma almost ineffaceable, which may actually compel the young convict after his release to revert to companionship where imprisonment is no disgrace, are worse yet. Slavery, banishment, prohibition to live in certain places or permission to reside only in others, interdicting residence in large cities for the young, all kinds

[1] Juvenile Offender, p. 212.

of individualization of punishment, sumptuary preceptors, mutilation, all preceded the modern prison, which seems to have been evolved from the monastic rule of sequestering recalcitrant monks in a cell, as early as the sixth century.[1] Perpetual solitude and silence by day and night is a crime against the soul for adults; but is still worse for the immature. Ameliorating the severities of life and shortening the term of detention for good conduct is one of the best of modern developments, and the increasing tendency to return to crime and to the bar of justice, which seems to bear some direct proportion to the comfort of prison life, is one of the worst. As Morrison well urges, the prisoner has all his needs provided for as if he were a child, but generally he has become a criminal simply because he could not satisfy these needs; hence the danger that a good prisoner will make a bad citizen because the personal, industrial, and social discipline is not such as to adjust him to life in society, and imprisonment is less effective for social security than it should be, and for adolescents is very inefficacious. All authorities agree that the age of responsibility and liability should be as late as is compatible with social welfare, and that even while awaiting trial great care should be exercised and special places provided for this detention.

For children all offenses are simply forbidden things, and the distinction between what is wrong or forbidden and what is criminal, and the perspective that differentiates between different crimes comes late, but moral comes even later than intellectual maturity. Again, if children are imprisoned young enough, so that they can return to school later, the fascination of their schoolmates and the imitation impulses endanger others. Young offenders, too, need exceptional care that their physical system should not deteriorate and become still more unfit to bear the strain of life than when they entered. As a class they are badly nourished and weakly, and this is a potent factor in recidivism. They should come out not only able, but disposed to do a regular day's work. Habits of industry are rare in this class, and regularity is an irksome yoke, and houses of detention of all kinds for the young should strive to develop habits of regular labor. Lack of occupation makes the mind as dead and apathetic as the surroundings are dull, and active and

[1] Morrison, p. 230.

stated effort is the only surety against this sad result. The closest relations with outside friends should be cultivated; especially the first hours and days of confinement are the golden time for reconciliations, when self-respect is dejected, and when, besides, memories of friends are most natural. The trouble is that prisons were made for adults, and all the institutions are primarily adapted for them, but as Morrison again wisely says, while the guardians of mature criminals need a disciplinary attitude, those of the young should cultivate an educative temper, and officers should, if possible, be parents, and of children of similar age. Hence on every ground differentiation of buildings, regimen, occupation, and supervision are needed. Administration should be tested not by conduct within, but its effects upon restoration to society. To minimize the great and never entirely avoidable dangers of the first period of liberty, gradual and conditional liberation has already proven its beneficence.

Professor Yoder [1] insists that there are no children incapable of being amended. He found that the age of most frequent commitments to reform schools in 10,000 cases was fifteen, and that the age did not differ for boys and girls. He was unable to determine whether incorrigibles leave school because of their own condition or that of the school, but deems it unfortunate that the age of transition from grammar to high school comes at the stress of adolescence. He is inclined to agree with Swift,[2] that a period of semicriminality is normal for all healthy boys; that those whose surroundings are bad will continue it, but others will grow away from it as they approach maturity. The incorrigible often seeks the society of younger children, whom he dominates, because he has a new passion for leadership which the teacher should give better direction. The instinct to be an initiative power needs appreciation and direction. The spiritual soil in which such have been trained is exhausted and they need transplanting. It is never so irksome to do over and over again things familiar. In many a schoolroom, a boy's incorrigibility saves him; the fussy martinet and the red tape of school are objects that provoke revolt

[1] The Incorrigibles. Journal of Childhood and Adolescence, Jan., 1902, pp. 22–34.

[2] Ped. Sem., March, 1901.

in the healthy soul. It is significant that sixteen is the age when children are most influenced by their teacher.[1] The boy feels that his day has come; he is becoming a man and the girl a woman. Just as gregarious animals are easiest tamed, so the very gang instinct itself is almost a cry of the soul to be influenced, and this instinct can be made to lead to the good as well as to the bad.

Adolescence is the best key to the nature of crime. It is essentially antisocial, selfishness, refusing to submit to the laws of altruism. As the social demand for a larger mutual helpfulness increases, prohibitions multiply. Hence the increase of juvenile crime, so deplored, is not entirely due to city life or growing youthful depravity, but also to the increasing ethical demands of society.[2]

De Fleury,[3] in his interesting discussion of fatigue, indolence, melancholy, anger, etc., believes that many of the distempers of youth are especially susceptible to the douche at different temperatures, to static electricity, to friction with the hair glove, massage, and sun and air cures, and that mechanical stimulation has great power in neurasthenic subjects to awaken vitality, especially when they are downcast and irritable and in the later stages of digestion. He pleads for a new kind of medical morals, and holds that pessimism or the sense that the sum of evil surpasses the sum of good is found in civilized man "in direct proportion to the learned notions or to the sensations of art accumulated in his brain, and in inverse proportion to the intellectual labor expended." The latter only expands self in a healthful way. Thus laziness tends to moral decay, and all weakness brings misery, and neuropathic symptoms need to be met by toning up the muscles. He believes it is possible, in ways hitherto unrealized, to supply new sources of human energy and to strengthen feeble minds to live with intensity, for morality does not consist in qualitative changes of states of mind, but in ardor and energy of living, and thus he holds to a higher hygiene that is to be the morals of the future, give a better normal tone, bring out latent qualities, and cure many moral perversities.

---

[1] Bell. Ped. Sem., Dec., 1900.

[2] A. C. Hall: Crime and Social Progress. N. Y., 1902, p. 393.

[3] Medicine and the Mind. London, 1900.

The causation of crime, which the cure seeks to remove, is a problem comparable with the origin of sin and evil. First, of course, comes heredity, bad antenatal conditions, bad homes, unhealthful infancy and childhood, overcrowded slums with their promiscuity and squalor, which are always near the border of lawlessness, and perhaps are the chief cause of crime. A large per cent of juvenile offenders, variously estimated but probably one-tenth of all, are vagrants or without homes, and divorce of parents and illegitimacy seem to be nearly equal as causative agencies. If whatever is physiologically wrong is morally wrong, and whatever is physiologically right is morally right, we have an important ethical suggestion from somatic conditions. There is no doubt that conscious intelligence during a certain early stage of its development tends to deteriorate the strength and infallibility of instinctive processes, so that education is always beset with the danger of interfering with ancestral and congenital tendencies. Its prime object ought to be moralization, but it can not be denied that in conquering ignorance we do not thereby conquer poverty or vice. After the free schools in London were opened there was an increase of juvenile offenders. New kinds of crime, such as forgery, grand larceny, intricate swindling schemes, were doubled, while sneak thieves, drunkards, and pickpockets decreased, and the proportion of educated criminals was greatly augmented.[1] To collect masses of children and cram them with the same unassimilated facts is not education in this sense, and we ought to confess that youthful crime is an expression of educational failure. Illiterate criminals are more likely to be detected, and also to be condemned, than are educated criminals. Every anthropologist knows that the deepest poverty and ignorance among primitive people are in nowise incompatible with honesty, integrity, and virtue. Indeed there is much reason to suspect that the extremes of wealth and poverty are more productive of crime than ignorance, or even intemperance. Educators have no doubt vastly overestimated the moral efficiency of the three R's and forgotten that character in infancy is all instinct; that in childhood it is slowly made over into habits; while at adolescence more than at any other period of life, it can be cultivated through ideals. The dawn of puberty, al-

[1] North American Review, May, 1899.

though perhaps marked by a certain moral hebetude, is soon followed by a stormy period of great agitation, when the very worst and best impulses in the human soul struggle against each other for its possession, and when there is peculiar proneness to be either very good or very bad. As the agitation slowly subsides, it is found that there has been a renaissance of either the best or the worst elements of the soul, if not indeed of both.

Although pedagogues make vast claims for the moralizing effect of schooling, I can not find a single criminologist who is satisfied with the modern school, while most bring the severest indictments against it for the blind and ignorant assumption that the three R's or any merely intellectual training can moralize. By nature, children are more or less morally blind, and statistics show that between thirteen and sixteen incorrigibility is between two and three times as great as at any other age. It is almost impossible for adults to realize the irresponsibility and even moral neurasthenia incidental to this stage of development. If we reflect what a girl would be if dressed like a boy and leading his life and exposed to the same moral contagion, or what a boy would be if corseted and compelled to live like a girl, perhaps we can realize that whatever rôle heredity plays, the youth who go wrong are, in the vast majority of cases, victims of circumstances or of immaturity, and deserving of both pity and hope. It was this sentiment that impelled Zarnadelli to reconstruct the criminal law of Italy, in this respect, and it was this sympathy that made Rollet a self-constituted advocate, pleading each morning for the twenty or thirty boys and eight or ten girls arrested every day in Paris.

Those smitten with the institution craze or with any extreme correctionalist views will never solve the problem of criminal youths. First of all, they must be carefully and objectively studied, lived with, and understood as in this country Gulick, Johnson, Forbush, and Yoder are doing in different ways, but each with success. Criminaloid youth is more sharply individualized than the common good child, who is less differentiated. Virtue is more uniform and monotonous than sin. There is one right and many wrong ways, hence they need to be individually studied by every paidological method, physical and psychic. Keepers, attendants, and even sponsors who have to do with these children should be educators with souls full of fatherhood and motherhood, and they should understand that the darkest criminal propensities are frequently offset by the very best qualities; that juvenile murderers are often very tender-hearted to parents, sisters, children, or pets;[1] they should understand that in the criminal constitution there are precisely the same ingredients, although perhaps differently compounded, accentuated, mutually controlled, etc., by the environment, as in themselves, so that to know all would, in the great majority of cases, be to pardon all; that the home sentiments need emphasis; that a little less stress of misery to overcome the effects of economic malaise and, above all, a friend, mentor, adviser are needed.

I incline to think that many children would be better and not worse for reading, provided it can be done in tender years, stories like those of Captain Kidd, Jack Sheppard, Dick Turpin, and other gory tales, and perhaps later tales like Eugene Aram, the ophidian medicated novel, Elsie Venner, etc., on the principle of the Aristotelian catharsis to arouse betimes the higher faculties which develop later, and whose function it is to deplete the bad centers and suppress or inhibit their activity. Again, I believe that judicious and incisive scolding is a moral tonic, which is often greatly needed, and if rightly administered would be extremely effective, because it shows the instinctive reaction of the sane conscience against evil deeds and tendencies. Special pedagogic attention should be given to the sentiment of justice, which is almost the beginning of personal morals in boys, and plays should be chosen and encouraged that hold the beam even, regardless of personal wish and interest. Further yet benevolence and its underlying impulse to do more than justice to our associates; to do good in the world; to give pleasure to those about, and not pain, can be directly cultivated. Truth-telling presents a far harder problem, as we have seen. It is no pedagogical triumph to clip the wings of fancy, but effort should be directed almost solely against the cowardly lies, which cover evil, and the heroism of telling the truth and taking the consequences is another of the elements of the moral sense, so complex, so late, and so often permanently crippled. The money sense by all the many means now used

[1] Holzendorff: Psychologie des Mordes.

for its development in school is the surest safeguard against the most common juvenile crime of theft, and much can be taught by precept, example, and moral regimen of the sacredness of property rights. The regularity of school work and its industry is a valuable moralizing agent, but entirely inadequate and insufficient by itself. Educators must face the fact that the ultimate verdict concerning the utility of the school will be determined, as Talleck well says, by its moral efficiency in saving children from personal vice and crime.

Wherever any source of pollution of school communities occurs, it must be at once and effectively detected, and some artificial elements must be introduced into the environment. In other words, there must be a system of moral orthopedics. Garofalo's [1] new term and principle of "temibility" is perhaps of great service. He would thus designate the quantum of evil feared that is sufficient to restrain criminal impulsion. We can not measure guilt or culpability, which may be of all degrees from nothing to infinity perhaps, but we can to some extent scale the effectiveness of restraint, if criminal impulse is not absolutely irresistible. Pain then must be so organized as to follow and measure the offense by as nearly a natural method as possible, while on the other hand the rewards for good conduct must also be more or less accentuated. Thus the problem of criminology for youth can not be based on the principles now recognized for adults. They can not be protective of society only, but must have marked reformatory elements. Solitude [2] which tends to make weak, agitated, and fearful, at this very gregarious age should be enforced with very great discretion. There must be no personal and unmotivated clemency or pardon in such a scheme, for, according to the old saw, if mercy pardon those who kill, it becomes a murderer; nor on the other hand should there be the excessive disregard of personal adjustments, and the uniformitarian, who perhaps celebrated his highest triumph in the old sentence, "kill all offenders and suspects for God will know his own," should have no part nor lot here. The philosopher Hartmann has a suggestive article advocating that penal colonies made up of transported criminals

---

[1] La Criminologie, p. 310.

[2] See its psychology and dangers well pointed out by M. H. Small: Psychical Relations of Society and Solitude. Ped. Sem., April, 1900, vol. vii, pp. 13–69.

should be experimented on by statesmen in order to put various theories of self-government to a practical test. However this may be, the penologist of youth must face some such problem in the organization of the house of detention, boys' club, farm, reformatory, etc. We must pass beyond the clumsy apparatus of a term sentence or the devices of a jury, clumsier yet, for this purpose; we must admit the principle of regret, fear, penance, material restoration of damage, and understand the sense in which, for both society and for the individual, it makes no practical difference whether experts think there is some taint of insanity, provided only that irresponsibility is not hopelessly complete.

In few aspects of this theme do conceptions of and practises in regard to adolescence need more radical reconstruction. A mere accident of circumstance often condemns to criminal careers youths capable of the highest service to society, and for a mere brief season of temperamental outbreak or obstreperousness exposes them to all the infamy to which ignorant and cruel public opinion condemns all those who have once been detected on the wrong side of the invisible and arbitrary line of rectitude. The heart of criminal psychology is here, and not only that, but I would conclude with a most earnest personal protest against the current methods of teaching and studying ethics in our academic institutions as a speculative, historical, and abstract thing. Here in the concrete and saliently objective facts of crime it should have its beginning, and have more blood and body in it by getting again close to the hot battle line between vice and virtue, and then only when balanced and sanified by a rich ballast of facts can it with advantage slowly work its way over to the larger and higher philosophy of conduct, which, when developed from this basis, will be a radically different thing from the shadowy, fantom, shablone speculations of many contemporary moralists, taught in our schools and colleges.

CHAPTER VI

SEXUAL DEVELOPMENT: ITS DANGERS AND HYGIENE IN BOYS

The bio-psychology of sexuality—Variability of parts—Pubertal changes in hair—Sexual elements—Mammæ—Uterus—Ovaries—Testes—Other parts—Castration and its moral and physical effects—Its justification—Self-abuse: its prevalence, its causes, and its mental and physical effects—The problem of masturbatic insanity—Sexual tension—The question of special sex nerves and centers; their hierarchy and order of development see psychology—Representative experiences of victims of self-abuse—The critical point in the development of the habit—Psychic and moral effect of spontaneous emissions—State of mind which leads youth to quacks—Unique opportunity for, and efficacy of, religion—Inadequacy of ethical teaching in cases—Ignorance and neglect of parents and preachers—Limited insight and knowledge of physicians—Devices of quackery and the extent of its influence—Proper food and regimen—Kind of instruction needed—Special methods of amelioration and of prevention.

For biology the plasmata in general and the protoplasms in particular, under many names and aspects, occupy a position of ever-increasing interest and preeminence. Unlike ether, the still more or less hypothetical background of all physical existence, protoplasm is a tangible reality accessible to many and ever more subtle methods of study, and like Schopenhauer's basal will to live, its all-dominant impulse is to progressive self-expression. It is the creator of the ascending series of types and species of plants and animals, which become its habits of self-formulation, although all that have so far existed do not yet fully express it. It unites successive generations into an unbroken continuum, so that they bud, the later from the earlier, each ontological link organizing a soma of gradually lessening vitality doomed to death, while it remains immortal in the phylum. Bonnet speaks of an unique animated fluid which the Architect of the universe has sown through living bodies as he has sown worlds through the celestial spaces. The most primitive and characteristic cellular expression of protoplasm is in the spermatozoa and ova (which it is now thought were themselves developed out of an indifferent or intermediate structure), the vast numbers of which, not only in the lower forms but in man himself, illustrate its fecundity. As these primitive sex elements differentiate one from the other, sex organs, secondary and ancillary to their needs in all their vast variety and beauty of form and exact adaptation to each other, throughout the plant and animal kingdom, are developed. Nerves and brains themselves, and all their functions, from the most elemental tropism toward light, air, food, gravity, etc., up through instinct to conscious soul, are the mouthpieces of germinant living substance to express its nature and needs and to light its way onward. Yet while the individual grows, thinks, and plans, his whole organism and life may have a higher and very different use for this primitive, vital substance than the ends which persons or races consciously propose or even than those which their instinctive life illustrates. History, and perhaps the whole life of all known or even possible species, may be but an incident in its development. Again there is growing reason to regard it as not only transcendent in this sense, but as a storehouse or reservoir of experiences, so that heredity itself may be a form of memory and nothing perhaps be ever lost. Thus as we watch under the microscope this marvelous substance that spins out filaments, foams, develops granules or films, vibrates, takes on or puts off various forms of organization in its ceaseless Heraclitic becoming, which even histological methods and stains but half reveal and half conceal, we can not repress some degree of the sentiment which declared the undevout astronomer mad, because we here contemplate the one unbroken physical source and origin of all life which makes its most diverse forms forever akin. As variations increase with the number of atoms in a molecule, there may be, according to Caley and Peirce, "billions or trillions of protoplasmic substances, and not one only, as was once assumed."

As most closely related to this great pleromal sea of life, abounding stand in the higher plants and animals the sexual organs, which in ancient phallicism and in the modern love of flowers are objects of great esthetic interest and curiosity. In them and their function, life reaches its maximal intensity and performs its supreme function. The *vita sexualis* is normally a magnificent symphony, the rich and varied orchestration of which brings the individual into the closest *rapport* with the larger life of the great Biologos, and without which his life would be a mere film or shadow. As this vast subject looms up to the psychologist and he begins to catch glimpses of its long-neglected wealth and beauty overgrown with foul and noxious fungoids and haunted by all the evil spirits that curse human life; as he clearly sees to what a degree art, science, religion, the home, the school, and civilization itself suffer from this degradation; as he understands the all-conditioning importance of normality of primary acts and organs and the hitherto unsuspected range of qualities that are now coming to reveal themselves as secondary sexual both in their origin and in their present deeper relationship, he realizes that it is his preeminent prerogative and duty, from which it would be base cowardice to shrink, to sound a cry of warning in terms plain enough if possible to shock both quacks and prudes, who have, the one perverted, and the other obscured, the plain path of life for adolescence.

I. The sexual organs make procreation surer, less wasteful, and probably far more hedonic as we ascend the scale of being. In the human fetus the testes can be detected as early as the sixth week, and at the close of the third month they can be discriminated from the ovaries. The genital tubercle from which the male glans is to grow can be seen by the tenth week. Minot [1] finds that the male and female organs have seven parts in common, while there are thirteen homologies which are slowly differentiated as the embryo becomes fully sexed. In hermaphrodites, which Duval and many since have studied, sexual differentiation which ought to take place in embryonic life has been incomplete, and sometimes, as in the still unparalleled case of Leport, who at sixteen was predominantly a girl and at sixty-five a man, the qualities of the two sexes are nearly balanced, but usually even in these cases one predominates. The testes of the frog grow around the ovaries, and one or the other is absorbed

[1] Human Embryology, p. 492.

as sex declares itself, and in many other cases we now know that the embryological truth of Plato's myth of the bifurcation of an originally bisexual man was a periphrastic adumbration. Geigel[1] found two kinds of developmental variability, one group being due to more or less rapidity in the evolution of the parts peculiar to each sex, which he referred to varying local nutritive activity, and another group differentiated by the very variable time of the disappearance of parts peculiar to the opposite sex, due, he thought, to circulatory and resorptive differences. In the animal and even plant series closely allied species have great variability of sex parts and functions, the same organs sometimes producing alternately eggs and spermatozoa, while lower down we find many creatures that may reproduce either by fission or division or sexually.

Dr. F. N. Seerley, who has examined over 2,000 normal young men as well as many young women, tells me that in his opinion individual variations in these parts are much greater even than those of face or form, and that the range of adult and apparently normal size and proportion as well as function, and of both the age and order of development, not only of each of the several parts themselves, but of all their immediate annexes, and in females as well as males, is far greater than has been recognized by any writer. This fact is the basis of the anxieties and fears of morphological abnormality, to be discussed later, and so frequent during adolescence. Normal development here is a physiological *sine qua non*, conditioning that of many traits of mind and body not usually recognized as sexual.

The significance of the normal evolution of these organs is seen in the great preponderance of defect due to both congenital conformation and to anomalies of evolution seen in defectives, among whom variations are still greater. In 507 delinquents examined by Marro,[2] over 10 per cent were abnormal in these organs as compared with 2 per cent among others. Out of 728 youthful epileptics and idiots studied

---

[1] Geigel, Richard. Ueber Variabilität in der Entwicklung der Geschlechtsorgane beim Menschen. Würzburg, 1883.

[2] La Puberté, p. 78.

by Bourneville and Sollier,[1] 262 had anomalies of these parts, a percentage which they call " enormously more " than that which was found among 299,270 conscripts from all classes, who were their bases of comparison. Varicocele, especially prevalent among young epileptics, hydrocele, epispadias, hypospadias, and other defects of the urinal passage, cryptochordias, and other testicular imperfections, especially on the left side, often complicated with hernia (130 cases), phimosis and other abnormalities of the prepuce, and various forms of arrest or defect, with occasional hypertrophies, both of structure and of function, that dwarf other lines of growth, are the chief troubles. It would be interesting to know how many of these cases had reproductive power.

Puberty literally means becoming hairy. Hair first develops in the pubic region at about fourteen in boys and thirteen in girls, generally before menstruation, later under the arm-pits just before the period of most rapid development of the breasts, and last comes the beard at the age of eighteen or nineteen. Tardiness or absence of the latter suggests arrest of the other later and higher qualities. Folk-lore proverbs and popular opinion warns us against beardless men. Marro (p. 79) publishes the following percentages of absence of beard at twenty years of age to show the difference between criminal and normal persons:

Assassins	16.2	Swindlers	4.3
Crime against persons	17.0	Thieves	11.0
Rape	8.3	Vagabonds	20.3
Brigands	12.0	Average	13.9
Incendiaries	16.6	Normal	1.5

Anomalies in the development of hair are common in defectives, but beard among bearded races seems a sign of mature virility, and although man may be gradually losing the hairy coat of his anthropoid ancestor, defect here is, at least now, a stigma of degeneration. The hair of the head often changes slightly in color and texture and may become straighter at puberty, and baldness and grayness increase fast at senescence. Vigor and beauty of hair and beard, and some think the quality and odor of their sebaceous

[1] Anomalies des Organes génitaux chez les Idiots et les Epileptiques. Prog. Med., 1888, p. 125.

glands, which, like all other glands, are in mysterious *rapport* with those involved in reproduction, are sexual charms. Beard and absence of hair on the body may be products of sexual secretion. The hair is normally at its best at the acme of sexual vitality. Its fetishisms then take their rise and its coiffure among savages is most elaborate. Just what this relation means in the present and in the evolutionary past is an unsolved problem.

The pubertal changes which take place in the male organs, besides those that are more obvious owing to their external condition, have received far less attention than has been bestowed by morphologists, physiologists, and gynecologists upon those of the female, and the sympathetic reverberations of these changes upon the whole organism are far less known. The corpora spongiosa, and still more the corpora cavernosa, increase to perhaps double their length and thickness, so that their vascularity and erethism is greatly augmented. The glans become larger and more sensitive, whether by increase in the size or number of the end bulbs and Pacinian corpuscles of touch and greater irritability of nerve centers, or by more local blood supply, is not known. The prepuce is more or less retracted on the glans and more mobile upon it, and grows more in circumference than in breadth or thickness. The glands of Tyson become active, and their odoriferous secretions, which in animals play an important rôle for sex, increase or sometimes now begin. The network of lymphatics grows more dense and active, and new dangers of uncleanliness and irritation, both of which may cause abnormal states, now arise. These dangers are so great and obvious that many primitive races have practised circumcision at this age as a preventive. The prostate glands and those of Cowper, as well as the seminal vesicles, develop in size and function.

The scrotum expands to more than twice its former size, the spermatic cord lengthens, the testes descend further and enlarge greatly. They also become more variable in size and activity with the conditions of the vita sexualis. The testes are developed in the abdomen, beginning just below the kidneys, and slowly migrate downward toward the scrotum during the later months of intra-uterine life.

Normally they grow at the same time. Arrest, both of descent and growth, and even atrophy and absence of one or both may occur, as the comprehensive monograph of E. Godard [1] shows, although mature function without descent may occur. Many hypotheses have been put forth to explain the descent, its relation to growth, to hernia, disease, abnormal secretions, all the many anomalies of form, and their re-ascent by excess or shock into the crural canal, the perineal region, or even to the iliac fossa. Non-descent, common to many animals, in man usually implies absence of function, and puberty is the last stage of life at which belated descent can be hoped for. They grow rapidly at adolescence to an average weight of 16 grams. Scrotic tonicity, which in part determines the degree of pendency of the testes, is in hardly less delicate *rapport* with states of brain, cord, and psyche than in the knee-jerk or the dilation and contraction of the iris. General debility or excessive function, like approaching old age, may cause relaxation, especially on the left side, which is lowest in most men, but artificial support is rarely necessary. The scrotic reflex is far more widely irradiated on the thighs and abdomen at puberty. The veins of the scrotum have few or no valves. For animals that go on all-fours and have no pendency, valves are unnecessary, but the upright position and pendency together are hard on these veins, and varicocele of more or less intensity and often transient is frequent shortly after adult size is attained. This is another cause of fears that are usually excessive, for this trouble has little and probably nothing whatever to do with excess of sexual function. Again, the motor-waves of the scrotum begin at this age and are analogous to the peristaltic action of the intestines, and like them reflect psychic states, and also probably general, and not merely special, sexual tension. They decline at senescence with the decrease of the secretions that are thus propelled along the epididymis and the long vas deferens. These changes have been superstitiously used for auguries of procreation, and all of them are often the basis of groundless fears. In few parts and functions of our bodies can Nature

---

[1] Études sur la Monochordie et la Cryptochordie, p. 164.

be more complacently trusted if allowed to work out her own way unmolested.

The chief physical fact of male puberty, about which all the other physical changes center, is that now true spermatozoids are formed. The seminiferous canals, hitherto round and smooth, become turgid by the development of large spermatophore cells which produce clusters of spermatozoa. The processes by which these latter arise within the walls of the canals has for a quarter of a century been a theme of continuous research, theory, and controversy. The primitive male cell, unlike the female cell which long remains stationary, undergoes many divisions before true sperm cells are formed. Geddes and Thompson prefer the following pedigree and nomenclature (p. 113): First, the primitive sex cell or male ovule; this is modified over into the mother sperm cell of spermatogonium; this divides into spermatocytes, and from these descend the spermatides or immature cells which differentiate into spermatozoa. The vast complexity and obscurity of these processes is only equaled by their importance.

When spermatozoa were first discovered by Hamm, a pupil of Leeuwenhoek, at Leyden, in 1677, they were thought to be parasites, and only near the middle of this century were their origin and function known. They are only about $\frac{1}{450}$ of an inch in diameter, and according to Lode[1] 226,257,000 are produced in both testicles per week, or 339,385,500,000 during thirty years of vigorous sexual life. This vast number seems a relict of the great fecundity of lower forms of life maintained, perhaps, because of their small size and the corresponding improbability of any single cell finding an ovum. Here, if anywhere in the human organism, life still remains a continuous cell division from one generation to another, and as in certain protozoan forms of life, there is no death and no corpse. Every other physical process and every act of life may be regarded as but the wriggle of flagella to bring these elements to their highest maturity before and after their union with ova, to effect that union under the most favorable terms, etc. At any rate, the spermatozoa and ova, the elements of which preexist in the

[1] Pflüger's Archiv, 1891.

infant body, but which come to maturity at puberty, are elements of a very different and far higher biological order than any other tissue or organ. To their interests, could we only know them, all others whatsoever should yield, and they might be regarded as in some sense the highest criteria of every act or mode of life, whatever our views of Weismann's theories.

It is not wholly the accumulation of sexual fluid in and its pressure on the walls of the vesicles that causes the first ejaculation by reflex action. Accessory secretions often precede, and the phenomena of pro-spermatogenesis, sometimes not without much pain, often precede functional maturity. The first spontaneous but perfectly normal activity of the sex organs at puberty constitute a group of psychophysical phenomena so new that great perturbations are often caused, upon which quacks know so well how to play by exciting morbid fears. Sometimes the testicular secretions, although abundantly produced, do not appear without, but are resorbed *in situ*, partly at least by the rich plexi of lymphatics which surround these canals, and this seems one of Nature's provisions to both aid and to utilize chastity. The influence of the presence of spermatic fluid upon the voice, muscular vigor, hair, growth, etc., are vast and obscure but very tempting fields for research and theory. Beunis thinks the first secretions of sperm begin between ten and fifteen, but contain no spermatozoa. These, Mantegazza thinks, do not normally appear, or at least ripen, before eighteen or twenty, but Bierent thought he found them in sixty cases at thirteen to fifteen, which conclusion agrees with that of Fredericq and Nuel, and from this he distinguishes three stages of adolescence: a premonitory, when spermatic secretions occur; a period of first ejaculation and menstruation usually marked by much perturbation; and third, the age, a year or more later, of maturity and reproductive power. This nearly corresponds with Marro's three stages of preparation, acceleration, and perfection of adolescent development.

II. Passing now to girls, traces of the mammæ, which give their characteristic name to the highest group of animals, first appear in man by the end of the second month of intra-uterine life. The mammæ and the nipple were developed by the grouping to one orifice of many glands slowly differentiated from those diffused over the dermal surface on which they open up to about the stage of the monotremes, traces of their old independence still being seen in slight pimple-like protuberances about the nipple and probably in supplementary mammæ. In their secretions these resemble the sebaceous, but in structure the sudoriferous glands. At first in the human female they secrete not milk but colostrum, and as Becquerel and Vernois have shown, there are more salts, butter, caseins, and solids before twenty, but the water and sugar ingredients increase after. The profound sympathy of the mammæ with the vita sexualis, both physically and psychically, is well known, and is established at this age when both their sensitiveness to touch and their secretions respond acutely to psychic and nervous influences.

Philogenetically they are evolved probably not from sebaceous but by specialized sweat glands. Up to ten or twelve years of age the internal structure and the outer form of the breasts is nearly the same for boys and for girls. At puberty they begin to undergo important modifications in females, and ever thereafter respond in the most sympathetic way to the changes in the pelvic molimena. Both the galactophores or glands and the supportive areolar tissue develop rapidly at this period, but the latter much preponderates until pregnancy, to which, in this respect, puberty is in a sense preparatory, when the former rapidly mature. Until eleven or twelve the glandular elements continue to divide in both sexes, but without forming true lobules. At this age, development, which it is very significant to note, is sometimes marked and even excessive in the male, and sometimes also retrogression occurs. In girls the circle around the nipple or the areola enlarges, and its distinctly pink color deepens, the nipple projects and grows firm, and the orifice of the separate glands appear as pimply projections, and its sensitiveness, measured by reaction to mechanical stimulation, increases. Fat also develops in the body of the breasts, and the alveoli enlarge and probably new ones are formed. The gland as a whole grows from one-half or three-fourths of an inch across and one-sixth of an inch in thickness, the size at which it remains in the male, to an average of about four and one-half inches wide and one-half an inch thick in the female. Arteries and veins also undergo adaptive enlargement. Very rarely there is a slight secretion and discharge at puberty, as sometimes in early infancy.

These are among the more variable parts of the body. Polymasty or supernumerary breasts occur about once in five hundred persons. These may be outside or above, but are generally caudad and suggestive of the rows of dugs in many higher vertebrates, but indeed may occur on almost any part of the trunk or even limbs. Charpy finds great individual differences beginning at puberty. The distance of the mammæ from each other increases somewhat in proportion to the curve of the thorax with well-marked, broad and round, especially long and pear-shaped, types often distinguished as racial differences, and varying with the form of the chest. The completeness of their development in structure no less than in function is also exceedingly variable, and is influenced by everything in the environment, including food, regimen, and occupation, error here tending to retard the later stages of their development. Few organs suffer more from avoidable cause of arrest, and one of the earliest of the long degenerative stages which mark the decay of ethnic stock is imperfect mammary function and inability to nurse offspring sufficiently.

The changes in the female organs of generation at puberty are very marked and of great complexity and importance. The mons is covered with hair, which, beginning in the central part, spreads slowly to its full and very variable extent, grows for several years in density, rigidity, and commonly takes on a darker hue. Adipose tissue is developed and the integument probably thickens. The labia majora also thicken by the same process, growing more over the labia minoria and reducing the rima. At no period of life are the outer labia so closely approximated, the vulva so entirely closed, and the inner parts so hidden, a result to which the rapid growth of the thighs at this age also contributes. The dartos tunic of unstriped muscular tissue is enlarged even more than the fat, nerves, and glands of the labia majora at puberty. The triangular apex of the minor labia protrude very slightly, changing to a darker hue, and the sebaceous glands of this part develop, while those of the nympha do so only in pregnancy. The distance from the fossa to the mons increases, and the marked racial difference in the position of the vaginal opening and of its direction, but slightly manifest before, now appear.

The pubertal growth of the clitoris is relatively about equal and very similar to that of the corresponding male organ. It acquires now its power of erectility. The genital corpuscles of Krause, and those of Finger, in which the nerves which stimulate reflex erectility end, no doubt undergo developmental changes. The urethral glands and the venous plexi of all the erectile tissues enlarge in all these parts, which together are the homologues of the prostate gland in man. The anterior tubercle of the vagina, however, which surrounds the meatus, diminishes at least relatively, while the vulvo-vaginal glands grow nearly to the size of an almond, and secrete reflexly upon excitation of the clitoris.[1] Much the same is true of the mucous secretions of the vestibulary and urethral follicles. Whether the acidity of these secretions is increased, or only their quantity, is unknown. The secretory function, too, of all these parts is augmented in a marked degree.

The vagina undergoes a great increase of both length and breadth. Its muscular tunic thickens, the mucous surfaces redden and grow active, and all the venous plexi enlarge as the circulation in these parts increases.

The uterus is small in children, but grows immensely on the approach of womanhood to forty or fifty grammes in weight, and also changes from a cylindrical to its characteristic pyriform shape. As the pelvic cavity enlarges it tips forward and its anteflexion is slightly diminished, its neck becomes relatively shorter, and the orifices toward the tubes become longer and more opened as the cavity grows larger. The arbor vitæ shows its structure, making its neck resemble the buccal orifice. The muscular walls increase greatly,

---

[1] See Bierent, La Puberté, 1896, pp. 104–121.

partly by enlargement of preexisting and partly by the development of new fibers, and the mucous surfaces undergo very important changes described elsewhere in the complex processes of nidification and menstruation.

The hymen grows in both thickness and tenacity, but there is hardly more individual variation in these respects than in size and form of its orifice. Probably its form changes at puberty from the previously simpler shape and is less often annular and more often corolliform, and it is often broken by several rarely symmetrical notches or lobes. From puberty its orifice enlarges slowly till full nubility. The bulbus vestibuli certainly, and probably the sphincter vaginæ, and Kobelt's pars intermedia, participate in the accelerated growth of this period. So too must the nerves, if we can infer from the great increase of sensitiveness.

Puech found that the ovaries grew from early girlhood in each of their three dimensions, and that there was a marked augmentation of rate at or near the dawn of puberty, but that their growth normally continued for some years afterward before they attained adult dimensions, the right always slightly leading the left. They grow soft and vascular, but weight increases in about the same proportion as size, or from about two or three grams before puberty to five or six at full maturity. Their growth in length is greater than in their vertical and transverse diameters. Up to ten the ovaries are at about the level of the iliac fossæ, but they become intrapelvic and more or less mobile at puberty, owing to their erectile function and the traction of the uterus and Fallopian muscles. A slight projection at a single point marks the ripening of the first Graafian follicle, the monthly rupture of which is later to scarify the previously smooth ovarian surfaces. The parenchyma of the ovaries from which the ovules germinate is not only enlarged, but becomes the center upon which the pubertal development of breasts and uterus is especially dependent. The medullary substance grows more than any other part of the ovarian tissue at puberty, and is enlarged much at the first menstruation and somewhat at each later one, when its color also changes to a dark slaty-red, due to normal congestion.

Since 1827, when von Baer discovered the ovum in man,

the existence of which had long been known in animals, there has been, as Auvard well says, a revolution in genital physiology. Ovulation is at least in some sense a secretion, although, unlike other glands, the ovaries and testes secrete living cells. The process is spontaneous, the ova emerging from the Graafian follicle at the surface of the ovaries, and being conveyed through them mainly by ciliary motions to the uterus. Normally the ovaries lay their eggs when the nest of uterine mucus is ready to receive and fix them if impregnated, although the latter is broken down and discharged if not needed. These two processes, however, are somewhat independent, for each may occur without the other, although normally they are almost as coincident as the special adjustment of the vocal cords and the stress of the breath used to produce phonation. The growth of the mucous surface is a monthly anabolic surplus upon which the ovum can live for a time. If it is not fertilized, these preparations are vain, and menstruation is an expression of their failure. When the cellular detritus from the inner wall of the uterus has passed off, the blood ceases, and in eight or ten days the lost lining is replaced, and the wounds in the ovaries caused by the bursting of the follicle and the liberation of the ova are healed, leaving, however, scars for each period. We have here, then, a striking case of the rejuvenation of the tissue by proliferation centering about reproduction, which may itself be considered as the very highest degree of this process. Here, too, we have atavistic suggestions of a great but now lost fecundity. In the two ovaries of a girl of eighteen there are estimated to be 72,000 primitive ova, of which, however, only about 400 mature during life, reaching an average size of $\frac{1}{127}$ of an inch.[1]

III. Andrews[2] has undertaken to describe the effects of castration on animals as follows: Wethers do not grow larger, but their wool is less oily and of more value, indicating sympathy of the testes with sebaceous glands. Cats grow larger, are fonder of petting, as if a secondary sex quality was increased, and remain good mousers. The

[1] Lee. American Text-Book of Physiology. pp. 887, 982.

[2] Am. Med. Jour., January, 1898.

horse grows larger if castrated young, suggesting the inverse ratio of individuation to genesis, but the bridle teeth are not modified as in the full male, indicating less vigor of jaw development and less power to bite. The calf is larger and taller than the bull, but his neck and fore-quarters, effective in sexual conflicts with other males, are smaller. His cerebellum increases, and his horns are longer and perhaps even thicker, but on the whole less powerful and dangerous than those of the bull. The pitch of the voice is higher, not in bellowing, to which he is more prone, but in lowing. The elks experimented on did not shed their horns, which are accessory sexual in function, as usual, but their tips were frozen in the severe winter, and when they came off numerous small sprouts grew in the spring, which were again nipped the next winter, until large bony knobs arose which, perhaps, if protected with care, would have attained a great size.

The influence of sex seems to extend in some mysterious way, which we do not understand, to that disappearance of cartilage which marks the cessation of bone growth. The general view since Haller was for a long time that castration weakened the force of growth. Springer[1] holds that nutritive activity is checked in eunuchs, and that they have especially small and arrested legs and thin thighs like old men. Lortet, however,[2] who has examined many eunuchs and extended his study to castrated animals, concludes that while their pelvic and thoracic regions are small, most bones of the arms, legs, feet, and fingers are long, slender, comparable with the bones of the ox, and often delicate, and that this is especially true of the legs. May it be that there is an inverse relation between length of limb, especially the femur, and relative size of pelvis and sexual vigor and maturity, and that disproportionate length of upper leg is a bad sign for maternity? This operation on the eunuchs of Cairo, even though it may have been performed in infancy, does not cause much differentiation till puberty, but they attain a stature of nearly two inches more than the average of their race.

---

[1] La Croissance, Paris, 1899.

[2] Comptes Rendus de l'Acad. des Sciences, April, 1890.

Lancaster[1] quotes a letter from "a well-known professor in a New England College," who spent years in the East among Nubian eunuchs, as follows: "There is no question that castration at an early age does in various ways modify physical development, though I do not think it modifies it so much as is commonly supposed. The difference most likely to be observed was in the voice. Castration does produce an immense effect, though an indirect one, upon the character. It is not the operation in itself, but its effects upon the mind. The mind broods over the fact that the body is reproductively impotent and is filled with morbid resentment and jealousy. No other physical deformity can so far distort and devilize the character. As far as I can judge, sex feelings exist unmodified by absence of the sexual organs. The eunuch differs from the man, not in the absence of sexual passion, but only in the fact that he can not fully gratify it. As far as he can approach a gratification of it, he does so. Often, maddened by a sense of impotence, he wreaks vengeance on the irresponsible object of which he is enamored. . . . The eunuchs have all the adolescent phenomena. I have watched, for example, boy-eunuchs of ten or eleven years, possibly younger. Early conscious, as they are, of their desexed condition, there was nothing apparent in their moods or pleasures different from other children of their race. They took the same delight in a perfume or a flower, or a pretty baby, as any other boy of their race would have done. The little eunuch is more inclined to solitude than almost any Western child, but perhaps no more than his compatriots. As to rebelling against authority, I have more than once seen a diminutive eunuch do that."[2]

Marro[3] insists on the close relation between the development of organs and the secondary sexual characteristics, and gives two interesting cases where the former atrophied and

---

[1] Psychology and Pedagogy of Adolescence, by E. G. Lancaster. Ped. Sem., July, 1897, vol. v, p. 61.

[2] Kroemer [Zeitsch. f. Psychopath., 135–52] and Krafft-Ebing [Psych. Arbeiten, ii., 189], recommend it guardedly for men in cases of sexual hyperæsthesia, but the latter thinks its beneficial effects are not apparent for a year or two.

[3] La Puberté. Bull. de la Soc. de Med. de Belgique, 1894, p. 1575.

the latter did not develop. History records the achievements of many eunuchs of great ability—the Marseilles philosopher, Favorino, the Egyptian general, Aristonicus, Narses, the general of Justinian, Salomon, one of the lieutenants of Belisarius, Haly, grand vizier of Soliman; but Marro thinks these are exceptions. Eunuchs, he holds, are precocious and never live to great age. The pulse is feeble, and they are prone to varicosities in the extremities and to periodic hemorrhoids, liver troubles, etc. Like animals thus mutilated, they are more docile. In Central Asia, Dr. G. Roberts reports that girls are often castrated to act the rôle of and sometimes to be sold for eunuchs. Mojon thinks that if this operation is performed upon the young, those bones not yet entirely hardened continue soft and growing. Osteomalacia, which is especially a disease of women, and consists in softening of the bones, is arrested by extirpation of the ovaries. Acromegalia, which is also closely connected with the sexual organs, and is marked by extraordinary development of the bones of the face and those of both the upper and lower extremities, sometimes causes girls to assume a virile aspect, the voice to deepen, and the breasts to shrink, the thyroid gland and the clitoris to increase, and the genesic desires, and perhaps the periods, to diminish. Marie, Souza-Leite, Tamburini, Tanzi, and Freund think this trouble closely connected with disorder of the genital functions at puberty. Indeed, some think that the terminal parts of the extremities grow first at puberty, the hands and feet becoming less graceful and magnified, and their muscles and even fat developing out of proportion to the rest of the body which makes up its due proportions later. If this be so, normal puberty would present anomalies similar to those of acromegalia.

Flood [1] thinks that if castrated young, man grows taller, fatter, and has a larger frame; that the hair on pubes and face does not grow; that the cheeks look round and prominent, and the chin is often double; that the voice of boys is higher, and that of girls lower. Harris [2] thinks eunuchs have longer legs, light pelvis, and are prone to be undeveloped

[1] Notes on the Castration of Idiot Children. Am. Jour. of Psy., vol. x, p. 296.
[2] Phila. Med. Jour., 1898.

in chest and arms, again like the ox, and their bones are not only longer but more hollow and so weaker. The skin of castrated negroes often grows several shades lighter colored, as if the color-type was weakened. Eunuchs are said to suffer less from gout and renal calculus, as if sex was inversely as this kidney function, have a weak, slow pulse, are prone to hemorrhoids, liver troubles, indicating concomitant decline of glandular vigor, rarely live to old age, and resemble animals thus operated upon which are more tractable and more easily domesticated.

The functional castration, practised among the Pueblo Indians to fit certain young men for religious ceremonies and also for pederasty, is performed by excessive abuse of this function in unmentionable ways till local paralytic impotence supervenes and becomes permanent, and the victims are reduced to the condition of "mugenados" or women-men, when the organs atrophy, the beard falls out, the voice grows feminine, and the breasts give milk. In China, where the Emperor used to keep 2,000 eunuchs, the operation removes all organs by a single stroke before adolescence, and the process is said to be fatal in only three per cent of the cases. It is practised by certain fanatical religious sects, notably the White Doves or Skoptzi, in Russia, to insure purity. They are described as a very vigorous people with many excellent qualities. Ablation of the ovaries, still practised in Bombay, suppresses the menses, makes the voice harsh, the breasts shrunken, the face hairy, the character forceful and masculine, and the form angular and unattractive.

In general, the psychic as well as the physical effects of castration are less the later the latter operation. The ox and gelding, as is known, do not entirely lose their libido, but it is greatly reduced. Guinard has shown that in two or three per cent of cases castration of horses does not prevent coition. In men libido of a falsetto kind may occur. Flood, who operated on twenty-six idiot boys, all but two of whom were under seventeen, and half under fourteen, reports sexual appetite missing in all but two cases, and in these being only spasmodic, although erections, and in one case masturbation, persisted slightly at intervals. In all instances temper was greatly improved, and there was less pugnacity, obstinacy, self-will, and more sympathy, altruism, and normal balance of emotion. Möbius,[1] who has given us the fullest history of the effects of castration, lays emphasis on the mental enfeeblement.

Facts in this field thus show the dependence of a very important group of not only physical but psychic qualities upon the presence of this quasi-gland, the loss of which seems to change both the intensity and the nature of character more than the loss of one and perhaps both legs, or any other removable part.

There has been much recent discussion in this country concerning the desirability of this operation. On the whole, the testimony seems conclusive that epileptic seizures may thus be made both less frequent and less severe. All but two of Flood's cases were epileptics, and only five were thought to need even diminished doses of bromide after the operation. Dr. W. O. Henry[2] designates as a crime of medical men their failure to urge legislation to prevent the marriage of criminals, or else to have them castrated. In 1897 a bill was introduced into the Michigan Legislature to insure the castration of inmates of the State Home for the Feeble-Minded and Epileptic before their discharge, in the case of those convicted of rape or of a felony for the third time, but it did not pass. The House Committee on Public Health of the Kansas Legislature lately reported favorably on a bill doing away with prison for rape and substituting castration, and was supported by the Social Purity League of Topeka. It has been claimed that ten other States would follow the lead of Kansas. Dr. Daniels, of Texas, and the late Dr. Wey, of Elmira, have urged castration for sexual perversion and for habitual criminals, and Dr. Boal, of Illinois,[3] recommended it and ovariotomy for the punishment of crime and the reformation of criminals. It has also been often urged of late, instead of lynching, for negroes who commit rape in the South.

This may well give us pause. The case of dangerous

---

[1] Ueber die Wirkung der Castration. Halle, 1903.

[2] Medical Herald, June, 1866.

[3] Jour. Am. Med. Ass'n, September, 1895.

idiots is certainly very different from that of criminals. Felony has no fixed meaning and varies greatly in different lands and in different States, and few jurists would venture to define it. It is heinous and used to involve loss of all possessions, but now often includes crimes punishable by death or imprisonment, and is sometimes due to excessive vigor in wrong directions which subjective inhibition or objective deterrents have not yet repressed, and which we may yet learn to divert to right directions. How far law should undertake human stirpiculture by such methods involves some of the deepest problems of biology, of the rights of personality and of society, and perhaps penal colonies or other new ways of treating crime, the possibility of new human varieties, etc.

This operation in maturity is far more serious, and according to Cabot[1] is very liable to be followed by mental disturbance as well as death when performed on the aged for enlarged prostate. While those subjected to it early in life practically lose the desire, this is far less abated in those operated on in later years. The extreme envy and jealousy charged to eunuchs may be due largely to their fidelity and zeal in defending the women in their charge.

When this operation in man occurs after puberty, normal congress but not fecundation is possible, and probably more often so in men than in animals. Glaevecke found that in females castrated after maturity sexual desire persisted in twenty-two per cent, was diminished in thirty-seven per cent, and extinguished in forty-one per cent. Jayle,[2] as the result of a *questionnaire*, reports that out of thirty-three cases of ovarian castration, desire was unchanged in eighteen, diminished in three, abolished in eight, increased in three; pleasure remained the same in seventeen, was diminished in one, abolished in nine, increased in five, and painful in six. In thirteen cases of utero-ovarian castration, desire was unchanged in three, diminished in two, abolished in one, and augmented in four, while pleasure remained the same in six, was increased in one, was hyperesthetic in one, and painful in one. Auto-suggestion that after the operation there

[1] Annals of Surgery, September, 1896.
[2] Rev. de Gyn., 1897, p. 403.

should be a change, he says, probably played a great rôle. This appetite often survives, and may even increase, after the menopause. Closely connected as the organs are with desire, they are not indispensable to it, but the need is more or less diffused throughout the entire organism. The agitation at puberty, as the individual prepares for the perpetuation of the species, is not only often not localized from lack of knowledge of organs and acts, but is general and not unlike hunger, which is not all located in the stomach but is the aggregate effect of the nutritive needs of all the cells and tissues. The glandular cells along the digestive tract are overcharged and need to function, as do overrested muscles; so "we love with our whole body and not a single anatomical element is disinterested in the function of reproduction," and the soul as well as the body has its needs.

Concerning early intersexual vice I have spoken in the last chapter. How this is complicated with social and physical disease two recent researches typically show. Baer,[1] in a very valuable study of twenty-two murderers, in Berlin, between the ages of fourteen and eighteen, notes none of Lombroso's anatomical signs, but finds most to be victims of the vicious sexual precocity characteristic of young criminals in large cities. The crime was in most instances revoltingly brutal and without remorse, and most such cases are deemed incorrigibly defective in their moral if not their intellectual nature. Caldo[2] finds that most prostitutes fall between the ages of fifteen and eighteen, which he terms the period of sexual vulnerability toward which chief effort should be directed. Diseased women are always more dangerous than diseased men, and this youthful class is most infectious. Into this vaster field I can not enter here.[3]

---

[1] Ueber jugendliche Mörder. Arch. f. Crim. Anthropol., Bd. xi, 1903.

[2] Vénéréologie Sociale. Le Progrès Méd., April 11, 1903.

[3] An interesting and valuable illustration of the awakening sense of responsibility in this field is seen in a comprehensive German report[1] based on 900 full answers to a six-page *questionnaire*, with 70 cases, showing the effects of church, plain speaking, and scientific literature on sex, association, and the dangers from soldiers, who

---

[1] Die geschlechtlich-sittlichen Verhältnisse der evangelischen Landbewohner im deutschen Reiche. 1. Band. Ostdeutschland. Von Pastor H. Wittenberg und Pastor Dr. E. Hückstädt. Leipzig, 1895, pp. 309 and 236.

IV. One of the very saddest of all the aspects of human weakness and sin is onanism, and to say that it is as important in treating adolescence as it is painful to consider is to say very much. Until recently it has been met on the one hand with either prudery and painstaking reticence or treated in terms of exaggerated horror, as in the "scare" and quack literature. It still requires a great degree of moral earnestness to discuss it with candor and the requisite plainness. One thing can safely be assumed, namely, that no one ever fell into the habit by reading a serious work upon it. A sentence of Stuart Mill's has been well quoted [1] concerning it, viz., "The diseases of society can be no more checked or healed than those of the body without publicly speaking of them." To ignore or deny the wide prevalence of the evil, in the way often done, is sometimes honest ignorance, but is also often affectation and even a form of hypocrisy and cant. While scientific discussion of the subject may not be meant for all the young, lest they form too poor an opinion of human nature, it is, in my judgment, imperative for educators, and one of the richest scientific quarries opened by the new psychology.

The vice, as we know from Aristophanes, Ovid, Horace, and others, abounded in ancient Greece and Rome. The treatise of Hippocrates, 380 B. C., which ascribed the chief causal rôle to the spinal cord and gave it a fatalistic tone, was not excelled in acumen by any work upon the subject until the epoch-making treatise by Tissot,[2] in 1760, which was classic in style and very important in its results. It sought to make headway against the nameless abuses and vices in France centering in the court of Louis XIV and XV. The works of Simon [3] and Lallemand [4] described the

are called the most corrupting agency. Unmarried officers are called the curse of young women. Parental neglect is the first cause of lapses. On the whole, this voluminous and very comprehensive report presents a sad monotone of iniquity, accented now and then by incidents of exceptional pathos.

[1] Die Masturbation. Eine Monographie für Aerzte und Pädagogen, von Dr. Med. Hermann Rohleder, Berlin, 1899, p. 319. One of the latest and best treatises on the subject.

[2] De l'Onanisme, Lausanne, 1760.

[3] Traité d'Hygiène appliqué à l'éducation de la Jeunesse, Paris, 1827.

[4] Des Pertes séminales involontaires, Paris, 1836–42.

consequences of self-abuse as terrible—diseases of the brain and cord, paralysis, dementia, blindness, tabes, etc., in ways truer to the needs of morality than to science. Indeed, salutary as were these works, their influence is still seen in the lurid effects of the vice as described in much of the current popular literature, and has tended to bring the serious efforts of science in this field into discredit. The two comprehensive treatises of Pouillet [1] brought us back to common sense. The fifth International Hygienic Congress at Budapest, in 1894, at which Cohn [2] read the outlines of his important treatise, almost marked an epoch in the frankness and scientific mode of treating the subject, as Fournier's [3] work had done in France. Tarnowsky, Rosenbach, Rohleder, Fürbringer, Löwenfeld, Hösslin, Ribbing, Moll, Lombroso, Krafft-Ebing, I. P. West, Hammond, and others have in recent years shed much light upon this subject and the broader one of *vita sexualis* in general. We shall, as far as practicable, confine ourselves to the adolescent aspects of the subject.

The first problem is the extent of the evil. Cohn proposed to send *questionnaires* to the best of the 21,000 German physicians and the 8,000 German students of medicine, requesting anonymous answers based upon their own school-memories and observations, but the scientific academy to which he appealed for the expenses of this research (some $1,500) has not yet responded. Until some such comprehensive investigation is made, it is impossible to determine the extent of the vice. Many hold, however, that it is the most wide-spread of all the popular diseases. Blaschko, a Berlin expert, estimated in 1893 that there were yearly in that city over 30,000 cases who consulted physicians, and that if, in the four student years reckoned by averages, every patient was a different person, every student was treated for diseases indicating excess. Rohleder, in an earlier work published in 1895, estimated that ninety per cent had practised it, and the next year concluded that about all men once at least in

[1] L'Onanisme chez l'homme, 1883. L'Onanisme chez la femme. Tr. from the sixth edition in eight numbers of the Med. Times and Register, 1896.

[2] Was kann die Schule gegen die Masturbation des Kindes thun, von Prof. Hermann Cohn, Berlin, 1894.

[3] De l'Onanisme, Paris, 1893.

their lives had been guilty. Berger[1] asserts the same. Tissot, in 1759, found every pupil in the *lycée* he investigated guilty. Benseman asserts its enormous prevalence in the English high schools. Moll quotes approvingly the phrase, "who denies it has forgotten," and Cohn is cynical enough to say, "If any one denies that he ever did it, he does it now." Dr. Seerley, of Springfield, Mass., found out of one hundred and twenty-five academic students, eight who satisfied him they had never indulged in it, and of three hundred and forty-seven who answered his questions, seventy-one denied having practised it. It was found to be practised without a single exception in a certain reform school known to the writer, where the inmates competed and the one who could consummate it oftenest daily was the object of a certain hero-worship. Because it is so dangerous, and liable to occur in individuals who lack stamina, it has its octopus-grasp in nearly all institutions for the defective classes. It is known to be practically ineradicable in institutions for the feeble-minded, and I have been told by heads of schools for deaf-mutes, and still more emphatically by officers of institutions for the blind, that in these—perhaps because they lack the normal quantum of sense stimuli and are less active and objective in their habits—it is peculiarly prevalent and tenacious.

F. S. Brockman[2] received two hundred and thirty-two replies from college and theological students at an average age of twenty-three and a half years, to the question, "What was the severest temptation of your school days?" One hundred and thirty-two specified masturbation, and ninety-two specified other sexual temptations, and these two together constituted five more than all other temptations combined. In forty-two papers only out of the two hundred and thirty-two was there no clear intimation of this form of temptation. "There were seventy-five who were guilty of masturbation after their conversion, and twenty-four after they had decided to become ministers." Some specified their struggles with this temptation at great length. Brockman sums up his conclu-

[1] Archiv für Psych., 1896.

[2] A study of the moral and religious life of two hundred and fifty-one students in the United States. Ped. Sem., vol. ix, p. 255.

sions as showing an alarming extent of this vice, a morbid state of mind thus occasioned, the stronghold which the habit still has, and the uniformity with which they blame their elders for not having warned them. The literature upon the various modes in which it is practised and the methods of imitation, contagion, and the seduction of younger by older boys is copious. We may well hope that these estimates are exaggerated, and the writer at least feels, as probably every reader will, a strong disposition to discredit with indignation all high estimates until they are forced home by statistics upon methods invulnerable to criticism. Yet it must be confessed that the whole literature of the subject attests that wherever careful researches have been undertaken, the results are appalling as to prevalence, and suggest that the Occident has little, if any, advantage over the sad records of the Orient, and that civilized man is on the whole, to say the least, no better, if not far worse, in this respect than his savage brother.

onanism

Strange to say, this perversion is not peculiar to man; for we have many and well-attested reports of its prevalence among monkeys, dogs, blood stallions, elephants, turkeys, etc., although in many of these cases the climax is not reached. Another sad chapter is that which describes it among children of tender years. There are well-authenticated cases where children of both sexes under two years of age have practised it, and far more cases are on record for still later childish years. In some cases it is taught by nurses, older children, or perverts; but there is abundant evidence that even with the very young, and still more with those older, the old view that it was not spontaneously learned, but due to example and moral infection, was wrong. It is one of the easiest and most spontaneous of all vices, and in very young children many now think it a disease more frequent among girls than boys. Some now believe that sucking the thumbs, fingers, rubber or other artificial nipples predisposes to it. It certainly does not need to be taught and may be spontaneous, although, in fact, it is probably in most cases contagious. All agree that the early years of puberty, from twelve to fourteen, are those in which it is most common. Sometimes an epidemic of mutualism, or some other form of it, devastates an entire school, and many cases are on record where its prevalence in these years passes all non-expert credence. During the teens the intensity and frequency of it in individual cases, particularly in those of sanguine and choleric temperament, is no less difficult to believe. It sometimes reaches a satyriasic and nymphomaniac degree, and many, if not most, of the perversions originate in these years.

Its causes are many and difficult to proportion. Prominent among these is precocious mental development and too much psychic and too little physical expression. In these cases the attention of the child, in the progress of self-knowledge of its own body, is certain to be instinctively directed, as a mere matter of curiosity, to its sexual parts, and this is very greatly favored by a sitting position, especially if long maintained, which of itself is a stimulus, and by absence of other intense interests. Even in those of perfervid fancy the habit is sometimes formed in complete ignorance of its meaning. With knowledge, it is a matter of the strength of will, and wherever mental overwork weakens this, it tends to that irritable weakness of the nervous system which makes the rankest ground for onanism. Whether the central nervous system acts most upon the organs or *vice versa*, a question much discussed, is no doubt largely an individual matter, for probably each affects the other, but in different degrees in different stages of development. Wherever children mature early in mind there is special danger of a wrong direction, and therefore need of all the methods of control. The temperament from which hysteria and epilepsy spring is volcanic, and makes perhaps the best natural psychic constitution for the development of this evil. The physical processes of first menstruation predispose to it, and with some instruction or instinctive foreboding of its evil, cause violent struggles of soul which are exhausting in themselves.

A long list of skin diseases—pruritus, eczema, urticaria, and various parasitic disorders like scabies—increase the dangers. A consumptive heredity is a powerful predisposing agent. This insidious disease seems to act on human nature like a worm upon fruit in producing premature ripeness and activity of the reproductive function. A long convalescence, piles, habitual constipation, irritating urinal deposits, malformation of the organs, idleness and laziness, weakness of will in general, and doubtless heredity, play important etiological rôles. Among the external causes are springtime, which is a peculiarly dangerous season, warm climates, improper clothes, rich food, indigestion, mental overwork, nervousness, habits of defective cleanliness, especially of a local kind, prolonged sitting or standing, too monotonous walking, sitting cross-legged, spanking, late rising, petting and indulgence, corsets that produce stagnation or hyperemia of blood in the lower part of the body, too great straining of the memory—the causal influences of all these are expatiated on in detail by Rohleder and others.

Prominent among predisposing causes are often placed erotic reading, pictures, and theatrical presentations. Cohn even pleads for an expurgated Bible and dictionary, and others would banish the Odes of Horace, the Satires of Juvenal, to say nothing of Martial and Terence, and forbid ballets. Certain drugs, like phosphorus, cocaine, opium, camphor, and inhalation of oxygen, are now known to have stimulating, while others, like digitalis, saltpeter, arsenic, have an opposite effect. Schiller protests against trousers-pockets for boys, as do others against feather-beds, while even horseback-riding and the bicycle have been placed under the ban by a few recent extremist writers. Indulgence in intoxicating drink without doubt predisposes to it, as does any physical or psychic difficulty in access to closets, solitude, certain perfumes, overeating, fondling, fur, and rocking-chairs.

In general, while for a healthy child under good influences the majority of these causes can be successfully defied, like other of the ultra-refinements of modern hygiene, the greater the liability of the disease the more necessary does it become to attend to the very slightest etiological motives. While some are more or less frigid to the great majority of these favoring influences, the delicate, nervous child may respond in more or less degree to them all, even the slightest; and it should never be forgotten that early adolescent years are sensitive to all matters pertaining to sex, even very remotely, to a degree that science probably does not yet recognize and about which the ordinary parent is densely ignorant and optimistic, and which the child himself does not begin to comprehend. The prurient often experiment with themselves in seeking assurance that function is normal, and this leads to manipulation and then to masturbation in the early teens, which is often carried on for a few years. The new sense of virility brings a certain deep elation that in coarser natures even becomes ostentatious and boastful before their mates, and sometimes especially before younger boys, with a vaunting feeling of superiority. The first orgasm, especially if forced at premature age, consists in a general and diffused glow and exhilaration of the sense of well-being even before emission is possible. This gives a heightened sense of the value of life, and a flush of ecstasy and joy that tinges the world with a glory that is far more than sensuous. But before this function is well developed the Nemesis of depression follows hard after these exaltations, and both states arouse thought and fancy in new directions and with a vividness unknown before. In bright, nervous children pubescence often dawns with almost fulminating intensity and suddenness, and sweeps the individual into pernicious ways long before moral or even intellectual restraints are operative. Excessive danger here is one of the penalties man pays for that inestimable tool of his development on to the human plane—the hand. The very definition of precocity involves inversion; the order of nascent periods has been reversed in both sequence and strength. Wherever this occurs the race deteriorates. Yielding to mere and gross sensuous pleasure shortens the growth period, and the only way to prolong it and attain an ever higher and fuller maturity for the race is by the plain old virtue of self-restraint. This is probably the field of most active and normal natural selection. The ascendant individual family or stock is the one that refuses to yield in excess to the temptation of the flesh, and the descendants are those whose instincts for selfish gratification preponderate over those of race-conservatism. These are the sins of the parents that are visited on their children, devitalizing, arresting their full development, and finally exterminating them. Honor to the unborn by parents is their chief claim to reverence by their children, and to enfeeble the power of hereditary transmission is worthy the contempt and curses which recent literature has often represented as felt by degenerates for those responsible for their existence. The invective of a decadent son upon a sire but for whose private vice he might have been well born, is as haunting and characteristic a note of our modern culture as was the curse of Atreus's time for ancient Greece.

In discussing the results of onanism, we must first of all recognize that the immediate and sensational effects often seriously believed in, and often purposely exaggerated for pedagogic effects, are not so immediate or disastrous as represented in both the popular and the earlier literature. The brain is not literally drained away; dementia, idiocy, palsy, and sudden death are not imminent, nor is there any peculiar infallible expression, attitude, or any other manifestation instantly recognizable by experts. Current impression to this effect has much to do in causing terror, shamefacedness, and some of the bashfulness and solitude sometimes seen.

Perhaps the most common psychic result is a sense of unworthiness, sin, pollution, and the serious diminution of self-respect, often instinctively covered or resisted by whimmish and boisterous self-assertion, or occasionally hidden by almost morbid scrupulousness and convictions of foreboding disaster or penalty. In what theologians have described as the conviction of sin, this plays an enormous and hitherto unappreciated rôle. Consciousness of a vice so hated and despised is a potent factor in youthful melancholia, taking away the joy of life, and sometimes plunging the victim into discouragement culminating in a sense of utter despair. It is one of the causes of most of the morbid types of self-consciousness or introspection. The struggle between what is felt to be right, pure, honorable, and the lusts of the flesh is always hard for sanity, so that the physical lassitude and the sense of inadequacy to meet the ordinary burdens of life are not infrequently overwhelming. Now there is resolution and confidence as nature repairs lesions and buttresses budding manhood and womanhood against undermining influences from her beneficent and inexhaustible storehouse of growth-energy, but a lapse plunges into the depths again, so that the cyclic psychoses of undue elevation and exaltation, succeeded by depression, are established. Struggles for absolute purity and perfection germane to this age are met by the influences that seem to spring from the prince of darkness and his abode. This dualism, which strains the unity of personality and makes hell-fires a subjective reality, divides the soul against itself and diverts energy otherwise available for study, exercise, and normal growth, and leads to many a battle with Apollyon absolutely unsuspected by all, so that many effects thought by many medical writers to be the results of physical laws are really due to the wear and tear of psychic struggles. Disciples of Dupenlin and Hartmann, like Mailouch, Kürnig, and others, make the highest human virtue to refrain from procreation, and not a few of them, in terms carefully guarded against the law, praise self-abuse, sexual perversity, abortion, etc., as midway between the supreme merit of perfect celibacy of body and soul and the *summum malum* of bringing children into the world. In every sane and moral mind the pessimistic cynicism of such views needs no refutation.

Prominent and preliminary in the study of effects is the problem whether self-abuse is more pernicious than excess in the natural way, and how the two differ. Here authorities are diametrically opposed. Some, especially those of a decade or two ago, have declared the effects to be the same, but now I find no competent authority who does not assert that abuse is far more injurious, and that in many ways; first, because it can be indulged in more readily, as the means are always at hand. This, of course, makes the dangers of excess far greater. Again, the stimulus is very different and more concentrated in time and place, and therefore tends to make the act more precipitate and convulsive. The evils of masturbation are due to the fact that, being unnatural, it requires greater excitement to produce the same effect; the action, moreover, is more specialized and limited; is less bound down to outer conditions, and can be more frequent; favors too early discharge and spermatorrhea and lacks the normality of gradual approach by the preliminary excitation of all the secondary sexual qualities of mind and body. All the irradiations of touch, sight, gradual approach, the long-circuit stimuli through the secondary sex qualities are lost, and the act is more brutal and descends far lower in the phylogenetic scale of animality. The normal act often produces an exaggerated self-feeling of maturity, of being especially favored, attractive, or perhaps irresistible, while abnormal acts impair self-respect and tend to a sense of shame and of being an outcast to the better self as well as to society. This, which I nowhere find mentioned in the medical writers, I deem central. Generally, either the form, presence, or more often some particular object connected with the other sex is imagined with the utmost intensity. What sight, hearing, touch, and other senses perform is now the result of the imagination, which is fevered and in the act made morbidly intense and acute, so that here I believe we have a glimpse of the cause, not only of the marvelous intensity of the lascivious fancy, but of certain of the morbid perversions which have never yet been explained. The imagination is subjected to a most excessive strain in order to produce the desired climax, and sometimes a ritual of forms becomes established and closely associated with the voluptuous sensations. This may be in the form of definite and specific pictures, so that some of the forms of erotic fetishism are begun, or it may take the form of almost ritualized acts, or again erotic zones may be developed. The psychic methods of arousing adequate stimuli always involve a realism of fancy of which youth is especially capable and prone at this age, and for this time and purpose place the imagination not only on the level of reality in vividness, but above it. This is especially seen in the sad and well-known cases of mental masturbation which are not infrequent. The reciprocal relations between this vice and certain of the perversions of the power of imagery in youth, showing how easily illusions and hallucinations may arise in this soil, where love and fancy normally celebrate their glorious nuptials, is one of the most inviting chapters I know in the whole range of the new psychology. Not only the relations of the mind and the body in general, but the connection of art and Eros, can here be approached with a rich casuistic, if largely morbid, material.

We know that, despite the enormous number of spermatozoa in the average individual, the loss of concentration of albumin, lecithin, peptones, etc., can be a great drain upon the system. Moreover, spermin is now thought to play a very important rôle in removing products of decomposition.

Spermin,[1] $C_5H_{14}N_2$, is found normally in considerable quantities in the testes, prostate, thymus, milt, ovaries, and the blood, and is thought to play an important rôle in the respiration of tissues. When dissolved, it advances interorganic oxidation, and is a ferment which helps to remove the products of the regressive metamorphoses of albuminous substances or leucomains (as, since Gautier, all nitrogenous intermediate products of such change are called which are not oxidized as far as urea). These are formed constantly in both normal and morbid states, and at least many of these are toxic, like ptomaines. The accumulation of these predisposes the system to infection and causes other diseases. Spermin, according to this view, removes these products by further oxidation, thus preventing disease. Its activity diminishes with the alkalescence of the blood. The administration of testicular and other extracts of spermin, orally or subcutaneously, has thus beneficent therapeutic effects, and the reduction of it by masturbation, excessive venery, or disease favors all the disorders due to the accumulation of the above products of decomposition. Nerve tissue is freshened and self-feeling increased, and, as the upholders of the spermin-therapeutics hold, without any aid from suggestion. No doubt individual differences in this, as in all other respects, are great, and there is every indication that every organ suffers from the excessive loss of this substance, which is perhaps the highest and most complex of all things in the physical world.

The old phrase, *post coitus triste*, is illustrated in excess of all forms, and especially in self-abuse. Weakness always brings more or less depression, and in some cases the physical exhaustion of muscles and nerves, if intensified by excess, brings pain and traces of convulsion, epilepsy, palpitation, and photophobia, differing according to individual predispositions and powers of resistance. Neurasthenia, cerebrasthenia, spinal neurasthenia, and psychic impotence generally result not more in the loss of fluid than from expenditure of physical force and often by tissues connected with the sympathetic

[1] A. Poehl: Einwirkung des Spermins auf den Staffumsatz. Zeits. f. klin. Med., 1894, p. 135 *et seq.*

system. Subjective light sensations, optical cramps, perhaps Basedow's disease, intensification of the patellar reflex, weak sluggishness of heart action and circulation seen in cold extremities, purple and dry skin, lassitude and flaccidity, clammy hands, anemic complexion, dry cough, and many digestive perversions can be often directly traced to this scourge of the human race. The onanistic psychosis seems especially to predispose to convulsive disorders like epilepsy, to which it is so akin, but weakness of memory and attention, paranoia, agitation, cachexia, various neuroses of the stomach which Preyer and Fournier have studied, dwarfing or hypertrophy of the organs themselves, and many of the lighter and transitory forms of psychic alienations, are produced.

One of the most direct moral effects is lying, secretiveness, and hypocrisy which conceals or denies a whole area of interests very real to the subject, and this is closely connected with cowardice, timidity, egoism, and frivolity. The power of pity and sympathy is often almost extinguished. Self-control and will-power, purposive self-direction, resolute ability to grapple with difficulties mental or physical, to carry work that is begun through to its completion, are certain to decline.

Sometimes from excessive prudery the opposite state of loss of modesty may follow excessive venery. The masturbator's heart, so often discussed, is weak like his voice. Dr. Seerley diagnoses a murmur which he thinks an almost infallible sign. Dr. G. Bachin describes the "masturbator's heart," based on six interesting cases.[1] The very rise of temperature during the act lapses to listlessness and frigidity, and clamminess afterward. Too great tension, which may predispose to convulsions and reach an almost epileptic degree, is followed by an exhaustion which makes all lesser excitations seem pale and uninteresting. One who has tasted these forbidden joys of youth has a languid appetite for the larger, if less fevered, pleasure of the intellect, of friendship, of high enthusiasms, and lapses to a *nil admirari* indifference which is one of the worst signs in youth.

---

[1] Deutsche Arch. f. klin. Med., 1895, p. 201 *et seq.*

These effects might perhaps be summed up as phenomena of arrest. Growth, especially in the moral and intellectual regions, is dwarfed and stunted. There are early physical signs of decrepitude and senescence. Gray hairs, and especially baldness, a stooping and enfeebled gait, the impulsive and narrow egoism which always goes with overindulgence, marks of early caducity which may crop out in retina, in cochlea, in the muscular or nervous system, in the stomach—all the troubles ascribed to this cause are distinctly senescent in their nature. Life has been lived out with abandon; its energies have been overdrawn, and its wheels have run down like the mainspring of a clock the regulator of which has been lost, so that the term " fast " has a profound biological significance.

While it can not, of course, be mathematically demonstrated, it is nevertheless probable that worse and earlier than any of these psychic effects are those that appear in the offspring. Beginning with the gradual descendance rather than ascendance of the long line of posterity in proportion as the evil has become more intense, its effects are manifest, nearer, perhaps, in the incomplete maturity of mind and body in the next generation; in persistent infantilism or overripeness of children. If more intense, it affects the number of posterity, the power to nurse offspring by the female, and finally ends in complete sterility, always the penalty of the excessive selfishness, the greatest and most unpardonable of all sins, where the individual uses up in his own life all the energy of which he is merely the pilot and guardian and which is meant to transmit life to countless generations. This enfeeblement, brain instability, and all the deciduous phenomena connected with this vice; the loss of higher interests; the easy fatigue; inertness of affection, make the marital and paternal office at best inadequate and all high enthusiasms impossible, even though it were, as Schopenhauer said, something which might be permissible in those too old to become parents. The whole problem is so difficult and at the same time so vital that we are all liable to the fallacy of the feeble mind which grasps a problem too large for it, viz., to have recourse to extreme superficial views and to lay undue emphasis upon special and partial causes, cures, or aspects of it. But although the best may be mistaken, let us not yield to the temptation of cowardice or psychic dishonesty, and ignore or deny its magnitude or importance. That here an immense problem looms up for all who study any department of the great science of man, whether his body or his mind, will now be generally recognized.

Another question much debated and of interest here is whether self-abuse itself can be the cause of a distinct type of insanity. The opinions of experts here have differed widely. Some believe its effects are seen only in forms of general deterioration and arrested development; others connect it in a more or less causal way with one or more of the morbid forms of sex perversion, or hold that it makes a psycho-physical soil which readily bears their dread fruit. Dr. Clark,[1] whose interesting demonstration that the act of self-abuse was attended by a rise of temperature of one or two degrees during the first half-hour, falling slowly later, and who thinks it rarely self-learned, doubts the existence of a true masturbatic insanity, although in those already insane some form of violence, blind fury, heightened automatisms, excited movements or efforts to escape often follow the act. Restlessness and constant mobility he holds to be in part a predisposition and sometimes an effect. Gowers thinks masturbation can properly be called a cause of epilepsy only if the arrest of the habit arrests the disease, but that the continuance of the disease after the arrest of the practise does not disprove causality, for, once established, the "conclusive habit" tends to continue. He inclines to think it more frequently causes untypical attacks than true epilepsy, and that self-abuse is a cause he does not doubt.

Spitzka[2] believes in masturbatic insanity, the onset of which he thinks marked by great variations of symptoms from day to day and week to week, now by destructiveness, now by lethargy, etc. At first the patient is listless in the morning and recuperates during the day; but in the late and hopeless stages the patient is best in the morning and grows silly, irritable, and lapses into progressive stupor toward night.

[1] Journal of Mental Science, 1888, p. 388.

[2] Journal of Mental Science, 1888, pp. 52 and 216.

Insanity due to masturbation he thinks five times as common among males as females, because for the latter Nature sets no limits. In persons of sound constitutions and heredity, it must be begun early and carried far to produce actual vesania, and he agrees with Clouston that quack advertisements produce nearly as much insanity by their appeals to fear and remorse as self-abuse itself. The symptoms are cerebral anemia, atonic muscles and expression, clammy hands, alternating spells of gluttony and anorexia, cowardice, suspecting the purity of all others, avoidance of rough, manly sports, neglect of toilet and dress, spells of sulks, pets and peevishness, *tædium vitæ*, outrageous selfishness, cunning self-accusation, cruelty, maliciousness, imperative ideas, morbid fear, strange somatic sensations, etc. Katatonia and cataleptic stupor may be episodes in insanity of this type. It differs from hebephrenia as original paranoia does from progressive dementia. The former is the ruin of an incomplete mental edifice, the latter is an edifice improperly founded and unsymmetrically completed. Spitzka considers sexual excess less dangerous, because self-abuse is begun earlier, can be carried to greater lengths, and is not limited, like the former, by the erector mechanism. The latter is usually attended by more or less of the noble emotion of love, masculine supremacy is asserted, and it is often felt to be an object of manly ambition while secret vice is only shameful, so that the moral effects of the two are almost antithetical.

Maudsley[1] thinks masturbatic can not always be distinguished from pubescent insanity, and that active alienation rarely results from self-abuse if the heredity is good. The vice he thinks most common and most severe in weak boys who have been most carefully protected, and been least among vigorous boys who have an abundance of other indulgences. The best help lies not in moral and religious appeals, but in stigmatizing it as dirty, sure to show in the face, etc., because vanity and a manly tone are often stronger than conscience. He regards the morbid mental symptoms from this cause as less serious if the habit breaks out early in pubescence before the sexual function has transformed the modes of thought and feeling, than if

[1] Pathology of Mind, p. 399 *et seq.*

it occurs later when sex has advanced further in its transformation of character. In a boy of seventeen or eighteen work is neglected, done in a slouchy and fitful way; he is moody, lazy, devoid of interest even in amusements, sullen, morose, self-sufficient, solitary, slovenly, or fastidious and exacting, hypochondriacal, and disposed to treat his imaginary ailments with special forms of exercise and diet. If it comes on later, society and especially ladies are shunned; there are fancied love sentiments and dramas with those very slightly known; physicians are consulted about imaginary symptoms or some sex problem. If the victim becomes engaged, he is even fuller of scruples about his fitness to marry, fears incompatibility or infidelity, like the heroes of Ibsen's Love's Comedy, that marriage degrades love, and so passes to new engagements. Sometimes his morality is superfine and scornful of the base ways of the world, while he is in thought and fact nasty and sensual. As a husband such an one is apt to be irascible, tyrannous, exacting, suspicious, and sometimes assaults and even murders result. As he does not really respect himself, he thinks he has lost the respect of others. The habit of self-abuse is less frequent and less hurtful in women.

Sturgis [1] believes that masturbation in some cases is the direct product of an hereditary tendency toward nervous and mental disorders, and that such a neurotic condition not only predisposes to this habit, but renders such subjects particularly prone to the evil effects which result from it. These, for the ordinary healthy young adult, he believes, as a rule, are very slight, although he estimates the percentage to be not less than eighty. Thus a great deal of the evil ascribed to this habit he holds exaggerated and overdrawn. The fright caused by belief in a derangement in this part of his nature is so common and great that he declares "that a large proportion of patients who consult the surgeon for treatment are really more hypochondriacs than sexual cripples; they dwell constantly upon the condition of these organs." Very little imagined change or peculiarity "produces a condition of nervous irritation which prevents them from thinking of anything else, and precludes them from pursuing their daily occupations with the ordinary

---

[1] Sexual Debility in Man, New York, 1900, p. 98 *et seq.*

zest and vigor with which they have been accustomed to perform their duties." Even where there is a slight real cause it would often play but a small rôle but for the mental disturbance thus produced.

Aristotle held that the testes maintained a tension of nerves and veins as a weaver's weight keeps his warp tight. Marro quotes a case of psychic impotence and melancholy due to lack of development of one testicle that was completely cured by an operation which inserted a silver one which the patient supposed normal. Two views are now prevalent to explain the close relation between these organs and the general vigor of the nervous system. One is that it is biologico-chemical and mediated by glandular secretions. This was held by Brown-Séquard and led to his spermal injections, and is strongly advocated by Poehl. Many men, especially in various stages of senescence, have reported great benefits from this treatment in increased energy for mental and physical work and in general buoyancy of spirits, but the opinion is now gaining ground that this is psychic and to a great extent due to suggestions. The other view is that it is dynamic and mediated by means of the nervous system and to some extent by consciousness. In the present state of our knowledge it is impossible to decide between these views; there may be truth in both. Certain it is, however, that the spermatozoa are very different from other testicular secretions, and that the two are, to quite an extent, independent variables. In his History of Medicine, Sprengel describes periods when the view, still met with among the ignorant, was felt in medical theory and practise that this fluid, like phlegm, might be noxious if allowed to accumulate. I have seen letters to quacks in which it was regarded as an excretion, and, like those of the bladder and intestines, something to be got rid of. I have conversed with at least four college students and graduates who held this view in both theory and practise and defended it. It hardly need be said that everything relevant that we know in biology and physiology indicates that nothing could be more false and pernicious.

While nothing is known of any special nerves mediating afferent sexual impressions, the reflex theory has long assumed special centers for sex activities. Gall thought the cerebellum the chief central organ of this function. Budge thought it in the lumbar cord, which was assumed to mediate erection and ejaculation. Luys urged the claim of the pons; Tarchanoff of the corpora quadrigemina, basing his conclusions upon experiments on the frog; Albertoni of the thalami from studies of the turtle, which did suggest their importance for the act of embracing. Magnan assumed a hierarchy of four centers, viz., the spinal, mediating immediate reflexes, as in the onanism of complete idiocy and perhaps identical with the centers of Budge; the posterior spinal cerebral, limited by the medulla and mediating visual images and instinctive and brutal orgasms evoked by sight; third, the anterior cerebro-spinal, mediating psychic influences, and finally the anterior part of the cerebral centers representing the state of ecstatics and entomaniacs. Loss of balance and harmony between these four accounts for all alterations and perversions. The center has also been placed in the olfactory region, and Roux thinks it is the Rolandic near the ending of the nerves of general sensibility.

Rowe[1] holds that the *primum movens* of sexual phenomena is not central but peripheral. He agrees with K. Ebing, Beaunis, Tarchanoff, and Delbeuf, that the genesic glands, and more specifically the seminal elements themselves, are the points of departure for sensations absolutely new at puberty which profoundly modify intelligence, habit, and character. The heart, lungs, legs, and even the fore brain and testicles of frogs can be removed without arresting copulation when it has been begun, while section of the seminal vesicles stops it at once. Dilating them with a neutral fluid starts up afferent nervous processes which create artificial desire. This latter thus rests on the impulse of organs to function. The well-established cases of precocious maternity before menstruation, and the frequency of sexual precocity in idiots, which Sollier has noted, show that the desire may, in exceptional cases, antedate the complete development of the organs, and is not therefore entirely dependent upon them.

Wherever the higher center is, it is the seat of the purely affective state which precedes any intellectual representation, which makes the profound metamorphoses of puberty, that may cause an indefinable malaise, to sometimes reach the in-

[1] J. Rowe: Psych. de l'Instinct Sexuel, Paris, 1899, p. 96.

tensity of an obsession. With enamored adults there is often, besides the desire of pleasure, the very different desire to find quietude and surcease of excitation. Representative sex life is a complex of many kinds of sensations and images differing vastly according to habit and association. Sexual need is most closely associated with sensation of the organs. In the sexual psychopathy, which is due to precocious need before organs are developed, this association is not effected. Later and with experience the need awakens the images, and following Roux's terminology, there is a sexual hunger, or conversely the images awaken the need and there is sexual appetite, and the primacy is now of one and now of the other. In the next stage the opposite sex is closely felt, but without personal preference, representing perhaps Magnan's spinal and posterior cerebral stage. Every comely girl and every boy are attractive to each other, but there should be no falling in love. Coquetting on one side and showing off on the other impel each sex to a higher ideal and make each a stimulus to the other. Next in the spinal and anterior cerebral stage sexual selection occurs, and here the imagination transcends and perhaps transforms reality; and finally in the anterior cerebral stage the ideal and the real meet in the realization of the needs of marriage and companionship.

Moll[1] assumes as the basis of sexual life two instincts, one which he calls contrectation or the tendency to touch, and the other the instinct of detumescence, or that to change—especially to discharge—the sexual organs, and from this he develops a theory which has much explanatory power for many abnormal phenomena. He agrees with Carus, and cites the philological indications gathered by Kleinpaul[2] to the same effect, that sexual life begins on a somatic basis with these two instincts, that there is a stage of relative undifferentiation in early puberty, and that it is at this point that heterosexuality makes itself manifest. At this time love, in the higher romantic and idealizing sense of the word, can also develop. With men this instinct, for physical reasons, is more in the foreground of consciousness, while women often give themselves to those

---

[1] See both his Libido Sexualis, Berlin, 1898, and Konträre Sexualempfindung, Berlin, 1899.

[2] Die Rätsel der Sprache.

they love with relative unconsciousness of the physical side, which is merged in higher psychic qualities. Havelock Ellis [1] lays great stress on the fact that these organs are by nature and in a primitive state, like the blossoms of flowers, thought most beautiful and an object of intense and concentrated interest and attention. Dress and modesty have tended to divert this interest into many unusual directions, and he suggests may have tended to homosexuality.

Whatever the analyses and localizations of the factors of this instinct, if not before, certainly and at the latest at early puberty, when the changes normal to that period supervene with attendant new sensations, these parts for a time, and especially in boys, play a great and hitherto not adequately recognized rôle in consciousness. Owing in part to the great variability of form, size, or function, or all together, very many boys suffer from the fear that they are abnormal in form and not infrequently life is for years overcast by apprehensions. Incidental comparisons with others made, for instance, in bathing, are very apt to suggest, as variability is so great, individual abnormality. Cases are given where several boys recently developed, on seeing others, have thought themselves deformed, and suffered acutely with manifold forebodings for the future. These fears often deepen into phobias when connected with the new activities normal to this period, and every variation is ascribed by a hypersensitive consciousness to abnormality of function or sin. From cases which might fill a small volume, I select here as typical one only, viz., that of a doctor of philosophy, prominent in his profession and a father of several healthful children, who writes in substance: [2]

The one greatest fear of all my boyhood was connected with my sexual organs; the big boys would expose us little ones, and said mine were too small. I began to brood over this, age eight; felt disgraced, and haunted with forebodings; one day there seemed a very slight inflammation, age twelve; I thought I had done a nameless sin, and prayed God to let me get well, which I soon did, but a morbid association between it and a hen's neck long persisted; I read literature on lost manhood, self-abuse, etc.; fancied I had all the diseases, and had committed the unpardonable sin; the first spontaneous emission

[1] The Psychology of Sex, vol. i, p. 109.

[2] See my Study of Fears, Am. Jour. of Psy., January, 1897, vol. viii, p. 225.

nearly paralyzed me, but although I found myself still alive, felt that my days were numbered; I corresponded with a quack, and later began to study my urine with great alarm, and found plenty of marks of disease; there were reddish and whitish settlings, lack of color and overcolor, strong smell and no smell, it was too clear, too thick, too copious, too scanty, or, worst of all, had an iridescent scum; when fourteen I gradually settled to the fact that I was sexually abnormal, might possibly live seven years, till twenty-one, and then find what I had heard was a sure cure in marriage; I found encouragement from quack advertisements, which said the wretched beings sometimes held out for years; I lived on, and people said I was in robust health, but it was years before I realized that I was perfectly normal; Bible passages greatly aggravated my fears, such as one in Deut. xxiii, and others; as I look back, my entire youth from six to eighteen was made miserable from lack of knowledge that any one who knew anything of the nature of puberty might have given; this long sense of defect, dread of operations, shame and worry has left an indelible mark.

Dr. Seerley tells me he sees one hundred cases a year of young men who deem their case hopeless. One typical youth of good heredity and otherwise normal decided that he would not go to college, was ruined, and must soon inevitably become insane. Another bought a revolver and planned, after a farewell visit to his mother in a distant town, to shoot himself in despair. Another selected a spot at the river where he would drown himself, which he prepared to do, but almost by accident met a physician who persuaded him after two hours that he was all right, when he went to work with renewed courage, and now seems entering upon a promising career. Another young man selected a cord, which he carried in his pocket for a long time, trying to muster courage to hang himself, because he could only disgrace his friends and his parents, who had made so many sacrifices for him. Another gave up a promising career and shipped on a long voyage, hoping to find this a cure. Another turned on the gas at night, but was discovered and saved in time, etc.

Perhaps masturbation is the most perfect type of individual vice and sin. Where practised, not by the old or by defectives as mitigations of the dangers of procreation for those unfit for it, but by the young, it is perhaps the purest illustration of mere sense pleasure bought at the cost of the higher life. It is destructive of that perhaps most important thing in the world, the potency of good heredity; it is the acme of selfishness;

it is the violation of the restraint perhaps most of all imperative, and yet all we know points to the conclusion that it is far more common among civilized than among savage races, owing in part to the postponement of marriage. The ideals of chastity are perhaps the very highest that can be held up to youth during this ever lengthening probationary period. This is the hard price that man must pay for full maturity. Idleness and the protected life of students increase temptation, so does overfeeding, which also increases sterility, so that enjoyment and the power of effective parenthood which God and nature united part company and at a certain variable period become inversely as each other. Although the facts in this chapter may lessen respect for our race and make us less hopeful of its future, the saving fact remains that the outburst of adolescent growth still precedes that of sexual maturity. If this interval were to lessen instead of to increase, so that the race tended, as do abnormal individuals in it, toward a development of the sexual function so premature and intense as to interfere with or obviate the increased rate of growth now normal, this would mean sure ethnic devolution.

V. Whatever the facts concerning the extent of this vice, spontaneous emissions are probably as universal for unmarried youth as menstruation for women. Ignorance of this fact, even by the virtuous and normal, causes an amount of mental anguish in young men perhaps as great as the physical suffering caused by lack of proper instruction to young women beginning their periods. This is not recognized, and even the realization of it is often an immediate and unspeakable relief to those who would be pure. Maturity often first announces itself by nightly experiences that rouse the soul to a state of great alarm, that settles to a brooding anxiety. First let us look at the facts as seen in those who are more mature in their sexual life. I have in my possession three records kept by three unmarried men not far from thirty of their nightly spontaneous discharges, one, the best on record, by a virtuous, active, able man whom I know well, lacking but six months of eight continuous years, and all of them doctors of philosophy, who believed themselves to be normal. The best of these records averages about three and a half such experiences per month, the most frequent being 5.14 for July, and the least frequent 2.28 for September for all the years taken together. There appears also a slight rise in April and another in November, with a fall in December. Frequency varies considerably in individuals. Here, too, we find a distinct psychic male cycle, but not a tendency to monthly groups, as in Nelson's case. On the upward curve there is growing vigor and euphoria and a progressive sense of the intensity of life, and after the climax a brief period of reduced energy. The variations of interval for the month are not great, and for the year in this best eight-year case the minimum number is thirty-seven and the maximum fifty. There is a spring and summer rise corresponding to the seasonal welling up of life. The variations in the amount or intensity of the climax seem to be quite as great as those in time. Fifty-nine per cent of all were of an interval of a week or less; forty per cent an interval of from one to four days; thirty-four per cent an interval of from eight to seventeen days, the longest being forty-two days. Poor condition, overwork and undersleep tend to infrequency. Early morning is the most common time. Special precautions tend to delay, but their influence seems temporary. In low conditions or with unusual frequency the crisis is followed by depression, although normally there is a sense of distinct relief. Thus in males there seems to be a normal curve.

Very interesting in these data is the suggestion of a rather sharp line between excess and defect, of which it would almost seem that there is a subtle and rather acute physiological sense or instinct, as if the body or the soul, or both, were endowed by nature with a guiding principle which can be developed as a regulative, but which is easily obscured. This orienting instinct, implanted it may be as a special conscience, appears to respond as exquisitely as a sensitive flame, and despite abnormal habits suggests an original anchorage that is still operative.

Of special significance are the records of dreams and psychic states connected with the orgasms. Sometimes the latter are so entirely lost that waking consciousness finds no trace of them, and they can only be verified by physical results. In other cases there is a full drama of mentation and feeling which can be recalled and written down with much detail. In by far the most cases, however, consciousness, even when the act causes full awakening from sleep, finds only scattered images, single words, gestures and acts, many of which would perhaps normally constitute no provocation. Many times the mental activity seems to be remote and incidental, and the mind retains in the morning nothing except perhaps a peculiar dress pattern, the shape of a finger nail, the back of a neck, the toss of a head, the movement of a foot, or the dressing of the hair. In such cases these images stand out for a time with the distinctness of a cameo and suggest that the origin of erotic fetishisms is largely to be found in sexual dreams. Very rarely is there any imagery of the organs themselves, but the tendency to irradiation is so strong as to reenforce the suggestion of so many other phenomena in this field that nature designs this experience to be long circuited and that it may give a peculiar ictus to almost any experience. Where waking occurs just afterward it seems at least possible that there may be much imagery that existed, but failed to be recalled to memory, possibly because the flow of psychic impressions was over very familiar fields, and this, therefore, was forgotten, while any eruption into new or unwonted channels stood out with distinctness. All these psychic phenomena, although very characteristic of man in his prime, are not so of the dreams of dawning puberty, which are far more vivid.

We have another very interesting suggestion of the tendency to irradiation in the fact that the inhibition nisus has become so frequent and strong before the end of the twenties. Before the mind is fully roused from slumber there is very often a blind impulsion to arrest the process or check it in almost any stage. Only in rare cases is this successful, so that sometimes the first waking experience is a sense of loss, waste, or regret. In still other although few cases, consciousness on awaking finds nothing but a vague, diffused glow of pleasure that mounts perhaps almost to ecstasy, a sense that life is immeasurably richer in enjoyment, that there are higher possibilities than it has ever entered into the soul before to conceive, that life has hitherto been on a low, dull plain, and that everything, or in other cases some one particular thing, has a charm or beauty about it hitherto unsuspected, as if the cerebrospinal system, on awakening, found itself impelled by the sympathetic system to a fulness and completeness of function which it had lost.

Of course more records and fuller ones are needed before anything better than tentative results can be gained, but the value of such data consists in part in the fact that they suggest the problem of how the reproductive function which maintains the race is originally related to the intellectual function which represents the experiences of the individual. In this field, which, so far as I know, is glimpsed here almost for the first time, it would be perilous to construct theories until more facts are forthcoming.

In his present state there is no doubt that man, in his best years, has normal spontaneous emissions far more frequently than is needful for the purposes of procreation, just as spermatozoa, as we have seen, are formed in vast and almost incalculable numbers. Probably in man, during his northward migration, the seasonal intensifications of this function were originally far greater than at present. Protection from wind and weather, the regulation of temperature, comfort, etc., like domesticity in the animal world, tend to obliterate seasonal rhythms, and it would appear also to substitute for these those of the sun's rotation, or especially of the moon and tides. If there have been tendencies to weekly rhythms, it is hard to bring them into relation with the long habit of rest one day in seven, where perhaps they belong in average male maturity. Moreover, if man was originally tropical, it would appear that seasonal differences would have been less and not over compensated by increasing adjustments by means of clothing, shelter, etc., as he penetrated northward; so that it is not impossible that the seasonal habit, which, as is well known, is found among races dwelling in the arctic regions, is itself derived from shorter periodicities instead of *vice versa*. The significance of this rhythm, the range or interval between its two extremes of tension and release, is no doubt of great individual and perhaps racial importance; while everything indicates that in general the longer the rhythm the better, and points to the one conclusion, that restraint is indispensable, and that during a period of more and more years in youth, if they are to mature well as civilization advances; and also that restraint is vastly easier with a normal nature than is often said by those who are neurotic or have tasted too much forbidden fruit. Periodicity is probably as much stamped upon sleep and dream life as upon that of sex. The facts show also even in this field, where all problems of the relations of body and soul and the primacy of either or the concomitancy of both are far more accessible than in that of the muscles and will, how purely and abstractly speculative and impossible of solution, as immortality itself, are such theories as that of Lange and James. The best diatheses are those that gravitate toward the tense state, that develop all the vicarious functions of diversion, work of body and mind, exposure, perhaps excessive fatigue, and that find out ways of utilizing sexual tension on many long circuits. Work and occupations of interest that absorb need to be developed during the critical years probationary to procreation, with reference to normality there. When we know how to keep tense and use tension in this field we shall have solved some of the fundamental problems of education in all its largest aspects. Some have thought they found utility in a regimen of imagery more or less lewd, as a back fire or mental inoculation against too frequent orgasms, while others, let us hope more normal and more truly, have thought they found it in impulses to conceptions which suffuse the soul with a higher eroticism of the good, the beautiful, and the true.

Now, self-abuse greatly complicates this experience, and makes this function vastly more labile, as indeed do lascivious thoughts, imagery, and especially anxiety. If secret vice is practised before, the later teens often bring revulsion. Wisdom from within and without has by this time developed a sense of self-condemnation or fear, and reform is attempted and often achieved, but increased tension and the stress of the past habit augment spontaneous pollution in sleep. This causes fear, sometimes amounting to terror, lest control be lost and life now given over into the hands of blind and lethal powers against which conscious will and resolution are of no avail. Masturbation is felt to be controllable and the victim feels that he can stop at any time, but spontaneous emissions give a sense of being powerless in the hands of fate. Free will is lost and the youth feels helplessly possessed by his automatism. This frequently brings a dumb despair that saps all the joy of life, may make it intolerable and lead to suicide. It is a little as if girls were led to feel when their periods come that they were in consequence of their own misdoings. The innate modesty of the young soul makes it all so sacredly secret that he can not muster courage to reveal his condition and appeal for help. Those to whom he should turn, who could inform and help by veiled hints and remote suggestions (for his apperception organs in this field give him prodigious understanding), are just those he feels it hardest to approach. Highly sensitized in every fiber, he fears censure or rebuke, and the very thought of that from those nearest and dearest he can not bear. The humiliation would be too great. Sometimes he tries to lead up to the topic indirectly, or tells his own troubles in the third person, or elaborately makes openings for conversation or instruction upon the subject, only to find that his elders feel positive reluctance to talk of it, or he asks directly only to find an ignorance equal to his own. Self-abuse is often common knowledge among mates, but not this involuntary experience. Thus he is twice helpless: he can do nothing to save himself, and he has learned that there is no help for him in his natural environment. There is no state or condition in life that the common phraseology of personal and hereditary sin and depravity fits so well as this. The young man is fighting the hottest battle of his life with the devil solitary and alone. Often his ill-judged and ignorant precautions themselves, and always and especially his concern, directly aggravate his troubles. Literature that treats of any aspect of sex, and often the worst sources of information only are accessible, is devoured with an avidity felt in no other subject. There is a great hunger to know the laws of life and reproduction. Every instinct impels to find again the right way. There is a self-loathing and loss of respect in the morning, and apprehension at night, that put a heavy strain on the nervous system, and that associate the exercise of this function, which should be the focus of all pleasant states of consciousness, with exquisitely painful emotions. These latter may rise to such strength as to even blight not only the prospects but the fruition of wedlock, and plant misery in the center of the garden of joy, bringing impotence, temporary and perhaps permanent, to natures that would otherwise be healthful.

It is in this state of mind that youth most needs father, pastor, mentor, or mature friend. He shrinks from the doctor, for that means fuller revelation, examination or full detection, but he seeks one who understands his trouble from afar, knows his symptoms in advance, has met many such cases, and will give him not general hygienic, religious or moral advice, but specific and especially material help. Doses and even appliances appeal to just his age, and so youth falls into the cunning web spread so alluringly for his unwary feet across the ways he most frequents. Lancaster[1] found a single New York broker who had 3,000,000 confidential letters written to advertising medical companies and doctors mostly by youth with their heart's blood and under assurances of secrecy, which are sold at fixed syndicate prices. I have bought 1,000 of them, and estimate that I could purchase at least 7,000,000 if I wished to go into this business, by addressing correspondence patients who had left other practitioners in this field discouraged but who were ready to try one more. That some try a fifth is shown by the fact that the stated price per thousand letters, guaranteed to have been sold but four times, is $5. In these announcements the young man finds his every symptom and experience, and many more enumerated and described.

When the soul has entered upon this gloomy pathway to Avernus, everything seems to help it onward and downward. The fact that these organs are so much in his consciousness greatly stimulates their activity on the principle that *ubi stimulus ibi affluxus*. In every part attended to, blood gathers, as all plethysmograph experiments show, and to these parts most of all. A mass of symptoms, half real and half imagined, accumulates and slowly becomes organized into a body of delusions. Ignorant of the wide range of normal variations in the male, boys observe themselves, sometimes very consciously and methodically, even with mirrors, worry over every peculiarity of size, direction, shape, unequal pendency of testes, laxity of the scrotum, position of the prepuce, crook or twist, bilateral asymmetry, shade and color, change of vascularity, and become anxious urinoscopists, and the first

[1] Psychology and Pedagogy of Adolescence. Ped. Sem., July, 1897, vol. v pp. 61–128.

spontaneous discharge produces psychic perturbations that are entirely unnatural and often wild. Cases of the slight varicocele, not uncommon, especially on the left side at this age, are often thought to be a product of vice and excessive functions, with which, in fact, it has no more to do than has the texture of the hair. Youth strongly desires to be sound and natural sexually. The changes normal at this age attract attention in all, and in those of unstable temperament and heredity the new consciousness centering in sex has many symptoms which are often brooded over very secretly and affect profoundly the whole tone of mind and body. His case is graver than he had fancied, but however serious, there is hope and, better yet, sure relief. He is told (and here I follow circulars of what are to-day the leading firms in this line) that if he is irritable, discouraged, fears his manhood is lost or imperiled, has bad dreams, or unreliable memory, pimples, blotches, is easily fatigued, is bashful in the presence of the other sex, has lascivious thoughts, fancies, etc., symptoms some of which are inseparable from this time of life, his intellectual fabric is in jeopardy. A white deposit is commonly found in the urine, which is partly a normal secretion of the kidneys and partly mucus discharged as constantly from the walls of the bladder as from the inner nasal or abdominal cavities. This, the quack labels a sign of premature decay. The coil of tubes of the epididymis is easily observable, and this is the seat of the inflammatory process of varicocele, and the subtlety with which these practitioners draw attention to what would often be unnoticed and describe it as morbid, is one of the many grave, moral indictments against them. Is one of the testes lower or larger than the other; are they pendant or tense, of different tint from that of the limbs; is the prepuce long, short, retracted, or covering the glans; is there a twist in the urinal stream; is the organ small, too flaccid, turgescent or oblique, curved or twisted; is there pruritus, moisture or dryness; are veins visible; is there peristaltic movement, a sense of heat or cold—all these are lurid danger signals, and there is no time to lose. Their victims are often told that emissions occur in the urine, and one so far juggles with anatomy as to say the vital fluid can be lost through the bowels. Every detail of form of each organ is described as abnormal, and every flush, twinge, pain, palpitation, freak of appetite, becomes a symptom of debility. No healthy man can read this "scare" literature without finding in himself a dozen ominous symptoms.

The victims thus enmeshed are sometimes sold placebos or harmless drugs, and if made well are really healed by faith or by alleviation of worry. Perhaps suggestion is never so potent as for those in this case. For many it may be true that as they believe so they are, and this leads me to think that the bread-pill theory and practise would often be benign here with the added psychic treatment suggested below. Bromides are sometimes given or general tonics sanctioned by the regular practise. Quacks well know the power of a name, and so call their nostrums by such suggestive names as sexine tablets, nerve seeds, Paris vital sparks, etc. Sometimes the drugs used are powerful erotics that aggravate and bring the hapless youth still more under the power of his blind and greedy guide. Most of the apparatus also is sold at exorbitant prices, that consume the savings of years and sometimes prompt to theft. Some are pencils, some catheters or tubes, the use of which may in rare medical cases do good, but the stated use of which is very exciting. Others sell wire springs, rubber, etc., to be wound about and prevent erethism or make it painful, which are always dangerous and frequently harmful; others offer so-called electric belts or suspensive apparatus. One "company" sells a glass cone and a rubber suction bulb, the vacuum thus produced causing an excitement, called by a physiologist far greater than that possible by any other known means, normal or abnormal.[1] A friend of the writer, an unusual specimen of physical purity and manhood and a physician, wrote recently in answer to an advertisement, that while he was otherwise thoroughly well, a hard worker, never had a doctor, and had an unusually healthy family, he had a marked feeling of inertia every morning when it was time to get up, and if he lifted a great weight with his maximal effort and in a stooping position, his eyes were sometimes momentarily blurred. The letter in response stated that the physician had called a special council for his case, which was a striking one of crypto-spermatorrhea, which perhaps might be not past cure if certain expensive medicines and apparatus were vigorously used within

[1] Here again I am indebted to Dr. Seerley.

thirty days. A visit later to this address revealed on a squalid house the name of a physician, on whose sign it was stated that his practise was by correspondence only and he could not be seen. A medical expert informs me that in some thousands of patients, not one thought they had received any benefit, but many confessed that their fear was so great that no price whatever would have deterred them.

It is painful to dwell upon such details, which could be easily multiplied indefinitely. Like many disagreeable themes, it is very rich for science, but the sole effort and desire here must be ethical, and to this end the extent and the reality of the evil must be understood. I will only briefly indicate a few cases believed to be typical. A young convert felt that he was losing his mind from nocturnal experiences, but found a motive to exceptional and incessant religious activity, so that in the short time left before he became an utter wreck he might do so much good and cling so close to God that it would be possible for him to be saved after his mind was gone. Another struggled for three years in the state above described before he could muster courage to write the doctor, had abandoned his purpose of entering the ministry because he felt unfit, finally staked the question of suicide on the results of the examination and conference that followed, and was found perfectly normal. Another, who had sought religion as a refuge and been converted, found that prayer and service for others could not help him, and so dropped out, gave up hope of ever having a home or family of his own, thought he had lost virility, and at last, after long brooding, visited a vile house to make the one experimental test of his life; nausea and high-keyed tension combined seemed to confirm his worst fears, but he was saved by a long, frank talk, and is now the proud and happy head of a promising young family. Another, who had not realized his ambition for studying in the high school, felt his intellect enfeebled from this cause, abandoned his plan of going to college, and enlisted as a common seaman in the navy, hoping to be cured by a life of hardship. His friends thought him a youth of singular ability and promise. A freshman, balked in his aspiration for purity, threw away his hopes of a career and resolved on a short life and a merry one, and, having means, became in fact the wreck he at first only fancied himself to be. One sought cure by early marriage, faltered and fled, almost at the church door, feeling his unworthiness. The honeymoon could not overcome the distaste for normal sexuality so often developed in some of these cases. A sound and vigorous talk by a medical sage at an opportune moment may vanquish these fixed obsessions of impotence and all be well.

VI. Passing now to sexual pedagogy and regimen, the world presents probably no such opportunity to religion, the moralist, teacher, the wise father, the doctor who is also a philosopher. There is no such state of utter plasticity, such hunger for vital knowledge, counsel, sound advice. Young men in other respects headstrong, obstinate, self-sufficient, and independent, are here guided by a hint, a veiled allusion, a chance word of wisdom. The wisest man I know in these matters and the most experienced, a physician and also a religious teacher, goes to audiences of young men at the end of the academic year, who have been unmoved by the best revivalists, who are losing power just in proportion as they neglect to know or prudishly ignore this field, and wins men by the score to both virtue and piety. I have sat at his feet and tried to learn the secret of his method. It is simple, direct, concise, and in substance this: In these overtense cases the mind must first of all be relieved of worry, and it must be explained that excessive anxiety and attention is the chief provocative of nocturnal orgasms. This is itself often a cure. Then the assurance that such experiences, varying greatly with different individuals in frequency, are normal, and that their entire absence would be ominous for sexual health, often comes as a gospel of joy to victims of ignorance, as does the knowledge that their case is common and not unique and exceptional. Personal examination by one who has seen thousands of cases and who can speak with an authority that commands confidence in most cases, reveals none of the grave or even mild ailments that had grown to such alarming proportions in the rank soil of youthful fancy. Diversion to objective interests or tasks that are active and absorbing, confirmation of wills that are not sufficiently established against occasional lapses by showing how fundamental sexual health and its irradiation are for domestic happiness, for a religious life and altruism, a few hygienic precepts concerning sleep, food, pure air, bathing, exercise and regularity, and perhaps a little carefully selected biological reading, and in many, if not most cases, a wondrous change is wrought. Some describe their experience as having a great burden rolled off, a strain or chain removed, they seem to walk on air, feel themselves men again, their strength renewed, look back with self-pity upon their former folly, etc.

Ethical culture alone is very inadequate, and preaching or evangelistic work that ignores this evil is unsuccessful. Religion best meets these needs because it deals, if true, with what most affects the life of the young and what is the tap-root of so much that is best in them. Youth takes to religion at this age as its natural element. True conversion is as normal as the blossoming of a flower. The superiority of Christianity is that its corner-stone is love, and that it meets the needs of this most critical period of life as nothing else does. It is a synonym of maturity in altruism, and a religion that neglects this corner-stone, that is not helpful in this crisis, that is not entered upon now inevitably, is wanting. He is a poor psychologist of religion and a worse Christian teacher who, whether from ignorance or prudery, ignores or denies all this, or leaves the young to get on as best they may. Sex is a great psychic power which should be utilized for religion, which would be an inconceivably different thing without it, and one of the chief functions of the latter in the world is to normalize the former. Error blights the very roots of piety in the heart, atrophies the home-making faculties, and kills enthusiasm and altruism. Their curves of ascent and decline rise and fall together both in age and in normality, and very many church communicants are not what they would be but for some psycho-physical handicap of this nature. But *ubi virus, ibi virtus*. God and nature are benign, and recuperative agencies, in these years so super-charged with vitality, in cases that seem desperate, often act *cito, certe et jucunde*. The very excess of the physiological fecundating power in man which caused man's fall is so abounding that it may work his cure. Grave psychic dyscrasias due to passional states generally seem to be completely outgrown, and even gonorrhea and its sometimes persistent sequel, gleet, can not usually long withstand nature's *vis reperatrix* if re-enforced by an hygienic habit of life.

That this department of sexual hygiene has been almost criminally neglected, none can doubt. Family physicians are almost never consulted by boys, and the great majority of doctors know almost nothing about the whole subject save the standard modes of treating a few specific diseases with overt symptoms; while clergymen, who should be spiritual and moral guides, know perhaps still less, and have often come to regard as superior ethical purity and refinement the sloth and cowardice that dreads to grapple with a repulsive and festering moral sore. While legislation is sadly needed for the protection of youth, instruction is no less imperative if the springs of heredity are to be kept pure. The blame rests mainly with the false and, I believe, morbid modesty so common in this country in all that pertains to sex. At Williams College, Harvard, Johns Hopkins, and Clark, I have made it a duty in my departmental teaching to speak very briefly but plainly to young men under my instruction, personally if I deemed it wise, and often, though here only in general terms, before student bodies, and I believe I have nowhere done more good, but it is a painful duty. It requires tact and some degree of hard and strenuous common sense rather than technical knowledge.

The medical cures of masturbation that have been prescribed are almost without number: bromide, ergot, lupin, blistering, clitoridectomy, section of certain nerves, small mechanical appliances, of which the Patent Office at Washington has quite a collection. Regimen rather than special treatment must, however, be chiefly relied on. Work reduces temptation and so does early rising, while excessive mental or physical effort easily fatigues before the power of resistance, caused by rapid growth, is acquired. Good music is a moral tonic. Lycurgus had the girls play before young men to stimulate them to their exercise; the Jesuits in Paraguay provided music to make the daily work of the Indians more tolerable and agreeable. Among the Romans it was forbidden to speak freely of things relating to sex in the presence of young men who still wore the *toga prætexta*, and Senator Manilus was condemned for kissing his wife in the presence of his daughter. Where the attention goes, innervation is roused and plethora may result.

The mystery of sex gives it a great attraction to youth. Kaan [1] thinks the study of sex organs and functions should begin in plants, and that thus the desire of learning is stimulated and sexual curiosity given an intellectual direction. Marro holds that young people should not be alone or build air castles, because the latter loosens the mental processes of association, while solitude and taciturnity are noxious, and when they appear adults should study their cause, for the latter often covers the slow incubation of morbid impulses. Goudin thinks early betrothal can be relied on to check the allurements of youthful roving loves.

Sexual activity is accompanied by increased internal heat and masturbators can bear surprising exposures to cold, but heat means precocity and exhaustion. Young Orientals who exercise marital functions at thirteen are worn out at thirty, and have recourse to aphrodisiacs. Yet cold is one of the best of all checks upon sexual excess, and in high latitudes venery is both later and less intense. The Spartan boys, when at twelve they exchanged the toga for the man's pallium, slept on straw or hay with no cover, and when fifteen slept on reeds. Marro has accomplished remarkable cures by cold hip baths applied many times a day, serving perhaps the purpose of Galen's lead plates. The strain is greatest upon youth vowed to monastic life, in whom sedentary habits and asceticism with insufficient exercise provoke error. Cold washing without wiping has special advantages.

Raciborski well calls this period a court of appeal or a day of judgment. Marro [2] advocates that the proper alimentation for this age is milk, bread, cereals, and vegetables rich in proteins and phosphorus, and little meat. Food must provide for the great consumption of hydrocarbonates, must give salt for the skeleton, albumin for the muscles, and fat for respiration; bread, milk, a little meat and fruits are good, while a diet of eggs, venison, aromas, coffee, and alcohol exaggerate dispositions now dangerous. He recommends a great deal of bathing and swimming, and even the vulgarized treatment of Kneipp, much of exercise, plenty of society, emulation, and rivalry. Marro also has a very strong belief in song to correct nervous

[1] Psychopathia Sexualis. [2] Med. Rev., July 22, 1894.

tensions and as a great autosuggestive power, and has striven to introduce it into reformatories for the young in Italy. He deems the acquisition of habits of work and the use of muscles, senses, and discipline, helpful; and would correct excessive presumption by due apprenticeship that brings a skill which develops self-confidence and satisfaction, but there must be struggle, effort, and perhaps conflict. Fear for girls at this stage is especially noxious, and, as Mosso has shown, diminishes sensibly the temperature.

There is also much to be said in favor of circumcision, at least for some. Since man assumed the upright position, and especially since he began to wear clothing, the part removed by this operation is less needed for protection, and has become a rudimentary organ with all the morbid tendencies these often exhibit. Arnold, an exceptionally experienced "Mohel," urges that the foreskin is a protection from frictional stimulation of the clothing, which may become a dangerous temptation if this natural covering be removed. The weight of opinion, however, is conversely that removal indurates the exposed surface, so that excitability is distinctly lessened. While uncleanliness is less common as intelligence and civilization increase, while the best medical thought now inclines to the view that its dangers have been much over-rated, and while the percentages of phimosis are less than have been assumed, what may perhaps be called, on the other hand, the psycho-neural arguments for circumcision, appear to the writer to have great force. The anal, urinal and general reflex disturbances relieved by the operation reduce liability to certain local diseases, while its undoubted restraining influence on self-abuse, its tendency to withhold from sexual excess, and generally to stabilize and give poise to and probably to prolong the *vita sexualis,* should still preserve for this rite a unique place among mutilations, unprejudiced by its possibly phallic origin or its historic association with barbarism. Moreover, other and more specific reasons in the physiological psychology of the topic, which can not be entered upon in a volume intended for general reading, incline me, although a Gentile of Gentiles, to favor circumcision, if individually prescribed and if safe-guarded by the anesthetics, antiseptics, and other resources of modern surgery.

Trousers should not be too highly drawn up by suspenders, as boys are so prone to do, but should be left loose and lax. They should be made ample, despite fashions often unhygienic. The irritation otherwise caused may be an almost constant stimulus. Undergarments for both sexes should be loose and well cut away, and posture, automatisms and acts that cause friction should be discouraged. Too great thickness of garments here is harmful in another way, for coolness is no less essential. Pockets should be placed well to the side and not too deep, and should not be kept too full, while habitually keeping the hands in the pockets should be discouraged. Modern garments are less favorable to health in this respect than those of classical antiquity, the Orient, or even to a great extent those of savage races. In some institutions certain, and in others all, boys must wear pants open only at the sides. The body in general, and especially the head, hands, and neck, should not be too warmly dressed in cold weather. Of course, the ungrown body has more surface in proportion to its bulk than that of a larger adult, but sufficient cold sends the blood inward to nourish the internal organs, stimulates greater activity and generates warmth. Rooms, too, should not be kept too warm. With plenty of good out-of-door air, high temperature is far less deleterious than in close rooms, where the atmosphere is not in motion and is loaded with carbon dioxide.

Beds should be rather hard and the covering should be light, because too much not only produces excessive heat, but presses upon the body and reduces the effectiveness of circulatory and respiratory processes. Too soft a bed develops a diathesis of sensuous luxury and tempts to remain too long after awakening, and just this hour is probably the most dangerous time of all. We may not agree with a recent Italian writer who says, boys that lie abed late are almost sure to be masturbators, but the habit of retiring and rising early is by far the best for eyes and nerves as well as for morals. One or more windows should always be open at night in the sleeping-rooms of adolescents, and the temperature kept as low as is compatible with health. Each should have at least a bed, if not a room to himself, but it should not be too remote and not too secluded from adult observation. Everything possible should be done to favor sleep as deep and sound in quality and usually as long in quantity as possible, and everything that seriously interferes with this end should be sedulously avoided, for in normal natures this conditions and is in direct proportion to the vigor of waking activities.

Some think, at least for girls, all that is needed can be taught by means of flowers and their fertilization, and that mature years will bring insight enough to apply it all to human life. Others would demonstrate on the cadaver so that in the presence of death knowledge may be given without passion. This I once saw in Paris, but can not commend for general use. An evil of such dimensions will be cured by no newly discovered method or specific, but only by courageous application for generations of the many means already known for strengthening the physical and moral nature. Some would merely give simple, direct, and honest answers to honest questions, being careful to go no further than to satisfy so much curiosity as had been aroused. Others would begin at eight or ten, before passion had awakened, and with no reserve tell everything by charts about the origin of life. Others would make it all mystic and symbolic, and some would leave all to nature or accidental sources of information. It seems clear and certain that in our modern life something should be taught, and that betimes. This should, I believe, be chiefly personal, and by fathers to sons and by mothers to daughters. It should be concise and plain, yet with all needed tact and delicacy in well-chosen words. It should be very brief, and not spun out like the well-meant and goody books on the subject that should be boiled down to about one-fiftieth their size and cost. This probably ought to be the most inspiring of all topics to teach, as to the truly pure in heart it is the most beautiful of all. In twilight, before the open fire, in the morning, in some hour of farewell, on a birthday, or any opportune confidential time, this most sacred topic could be rescued from evil or be given abiding good associations. The self-knowledge imparted that makes for health is perhaps almost the culminating function and duty of parenthood. It may be that in the future this kind of initiation will again become an art, and experts will tell us with more confidence how to do our duty to the manifold exigencies, types and stages of youth, and instead of feeling baffled and defeated, we shall see that this age and theme is the supreme opening for the highest pedagogy to do its best and most transforming work, as well as being the greatest of all opportunities for the teacher of religion.

A physician, who does not betray his identity, elaborates in a pamphlet an address he gave at the fifty-ninth session of the American Medical Association [1] which was heartily approved by eight well-known practitioners who discussed it. It was in the form of an address to adolescent boys. He says, if a boy friend boasts to you of his sexual experience with girls, "drop acquaintance with that boy at once; he is trying to corrupt your mind by lying to you." If a boy in an unguarded moment tries to entice you to masturbatic experiments, he insults you. "Strike him at once and beat him as long as you can stand," etc. Forgive him in your mind, but never speak to him again If he is the best fighter and beats you, take it as in a good cause. If a man scoundrel suggests indecent things, "slug him with a stick or a stone or anything else at hand." Give him a scar that all may see, and if you are arrested, tell the judge all and he will approve your act, even if it is not lawful. If a villain shows you a filthy book or picture, snatch it and give it to the first policeman you meet and help him to find the wretch. If a vile woman invites you, and perhaps tells a plausible story of her downfall, you can not strike her, but think of a glittering, poisonous snake. She is a degenerate and probably diseased, and even a touch may poison you and your children. He explains briefly the working of gonotoxin, when it begins and when it reaches heart, kidneys, joints, eyes, brain, etc., describes buboes and chancre, and explains the horrors of the latter, warns against all doctors who advertise, and tells of their methods.

The literature upon this topic falls into several classes. 1. Anthropological, treating of the sexual life of primitive people, like Ploss, and shading down to Jennings, Furlong, and writers on phallicism. That traces of the latter—if, as is often assumed, it was general—have been carefully scored away, makes the subject tempting to mystics who see its symbols in everything upright or circular. Despite the extravagances of this school, it must be admitted that their claims for the pervasiveness and wide and fantastic irradiations of sex symbolism have some support, or at least analogy, in the prurient fancy of a certain stage and class of youth to-day whose sensitiveness is so hypertrophied that they see indecent allusions in almost every form, act, and word. 2. The studies of abnormal phenomena, like those of Tarnowsky, Krafft-Ebing, Ellis, etc. Here, as always, morbid are often normal phenomena magnified, and from the literature of this class that should be unread save by the expert, I draw this momentous inference, that I have nowhere found stated, viz., *that there is almost no feature, article of dress, attitude, act, or even animal or perhaps object in nature, that may not have to some morbid soul specialised erogenic and erethic power.* If this be true even to any considerable extent, it shows that the eroticism may be cut loose from its natural excitants and be provoked by even remote accessories, and suggests the profoundly significant conclusion that esthetic pleasure in general is in considerable part of sexual origin,

---

[1] The Boys' Venereal Peril. Chicago, 1903, p. 35. See also Harvard: Monograph, The Venereal Peril; and Fournier's address to sons on attaining their eighteenth year.

and also that love is not only the strongest but also the most plastic of all the sentiments, and if not trained to the very highest possible objects may grovel to the lowest. 3. Studies of normal sexual psychology, like those of Finck, Scott, Gulick, Bell, and also Ellis. 4. The vast biological literature. 5. That of warning, like Storer, Howe, M. W. Allen, Sperry, Blackwell, Warren, Richmond, Stall, Wilcox, Wilder, and Morley. Most of these are too long; however, some, written by well-intentioned religious people, have had wide sale and brought their authors great gain, and perhaps on the whole they do good. Even these groups do not include works like Ch. Feré, Auvard, Marwedel, Duckelmann, Gamble, Dantec, Bauer, Rowe, and, perhaps best of all, Ch. Wagner's Youth.

CHAPTER VII

PERIODICITY

Periodicity in animals—Relation to seasons and length of life—Age of first menstruation and its relations to climate and social status—Precocity—Ideas and practises among savages—Psychic changes during the lunar month—Theories of the nature of menstruation—Wave theories—Irradiation in other parts—Changes in the blood, secretions, pulse, etc.—Psychic states in normal and morbid girls—Menstrual irregularities of excess and defect—Relation to crime and insanity—Cases—Relations to tide and moon—Corresponding rhythms in men—Present transitional stage of gynecology—Needs and regimen—Importance for psychology—Lessons for education.

PERIODS of rut or œstrus are frequent and regular in many of the higher animals:[1] monkey, mare, buffalo, zebra, hippopotamus, four weeks; sow, fifteen to eighteen days; sheep, two weeks; dog, nine to ten days. In the latter, according to Ketterer, mucous congestion, rupture, extravasation and degeneration of tissues, very like those processes in the human female, occur. In wild animals these periods are seasonal, usually occurring in the spring, and are in abeyance during the rest of the year. In extremely northern latitudes the return of long days and warm weather is marked by an outburst of venery, which becomes almost a rage, in which all the glands share, although during the cold arctic night this function is almost suspended. Traces of the old seasonal rhythm are still seen in women by tables showing a greater frequency of conceptions in May and June, and by the fact that statistics attest that the farther south we go the earlier the maximum of spring impregnations occur. Domestication with the increased regularity and abundance of food and protection has increased the frequency of these periods. Civilization has had a similar effect in rendering them more pronounced among women. Menstrual phenomena seem to be more and more marked as we pass up the scale. Lee says "it

[1] See the valuable presentation of this subject by F. S. Lee in the Am. Text-Book of Physiology, p. 898 *et seq.*, and *passim.*

is wholly probable that the menstrual periods of women are homologous of the frequent reproductive periods of the lower forms." Similarly, I think, we may interpret the vast number of ova and spermatozoa to be a survival in man of the enormous fecundity of lower species.

Heape[1] has studied with unusual care the menstruation and ovulation of a number of specimens, each of two species of monkey, the *Macacus rhesus* and the *Semopithecus entellus*. Their periods are marked by congestion of the skin of the abdomen, legs and tail, nipples, vulva, and face, together with regular flow of blood, detritus, etc. These animals have a definite breeding season, differing in different parts of India, but in the non-breeding season ovulation does not occur with menstruation, but is practically suspended. In seventeen cases there was no sign of a recent rupture of a follicle, although the other phenomena occurred. Heape thinks the human species once had a breeding season, and that traces of this remain in those periods of the female unfavorable to conception, and that at least ovulation is independent of the menses and may be suspended, the latter remaining regular as usual with no external sign that the most essential part of the function has ceased. It is remarkable that there was no trace of blood clot in the ruptured follicle of monkeys, although this is so distinct in the human female. In these species the periods occurred each month, and lasted about four days; and although breeding occasionally occurred at all seasons, spring had the marked preference, so that the time of gestation does not vary greatly from that of the human species. These valuable and detailed studies were chiefly histological, and shed no light on the phenomena attending the first onset of the period, but show that not only in the tolerable degree of regularity

Animal.	Age of adolescence.	Length of life.
Dormouse	3 months	4–5 years.
Guinea-pig	7 months	6–7 years.
Lop rabbit	8 months	8 years.
Cat	1 year	12 years.
Goat	1 year and 3 months	12 years.
Fox	1 year and 6 months	13–14 years.
English cattle	2 years	18 years.
Large dogs	2 years	15–20 years.
Horses	4 years and 6 months	30 years.
Hog	5 years	30 years.
Hippopotamus	5 years	30 years.
Lion	6 years	30–40 years.
Arab horse	8 years	40 years.
Camel	8 years	40 years.
Elephant	30 years	100 years.

[1] Proceedings of the Royal Society, vols. liv, lviii, lx, 1890, 1894, 1896, and Philos. Trans., vol. clxxxv.

found here, but also in the nature of the discharge and the dangers attending the removal to cold climates, and particularly in all the details of the internal processes, analogies to man vastly predominate over differences. So far as it marks the advent of possible parenthood, the table Chamberlain computes (The Child, 1900, p. 8) is suggestive. (See preceding page.)

In cows it occurs every three weeks; in the hippopotamus, the guenon, and many apes, it is monthly. A baboon averaged six weeks, but the intervals were more frequent in late autumn and winter than in summer. In the chimpanzee, Keith says it occurs every twenty-three to twenty-four days, but in most animals it frequently undergoes great seasonal variation.

The first onset of menstruation in the human female is very varied. Sometimes it is slight and so gradual as to be almost unobserved, and from the first period is regular. In other cases it is preceded by nervousness, febrile symptoms, and pain. The interval may be at first two or three months, and a year or two passes before regularity is established. Sometimes periodic pain and perhaps leucorrhœa precede the first flow, and the latter when it arrives is copious, and perhaps with cramps, hysteria, chlorosis, etc. These cases are not so rare as to be necessarily pathological.[1]

I. Age determinations show a wide range of both individual and racial variations. Basset found the average age of first menstruation in 4,815 cases in northern Europe sixteen years and three months; for 1,655 cases in southern and Oriental lands, twelve years and seven months; and for 10,254 cases in temperate lands, fifteen years. In 261 Italian girls, Marro found first period in 61 cases at the age of 14, 54 at 15, 40 at 16, 34 at 13, 29 at 16, 16 at 12, 12 at 18, etc. From many other observations of rather small numbers he thinks the above distribution of age about normal. Pagliani showed that in country girls the first menstruation is more likely to occur in the spring than at other seasons.

Other comprehensive studies [2] are as follows:

Meyer, Germany. 6,000 observations.		Kakuskine, Russia.		Meyer, Germany, 6,000 observations.		Kakuskine, Russia.	
Rich......	15.51	Rich.......	13.0	City.......	15.98	City........	14.9
Poor......	16.31	Poor	13.0	Country...	14.20	Country	15.3

[1] L. Meyer: Der Menst. Process, Stuttgart, 1890, p. 16 *et seq.*

[2] La Femme Criminelle, par Lombroso et Ferrero, Paris, 1896, p. 37 *et seq.*

In Hanover 2,129 observations showed for cities an average age of 16.76 and for the country 17.03. Tarnowski gives the average age of 5,000 cases in Russia as 16 years; Haeker in Munich found it 16 to 17; Boismont in Paris found it 14 to 15, or averaging 14.4. In Parma, Calderini (277 cases) found it most frequent at 15, next at 14, then 16 and 13. Pagliani found 280 cases at 14, 219 at 15, 205 at 13, 116 at 12, 89 at 16, 55 at 17, 14 at 18, 7 at 11, and 20 at 10. According to DuBois and Payot, in warm climates the age is from 11 to 14; in temperate climates from 13 to 16; and in cold climates from 15 to 18. In Italy half of those who menstruate at 13 are blondes, and only one-fifth brunettes.

At twelve American institutions reporting to the Massachusetts Labor Bureau and representing 1,290 girls, the average age of menstruation was 13.62. Krieger, in Berlin, reporting on 6,550 cases, places this period at the beginning of the fifteenth year. Kennedy, basing on 225 girls in the United States, places it at 13.7. A. F. Currier reports 14.5 years as the average age of 200 cases. Lancaster found 78 American girls averaging 13.6. Tuckerman, in New York city, found 81 cases averaging from 14 to 15. In Vienna, Scukits places it at 15 years 8½ months. Whitehead fixes upon 16 in England, Weber 14½. Tilt thinks it is a little over 13 in hot countries, over 14 in temperate, and over 15 in cold climates. Chadwick fixes the average age at 14½ in U. S. A., light-haired preceding dark-haired girls from one to two years.

One of the most instructive studies of the age of first menstruation is that of Lullies,[1] based on 3,000 Prussian girls. Although more cases occur at fifteen than any other year, or $\frac{17}{67}$ of all, the average age obtained by dividing the sum of the ages of all by the number of cases gives about sixteen. Nearly all such tables show that large girls menstruate earlier than those of small or average size. Lullies thinks, in opposition to most earlier observers, that the strong begin this function later than the weak. Nearly all agree that blondes precede brunettes. Thus, first of all, come large weak blondes, and last come the middle- or small-sized strong brunettes. Despite sev-

[1] Ueber die Zeit des Eintritts der Mens., nach Angabe von 3,000 Schwangerern, etc. Thesis, Königsburg, 1886.

eral tables to the contrary, Lullies thinks country girls are at least six months later than city girls. In eighty-three per cent of all the cases the periods were regularly established at once, and in seventeen they were irregular for a time. The average duration of the flow of those in whom it occurred regularly was 4.79 days. Seven and especially eight days are unusually frequent.

Lullies's Table for Prussia.

YEAR.		Per cent of all.
10	6, or 1 in 600, or	0.17
11	16, or 1 in 187, or	.53
12	81, or 1 in 37, or	2.70
13	279, or 1 in 11, or	9.30
14	476, or 1 in 6, or	15.87
15	529, or 1 in 5, or	17.63
16	458, or 1 in 7, or	15.27
17	470, or 1 in 7, or	14.00
18	275, or 1 in 11, or	9.17
19	242, or 1 in 12, or	8.07
20	122, or 1 in 25, or	4.07
21	55, or 1 in 54, or	1.83
22	19, or 1 in 158, or	.63
23	15, or 1 in 200, or	.05
24	4, or 1 in 750, or	.13
25	1, or 1 in 3,000, or	.03
26	1, or 1 in 3,000, or	.03
27	1, or 1 in 3,000, or	.03
28	1, or 1 in 3,000, or	.03

Dr. Joubert[1] thinks, with Playfair, that the influence of climate on menstruation has been exaggerated, and constructs a table to show that racial differences are slight if other conditions are similar. Precocity, he thinks, is due to too early knowledge and sexual excitement, and he lays great stress on the contrast between the ignorance in which European girls are raised and the utter want of domestic privacy in the East. Everything is seen and known in India by girls at eight or ten, and the sexual excitement to which child-brides are subjected is a potent factor. Weber lays stress upon race more than climate. Krieger thinks the mode of life has less influence than altitude above the sea. Mosca thinks that it is earlier in higher classes, latest in peasants, and intermediate among clergy, merchants, etc. Weber suggests that students, actresses, and teachers report earliest ages.

[1] The Supposed Influence of Tropical Climate on Menstruation: C. H. Joubert. Indian Med. Gazette, Calcutta, April, 1895, p. 129.

Raciborski[1] compiled with indefatigable industry the following table on the relation of the average temperature and of latitude to puberty:

PLACE.	Temperature C.°	Beginning of Menstruation.			Latitude.
So. Asia	25.6	12	10	27	18° 56′ — 22° 35′
Corfu	18.	14	0	0	39° 38′
Toulon	16.75	14	0	5	43° 7′ 28″
Montpellier	15.30	14	1	26	43° 36′
Florence	15.3	14	6	1	43° 47′
Marseilles	14.75	13	7	24	43° 17′ 52″
Nîmes	14.32	14	3	2	43° 50′
Madrid	14.02	15	0	13	40° 25′ (39–43)
Lyons	12.44	15	5	16	45° 45′ 45″
Sables d'Olonne	12.25	14	8	11	46° 29′ 48″
Rouen	11.57	14	9	3	49° 26′ 29″
London	11.04	14	9	19	51° 31′
Paris	10.50	14	11	9	48° 50′ 13″
Vienna	10.1	15	8	15	48° 13′
Strassburg	9.80	15	3	11	48° 30′
Göttingen	9.1	16	0	10	51° 32′
Manchester	8.7	15	2	14	58° 29′
Copenhagen	8.2	16	9	25	55° 41′
Warsaw	7.5	15	9	0	52° 13′
Berlin	7.03	16	1	5	52° 30′
Stockholm	5.6	15	8	0	59° 21′
Christiania	5.6	16	1	15	59° 54′
Kazan	2.2	15	3	20	55° 48′
Lapland	0	16	7	27	68°

In a late paper Engelmann reaches remarkable conclusions concerning the age of first menstruation on the Western continent. From Matthews's study of sub-arctic Indians, and from his and others' data for Eskimos (12.6) and Robertson's study of plantation negroes in Jamaica and Barbados (15.6), etc., he infers "an early puberty at the pole and retarded development near the equator, conditions diametrically opposed to what has hitherto been accepted."[2] He also finds American women "very much more precocious than the women of other continents in the same region of the temperate zone, more precocious than the peoples from whom they have sprung, an average of 14 on this continent and 15.5 in Europe." The native American is more precocious than the American born

[1] Traité de la Menstruation, 1868, p. 200.

[2] The Age of First Menstruation in the North American Continent. Trans. of the Am. Gyn. Soc., 1901.

of foreign parents, and only one year behind his average for southern climates. Climate here has practically no influence; race, very little. This is due chiefly to mentality and nerve stimulation, which also hastens the development of the red and black races. Here, too, he finds the difference between the development of girls of the refined and those of the laboring classes to average less than half a year, so that this change takes place here nearer the same age in all classes, and also there is found to be less individual difference. One of Engelmann's curves gives American girls at 14, Irish at 15, and German at 16. The influence of social state and race, which seems established at least in Europe, often appears on this continent to be overridden by that of nerve strain. The *milieu* stimulates "the psychic phenomena reverberating clearly in the genital plexus," suggesting that the influence of environment is greater in this respect than that of heredity. If this be so, a cold climate must be ranked with, and not against, mentality as a cause of acceleration, and it would seem to follow that education in a temperate or subarctic zone is more productive of precocity than in the south, and if general nervous stimulus is the cause, the same schooling is more dangerous in the city than in the country.

In rare cases this function may be very premature. Dr. Peeples[1] reports a case of a primipara where the child was beautiful, well grown, and in the best of health, with breasts and reproductive organs remarkably well developed, having a full and proficiently studied menstruation at the age of five days. Dr. I. W. Irons[2] reports a girl seven days old who menstruated from December to August, the period during which it was under observation, regularly. Dr. P. E. Plumb[3] deports a healthy girl who began to menstruate at the age of six weeks and continued to do so every six weeks for ten months, or up to the date of this report. Dr. Howe[4] describes a case where menstruation began at three, continued regularly for six periods, then stopped for eight months and

---

[1] Dr. D. L. Peeples: New York Med. Jour., March 30, 1885.
[2] N. Y. Med. Jour., August 15, 1896.
[3] N. Y. Med. Jour., July 5, 1897.
[4] Brit. Med. Jour., part i, vol. ii, 1896, p. 653.

resumed. The child was otherwise normal, but looked four or five years older, and had marked sexual development of a child still older. Dr. Price[1] describes a remarkable case of a girl of six years and seven months who was mature apparently in every respect. Some features of puberty were observed at eighteen months—pubic and axillary hair—and menstruation occurred early in the fourth year. In reporting a case of menstrual precocity at the age of four years and nine months, Dr. Seuvre[2] takes occasion to gather a few facts from literature and from his own observations to refute the general impression that precocity usually goes with early cessation of the powers of maternity. His own view is, that the earlier the sex function develops in girls the later it continues and the greater the probability of numerous progeny. Often at least such persons continue to bear children to an advanced age. Similar cases could easily be greatly multiplied.

Instead of being seen to be the inflorescence of the human plant, like its analogues, the blossoms and ripeness of the vegetable and rut in the animal world, both its first and its subsequent appearance have been regarded with great awe and generally with aversion. Among some primitive races[3] women wear a special costume, badge, or symbol at the first, and often at subsequent monthly periods. The forms and ceremonies that mark the advent of this sign of maturity are very diverse, and often initiations are severe and are intended to drive out the demon of uncleanness. Tattooing, isolation, many local operations, fasting, close confinement, nauseous food, etc., show that these phenomena have generally seemed to primitive hygiene not only mysterious, but that, analogous though it seems to heat in animals when the male is especially attracted, it has had a repellent effect upon man. The old idea was that this function was a periodic purification to rid the body and soul of a previous contamination of original sin. Woman's reserve, too, is increased rather than diminished at these periods, and many superstitions of infection and contagion augment this mutual withdrawal and perhaps taboo. Every-

[1] New Orleans Med. and Surg. Jour., August, 1896, p. 104.
[2] Union Med. de Nord. Est., January 30, 1897.
[3] Ploss: Das Weib, pp. 228–285.

thing known upon this subject seems to indicate that these repellent tendencies are very ancient as well as universal, so that it is impossible to determine how much is due to the accumulated effects of immemorial usage, and whether, e. g., the depression and perhaps even the psychic and physical pains may be inherited effects of the ages of ostracism and cruelty suffered at these times. What we are coming to know from recent studies of hysteria of its metamorphic nature, and the readiness with which psychalgia passes to somatalgia, and even *vice versa*, inclines the writer to the view that in the psycho-sensory changes of the lunar months modern women recapitulate atavistically the effect of ages of such error and misuse, and that few, if any, topics in the whole biopsychic field are as interesting, tantalizingly baffling though they are, for all who have fully adopted the genetic standpoint, as the phenomena and usages that center about the *menstrum virginis primum* and the subsequent catamenia with the attendant magic, superstitions, usages, surprises, and all that early writers comprised under the term parthenologia.

II. Precisely what menstruation is, is not yet very well known. It was not long ago held that in the human female it can not be the homologue of œstrus in animals, because women then have no desire, and men are repelled. Desire has been held to be relieved by the flow, which Wiltshire held was more sanguineous the higher the animal. Dr. Elizabeth Blackwell says the flow itself is a competent relief of sex feeling, and Icard thought that thus virginity was safeguarded. Havelock Ellis [1] boldly champions the view that normally the desire and flow coincide in time, and has gathered statements of women confirming this view. The facts on which the aversion theory rests, he thinks, are superposed by convention upon and belie nature. If ardor is not present, it may be due to languor produced by the process, conformity to custom, or to fear of arousing disgust in man, who superstitiously thinks it dangerous for him or for the offspring. Here again, if this view is correct,

[1] In his valuable chapter on Sexual Periodicity, in his Psychology of Sex, 1900, p. 53 *et seq.* See also Menstruation et Fécondation Physiologique et Patho logique. A. Auvard, Paris, 1895.

our race has rebelled against its own nature, and in this instance the medieval Church aided the revolt. Indeed, just as savages magnify, but civilized races hide and minimize, the organs as centers of attraction, as Moll says has occurred in secondary sex qualities like the beard, so it may be menstruation is now magnified in importance by the attention it receives, and in an age that considers it less it will lapse to a less regarded and therefore normal place. In very rare cases, apparently normal (Ellis, p. 54), it may all be absent.

Raciborski's careful and still valuable work [1] on puberty in girls, that was stimulated by a prize offered by the Royal Academy for the best memoir on the physiology of menstruation and its relation to diseases, and Bouchet's treatise [2] upon this subject, marked the first advance that had been made since Aristotle and Pliny. Considering the methods at his disposal, Raciborski's contributions to the subject were remarkable and almost epoch-making. He investigated the influence of climate, temperament, race, urged the very great impressionability of the sex organs to music, the development of the Graafian follicles, the action of different emmenagogues, and treated Malthusianism also with great sagacity, the improvement of public morality by early marriage, senescence, superfœtation, hygiene, etc. In 1852 Tilt found that of 1,000 girls twenty-five per cent were totally unprepared. Many were frightened, thought themselves wounded, washed in cold water, etc. Laborde [3] assumed that woman is what she is by virtue of the uterus, thought menstruation a peculiar erectile process, wondered that man did not share it, and sought to trace a *rapport* between the diseases of puberty and those most liable to occur at the menopause.

Bassat,[4] in his comprehensive thesis, to which a valuable and copious bibliography is appended, defines puberty in woman not as the period of the development of pubic hair, as the etymology of the word suggests, but as the age of the growth which accompanies the maturation and escape of the

[1] La Puberté chez la Femme, 1844, p. 520.

[2] Théorie de l'Ovulation Spontanée, 1847.

[3] Quelques Considérations sur la Puberté chez la Femme et sur la Menopause. Thèse, Paris, 1860.

[4] Étude sur la Puberté chez la Femme. Montpellier, 1867, p. 134.

ovule, and his motto is, "The whole woman is in the ovaries." The girl ceases the play of a child, seeks solitude and indulges in reverie and contemplation, is joyous and sad by turns. A new timidity and modesty appears; she seeks strong and more special friendships with her companions, or would forget all else in a more ardent love of her mother. These, however, do not satisfy her, and she is joyous and sad by turns. The other sex seems more beautiful and attractive, and yet perhaps there is a new shyness in the presence of young men. Increased sensibility, more blushing, vague desires, emptiness of heart, and sometimes a disposition to follow and perhaps brood on the changes which occur in body and soul with introspection, curiosity, and perhaps awe, are noted. There are often obscure symptoms of disease of mind and body, which threaten, but only in a minority of cases become overt, and nature usually is able to slowly establish a normal rhythm between plethora and anemia on which the hygienic and moral future depend. Each sense is more acute, the imagination more lively, reveries more frequent. In dress she blossoms into colors, a new moral hygiene is slowly added, more manifold exercises are needed, and increased rest in sleep, for there is great feebleness at this plastic age. This paper shows how far knowledge of this subject had progressed before what may be called the modern period.

But we are not here concerned with the history of the topic. Both physiologists and gynecologists differ widely both as to the causes and nature of menstruation. Some ascribe the chief or primal rôle to the ovaries, some to uterine processes, some to the nerves; and it is certain that the first two can and often do act independently of each other. Current views, which seem to the writer as no longer incapable of harmonization in our higher synthesis, may be summarized from their leading representatives as follows:

Most widely held now is probably the theory of Pflüger's, that the significance of menstruation is not to escape plethora, but to denude a fresh uterine surface to which the egg, if impregnated, can graft itself. The constant ovarian growth causes a reflex stimulation which tumefies the uterus and probably also matures a Graafian follicle. Both ovulation and the monthly flow, while very distinct phenomena, either of which may occur without the other, are yet both due to this congestion. By one process the nest is prepared, by the other the egg is laid in it. If the ovum is fertilized and attaches itself to the thickened uterine wall, then the menstrual decidua become the decidua of pregnancy, and are not detached till parturition, of which menstruation is the homologue and forerunner.[1] Pflüger thus holds that menstruation and ovulation have thus only a reflex connection, and that the former is a periodic wounding of the surface in order that the ovum may be more readily attached to it.[2] This view is not inconsistent with that which Virchow was the first to suggest, that every monthly illness is a pregnancy on a small scale. Aveling long ago pointed out the difference and similarities between a womb and a nest, and considered menstruation as infecund oviposition. Changes in the uterine mucus, he thought preparatory nidification. The decidua were nidal and nidation could come on independently of the ovaries. Occasionally the nest was ready too soon or in vain, and at other times was unfinished and too early. Hypernidation sometimes may be due to decline of nutrition, and may cause sterility. The nest may be expelled whole.[3] Jacobi thinks it the homologue of parturition and perhaps an ontogenetic relict of the frequent births of lower forms.

Lowenthal[4] thinks that the unfertilized ovum causes the menstrual decay of tissue which its impregnation prevents, and opposes the idea that the relation between these two events is merely temporal. On this view the periodicity of the hemorrhages depends on the duration of the extra follicular life power of the imbedded but unimpregnated egg. Menstrual hemorrhage, he thinks, is not physiological, but the natural effect of the non-impregnation and consequent death of the ovum, and must be regarded like other pathological bleedings and the flux be reduced to a minimum, so that amenorrhea is not always a disease and diapedism is the least morbid way. King[5] also thinks menstruation a pathological process, and that women live abnormally in sex. Nature requires them to bear children throughout their sexual life,

---

[1] See Am. Text-Book of Physiology, p. 399. Also, Lee: Reproduction, p. 898.

[2] Untersuchungen, 1865.

[3] Nidation in the Human Female. Obstet. Journal of Great Britain and Ireland, July, 1874, p. 209.

[4] Eine neue Deutung des Menst. Processes. Arch. f. Gynäcol., 1889, pp. 169–261.

[5] Am. Jour. of Obstet., 1875.

and thus to mostly escape menstruation. Stemham[1] says, on the contrary, that it is a physiological adaptation of a special kind to keep the uterus in functional health, and while it is pathological in bleeding and degeneration, it is otherwise essentially normal, and no more abnormal than the excessive production of ova. It seems to be an adjustment, so that there shall be times favorable and others unfavorable for conception.

Oliver[2] approached the subject in a somewhat unique and philosophical way by assuming that the molecular world is in a condition of highly sensitized vital trepidation, and that equilibrium is the outcome of inherent powers of adaptation. Both structural and functional integrity are maintained in the animal body by the dependence of organs upon each other, and every tissue and part is thus in a relation of vicarious compensation, and this is a fundamental law. All double organs compensate, growing and doing extra work if the other is incapacitated. Uterine changes are anticipated by spontaneous ones in the nerve-centers, perhaps in the oblongata, so that neural symptoms may grow and be quite developed without the common physical changes. The periodic death of the endometrium does not start in the mucous membrane, is not the analogue of the loss and reproduction of limbs, the shedding of its skin by the serpent, moulting, etc. There are frequently monthly disturbances of the psyche with menstruation, and epilepsy is the disease which most effects it. This nervous rhythm, as it were out toward the next generation, is due to some gradual but unknown vital energy which is primary. Ovulation he too saw to be a process quite distinct and apart.

Westphalen[3] believed that he had decided finally the question whether menstruation is a shedding of the outer mucous layer and the consecutive regeneration of its mucous. He concludes, first, that diffuse fine granular infiltration of fat is at all times a frequent finding in normal uterine mucous and is in no causal relation to bleeding; second, that the shed tissue undergoes fatty degeneration; third, at the end of the period there is an increased tendency to fatty metamorphosis of the protoplasm in the upper mucous membrane. This fatification is not death of the part, for it can be resorbed. As to whether in different phases of menstruation the conditions for the insertion of an egg are differently favorable, and what time is most so, is not yet solvable. From his studies upon extirpations and scrapings of fifty cases, he concludes that the cells, especially those of the epithelium, are renewed by indirect cell division periodically from six to eighteen days after the beginning of menstruation, and from the eighteenth day onward no proliferation occurs. The decidua are simply decadent

[1] Menst. und Ovulation in ihre gegenständliche Beziehungen. Gekrönte Preisschrift, Leipzig, 1890.

[2] Menstruation: Its Nerve Origin not a shedding of Mucous Membrane. Jour. of Anatomy and Physiology, 1886–67, p. 378.

[3] Zur Physiol. der Menstr. Arch. f. Gynäcol., 1896, p. 35.

growths, broken down and removed after they are dead by gravity, a process made easy and economical by man's upright position.

It seems that man's self-domestication has had upon his own species the same result of increased fecundity and more frequent reproductive periods that it has had upon domesticated plants and animals. Menstrual phenomena seem more pronounced in the higher forms of animal life, and it has even been suggested that we may infer that in woman they will increase as civilization advances.

Reinl[1] held menstruation a result of a periodical disturbance of the entire circulatory system, and describes a growing contraction of vessels alternating with hyperæmia, which is greatly accentuated by puberty. He believed in the existence of this rhythmic period in men, children, and old people as well as during pregnancy and lactation. Degeneration and removal of the ovaries does not affect the form of this wave, and menstruation is only one manifestation of it. The wave may take many forms and even be reversed in pathological cases.

Dr. O. W. Johnston[2] may be cited as the best representative of the neuro-ovulation theory. The ovaries are active before birth and continue to form follicles as long as the woman lives. She ripens probably four or five a year, but this has nothing to do with rut. The latter in animals occurs when they are at the very top of their condition and never when they have all they can do to live. As civilization has overcome climate, man may be said to be always at his best. Thus deer rut in the fall, birds in the spring, etc. All animals have desquamation times after the procreative periods, when hair, antlers, etc., are shed. Sex ornaments are akin to the manufacture and decay of the endometrium, as are feathers, papillæ, and other sex decorations, arising as they do from the same embryonic layer. Thus we have here only a special case of karyokinetic growth and of the regeneration of tissue by which all wear and tear is supplied. Remak's view, that

---

[1] Die Wellenbewegung der Lebensprocesses des Weibes. Samml. klin. Vorträge Gynäcol., No. 67 (whole No. 243).

[2] Relation of Menstruation to Other Reproductive Functions. Am. Jour. of Obstetrics, 1895, p. 33.

the sensory motor system comes from the epiblast; the muscles, bones, excretory, secretory, and generative organs from the mesoblast; while the hypoblast is largely nutritive, is said to favor this standpoint.

The first really careful curves of temperature were plotted by Dr. Stephenson,[1] while Dr. Jacobi established the first proof of a nutritive wave. The pulse tension curve culminating a few days before menstruation is generally accepted as another part of the well-marked curve of vital energy. Stephenson held that equal parts of the curve were below and above the line; that they varied with individuals; that the temperature wave was most uniform in its rise and fall, and that the waves were more or less independent of each other.

This wave may be further described as follows: From about seventeen days after the cessation of the flow, the pelvis is anemic and the curve is a low level plateau with few and slight modifications and but a very gradual ascent. On or near the eighteenth day the rise is distinct and increasingly rapid, reaching its greatest angle of ascent about the twenty-third day, and continuing to augment till hydrostatic pressure causes local hemorrhage, when the pressure falls rapidly and the process is repeated twenty-eight days later.[2] This view may perhaps harmonize with the older conception of the dominance of the uterine nerve plexi as a sort of pelvic brain, analogous to the solar plexus, often called the abdominal brain. This uterine center would thus be a sort of telephonic switchboard, and hysteria would be due to derangement of its connections. In addition to the above blood pressure curve, there is a closely coinciding urea wave and a carbonic acid wave, the ash and smoke respectively of the combustion of the products of a hyperanabolic activity. These are indexes of the increased oxidation just preceding the flux necessary to get rid of the albuminoid surplus in the blood, produced because every normal female constantly produces food for two. Menstruation is a vast improvement upon the way in which this surplus in the endometrium, de-

---

[1] On the Menstrual Wave. Am. Jour. of Obstetrics, 1882, vol. xv, p. 287.

[2] Pathol. Aspects of the Stephenson Wave. O. W. Johnston, M.D., Amer. Jour. Obstet., vol. xxxi, 1895, p. 662.

posited there for the manufacture of the placenta, was got rid of by slow absorption before the erect position was attained.

The Stephenson wave [1] thus best explains vicarious menstruation. It is a process in upright animals akin to moulting or yearly loss of horns, hair, etc., and is a great biologic advance over the process so common among the lower animals of slowly removing the endometrium through the lymphatics. If there is obstruction, the wave is thrown to whatever point of the system is weakest. Every trouble in woman, which is aggravated or relieved at the same point of the menstrual wave, be it trough or crest, demands that special attention be given to the pelvis. Dr. Johnston found these periodicities in many cases of indigestion, constipation, liver symptoms, glycosuria, certain inflammation and congestion and Bright's disease, Basedow's disease, loss or weakness of voice, tinnitus aurium, amblyopia, choked disk, many brain troubles, etc., which are really inexplicable without knowledge of this wave, the detection of which, Dr. Johnston thinks, " is equaled in its benefits to our calling only by Harvey's immortal discovery." About five days after the onset of the flow is the best time to perform surgical operations in the anemic trough of the wave. Just what of all the great number of periodic phenomena are causative, concomitant, or resultant, can not yet be told. If this author is right, that only five ova ripen each year, it would seem that the ovarian factor is less central than has been thought. He too holds that there are traces of such a wave observant in males.

The curve on p. 488, from Engelmann,[2] illustrates almost equally well the rise and fall of pulse, temperature, blood pressure, muscular force, pulmonary capacity, morbid nervous symptoms, like the hystero-neuroses and the anatomical changes which he found in the uterine mucosa. This wave does not represent the amount or degree, but only the time of these undulations, the numbers being the days of the mensal period and the shaded days those of the flux.

The cyclic theory in its various forms assumes nervous centers in the walls of the blood vessels, which slowly elab-

[1] The Clinical Importance of the Menstrual Wave, by C. A. Johnston, M. D. Gynecol. Trans., 1896, p. 57.

[2] The American Girl of To-day. Am. Physical Ed. Rev., November, 1901.

orate power and contract the arterial muscular coats, acting partly by their own law and partly dependent upon higher nerve-centers, and thus cause a slight elevation of pressure throughout the entire body, till in certain parts best adapted thereto anatomically the hemorrhage occurs when the vascular tension becomes sufficiently high. Even in pregnancy traces of these periods often continue, and miscarriages are more liable at such times. No surgical operation during or just preceding the monthly epoch should be performed. Vicarious menstruation is not uncommon and flow of blood is

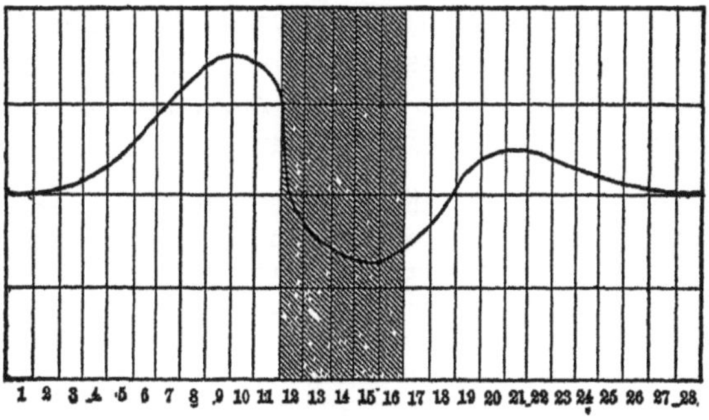

then harder to stanch. Sleep, hibernation, peristaltic action, the uterine contractions once every two to thirty minutes, are at root, like menstrual periodic muscular phenomena, of nervous origin. Prepubertal growth is hypertrophy of certain tissues dominated by trophic nerves, which must thus first undergo structural development, and then indirectly, by affecting circulation, cause the larynx, pelvis, and probably the vascular muscles, walls, etc., to grow. Motility does not ultimately reside in the non-striated muscles any more than it was thought to reside in the voluntary muscles in the days when the doctrine of independent muscular irritability prevailed. Congestion thus not only precedes, but actually causes the flow. Growth and nutrition are thus not purely vegetative, but are indirectly influenced by nerves. This view, it is claimed, affords a principle large enough to explain erection, vicarious menstruation, the flushing in hemorrhage of capillary birthmarks, excessive swelling, varicose veins, nosebleed, spitting blood, enlargement of the thyroid gland

and spleen, puffiness, and dark coloration under the eye, and in rare cases where this interesting phenomenon is seen, stigmatization and cutaneous extravasation.

Dr. Schmey[1] pleads for a higher standpoint concerning menstruation, and assumes monthly plethora in both sexes. In men wounds often bleed periodically. Hemorrhages from the lungs are often monthly, as are hemorrhoidal and other sores. Senator demonstrated menstrual hyperemia of the liver. Both menstruation and ovulation are signs of a periodic fulness of blood in both sexes, at the height of which in woman the Graafian follicle is likely to be emptied and menstruation to occur. There is a cyclic change in the total amount of blood, and menstruation is a chance symptom due to the sensitiveness of the mucous membrane of the uterus. The lunar tide theory he thought suggestive.

On the basis of careful clinical studies upon the metabolism of menstruation, F. Schröder[2] found that in both urine and feces less nitrogen was excreted from the system during these periods than during the rest of the month, while nutrition remained the same. This means, of course, less decomposition of albumin and the formation of less urea. The monthly hemorrhage is thus attended by the accumulation of nitrogen in the system, and not, as previous very tentative experiments on animals had indicated, by the increased decomposition of albumin. In these periodic and complementary groups of processes the blood loses albumin, but the cells of the body demand less of it, all processes thus adapting themselves to the needs of the sexual life. It is surprising to see how many of the studies of the menstrual curve of urea, nitrogen, and temperature failed to take account of either food or feces, and are therefore of almost no value. Whether all the monthly variables in the life of woman can be connected with the catamenia is also rarely considered.

Marro[3] thinks that during the menstrual epoch the girl exhales less carbonic acid; eliminates less urea and sulphuric acid. Calcic phosphate is eliminated in less quantities.

Silva[4] made very careful observations, although only on a few cases, from which he concludes that the alkaline reaction of the blood in normal girls is less during menstruation; that the influence of elec-

---

[1] Zur Theorie der Menst. u. z. Behandlung einiger Mens. Störungen. Therapeut. Monatshefte, February, 1897, p. 93.

[2] Stoffwechsel während der Menst. Zeitsch. klin. Med., 1894, pp. 72–90; see also Annali di Freniatria. Turin, 1895.

[3] Annali di Freniatria. Turin, 1898.

[4] Contribution à l'Étude de la Physio-pathologie de la Menst. Arch. Ital de Biol., 1896, p. 435.

tric stimulation of the vaso-motor system is slight during the flux, but exquisite during the rest of the month. The same he finds true for the influence of heat and cold. Reaction time was slower and feebler. Respiration was more irregular and less affected by external stimulation. During the flow a strong stimulus less readily changed the costal to the abdominal type of respiration. Silva holds that the vaso-motor state which is the chief defense against bacteria has a real effect upon the organism's power of resistance; that the chemotactic action of the leucocytes probably does not affect the state of the vessels, and that in low nutrition the organism is easily impregnated by poison. Menstruation he regards as somewhat like pyrexia, and calls it an embryonal puerperal process. The bactericide power of serum diminishes with alkalinity, which increases the consumption of albumin; and *vice versa,* immunized animals have more alkalinity. This comports with Schröder's view that during menstruation the urine and feces excrete about one half less azote, its budget measuring the loss of albumin.

Normally the pulse rate increases and the vascular tension rises as the period approaches, the minimal point being a few days after the cessation of the flow and the maximum just before. Temperature may increase before the flow as much as half a degree F. The amount of urine is increased, while the urea increases just before and after, but perhaps falls off a trifle during the flux. The thyroid and parotic glands and breasts are swollen, and the Fallopian tubes congested. Finklestein showed a concentric narrowing of the field of vision beginning one to three days before, and culminating on the third or fourth day of menstruation, and vanishing three or four days later. His perimetric tests showed this narrowing of the field for red, blue, green, and yellow, as well as for white, while distinctness of vision in the central field was also slightly impaired. Traces of pigmentation, so marked at this period in the anal regions in some monkeys, where it is very brilliant, are seen under the eyes and around the nipples and sometimes on the renal parts. An odor quite distinct from that peculiar to the organs, and aromatic, is often noticed, and the voice may grow dull and flat. Women are more easily hypnotized, more prone to jealousy, ill-temper, and confessionism, can make less accurate and energetic movements, and mental activities are less brilliant, while these powers are at their best at the time of strongest genitive impulses and greatest conceptive power.

The total period of twenty-eight days may, according to Minot, be approximately divided as follows: tumefaction of the mucosa and its attendant phenomena, five days; menstrual flux, four days; restoration of the mucosa, seven days; resting period, twelve days. In a sense, as Ellis [1] says, a woman during her reproductive life is always engaged in menstruating. Everything she does or says must be judged by its exact position in this cycle which permeates her whole physical and psychical organism; and especially in unbalanced and neurotic persons, even guilt for crime is lessened, so that in criminal trials this should always be considered. This is in distinct opposition to views like those of Miss F. P. Cobbe and Mrs. Fawcett, the latter of whom declares, in contradiction to Mr. Harrison's statement, that nearly "all women are subject to functional interruptions absolutely incompatible with the highest forms of continuous pressure," that "the ordinary healthy woman is as fit for work every day of her life as the ordinary healthy man." Miss E. B. Gamble asserts that these eternal wounds of love and their cicatrization, which may even account for woman's smaller size as compared with man, which fill the month with a drama which has a new motive each day, and often makes her an invalid one-fifth of the time, are normally pathological, and due in some way, she does not attempt to explain, to long ages of man's brutality.

Although every recurrent period has the closest *rapport* with the neuro-psychic functions, the few first and last menstruations have a far greater influence upon the brain and soul than do those when the sexual rhythm is best established. The psychoses caused by the former are often acute and stormy. The first periods are often very irregular in time, sometimes occurring once in three to five months, one in two years, or even more.[2] This has a very disturbing effect upon the organism. Esquirol thought one-sixth of all psychic diseases in women were influenced if not caused by menstruation. A similar view also led Morel to ascribe great

---

[1] On these points see Ellis: Man and Woman, p. 251 *et seq.*, also p. 247.

[2] P. I. Kovalevski: Des Menstruations-Zustand und der Mens. Psychosen. Med. Wochensch., St. Petersburg, 1894, p. 216 *et seq.*

etiological importance in insanity to the way in which first menstruation was established. Headache, tearfulness, irritability, relaxation, and indisposition often appear two or three days before the illness is due; and often these symptoms are repeated every twenty-eight to thirty-two days, three or four days before the flux appears; or again after the latter has once appeared, six months may elapse before another occurs, while the above nervous symptoms occur monthly.

The normal woman in her prime, no matter how healthy, is more sensitive, more prone to depression, excitable, moody, feels more fatigued, distracted, suffers pain more or less intense in different parts of the body, especially in the head, is liable to discontent, quarrelsomeness, unstable in appetite and sleep, disappointed, feels oppressed, and can do less work with mind and body. She is liable to nausea, palpitation, paranœa and hyperæsthesia, a feeling of heaviness of body, sick headache, partial and temporary paresis, prosopalgia, fickleness, changes from elation to depression, local chills and flushes, etc. These symptoms gradually diminish and finally the "rules" cease. Then "the woman is born anew. She is vigorous, energetic, joyful, well. Her soul is clean and ready for ceaseless work." The pains were those of childbirth on a small scale. We might say that in the one case the race is renewed through pain; in the other, the individual. She is now at the very top of her condition, most brilliant, beautiful, attractive to men, and most attracted to them. Before, she needed the greatest tenderness, delicacy, and sympathy, but gradually, as the month advances she becomes more independent and often a little less dominated by her affections. These processional changes in a strong and healthy nature have something of the magnificence and awfulness of Nature's primitive revelation.

During just the time when savages isolate woman and call her unclean, she is really in her fullest flower and glory, and she must begin by reenforcing her self-respect at this period. She must have freedom to control the entire environment, and thus, perhaps, to some extent, the time of her month. With the birth of the function at adolescence comes one of the most wondrous of all instincts, namely, just how to best care for herself. This has been enfeebled and now needs more or less help. Man can never understand this, and to him she may always seem somewhat more unique and strange then. The nerves, feelings, and the muscles need a regimen varying in individual women more, perhaps, than the whole range of male variability. In this women differ from each other more than they differ from man. Into this field I can not enter; but happy she who, at twenty-five, has really achieved freedom, intelligence, and true self-knowledge. During the first few days she is introverted to strange sensations which ideally are not painful, but deliciously and sometimes almost ecstatically charming. The volume of her emotional life is greatest, as is its depth and range. Then, actually though unconsciously, if entirely healthful, she is more attractive to man; and as the wave of this great cosmic pulse which makes her live on a slope passes, her voice, her eye, complexion, circulation, and her very dreams are more brilliant. She feels her womanhood and glories in it like a goddess. Her toilet is never so detailed, even where it is most hidden, to any other eye than her own. The flow itself has been a pleasure and the end of it is a slight shock. The instinct to conceal is a part of female coyness, which is directed only toward others, and she is most of all reserved toward any chosen one. In the earliest stirrings of the adolescent ferment, she has first dreamed of some ideal of manhood and is altruistic, and only later comes the conception of selfhood. Solitude and the country develop ideals of others, and society and the city tend toward the self-center. So far from ever having wished herself a male, she exults in her womanhood as something superior, and feels it worthy of love, reverence, protection, care, and service. In early adolescence her impulse is to make herself absolutely perfect. When her cycle is complete, her whole life must be regulated to prepare for the next. She develops new sentiments, instincts, and insights, is a charm to herself and both a fascination and a study for others; and because these days are not all on a dull, prosaic level, her life is larger and explores all the possibilities of humanity, so that she is less in need of supplementing her own individual limitations by the study of the alien lessons of the schools. So much comes to her by intuition and experience that her way of wisdom is larger and must always seem more esoteric and mystic to man. Thus she illustrates the type of wholeness, rather than halfness, which a German scholar has suggestively described.[1]

Every day of the twenty-eight she is a different being, and the wide range of circumnutation which explores the pleasures and pains of life, its darkness and its light, its depressive and exalted states, its hopes and fears, its sense of absolute dependence and of independence, sometimes almost to the declaration of war of sex against sex, reveals her as a more generic creature than man, less consistent than he if we compare days or hours, more so if we compare months as the units of her life. Is all this health or disease, normal or abnormal, or half-way between, is a question often asked, but which can not be answered till we know whether the human race realizes its ideal. This phenomenon has, perhaps, had very much to do in the development of the persistent conception that man is suffering from the effects of great calamity or error in the remote and forgotten past, that has perverted and left its mark upon his nature.

Very different are the phenomena in girls handicapped by morbid nervous periodicity. All the preliminary symptoms are exaggerated. On or near the culminating day of first menstruation, a slight shock, joy, or pain, may cause an hysterical outbreak, and if the normal menstrual endeavors are thwarted, abnormal molimina are intensified. Each stage of the month has its onset of feelings, thoughts, perhaps acts, psychic scenery and color generally, and sometimes the doubts, disturbances, and comparisons of one stage from the standpoint of another, cloud not only the future but may tend to nervous and even mental weakness. There is a man- and school-bred kind of logical consistency to impose which upon her is an outrage to her nature. More often in such cases the impulses of each stage may break away from control by the others, and impulsiveness, epileptic symptoms, senseless terrors, præcordial anxiety, pyromania, the assumption of an alien rôle, grave illness, one-half of which is real and the other half sometimes consciously feigned, and some-

[1] Die Ganzen und die Halben: Zwei Menschheitstypen. Deuts. Rundschau, August, 1900, pp. 213–242.

times honestly fancied, may occur. Hysteria, more often in its mild form of uncontrollable weeping, laughing, or globus hystericus, often makes its first appearance at the time of first menstruation. Slight epilepsy in the form of brief fainting fits is liable. The girl falls, perhaps with a cry, has cramps, staring eyes, rapid pulse for a few minutes and recovers, and then is as usual till the next period. First menstruations after childbirth and those at the beginning of sexual life are often attended by similar psychic symptoms. Occasionally it may cause improvement of specific troubles, e. g., of chorea, and when it first appears as something unknown and unexpected, the dangers to psychic equilibrium are greater, as also when there is a tendency to specific diseases, as of the lungs, heart, etc.

The effects of menstruation upon previously existing morbid mentation and of the cessation of periods upon the onset of disease and its return with convalescence, do not indicate, as is usually thought, a causal relation between the two, but rather both are perhaps concurrent and independent effects of the same cause, like exhaustion and rest. Sometimes, indeed, the beginning and end of this period have no effect on the progress of psychic disease. Selager, Schröder, Krafft-Ebing, and Algeri think it intensifies; and Marci and Kovalevski hold that it may often even mitigate the intensity of insane states. Abnormal brain conditions, then, must be regarded as concurrent symptoms of anomalous menstruation, and not as the cause of it. Periodicity with similarity of symptoms on successive months, brief duration and recovery, circular insanity with attending depression or exaltation, and obscenity in word or act, often indicate that the perversity is of menstrual origin. Sometimes, on the other hand, mental disturbance seems the direct and immediate effect of arrest or excess of flux. Some psychoses are vicarious for menstruation.

Very characteristic, although rare, are cases of vicarious puerperal bleeding at the nose, stomach, and elsewhere.[1] This is far less alarming and far less common than periodic hemorrhages near the meno-

[1] See a good typical case in a girl of fourteen, in the New Zealand Medical Journal, 1895, p. 157.

pause.[1] It may be in some respects compared with so-called pregnant menstruation, which is really pathological bleeding and perhaps about as infrequent.[2] This strange reciprocity is complicated by the curious clinical fact that mental disturbance should be much more frequent at the natural period of the climacteric than when the menstrual function is suddenly inhibited by accidental cause.[3] Meyer urges that the causes of abnormalities and their results are "not to be sought alone, and indeed not predominantly in the sex organs, but in every organ of the body."

Menstrual irregularities which seem to be everywhere increasing are usually grouped under three heads: disorders of defect, or amenorrhea; of excess, or metrorrhagia; of perversion, or dysmenorrhea.

(*a*) Amenorrhea may be partial, involving action of the ovaries only. In such cases the monthly flux may be regular and normal in both quantity and quality, but ovulation does not occur. On the other hand, the ovaries may do their part, but the uterus remains inactive. In such cases the discharge does not occur. These main defects, as well as under-functioning of the Fallopian tubes and vagina, may of course occur in all degrees, from complete absence up to normal activity, and even be well-proportioned in amount and properly connected in time. Non-ovulation is very hard to diagnose, so that suppression of the flow is the chief fact. The latter may be temporary or prolonged; so complete that almost none of the characteristic sensations or symptoms are felt, or the flow may be only a slightly paler color, at a little longer interval or with reduction in quantity. In such cases supplementary hemorrhages often occur. Puech, whose statistics are still the best, found these complementary escapes of blood to occur in the order of frequency as follows: most often it is vomited from the stomach, next most frequently it escapes from the breasts, then come hemorrhages from the lungs, throat, mouth, nosebleed, discharges from the lower limbs, trunk, back, walls of the thorax; intestinal piles, swollen gums or eyelids, lacrymal glands, urine, hands, hair, ears, umbilicus, salivary glands, cheeks, etc., may bleed. Indeed, spontaneous supplemental hemorrhages may occur almost anywhere or produce congestion in any organ.

The causes of suppression, besides the chief uteropathies and pregnancy, are many, some well-established and others obscure. Of all these processes the ovaries are, biologically considered, the center and soul, so that any trouble here causes hesitation or crepuscular menstruation, and may slowly and entirely check it, as is seen in cases where the ovaries have been removed. Among the non-genital causes of partial or total suppression, chlorosis and anemia are very common. Consumption has a gradually suppressive effect; so does obesity, and several urinal and sexual abnormalities. Strong or sudden emotion

[1] Cincinnati Lancet-Clin., September 26, 1896.

[2] Levy. Archiv f. Gyn., Bd. 15, pp. 361–383.

[3] Barus. Scalpel, July, 1896.

can prevent or almost momentarily arrest the flux, and psychic states have an immediate and profound influence in both increasing and diminishing it. The face itself, which grows pale or flushed with every change of sentiment, and reflects each effect of pleasure or pain, says Auvard in substance, responds no more delicately to every change of moral and intellectual states than do organs involved in menstruation. Fear, whether sudden or chronic, great dread or desire of pregnancy in young married women, certain hysterical manifestations, study or worry about lessons, bad air, constrained positions, improper or fluctuating temperatures either local or general, change of diet, of regimen, environment, the honeymoon, medication, many unknown and idiopathic causes, may lead to the same results. The treatment of so complex a disorder, it need scarcely be said, should be mainly directed to the removal of its cause, and can be completely restorative only when taken before bad menstrual habits have been too long confirmed or too far advanced.

(*b*) Metrorrhagia, or excessive menstruation, may appear in abnormal hemorrhages from almost any part of the genital organs. If the female organs in all their varied functions, including parturition, are more prone to hemorrhages than those of the male, the former bear the loss of blood far better and seem to have greater spontaneous styptic or stanching power, and woman's more anabolic activities make all loss good sooner and with greater ease than does the male organism. Excess may appear in quantity, duration, and frequency, and these forms often have an intimate reciprocity. At the pubertal instauration of the periods, as well as at the menopause, various forms of excess are liable. Excluding local mechanical causes and also those due to changes in the composition of the blood, certain cardiac affections, neuralgia and many psychic states and processes, cause uterine congestion, and may aggravate any or all of the factors of menstruation. Abdominal compression is prominent among the disturbances that cause aggravation of these disorders. All such forms of excessive activity of course involve loss of vital energy and keep the unfortunate subject on a low plane of vigor and emotional tone, check the later stages of mental and bodily growth, and impair the power of normal procreation, and often before the danger is fully realized condemn girls to a life of semi-invalidism that might have been avoided by a little more care and wisdom at the critical time when these functions were being first established and regulated.

(*c*) Dysmenorrhea, the third form of abnormality, is often marked by colic, which is to the smooth or involuntary what cramp is to the striated or voluntary muscles. The normal contraction of the uterine muscles is not perceived, but their painful action is analogous to the discomfort of indigestion, colic of the kidneys, or palpitation of the heart. Many varieties and symptom-groups have been proposed, but most features are common to all forms. The pain is intermittent, like the contractions which cause it. It is ill-defined as lumbar, abdominal, hypogastric, crural, etc. It is worst just at the time of the discharge or just before, and often hinders sleep. The flux may be serous or clotted, may contain villosities, the detritus of decaying tissue, or it may be scanty and thin. The importance of these pseudo-menstruations, says Auvard, is secondary, and they may be more frequent than is suspected in less observed normal cases. Sometimes the pain at the crisis is so great that the next recurrence is dreaded almost like parturition, and its discomforts anticipated by those endowed with vivid imagination. Often such accompaniments as bad breath, flushes and pallor, and faintness are watched for with apprehensions, which may themselves become a cause of depression or debility. The source of this, as of all the other genetopathies, may be congenital or even hereditary, but very often its origin is in the nervous system. The tubes, ovaries, or vagina, as well as the uterus, may contribute to dysmenorrhea.

Many of the disturbances, which are hardly less complex or manifold than the causes of sterility, have been themes for clinical, surgical, and physiological study, and together make up a rich body of data which constitutes the science of the gynecologists and fills their journals. But some plain and simple statement of the significance and dangers of these periods should be an essential part of the educational equipment of every girl on or before reaching this age.

Dr. C. Clark[1] held that there were no forms of insanity expressive of particular types of menstrual irregularity. Irritability, depression, and stupor, the three types of psychic reflex from this can not be ascribed to special forms of it. Icard[2] has constructed a table of great value, although based upon only three hundred and forty-nine cases, indicating the relative frequency of various forms of psychic perversion obviously menstrual in character. Most common is a group of disorders of middle life, which he designates somewhat collectively as acute mania and impulsive and nameless delirium. Next most common come religious delusions, quite frequent near the menopause. Then follow in order of frequency, suicidal impulses, most of which are in middle life, genesic excitation, melancholia, homicidal impulses, illusion and hallucination, pyromania most frequent at puberty, kleptomania, dipsomania, spells of jealousy, lying, and calumny. Icard concludes that the menstrual function in these cases, where predisposition exists, creates a psychological state, varying

[1] Jour. of Mental Science, 1888, p. 386.

[2] La Femme pendant la Période Menstruelle, par D. G. Icard, Paris, 1890, p. 283.

all the way from simple moral malaise or disquietude to positive alienation, with complete loss of reason, morality, and responsibility. In such cases, those who know most will pardon most. Wherever crime occurs in such states, he would persistently raise the question of legal accountability. The sympathies between the brain and reproductive organs are far more intimate than has hitherto been suspected. Even hysteria, epilepsy, chorea, chlorosis, and exophthalmic goître are classified among the neuroses of menstruation. Abnormality of this function is a predisposing cause to any of the obvious disturbances that heredity or the nature of any other troubles of body or mind may determine. It is impossible to ascertain whether psychic disturbances have a more immediate and profound effect on menstrual disorders or *vice versa*, but the relation of body and mind is nowhere more intimate than here, and a psychology that does not take careful account of this is defective.

In an important article,[1] a large number of cases of crime in the menstrual state are quoted from Krafft-Ebing, Tuke, Pellmann, Westphal, Mabille, Girand, and others. As typical as any are the following:

Z., a peasant woman, aged twenty-two, set fire to her own hut. Up to the age of ten she was normal, but afterward led a hard life; menstruation began at sixteen and was attended by pain in the head and collapse. She married at twenty, but was childless. During the summer preceding her crime the courses ceased, but in their place came præcordial anxiety and irritation, headache, restlessness, loss of sleep, and nameless dread. Her husband's relatives beat her, and she was thought stubborn during her periods. For a supposed neglect due to her confused state she was beaten on the head, and broke out into a fit of anger that made her violent but unconscious. When the family had retired and she had come to herself, she imagined assaults and other terrible things, and finally fired the roof and felt great satisfaction. On hearing the alarm she aroused her husband and helped to extinguish the flames. On the same night menstruation appeared and she felt reborn to a new life. All her troubles ceased and she confessed everything openly.

Another case was a twenty-year-old daughter of a professor, well-bred and trained but of nervous heredity, and who had convulsions in childhood but no disease. With the first menstruation at fourteen came great access of fear, which she could not account for or define the

[1] The Menstrual State and Psychoses, by P. I. Kovalevski. Russian Archiv Psychiatrie. Kharkov, 1894, pp. 73–131.

object of. She was restless, ran from place to place, sobbed, prayed, but when she knelt blasphemous words forced themselves into her mind in connection with the Blessed Virgin, Jesus and his saints, until she beat her head against the wall and tried to spring from the window and choke herself. She understood well that it was all disease, but it drove her to resolve on suicide. This state lasted about three or four days and ceased with the flow, when she became again cheerful, only to renew all these symptoms with great exactness in twenty-eight days, the first being the most painful. Thus in a year and a half there were fifteen such attacks, till at last under treatment the psychical troubles ceased, slight symptoms of which were felt two years later on bereavement. These attacks were severest in September, October, November, and March, and during the summer were mitigated into the form of sleeplessness, uneasiness, and desolate and depressive states of mind. This condition in the many cases of which this is typical usually continues up to the climacteric.

H. Ellis[1] says, "whenever a woman commits a deed of criminal violence it is extremely probable that she is at her monthly periods." Clouston says more specifically, "the melancholiacs are more depressed, the maniacal more restless, the delusional more under the influence of their delusions in their conduct, those subject to hallucinations have them more intensely, the impulsive cases are more uncontrollable, the cases of stupor more stupid, and the demented tend to be excited," at these periods. The matter is by no means so simple, however. Näcke[2] concludes from a careful study of ninety-nine cases of chronic psychoses, that in regularity and all other respects these periods do not materially differ from those of normal people, and that this influence on the course of such disturbances is relatively slight and inconstant. In sixty-five cases, no influence whatever could be detected. Even abnormalities in these functions had no greater influence than on the sane.

Kiernan[3] attempts to elaborate and further illustrate Moll's conception of mixoscopic adolescent states. When the factors that make up the ego are disjointed, primitive instincts often arise and new direc-

[1] Man and Woman, p. 254.

[2] Die Menst. u. ihre Einfluss bei chron. Psychosen. Arch. f. Psychiatrie, 1896, vol. xxviii, No. 1, p. 169.

[3] See articles in the Alienist and Neurologist, beginning May, 1903, entitled Mixoscopic Adolescent Survivals in Art, Literature, and Pseudo-Ethics.

tions are taken. Religious ecstasy may become associated with salacity. Algophily may become love of seeing pain in others or of suffering it one's self. New relations between the cerebral and reproductive system are common. Gross ideas of sex in people of blameless lives; the intensification of lust which may grow with jealousy; hypersensitiveness, as, for instance, "the nervous bladder"; philistine conventions beside erotic imaginations; prurience in prudery; the venting of sexual unrest in very eccentric ways, as in the case of Viola Larsen, who leaped into notoriety in the West by stealing, which she described as wildly intoxicating, delicious, beautiful, wonderful, a girl who early burned for fame and took delight in many kinds of strange antics—these symptoms illustrate mixoscopia. The rapture of being plunged into the waves of that great ocean of feeling which underlies our daily life in order to intensify consciousness and feel energy; the indulgence of pungent sexual argot; in "furtively sniggering over indecency"; the depression of the habitual motives of modesty into the realms of the unconscious; the "auto-erotism of the Narcissus type" which sometimes appears as a result of excessive use of the mirror, are further outcrops.

Gall thought there were periodic changes in men at puberty analogous to the twenty-eight-day periods in women. This he held was noticed chiefly in approaching senescence, especially in the feeble. Their complexions grow dull, the perspiration changes, digestion is poorer, and there may be periodic sadness, discomfort, and inability to work.

Sanctonius, Keill, and Laycock long ago held this view.[1] Clark thinks temperature, and Hammond says nosebleed, headache, excess of uric acid, and Clouston that the nisus generativus, show monthly rhythm; Ellis[2] rather inclines to accept a three-and-a-half day period as the unit, with weekly and fortnightly cycles, seen perhaps also in pulse, rate of respiration and weight, although even his very interesting case of Perry-Coste hardly favors a strictly lunar period. We should expect that such a fundamental rhythm, if it existed, would be overlaid by many social and auto-suggestions. This rhythm may precede and survive sexual life, and menstruation itself may be a special and secondary outcrop of a more basal rhythm that extends from the cradle to the grave in both sexes.

The spells of discomfort, distraction, irascibility, and depression in males thought to be of this character are probably much more common than is generally supposed. Young and

---

[1] See Gould and Pyle: Anomalies and Curiosities of Medicine, p. 28.

[2] Psychology of Sex, p. 73 *et seq.*, and Appendix B, p. 251.

robust men and adolescents are often subject to recurrent periods of wakefulness, which often coincide with the full moon, and may be due to its light. Indeed, Mantegazza holds that the menstrual periods were established because moonlight nights were favorable to courtship, and later, when the rhythm was well established, they became independent of lunar periods. The Sabbath had a great influence in fixing the twenty-eight-day period. Koster (Periodische Irresein) thinks that nearly all periods in periodic disease are compounded of various multiples of seven days, and that the anomalistic period of physiological month of twenty-eight days makes a veritable tide in the health of man, so independent of sea tides that Darwin's suggestion of these as causative of the menstrual rhythm is unnecessary. The moon is 47–55 thousand miles nearer the earth in perigee than in apogee, and exerts nearly one-sixth greater magnetic and gravitational effect upon the earth. Kern, in his treatment of periodic psychoses, thinks most of those with prominent psychic symptoms develop at adolescence. Sometimes melancholy and mania succeed each other with lucid intervals, in great regularity. Where there is much variation averages sometimes bring it out, and where other, e. g., seasonal periods are more prominent, this rhythm is nevertheless present. Bartel, who ascribed one-third of the cases of female insanity to this cause, classifies periodic diseases into those which do and those which do not coincide with the mensal unit of time.

Nelson,[1] who was a good dreamer, and whose methods and results are so far the best, habituated himself to recording immediately, without rising from bed, all his dreams and computing them by a method designed to show the amount of dream energy each night for thirty months, and found a distinct mensal period. His sexual activity during sleep, measured by involuntary emissions or "ekboles," showed a still more marked monthly rhythm. His major climax also was near the summer solstice, near which Döring's curves show the maximal number of conceptions.

It is singular that a process eternally and regularly repeated in the life of woman has never been regarded as quite normal

---

[1] A Study of Dreams. Am. Jour. of Psy., vol. i, p. 367.

or physiological. It is somewhat less unaccountable that it should have been everywhere considered as a badge of inferiority or a basis of exclusion or disgust. In accepting this view woman has exposed herself to the constant temptation to a dissimulation that too often becomes constitutional, by trying in every way to conceal it, even though she aggravate its dangers by efforts she should not then put forth. This lack of candor and naturalness must affect character in the direction of frankness and honesty. On the other hand, this aversion has been, as we saw, favorable so far as it tended to secure seclusion and rest, so that in this respect superstition did the work of science. This strange chronometry, in mysterious *rapport* with moon, tides, reproduction, race, climate, and all the environment in its every item, has contributed not a little among many savages to make woman an object of superstitious awe; and even if it has had nothing to do with keeping her stature inferior to man's, has made her more many-sided, so that she may have thus been better able to reduce his polygamous instincts by becoming herself in the course of the month several different kinds of person and appealing by turns to his pity, his passion, and ruling him now by sympathy, now by service, now by admiration, while her repertory of changes gives her an added charm and ever-stimulating interest.

Ever since Hippocrates the period of first menstruation has been thought to be very critical for the development of the nervous system. The entire genital organism is congested; the volume of the uterus and ovaries increases; the Fallopian tubes grow turgescent; the breasts are enlarged and tender; the thyroid gland swells; the nerves are tense and irritable; from 250 to 500 grams of venous and often clotted blood are lost normally, and this of itself in girls not properly instructed may cause great alarm, aggravated, as it often is, by idiopathic horror of blood, which indeed it may cause, and which may still more prompt unhygienic and even dangerous modes of concealment, removal, stanching, etc. It may thus lay deep in the nervous system, the foundation of psychic perturbations at every period. Few more pitiable objects exist in nature than a girl, especially if nervous or overworked, who must encounter this experience for the first time, uninstructed or alone. The quality of motherhood has nowhere a more crucial test than in meeting the needs of this epoch. The individual variations are so very wide that every girl should be a special case by herself, and all reasoning from one person to another is apt to be fallacious. All of the physical and psychic phenomena are peculiarly prone to abnormal defect or perversion, and for a considerable time everything that in the least degree jeopards the harmony and balance of the many factors involved in the settled establishment of regularity and normality should give way. Now begins a great and ineradicable difference between the physical and psychic life of woman and that of man.

Gynecology is by general consent the largest, with the possible exception of neurology, of all the specialties of medicine. Few departments of the profession are more important, and it can boast some of the greatest and noblest of practitioners. But the limitations in this field are peculiar. They are seen in the complacency in partial views that ascribe everything to some one simple theory which is utterly inadequate to the subtleties of nature—nerve cycle, endometric degeneration, ovulation as primal and all-conditioning in menstruation, or make pelvic anomalies, or metritis, or engorgement of the base, the keystone of the arch. The diversity of theories is probably not so wide as the range of individual variations, and while the latter graduate into each other by imperceptible gradations, the former remain rigid and unmediated, and their representatives sometimes resemble hostile camps. So in treatment, what Dr. Jacobi[1] said eighteen years ago, is still too true. Some prefer the knife, others the cautery, others the curette and irrigation with lotions or tamponing, others supports, internal and external, pessaries, etc. In the present confusion, the chief points of safety should be to avoid heroic or premature treatment until we know more what constitutes excess or chronicity; what is the pathological significance of versions, catarrh, inflammations; until discussions concerning the nature of the disease are at least as discriminating and animated as those concerning treatment. There is a classic treatment of certain diseases like pneumonia, typhoid, and nephritis, but the whole field of uterine troubles has been, and still is, one of great distraction and uncertainty.

---

[1] Studies in Endometritis. Am. Jour. of Obstetrics, 1885, vol. xviii. Seven valuable articles.

There are now, happily, signs of a reaction against the recent excessively surgical tendency, which has been too dominant, toward a large view of the whole life of woman. Specialists are beginning to realize that they must broaden their view from the pathology of her organs, till lately so often doomed, if she once consulted them, to the entire problem of regimen, and know at least as much about woman as about her pelvic diseases. Indeed, not a few experts are beginning to recognize that this larger field is relatively unknown to them, and that they must begin the study of the new or higher gynecology with something like a Socratic confession of ignorance. As long as they hold any exclusive theory which consigns to either ovaries, uterus, tubes, or central nervous system, the exclusive dominance, or assume that either the psyche or soma is always primal or causal, little progress can be made. Each of the modern views is partially correct and must always be considered as a possible aspect of each case.

To understand a woman's body and soul is a larger problem than to understand a man's. It is true of her more than of him, that to know a part we must know the whole; first, because her nature is more generic and less specific, and, second, because reproduction, the deepest secret of animate nature, plays a larger rôle in her life. Illness constitutes a greater element of her existence and is in a sense more a part of her. Each woman is a more adequate representative of her sex than a man is of his, so that to know one well more involves knowing all; hence experts and specialists, apparatus and particular processes, while often helpful, are more liable to be an insult to the deeper laws of her being. Our medical science, our psychology, and our philosophy are still inadequate to answer the questions her nature propounds. If the male doctor could occasionally be a woman, as Plato thought he should be sickly to more sympathetically understand those with whom he deals, this would avail much, but might reveal more new problems than answers to old ones, for, despite the great and real recent advances, it is not unlikely that modern woman, with her progressive complexity and sensitiveness, is evolving new symptoms and disorders yet faster. Perhaps it is this that has kept gynecologists so bound down to pressing needs as they arise that they have had little time to generalize on the facts within their ken, and little strength to rebase their practises upon larger views of woman's nature. Perhaps our medical schools, now happily becoming endowed, have not hitherto been able to do their duty in the lines of research that are so inviting here. American woman is herself unique enough to furnish many special problems that almost cry out for investigation. Her status is changing more rapidly here than elsewhere, and the future of our race depends on whether for good or for ill, but this we can not clearly see till medicine broadens, here at least where need is greatest, to include anthropology, and all study of woman's diseases is made on a broad background of biology and heredity.

No one who has once abandoned himself to the fascination and suggestiveness that all parts of this field are now acquiring can fail to hope that a new and higher synthesis is impending which will not coordinate menstruation with pregnancy, and adolescence with senescence, but will bring together the results of the changes in the quantity, pressure, and alkalinity of the blood, in pulse rate, in the rhythm of output of carbonic acid and urea, temperature, nerve tension in brain, medulla, cord, and pelvic plexus and ovaries; homologize the loss of the endometrium and its regeneration with the moulting and subsequent reproduction of new organs; correlate normal with morbid changes; and show the true relation of these processes to pubertal growth on the one hand and to sexual desire on the other, as well as to fecundity. It is also apparent that the key that is to unlock the secret of all these relations is to be found in the biogenetic field. That the challenge that this condition now issues to science will soon be taken up more successfully and its difficulties overcome, we must hope. It is certain that any marked advance here will mark an epoch in our knowledge of both man's body and soul, and, what is more vital, will help us to bring the future mothers of our race to a better discharge of their functions.

Meanwhile we must hold fast to the basal fact that this process must be absolutely normal and complete in all its details or the mental and physical well-being of woman is jeopardized, and that a healthful performance of this function is essential to a well-balanced mind. If every organ has an independent nervous mechanism, these must be combined with reciprocal interaction from a rhythmically pulsating center as real as that which controls respiration or heart-beat. Ophthalmology has vastly widened its scope in recent years by entering the school and doing a great preventive work for the young. Gynecology should profit by this example. Woman's sphere has vastly widened of late, yet she is not equipped for the boundless field opening before her, but is handicapped by needless fashion and inveterate habits of antihygienic life. Vital as the distinction may be for diagnosis, it is often impossible to tell whether the mental symptoms are caused by defective menstruation or *vice versa*. The whole problem of the relation of the mind and body is here involved.

It is frequently assumed that among individuals of the same race and environment an early beginning goes with a late cessation of menstruation, and in individual cases this is demonstrated, as is the fact that a retardation of the development of this function goes with early senescence. In general, the former at least must be regarded as exceptional. Commonly, if it is accelerated prematurely it is followed by early involution, as women in hot climates are often old at thirty. In the main it is probable that those who mature late age late. It would certainly seem as if the interests of racial advancement required at least a progressively later ripening, if not a later decay, and that most effective propagation be kept near the acme of maturity. The duration of this best age for offspring may not increase or decrease concomitantly with that of menstruation, but may fall within its limits by a variable interval.[1]

In fine, puberty for a girl is like floating down a broadening river into an open sea. Landmarks recede, the water deepens and changes in its nature, there are new and strange forms of life, the currents are more complex, and the phenomena of tides make new conditions and new dangers. The bark is frail, liable to be tossed by storms of feeling, at the mercy of wind and wave, and if without chart and compass and simple rules of navigation, aimless drifting in the darkness of ignorance, amidst both rocks and shoals, may make of the

[1] The curves on p. 508 will aid us in stating the many unsolved problems here. The lower line represents the age of first menstruation; line 2, the age capable of producing viable children; line 3, the age of most effective heredity. The three

weak or unadvised wrecks or castaways. The change itself is exciting, and half knowledge or popular and perhaps prurescent fallacies only augment instead of allaying the strain. Four or five days a month for some thirty years the girl's system will be depleted, and there will be lassitude with peculiar susceptibility to physical or mental shock, and complex problems of regimen that even with the best instruction must receive a large residuary personal solution. Shall she withdraw, and make or accept excuses which seem to her a kind of implicit confession which is so hard even to those nearest her? Does she show or

---

curves are schematic representations of the fertile age, of which *a* pictures early maturity and decay with deficient effectiveness; *b* represents later maturity and prolonged fertility; *c* a late short period of very effective productivity. The short lines just above each curve represent children 7, 9, and 4 in number, progressivity being their upward direction. Thus the first and last child of *a* are decadent; the second and sixth, which are horizontal, just maintain the status of the parent; the third and fifth add a little, and the fourth adds most, while the four children of *c* are all progressive. Frequency is greatest in *a* and least in *c*, which excels also in regularity of interval. While such a curve might be constructed for any fertile mother who had already reached the menopause, or, better yet, for a fertile grandmother, in point of fact we can not construct any part of such a general curve

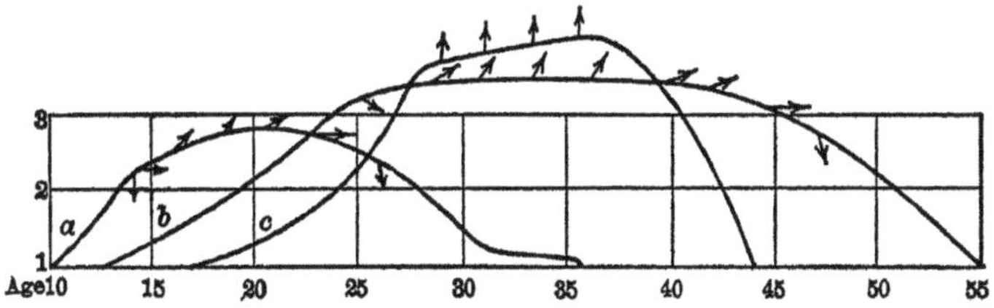

from any other given part of it. We do not know whether those who begin to menstruate late attain full fertility sooner or later or within the same interval as those who begin early. Perhaps curve *b* should be very steep at first and reach line 3 almost as soon as does curve *a*, instead of crossing it at a greater interval than it rises from line 1. Perhaps curve *c* is not the one that ascends highest, and perhaps it, and not *b*, is most prolonged at its greatest altitude. Curve *a* may really fall later than does *c*. Statistics of viability of offspring suggest quite an interval between lines 1 and 2, and we have every reason to believe that the period of prenubility and adolescence should be prolonged above the latter, but above line 3 we have no clue save that of vague popular impression or abstract theory. Whether, and, if so, how long, the curve becomes horizontal on top, or whether those that reach the highest level do so latest and decline earliest, as is often commonly assumed among the educated classes, or whether nature decrees that, to do the very best that birth can do for offspring, preparation must be begun early rather than late, we are ignorant.

can she conceal her state at least from strangers, or will they suspect, or must she make an effort to be natural? Shall she accept corsets, long and heavy skirts, the rush, crush, and bustle of social obligations? Shall she seek the information or advice she feels the need of, and how and of whom? There is almost always some pain, reflex or direct, and this is a nervous handicap which may tend to feverish instability. After a few periods and a little knowledge she often learns to be more or less anxious about either regularity, duration, or quantity, or all, and practises little expedients, stumbling onward in the pathway of self-knowledge. In the dim depths of her soul she vaguely feels how paramount this function is, especially in its initial stage of incipiency, at least for her good looks, spirits, and ease of daily duties, but at the same time she infers from observation of others, and perhaps from the very paucity of information given her, that the less concession made to this instinctive sense of its importance, or to her feelings or her sense of waning vigor, the better. The change in her own psychic state naturally suggests that the periods are all-conditioning, but the sentiment of her environment is to ignore them as unimportant if not shameful. She may have experienced a nervous shock at the first flow, or suffered, as experts tell us so many still do, from applying cold water as if to stanch a wound, or been the victim of unusual exposure or activity at the critical time; or, as our returns show, she not infrequently tides herself over by unwonted coffee, tea, or even vinegar or tablets of various kinds, that often acquire unsuspected vogue in school circles, where such expedients occasionally are almost comparable to the errors of incompetent obstetricians later, which Engelmann says furnish the gynecologist half his patients, or the fad of operation when, for a period just closing, experts were "blinded by the glitter of the surgeon's knife." Everywhere, whether in the profession or among adolescents, the greater a non- or half-understood subject like this is felt to be, the more rankly fads and extreme and special theories and practises arise and flourish for a season. This phenomenon of *fides quaerens intellectus* is nowhere so well illustrated as in every aspect of sex, and is itself a most tempting psychological theme.

But my point here is one I have nowhere seen stated, viz., that menstruation now forces a most challenging set of questions, conscious and unconscious, upon the girl's mind, that of themselves constitute a great strain and demand for some time a good share of all her power of mentation. Because her puberty is shorter and its manifestation more ostensive and the function now born more central for her life than for the boy, this psychic incubation is more important if she would emerge into full womanhood unscathed. Perhaps to this we must add another unnoticed factor, viz., fully assimilated knowledge that immediately becomes a part of life is strength, but that which is undigested and not transformed into carrying power, but is a burden to be carried in memory, is an added cause of tension and fatigue. It devitalizes, augments worry, and if there is no introspection may be permanently de-educational. Because girls accept with more patience than boys learning that is merely conventional, they are especially exposed at this period of conformity to harm by pedagogic fooleries that have only a factitious school value, and to be victimized by spurious mental interests just when real ones would steady them, in their time of greatest danger from emotional instability. Vital and normal intellectual work and zest has a power already manifestly hygienic, but with possibilities in this direction needing, and therefore certain of, great further development. That concessions are progressively, if unconsciously, made with the increasing feminization of American schools is seen, happily for the girls but unhappily for the boys, in both the matter, method, and quantity of work.

Savagery has great advantage even over modern educational life in that it everywhere recognizes the need of seclusion. The tepee, or booth, or grot, so commonly set apart for menstruant girls, often purposely built so low that they can not stand but are forced to sit or lie down, suggests so far sound ideas of health, although other requirements are often deleterious. In many ancient civilizations withdrawal was divinely ordained and enforced by penalties. False as was the idea of uncleanness or contamination, in practise it wrought good. While of all influences right muscular exercise can best smooth out this wave, even it must cease for a time at the onset of puberty when the organism first enacts the minimized pantomime of parturition, as children rehearse in play with toys and dolls the serious business of life. This system at least did not turn out either the hectic or the faded fraud that once was proud of semi-invalidism as a delicacy that was thought to be interesting, and later cultivated the Grecian bend, which is its instinctive posture, and now is content with a nervous sprightliness and vivacity as if restlessness were brilliancy.[1]

Instead of shame of this function girls should be taught the greatest reverence for it, and should help it to normality by regularly stepping aside at stated times for a few years till it is well established and normal. To higher beings that looked down upon human life as we do upon flowers, these would be the most interesting and beautiful hours of blossoming. With more self-knowledge woman will have most self-respect at this time. Savagery reveres this state and it gives to woman a mystic awe. That after the almost universal pubescent initial seclusion practised among primitive people it is so commonly ignored, is perhaps one cause of tribal arrest or decline. Civilization differentiates the sexes in nearly every respect. The time may come when we must even change the divisions of the year for woman, leaving to man his week and giving to her the same number of Sabbaths per year, but in groups of four successive days per month. But Sabbaths they should remain —days, superior to others, devoted to leisure, to higher over-thoughts, religious sentiments and suggestive of a lost paradise, the idea of a more precise expression of her nature and needs at this time than the weekly cycle man accepted for his norm from his God and has imposed on woman. When woman asserts her true physiological rights she will begin here, and will glory in what, in an age of ignorance and sense, man made her think to be her shame. The pathos about the leaders of woman's so-called emancipation is that they, even more than those they would persuade, accept man's estimate of this state, disapprove, minimize, and perhaps would eliminate if they could the very best thing in their nature. In so doing it is the feminists, who

---

[1] See Engelmann: The Health of the American Girl, Trans. of So. Surgical and Gynecological Association, 1890. Hatfield: Dynamics of School Puberty, Jour. of Am. Med. Ass'n, November, 1899. L. Meyer: Der Menstruations Process, Stuttgart, 1890. R. H. Smith: Preventive Gynecology, Am. Jour. of Obstetrics, May, 1900. Schaeffer: Einfluss der Psychosen auf den Menstruations Vorgang, Allg. Zeitsch. f. Psychiatrie, 1893, p. 976 *et seq.* Axel-Key: Die Pubertäts Entwickelung, Verhandl. d. Internat. med. Cong., Berlin, 1890, p. 67.

are still apishly servile to man even in one of his greatest mistakes, which has done woman most wrong. She will not profane her own Sabbath of biological ordination, but will keep it holy as to the Lord, for he has hallowed it as a day of blessing from on high. Those interested in Sabbath psychology and pedagogy can find no better suggestions for its right keeping than those written in the language of woman's needs. This is one of the several reasons why she is more religious by nature than man, because at these seasons her frame of mind inclines her to a natural piety and sense of dependence and of being an organism in the hands of a higher power. Details for its better observance, attitudes and exercises of soul make a suggestive theme for noble women, who are emancipated from the man-aping fashion now just beginning to wane, and will no doubt sometime be wrought out. It will not be a Lord's day of Puritan severity or of ancient taboos, but of joy and pride, and those first rightly initiated into its observance will learn to look forward to its recurrence with pleasure, and later in life will look back to the months and years of their novitiate and all its glow of idealism and aspiration somewhat as Jehovah's people remembered the precious promises of old.

CHAPTER VIII

ADOLESCENCE IN LITERATURE, BIOGRAPHY, AND HISTORY

I. Plato's boys—Neoptolemus and Telemachus—Aristotle's description of youth. II. The disciples of Jesus—Youth of the saints—The age of chivalry. III. General characterization and results of the study of description of youth in biography and literature. IV. Men of Science V. Literary women. VI. Difference between the accounts given of their adolescence by men and women—Literary men: English, American, German, and French.

ROMANCE, poetry, and biography furnish many admirable descriptions of the psychic states and changes characteristic of every stage of the ephebic transformation, and now, before passing to a more detailed account of its normal aspects, it may be well to pause and consider a few silhouettes of representative types, beginning with the Greeks, whose athletic ideals and regimen of it were described in Chapter III. These cases, like returns to *questionnaires*, are in part either data or illustrations for some of the conclusions of later chapters in which they are often cited.

I. The Platonic dialogues are among the best of all literary sources for the study of the pedagogy of adolescence. After many years of teaching them and reading Jowett in seminary classes, it is ever clearer to me that some of the best of them owe much of their charm to the noble love of adolescent boys. At most of the dialogues one or more of them were present, and Socrates found much of his inspiration in them. In the Laws, where only old men appear, in the Timæus, the Cratylus, the Crito, and perhaps the Critias alone, among the authentic dialogues and in the lesser Hippias, it appears that no youth were present, and most of these, especially the longer of them, by general consent are the most uninteresting, if not tedious, to modern taste. Of the twenty-seven dialogues, which Jowett accepts, with about one hundred and ten characters, twelve or fourteen are obviously adolescents, although not all of them stand out very clearly.

Charmides is perhaps the most glorious of all Plato's boys. He appears in the Palæstra, where the dialogue which bears his name is held, drawn to the conversation of the sages concerning temperance. His friend and lover, Chærephon, a crazy-brained, impetuous young man, had pronounced him the reigning beauty of the day, whom all his companions loved, and he was always followed by a train of admirers. "There was not one, not even the smallest, who looked in any other direction; all gazed upon him as upon some sacred statue." He was said to be yet fairer in form than in face. There was a flutter when he entered, and all made place to have him sit beside them. "All the world seemed enamored of him, and amazement and confusion reigned when he entered." His soul was found to be as beauteous as his body, so that he best illustrates the Greek ideal of a fair soul in a fair body. As Socrates delicately proceeds to strip and cure his soul by conversing with him on temperance, the chief Greek virtue, he appears an almost ideal illustration of this also.

Lysis seems, with his shyness, impulsiveness, and artless candor, his insatiable eagerness to hear more, perhaps the youngest of Plato's boys. He, too, is of noble birth, and is found in the Palæstra with his pugnacious friend, Menexenus, and his praiser and idolizer, Hippothales. Among his mates, all in festive array, having just offered sacrifice and playing at knuckle-bones, Lysis, with a chaplet on his head, was preeminent among all the rest for beauty of form and grace of action. Socrates, with characteristic sympathy, easily engages him in conversation. Your parents love you and want you to be happy, but do they gratify all your wishes? When he replies No, that even his father's hirelings can drive the horses which he can not, Socrates expresses surprise, but leads on to the truth that men are trusted in things they know. The dialogue on the nature of friendship is given added zest by the concealed presence of Lysis's unwelcome lover.

Cleinias in the Euthydemus is a youth exposed to the rough horse-play of the eristic sluggers, who teach wisdom and also fighting in heavy armor, until Socrates must repeatedly come to his rescue and give him encouragement. He is a lad of illustrious name, in whose future all Athens felt a deep interest. Socrates seeks to relieve him from his painful bewilderment that he may form sound opinions and no longer need the Sophists or any one to teach him, and finally leads up to the conclusion that as wisdom is the only good he must become a lover of it or a philosopher. " That I will," concludes Cleinias.

These " figures upon whom our attention centers belong to the flower of Athenian youth, and bear that stamp of breeding which seems to have been a birthright of noble parentage, which goes far to justify the aristocratic predilections of Plato. Free from concern as to their own reputation, they have no thought of concealing the ' wonder,' which Socrates prizes as an ' affection peculiar to the philosophical mind.' All alike display a charming simplicity and genuineness, which are the more remarkable because of the admiration lavished upon them by young and old. It speaks well for healthfulness and symmetry of Hellenic influence that a universal adoration, partaking almost of a religious character, has imparted to them no trace of vanity or self-consciousness, the taint of which must have inevitably diminished their zeal in the pursuit of truth."

Meno is another golden youth, highly sophisticated, charged to overflowing with the finished definition philosophy of the nihilistic Gorgias, whose sophistic half-knowledge Socrates so well exposes, who is so examined as to show the fallacy of this tendency of thought, and is almost tenderly taught that virtue can be imparted by no such method. At first Meno has no idea of any general conception of virtue, but only of that of a man, or woman, of every age and state. Then he conceives it as delighting in things honorable with the power to get them. When this definition is upset, he complains that Socrates acts on his mind like a torpedo shock. To others he can talk well of virtue, but in his presence he is perplexed. Every soul has a germ of latent knowledge, and from one of Meno's slaves, also a boy, the Pythagorean theorem is elicited and the doctrine of the preexistence of the soul inferred therefrom. In this sense virtue is teachable, but alas! there are no teachers. The character of Meno has little to do with the Meno of history. He is a spoiled child of fortune, eager to learn from any one, and Socrates's cross-examination, which is half playful, shows forth the shortcomings of his teachers who had neglected dialectics.

Ion, the rhapsode, who had just won the first prize for his

impassioned recitations of Homer, is also a youth, and his discussion with Socrates on inspiration and sacred madness, in which his teacher reaches the well-known conclusion that poets are sacred persons who should be treated with respect, but are touched with madness and should not be tolerated in a well-ordered state, must also have acted as a shock upon this elocutionist's transparent childlike enthusiasm. His assumption that by being always in the good company of Homer, to whom his skill was restricted, brightening up when he is mentioned and growing sleepy when others are discussed, he participated more or less in the creative power of his author, and could even judge of war, medicine, and prophecy, as well as experts, falls prostrate. It would be interesting to know the sequel of this shock.

Polus is an impetuous youth, a runaway colt, bad-mannered, violent, angry at first, having never heard the other side, fascinated and astounded by the rhetoric of his master and ready to maintain his position against the world. As Socrates develops the view that rhetoric is flattery; is a "shadow of a part of politics"; the evil-doers are more miserable if they escape than if they suffer penalty, Polus laughs outright, but early in the dialogue he heeded Socrates's injunction to be less prolix, and almost seems to acquiesce in the end that it is better to suffer than to do injustice.

Philebus, confused as youth so often is concerning the relation of pleasure to goodness and wisdom, and his friend, Protarchus, the noble son of Callias, inspire one of the best expositions of this favorite Socratic topic. Philebus, who had been his teacher and perhaps his lover, had left him still a partizan of pleasure, but had not taught him that pleasure, like color, is both one and many. The problem of pleasure, always a burning one with youth, is implicated with that of the infinite and the finite, the one and the many; and its ethical nature and the relations to knowledge and to the good are taught in a way suggestive to modern pedagogical methods in college philosophy.

The most radiant and conscious boy beauty of all the more or less juvenile interlocutors of Socrates was Alcibiades, who first appears in the brief and doubtful dialogue bearing his name. Here he is very young and about to enter public life, and would persuade the people, but of what and to what end? Socrates leads him to say that he would seek justice rather than wealth or power. Only the virtuous deserve freedom. "Are you free?" and he replies, "I feel that I am not, but I hope, Socrates, that by your aid I may become free, and from this day forward I will never leave you." We have another glimpse of this favorite in the Protagoras, where we are told his beard is just appearing. In the Symposium he seems in the early twenties, and intrudes intoxicated and with his followers into the assemblage, lawless, a lion's whelp, but already known as one of the ablest and most gifted of all Greeks. He tells of his vain effort to ensnare Socrates, the Silenus-faced master of dialectics, by his homosexual blandishments, and then proceeds to the most brilliant eulogy of his character. Here his own traits are well set off by those of the other fair youth, Agathon, whose encomium on love is an almost dithyrambic praise of the gods for his gifts.

In the Republic, Polimarchus, who appears in the early part of the dialogue, is a frank, impetuous youth, who would detain Socrates by force and compel him to tell him what he knows about women and children. Like his father, Cephalus, he is "limited in his point of view and represents the proverbial stage of morality, which has rules of life rather than principles." He has not felt the charm of the Sophists, and is so confused by Socrates that he hardly knows what he says. In the Protagoras, the most dramatic of the dialogues, Hippocrates, with youthful ardor, pounds upon Socrates's door before dawn to make the momentous announcement that Protagoras the Great is in town at the house of Callias. Socrates knew his "courageous madness," and could hardly restain him from almost making an assault upon the great sophister to relieve him of some of his wisdom. At first the youth is fascinated by being told that he will be made an ever better and wiser man, but perpends as his hero is entangled in the meshes of Socrates, and as his unfitness to train the flower of Athenian youth and to receive their pay is exposed. In the Statesman, an unknown or fictitious "Young Socrates" is a somewhat wooden responder throughout. In the Parmenides, Socrates himself appears to be rather young and attacks the paradoxes of Zeno with great subtlety. Phaedo, in the dialogue of that name, although he is a beloved disciple and says nothing, is evidently young as is the madman, Apollodorus, who is emotional and whose grief is violent. In the Phaedrus, Isocrates is still young and full of promise. They are in the country, and fittingly end the discussion of the relation of rhetoric to dialectics, with a prayer to Pan for inner beauty of soul. Euthryphro, the religionist and definer of piety as doing as he does or doing what is dear to the gods, is thought by some to be a youth.

Theætetus is an adolescent Socrates of unattractive exterior, and who might be described as that weird English poet, Francis Thompson, speaks of a plain but gifted lady, whose countenance one could not see for her soul. He is introduced to us as striving to accomplish the Hercules labor of passing from mathematics to metaphysics, and seeking, like some ingenuous academic students of our day, to make an Hegelian voyage of discovery to find out what knowledge really is. Socrates can hardly treat seriously the callow but earnest poetic passion of his ephebic ectype. With characteristic irony he is drawn out and lured on, each crude definition being welcomed with a gratitude sometimes effusive, till on second thought the inevitable little scruple arises which shows its inanity. When told that knowledge is sense perception, the master reflects that a tadpole, a pig, or a dog-faced baboon may then have true knowledge; and when at last true opinion rightly defined is proposed as the best description of it, doubts thicken as the thought-midwife perpends, till the pupil is told that there is no escape from the domain of the god of flux and Herakleitic motion, and that his mind will be the better for being rid of the embryo ideas of which it has just been delivered, and that they are of no value, but should be exposed like monstrous births. The end of the prolonged dialectics of the Theætetus, like that of the other dialogues of search, is negative and almost collapsing, and the moral is an at least tentative but most tonic confession of nescience. He appears again in the Sophist, but is no longer young.

Although Socrates abhors every form of afflatus, he is strangely drawn toward ingenuous boyhood, as if by its very *naïveté*. It is perhaps precisely because he would despoil them of their unconsciousness and elevate their mental impulses to the plane of reason. In a land and age of unnatural lust, he passionately strove to seduce youth only to wisdom and to discourse solely of high themes, striving to do and suffer nothing base, knowing that to love boys is the key to their education. Their presence and the duty of adults to inspire and set noble examples turn the discourse to high thoughts and glorious deeds. While he felt it his mission to give no information but only to kindle latent genius and turn the soul toward truth, his amplest theme, and that perhaps wherein his thoughts ran deepest, was that in which youth has a strange zest—love. All who strive are lovers; and the only true love is of knowledge and virtue and the deathless beautiful-good, which is so impersonal and pure that wisdom-love is a kind of dying. And yet it was precisely the charge of corrupting youth which seems to have had great, if not chief, weight in his condemnation. In the Apology, he exhorts the Athenians to trouble his sons as he has troubled them, if they prefer riches to virtue, or think themselves something when they are nothing. He was commissioned by the oracle to find a wiser man than he, and therefore had to expose pretended wisdom, and was obliged to meet the "stock accusation" of free-thinking and atheism, when all others failed. But, as represented in Plato, he has always remained an ideal teacher of philosophy to the adolescent mind. It should also be added that the Platonic myths are pedagogic masterpieces, precisely suited to this stage of psychic development when sentiment is three-fourths of life, and symbolism and parable are perhaps chief among the methods of reason. Altogether Plato presents most of the chief types of ephebic perplexity and the elucidation of each, as if he considered it one of his chief missions to be a true intellectual midwife, presiding over the new birth of the soul. Those who best know Plato will most fully realize how far inferior our own age still is in understanding the real nature of youth and in the development of the right means of ministering to its needs. Greek superiority in this respect may have been largely due to the fact that the race and age represented a more youthful stage of development than does our own. Could Socrates and Plato but come again to the philosophical classes of our modern colleges and universities, would they find us modern teachers of wisdom anything more than modern Sophists? and if not, as I often fear, what would their great insight into the mental and moral nature and needs of adolescent mind and life suggest as the same reform they wrought, put into the language of our modern life and needs?

Neoptolemus is, in the opinion of Professor Gildersleeve, next to Telemachus, the most interesting of the Greek characterizations of youth, "not only young, but young for his years."

Sophocles introduces this son of Achilles as the tool of Ulysses in beguiling Philoctetes to leave his lonely island of Lemnos, where he had passed nine weary years in pain from his gangrene wound, and bring with him the wondrous bows and arrows bequeathed him by Hector, for an oracle had revealed that Troy could never fall but by the bow of Hercules and with the aid of a son of Achilles. Neoptolemus was a mere boy in far-off Phthiotis when the hero was deserted, and so was guileless of this treachery. Ulysses lands with him; explores the double-mouthed cave, keeping himself in the background for fear of the poisoned arrows and sending Neoptolemus ahead, who finds the bed of leaves, the rags for dressing the wounded foot, and only at the last moment, when it is too late to withdraw, the man of many wiles explains to the youth his rôle. He must pretend to have been deprived of the arms of his father, Achilles, by Ulysses, upon whom he must heap reproach, and state that, stung by insult, he is on the way home and will give Philoctetes a safe passage to his own land. The youth at first revolts at this treachery, which even in word he loathed to hear, for his nature was not made for crooked guile, although for the great end of conquering Troy he would take the man by force. Failure is better than a foul success. Thus he is "gallant, impetuous, open, chivalrous, the true son of the ideal knight of Greek romance," who detested "as the gates of hell" one who dared think one thing and say another. At last, however, the plausible Ulysses wins against the better feelings of his comrade, as if their end would sanctify any means. When Philoctetes approached painfully, Neoptolemus acts the rôle ascribed him and tells his tale and reports the news of Troy. He begs to be taken home; Neoptolemus does the by-play of hesitation, and at last pretends reluctant assent. Other messengers from Ulysses arise and seek to hurry them, representing that Neoptolemus is pursued, and as they approach the ship Philoctetes has one of his paroxysms of agony, begs his friend to smite off his limb, and bids him hold his bow and arrows during the slumber that must follow such pain, and into which, like a death-trance, the sufferer soon sinks. Before he awakes, the better nature of Neoptolemus has conquered. The interest in the Greek cause and his personal renown, prophesied in the capture of Troy, are weighed in the balance and found wanting, and he confesses his abominable rôle and how noisome and base he has been by deserting his own true self. At first he would not give back the weapons, however, and when he makes a motion to restore the bow Ulysses intervenes. At last Neoptolemus makes up his mind to "do the right, come what may." The glory of taking Troy will be bought at too high a price if self-respect is lost. He braves Ulysses with his sword; gives Philoctetes back his weapons; and only the intervention of Hercules in the air saves the life of Ulysses. This struggle between interest and duty constitutes the tragic interest in the drama, and in the sequel, in the glory of his father's armor, it is this pyrrhic or red-haired youth who leads the Greeks to the storm and sack of the city by night, while the Trojans slept or held council. The last glimpse of the young hero appears in the Andromache of Euripides, where the Argive prince is put out of the way for coveting Hermione.

Perhaps the fullest portrayal of adolescence in which Greek life and Greek ideals are symmetrically mingled is that of Telemachus, the only son of Ulysses, to whom a large part of the first four books of the Odyssey is devoted.

He is represented as a rather tame, home-staying, and affectionate son, who had to have strength put into his heart by a visit of Minerva, who roused him from his perhaps Hamlet-like musings by the hearthstone of his mother, Penelope, as to whether his father would return and take vengeance on the insolent suitors. The young prince, stirred by this visit of divine wisdom, awoke to his responsibilities, took his place again among the revelers, a changed man, reminded his mother that the loom and distaff were woman's kingdom and that his father's place now belonged to him, and warned the suitors to leave. In the council of the rulers the next day his mien showed forth a new majesty in contrast with his former supineness. He appealed to the gods for vengeance, but when mocked wandered to the seashore, prayed his guardian goddess to show him forth the true son of his father, and was helped by her on his voyage to find him to the consternation of the suitors at his bold step, to the grief of his mother, now twice bereaved, and the dismay of his old nurse, Euryclcia.

Fénelon amplifies the story of his search for his father in his well-known tale, which has for some generations been a standard text-book in French, especially for young ladies, and which is a kind of Wilhelm Meister or typical adolescent experience for a prince in classical times. Perhaps no work even of antiquity describes with such detail and fidelity to nature the stirrings of youthful impulses and their masterly guidance by Mentor. Fénelon drew richly upon all the resources of Greek culture. His hero, by the aid of his guide, resists the wiles of Calypso, and even his passion for her nymph, Eucharis, is controlled. He becomes a slave in Ethiopia, but compels the love and admiration of all about him, even of his cruel master. He is urgently offered the crown of Crete, establishes a new government at Salentum, seeks Ulysses through the dreary realms of Tartarus, falls in love with Antiope, whom he rescues from a wild boar, teaches good government to a reprobate prince, is always wisely counseled, and at last, just before meeting his father, is given final parting counsel by Mentor, who now bids him farewell, assuring him that his apprenticeship to life is complete and he must now guide his own actions. Homer completes the tale in the seventh book with his return from Sparta to Ithaca. When his father's rags fell off and royal robes took their place and he was at last convinced of his identity, the suitors planned vengeance, and while Ulysses plied his wondrous bow Telemachus by his side dealt death to them with his spear.

Aristotle has given the best ancient characterization of youth. He says:

The young are in character prone to desire and ready to carry any desire they may have formed into action. Of bodily desires it is the sexual to which they are most disposed to give way, and in regard to sexual desire they exercise no self-restraint. They are changeful, too, and fickle in their desires, which are as transitory as they are vehement; for their wishes are keen without being permanent, like a sick man's fits of hunger and thirst. They are passionate, irascible, and apt to be carried away by their impulses. They are the slaves, too, of their passion, as their ambition prevents their ever brooking a slight and renders them indignant at the mere idea of enduring an injury. And while they are fond of honor, they are fonder still of victory; for superiority is the object of youthful desire, and victory is a species of superiority. Again, they are fonder both of honor and of victory than of money, the reason why they care so little for money being that they have never yet had experience of want, as the saying of Pittacus about Amphiaraus puts it. They are charitable rather than the reverse, as they have never yet been witnesses of many villainies; and they are trustful, as they have not yet been often deceived. They are sanguine, too, for the young are heated by Nature as drunken men by wine, not to say that they have not yet experienced frequent failures. Their lives are lived principally in hope, as hope is of the future and memory of the past; and while the future of youth is long, its past is short; for on the first day of life it is impossible to remember anything, but all things must be matters of hope. For the same reason they are easily deceived, as being quick to hope. They are inclined to be valorous, for they are full of passion, which excludes fear, and of hope, which inspires confidence, as anger is incompatible with fear, and the hope of something good is itself a source of confidence. They are bashful, too, having as yet no independent standard of honor and having lived entirely in the school of conventional law. They have high aspirations; for they have never yet been humiliated by the experience of life, but are unacquainted with the limiting force of circumstances; and a great idea of one's own deserts, such as is characteristic of a sanguine disposition, is itself a form of high aspiration. Again, in their actions they prefer honor to expediency, as it is habit rather than calculation which is the rule of their lives, and, while calculation pays regard to expediency, virtue pays regard exclusively to honor. Youth is the age when people are most devoted to their friends or relations or companions, as they are then extremely fond of social intercourse and have not yet learned to judge their friends, or indeed anything else, by the rule of expediency. If the young commit a fault, it is always on the side of excess and exaggeration in defiance of Chilon's maxim (μηδὲν ἄγαν); for they carry everything too far, whether it be their love or hatred or anything else. They regard themselves as omniscient and are positive in their assertions; this is, in fact, the reason of their carrying everything too far. Also their offenses take the line of insolence and not of meanness. They are compassionate from supposing all people to be virtuous, or at least better than they really are; for as they estimate their neighbors by their own guilelessness, they regard the evils which befall them as undeserved. Finally, they are fond of laughter and consequently facetious, facetiousness being disciplined insolence.[1]

II. Keim, who has written one of the most comprehensive and scholarly of all the lives of Jesus, thinks that many, if not most, of his disciples, when he chose them, were adolescents. He says:

Though some of the disciples, as well as of the women, may have been married, yet an age of not much more than twenty years is plainly indicated in the case of the four first called, notably of the sons of Zebedee, and also of James the younger, of the youth in Judæa and Gethsemane, nay, indeed, of most of them, for they are represented as coming directly from the houses of their parents, and Jesus cautions them against preferring their parents to their Teacher, against jealous fancies and ebullitions of temper, and administers to them truly paternal censures. Just such an attitude was assumed by the Scribes toward "the young"; and thus might Jesus hope—as did Luther in more modern times—to win the old and to tear up the deeply rooted Pharisaic bondage, by means of the fresh and vigorous youths whom Judaism itself looked upon as the guard of the coming Messiah. He might also hope to find in youth the next neighbor to that innocent and humble childlikeness to which he could promise and give the kingdom of heaven.[2]

---

[1] Welldon: Rhetoric of Aristotle. New York, 1886, pp. 164–166.

[2] Keim, Theodor: The History of Jesus of Nazara. Translated by Arthur Ransom. London, 1877, vol. iii, p. 279.

A radically different type and ideal of adolescence arose in the early Christian Church and persisted for centuries. The mental life was in many ways narrowed and impoverished by the intense struggles for purity of body and soul which the new religion had inspired. Instead of the harmony between them that pervaded Greek thought, soul and body were now violently sundered, and asceticism assumed that the transient life of the body must be subordinated to the eternal life of the spirit, and mortification of the flesh, visions, and ecstatic communion with the divine were the ideals. The most precious and abundant data for illustrating this new attitude are fortunately at hand.

The first two volumes of the Acta Sanctorum, or Lives of the Saints, by the Bollandists or Jesuit editors, appeared in 1643. Each contained twelve hundred pages in close print and double columns, and both were devoted to the Saints of January. Seven folios were devoted to May, eight to September, and ten to October. Fifty-seven volumes had appeared in 1861. The new Belgian edition, finished in 1875, contained sixty-one folio volumes. Baring-Gould has selected about thirty-six hundred lives, mainly but not entirely from this source, and presented them to us in twelve volumes, one for each month.[1] He has eliminated many of the most improbable incidents. The various calendars and martyrologies and modes of apotheosis have all been considered, but are not fully treated by the English editor. Indeed, comparatively few saints have received formal canonization at Rome itself.

Although the historical character of the records may be questioned, in detail, they show how strong were the motives that impelled young men and women of all stations to take religious vows and enter upon lives of sanctity. Hence, monotonous as these lives seem to a persevering reader, they are a precious thesaurus of data showing the profound impression which the medieval Church made upon the heart and mind of youth. Some intimation of this may be given by a list of names and incidents, as copious as our limits permit, taken almost at random to be the more representative.

---

[1] The Lives of the Saints, by S. Baring-Gould. Third edition, 1877.

Theckla, so romantically enamored of St. Paul in the apocryphal Acts of Paul and Theckla, was seventeen or eighteen.

St. Martian (A. D. 300) at eigtheen retired to a mountain near Cæsarea, where he lived for twenty-five years among holy solitaries, resisting incredible temptations, especially from women.

St. Agnes (303) was but thirteen, Augustine says, when she died, a martyr of purity and chastity. Rich and beauteous, she repulsed her lovers and overcame temptations.

St. Julian (310), of noble birth but precocious piety, when called to marry at eighteen refused for love of the devout life, but being compelled, chose Basilissa, and they kept together for life the vows of purity made in the nuptial chamber, with a supernatural odor of flowers although in midwinter.

St. Antony (356), of noble birth, well reared and exclusive, longed to dwell simply, being content to understand the blessed Word. At eighteen, meditating on the way to church how the Apostles had left all, he heard, "If thou wilt be perfect, go and sell that thou hast," etc. This he did and made himself poor, taking no thought for the morrow, praying continually, and observing that if any man will not work neither shall he eat.

St. Hilarion (died 371) was reared among idolatrous Romans and well trained in grammar and rhetoric. He early turned from the madness of the circus, the blood of the arena, and the luxury of the theater, and was filled with longing to visit St. Antony in the desert. As soon as he saw him he changed his dress and the order of his life, became prayerful and humble, and returning gave away all he had. "Naked, but armed in Christ," he entered the desert at the age of fifteen and rejoiced in the terrible solitude and hardships, so that the devil who tempted his senses and tried to wear him out with hunger and thirst, cold, and horrid dreams of beasts and women, was himself finally tormented by finding that he was conquered by a boy, who at sixteen built a little cell, 4 × 5, not unlike a tomb, which is still shown.

St. Ephraem the Syrian (378) was a wild boy and indulged in various escapades, but at eighteen felt remorse, was baptized, and began to discipline his body and soul with great severity, fasting and lying on the bare ground all night in prayer.

St. Artemas was in a heathen school, but his heart was full of faith. When the master threatened, he defied, until his schoolmates stabbed him to death with the iron pens used on their wax tablets.

St. Martin of Tours (401) was attracted in boyhood to a monastic life, though his parents were heathen. His father enrolled him in the army at fifteen. Here in the Roman camp he learned faithfulness and hardihood. At eighteen, one bitter winter's day, he saw a beggar naked, and cut his mantle in two and gave him half; but the next night he saw a vision of Jesus Christ on his throne, surrounded by a host of heaven, wearing his half mantle. Now his poor beadsmen wear as their livery a mantle half red and half white.

St. John Chrysostom (407) was carefully trained by his pious mother, and only her gentle influence restrained him from becoming a monk till she died, when he entered a cave till his health failed, and then he became a preacher.

St. Euphrasia (410) became austere at twelve and refused marriage, but her "youthful spirits and passions were in effervescence and she was cruelly tormented with vain imaginations and temptations"; humiliated herself by obedience to degrading commands, and gave away her property to the poor. Unlike many saints, she was denied martyrdom, but had special power of working miracles.

St. Euphrosyne (470) at twelve was taught by her father, and the fame of her good sense and beauty was wide-spread. At eighteen, visiting a monastery, "her heart began to be solicitous in the fear of God," and she soon had her head shorn and entered upon the devout life.

St. Benedict (543), of illustrious birth, was scarcely fourteen when he renounced fortune, family, and worldly joy, plunged into wild gorges over savage hills, put on monastic habit of skin, and took up his abode in a dark and inaccessible cave, drawing up each day with a cord, when warned by a bell, the loaf which a friend provided. Here he lived three years, and when shepherds found him was thought a wild beast till he instilled grace into their rustic souls. He was strongly tempted to voluptuousness, but stripping himself naked rolled in a clump of thorns and briers "till his body was all one wound, but also till he had extinguished forever the eternal fire which inflamed him even in the desert."

St. Kentigern's (601) childhood abounds in legends. Robins perched upon his head and twittered as he chanted the songs of David, and when killed, revived when he made the sign of the cross over them. He early betook himself to a cave.

St. Columbanus (615) was well trained in the classics, but early resolved on the ascetic. Dreadful were his struggles to forget the pretty faces, bright eyes, and winning ways of the Irish girls, which were a great snare to his studies, so that he finally decided to fly from them to solitude, though to do so he had to step over the prostrate body of his weeping mother.

St. Walaric (619), among the volcanic caves of Auvergne, learned letters from a psalter while pasturing his sheep. His cravings to know more of the Great Shepherd gave him no rest, and he fled to a monastery, carrying with him "the freshness of his mountain air, the sweetness of his thyme, and became a paragon of modesty, sweetness, and gentleness."

St. Isidore (636), with the exquisite sensitiveness of youth, one day when he had run away from school saw where the dropping water had worn a stone, and the sight was to him what the Bow-Bells were later to Whittington. Dull as he was, with diligence he became an accomplished scholar. These drops were God's messengers and gave to Spain an historian, and to the Church a doctor.

St. Cuthbert (687) was a shepherd-boy of rare vigor and boldness, but prayerful and clearly a visionary. At fifteen he had begun his career as a knight attended by a squire, and when he entered the cloister showed rare aptitude for cenobitic life, surpassing all others in study, prayer, vigil, and labor, traveling and preaching far and near.

St. Werburga (eighth century), well reared and preferring Church offices to the giddy whirl of pleasure, early resolved to devote herself to virginal purity. Her beauty drew crowds of suitors, wealthy and famous, but all her affections were weaned from earthly things and fixed on God.

St. Notker Balbulus (912) stammered, but excelled in music. The school songs at St. Gall had grown very corrupt, "for Alpine bodies with their thundering voices are not adapted to sweet modulations of tone." His youthful soul was absorbed in the rhythm, cadence, and words of Church music, which he reformed and to which he made great additions.

St. Dunstan (968) had a wondrous dream, when a boy, that he was driving off dogs, and rushed on to the roof of the church and nearly fell. He did not clearly recall it, but was afterward changed. As a page at court, his jealous mates ducked him and set the dogs on him. He fell desperately in love with a beautiful girl and repelled the entreaty of his friends that he should renounce her for the woolen smock of a monk, but soon a violent and irritating eruption impelled him to the Church. After saying the first versicles at Compline, a great stone fell near him, but the devil missed his aim. When he hung his harp near a window, it played faint Æolian music as a presage of his greatness and sanctity.

St. Peter Damiani (1072) as a boy was treated almost like a slave and made a swineherd, but was finally sent to scool. Here, to arm himself against the allurements of the devil, he began to wear a rough hair shirt under his clothes, and when temptations of concupiscence arose, would leave his bed and plunge into the river. He gave to the poor all he had.

St. Anselm (1109) in boyhood felt the common attractions of his age for monastic life. Then came a reaction for pleasure that banished religion and even his early love of study, especially when his Christian mother, who had been a great restraint upon him, died, "the ship of his heart lost its anchor and drifted off altogether into the waves of the world." His father's harshness drove him from home, but finally he followed Lanfranc to Bec, and his remarkable life was lived out as the world knows.

St. Bernard (1153) at the age of twelve had a vision in which his just dead mother urged him to become a monk, but his mind was expanding; the schools of Paris were stimulating; philosophy began to weave its wondrous spell; and it was only after a long struggle that he was able to "quell the fervent straining of his mind for intellectual activity" and condemn it to bondage to the soul, whose welfare alone he resolved to cultivate. So, persuading a brother to desert his young wife, they fled to the desert and cloister.

St. Hildegund (1158) lost her clothes one night and had to put on those of a boy, which she came to retain all her life because of the freedom and protection they afforded her. She was hung and left for dead, but cut down, and had a strange vision. She was page and servant, but studied; received the tonsure; became a novice, and until her death no one knew her sex.

St. Ven (1158) early dedicated her soul and body to God and resisted her parents' efforts to make her marry. At the wedding, when asked if she would take this man, cried out before the whole church that she would not. When force was used and preparations again made, it was found that she had cut off her nose. Thus she had her way.

The austerities of St. Godrick (1170) knew no bounds. He lived on roots, leaves, flowers, and berries, and offered the food his friends brought him in the wilderness to ravens. He watched, fasted, and scourged himself; sat even in winter in the cold waters where he had hollowed a natural bath of a sunk barrel; tilled a scrap of ground and ate his grain mingled with ashes. When asked to tell of his life, he declared he was a "gross rustic, an unclean liver, an usurer, a cheat, a perjurer, a flatterer, a wanderer, pilfering and greedy; now a dead flea, a decayed dog, a vile worm; not a hermit, but a hypocrite; not a solitary, but a gad-about in mind; a devourer of alms, dainty over good things, greedy and negligent, lazy and snoring, ambitious and prodigal, one who is not worthy to serve others, and yet every day beats and scolds those who serve him—this, and worse than this, you may write of Godrick." "Then he was silent as one indignant," says his biographer, "and I went off in some confusion," and the grand old man was left to himself and to his God.

St. Dominic (1221) as a babe would creep from his soft couch to lie on the hard ground; was trained as a student, and at fifteen entered the University of Palencia, but in a famine sold his clothes and then his books to feed the poor, for he said, "How can I pursue dead parchment when breathing men are perishing?" So simple and pure of heart was he that he could find innocent pleasure "in the bright prattle of young girls rather than in the querulous gossip of old women; but the sweet flower of his childlike modesty was never injured, as it never need be, by such associations."

St. Christina the Wonderful (1224) was orphaned at fifteen and fell down in a fit; was laid out and taken on a bier, but in the midst of the funeral jumped from her coffin, ran after the mourners in her winding-sheet, and climbed up a pillar to the roof, where she sat "like a bird." In her trance she had been carried to hell and then to purgatory, where she saw many acquaintances and friends, whom she warned and sought to liberate by doing all the absurd penances by which her friends' souls had found purgation in her vision. She had a hysterical loathing of the scent of mankind, especially of peasants, to avoid which she was wont to climb tree-tops and the summit of church towers, sometimes balancing herself beside the weathercock. She would plunge into fire and scatter brands with her feet; dive under the sluice of a mill-wheel and go through the conduit; would suspend herself dangling between the corpses of criminals on the gibbet; scald herself with hot water; coil herself into a ball and straighten herself out with marvelous flexibility.

St. Francis of Assisi (1226) as a child acquired the French tongue so easily that it seemed a miracle, although he did not speak it correctly. In early youth he was almost miserly; loved eating and drinking and cheerful society; and finally developed a taste for arms, but met a poor warrior vilely clad, to whom he gave his armor, being rewarded by a better one in a dream at night. He fell ill and heard a voice saying, "Francis, whom does it profit most to follow, the master or the servant?" And he replied, "Lord, what wilt Thou have me to do?" He gave up drinking, frolic, music, laughter, and wooed the muse of charity and self-denial.

St. Elizabeth of Hungary (1231) was espoused to Prince Ludwig when she was nine and he fifteen, but she was wretchedly treated by his mother Sophia. At a ceremonial before the crucifix she took off her coronet and knelt weeping in an ecstasy of devotion despite rude reproof. At ten, having thrice drawn St. John by lottery, he was chosen as her patron saint. She dreamed that she was visited by her dead mother. She was long tormented by cruel hints that her prince was tired of her and would never return, although he was true and wedded her when she was fifteen, after which she devoted herself to the poor, giving from her own stock of clothing, miraculously renewed, and for years subject to the influence of an inquisitor, Conrad of Marburg. She died at the age of twenty-four.

St. Edmund (1242), when on his way to school, saw a beautiful boy who greeted him by name, who proved to be the child Jesus, and was told to write this name on his brow with his finger each night and he would be kept from sudden death. Seeing a flock of rooks, he made the sign of the cross and they flew off, and he saw that they were devils waiting to carry off the souls of sinners. In his teens the daughter of his host fell in love with him and stole into his room by night, but he grasped his birch rod and covered her back with purple wheals, which she had to endure, lest if she screamed her parents would find her out.

St. Clara (1253) in the middle teens heard the great Francis, and his voice and enthusiasm thrilled her heart and filled her with the vehemence of love and a passion of devotion that nothing could quench in after years. She had dedicated her life to the mendicants, and when she was eighteen the Bishop's eye rested upon her in the cathedral, modest, bashful, standing back and without a palm, and to the amazement of all he stepped down and handed her one. This was her consecration. She fell on her knees before the barefoot friars; tore off her jewels, brocade, and velvet; bowed her head to the shears and received the coarse gray; and enrolled herself among the champions of poverty. Thus, despite the entreaties of her friends, she persisted in the ascetic life and proceeded to develop her order—The Poor Clares.

St. Peter Nolasco (1256) had an early passion for matin soon after midnight and for charity. At fifteen, orphaned and rich, he began to strengthen in himself the Christian graces. Being urged to marry, he cast himself before the crucifix all night and vowed his patrimony to the Church and himself to celibacy.

St. Juliana (1258) fasted as a child, and when punished by an order to kneel a few minutes in the snow, did so so gladly that it was seen that she was born for a life of austerity. At fourteen, hearing the first strains of the Vexilla Regis, she shook with emotion; tears flowed, and she gave all her wealth and her life in exchange for the veil; and at sixteen began to have visions, and later became a famous Superior.

St. Louis (1270). This hero and ideal of youth, who pushed the virtues of king, hero, and man combined to so high a point, "allying the majesty of the throne with the holiness of the Gospel and the humiliations of penance," succeeded his father at the age of twelve. At fourteen he submitted to a hard tutor, who beat him. His expression was so sweet that none could see him without love. His gentleness, sympathy, passionate love of justice, truth, and honor awakened very early. He observed all fasts; would taste fruit but once a year; wore sackcloth next his skin; submitted to the cruel discipline of wire; walked on pilgrimages with bleeding feet; washed those of beggars; and even bore reproaches with meekness.

St. Ambrose of Sienna (1287) carved little crosses; imitated processions; furnished a room, where he lodged pilgrims; washed their feet; took them to mass; visited hospitals and prisons until the age of seventeen, when he entered the Dominican Order and went to Cologne to study with Albertus Magnus and St. Thomas.

The Blessed Oringa (1310), a peasant girl, so kind that her cows became docile and obeyed her voice in all things, refused marriage; disguised her beauty with walnut juice, took service, and was devoted to ecstasy and prayer.

St. Frances of Rome (1440) from childhood longed for the convent, and when at twelve she learned that her father had promised her hand to a nobleman of great wealth and virtue was overwhelmed with grief and with great difficulty was persuaded by her director to yield. But her husband encouraged and even venerated her sanctity, and her life brought many to the true faith.

St. Colette (1447) at the age of seven yearned for the cloister; made herself a little oratory in the back yard where she spent hours in communion with God, and to this she fled to escape her youthful companions. She always gave her food to the poor, and at twenty-two became a voluntary recluse in an anchorite cell built against the church wall.

St. Catharine (1463) at eleven joined the Order of Poor Clares and entered its convent. Her fervor of soul, gentleness, and obedience, long hours of prayer, cheerfulness, and power to resist temptation were themselves almost miraculous.

The Blessed Veronica (1497) worked in the fields all day and tried to study her primer at night until the first apparition of the Virgin told her to leave study and learn but three letters—white for purity, black for the dead world, and red for meditation on the passion, and thus she advanced on the way of perfection.

St. Francis of Paula (1508), at twelve in a convent, voluntarily denied himself the use of linen and meat; soon withdrew a mile from town to a cave in the face of a rock, where at fifteen he shut himself up with no bed than the rock, and no food but herbs and what his friends sometimes brought. Before he was twenty others had joined him, and the neighbors had built three cells and a chapel, where they sang God's praises, and a priest joined them and a new order was founded. His later history fills an important place.

St. Theresa's (1585) father delighted in books and bought them in Spanish that his children might read. Her mother was an invalid. The children's minds were steeped in the lives of the saints, and they once started for Morocco in the hope of being martyred. When Theresa was twelve her mother died, and with prayers and tears she adopted the Sovereign Virgin to be her mother, who afterward took care of her. She read romance secretly from her father, and much injured her modesty and caused her many hours of prayer by day and night. She was vain of her hair and hands and fond of perfumes. Her chosen friend was flighty and vain. At fourteen she was removed to a convent, where at first she was very unhappy, but soon grew tired of her vanities, confessed often, became beloved though was tempted of the devil. After eighteen months she fell ill and stayed with her uncle, who was very religious. She suffered from fevers and fainting fits, and longed to enter a religious order against her father's will, and at seventeen ran away and did so. At eighteen she became a novice in the Carmelite House of the Incarnation. The change injured her health, and she sought to convert a fallen priest, but soon had a cataleptic fit, which lasted four days, and at one time she was thought dead. She had bitten her tongue, and was full of nervous and hysterical pains. She had a vision of the Lord, who looked angrily at her. She perpetually changed her confessors. After reading Augustine's Confessions, her hysteria took the form of ecstasy and vision, and she at last found a confessor, who told her these raptures came from God, and she must henceforth converse with angels. Once she saw a seraph stab her with a dart whose point burned with fire. She often saw our Lord, gazing at his wondrous beauty and sweetness, as she said, "with his most lovely and divine mouth." Very vividly she saw and described the place the devils had prepared for her. Whenever she saw any one she liked, her instant and consuming desire was that he should give himself to God. She soon began to form her first convent of discalced monks, and in

1582, when she died, had established sixteen of these foundations. Nine months later her body was found "perfect and uncorrupted." Seven years later it was hardly changed save a few parts that had been cut off for relics. Now her dead heart at Avila glows at times with such ardor and devotion as to break a glass ball under which it is preserved. At Naples her scapula, at Paris a lump of her flesh, at Craco two large slices "highly scented," at Rome her right foot, at Lisbon her left arm, at Seville her fingers are venerated.

St. Rose of Lima (1617) was named from her complexion, and so added the name Mary. When playing with her brother, he plastered her long, rich, brown hair with mud, and when she sulked he said, "You little know what a frizzling girl's hairs get in hell-fire if they are vain of them." So, although she was but five, she shaved her head, to the grief and horror of her parents. Later, when in festivals she had to wear wreaths and garlands of flowers, she proceeded to bind thorns into them. When her mother required her to sleep in gloves to make her hands soft, she inserted nettles, till they were blotched and inflamed. When she had a cold and plasters were applied, she would not remove them till the skin fell off. When her fingers were admired, she rubbed them with lime till they were useless for thirty days. She pulled the flocks from her pillows and stuffed them with chips; wore a crown of ninety-nine thorns, as she is represented in art, and was mystically married to the Infant Jesus.

St. Francis of Sales (1622) at the age of eleven implored permission to take the tonsure. At seventeen his conscience awoke and he felt that he was not in a state of grace, and prayed in anguish for six weeks, when at last near death his eye caught sight of the famous prayer of St. Bernard. He vowed chastity, and the clouds lifted and God's favor was shown.

St. Vincent of Paul (1660) was a peasant's child watching sheep and swine, but would secretly climb into an oak to say his prayers. Later he found the hollow of a tree and used it as a cell, and this was the manner of his call.

The knightly ideals and those of secular life generally during the middle ages and later were in striking contrast to all this; in some respects they were like those of the Greeks. Honor was the leading ideal, and muscular development and that of the body were held in high respect; so that the spirit of the age fostered conceptions not unlike those of the Japanese Bushido (Chapter III). Where elements of Christianity were combined with this we have the spirit of the pure chivalry of King Arthur and the Knights of the Round Table, which affords perhaps the very best ideals for youth to be found in history, as we shall see more fully later.

In a very interesting paper, entitled Shakespeare and Adolescence, Dr. M. F. Libby[1] very roughly reckons "seventy-four interesting adolescents among the comedies, forty-six among the tragedies, and nineteen among the histories." He selects "thirty characters who, either on account of direct references to their age, or because of their love-stories, or because they show the emotional and intellectual plasticity of youth, may be regarded as typical adolescents." His list is as follows: Romeo, Juliet, Hamlet, Ophelia, Imogen, Perdita, Arviragus, Guiderius, Palamon, Arcite, Emilia, Ferdinand, Miranda, Isabella, Mariana, Orlando, Rosalind, Biron, Portia, Jessica, Phebe, Katharine, Helena, Viola, Troilus, Cressida, Cassio, Marina, Prince Hal, and Richard of Gloucester. The proof of the youth of these characters, as set forth, is of various kinds, and Libby holds that besides these, the sonnets and poems perhaps show a yet greater, more profound and concentrated knowledge of adolescence. He thinks Venus and Adonis a successful attempt to treat sex in a candid, naive way, if it be read as it was meant, as a catharsis of passion, in which is latent a whole philosophy of art. To some extent he also finds the story of the Passionate Pilgrim "replete with the deepest knowledge of the passions of early adolescence." The series culminates in Sonnet 116, which makes love the sole beacon of humanity. It might be said that it is connected by a straight line with the best teachings of Plato, and that here humanity picked up the clue, lost, save with some Italian poets, in the great interval.

III. In looking over current biographies of well-known modern men who deal with their boyhood, one finds curious extremes. On the one hand are those of which Goethe's is a type, where details are dwelt upon at great length with careful and suggestive philosophic reflections. The development of his own tastes, capacities, and his entire adult consciousness was assumed to be due to the incidents of childhood and youth, and especially the latter stage was to him full of the most serious problems essential to his self-knowledge; and in the story of his life he has exploited all available resources of

[1] Ped. Sem., June, 1901.

this genetic period of storm and stress more fully perhaps than any other writer. At the other extreme, we have writers like Charles Dudley Warner,[1] a self-made man, whose early life was passed on the farm, and who holds his own boyhood there in greater contempt than perhaps any other reputable writer of such reminiscences. All the incidents are treated not only with seriousness, but with a forced drollery and catchy superficiality which reflect unfavorably at almost every point upon the members of his household, who are caricatured; all the precious associations of early life on a New England farm are not only made absurd, but from beginning to end his book has not a scintilla of instruction or suggestion for those that are interested in child life. Aldrich [2] is better, and we have interesting glimpses of the pet horse and monkeys, of his fighting the boy bully, running away, and falling in love with an older girl whose engagement later blighted his life. Howells,[3] White,[4] Mitter,[5] Grahame,[6] Heidi,[7] and Mrs. Burnett,[8] might perhaps represent increasing grades of merit in this field in this respect.

Yoder,[9] in his interesting study of the boyhood of great men, has called attention to the deplorable carelessness of their biographers concerning the facts and influences of their youth. He advocates the great pedagogic influence of biography, and would restore the high appreciation of it felt by the Bolandists, which Comte's positivist calendar, that renamed all the days of the year from three hundred and sixty-five such accounts in 1849, also sought to revive. Yoder selected fifty great modern biographies, autobiographies preferred, for his study. He found a number whose equipment and momentum have been strikingly due to some devoted aunt, and that give many glimpses of the first polarization of genius in the direction in which fame is later achieved. He holds that while the great men excelled in memory, that imagination is perhaps still more a youthful condition of eminence, magnifies the stimulus of poverty, the fact that elder sons become prom-

[1] Being a Boy. [2] Story of a Bad Boy. [3] A Boy's Town.
[4] Court of Boyville. [5] The Spoilt Child. [6] The Golden Age.
[7] Frau Spyri. [8] The One I Knew Best of All.
[9] The Study of the Boyhood of Great Men. Ped. Sem., October, 1894, vol. iii, pp. 134–156.

inent nearly twice as often as younger ones, and raises the question whether too exuberant physical development does not dull genius and talent.

One striking and cardinal fact never to be forgotten in considering its each and every phenomenon and stage is that the experiences of adolescence are extremely transitory and very easily forgotten, so that they are often totally lost to the adult consciousness. Lancaster[1] observes that we are constantly told by adults past thirty that they never had this and that experience, and that those who have had them are abnormal; that they are far more rare than students of childhood assert, etc. He says, " Not a single young person with whom I have had free and open conversation has been free from serious thoughts of suicide," but these are forgotten later. A typical case of many I could gather is that of a lady, not yet in middle life, precise and carefully trained, who, on hearing a lecture on the typical phases of adolescence, declared that she must have been abnormal, for she knew nothing of any of these experiences. Her mother, however, produced her diary, and there she read for the first time since it was written, beginning in the January of her thirteenth year, a long series of resolutions which revealed a course of conduct that brought the color to her face, that she should have found it necessary to pledge not to swear, lie, etc., and which showed conclusively that she had passed through about all the phases described. These phenomena are sometimes very intense and may come late in life, but it is impossible to remember feelings and emotions with definiteness, and these now make up a large part of life. Hence we are prone to look with some incredulity upon the immediate records of the tragic emotions and experiences typical and normal at this time, because development has scored away their traces from the conscious soul.

There is a wall around the town of Boyville, says White,[2] in substance, which is impenetrable when its gates have once shut upon youth. An adult may peer over the wall and try to ape the games inside, but finds it all a mockery and himself

---

[1] The Vanishing Character of Adolescent Experiences. North Western Mo., June, 1898, vol. viii, p. 644.

[2] The Court of Boyville, by William Allen White. New York, 1899. p. 358.

banished among the purblind grown-ups. The town of Boyville was old when Nineveh was a hamlet; it is ruled by ancient laws; has its own rulers and idols; and only the dim, unreal noises of the adult world about it have changed.

In exploring such sources we soon see how few writers have given true pictures of the chief traits of this developmental period, which can rarely be ascertained with accuracy. The adult finds it hard to recall the emotional and instinctive life of the teens which is banished without a trace, save as scattered hints may be gathered from diaries, chance experiences, or the recollections of others. But the best observers see but very little of what goes on in the youthful soul, the development of which is very largely subterranean. Only when the feelings erupt in some surprising way is the process manifest. The best of these sources are autobiographies, and of these only few are full of the details of this stage. Just as in the mythic prehistoric stage of many nations there is a body of legendary matter, which often reappears in somewhat different form, so there is a floating plankton-like mass of tradition and storiology that seems to attach to eminence wherever it emerges and is repeated over and over again, concerning the youth of men who later achieve distinction, which biographers often incorporate and attach to the time, place, and person of their heroes.

As Burnham[1] well intimates, many of the literary characterizations of adolescence are so marked by extravagance, and sometimes even by the struggle for literary effects, that they are not always the best documents, although often based on personal experience. Confessionalism is generally overdrawn, distorted, and especially the pains of this age are represented as too keen. Of George Eliot's types of adolescent character, this may best be seen in Maggie Tulliver, with her enthusiastic self-renunciation, with "her volcanic upheavings of imprisoned passions," with her "wide, hopeless yearning for that something, whatever it was, that was greatest and best on this earth," and in Gwendolen, who, from the moment she caught Deronda's eye, was "totally swayed in feeling and action by the presence of a person of the other sex whom she

[1] The Study of Adolescence. Ped. Sem., vol. i, p. 174 *et seq.*

had never seen before." There was "the resolute action from instinct and the setting at defiance of calculation and reason, the want of any definite desire to marry, while all her conduct tended to promote proposals." Exaggeration, although not the perversions of this age often found in adult characterizations, is a marked trait of the writings of adolescents, whose conduct meanwhile may appear rational, so that this suggests that consciousness may at this stage serve as a harmless vent for tendencies that would otherwise cause great trouble if turned to practical affairs. If Harmodius and Aristogeiton, the adolescent tyrant slayers of Greece, had been theorists, they might have been harmless on the principle that its analysis tends to dissipate emotion.

Lancaster[1] gathered and glanced over a thousand biographies, from which he selected 200 for careful study, choosing them to show different typical directions of activity. Of these, 120 showed a distinct craze for reading in adolescence; 109 became great lovers of nature; 58 wrote poetry; 58 showed a great and sudden development of energy; 55 showed great eagerness for school; 53 devoted themselves for a season to art and music; 53 became very religious; 51 left home in the teens; 51 showed dominant instincts of leadership; 49 had great longings of many kinds; 46 developed scientific tastes; 41 grew very anxious about the future; 34 developed increased keenness of sensation or at least power of observation; in 32 cases health was better; 31 were passionately altruistic; 23 became idealists; 23 showed powers of invention; 17 were devoted to older friends; 15 would reform society; 7 hated school. These, like many other statistics, have only indicative value, as they are based on numbers that are not large enough and upon returns not always complete.

A few typical instances from Lancaster must here suffice. Savonarola was solitary, pondering, meditating, felt profoundly the evils of the world and need of reform, and at twenty-two spent a whole night planning his career. Shelley during these years was unsocial, much alone, fantastic, wan-

[1] Lancaster: The Psychology and Pedagogy of Adolescence. Ped. Sem., July, 1897, vol. v, p. 106.

dered much by moonlight communing with stars and moon, was attached to an older man. Beecher was intoxicated with nature, which he declared afterward to have been the inspiration of his life. George Eliot had a passion for music at thirteen and became a clever pianist. At sixteen she was religious, founded societies for the poor and animals, and had flitting spells of misanthropy. Edison undertook to read the Detroit Free Library through, read fifteen solid feet as the books stand on the shelves, was stopped, and says he has read comparatively little since. Tolstoi found the aspect of things suddenly changed. Nature put on a new appearance. He felt he might commit the most dreadful crimes with no purpose save curiosity and the need of action. The future looked gloomy. He became furiously angry without cause; thought he was lost; hated by everybody, was perhaps not the son of his father, etc. At seventeen he was solitary, musing about immortality, human destiny, feeling death at hand, giving up his studies, fancying himself a great man with new truths for humanity. By and by he took up the old virtuous course of life with fresh power, new resolutions, with the feeling that he had lost much time. He had a deep religious experience at seventeen and wept for joy over his new life. He had a period before twenty when he told desperate lies, for which he could not account, then a passion for music, and later for French novels. Rousseau at this age was discontented, immensely in love, wept often without cause, etc. Keats had a great change at fourteen, wrestling with frequent obscure and profound stirrings of soul, with a sudden hunger for knowledge which consumed his days with fire, and "with passionate longing to drain the cup of experience at a draft." He was "at the morning hour when the whole world turns to gold." "The boy had suddenly become a poet." Chatterton was too proud to eat a gift dinner, though nearly starved, and committed suicide at seventeen for lack of appreciation. John Hunter was dull and hated study, but at twenty his mind awoke as did that of Patrick Henry, who before was a lonely wanderer, sitting idly for hours under the trees. Alexander Murray awoke to life at fifteen and acquired several languages in less than two years. Gifford was distraught for lack of reading, went to sea at thirteen, became a shoemaker, studying algebra late at night, was savagely unsociable, sunk into torpor from which he was roused to do splenetic and vexatious tricks, which alienated his friends. Rittenhouse at fourteen was a plowboy, covering the fences with figures, musing on infinite time and space. Benjamin Thompson was roused to a frenzy for sciences at fifteen; at seventeen walked nine miles daily to attend lectures at Cambridge; and at nineteen married a widow of thirty-three. Franklin had a passion for the sea; at thirteen read poetry all night; wrote verses and sold them on the streets of Boston; doubted everything at fifteen; left home for good at seventeen; started the first public library in Philadelphia before he was twenty-one. Robert Fulton was poor, dreamy, mercurial, devoted to nature, art, and literature. He became a painter of talent, then a poet, and left home at seventeen. Bryant was sickly till fourteen and became permanently well thereafter; was precociously devoted to nature, religion, prayed for poetic genius and wrote Thanatopsis before he was eighteen. Jefferson doted on animals and nature at fourteen, and at seventeen studied fifteen hours a day. Garfield, though living in Ohio, longed for the sea, and ever after this period the sight of a ship gave him a strange thrill. Hawthorne was devoted to the sea and wanted to sail on and on forever and never touch shore again. He would roam through the Maine woods alone; was haunted by the fear that he would die before twenty-five. Peter Cooper left home at seventeen; was passionately altruistic; and at eighteen vowed he would build a place like his New York Institute. Whittier at fourteen found a copy of Burns, which excited him and changed the current of his life. Holmes had a passion for flowers, broke into poetry at fifteen, and had very romantic attachments to certain trees in particular. J. T. Trowbridge learned German, French, and Latin alone before twenty-one; composed poetry at the plow and wrote it out in the evening. Joseph Henry followed a rabbit under the Public Library at Albany, found a hole in the floor that admitted him to the shelves, and, unknown to any one, he read all the fiction the library contained, then turned to physics, astronomy, and chemistry, and developed a passion for the sciences. He was stage-struck, and became a good amateur actor. H. H. Boyesen was thrilled by nature and by the thought that he was a Norseman. He had several hundred pigeons, rabbits, and other pets; loved to be in the woods at night; on leaving home for school was found with his arms around the neck of a calf to which he was saying good-by. Maxwell, at sixteen, had almost a horror of destroying a leaf, flower, or fly. Jahn found growing in his heart, at this age, an inextinguishable feeling for right and wrong—which later he thought the cause of all his inner weal and outer woe. When Nansen was in his teens he spent weeks at a time alone in the forest, full of longings, courage, altruism, wanted to get away from every one and live like Crusoe. T. B. Reed, at twelve and thirteen, had a passion for reading; ran away at seventeen; painted, acted, and wrote poetry. Cartwright, at sixteen, heard voices from the sky saying, "Look above." "Thy sins are forgiven thee." Herbert Spencer became an engineer at seventeen, after one idle year. He never went to school, but was a private pupil of his uncle. Sir James Mackintosh grew fond of history at eleven; fancied he was the Emperor of Constantinople; loved solitude at thirteen; wrote poetry at fourteen; and fell in love at seventeen. Thomas Buxton loved dogs, horses, and literature, and combined these while riding on an old horse. At sixteen he fell in love with an older literary woman, which aroused every latent power to do or die, and thereafter he took all the school prizes. Scott began to like poetry at thirteen. Pascal wrote treatises on conic sections at sixteen and invented his arithmetical machine at nineteen. Nelson went to sea at twelve; commanded a boat in peril at fifteen, which at the same age he left to fight a polar bear. Banks, the botanist, was idle and listless till fourteen, could not travel the road marked out for him; when coming home from bathing, he was struck by the beauty of the flowers and at once began his career. Montcalm and Wolfe both distinguished themselves as leaders in battle at sixteen. Lafayette came to America at nineteen, thrilled by our bold strike for liberty. Gustavus Adolphus declared his own majority at seventeen and was soon famous. Ida Lewis rescued four men in a boat at sixteen. Joan of Arc began at thirteen to have the visions which were the later guide of her life.

Mr. Swift has collected interesting biographical material[1] to show that school work is analytic, while life is synthetic, and how the narrowness of the school enclosure prompts many youth in the wayward age to jump fences and seek new and more alluring pastures. According to school standards, many were dull and indolent, but their nature was too large or their ideals too high to be satisfied with it. Wagner at the Nikolaischule at Leipzig was relegated to the third form, having already attained to the second at Dresden, which so embittered him that he lost all taste for philology and, in his own words, "became lazy and slovenly." Priestley never improved by any systematic course of study. W. H. Gibson was very slow and was rebuked for wasting his time in sketching. James Russell Lowell was reprimanded, at first privately and then publicly, in his sophomore year "for general negligence in themes, forensics, and recitations," and finally suspended in 1838 "on account of continued neglect of his college duties." In early life Goldsmith's teacher thought him the dullest boy she had ever taught. His tutor called him ignorant and stupid. Irving says that a lad "whose passions are not strong enough in youth to mislead him from that path of science which his tutors, and not his inclinations, have chalked out, by four or five years' perseverance, will probably obtain every advantage and honor his college can bestow. I would compare the man whose youth has been thus passed in the tranquility of dispassionate prudence, to liquors that never ferment, and, consequently, continue always muddy." Huxley detested writing till past twenty. His schooling was very brief, and he declared that those set over him "cared about as much for his intellectual and moral welfare as if they were baby farmers." Humphry Davy was faithful but showed no talent in school, having "the reputation of being an idle boy, with a gift for making verses, but with no aptitude for studies of a graver sort." Later in life he considered it fortunate that he was left so much to himself. Byron was so poor a scholar that he only stood at the head of the class when, as was the custom, it was inverted, and the bantering master repeatedly said to him, "Now, George, man, let me see how soon you'll

[1] Standards of Efficiency in School and in Life. Ped. Sem., March, 1903.

be at the foot." Schiller's negligence and lack of alertness called for repeated reproof, and his final school thesis was unsatisfactory. Hegel was a poor scholar, and at the university it was stated "that he was of middling industry and knowledge but especially deficient in philosophy." John Hunter nearly became a cabinetmaker. Lyell had excessive aversion to work. George Combe wondered why he was so inferior to other boys in arithmetic. Heine agreed with the monks that Greek was the invention of the devil. "God knows what misery I suffered with it." He hated French meters, and his teacher vowed he had no soul for poetry. He idled away his time at Bonn, and was "horribly bored" by the "odious, stiff, cut-and-dried tone" of the leathery professors. Humboldt was feeble as a child and "had less facility in his studies than most children." "Until I reached the age of sixteen," he says, "I showed little inclination for scientific pursuits." He was essentially self-taught, and acquired most of his knowledge rather late in life. At nineteen he had never heard of botany. Sheridan was called inferior to many of his schoolfellows. He was remarkable for nothing but idleness and winning manners, and was "not only slovenly in construing, but unusually defective in his Greek grammar." Swift was refused his degree because of "dulness and insufficiency," but given it later as a special favor. Wordsworth was disappointing. General Grant was never above mediocrity, and was dropped as corporal in the junior class and served the last year as a private. W. H. Seward was called "too stupid to learn." Napoleon graduated forty-second in his class. "Who," asks Swift, "were the forty-one above him?" Darwin was "singularly incapable of mastering any language." When he left school, he says, "I was considered by all my masters and by my father as a very ordinary boy, rather below the common standard in intellect. To my deep mortification, my father once said to me, 'You care for nothing but shooting, dogs, and rat-catching, and you will be a disgrace to yourself and to all your family.'" Harriet Martineau was thought very dull. Though a born musician, she could do absolutely nothing in the presence of her irritable master. She wrote a cramped, untidy scrawl until past twenty. A visit to some very brilliant cousins at the age of sixteen had much to do in arousing her backward nature. At this age Pierpont Morgan wrote poetry and was devoted to mathematics. Booker T. Washington, at about thirteen or fourteen (he does not know the date of his birth), felt the new meaning of life and started off on foot to Hampton, five hundred miles away, not knowing even the direction, sleeping under a sidewalk his first night in Richmond. Vittoria de Feltre, according to Dr. Burnham, had a slow, tardy development, lingering on a sluggish dead level from ten to fourteen, which to his later unfoldment was as the barren, improving years sometimes called the middle ages, compared with the remainder which followed when a new world-consciousness intensified his personality.

Lancaster's summaries show that of 100 actors, the average age of their first great success was exactly 18 years. Those he chose had taken to the stage of their own accord, for actors are more born than made. Nearly half of them were Irish, the unemotional American stock having furnished far less. Few make their first success on the stage after 22, but from 16 to 20 is the time to expect talent in this line, although there is a second rise in his curve before and still more after 25, representing those whose success is more due to intellect. Taking the average of 100 novelists when their first story met with public approval, the curve reaches its highest point between 30 and 35. Averaging 53 poets, the age of most first poems published falls between 15 and 20. The average age of first publication that showed talent he places at 18, which is in striking contrast with the average age of the first patent of inventors, which is 33 years.

A still more striking contrast is that between 100 musicians and 100 professional men. Music is by far the most precious and instinctive of all talents. The average age when marked talent was first shown is a little less than 10 years, 95 per cent showed rare talent before 16, while the professional men graduated at an average age of 24 years and 11 months, and 10 years must be added to mark the point of recognized success. Of 53 artists, 90 per cent showed talent before 20, the average age being 17.2 years. Of 100 pioneers who made their mark in the Far West, leaving home to seek fortunes near the frontier, the greatest number departed before they were 18. Of 118 scientists, Lancaster estimates that their life interest first began to glow on the average a little before they were 19. In general, those whose success is based on emotional traits antedate by some years those whose renown is more purely in intellectual spheres, and taking all together, the curves of the first class culminate between 18 and 20.

IV. While men devoted to physical science, and their biographers, give us perhaps the least breezy accounts of this seething age, it may be, because they mature late, nearly all show its ferments and its circumnutations, as a few almost random illustrations clearly show:

Tycho Brahe, born in 1546 of illustrious Danish stock, was adopted by an uncle, and entered the University of Copenhagen at thirteen, where multiplication, division, philosophy, and metaphysics were taught. When he was fourteen an eclipse of the sun occurred, which aroused so much interest that he decided to devote himself to the study of the heavenly bodies. He was able to construct a series of interesting instruments on a progressive scale of size, and finally to erect the great Observatory of Uraniberg on the Island of Hven. Strange to say, his scientific conclusions had for him profound astrological significance. An important new star he declared was "at first like Venus and Jupiter, and its effects will therefore first be pleasant; but as it then became like Mars, there will next come a period of wars, seditions, captivity, and death of princes, and destruction of cities, together with dryness and fiery meteors in the air, pestilence, and venomous snakes. Lastly, the star became like Saturn, and thus will finally come a time of want, death, imprisonment, and all kinds of sad things!" He says that "a special use of astronomy is that it enables us to draw conclusions from the movements in the celestial regions as to human fate." He labored on his island twenty years. He was always versifying, and inscribed a poem over the entrance of his underground observatory, expressing the astonishment of Urania at finding in the interior of the earth a cavern devoted to the study of the heavens.

Galileo[1] was born in 1564 of a Florentine noble, who was poor. As a youth he became an excellent lutist, then thought of devoting himself to painting, but when he was seventeen studied medicine, and at the University of Pisa fell in love with mathematics.

Isaac Newton,[2] born in 1642, very frail and sickly, solitary, had a

[1] See The Private Life of Galileo. Anon. Macmillan, 1870

[2] See Brewster's Life of Newton.

very low place in the class lists of his school; wrote poetry, and at sixteen tried farming. In one of his university examinations in Euclid he did so poorly as to incur special censure. His first incentive to diligent study came from being severely kicked by a high class boy. He then resolved to pass him in studies, and soon rose to the head of the school. He made many ingenious toys and windmills; a carriage, the wheels of which were driven by the hands of the occupants, and a clock which moved by water; curtains, kites, lanterns, etc.; and before he was fourteen fell in love with Miss Storey, several years older than himself. He entered Trinity College at Cambridge at eighteen.

Flamsteed, born in 1646, as a youth was very fond of highly imaginative romances, but at twelve resolved to leave the wilder ones and read only those which it was possible to picture. By fifteen his reading craze had taken him through Plutarch's Lives, Tacitus, etc., but he made no progress in arithmetic before he was ten. Up to eighteen he was sickly, and had to live in the chimney corner in winter. At nineteen, in despair his father took him to a quack, who "touched and stroked him," but gradually thereafter he grew better; investigated the methods of casting a nativity, but later found astrology not definite enough.

William Herschel, born in 1738, at the outbreak of the Seven Years' War, when he was eighteen, was a performer in the regimental band, and after a battle passed a night in a ditch and escaped in disguise to England, where he eked out a precarious livelihood by teaching music. He supported himself until middle age as an organist. In much of his later work he was greatly aided by his sister Caroline. When he discovered a sixth planet he became famous, and devoted himself exclusively to astronomy, training his only son to follow in his footsteps, and dying in 1822.

Agassiz[1] at twelve had developed a mania for collecting. He memorized Latin names, of which he accumulated "great volumes of MSS.," and "modestly expressed the hope that in time he might be able to give the name of every known animal." At fourteen he revolted at mercantile life, for which he was designed, and issued a manifesto planning to spend four years at a German university, then in Paris, when he could begin to write. Books were scarce, and a little later he copied, with the aid of his brother, several large volumes, and had fifty live birds in his room at one time.

At twelve Huxley[2] became an omnivorous reader, and two or three years later devoured Hamilton's Logic and became deeply interested in metaphysics. At fourteen he saw and participated in his first post-mortem examination, was left in a strange state of apathy by it, and dates his life-long dyspepsia to this experience. His training was irregular; he taught himself German with a book in one hand

[1] His Life and Work, by C. F. Holder.

[2] Life and Letters of Thomas H. Huxley, by his son Leonard Huxley.

while he made hay with the other; speculated about the basis of matter, soul, and their relations, on radicalism and conservatism; and reproaches himself that he does not work and get on enough. At seventeen he attempted a comprehensive classification of human knowledge, and having finished his survey, resolved to master the topics one after another, striking them out from his table with ink as soon as they were done. "May the list soon get black, although at present I shall hardly be able, I am afraid, to spot the paper." Beneath the top skimmings of these years he afterward conceived seething depths working beneath the froth, but could give hardly any account of it. He undertook the practise of pharmacy, etc.

The great surgeon Billroth (1829-94), a man of immense energy, illustrates strikingly a second vocation remote from that in which his fame was achieved. As a youth he desired to devote himself to music for life. He felt himself to be, as he said, "truly a child of music and the stage." Music, says Hemmeter,[1] remained his tried and beloved companion until the end of his days. Not only did he play violin and piano well, but was at work for many years upon his volume, Wer ist Musikalisch, only part of which was published during his life, and which is one of the most suggestive works ever written upon what might be called the physiological psychology of music.

Carl Gegenbaur,[2] in his autobiography, describes the effect of his father's removal to a beautiful country region when the son was twelve, how deeply the lovely face of nature impressed him in the trips he often made, and how susceptible his soul was to the influences of the good Catholic pastor. He had no pleasant memories of his gymnasial life, because of its extreme severity, and the vacations too brief for his loved excursions. In these, although ostensibly for the purpose of hunting, he was collecting and dissecting small animals; making a flower calendar; filling his hunting pouch with roots; studying local myths, heraldry, medieval history, and other allotria, and engaging in patriotic celebrations; but at nineteen had found his direction in the medical course of the university, where he, too, had a slight religious *Aufklarung*, but not enough to cause him to break permanently with the old associations.

V. Women with literary gifts perhaps surpass men in their power to reproduce and describe the great but so often evanescent ebullitions of this age; perhaps because their later lives, on account of their more generic nature, depart less from this totalizing period, or because, although it is psychologically shorter than in men, the necessities of earn-

---

[1] Theodor Billroth, Musical and Surgical Philosopher. Johns Hopkins Hospital Bull., December, 1900, No. 117.

[2] Ererbtes und Erstrebtes. Leipzig, 1901.

ing a livelihood less frequently arrest its full development, and again because they are more emotional, and feeling constitutes the chief psychic ingredient of this stage of life, or they dwell more on subjective states.

Manon Philipon (Madame Roland) was born in 1754. Her father was an engraver in comfortable circumstances. Her earliest enthusiasm was for the Bible and Lives of the Saints, and she had almost a mania for reading books of any kind. In the corner of her father's workshop she would read Plutarch for hours, dream of the past glories of antiquity, and exclaim, weeping, "Why was I not born a Greek?" She desired to emulate the brave men of old.

Books and flowers aroused her to dreams of enthusiasm, romantic sentiment, and lofty aspiration. Finding that the French society afforded no opportunity for heroic living, in her visionary fervor she fell back upon a life of religious mysticism, and Xavier, Loyola, St. Elizabeth, and St. Theresa became her new idols. She longed to follow even to the stake those devout men and women who had borne obloquy, poverty, hunger, thirst, wretchedness, and the agony of a martyr's death for the sake of Jesus. Her capacities for self-sacrifice became perhaps her leading trait, always longing after a grand life like George Eliot's Dorothea Brooke. She was allowed at the age of eleven to enter a convent, where, shunning her companions, she courted solitude apart, under the trees, reading and thinking. Artificial as the atmosphere was here, it no doubt inspired her life with permanent tenderness of feeling and loftiness of purpose, and gave a mystic quality to her imagination. Later she experienced to the full the revulsion of thought and experience which comes when doubt reacts upon youthful credulity. It was the age of the encyclopedia, and now she came to doubt her creed and even God and the soul, but clung to the Gospels as the best possible code of morals, and later realized that while her intellect had wandered her heart had remained constant. At seventeen she was, if not the most beautiful, perhaps the noblest woman in all France, and here the curtain must drop upon her girlhood. All her traits were, of course, set off by the great life she lived and the yet greater death she died.

Gifted people seem to conserve their youth and to be all the more children, and perhaps especially all the more intensely adolescents, because of their gifts, and it is certainly one of the marks of genius that the plasticity and spontaneity of adolescence persists into maturity. Sometimes even its passions, reveries, and hoydenish freaks continue. In her

Histoire de ma vie, it is plain that George Sand inherited at this age an unusual dower of gifts. She composed many and interminable stories, carried on day after day, so that her confidants tried to tease her by asking if the prince had got out of the forest yet, etc. She personated an echo and conversed with it. Her day-dreams and plays were so intense that she often came back from the world of imagination to reality with a shock. She spun a weird zoological romance out of a rustic legend of *la grande bête.*

When her aunt sent her to a convent, she passed a year of rebellion and revolt, and was the leader of *les diables*, or those who refused to be devout, and engaged in all wild pranks. At fifteen she became profoundly interested in the lives of the saints, although ridiculing miracles. She entered one evening the convent church for service, which was an act of disobedience, without permission. The mystery and holy charm of it penetrated her; she forgot everything outward and was left alone, and some mysterious change stole over her. She "breathed an atmosphere of ineffable sweetness" more with the mind than the senses; had a sudden indescribable perturbation; her eyes swam; she was enveloped in a white glimmer, and heard a voice murmur the words written under a convent picture of St. Augustine, *Tolle, lege*, and turned around thinking Mother Alicia spoke, but she was alone. She knew it was an hallucination, but saw that faith had laid hold of her, as she wished, by the heart, and she sobbed and prayed to the unknown God till a nun heard her groaning. At first her ardor impelled her not only to brave the jeers of her madcap club of harum-scarums and tomboys, but she planned to become a nun, until this feverish longing for a recluse life passed but left her changed.[1]

When she passed from the simple and Catholic faith of her grisette mother to the atmosphere of her cynical grandmother at Nohant, who was a disciple of Voltaire, she found herself in great straits between the profound sentiments inspired by the first communion and the concurrent contempt for this faith instilled by her grandmother for all these mummeries through which, however, for conventional reasons she was obliged to pass. Her heart was deeply stirred, and yet her head holding all religion to be fiction or metaphor, it occurred to her to invent a story which might be a religion or a religion which might be a story into any degree of belief in which she could lapse at will. The name and the form of her new deity was revealed to her in a dream. He was Corambé, pure as Jesus, beautiful as Gabriel, as graceful as the nymphs and Orpheus, less austere than the Christian God, and as much woman as man, because she could best understand this sex from her love for her mother. He appeared in many aspects

[1] See also Sully: A Girl's Religion. Longmans' Mag., 1890, p. 89.

of physical and moral beauty; was eloquent, master of all arts, and above all of the magic of musical improvisation; loved as a friend and sister, and at the same time revered as a god; not awful and remote from impeccability, but with the fault of excess of indulgence. She estimated that she composed about a thousand sacred books or songs developing phases of his mundane existence. In each of these he became incarnate man on touching the earth, always in a new group of people who were good, yet suffering martyrdoms from the wicked known only by the effects of their malice. In this "gentle hallucination" she could lose herself in the midst of friends and turn to her hero deity for comfort. There must be not only sacred books, but a temple and ritual, and in a garden thicket, which no eye could penetrate, in a moss-carpeted chamber she built an altar against a tree-trunk, ornamented with a wreath hung over it. Instead of sacrificing, which seemed barbaric, she proceeded to restore life and liberty to butterflies, lizards, green frogs, and birds, which she put in a box, laid on the altar, and "after having invoked the good genius of liberty and protection," opened it. In these mimic rites and delicious reveries she found the germs of a religion that fitted her heart. From the instant, however, that a boy playmate discovered and entered this sanctuary, "Corambé ceased to dwell in it. The dryads and the cherubim deserted it," and it seemed unreal. The temple was destroyed with great care, and the garlands and shells were buried under the tree.[1]

Adeline, Countess Schimmelmann,[2] was born in 1854 in a Danish castle. Her education was very careful; her character strong and early developed. As a girl of ten she was fond of climbing trees, bathing, fishing, and rowing; was early impressed by Schnorr's great Bible pictures, by the death of her grandmother, and especially by a horrible murder of his whole family by a desperate man, who denied his guilt, and

---

[1] Sheldon (Institutional Activities of American Children; Am. Jour. of Psychol., vol. ix, p. 434) describes a faintly analogous case of a girl of eleven, who organized the worship of Pallas Athena on two flat rocks, in a deep ravine by a stream where a young sycamore grew from an old stump, as did Pallas from the head of her father Zeus. There was a court consisting of king, queen and subjects, and priests who officiated at sacrifices. The king and queen wore goldenrod upon their heads and waded in streams attended by their subjects; gathered flowers for Athena; caught crayfish which were duly smashed upon her altar. "Sometimes there was a special celebration, when, in addition to the slaughtered crayfish and beautiful flower decorations, and pickles stolen from the dinner-table, there would be an elaborate ceremony," which because of its uncanny acts was intensely disliked by the people at hand.

[2] Glimpses of My Life. New York, 1896, p. 210.

for whom she prayed daily. Just before his execution he confessed his guilt and experienced religion, all, as she felt, in answer to her prayers. She grew profoundly religious, although such topics were carefully avoided in her family. At fifteen she was confirmed, and her whole religious nature very greatly deepened, but she entered the gay life of her home and soon was presented at court, and for eighteen years was maid of honor to the German Empress Augusta, by whose character she was greatly impressed.[1]

Louisa Alcott's romantic period opened at fifteen, when she began to write poetry, keep a heart journal, and wander by moonlight, and wished to be the Bettine of Emerson,

---

[1] Her subsequent life was entirely dominated by momentum of this period, and her eccentricities were only its persistence into maturity. By the death of her father, she became possessed of a considerable fortune and then resolved to devote herself to the work of charity, beginning among the wild and abandoned sailors and fishermen of the Pomeranian shore. She adopted two boys of low birth, one of them nearly idiotic, who followed her wherever she went, and on whom she lavished great care and attention. She built and personally conducted a seaman's home at Goehren, often cooking and furnishing food for body and soul. Her piety was so extreme and her charity so great, that her relatives, failing to abate them, had her sequestered in an insane asylum, where she remained for some months amid great hardships and indignities before her sanity was entirely vindicated, when she returned to her good works in Berlin among the lowest classes, where her life was several times in extreme danger. She had a great desire to save one soul for each of the magnificent diamonds in a necklace which she possessed. The wider field of her mission for which she is still laboring and collecting money is the fishermen of the Baltic, the sailors of all nations in European ports, and the distressed and troubled elements of society everywhere. Efforts were made to prove her an anarchist, but these, too, were abortive. She imagines a future brotherhood of the sea reared by pious bequests. Failing in the primal sensations of wife and mother and needing an atmosphere of warmth, with an overflowingly good heart and a sound head, disdaining the soft life of a great lady, she determined to love Jesus and devote herself to his work. In this she was sustained by her friend, the good pastor Funcke. As sovereign over her fishermen, their worship and admiration were better to her than a satin bed. She was able to forbid them whisky. During the dreadful winter of 1891–92 in Berlin, she penetrated into an insurgent mob of laborers the police dared not approach, at the peril of her life; distributed money; prayed inwardly, and then preached Jesus; sang hymns; sold her country house to buy a supply yacht from which to distribute provisions and Bibles in the North Sea; sought to break the monopolies that ground the fishermen; in one year visited five hundred vessels and distributed twenty thousand Bibles and other religious books. Her work has been chiefly with rough men. She loves the masculine element and evokes the healthful chivalry of men, and does all in the service of "My Jesus." Her work may not be permanent, but it is beneficent.

in whose library she foraged; wrote him letters which were never sent; sat in a tall tree at midnight; left wild flowers on the doorstep of her master; sang Mignon's song under his window; and was refined by her choice of an idol. Her diary was all about herself.

If she looked in the glass at her long hair and well-shaped head, she tried to keep down her vanity; her quick tongue, moodiness, poverty, impossible longings, made every day a battle until she hardly wished to live, only something must be done, and waiting is so hard. She imagined her mind a room in confusion which must be put in order; the useless thought swept out; foolish fancies dusted away; newly furnished with good resolutions. But she was not a good housekeeper; cobwebs got in, and it was hard to rule. She was smitten with a mania for the stage, and spent most of her leisure in writing and acting plays of melodramatic style and high-strung sentiment, improbable incidents, with no touch of common life or sense of humor, full of concealments and surprises, bright dialogues, and lofty sentiments. She had much dramatic power and loved to transform herself into Hamlet and declaim in mock heroic style. From sixteen to twenty-three was her apprenticeship to life. She taught, wrote for the papers, did housework for pay as a servant, and found sewing a pleasant resource because it was tranquillizing, left her free, and set her thoughts going.

Mrs. Burnett,[1] like most women who record their childhood and adolescent memories, is far more subjective and interesting than most men. In early adolescence she was never alone when with flowers, but loved to "speak to them, to bend down and say caressing things, to stoop and kiss them, to praise them for their pretty ways of looking up at her as into the eyes of a friend and beloved. There were certain little blue violets which always seemed to lift their small faces childishly, as if they were saying, 'Kiss me; don't go by like that.'" She would sit on the porch, elbows on knees and chin on hands, staring upward, sometimes lying on the grass. Heaven was so high and yet she was a part of it and was something even among the stars. It was a weird, updrawn, overwhelming feeling as she stared so fixedly and intently that the earth seemed gone, left far behind. Every hour and moment was a wonderful and beautiful thing. She felt on speaking terms with the rabbits. Something was happening in the leaves which waved and rustled as she passed. Just to walk, sit, lie around out of doors, to loiter, gaze, watch with a heart fresh as a young dryad, following birds, playing hide-and-seek with the brook—these were her halcyon hours.

With the instability of genius, Beth[2] did everything suddenly.

[1] The One I Know Best of All. A Memory of the Mind of a Child. By Frances Hodgson Burnett. New York, 1893.

[2] The Beth Book.

When twelve or thirteen she had grown too big to be carried, pulled, or pushed; she suddenly stood still one day, when her mother commanded her to dress. She had been ruled before by physical force, but her will and that of her mother were now in collision, and the latter realized she could make her do nothing unless by persuasion or moral influence. Being constantly reproved, scolded, and even beaten by her mother, Beth one day impulsively jumped into the sea and was rescued with difficulty. She had spells of being miserable with no cause. She was well and happy, but would burst into tears suddenly, which seemed often to surprise her. Being very sensitive herself, she was morbidly careful of the feelings of others and incessantly committed grave sins of insincerity without compunction in her effort to spare them. To those who confided in her abilities, praised her, and thought she could do things, her nature expanded, but her mother checked her mental growth over and over, instead of helping her, by saying, "Don't try, you can't do it," etc.

Just before the dawn of adolescence she had passed through a long period of abject superstition largely through the influence of a servant. All the old woman's signs were very dominant in her life. She even invented methods of divination, as, "if the boards do not creak when I walk across the room I shall get through my lessons without trouble." She always preferred to see two rooks together to one, and became expert in the black arts. She used to hear strange noises at night for a time, which seemed signs and portents of disaster at sea, fell into the ways of her neighbors, and had more faith in incantations than in doctors' doses. She not only heard voices and very ingeniously described them, but claimed to know what was going to happen and compared her forebodings with the maid. She "got religion" very intensely under the influence of her aunt, grew poor, lost her appetite and sleep, had heartache to think of her friends burning in hell, and tried to save them.

Beth never thought at all of her personal appearance until she overheard a gentleman call her rather nice-looking, when her face flushed and she had a new feeling of surprise and pleasure, and took very clever ways of cross-examining her friends to find if she was handsome. All of a sudden the care of her person became of great importance, and every hint she had heard of was acted on. She aired her bed, brushed her hair glossy, pinched her waist and feet, washed in buttermilk, used a parasol, tortured her natural appetite in every way, put on gloves to do dirty work, etc.

The house always irked her. Once stealing out of the school by night, she was free, stretched herself, drew a long breath, bounded and waved her arms in an ecstasy of liberty, danced around the magnolia, buried her face in the big flowers one after another and bathed it in the dew of the petals, visited every forbidden place, was particularly attracted to the water, enjoyed scratching and making her feet bleed and eating a lot of green fruit. This liberty was most precious, and all through a hot summer she kept herself healthy by exercise in the moonlight. This revived her appetite, and she ended these night excursions by a forage in the kitchen. Beth had times when she hungered for solitude and for nature. Sometimes she would shut herself in her room, but more often would rove the fields and woods in ecstasy. Coming home from school, where she had long been, she had to greet the trees and fields almost before she did her parents. She had a great habit of stealing out often by the most dangerous routes over roofs, etc., at night in the moonlight, running and jumping, waving her arms, throwing herself on the ground, rolling over, walking on all-fours, turning somersaults, hugging trees, playing hide-and-seek with the shadow fairy-folk, now playing and feeling fear and running away. She invoked trees, stars, etc.

Beth's first love affair was with a bright, fair-haired, fat-faced boy, who sat near her pew Sundays. They looked at each other once during service, and she felt a glad glow in her chest spread over her, dwelt on his image, smiled, and even the next day felt a new desire to please. She watched for him to pass from school. When he appeared, "had a most delightful thrill shoot through her." The first impulse to fly was conquered; she never thought a boy beautiful before. They often met after dark, wrote; finally she grew tired of him because she could not make him feel deeply, sent him off, called him an idiot, and then soliloquized on the "most dreadful grief of her life." The latter stages of their acquaintance she occasionally used to beat him, but his attraction steadily waned. Once later, as she was suffering from a dull, irresolute feeling due to want of a companion and an object, she met a boy of seventeen, whose face, like her own, brightened as they approached. It was the first appearance of nature's mandate to mate. This friendly glance suffused her whole being with the "glory and vision of love." Religion and young men were her need. They had stolen interviews by night and many an innocent embrace and kiss, and almost died once by being caught. They planned in detail what they would do after they were married, but all was taken for granted without formal vows. Only when criticized did they ever dream of caution and concealment, and then they made elaborate parades of ignoring each other in public and fired their imaginations with thoughts of disguises, masks, etc. This passion was nipped in the bud by the boy's removal from his school.

In preparing for her first communion, an anonymous writer[1] became sober and studious, proposing to model her life on that of each fresh saint and to spend a week in retreat examining her conscience with a vengeance. She wanted to revive the custom of public confession and wrote letters of penitence and submission, which she tore up later, finding her mind not "all of a piece." She lay prostrate on her prie-dieu weeping from ecstasy, lying on the rim of heaven held by angels, wanting to die, now bathed in bliss or aching intolerably with spiritual joy, but she was only twelve and her old nature often

---

[1] Autobiography of a Child. London, 1899, p. 255.

reasserted itself. Religion at that time became an intense emotion nourished on incense, music, tapers, and a feeling of being tangible. It was rapturous and sensuous. While under its spell, she seemed to float and touch the wings of angels. Here solemn Gregorian chants are sung, so that when one comes back to earth there is a sense of hunger, deception, and self-loathing. Now she came to understand how so many sentimental and virtuous souls sought oblivion in the narcotic of religious excitement. Here at the age of twelve youth began and childhood ended with her book.

Pathetic is the account of Helen Keller's effort to understand the meaning of the word love in its season.[1]

Is it the sweetness of flowers? she asked. No, said her teacher. Is it the warm sun? Not exactly. It can not be touched, "but you feel the sweetness that it pours into everything. Without love, you would not be happy or want to play. The beautiful truth burst upon my mind. I felt that there were invisible lines stretched between my spirit and the spirit of others." This period seems to have come gradually and naturally to this wonderful child, whose life has been perhaps the purest ever lived and one of the sweetest. None has ever loved every aspect of nature accessible to her more passionately, or felt more keenly the charm of nature or of beautiful sentiments. The unhappy Frost King episode has been almost the only cloud upon her life, which unfortunately came at about the dawn of this period, that is perhaps better marked by the great expansion of mind which she experienced at the World's Fair in Chicago in 1893, when she was thirteen. About this time, too, her great ambition of going to college and enjoying all the advantages that other girls did, which, considering her handicap, was one of the greatest human resolutions, was strengthened and deepened. The fresh, spontaneous, and exquisite reactions of this pellucid mind, which felt that each could comprehend all the experiences and emotions of the race and that chafes at every pedagogical and technical obstacle between her soul and nature, and the great monuments of literature, show that she has conserved to a remarkable degree, which the world will wish may be permanent, the best impulses of this golden age.

Marie Bashkirtseff,[2] who may be taken as one of the best types of exaggerated adolescent confessionalists, was of rich and noble birth, and began in 1873, at the age of twelve, to write a journal that should be absolutely true and frank, with no pretense, affectation, or concealment. The journal continues until

[1] The Story of My Life. By Helen Keller. New York, 1903, p. 30.

[2] Journal of a Young Artist. New York, 1889, p. 434.

her death, October, 1884, at the age of twenty-three. It may be described as in some sense a feminine counterpart of Rousseau's confessions, but is in some respects a more precious psychological document than any other for the elucidation of the adolescent ferment in an unusually vigorous and gifted soul. Twice I have read it from cover to cover and with growing interest.

At twelve she is passionately in love with a duke, whom she sometimes saw pass but who had no knowledge of her existence, and builds many air castles about his throwing himself at her feet and of their life together. She prays passionately to see him again, would dazzle him on the stage, would lead a perfect life, develop her voice, and would be an ideal wife. She agonizes before the glass on whether or not she is pretty, and resolves to ask some young man, but prefers to think well of herself even if it is an illusion; constantly modulates over into passionate prayer to God to grant all her wishes; is oppressed with despair; gay and melancholy by turn; believes in God because she prayed Him for a set of croquet and to help her to learn English, both of which He granted. At church some prayers and services seem directly aimed at her; Paris now seems a frightful desert, and she has no motive to avoid carelessness in her appearance. She has freaky and very changeable ideas of arranging the things in her room. When she hears of the duke's marriage she almost throws herself over a bridge, prays God for pardon of her sins, and thinks all is ended; finds it horrible to dissemble her feelings in public; goes through the torture of altering her prayer about the duke. She is disgusted with common people, harrowed by jealousy, envy, deceit, and every hideous feeling, yet feels herself frozen in the depth, and moving only on the surface. When her voice improves she welcomes it with tears and feels an all-powerful queen. The man she loves should never speak to another. Her journal she resolves to make the most instructive book that ever was or ever will be written. She esteems herself so great a treasure that no one is worthy of her; pities those who think they can please her; thinks herself a real divinity; prays to the moon to show her in dreams her future husband, and quarrels with her photographs.

In some moods she feels herself beautiful, knows she shall succeed, everything smiles upon her and she is absolutely happy, and yet in the next paragraph the fever of life at high pressure palls upon her and things seem asleep and unreal. Her attempts to express her feelings drive her to desperation because words are inadequate. She loves to weep, gives up to despair, to think of death, and finds everything transcendently exquisite. She comes to despise men and wonder whether the good are always stupid and the intelligent always false and saturated with baseness, but on the whole believes that some time or other she is destined to meet one true, good, and great man. Now she is inflated with pride of her ancestry, her gifts, and would subordinate everybody and everything; she would never speak a commonplace word, and then again feels that her life has been a failure and she is destined to be always waiting. She falls on her knees sobbing, praying to God with outstretched hands as if He were in her room; almost vows to make a pilgrimage to Jerusalem one-tenth of the way on foot; to devote her money to good works; lacks the pleasures proper to her age; wonders if she can ever love again. On throwing a bouquet from a window into a crowd in the Corso, a young man choked so beautifully a workman who caught it that by that one act of strangling and snatching the bouquet she fell in love. The young man calls and they see each other often. Now she is clad from head to foot in an armor of cold politeness, now vanity and now passion seem uppermost in their meetings. She wonders if a certain amount of sin, like air, is necessary to a man to sustain life. Finally they vow mutual love and Pietro leaves, and she begins to fear that she has cherished illusions or been insulted; is tormented at things unsaid or of her spelling in French. She coughs and for three days has a new idea that she is going to die; prays and prostrates herself sixty times, one for each bead in her rosary, touching the floor with her forehead every time; wonders if God takes intentions into account; resolves to read the New Testament, but can not find one and reads Dumas instead. In novel-reading she imagines herself the heroine of every scene; sees her lover and they plan their mode of life together and at last kiss each other, but later she feels humiliated, chilled, doubts if it is real love; studies the color of her lips to see if they have changed; fears that she has compromised herself; has eye symptoms that make her fear blindness. Once on reading the Testament she smiled and clasped her hands, gazed upward, was no longer herself but in ecstasy; she makes many programs for life; is haunted by the phrase "we live but once"; wants to live a dozen lives in one, but feels that she does not live one-fourth of a life; has several spells of solitary illumination. At other times she wishes to be the center of a salon and imagines herself to be so. She soars on poets' wings, but often has hell in her heart; slowly love is vowed henceforth to be a word without meaning to her. Although she suffers from *ennui*, she realizes that women live only from sixteen to forty and can not bear the thought of losing a moment of her life; criticizes her mother; scorns marriage and child-bearing, which any washerwoman can attain, but pants for glory; now hates, now longs to see new faces; thinks of disguising herself as a poor girl and going out to seek her fortunes; thinks her mad vanity is her devil; that her ambitions are justified by no results; hates moderation in anything; would have intense and constant excitement or absolute repose; at fifteen abandons her idea of the duke but wants an idol, and finally decides to live for fame; studies her shoulders, hips, bust, to gauge her success in life; tries target-shooting, hits every time and feels it to be fateful; at times despises her mother because she is so easily influenced by her; meets another man whose affection for her she thinks might be as reverent as religion and who never profaned the purity of his life by a thought, but finally drops him because the possible disappointment would be unbearable; finds that the more unhappy any one is for love of us the happier we are; wonders why she has weeping spells; wonders what love that people talk so much about really is, and whether she is ever to know. One night, at the age of seventeen, she has a fit of despair, which vents itself in moans until arising, she seizes the dining-room clock, rushes out and throws it into the sea, when she becomes happy. "Poor clock!"

At another time she fears she has used the word love lightly and resolves to no longer invoke God's help, yet in the next line prays Him to let her die as everything is against her, her thoughts are incoherent, she hates herself and everything is contemptible; but she wishes to die peacefully while some one is singing a beautiful air of Verdi. Again she thinks of shaving her head to save the trouble of arranging her hair; is crazed to think that every moment brings her nearer death; to waste a moment of life is infamous, yet she can trust no one; all the freshness of life is gone; few things affect her now; she wonders how in the past she could have acted so foolishly and reasoned so wisely; is proud that no advice in the world could ever keep her from doing anything she wished. She thinks the journal of her former years exaggerated and resolves to be moderate; wants to make others feel as she feels; finds that the only cure for disenchantment with life is devotion to work; fears her face is wearing an anxious look instead of the confident expression which was its chief charm. Impossible is a hideous, maddening word; to think of dying like a dog as most people do and leaving nothing behind is a granite wall against which she every instant dashes her head. If she loved a man, every expression of admiration for anything or anybody else in her presence would be a profanation. Now she thinks the man she loves must never know what it is to be in want of money and must purchase everything he wishes; must weep to see a woman want for anything, and find the door of no palace or club barred to him. Art becomes a great shining light in her life of few pleasures and many griefs, yet she dares hope for nothing.

At eighteen all her caprices are exhausted; she vows and prays in the name of the Father, Son, and Holy Ghost for her wishes. She would like to be a millionaire, get back her voice, obtain the *prix de Rome* under the guise of a man and marry Napoleon IV. On winning a medal for her pictures she does nothing but laugh, cry, and dream of greatness, but the next day is scolded and grows discouraged. She has an immense sense of growth and transformation, so that not a trace of her old nature remains; feels that she has far too much of some things and far too little of others in her nature; sees defects in her mother's character, whose pertinacity is like a disease; realizes that one of her chief passions is to inspire rather than to feel love; that her temper is profoundly affected by her dress; deplores that her family expect her to achieve greatness rather than give her the stimulus of expecting nothing; declares that she thinks a million thoughts for every word that she writes; is disgusted with and sometimes absolutely hates herself. At one time she coquets with Kant, and wonders if he is right that all things exist only in the imagination; has a passion for such "abracadabrante follies" that seem so learned and logical, but is grieved to feel them to be false; longs to penetrate the intellectual world, to see, learn, and know everything; admires Balzac because he describes so frankly all that he has felt; loves Fleury, who has shown her a wider horizon; still has spells of admiring her dazzling complexion and deploring that she can not go out alone; feels that she is losing her grip on art and also on God, who no longer hears her prayers, and resolves to kill herself if she is not famous at thirty.

At nineteen, and even before, she has spells of feeling inefficient, cries, calls on God, feels exhausted; is almost stunned when she hears that the young French prince about whom she has spun romances was killed by the Kaffirs; feels herself growing serious and sensible; despises death; realizes that God is not what she thought, but is perhaps Nature and Life or is perhaps Chance; she thinks out possible pictures she might paint; develops a Platonic friendship for her professor; might marry an old man with twenty-seven millions, but spurns the thought; finds herself growing deaf gradually, and at nineteen finds three gray hairs; has awful remorse for days, when she can not work and so loses herself in novels and cigarettes; makes many good resolutions and then commits some folly as if in a dream; has spells of reviewing the past. When the doctor finds a serious lung trouble and commands iodine, cod-liver oil, hot milk and flannel, she at first scorns death and refuses all, and is delighted at the terror of her friends, but gradually does all that is necessary; feels herself too precocious and doomed; deplores especially that consumption will cost her her good looks; has fits of intense anger alternating with tears; concludes that death is annihilation; realizes the horrible thought that she has a skeleton within her that some time or other will come out; reads the New Testament again and returns to belief in miracles and prayer to Jesus and the Virgin; distributes one thousand francs to the poor; records the dreamy delusions that flow through her brain at night and the strange sensations by day. Her eye symptoms cause her to fear blindness again; she grows superstitious, believing in signs and fortune-tellers; is strongly impelled to embrace and make up with her mother; at times defies God and death; sees a Spanish bull-fight and gets from it a general impression of human cowardice, but has a strange intoxication with blood and would like to thrust a lance into the neck of every one she meets; coquets a great deal with the thought of marriage; takes up her art and paints a few very successful pictures; tries to grapple with the terrible question, "What is my unbiased opinion concerning myself?" pants chiefly for fame. When the other lung is found diseased the diary becomes sometimes more serious, sometimes more fevered; she is almost racked to find some end in life; shall she marry, or paint? and at last finds much consolation in the visits of Bastien-Lepage, who comes to see her often while he is dying of some gastric trouble. She keeps up occasional and often daily entries in her journal until eleven days before her death, occurring in October, 1884, at the age of twenty-three, and precipitated by a cold incurred while making an open-air sketch.

The confessional outpourings of Mary MacLane[1] constitute a unique and valuable adolescent document, despite the fact that it seems throughout affected and written for effect; however, it well illustrates a real type, although perhaps hardly possible save in this country, and was inspired very likely by the preceding.

She announces at the outset that she is odd, a genius, an extreme egotist; has no conscience; despises her father, "Jim MacLane of selfish memory"; loves scrubbing the floor because it gives her strength and grace of body, although her daily life is an "empty damned weariness." She is a female Napoleon passionately desiring fame; is both a philosopher and a coward; her heart is wooden; although but nineteen, she feels forty; desires happiness even more than fame, for an hour of which she would give up at once fame, money, power, virtue, honor, truth, and genius to the devil, whose coming she awaits. She discusses her portrait, which constitutes the frontispiece; is glad of her good strong body, and still awaits in a wild, frenzied impatience the coming of the devil to take her sacrifice, and to whom she would dedicate her life. She loves but one in all the world, an older "anemone" lady, once her teacher. She can not distinguish between right and wrong; love is the only thing real which will some day bring joy, but it is agony to wait. "Oh, damn! damn! damn! damn! every living thing in the world!—the universe be damned!" herself included. She is "marvelously deep," but thanks the good devil who has made her without conscience and virtue so that she may take her happiness when it comes. Her soul seeks but blindly, for nothing answers. How her happiness will seethe, quiver, writhe, shine, dance, rush, surge, rage, blare, and wreak with love and light when it comes!

The devil she thinks fascinating and strong, with a will of steel, in conventional clothes, whom she periodically falls in love with and would marry, and would love to be tortured by him. She holds imaginary conversations with him. If happiness does not come soon she will commit suicide, and she finds rapture in the thought of death. In Butte, Montana, where she lives, she wanders among the box rustlers, the beer jerkers, biscuit shooters, and plunges out into the sand and

---

[1] The Story of Mary MacLane. By herself. Chicago, 1902, p. 322.

barrenness, but finds everything dumb. The six tooth-brushes in the bathroom make her wild and profane. She flirts with death at the top of a dark, deep pit, and thinks out the stages of decomposition if she yielded herself to Death, who would dearly love to have her. She confesses herself a thief on several occasions, but comforts herself because it was given to the poor. Sometimes her "very good legs" carry her out into the country, where she has imaginary love confabs with the devil, but the world is so empty, dreary, and cold, and it is all so hard to bear when one is a woman and nineteen. She has a litany from which she prays in recurrent phrases, "Kind devil, deliver me"—as, e. g., from musk, boys with curls, feminine men, wobbly hips, red note-paper, codfish-balls, lisle-thread stockings, the books of A. C. Gunter and Albert Ross, wax flowers, from soft old bachelors and widowers, from nice young men, tin spoons, false teeth, thin shoes, etc. She does not seem real to herself, everything is a blank. Though she doubts everything else, she will keep the one atom of faith in love and the truth that is love and life in her heart. When something shrieks within her, she feels that all her anguish is for nothing and that she is a fool. She is exasperated that people call her peculiar, but confesses that she loves admiration; she can fascinate and charm company if she tries; imagines an admiration for Messalina. She most desires to cultivate badness when there is lead in the sky. "I would live about seven years of judicious badness, and then death if you will." "I long to cultivate the element of badness in me." She describes the fascination of making and eating fudge; devotes a chapter to describing how to eat an olive; discusses her figure. "In the front of my shirt-waist there are nine cambric handkerchiefs cunningly distributed." She discusses her foot, her beautiful hair, her hips; describes each of the seventeen little engraved portraits of Napoleon that she keeps, with each of which she falls in love; vows she would give up even her marvelous genius for one dear, bright day free from loneliness. When her skirts need sewing, she simply pins them; this lasts longer, and had she mended them with needle and thread she would have been sensible, which she hates. As she walks over the sand one day she vows that she would like a man to come so be that he was strong and a perfect villain, and she would pray him to lead her to what the world calls her ruin. Nothing is of consequence to her except to be rid of unrest and pain. She would be positively and not merely negatively wicked. To poison her soul would rouse her mental power. "Oh, to know just once what it is to be loved!" "I know that I am a genius more than any genius that has lived," yet she often thinks herself a small vile creature for whom no one cares. The world is ineffably dull, heaven has always fooled her, and she is starving for love.

Ada Negri illustrates the other extreme of genuineness and is desperately in earnest.[1] She began to teach school in a squalid, dismal

[1] Fate. Tr. by A. M. Von Blomberg, Boston, 1898.

Italian village, and to write the poetry at eighteen that has made her famous. She lived in a dim room back of a stable, up two flights, where the windows were not glass but paper, and where she seems to have been, like her mother, a mill hand before she was a teacher. She had never seen a theater, but had read of Duse with enthusiasm; had never seen the sea, mountains, or even a hill, lake, or large city, but she had read of them. After she began to write, friends gave her two dream days in the city. Then she returned, put on her wooden shoes, and began to teach her eighty children how to spell. The poetry she writes is from the very heart of her own experience.

She craved "the kiss of genius and of light," but the awful figure of misfortune with its dagger stood by her bed at night. She writes:

> "I have no name—my home a hovel damp;
> I grew up from the mire;
> Wretched and outcast folk my family,
> And yet within me burns a flame of fire."

There is always a praying angel and an evil dwarf on either side. The black abyss attracts her, yet she is softened by a child's caress. She laughs at the blackest calamities that threaten her, but weeps over thin, wan children without bread. Her whole life goes into song. The boy criminal on the street fascinates her and she would kiss him. She writes of jealousy as a ghost of vengeance. If death comes, she fears "that the haggard doctor will dissect my naked corpse," and pictures herself dying on the operating-table like a stray dog, and her well-made body "disgraced by the lustful kiss of the too eager blade" as, "with sinister smile untiring, they tear my bowels out and still gloat over my sold corpse, go on to bare my bones and veins at will, wrench out my heart," probe vainly for the secrets of hunger and the mystery of pain, until from her "dead breast gurgles a gasp of malediction." Much of her verse is imprecation. "A crimson rain of crying blood dripping from riddled chests" of those slain for liberty falls on her heart; the sultry factories where "monsters of steel, huge engines, snort all day," and where the pungent air poisons the blood of the pale weaver girls; the fate of the mason who fell from a high roof and struck the stone flagging, whose funeral she attends, all inspire her to sing occasionally the songs of enfranchised labor. Misery as a drear, toothless ghost visits her, as when gloomy pinions had overspread her dying mother's bed, to wrench with sharp nails all the hope from her breast with which she had defied it. A wretched old man on the street inspires her to sing of what she imagines is his happy though humble prime. There is the song of the pickaxe brandished in revolution when mobs cry "Peace, labor, bread," and in mines of industry beneath the earth. She loves the "defeated" in whose house no fire glows, who live in caves and dens, and writes of the mutilation of a woman in the factory machinery. At eighteen years "a loom, two handsome eyes that know no tears, a cotton dress, a love, belong to me." She is inspired by a master of the forge beating a red-hot bar, with his bare neck swelled. He is her demon, her God, and her pride in him is ecstasy. She describes jealousy of two rival women, so intense that they fight and bite, and the pure joy of a guileless, intoxicating, life-begetting first kiss. She longs for infinite stretches of hot, golden sand, over which she would gallop wildly on her steed; anticipates an old age of cap and spectacles; revels in the hurricane, and would rise in and fly and whirl with it adrift far out in the immensity of space. She tells us "of genius and light I'm a blithe millionaire," and elsewhere she longs for the everlasting ice of lofty mountains, the immortal silence of the Alps; sings of her "sad twenty years," "how all, all goes when love is gone and spent." She imagines herself springing into the water which closes over her, while her naked soul, ghostly pale, whirls past through the lonely dale. She imprecates the licentious world of crafty burghers, coquettes, gamblers, well-fed millionaires, cursed geese and serpents that make the cowardly vile world, and whom she would smite in the face with her indignant verse. "Thou crawlest and I soar." She chants the champions of the spade, hammer, pick, though they are ground and bowed with toil, disfigured within, with furrowed brows She pants for war with outrage and with wrong; questions the abyss for its secret; hears moans and flying shudders; and sees phantoms springing from putrid tombs. The full moon is an old malicious spy, peeping stealthily with evil eye. She is a bird caught in a cursed cage, and prays some one to unlock the door and give her space and light, and let her soar away in ecstasy and glory. Nothing less than infinite space will satisfy her. Even the tempest, the demon, or a malevolent spirit might bear her away on unbridled wings. In one poem she apostrophizes Marie Bashkirtseff as warring with vast genius against unknown powers, but who now is in her coffin among worms, her skull grinning and showing its teeth. She would be possessed by her and thrilled as by an electric current. A dwarf beggar wrings her heart with pity, but she will not be overwhelmed. Though a daring peasant, she will be free and sing out her pæan to the sun, though amid the infernal glow of furnaces, forges, and the ringing noise of hammers and wheels.

VI. Literary men who record their experiences during this stage seem to differ from women in several important respects. First, they write with less abandon. I can recall no male MacLanes. A Bashkirtseff would be less impossible, and a Negri with social reform in her heart is still less so. But men are more prone to characterize their pubic metamorphoses later in life, when they are a little paled, and perhaps feel less need of confessionalism for that reason. It would, however, be too hazardous to elaborate this distinction too far. Secondly and more clearly, men tend to vent their ephebic calentures more in the field of action. They would break the old moorings of home and strike out new careers, or vent their souls in efforts and dreams of reconstructing the political, industrial, or social world. Their impracticalibilities are more often in the field of practical life and remoter from their own immediate surroundings. This is especially true in our practical country, which so far lacks subjective characterizations of this age of eminent literary merit, peculiarly intense as it is here. Thirdly, they erupt in a greater variety of ways, and the many kinds of genius and talent that now often take possession of their lives like fate are more varied and individual. This affords many extreme contrasts, as, e. g., between Trollope's pity for, and Goethe's apotheosis of his youth; Mill's loss of feeling, and Jeffries's unanalytic, passionate outbursts of sentiment; the esthetic ritualism of Symonds, and the progressive religious emancipation of Fielding; the moral and religious supersensitiveness of Oliphant, who was a reincarnation of medieval monkhood, and the riotous storminess of Müller and Ebers; the abnormalities and precocity of De Quincey, and the steady, healthful growth of Patterson; the simultaneity of a fleshly and spiritual love in Keller and Goethe, and the duality of Pater, with his great and tyrannical intensification of sensation for nature and the sequent mysticity and symbolism. In some it is fulminating but episodic, in others gradual and lifelong like the advent of eternal spring. Fourth, in their subjective states women outgrow less in their consciousness, and men depart farther from their youth, in more manifold ways. Lastly, in its religious aspects, the male struggles more with dogma, and his enfranchisement from it is more intellectually belabored. Yet, despite all these differences, the analogies between the sexes are probably yet more numerous, more all-pervasive. All these biographic facts reveal nothing not found in *questionnaire* returns from more ordinary youth, so that for our purposes they are only the latter, writ large because superior minds only utter what all more inwardly feel. The arrangement by nationality which follows gives no yet adequate basis for inference unless it be the above American peculiarity.

In his autobiography from 1785–1803, De Quincey[1] re-

[1] Confessions. Part I. Introductory Narrative.

membered feeling that life was finished and blighted for him at the age of six, up to which time the influence of his sister three years older had brooded over him.

His first remembrance, however, is of a dream of terrific grandeur before he was two, which seemed to indicate that his dream tendencies were constitutional and not due to morphine, but the chill was upon the first glimpse that this was a world of evil. He had been brought up in great seclusion from all knowledge of poverty and oppression in a silent garden with three sisters, but the rumor that a female servant had treated one of them rudely just before her death plunged him into early pessimism. He felt that little Jane would come back certainly in the spring with the roses, and he was glad that his utter misery with the blank anarchy and confusion it brought could not be completely remembered. He stole into the chamber where her corpse lay, and as he stood, a solemn wind, the saddest he ever heard, that might have swept the fields of mortality for a thousand centuries, blew, and that same hollow Memnonian wind he often had heard since, and it brought back the open summer window and the corpse. A vault above opened into the sky, and he slept and dreamed there, standing by her, he knew not how long; a worm that could not die was at his heart, for this was the holy love between children that could not perish. The funeral was full of darkness and despair for him, and after it he sought solitude, gazed into the heavens to see his sister till he was tired, and realized that he was alone. Thus, before the end of his sixth year, with a mind already adolescent, although with a retarded body, the minor tone of life became dominant and his awakening to it was hard.

As a penniless schoolboy wandering the streets of London at night, he was on familiar and friendly terms of innocent relationship with a number of outcast women. In his misery they were to him simply sisters in calamity, but he found in them humanity, disinterested generosity, courage, and fidelity. One night, after he had walked the streets for weeks with one of these friendless girls who had not completed her sixteenth year, as they sat on the steps of a house, he grew very ill, and had she not rushed to buy from her slender purse cordials and tenderly ministered to and revived him, he would have died. Many years later he used to wander past this house, and he recalled with real tenderness this youthful friendship; he longed again to meet the "noble-minded Ann ——" with whom he had so often conversed familiarly "more Socratico," whose betrayer he had vainly sought to punish, and yearned to hear from her to convey to her some authentic message of gratitude, peace, and forgiveness.

His much older brother came home in his thirty-ninth year to die. He had been unmanageable in youth and his genius for mischief was an inspiration, yet he was hostile to everything pusillanimous, haughty, aspiring, ready to fasten a quarrel on his shadow for running before, at first inclined to reduce his boy brother to a fag, but finally before his death became a great influence in his life. Prominent were the fights between De Quincey and another older brother on the one hand and the factory crowd of boys on the other, a fight incessantly renewed at the close of factory hours, with victory now on one and now on the other side; fought with stones and sticks, where thrice he was taken prisoner, where once one of the factory women kissed him, to the great delight of his heart. He finally invented a kingdom like Hartley Coleridge, called Gom Broon. He thought first that it had no location, but finally because his brother's imaginary realm was north and he wanted wide waters between them, his was in the far south. It was only two hundred and seventy miles in circuit, and he was stunned to be told by his brother one day that his own domain swept south for eighty degrees, so that the distance he had relied on vanished. Here, however, he continued to rule for well or ill, raising taxes, keeping an imaginary standing army, fishing herring and selling the product of his fishery for manure, and experiencing how "uneasy lies the head that wears a crown." He worried over his obligations to Gom Broon, and the shadow froze into reality, and although his brother's kingdom Tigrosylvania was larger, his was distinguished for eminent men and a history not to be ashamed of. A friend had read Lord Monboddo's view that men had sprung from apes, and suggested that the inhabitants of Gom Broon had tails, so that the brother told him that his subjects had not emerged from apedom and he must invent arts to eliminate the tails. They must be made to sit down for six hours a day as a beginning. Abdicate he would not, though all his subjects had three tails apiece. They had suffered together. Vain was his brother's suggestion that they have a Roman toga to conceal their ignominious appendages. He was greatly interested in two scrofulous idiots, who finally died, and feared that his subjects were akin to them.

John Stuart Mill's Autobiography presents one of the most remarkable modifications of the later phases of adolescent experience. No boy ever had more diligent and earnest training than his father gave him or responded better. He can not remember when he began to learn Greek, but was told that it was at the age of three. The list of classical authors alone that he read in the original, to say nothing of history, political, scientific, logical, and other works before he was twelve, is perhaps unprecedented in all history. He associated with his father and all his many friends on their own level, but modestly ascribes everything to his environment, insists that in natural gifts he is rather below than above par, and declares that everything he did could be done by every boy of average capacity and healthy physical constitution. His father made the Greek virtue of temperance or moderation cardinal, and thought human life "a poor thing at best after the freshness of youth and unsatisfied curiosity had gone by." He scorned "the intense" and had only contempt for strong emotion.

In his teens Mill was an able debater and writer for the quarterlies, and devoted to the propagation of the theories of Bentham, Ricardo, and associationism. From the age of fifteen he had an object in life, viz., to reform the world. This gave him happiness, deep, permanent, and assured for the future, and the idea of struggling to promote utilitarianism seemed an inspiring program for life. But in the autumn of 1826, when he was twenty years of age, he fell into "a dull state of nerves," where he could no longer enjoy, and what had produced pleasure seemed insipid; "the state, I should think, in which converts to Methodism usually are when smitten by their first 'conviction of sin.' In this frame of mind it occurred to me to put the question directly to myself: 'Suppose that all your objects in life were realized; that all the changes in institutions and opinions which you are looking forward to could be completely effected at this very instant; would this be a great joy and happiness to you?' And an irrepressible self-consciousness distinctly answered, 'No.' At this my heart sank within me: the whole foundation on which my life was constructed fell down. All my happiness was to have been found in the continual pursuit of this end. The end had ceased to charm, and how could there ever again be any interest in the means? I seemed to have nothing left to live for. At first I hoped that the cloud would pass away of itself, but it did not. A night's sleep, the sovereign remedy for the smaller vexations of life, had no effect on it. I awoke to a renewed consciousness of the woful fact. I carried it with me into all companies, into all occupations. Hardly anything had power to cause me even a few minutes' oblivion of it. For some months the cloud seemed to grow thicker and thicker. The lines in Coleridge's Dejection—I was not then acquainted with them—exactly described my case:

"A grief without a pang, void, dark and drear,
A drowsy, stifled, unimpassioned grief,
Which finds no natural outlet or relief
In word, or sigh, or tear."

"In vain I sought relief from my favorite books, those memorials of past nobleness and greatness from which I had always hitherto drawn strength and animation. I read them now without feeling, or with the accustomed feeling minus all its charm; and I became persuaded that my love of mankind, and of excellence for its own sake, had worn itself out. I sought no comfort by speaking to others of what I felt. If I had loved any one sufficiently to make confiding my griefs a necessity, I should not have been in the condition I was. I felt, too, that mine was not an interesting or in any way respectable distress. There was nothing in it to attract sympathy. Advice, if I had known where to seek it, would have been most precious. The words of Macbeth to the physician often occurred to my thoughts. But there was no one on whom I could build the faintest hope of such assistance. My father, to whom it would have been natural to me to have recourse in any practical difficulties, was the last person to whom, in such a case as this, I looked for help. Everything convinced me that he had no knowledge of any such mental state as I was suffering from, and that even if he could be made to understand it, he was not the physician who could heal it. My education, which was wholly his work, had been conducted without any regard to the possibility of its ending in this result, and I saw no use in giving him the pain of thinking that his plans had failed, when the failure was probably irremediable, and, at all events, beyond the power of his remedies. Of other friends, I had at that time none to whom I had any hope of making my condition intelligible. It was, however, abundantly intelligible to myself, and the more I dwelt upon it the more hopeless it appeared."

He now saw what had hitherto seemed incredible, that the habit of analysis tends to wear away the feelings. He felt "stranded at the commencement of my voyage, with a well-equipped ship and a rudder, but no sail; without any real desire for the ends which I had been so carefully fitted out to work for: no delight in virtue, or the general good, but also just as little in anything else. The fountains of vanity and ambition seemed to have dried up within me as completely as those of benevolence." His vanity had been gratified at too early an age, and, like all premature pleasures, they had caused indifference, until he despaired of creating any fresh association of pleasure with any objects of human desire. Meanwhile, dejected and melancholy as he was through the winter, he went on mechanically with his tasks; thought he found in Coleridge the first description of what he was feeling; feared the idiosyncrasies of his education had made him a being unique and apart. "I asked myself if I could or if I was bound to go on living, when life must be passed in this manner. I generally answered to myself that I did not think I could possibly bear it beyond a year." But within about half that time, in reading a pathetic passage of how a mere boy felt that he could save his family and take the place of all they had lost, a vivid conception of the scene came over him, and he was moved to tears. From that moment his burden grew lighter. He saw that his heart was not dead and that he still had some stuff left of which character and happiness were made; and although there were several later lapses, some of which lasted many months, he was never again as miserable as he had been.

These experiences left him changed in two respects. He had a new theory of life, having much in common with the anti-self-consciousness theory of Carlyle. He still held happiness the end of life, but thought it must be aimed at indirectly and taken incidentally. The other change was that for the first time he gave its proper place to internal culture of the individual, especially the training of the feelings which became now cardinal. He realized and felt the power of poetry and art; was profoundly moved by music; fell in love with Wordsworth and with nature; and his later depressions were best relieved by the power of rural beauty, which wrought its charm not because of itself but by the states and feelings it aroused. His ode on the intimations of immortality showed that he also had felt that the first freshness of youthful joy was not lasting, and had sought and found compensation. He had thus come to a very different standpoint from that of his father, who had up to this time formed his mind and life, and developed on this basis his unique individuality.

Laurence Oliphant[1] was born in 1829. When he was twelve, "with all his faculties and his whole being agog for novelty and incident," he traveled alone from England to the East and had no more systematic education. But his active mind was immensely stimulated by his mother, only eighteen years older than himself. By seventeen he was a confirmed "rolling stone," and he never ceased his roving habits. He remained an adolescent all his life. He was intensely interested by turns in all sorts of political, social, artistic, military, and religious matters, and a citizen of three continents.[2]

---

[1] Memoir of the Life of Laurence Oliphant and of Alice Oliphant, his Wife. By Margaret O. W. Oliphant. 2 vols. New York, 1891.

[2] In 1867, when he was thirty-eight, already well known as a somewhat Bohemian litterateur, he met a zealot preacher itinerating in England and followed him to America, to the consternation of his friends, to join a community at Brockton or Salem or Erie to "live the life." He was sent to sleep in a loft; to clean a large cattle stable, wheel dirt and rubbish; could speak to no one; and his food was conveyed to him by a silent messenger. The "infernals" were often active and infested many, who were brought to Harris, the leader, who could cast out devils. To bind evil spirits, it was sometimes necessary for victims to be robbed of their sleep. Men were assorted in groups according as their magnetism helped or hindered each other, for all were batteries of unseen force. Families were broken up that love for the race might supplant that for the individual. For three years Oliphant led the life of a hard laborer. He was a teamster and "cadged strawberries" along the railroad, for all must serve a two years' novitiate. His delicate mother, Lady Oliphant, followed her son, and laying aside all the habits of her life, washed, scrubbed, cooked, and cleaned house; but though in the same community, could see her son, in whom her life was bound up and whose every serious thought she shared, only as other members of the community. After three years, in 1870, Oliphant returned and curiously dropped into the same place in society that he had held be-

Jeffries, when eighteen, began his Story of My Heart, which he said was an absolutely true confession of the stages of emotion in a soul from which all traces of tradition and learning were erased, and which stood face to face with nature and the unknown.

His heart long seemed dusty and parched for want of feeling, and he frequented a hill, where the pores of his soul opened to a new air. "Lying down on the grass, I spoke in my soul to the earth, the sun, the air, and the distant sea. . . . I desired to have its strength, its mystery and glory. I addressed the sun, desiring the sole equivalent of his light and brilliance, his endurance, and unwearied race. I turned to the blue heaven over, gazing into its depth, inhaling its exquisite color and sweetness. The rich blue of the unobtainable flower of the sky drew my soul toward it, and there it rested, for pure color is the rest of the heart. By all these I prayed. I felt an emotion of the soul beyond all definition; prayer is a puny thing to it." He prayed by the thyme; by the earth; the flowers which he touched; the dust which he let fall through his fingers; was filled with "a rapture, an ecstasy, an inflatus. With this inflatus I prayed. . . . I hid my face in the grass; I was wholly prostrated; I lost myself in the wrestle. . . . I see now that what I labored for was soul life, more soul learning." After gazing upward he would turn his face into the

---

fore. Still enthusiastic in his admiration of Harris, he urged that men must forsake all for the cross and be drudges and martyrs in the modern sense of the word in order to embody heavenly ideas. Both had found peace and content in this community and its spiritual atmosphere, although he slept on straw over a stable, rose at four to clean and feed horses, and worked till eight to thrash the devil out of him. He still regarded Brockton as the ideal of society. Soon after returning, a little sobered from his first elation, he met in Paris the beautiful and accomplished Alice le Strange, descended from a long line of country gentlefolk. She was a fine musician, full of inexplicable charm, vivacity, and beauty, and had already tasted all the applause of society until, like Edward Irving, she wanted something larger and more authoritative. It was almost love at first sight, and in 1872 they were betrothed, despite the protest of her friends. He infected her with love of his American scheme, and when, after some postponements, they were married, she entered enthusiastically into his plans, and even placed the whole of her property in the hands of Harris. The year 1873 found him with mother and wife back at Brockton under the "father," who separated husband and wife, and finally sent Alice to his new settlement in California. After some wandering on his part, during which he tried to exploit the Dead Sea for its chemical and mineral deposits, if only the Sultan had consented, the husband and wife were reunited. They went to Egypt, then to Palestine, always writing and scheming, and composing one strange book, "Synpneumata," in common, till at last, in 1878, she died; her spirit remained with her devoted, adventurous, and visionary husband, who married again in 1888, and died shortly after.

grass, shutting out everything with hands each side, till he felt down into the earth and was absorbed in it, whispering deep down to its center. Every natural impression, trees, insects, air, clouds, he used for prayer, "that my soul might be more than the cosmos of life." His "Lyra" prayer was to live a more exalted and intense soul life; enjoy more bodily pleasure and live long and find power to execute his designs. He often tried, but failed for years to write at least a meager account of these experiences. He felt himself immortal just as he felt beauty. He was in eternity already; the supernatural is only the natural misnamed. As he lay face down on the grass, seizing it with both hands, he longed for death, to be burned on a pyre of pine wood on a high hill, to have his ashes scattered wide and broadcast, to be thrown into the space he longed for while living, but he feared that such a luxury of resolution into the elements would be too costly. Thus his naked mind, close against naked mother Nature, wrested from her the conviction of soul, immortality, deity, under conditions as primitive as those of the cave man, and his most repeated prayer was, "Give me the deepest soul life."

In other moods he felt the world outré-human, and his mind could by no twist be fitted to the cosmos. Ugly, designless creatures caused him to cease to look for deity in nature, where all happens by chance. He at length concluded there is something higher than soul and above deity, and better than God, for which he searched and labored. He found favorite thinking places, to which he made pilgrimages, where he "felt out into the depths of the ether." His frame could not bear the labor his heart demanded. Work of body was his meat and drink. "Never have I had enough of it. I wearied long before I was satisfied, and weariness did not bring a cessation of desire, the thirst was still there. I rode; I used the ax; I split tree-trunks with wedges; my arms tired, but my spirit remained fresh and chafed against the physical weariness." Had he been indefinitely stronger, he would have longed for more strength. He was often out of doors all day and often half the night; wanted more sunshine; wished the day was sixty hours long; took pleasure in braving the cold so that it should be not life's destroyer but its renewer. Yet he abhorred asceticism. He wrestled with the problem of the origin of his soul and its destiny, but could find no solution; revolted at the assertion that all is designed for the best; "a man of intellect and humanity could cause everything to happen in an infinitely superior manner." He discovered that no one ever died of old age, but only of disease; that we do not even know what old age would be like; found that his soul is infinite, but lies in abeyance; that we are murdered by our ancestors and must roll back the tide of death; that a hundredth part of man's labor would suffice for his support; that idleness is no evil; that in the future nine-tenths of the time will be leisure, and to that end he will work with all his heart. "I was not more than eighteen when an inner and esoteric meaning began to come to me from all the visible universe, and indefinable aspirations filled me."

Interesting as is this document, it is impossible to avoid the suspicion that the seventeen years which intervened between the beginning of these experiences and their final record, coupled with the perhaps unconscious tendency toward literary effect, detract more or less from their value as documents of adolescent nature.

Mr. H. Fielding, author of The Soul of a People, has since written a book[1] in which, beginning with many definitions of Christianity, weighing the opinion of those who think all our advance is made because of, against those who think it in spite of Christianity, he proceeds to give the story of a boy, probably himself, who till twelve was almost entirely reared by women and with children younger than himself.

He was sickly, and believed not in the Old but in the New Testament; in the Sermon on the Mount, which he supposed all accepted and lived by; that war and wealth were bad, and learning apt to be a snare; that the ideal life was that of a poor curate, working hard and unhappy. At twelve he went to a boarding-school, passed from a woman's world into a man's, out of the New Testament into the Old, out of dreams into reality. War was a glorious opportunity, and all followed the British victories, which were announced publicly. Big boys were going to Sandhurst or Woolwich; there were parties; and the school code never turned the other cheek. Wars were God's storms, stirring stagnant natures to new life; wealth was worshiped; certain lies were an honor; knowledge was an extremely desirable thing—all this was at first new and delightful, but extremely wicked. Sunday was the only other Old Testament rule, but was then forgotten. Slowly a repugnance of religion in all its forms arose. He felt his teachers hypocrites; he raised no alarm, " for he was hardly conscious that his anchor had dragged or that he had lost hold " of it forever. At eighteen he read Darwin and found that if he were right Genesis was wrong; man had risen, not fallen; if a part was wrong, the whole was. If God made the world, the devil seemed to rule it; prayer can not influence him; the seven days of creation were periods, Heaven knows how long. Why did all profess and no one believe religion? Why is God so stern and yet so partial, and how about the Trinity? Then explanations were given. Heaven grew repulsive, as a place for the poor, the maimed, the stupid, the childish, and those unfit for earth generally.

Faiths came from the East. " The North has originated only Thor, Odin, Balder, Valkyres." The gloom and cold drive man into himself; do not open him. In the East one can live in quiet solitude, with no

[1] The Hearts of Men. London, 1891, p. 324.

effort, close to nature. The representatives of all faiths wear ostentatiously their badges, pray in public, and no one sneers at all religions. Oriental faiths have no organization; there is no head of Hinduism, Buddhism, or hardly of Mohammedanism. There are no missions, but religion grows rankly from a rich soil, so the boy wrote three demands: a reasonable theory of the universe, a workable and working code of conduct, and a promise of something desirable hereafter. So he read books and tried to make a system.

On a hill, in a thunder-storm in the East, he realized how Thor was born. Man fears thunder; it seems the voice of a greater man. Deny eyes, legs, and body of the Deity, and nothing is left. God as an abstract spirit is unthinkable, but Buddhism offers us no God, only law. Necessity, blind force, law, and a free personal will, that is alternative. Freedom limits omnipotence; the two can never mix. "The German Emperor's God, clanking round the heavenly mansions wearing a German *Pickelhaube* and swearing German oaths," is not satisfactory. Man's God is what he admires most in himself; he can be propitiated, hence atonement; you can not break a law, but you can study it. Inquiry, not submission, is the attitude. Perhaps both destiny and freedom are true, but truth is for the sake of light.

Thor had no moral code; the Greeks were unmoral. Jehovah at first asked only fear, reverence, and worship. This gives no guide to life. Most codes are directed against a foe and against pain. Truth, mercy, courtesy—these were slowly added to reverence; then sanitary rules, hence castes. Two codes, those of Christ and Buddha, tower above all others. They are the same in praising not wealth, greatness, or power, but purity, renunciation of the world, as if one fitted one's self for one by being unfitted for the other world.

Is heaven a bribe? Its ideals are those of children, of girl angels, white wings, floating dresses, no sheep, but lambs. "Surely there is nothing in all the world so babyish." One can hardly imagine a man with a deep voice, with the storm of life beating his soul, amid those baby faces. If happiness in any act or attitude is perfect, it will last forever. Where is due the weariness or satiety? But if happiness be perfect, this is impossible; so life would be monotony akin to annihilation. But life is change, and change is misery. There is effort here, but there will be none in the great peace that passes understanding; no defeat, therefore no victory; no friends, because no enemies; no joyous meetings, because no farewells. It is the shadows and the dark mysteries that sound the depths of our hearts. No man that ever lived, if told that he could be young again or go to any heaven, would choose the latter. Men die for many things, but all fear the beyond. Thus no religion gives us an intelligible First Cause, a code or a heaven that we want. The most religious man is the peasant listening to the angelus, putting out a little *ghi* for his God; the woman crying in the pagoda. Thus we can only turn to the hearts of men for the truth of religion.

Anthony Trollope's autobiography is pitiful. He was poor and disliked by most of his masters and treated with ignominy by his fellow pupils.

He describes himself as always in disgrace. At fifteen he walked three miles each way twice a day to and from school. As a sizar he seemed a wretched farmer's boy, reeking from the dunghill, sitting next the sons of big peers. All were against him, and he was allowed to join no games,and learned, he tells us, absolutely nothing but a little Greek and Latin. Once only, goaded to desperation, he rallied and whipped a bully. The boy was never able to overcome the isolation of his school position, and while he coveted popularity with an eagerness which was almost mean, and longed exceedingly to excel in cricket or with the racquet, was allowed to know nothing of them. He remembers at nineteen never to have had a lesson in writing, arithmetic, French, or German. He knew his masters by their ferules and they him. He believes that he has "been flogged oftener than any human being alive." "It was just possible to obtain five scourgings in one day at Winchester, and I have often boasted that I have obtained them all." Prizes were distributed prodigally, but he never got one. For twelve years of tuition, he says, "I do not remember that I ever knew a lesson."

At this age he describes himself as "an idle, desolate hanger-on . . . without an idea of a career or a profession or a trade," but he was tolerably happy because he could fancy himself in love with pretty girls and had been removed from the real misery of school, but had not a single aspiration regarding his future. Three of his household were dying of consumption, and his mother was day nurse, night nurse, and divided her time between pill-boxes and the ink-bottle, for when she was seventy-six she had written one hundred and forty volumes, the first of which was not written till she was fifty.

Gradually the boy became alive to the blighted ambition of his father's life and the strain his mother was enduring, nursing the dying household and writing novels to provide a decent roof for them to die under. Anthony had got his position without an examination; knew no French nor science; was a bad speller and worse writer, and could not have sustained an examination on any subject. Still he could not bear idleness, and was always going about with some castle in the air firmly built in his mind, carrying on for weeks and years the same continuous story; binding himself down to certain laws, proprieties, and unities; always his own hero, excluding everything violently improbable. To this practise, which he calls dangerous and which began six or seven years before he went to the post-office, he ascribes his power to maintain an interest in a fictitious story and to live in an entirely outside imaginative life. During these seven years he acquired a character of irregularity and grew reckless.

Mark Pattison[1] shows us how his real life began in the middle

[1] See his Memoirs. London, 1855.

teens, when his energy was "directed to one end, to improve myself"; "to form my own mind; to sound things thoroughly; to be free from the bondage of unreason and the traditional prejudices which, when I first began to think, constituted the whole of my mental fabric." He entered upon life with a "hide-bound and contracted intellect," and depicts "something of the steps by which I emerged from that frozen condition." He believes that to "remember the dreams and confusions of childhood and never to lose the recollection of the curiosity and simplicity of that age, is one of the great gifts of the poetic character," although this, he tells us, was extraordinarily true of George Sand, but not of himself. From the age of twelve on, a Fellowship at Oriel was the ideal of his life, and although he became a commoner there at seventeen, his chief marvel is that he was so immature and unimpressionable.

Mark Rutherford[1] learned little at school, save Latin and good penmanship, but his very life was divided into halves—Sundays and week days—and he reflects at some length upon the immense dangers of the early teens; the physiological and yet subtler psychic penalties of error; callousness to fine pleasures; hardening of the conscience; and deplores the misery which a little instruction might have saved him. At fourteen he underwent conversion, understood in his sect to be a transforming miracle, releasing higher and imprisoning lower powers. He compares it to the saving of a mind from vice by falling in love with a woman who is adored, or the reclamation of a young woman from idleness and vanity by motherhood. But as a boy he was convinced of many things which were mere phrases, and attended prayer-meetings for the clanship of being marked off from the world and of walking home with certain girls. He learned to say in prayer that there was nothing good in him; that he was rotten and filthy and his soul a mass of putrefying sores, but no one took him at his word and expelled him from society, but thought the better of him. Soon he began to study theology, but found no help in suppressing tempestuous lust, in understanding the Bible, or getting his doubts answered, and all the lectures seemed irrelevant chattering. An infidel was a monster whom he had rarely ever seen. At nineteen he began to preach, but his heart was untouched till he read Wordsworth's lyrical ballads, and this recreated a living God for him, melted his heart to tears, and made him long for companionship; its effect was instantly seen in his preaching, and made him soon slightly suspected as heretical.[2]

[1] See his Autobiography, edited by Reuben Shapcott. 2 vols. London, 1881.

[2] The rest of the two volumes is devoted to his further life of a dissenting minister, who later became something of a literary man; relating how he was slowly driven to leave his little church, how he outgrew and broke with the girl to whom he was engaged, whom he marvelously met and married when both were well on in years, and how strangely he was influenced by the free-thinker Mardon and his remarkable daughter. All in all it is a rare study of emancipation.

John Addington Symonds, in his biography, describes his "insect-like" devotion to creed in the green infancy of ritualism. In his early teens at boarding-school he and his mates, with half sincerity, followed a classmate to compline, donned surplices, tossed censers, arranged altars in their studies, bought bits of painted glass for their windows, and illuminated crucifixes with gold dust and vermilion. When he was confirmed, this was somewhat of an epoch. Preparation was like a plowshare, although it turned up nothing valuable, and stimulated esthetic and emotional ardor. In a dim way he felt God near, but he did not learn to fling the arms of the soul in faith around the cross of Christ. Later the revelation he found in Plato removed him farther from boyhood. He fell in love with gray Gothic churches, painted glass, organ lofts, etc.

Walter Pater has described phases of ferment, perhaps largely his own, in the character of Florian Deleal; his rapture of the red hawthorn blossoms, "absolutely the reddest of all things," an experience with which all red things in art later reminded him; his times of "seemingly exclusive predominance of interest in beautiful physical things, a kind of tyranny of the senses"; and his later absorbing efforts to estimate the proportion of the sensuous and ideal, assigning most importance to sensible vehicles and occasions; associating all thoughts with touch and sight as a link between himself and things, till he became more and more "unable to care for or think of soul but as in an actual body"; comforted in the contemplation of death by the thought of flesh turning to violets and almost oppressed by the pressure of the sensible world, his longings for beauty intensifying his fear of death. He loved to gaze on dead faces in the Paris Morgue, although the haunt of them made the sunshine sickly for days, and his long fancy that they had not really gone nor were quite motionless, but led a secret, half fugitive life, freer by night, and perhaps dodging about in their old haunts with no great good-will toward the living, made him by turns pity and hate the ghosts who came back in the wind, beating at the doors. His religious nature gradually yielded to a mystical belief in Bible personages in some indefinite place as the reflexes and patterns of our nobler self, whose companionship made the world more satisfying. There was "a constant substitution of the typical for the actual," and angels might be met anywhere. "A deep mysticity brooded over real meetings and partings," marriages, and many acts and accidents of life. "The very colors of things became themselves weighty with meanings," or "full of penitence and peace." "For a time he walked through the world in a sustained, not unpleasurable awe generated by the habitual recognition, beside every circumstance and event of life, of its celestial correspondent."

In D. C. Boulger's Life of General Charles Gordon[1] he records how, like Nelson Clive, his hero was prone to boys' escapades and outbreaks that often made him the terror of his superiors. He was

[1] London, 1896, vol. i.

no bookworm, but famous as the possessor of high spirits, very often involved in affairs that necessitated discipline, and seemed greatly out of harmony with the popular idea of the ascetic of Mount Carmel. As a schoolboy he made wonderful squirts "that would wet you through in a minute." One Sunday twenty-seven panes of glass in a large storehouse were broken with screws shot through them by his cross-bow "for ventilation." Ringing bells and pushing young boys in, butting an unpopular officer severely in the stomach with his head, and taking the punishment, hitting a bully with a clothes-brush and being put back six months in the Royal Military Academy at Woolwich; these are the early outcrops of one side of his dual character. Although more soldier than saint, he had a very cheery, genial side. He was always ready to take even the severest punishment for all his scrapes due to excessive high spirits. When one of his superiors declared that he would never make an officer, he felt his honor touched, and his vigorous and expressive reply was to tear the epaulets from his shoulders and throw them at his superior's feet. He had already developed some of the rather moody love of seclusion that was marked later, but religion did not strike him deeply enough to bring him into the Church until he was twenty-one, when he took his first sacrament. On one occasion he declined promotion within his reach because he would have had to pass a friend to get it. He acted generally on his impulses, which were perhaps better than his judgments, took great pleasure in corresponding on religious topics with his older sister, and early formed the habit of excessive smoking which gravely affected his health later. His was the rare combination of inner repose and confidence, interrupted by spells of gaiety.

Williamson, in his Life of Holman Hunt, tells us that at thirteen he was removed from school as inapt in study. He began to spend his time in drawing in his copybooks. He was made clerk to an auctioneer, who fortunately encouraged his passion, and at sixteen was with a calico printer. Here he amused himself by drawing flies on the window which his employer tried to brush off. There was the greatest home opposition to his studying art. After being rejected twice, he was admitted at seventeen to the Academy school as a probationer, and the next year, in 1845, as a student. Here he met Millais and Rossetti and was able to relieve the strain on his mind which the worry of his father concerning his course caused him, and very soon his career began.

At thirteen Fitzjames Stephen[1] roused himself to thrash a big boy who had long bullied him, and became a fighter. In his sixteenth year he grew nearly five inches, but was so shy and timid at Eton that he says, "I was like a sensible grown-up woman among a crowd of rough boys"; but in the reaction to the long abuse his mind was steeled against oppression, tyranny, and every kind of unfairness. He read Paine's Age of Reason, and went "through the Bible as a

[1] See his Life. By his brother, Leslie Stephen. London, 1895.

man might go through a wood, cutting down trees. The priests can stick them in again, but they will not make them grow."

Dickens has given us some interesting adolescents. Miss Dingwall, in Sketches by Boz, "very sentimental and romantic"; the tempery young Nickleby, who at nineteen thrashed Squeers; Barnaby Rudge, idiotic and very muscular; Joe Willet, persistently treated as a boy till he ran away to join the army and married Dolly Varden, perhaps the most exuberant, good-humored, and beautiful girl in all the Dickens gallery; Martin Chuzzlewit, who also ran away, as did David Copperfield, perhaps the most true to adolescence because largely reminiscent of the author's own life; Steerforth, a stranger from home and his victim, Little Emily; and to some extent Sam Weller, Dick Swiveller, the Marchioness, young Podsnap, the Artful Dodger and Charley Bates, while Oliver Twist, Little Nell, and Little Dorrit, Joe and Turveydrop in Bleak House, and Paul Dombey, young as they were, show the beginning of the pubescent change. Most of his characters, however, are so overdrawn and caricatured as to be hardly true to life.[1]

In the Romance of John Inglesant, by J. H. Shorthouse, we have a remarkable picture of an unusually gifted youth, who played an important rôle in the days of Cromwell and King Charles, and who was long poised in soul between the Church of Rome and the English party. He was very susceptible to the fascination of superstition, romance, and day-dreaming, and at eleven absorbed his master's Rosicrucian theories of spiritual existence where spirits held converse with each other and with mankind. A mystic Platonism, which taught that Pindar's story of the Argo was only a recipe for the philosopher's stone, fascinated him at fourteen. The philosophy of obedience and of the subjection of reason to authority was early taught him, and he sought to live from within, hearing only the divine law, as the worshipers of Cybele heard only the flutes. His twin brother Eustace was an active worldling, and soon he followed him to court as page to the Queen, but delighted more and more in wandering apart and building air castles. For a time he was entirely swayed and his life directed by a Jesuit Father, who taught him the crucifix and the rosary. At sixteen the doctrine of divine illumination fascinated him. He struggled to find the path of true devotion; abandoned him-

[1] See the very impressive account of Dickens's characterization of childhood and youth, and of his great but hitherto inadequately recognized interest and influence as an educator. By James L. Hughes, New York, 1901, p. 319.

self to extremely ritualistic forms of worship; dabbled a little in alchemy and astrology to help develop the divine nature within him and to attain the beatific vision. Soon he was introduced to the " Protestant nunnery," as it was called, where the venerable Mr. Ferran, a friend of George Herbert's, was greatly taken by Inglesant's accomplishments and grace of manner. Various forms of extremely High Church yet Protestant worship were celebrated here each day with great devotion, until he became disgusted with Puritanism and craved to participate in the office of mass. At this point, however, he met Mr. Hobbes, whose rude but forcible condemnation of papacy restrained him from casting his lot with it. At seventeen he saw one night a real apparition of the just executed Strafford. The last act of his youth, which we can note here, was soon after he was twenty, when he fell in love with the charming and saintly Mary Collet. The rough Puritan Thorne had made her proposals at which she revolted, but she and Inglesant confessed love to each other; she saw, however, that they had a way of life marked out for themselves by an inner impulse and light. This calling they must follow and abandon love, and now John plunged into the war on the side of the King.

W. J. Stillman[1] has written with unusual interest and candor the story of his own early life. As a boy he was frenzied at the first sight of the sea; caught the whip and lashed the horses in an unconscious delirium, and always remembered this as one of the most vivid experiences of his life. He had a period of nature worship. His first trout was a delirium, and he danced about wildly and furiously. He relates his very vivid impressions of the religious orthodoxy in which he was reared, especially revival sermons; his occasional falsehoods to escape severe punishment; his baptism at ten or eleven in a river in midwinter; the somberness of his intellectual life, which was long very apathetic; his phenomenal stupidity for years; his sudden insurrections in which he thrashed bullies at school; his fear that he should be sent home in disgrace for bad scholarship; and how at last, after seven years of dulness, at the age of fourteen, "the mental fog broke away suddenly, and before the term ended I could construe the Latin in less time than it took to recite it, and the demonstrations of Euclid were as plain and clear as a fairy story. My memory came back so distinctly that I could recite long poems after a single reading, and no member of the class passed a more brilliant examination at the end of the term

[1] The Autobiography of a Journalist. 2 vols. Boston, 1901.

than I; and at the end of the second term I could recite the whole of Legendre's geometry, plane and spherical, from beginning to end without a question, and the class examination was recorded as the most remarkable which the academy had witnessed for many years. I have never been able to conceive an explanation of this curious phenomenon, which I record only as of possible interest to some one interested in psychology."

A. Bronson Alcott[1] was the son of a Connecticut farmer. He began a diary at twelve; aspired vainly to enter Yale, and after much restlessness at the age of nineteen left home with two trunks for Virginia to peddle on foot, hoping to teach school. Here he had a varying and often very hard experience for years.

Horace Bushnell's[2] parents represented the Episcopal and liberal Congregational Church. His early life was spent on a farm and in attending a country academy. He became profoundly interested in religion in the early teens and developed extreme interest in nature. At seventeen, while tending a carding machine, he wrote a paper on Calvinism. At nineteen he united with the church, and entered Yale, when he was twenty-one, in 1823. Later he tried to teach school but left it, declaring he would rather lay stone wall, worked on a journal but withdrew, finding it a terrible life, studied law for a year, became a tutor at Yale, experienced a reconversion and entered the ministry.

A well-known American, who wishes his name withheld, writes me of his youth as follows:

"First came the love of emotion and lurid romance reading. My mind was full of adventure, dreams of underground passages, and imprisoned beauties whom I rescued. I wrote a story in red ink, which I never read, but a girl friend did, and called it magnificent. The girl fever, too, made me idealize first one five years older than I, later another three years older, and still later one of my own age. I would have eaten dirt for each of them for a year or two; was extremely gallant and the hero of many romances for two, but all the time so bashful that I scarcely dared speak to one of them, and no schoolmate ever suspected it all. Music also became a craze at fourteen. Before, I had hated lessons, now I was thrilled and would be a musician, despite my parents' protests. I practised the piano furiously; wrote music and copied stacks of it; made a list of several hundred pieces and tunes, including everything musical I knew; would imagine a crowded hall, where I played and swayed with fine airs. The vast assembly applauded and would not let me go, but all the time it was a simple piece and I was a very ordinary player. At fifty years this is still a relic. I now in hours of fatigue pound the piano and dream-

[1] See his Life and Philosophy, by Sanborn and Harris.

[2] Theodore F. Munger: Life of Horace Bushnell. Boston, 1899.

ily imagine dazed and enchanted audiences. Then came oratory, and I glowed and thrilled in declaiming Webster's Reply to Hayne, Thanatopsis, Byron's Darkness, Patrick Henry, and best of all The Maniac, which I spouted in a fervid way wearing a flaming red necktie. I remember a fervid scene with myself on a high solitary hill with a bald summit two miles from home, where I once went because I had been blamed. I tried to sum myself up, inventory my good and bad points. It was Sunday, and I was keyed up to a frenzy of resolve, prayer, idealization of life; all grew all in a jumble. My resolve to go to college was clinched then and there, and that hill will always remain my Pisgah and Moriah, Horeb and Sinai all in one. I paced back and forth in the wind and shouted, 'I will make people know and revere me; I will do something'; and called everything to witness my vow that I never again would visit this spot till all was fulfilled." "Alas!" he says, "I have never been there since. Once, to a summer party who went, I made excuse for not keeping this rendezvous. It was too sacramental. Certainly it was a very deep and never-to-be-forgotten experience there all alone, when something of great moment to me certainly took place in my soul."

In the biography of Frederick Douglass[1] we are told that when he was about thirteen he began to feel deeply the moral yoke of slavery and to seek means of escaping it. He became interested in religion, was converted, and dreamed of and prayed for liberty. With great ingenuity he extracted knowledge of the alphabet and reading from white boys of his acquaintance. At sixteen, under a brutal master he revolted and was beaten until he was faint from loss of blood, and at seventeen he fought and whipped the brutal overseer Covey, who would have invoked the law, which made death the punishment for such an offense, but for shame of having been worsted by a negro boy and from the reflection that there was no profit from a dead slave. Only at twenty did he escape into the new world of freedom.

Jacob Riis[2] "fell head over heels in love with sweet Elizabeth" when he was fifteen and she thirteen. His "courtship proceeded at a tumultuous pace, which first made the town laugh, then put it out of patience and made some staid matrons express the desire to box my ears soundly." She played among the lumber where he worked, and he watched her so intently that he scarred his shinbone with an adze he should have been minding. He cut off his forefinger with an ax when she was dancing on a beam near by, and once fell off a roof when craning his neck to see her go round a corner. At another time he ordered her father off the dance-floor, because he tried to take his daughter home a few minutes before the appointed hour of midnight. Young as he was, he was large and tried to run away to join the army, but finally went to Copenhagen to serve his apprenticeship with a builder, and here had an interview with Hans Christian Anderson.

---

[1] By C. W. Chestnutt. [2] The Making of an American.

Ellery Sedgwick tells us that at thirteen the mind of Thomas Paine ran on stories of the sea which his teacher had told him, and he attempted to enlist on the privateer Terrible. He was restless at home for years, and shipped on a trading vessel at nineteen.

Indeed, modern literature in our tongue abounds in this element, from Childe Harold to the second and third long chapters in Mrs. Ward's David Grieve, ending with his engagement to Lucy Purcell; Thackeray's Arthur Pendennis and his characteristic love of the far older and scheming Fanny Fotheringay; David in Allen's Reign of Law, who read Darwin, was expelled from the Bible College and the Church, and finally was engaged to Gabrielle; and scores more might be enumerated. There is even Sonny,[1] who, rude as he was and poorly as he did in all his studies, at the same age when he began to keep company, "tallered" his hair, tied a bow of ribbon to the buggy whip, and grew interested in manners, passing things, putting on his coat and taking off his hat at table, began to study his menagerie of pet snakes, toads, lizards, wrote John Boroughs, helped him and got help in return, took to observing, and finally wrote a book about the forest and its occupants, all of which is very *bien trouvé* if not historic truth.

Two singular reflections always rearise in reading Goethe's autobiographical writings: first, that both the age and the place, with its ceremonies, festivals, great pomp and stirring events in close quarters in the little province where he lived, were especially adapted to educate children and absorb them in externals; and, second, that this wonderful boy had an extreme propensity for moralizing and drawing lessons of practical service from all about him. This is no less manifest in Wilhelm Meister's apprenticeship and travels, which supplements the autobiography. Both together present a very unique type of adolescence, the elaborate story of which defies epitome. From the puppet craze well on into his precocious university life it was his passion to explore the widest ranges of experience and then to reflect, moralize, or poetize upon them. Perhaps no one ever studied the nascent stages of his own life and elaborated their every incident with such careful observation and analysis. His peculiar diathesis enabled him to conserve their freshness on to full maturity, when he gave them literary form. Most lack power to fully utilize their own experience even for practical self-knowledge and guidance, but with Goethe nothing was wasted from which self-culture could be extracted.

---

[1] Sonny. Ruth McEnery Stuart. New York, 1896.

Goethe's first impression of female loveliness was of a girl name Gretchen, who served wine one evening, and whose face and form followed him for a long time. Their meetings always gave him a thrill of pleasure, and though his love was like many first loves, very spiritual and awakened by goodness and beauty, it gave a new brightness to the whole world, and to be near her seemed to him an indispensable condition of his being. Her *fiancé* was generally with her, and Goethe experienced a shock in finding that she had become a milliner's assistant, for although, like all natural boys of aristocratic families, he loved common people, this interest was not favored by his parents. The night following the coronation day several were compelled to spend in chairs, and he and his Gretchen with others slept, she with her head upon his shoulder, until all the others had awakened in the morning. At last they parted at her door, and for the first and last time they kissed but never met again, although he often wept in thinking of her. He was terribly affronted to fully realize that, although only two years older than himself, she should have regarded him as a child. He tried to strip her of all loving qualities and think her odious, but her image hovered over him. The sanity of instinct innate in youth prompted him to lay aside as childish the foolish habit of weeping and railing, and his mortification that she regarded him somewhat in the style of a nurse gradually helped to work his cure.

He was very fond of his own name, and, like young and uneducated people, wrote or carved it anywhere; later placed near it that of a new love, Annette, and afterward on finding the tree he shed tears, melted toward her, and made an idyl. He was also seized with a passion of teasing her and dominating over her devotedness with wanton and tyrannical caprice, venting upon her the ill humor of his disappointments, and grew absurdly jealous and lost her after she had borne with him with incredible patience and after terrible scenes with her by which he gained nothing. Frenzied with his loss, he began to abuse his physical nature and was only saved from illness by the healing power of his poetic talent; the Lover's Caprice was written with the impetus of a boiling passion. In the midst of many serious events, a reckless humor which was due to excess of life developed which made him feel himself superior to the moment, and even to court danger. He played tricks, although rarely with premeditation. Later he mused much upon the transient nature of love and the mutability of character; the extent to which the senses could be indulged within the bounds of morality; he sought to rid himself of all that troubled him by writing song or epigram about it, which made him seem frivolous and prompted one friend to seek to subdue him by means of church forms, which he had severed on coming to Leipzig. By degrees he felt an epoch approaching when all respect for authority was to vanish, and he became suspicious and even despairing with regard to the best individuals he had known before, and grew chummy with a young tutor whose jokes and fooleries were incessant. His disposition fluctuated between gaiety and melancholy, and Rousseau attracted him. Meanwhile his health declined until a long illness, which began with a hemorrhage, caused him to oscillate for days between life and death, and convalescence, generally so delightful, was marred by a serious tumor. His father's disposition was stern, and he could become passionate and bitter, and his mother's domesticity made her turn to religion, so that on coming home he formed the acquaintance of a religious circle. Again Goethe was told by a hostile child that he was not the true son of his father. This inoculated him with a disease that long lurked in his system and prompted various indirect investigations to get at the truth, during which he compared all distinguished guests with his own physiognomy to detect his own likeness.

Up to the Leipzig period he had great joy in wandering unknown, unconscious of self, but he soon began to torment himself with an almost hypertrophied fancy that he was attracting much attention; that others' eyes were turned on his person to fix it in their memories; that he was scanned and found fault with, and hence he developed a love of the country, of the woods and solitary places, where he could be hedged in and separated from all the world. Here he began to throw off his former habit of looking at things from the art standpoint and to take pleasure in natural objects for their own sake. His mother had almost grown up to consciousness in her two oldest children, and his first disappointment in love turned his thought all the more affectionately toward her and his sister, a year younger. He was long consumed with amazement over the newly awakening sense impulse that took intellectual forms and the mental needs that clothed themselves in sense images. He fell to building air castles of opposition lecture courses and gave himself up to many dreams of ideal university conditions. He first attended lectures diligently, but suffered much harm from being too advanced; learned a great deal that he could not regulate, and was thereby made uncomfortable; grew interested in the fit of his clothes, of which hitherto he had been careless; he was in despair at the uncertainty of his own taste and judgment, and almost feared he must make a complete change of mind, renouncing what he had hitherto learned, and so one day in great contempt for his past burned up his poetry, sketches, etc.

He had learned to value and love the Bible, and owed his moral culture to it. Its events and symbols were deeply stamped upon him, so without being a pietist he was greatly moved at the scoffing spirit toward it which he met at the university. From youth he had stood on good terms with God, and at times he had felt that he had some things to forgive God for not having given better assistance to his infinite good-will. Under all this influence he turned to cabalism and became interested in crystals and the microcosm and macrocosm, and fell into the habit of despairing what he had been and believed just before. He conceived a kind of hermetical or neoplatonic godhead creating in more and more eccentric circles, until the last, which rose in contradiction, was Lucifer to whom creation was committed. He first of all imagined in detail an angelic host, and finally a whole theology was wrought out *in petto*. He used a gilt ornamented music-stand as a kind of altar with fumigating pastils for incense, where each morning God was approached by offerings until one day a conflagration put a sudden end to these celebrations.

Hans Andersen,[1] the son of a poor shoemaker, taught in a charity school at the dawn of puberty; vividly animated Bible stories from pictures painted on the wall; was dreamy and absent-minded; told continued stories to his mates; at confirmation vowed he would be famous, and finally at fourteen left home for Copenhagen, where he was violently stage-struck and worked his way from friendship with the bill-poster to the stage as page, shepherd, etc.; called on a famous dancer, who scorned him, and then, feeling that he had no one but God to depend on, prayed earnestly and often. For nearly a year, until his voice broke, he was a fine singer. He wet with his tears the eyes of a portrait of a heartless man that he might feel for him. He played with a puppet theater and took a childish delight in decking the characters with gay remnants that he begged from shops; wrote several plays which no one would accept; stole into an empty theater one New Year's day to pray aloud on the middle of the stage; shouted with joy; hugged and kissed a beech-tree till people thought him insane; abhorred the thought of apprenticeship to Latin as he did to that of a trade, which was a constant danger; and was one of the most dreamy and sentimental, and by spells religious and prayerful, of youth.

Georg Ebers[2] remembered as a boy of eleven the revolution of '48 in Berlin, soon after which he was placed in Froebel's school at Keilhau. This great teacher, with his noble associates, Middendorf, Barop, and Langekhal, lived with the boys; told the stirring stories of their own lives as soldiers in the war of liberation; led their pupils on long excursions in vacation, often lasting for months, and gave much liberty to the boys, who were allowed to haze not only their new mates but new teachers. This transfer from the city to the country roused a veritable passion in the boy, who remained here till he was fifteen. Trees and cliffs were climbed, collections made, the Saale by moonlight and the lofty Steiger at sunset were explored. There were swimming and skating and games, and the maxim of the school, *"Friede, Freude, Freiheit,"* was lived up to. The boys hung on their teachers for stories. The teachers took their boys into their confidence for all their own literary aims, loves, and ideals. One had seen the corpse of Körner and another knew Prohaska. "The Roman postulate that knowledge should be imparted to boys according to a thoroughly tested method approved by the mature human intellect and which seems most useful to it for later life" was the old system of sacrificing the interests of the child for those of the man. Here childhood was to live itself out completely and naturally into an ever-renewed paradise. The

---

[1] The Story of My Life.

[2] The Story of My Life from Childhood to Manhood.

temperaments, dispositions, and characters of each of the sixty boys were carefully studied and recorded. Some of these are still little masterpieces of psychological penetration, and this was made the basis of development. The extreme Teutonism cultivated by wrestling, shooting, and fencing, giving each a spot of land to sow, reap, and shovel, and all in an atmosphere of adult life, made an environment that fitted the transition period as well as any that the history of education affords. Every tramp and battle were described in a book by each boy. When at fifteen Ebers was transferred to the Kottbus Gymnasium, he felt like a colt led from green pastures to the stable, and the period of effervescence made him almost possessed by a demon, so many sorts of follies did he commit. He wrote " a poem of the world," fell in love with an actress older than himself, became known as foolhardy for his wild escapades, and only slowly sobered down.

In Gottfried Keller's Der grüne Heinrich, the author, whom R. M. Meyer calls " the most eminent literary German of the nineteenth century," reviews the memories of his early life. This autobiography is a plain and very realistic story of a normal child, and not adulterated with fiction like Goethe's or with psychoses like Rousseau or Bashkirtseff. He seems a boy like all other boys, and his childhood and youth were in no wise extraordinary. The first part of this work, which describes his youth up to the age of eighteen, is the most important, and everything is given with remarkable fidelity and minuteness. It is a tale of little things. All the friendships and loves and impulses are there, and he is fundamentally selfish and utilitarian; God and nature were one, and only when his beloved Anna died did he wish to believe in immortality. He, too, as a child, found two kinds of love in his heart—the ideal and the sensual, very independent—the one for a young and innocent girl and the other for a superb young woman years older than he, pure, although the personification of sense. He gives a rich harvest of minute and sagacious observations about his strange simultaneous loves; the peculiar tastes of food; his day-dream period; and his rather prolonged habit of lying, the latter because he had no other vent for invention. He describes with great regret his leaving school at so early an age; his volcanic passion of anger; his self-distrust; his periods of abandon; his passion to make a success of art though he did not of life; his spells of self-despair and cynicism; his periods of desolation in his single life; his habit of story-telling; his wrestling with the problem of theology and God; the conflict between his philosophy and his love of the girls, etc.

From a private school in Leipzig, where he had shown all a boy's tact in finding what his masters thought the value of each subject they taught; where he had joined in the vandalism of using a battering-ram to break a way to the hated science apparatus and to destroy it, feeling that the classical writers were overpraised; and where at the age of sixteen he had appeared several times in public as a reciter of his own poems, Max Müller returned to Leipzig and entered upon the freedom of university life there at the age of seventeen. For years his chief enjoyment was music.[1] He played the piano well, heard everything he could in concert or opera, was an oratorio tenor, and grew more and more absorbed in music, so that he planned to devote himself altogether to it and also to enter a musical school at Dessau, but nothing came of it. At the university he saw little of society, was once incarcerated for wearing a club ribbon, and confesses that with his boon companions he was guilty of practises which would now bring culprits into collision with authorities. He fought three duels, participated in many pranks and freakish escapades, but nevertheless attended fifty-three different courses of lectures in three years. When Hegelism was the state philosophy, he tried hard to understand it, but dismissed it with the sentiments expressed by a French officer to his tailor, who refused to take the trousers he had ordered to be made very tight because they did not fit so closely that he could not get into them. Darwin attracted him, yet the wildness of his followers repelled. He says, "I confess I felt quite bewildered for a time and began to despair altogether of my reasoning powers." He wonders how young minds in German universities survive the storms and fogs through which they pass. With bated breath he heard his elders talk of philosophy and tried to lay hold of a word here and there, but it all floated before his mind like mist. Later he had an Hegelian period, but found in Herbart a corrective, and at last decided upon Sanskrit and other ancient languages, because he felt that he must know something that no other knew, and also that the Germans had then heard only the after-chime and not the real striking of the bells of Indian philosophy. From twenty his struggles and his queries grew more definite, and at last, at the age of twenty-two, he was fully launched upon his career in Paris, and later went to Oxford.

At thirteen Wagner[2] translated about half the Odyssey voluntarily; at fourteen began the tragedy which was to combine the grandeur of two of Shakespeare's dramas; at sixteen he tried "his new-fledged musical wings by soaring at once to the highest peaks of orchestral achievement without wasting any time on the humble foot-hills." He sought to make a new departure, and, compared to the grandeur of his own composition, "Beethoven's Ninth Symphony appeared like a simple Pleyel Sonata." To facilitate the reading of his astounding score, he wrote it in three kinds of ink—red for strings, green for the wood-wind, and black for the brass instruments. He writes that this overture was the climax of his absurdities, and although the audience before which an accommodating orchestra played it were disgusted and the musicians were convulsed with laughter, it made a deep impression upon the author's mind. Even after matriculating at the university he abandoned himself so long to the dissipations common to student life before the reaction came that his relatives feared that he was a good-for-nothing.

---

[1] My Autobiography, p. 106.

[2] Wagner and His Works. By Henry T. Finck.

In his Hannele, Hauptmann, the dramatist, describes in a kind of dream poem what he supposed to pass through the mind of a dying girl of thirteen or fourteen, who does not wish to live and is so absorbed by the "Brownies of her brain" that she hardly knows whether she is alive on earth or dead in heaven, and who sees the Lord Jesus in the form of the schoolmaster whom she adores. In her closing vision there is a symbolic representation of her own resurrection. To the passionate discussions in Germany, England, and France, whether this character is true to adolescence, we can only answer with an emphatic affirmative; that her heaven abounds in local color and in fairy-tale items, that it is very material, and that she is troubled by fears of sin against the Holy Ghost, is answer enough in an ill-used, starving child with a fevered brain, whose dead mother taught her these things.

Saint-Pierre's Paul and Virginia is an attempt to describe budding adolescence in a boy and girl born on a remote island and reared in a state of natural simplicity. The descriptions are sentimental after the fashion of the age in France, and the pathos, which to us smacks of affectation and artificiality, nevertheless has a vein of truth in it. The story really begins when the two children were twelve, and the description of the dawn of love and melancholy in Virginia's heart, for some time concealed from Paul, of her disquiet and piety, of the final frank avowal of eternal love by each, set off by the pathetic separation, and of the undying love, and finally the tragic death and burial of each—all this owes its charm, for the many generations of readers since it was written, to its merits as an essentially true picture of the human heart at this critical age. This work and Rousseau have contributed to give French literature its peculiar cast in its description of this age.

"The first explosions of a combustible constitution" in Rousseau's precocious nature were troublesome, and he felt premature sensations of erotic voluptuousness, but without any sin. He longed "to fall at the feet of an imperious mistress, obey her mandates or implore pardon." He only wanted a lady to become a knight errant. At ten he was passionately devoted to a Mlle. Vulson, whom he publicly and tyrannically claimed as his own and would allow no other to approach. He had very different sensuous feelings toward Mlle. Goton, with whom his relations were very passionate, though pure. Absolutely under the power of both these mistresses, the effects they produced upon him were in no wise related to each other. The former was a brother's affection with the jealousy of a lover added, but the latter a furious, tigerish, Turkish rage. When told of the former's marriage, in his indignation and heroic fury he swore never more to see a perfidious girl. A slightly neurotic vein of prolonged ephebeitis pervades much of his life.

"In order to comprehend a religion," said Renan, "one must have believed in it and have left it." He bade the Church farewell in 1845, emancipated at fifteen, which "is the critical age for faith in French education."[1] He could not "commit the sacrilege of serving a God who still possessed his heart but no longer mastered his reason. Leaving religious illusion behind, he remembered all its magic spells and all its evasions, but also all its charm and all its benefit." He vowed always to love the ideal Jesus, whatever view he took of his nature. Even if he should abandon him, it would be to him a pleasing but most costly sacrifice. He was greatly troubled before he was eighteen by the persistent query, whether or not holding these views he was a Christian; and at this age he was initiated into Goethe and Herder and felt that "he was entering a temple." His confession, really and substantially written in 1848, when he was overflowing with illusions and enthusiasm, seemed to him later, when he saw that his "life had always been governed by a faith which he no longer possessed," the product of an entirely natural state, yet living solely in his fevered intellect. Like Müller, he turned to philology, because he thought it the basis for philosophy.

Pierre Loti's Story of a Child was written in the author's old age and contains hardly a fact, but it is one of the best of inner autobiographies, and is nowhere richer than in the last chapters, which bring the author down to the age of fourteen and a half. He vividly describes the new joy at waking, which he began to feel at twelve or thirteen; the clear vision into the bottomless pit of death; the new, marvelous susceptibility to nature as comradeship with boys of his own age was lacking; the sudden desires from pure bravado and perversity to do something unseemly, e. g., making a fly omelet and carrying it in a procession with song; the melting of pewter plates and pouring them into water and salting a wild tract of land with them; organizing a band of miners, whom he led as if with keen scent to the right spot and rediscovered his nuggets, everything being done mysteriously and as a tribal secret. Loti had a new feeling for the haunting music of Chopin, which he had been taught to play but had not been interested in; his mind was inflamed, by a home visit of an older brother, with the idea of going to the South Sea Islands, and this became a long obsession which finally led him to enlist in the navy, dropping, with a beating heart, the momentous letter into the post-office after long misgivings and delays. He had a superficial and a hidden self, the latter somewhat whimsical and perhaps ridiculous, shared only with a few intimate friends for whom he would have let himself be cut into bits. He believes his transition period lasted longer than with the majority of men, and during it he was carried from one extreme to another; had rather eccentric and absurd manners, and touched most of the perilous

[1] Darmesteter: Selected Essays, p. 186.

rocks on the voyage of life. He had an early love for an older girl whose name he wrote in cipher on his books, although he felt it a little artificial, but believed it might have developed into a great and true hereditary friendship, continuing that which their ancestors had felt for many generations. The birth of love in his heart was in a dream after having read the forbidden poet, Alfred de Musset. He was fourteen, and in his dream it was a soft, odorous twilight. He walked amid flowers seeking a nameless some one whom he ardently desired, and felt that something strange and wonderful, intoxicating as it advanced, was going to happen. The twilight grew deeper, and behind a rose-bush he saw a young girl with a languorous and mysterious smile, although her forehead and eyes were hidden. As it darkened rather suddenly, her eyes came out, and they were very personal and seemed to belong to some one already much beloved, who had been found with "transports of infinite joy and tenderness." He woke with a start and sought to retain the phantom, which faded. He could not conceive that she was a mere illusion, and as he realized that she had vanished he felt overwhelmed with hopelessness. It was the first stirring "of true love with all its great melancholy and deep mystery, with its overwhelming but sad enchantment—love which like a perfume endows with a fragrance all it touches."

It is, I believe, high time that ephebic literature should be recognized as a class by itself, and have a place of its own in the history of letters and in criticism. Much of it should be individually prescribed for the reading of the young, for whom it has a singular zest and is a true stimulus and corrective. This stage of life now has what might almost be called a school of its own. Here the young appeal to and listen to each other as they do not to adults, and in a way the latter have failed to appreciate. Again, no biography, and especially no autobiography, should henceforth be complete if it does not describe this period of transformation so all-determining for future life to which it alone can often give the key. To rightly draw the lessons of this age not only saves us from waste ineffable of this rich but crude area of experience, but makes maturity saner and more complete. Lastly, many if not most young people should be encouraged to enough of the confessional private journalism to teach them self-knowledge, for the art of self-expression usually begins now if ever, when it has a wealth of subjective material and needs forms of expression peculiar to itself.

Lightning Source UK Ltd.
Milton Keynes UK
UKHW040902170119
335676UK00001B/7/P

9 781443 723961

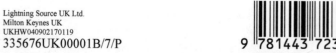